BIOINFORMATICS

METHODS OF
BIOCHEMICAL ANALYSIS

Volume 39

BIOINFORMATICS
A PRACTICAL GUIDE TO THE ANALYSIS OF GENES AND PROTEINS

EDITED BY

Andreas D. Baxevanis
Genome Technology Branch
National Human Genome Research Institute
National Institutes of Health
Bethesda, Maryland

B. F. Francis Ouellette
National Center for Biotechnology Information
National Institutes of Health
Bethesda, Maryland

WILEY-INTERSCIENCE
A JOHN WILEY & SONS, INC., PUBLICATION
New York / Chichester / Weinheim / Brisbane / Singapore / Toronto

Library of Congress Cataloging-in-Publication Data:
Bioinformatics : a practical guide to the analysis of genes and
  proteins / edited by Andreas Baxevanis and B.F. Francis Ouellette.
      p.   cm.
    Includes index.
    ISBN 0-471-19196-5 (pbk. : alk. paper) ISBN 0-471-32441-8 (cloth : alk. paper)
    1. Nucleotide sequence—Databases.   2. Amino acid sequence—
Databases.   3. Genes—Analysis—Data processing.   4. Proteins—
Analysis—Data processing.   I. Baxevanis, Andreas.   II. Ouellette,
B.F. Francis.
  QP620.B566   1998
  572.8'633—dc21   97-39019
                                                      CIP

Printed in the United States of America.

10 9 8 7 6 5 4 3 2 1

ADB dedicates this book to his mother, Anastasia, and to the memory of his father, Demetrios. Their wisdom and love have served as his guiding force throughout life.

BFFO dedicates this book to the memory of Angelos Kalogeropoulos, a friend and bioinformatician whose presence is greatly missed.

PREFACE

The last decade has seen a veritable explosion in the amount of raw information generated by molecular biologists worldwide. Coming to grips with this cascade of information has now become for many a full-time vocation, in contrast to the not-too-distant past when such analyses were practiced primarily by disgruntled graduate students who preferred handling a pipette to banging at a keyboard. The burgeoning field of bioinformatics, loosely defined at the intersection of molecular and computational biology, has given rise to numerous important discoveries and holds the promise of revealing even more of nature's secrets. For many, the attraction to bioinformatics rests in its newness as an untamed area of biology. For others, the attraction lies elsewhere—between the reductionist's fondness for details at the chemical level and the phylogeneticist's elation at understanding relationships within the parade of kingdoms.

Those with a conversational knowledge of bioinformatics have heralded its virtues broadly, calling it everything from the magic bullet that will cure all infirmities known to man to a brute-force powertool for dismantling sequence data to simply a sexy way to do science. In reality, bioinformatics is a new way to do hard, meaningful work. The field is one of methods that are constantly in flux and not fully developed, not unlike the early, golden years of biochemistry when the methods of choice involved melting and spinning a target biomolecule, in contrast to the much finer and more delicate methods available in the lab today. In the race to push bioinformatics along, however, a number of high-profile movers and shakers have conspired to downgrade bioinformatics from being a science in its own right to merely a function that can be done by buying the right kit. What keeps this field centered is the academic user community itself, whether the members are at private universities or at government-sponsored research centers. The significant advances being made in bioinformatics rest here, ranging from gathering and curating the raw data to developing new and elegant methods for examining the data, all in an open environment where information and expertise are freely shared. The bioinformatics community is unique in that, outside of the commercial sector, the *esprit de corps* is much more open than in many of the competitive arenas in biology. It is from this last thought that this book takes its inspiration, in enabling scientists who wish to know more about how to do sequence analysis to jump aboard and experience the ride that has enthralled so many. Through this book, we hope that the reader will come to appreciate the rigor of these methods and to understand that, not unlike the laboratory, the running of controls and the realization of what the methods can and cannot do are of the utmost importance. Most of all, we encourage the readers to just simply play.

There are many individuals we both thank, without whose efforts this volume would not have become a reality. First and foremost, our thanks go to the all the authors whose individual contributions make up this book. The combination of expert and professional view-points, coupled with general good-naturedness even under tight time constraints, has made working with these men and women a pleasure.

Inasmuch as a good portion of this book is devoted to the tools and databases developed at the National Center for Biotechnology Information (NCBI) at the NIH, we thank the all the members of the NCBI team for their hard work and dedication to maintaining the public databases under their charge and, more importantly, for making the data in those databases both of the highest quality and easily accessible to the scientific community. The computational biology community in general has been very generous with the fruits of its labor, making freely accessible tools and specialized databases without which elementary sequence analysis could not take place. We thank all those who have undertaken such projects, including those not specifically mentioned in this volume, for making possible many significant advances in this new age of sequence-based biology.

We also thank our editor, Ann Boyle, for her patience, encouragement, and support. This book marked a lot of firsts for us, so in the process of learning the ins and outs, we also developed a very strong friendship with her. We look forward to working with her again in the future.

From BFFO: I would like to acknowledge the constant support, love, and trust provided by my spouse, Nancy Ryder. Her respect for this work, as well as her having given me the space such an effort required, is beyond our vows, and I can only love her more for it. I also thank Mark Boguski, who invited me to the NCBI four years ago. Mark continues to direct my attention to a variety of new and interesting projects, and his continued enthusiasm and interest will always be inspirational to me.

And from ADB: My heartfelt thanks for the unbounded support and encouragement provided by David Landsman. My friendship with David began many years ago, when he was willing to take on as a post-doc a physical biochemist with little knowledge of what a brand-new field called bioinformatics was all about. I don't think either of us would have guessed back in 1992 that our teaching and research collaborations would lead to the writing of a textbook. Without his strong influence on how to think about computational biology, with the emphasis on *biology,* this book would not have been possible.

Andreas D. Baxevanis
B.F. Francis Ouellette

CONTENTS

Preface   vii

Contributors   xiv

1   The Internet and the Biologist   1
Andreas D. Baxevanis

Internet Basics / 1
Connecting to the Internet / 3
Electronic Mail / 4
File Transfer Protocol / 7
Gopher / 8
The World Wide Web / 8
References / 15

2   The GenBank Sequence Database   16
B. F. Francis Ouellette

Introduction / 16
Primary and Secondary Databases / 19
Format vs. Content: Computers vs. Humans / 20
The Database / 21
The GenBank Flatfile: A Dissection / 22
Conclusions / 33
References / 33
Appendices: Database File Formats / 35
    Appendix 2.1 Example of an GenBank (or DDBS) Record / 35
    Appendix 2.2 Example of an ASN.1 Record / 36
    Appendix 2.3 Example of an EMBL Record / 42
    Appendix 2.4 Example of a GenBank Summary File / 44

3   Structure Databases   46
Christopher W. V. Hogue and Stephen H. Bryant

Introduction to Structures / 46
PDB: Protein Data Bank at Brookhaven National Laboratories / 49
MMDB: Molecular Modeling Database at NCBI / 56

Structure File Formats / 58
Visualizing Structural Information / 60
Database Structure Viewers / 68
Can't Find a Published Structure? / 70
References / 71
Monographs / 72

4 Sequence Analysis Using GCG   **74**

Barbara A. Butler

Introduction / 74
The Wisconsin Package / 75
Databases That Accompany the Wisconsin Package / 75
The SeqLab Environment / 76
Analyzing Sequences with Operations and Wisconsin Package Programs / 80
Viewing Output / 81
Monitoring Program Progress and Troubleshooting Problems / 83
Annotating Sequences and Graphically Displaying Annotations in the SeqLab
     Editor / 83
Saving Sequences in the SeqLab Editor / 85
Examples of Analyses That Can Be Undertaken in SeqLab / 85
Extending SeqLab by Including Programs That Are Not Part of the Wisconsin
     Package / 91
References / 91
Appendix / 93

5 Information Retrieval from Biological Databases   **98**

Andreas D. Baxevanis

Retrieving Database Entries: The Retrieve Server / 99
Integrated Information Retrieval: The Entrez System / 101
Integrated Information Access: The Query Server / 111
Sequence Databases Beyond NCBI / 115
Medical Databases / 118
References / 120

6 The NCBI Data Model   **121**

James M. Ostell and Jonathan A. Kans

Introduction / 121
Pubs: Publications or Perish / 125
Seqids: What's in a Name? / 129
Bioseq: Sequences / 132
BioseqSets: Collections of Sequences / 135
Seq-annot: Annotating the Sequence / 136
Seq-descr: Describing the Sequence / 140
Using the Model / 141
Conclusions / 143
References / 144

7 Sequence Alignment and Database Searching   **145**

Gregory D. Schuler

Introduction / 145
The Evolutionary Basis of Sequence Alignment / 146
The Modular Nature of Proteins / 148
Optimal Alignment Methods / 150
Substitution Scores and Gap Penalties / 151
Statistical Significance of Alignments / 155
Database Similarity Searching / 156
FASTA / 159
BLAST / 160
Low-Complexity Regions / 166
Repetitive Elements / 166
Conclusions / 169
References / 170

8 Practical Aspects of Multiple Sequence Alignment   **172**

Andreas D. Baxevanis

Progressive Alignment Methods / 173
Motifs and Patterns / 176
Presentation Methods / 184
References / 188

9 Phylogenetic Analysis   **189**

Mark A. Hershkovitz and Detlef D. Leipe

Elements of Phylogenetic Models / 190
Phylogenetic Data Analysis: Alignment, Substitution Model Building,
    Tree Building, and Tree Evaluation / 191
Building the Data Model (Alignment) / 191
Determining the Substitution Model / 197
Tree-Building Methods / 206
Searching for Trees / 211
Rooting Trees / 212
Evaluating Trees and Data / 213
Phylogenetics Software / 217
Some Simple Practical Considerations / 225
Acknowledgments / 227
References / 227

10 Predictive Methods Using Nucleotide Sequences   **231**

James W. Fickett

Framework / 232
Masking Repetitive DNA / 232
Database Searches / 234
Codon Bias Detection / 234

Detecting Functional Sites in the DNA / 236
Integrated Gene Parsing / 238
Finding tRNA Genes / 238
Future Prospects / 241
Acknowledgments / 243
References / 243

11   Predictive Methods Using Protein Sequences   **246**

Andreas D. Baxevanis and David Landsman

Protein Identity Based on Composition / 247
Physical Properties Based on Sequence / 250
Secondary Structure and Folding Classes / 252
Specialized Structures or Features / 257
Tertiary Structure / 262
References / 265

**12   Of Mice and Men: Navigating Public Physical Mapping
        Databases**   **268**

Lincoln D. Stein

Types of Physical Map / 269
Genome-Wide Maps from Large Community Databases / 271
Genome-Wide Maps from Individual Sources / 278
Chromosome-Specific Human Maps / 291
Mouse Mapping Resources / 294
References / 297

13   ACEDB: A Database for Genome Information   **299**

Sean Walsh, Mary Anderson, and Samuel W. Cartinhour

General Features of ACEDB / 299
Sequence Analysis in ACEDB / 305
Miscellaneous Analysis Functions / 315
Acknowledgments / 316

14   Submitting DNA Sequence to the Databases   **319**

Jonathan A. Kans and B. F. Francis Ouellette

Introduction / 319
Where to Submit? / 320
What to Submit? / 321
How to Submit on the World Wide Web / 324
How to Submit with Sequin / 326
EST/STS/GSS / 348
Genome Centers / 348
Updates / 350

Concluding Remarks / 351
Acknowledgments / 351
References / 353

Appendix 1: Glossary   **355**

Appendix 2: Sample Sequence File Formats   **359**

Index   **363**

CONTRIBUTORS

Mary Anderson, Nottingham *Arabidopsis* Stock Centre, School of Biological Sciences, Nottingham University, Nottingham, United Kingdom

Andreas D. Baxevanis, Genome Technology Branch, National Human Genome Research Institute, National Institutes of Health, Bethesda, Maryland

Stephen H. Bryant, National Center for Biotechnology Information, National Library of Medicine, National Institutes of Health, Bethesda, Maryland

Barbara A. Butler, Genetics Computer Group, Inc., Oxford Molecular Group, Madison, Wisconsin

Samuel W. Cartinhour, Crop Biotechnology Center, Department of Biochemistry and Biophysics, Texas A&M University, College Station, Texas

James W. Fickett, SmithKline Beecham Pharmaceuticals, King of Prussia, Pennsylvania

Mark A. Hershkovitz, National Center for Biotechnology Information, National Library of Medicine, National Institutes of Health, Bethesda, Maryland

Christopher W. V. Hogue, Samuel Lunenfeld Research Institute, Mt. Sinai Hospital, Toronto, Ontario, Canada

Jonathan A. Kans, National Center for Biotechnology Information, National Library of Medicine, National Institutes of Health, Bethesda, Maryland

David Landsman, National Center for Biotechnology Information, Computational Biology Branch, National Library of Medicine, National Institutes of Health, Bcthesda, Maryland

Detlef D. Leipe, National Center for Biotechnology Information, National Library of Medicine, National Institutes of Health, Bethesda, Maryland

James M. Ostell, National Center for Biotechnology Information, National Library of Medicine, National Institutes of Health, Bethesda, Maryland

B. F. Francis Ouellette, National Center for Biotechnology Information, National Institutes of Health, Bethesda, Maryland

Gregory D. Schuler, National Center for Biotechnology Information, National Library of Medicine, National Institutes of Health, Bethesda, Maryland

Lincoln D. Stein, Cold Spring Harbor Laboratory, Cold Spring Harbor, New York

Sean Walsh, Nottingham Arabidopsis Stock Centre, School of Biological Sciences, Nottingham University, Nottingham, United Kingdom

1

The Internet and the Biologist

Andreas D. Baxevanis

Genome Technology Branch
National Human Genome Research Institute
National Institutes of Health
Bethesda, Maryland

With the explosion of sequence and structural information available to researchers, the field of bioinformatics, or more properly, computational biology, is playing an increasingly large role in the study of fundamental biomedical problems. The challenge facing computational biologists, especially in light of the vast amount of data being produced by the Human Genome Project and other sequencing efforts, will be to aid in gene discovery and in the design of molecular modeling, site-directed mutagenesis, and experiments of other types that can potentially reveal previously unknown relationships with respect to the structure and function of genes and proteins.

Before embarking on any practical discussion of computational methods in solving biological problems, it is necessary to lay the common groundwork that will enable users to both access and implement the algorithms and tools discussed in this book. We begin with a review of the Internet and its terminology, discussing as well four major Internet protocol classes, without becoming overly engaged in the engineering minutiae underlying these protocols. A more in-depth treatment on the inner workings of these protocols may be found in a number of well-written reference books intended for the lay audience (Falk, 1994; Krol, 1994).

INTERNET BASICS

Despite the impression that it is a single entity, the Internet is actually a network of networks, composed of over 20,000 interconnected local and regional networks in over 100 countries. While work on remote communications began in the early 1960s, the true origins of the Internet lie with a research project on networking at the Advanced Research Projects

Bioinformatics: A Practical Guide to the Analysis of Genes and Proteins
Edited by A.D. Baxevanis and B.F.F. Ouellette
ISBN 0-471-19196-5, pages 1–15.   Copyright © 1998 Wiley-Liss, Inc.

Agency of the U.S. Department of Defense in 1969 named ARPANET. The original ARPANET connected four nodes on the West Coast, with the immediate goal of being able to transmit information on defense-related research between laboratories. A number of different network projects subsequently surfaced, with the next landmark developments coming over 10 years later. In 1981 BITNET ("Because It's Time") was introduced, providing point-to-point connections between universities for the transfer of electronic mail and files. In 1982 ARPA introduced the Transmission Control Protocol (TCP) and the Internet Protocol (IP); TCP/IP allowed different networks to be connected to and communicate with one another, creating the system in place today. A number of references chronicle the development of the Internet and communications protocols in detail (Froehlich and Kent, 1991; Krol, 1994; Quarterman, 1990). Most users, however, are content to leave the details of *how* the Internet works to their systems administrators; the relevant fact to most is that it *does* work.

Once the machines on a network have been connected to one another, there needs to be an unambiguous way to specify a single computer so that messages and files actually find their intended recipient. To accomplish this, all machines directly connected to the Internet have an *IP number*. IP addresses are unique, identifying one and only one machine. The IP address is made up of four numbers separated by periods; for example, the IP address for the main file server at the National Center for Biotechnology Information (NCBI) at the National Institutes of Health is 130.14.25.1. The numbers themselves represent, from left to right, the domain (130.14 for the NIH), subnet (.25 for the National Library of Medicine at NIH), and machine itself (.1). While the use of IP numbers aids the computers in directing data, it is obviously very difficult for users to remember these strings, so IP addresses often have associated with them a *fully qualified domain name* (FQDN) that is dynamically translated in the background by *domain name servers*. Going back to the NCBI example, rather than use `130.14.25.1` to access the NCBI computer, a user could instead use `ncbi.nlm.nih.gov` and achieve the same result. Reading from left to right, notice that the IP address goes from least to most specific, while the FQDN equivalent goes from most specific to least. The name of any given computer can then be thought of as taking the general form *computer.domain,* with the top-level domain (the portion coming after the last period in the FQDN) falling into one of the six broad categories shown in Table 1.1. Outside the United States, the top-level domain names are instead replaced with a two-letter code specifying the country in which the machine is located (e.g., .ca for Canada and .uk for the United Kingdom).

TABLE 1.1 Top-Level Domain Names

AMERICAN TOP-LEVEL DOMAIN NAMES

.com	Commercial site
.edu	Educational site
.gov	Government site
.mil	Military site
.net	Gateway or network host
.org	Private (usually not-for-profit) organizations

EXAMPLES OF TOP-LEVEL DOMAIN NAMES OUTSIDE THE UNITED STATES

.ca	Canadian site
.ac.uk	Academic site in the United Kingdom
.co.uk	Commercial site in the United Kingdom

The most concrete measure of the size (and, thereby, the success) of the Internet lies in actually counting the number of machines physically connected to it. Network Wizards regularly counts these machines, or *hosts,* by launching a probe that hits as many hosts as it can find, returning the results of the probe to the launching computer. The rate of growth of the number of hosts has been phenomenal, having a doubling time of approximately 12 months; the total number of hosts currently stands in excess of 12 million. Most of this growth has come from the commercial sector, capitalizing on the growing popularity of new, multimedia platforms for advertising and communications such as the World Wide Web (Figure 1.1). The numbers presented in these surveys should be interpreted by comparing them to each other rather than in absolute terms, since many hosts will not be found by the probe. For example, many machines are situated behind corporate firewalls that block communications between the company and the outside world for security reasons; other machines, particularly home computers, are connected through the Internet transiently, via modem. The results of the Network Wizards search are then best thought of as representing the minimum size of the Internet at any given time.

CONNECTING TO THE INTERNET

Users who cannot plug their computers directly onto the Internet via an Ethernet, 10BaseT, or similar type of connection have two primary ways of accessing the Net: through *online services* or *Internet service providers* (ISPs). Online services, such as America Online

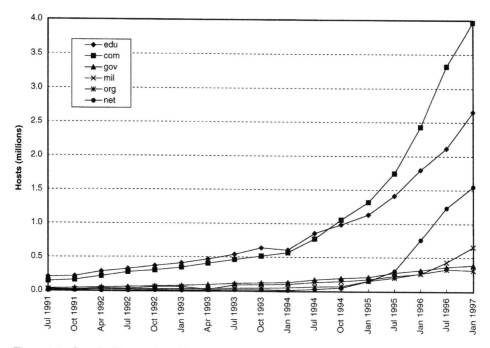

Figure 1.1 Growth of the number of Internet hosts as measured by domain. The total number of Internet hosts is in excess of 12 million, with the number of commercial (.com) sites first surpassing the number of educational (.edu) sites in 1994. [Data Network Wizards (*http://www.nw.com*).]

(AOL), CompuServe, and Prodigy, offer a large number of interactive digital services, including information retrieval, electronic mail (e-mail), bulletin boards, and "chat rooms," where users who are online at the same time can converse about any number of subjects. While the online services now provide access to the World Wide Web, most of the features and services available through these systems reside in a proprietary, closed network—once a connection has been made between the user's computer and the online service, one can access the special features, or content, of these systems without ever leaving the online system's host computer. Specialized content can range from access to online travel reservation systems to encyclopedias that are constantly being updated—items that are not available to nonsubscribers to the particular online service. The focus on in-house content comes at a price; most of the services impose hourly charges for use, charges that can rack up fairly quickly with even moderate use.

Internet service providers take the opposite tack. Instead of focusing on providing content, the ISPs provide the tools necessary for users to send and receive e-mail, upload and download files, and navigate around the World Wide Web, finding information at remote locations. Although major players here include large firms such as AT&T and MCI, the absence of a requirement to provide content has resulted in the rapid growth of a cottage industry, with many small, local firms providing reliable connections to the Internet. One such ISP is ClarkNet, located outside of Baltimore, Maryland. From humble beginnings as a bank of modems in the barn of a 500-acre farm, ClarkNet has grown in both size and quality to become one of the country's top-ranked regional service providers. The major advantage of ISPs is connection speed; often the smaller providers offer faster connection speeds than can be had from the online services. Most ISPs charge a monthly fee for unlimited use.

The line between online services and ISPs has begun to blur in the favor of the online services. AOL recently changed its pricing structure to a monthly flat fee rather than an hourly rate, so for the same cost charged by many ISPs, users can obtain all the proprietary content found on AOL as well as all the Internet tools available through ISPs. The extensive AOL network puts access to AOL as close as a local phone call in most of the United States, providing access to e-mail no matter where the user is located, a feature small, local ISPs cannot match. Developments such as this, coupled with the move of local telephone and cable companies into providing Internet access through new, faster fiber optic networks, foretell major changes in how people will access the Net in the future, changes that should favor the end user both in price and performance.

ELECTRONIC MAIL

Most people are introduced to the Internet through the use of electronic mail, or *e-mail*. The use of e-mail has become practically indispensable in many settings owing to its convenience as a medium for sending, receiving, and replying to messages. Its advantages are many:

- It is much quicker than the postal service or "snail mail."
- Messages tend to be much clearer and more to the point than is the case in typical telephone or face-to-face conversations.
- Recipients have more flexibility in deciding whether a response needs to be sent immediately, relatively soon, or at all, giving individuals more control over workflow.

- It provides a convenient method by which messages can be filed or stored.
- There is little or no cost involved in sending an e-mail message.

While these and other advantages have pushed e-mail to the forefront of interpersonal communication in both industry and the academic community, users should be aware of two major disadvantages. First is the issue of security. As mail travels toward its recipient, it may pass through a number of remote nodes, at any one of which the message may be intercepted and read by someone with high-level access, such as a systems administrator. Second is the issue of privacy. In industrial settings, E-mail is often considered to be an asset of the company for use in official communication only and, as such, is subject to monitoring by supervisors. The opposite is often true in academic, quasi-academic, or research settings; for example, National Institutes of Health policy encourages personal use of e-mail within the bounds of certain published guidelines. The key words here are "published guidelines"; no matter what the setting, users of e-mail systems should always find out their organization's policy regarding appropriate use confidentiality so that they may use the tool properly and effectively. An excellent, basic guide to the effective use of e-mail (Lamb and Peek, 1995) is highly recommended.

Sending E-Mail

E-mail addresses take the general form *user@computer.domain,* where *user* is the name of the individual user and *computer.domain* specifies the actual computer the e-mail account is located on. Like a postal letter, an e-mail message is comprised of an *envelope* or *header,* showing the e-mail addresses of sender and recipient, a line indicating the subject of the e-mail, and information about how the e-mail message actually traveled from the sender to the recipient. The header is followed by the actual message, or *body,* analogous to what would go inside a postal envelope. Figure 1.2 illustrates all the components of an e-mail message.

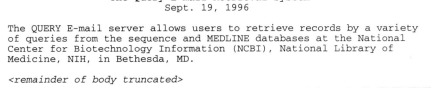

Figure 1.2 Anatomy of an electronic mail (e-mail) message (relevant components are indicated). This message is an automated reply to a "help" message sent to the NCBI Query server.

E-mail programs vary widely, depending on both the platform and the needs of the users. Most often, the characteristics of the local area network (LAN) dictate what types of mail program can be used, and the decision is often left to systems administrators rather than individual users. Among the most widely used e-mail packages with a graphical user interface are Eudora for the Macintosh and Microsoft Exchange for the Mac, Windows, and UNIX platforms. Text-based e-mail programs, which are accessed by logging in to a UNIX-based account, include Elm and Pine.

Newsgroups

In the example in Figure 1.2, the e-mail message is being sent to a single recipient. One of the strengths of this system is that a single piece of e-mail can be sent to a large number of people. The first mechanism for doing this depends on *aliases:* a user can define a group of people within his or her mail program and give the group a special name, or alias. Instead of using the individual e-mail addresses for all the people in the group, the user can just send the e-mail to the alias name, and the mail program will handle broadcasting the message to each person in that group. Setting up alias names is a tremendous time-saver, even for small groups; it also ensures that all members of a given group actually receive all e-mail messages intended for the group.

Newsgroups comprise the second mechanism for broadcasting an e-mail message. This model works slightly differently in that the list of e-mail addresses is compiled and maintained on a remote computer through subscriptions, much like the list of subscribers used by a magazine. For example, the BIOSCI newsgroups are among the most highly trafficked newsgroups, offering a forum for discussion or the exchange of ideas in a wide variety of biological subject areas. To begin receiving the messages posted to the automated sequencing discussion group within BIOSCI, a user would send a message to *biosci-server @net.bio.net* with the word `subscribe autoseq` in the body of the message. Then all postings to that group will go to the new subscriber, who will be able to participate in the discussions. A user who wished to be removed from the group would send to the same address a message reading `unsubscribe autoseq`. For more information on BIOSCI, including a complete list of discussion groups, send an e-mail message to *biosci-server@net.bio.net;* leave the subject line blank and place the words `info faq` in the body of the message. The BIOSCI server will then return a copy of the Frequently Asked Questions (FAQ) in response, with detailed information on each newsgroup overseen by BIOSCI.

As with postal mail, there has been a recent upsurge in junk e-mail, or "spam," from companies that compile bulk lists of e-mail addresses for use in commercial promotions. Since most of these lists are compiled from online registration forms and similar sources, the best way to remain off these bulk e-mail lists is to be selective in giving out your e-mail address. Most newsgroups keep their e-mailing lists confidential; if in doubt and if this is a concern, ask.

E-Mail Servers

So far, the discussion has centered on sending messages, whether it be to one recipient or many. It is also possible to use e-mail as a mechanism for making predictions or retrieving records from biological databases. Users can send e-mail messages in a format defining the action to be performed to remote computers known as *servers;* the servers will then perform the desired operation and e-mail back the results. Figure 1.2 shows the results of such an e-mail request, using the Query e-mail server at NCBI as an example. While this method is not interactive, it does place the responsibility for hardware maintenance and software upgrades on the persons maintaining the server, allowing users to concentrate on their results instead of on programming. The use of a number of e-mail servers is discussed in greater detail in context in later chapters. An excellent, up-to-date list of e-mail servers is maintained by Amos Bairoch of the University of Geneva; this list can be obtained by anonymous file transfer protocol (described below) at *expasy.hcuge.ch,* moving to the */databases/info* directory, and downloading the file *serv_ema.txt*. For most of these servers, sending the message `help` to the server e-mail address will return a detailed set of instructions for using that server, including the proper format for queries.

FILE TRANSFER PROTOCOL

Despite the many advantages of e-mail in transmitting messages, experienced users have no doubt experienced frustration in trying to transmit files, or *attachments*. The mere fact that a file can be attached to an e-mail message and sent does not mean that the recipient will be able to detach, decode, and actually use the attached file. While more cross-platform e-mail packages such as Microsoft Exchange are being developed, the use of different e-mail packages by people at different locations means that sending files via e-mail is not an effective, foolproof method, at least in the short term. One solution to this problem is through the use of a *file transfer protocol,* or FTP. The workings of FTP are quite simple: a connection is made between a user's computer (the *client*) and a remote server, and that connection remains in place for the duration of the FTP session. File transfers are very fast, at rates on the order of 5–10 kilobytes per second, with speeds varying with the time of day, the distance between the client and server machines, and the overall traffic on the network.

To make an FTP connection and transfer files, a user must have a computer account on the remote server. The academic community makes many files and programs freely available, however, and access to those files does not require having an account on each and every machine where these programs are stored. Instead, connections are made using a system called *anonymous FTP*. Under this system, the user connects to the remote machine, and instead of entering a username/password pair, types `anonymous` as the username and the individual's e-mail address in place of a password. The server's systems administrator can use the client's e-mail address to compile access statistics that may, in turn, be of use to those actually providing the public files or programs. An example of an anonymous FTP session using UNIX is shown in Figure 1.3.

Even though FTP actually occurs within the UNIX environment, Macintosh and PC users can use programs that rely on graphical user interfaces (GUI, pronounced "gooey") to navigate through the UNIX directories on the FTP server. Users need not have any knowledge of UNIX commands to download files; instead, they select from pop-up menus and point and click their way through the UNIX file structure. The most popular FTP program on the Macintosh platform for FTP sessions is Fetch. A sample Fetch window is shown in Figure 1.4 to illustrate the difference between using a GUI-based FTP program and the equivalent UNIX FTP in Figure 1.3. As with the e-mail servers, Amos Bairoch maintains an extensive list of molecular biology FTP servers. This list can be obtained by connecting to *expasy.hcuge.ch,* moving to the */databases/info* directory, and downloading the file *serv_ftp.txt*.

```
$ ftp ftp.bio.indiana.edu
Connected to magpie.bio.indiana.edu.
220-
220 firefly FTP server (Version wu-2.4(2) Sat Nov 23 08:51:39 EST 1996)
ready.
Name: anonymous
331 Guest login ok, send your complete e-mail address as password.
Password: ••••••••••••••••
230-                     Welcome to IUBIO archive!
230-
230-  This is a user-supported archive for biology software and data.
230-
230-       See the file Archive.Doc for details of this archive.
230-
230-    Report problems, uploads and other matters via e-mail to
230-                    archive@bio.indiana.edu.
230-
Remote system type is UNIX.
Using binary mode to transfer files.
ftp> cd /molbio/align
250 CWD command successful.
ftp> get clustalw.hqx
local: clustalw.hqx remote: clustalw.hqx
200 PORT command successful.
150 Opening BINARY mode data connection for clustalw.hqx (504232 bytes).
226 Transfer complete.
504232 bytes received in 4.34 seconds (113.43 Kbytes/s)
ftp> quit
221 Goodbye.

$
```

Figure 1.3 Using UNIX FTP to download a file. An anonymous FTP session is established with the molecular biology FTP server at the University of Indiana to download the ClustalW alignment program.

GOPHER

Once having entered a particular directory, a user working with FTP can see only the names of directories or files. To actually view what is within those files, the user must physically download them onto a local computer. To save time, researchers at the University of Minnesota developed a system through which text documents can be viewed without actually being downloaded. This program, named *Gopher* in honor of the school's mascot, is one of the first examples of a *distributed document delivery system,* a special type of interactive, client–server application.

Gopher is easy to use because a user does not need to know the physical location or address of the information being sought. All the information stored at various Gopher sites is organized in a defined hierarchy through which users can travel by clicking a mouse. Users can also travel from Gopher site to Gopher site throughout the Internet via interconnections known as *Gopher holes* in a similar point-and-click fashion. The main Macintosh application used for Gopher travel is TurboGopher, illustrated in Figure 1.5.

THE WORLD WIDE WEB

Gopher circumvents a lot of the problems involved in disseminating information easily, but it is limited to distributing text. Conceptually, though, Gopher provided an important shift in thinking that led to the development of the next generation of document delivery system,

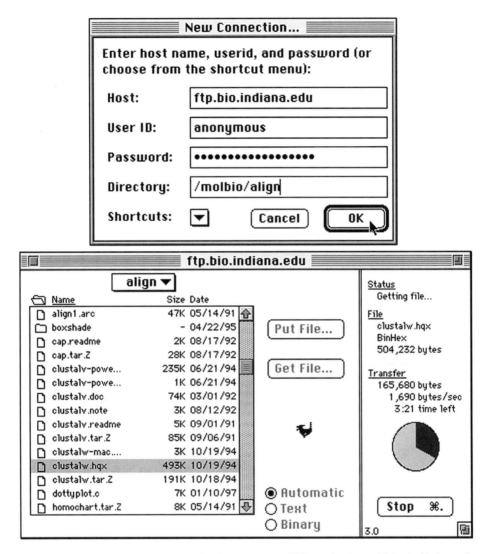

Figure 1.4   Using Fetch to download a file. An anonymous FTP session is established with the molecular biology FTP server at the University of Indiana (*top*) to download the ClustalW alignment program (*bottom*). Notice the difference between this GUI-based program and the UNIX equivalent illustrated in Figure 1.3.

one that could also deliver images, sounds, and videos. Research begun in 1989 at the European Nuclear Research Council (CERN) provided the groundwork for the World Wide Web, a then-new medium that could handle various types of non-text-based media.

Navigation

As with Gopher, navigation on the Web does not require advance knowledge of the location of the information being sought. Instead, users can navigate by clicking on specific text, buttons, or pictures. These clickable items are collectively known as *hyperlinks*. Once a hyperlink has been clicked, the user is taken to another Web location but, unlike the

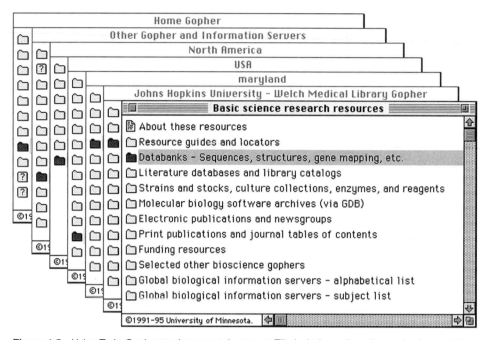

Figure 1.5   Using TurboGopher to view a text document. Tiled windows show the navigation path that was taken to find the shown document, starting at the "Home Gopher" at the University of Minnesota and ending at the Welch Medical Library at the Johns Hopkins University. Navigation does not require knowledge of the address or location of the information being sought; instead the search proceeds via a series of menus organized in a hierarchical fashion.

Gopher paradigm, the new location does not have to be the next location up or down in a hierarchy. Instead, the hyperlink can take the user to another Web location at the same site or half-way around the world. Each document displayed on the Web is called a *Web page*, and all the Web pages on a particular server are collectively called a *Web site*. Navigation strictly through the use of hyperlinks has been nicknamed *Web surfing*.

Users can take a more direct approach to finding information by entering a specific address. One of the strengths of the Web is that the programs used to actually view Web pages (appropriately termed *browsers*) can be used to visit Gopher and FTP sites as well as Web sites, somewhat obviating the need for separate Gopher or FTP applications. Thus a unified naming convention was introduced that would indicate to the browser program both the location of the remote site and, more importantly, the *type* of information at that remote location, so that the browser could properly display the data. These standard-form addresses are known as *uniform resource locators*, or URLs, and take the general form *protocol://computer.domain*, where protocol specifies the type of site and computer.domain specifies the location (Table 1.2). The *http* in a Web URL stands for *hypertext transfer protocol*, the method used in transferring Web files from the host computer to the client.

The Browser Wars

Browsers used to look at Web pages are client–server applications that connect to a remote site, download the requested information at that site, display the information on the user's

TABLE 1.2 Uniform Resource Locator (URL) Format for Each Type of Transfer Protocol

General form	*protocol://computer.domain*
FTP site	*ftp://ftp.ncbi.nlm.nih.gov*
Gopher site	*gopher://gopher.iubio.indiana.edu*
Web site	*http://www.nhgri.nih.gov*

monitor, and then disconnect from the remote host. The information retrieved from the remote host is in a platform-independent format called *hypertext markup language,* or HTML. HTML code is strictly text-based, and any associated graphics or sound for that document exist as *separate,* common-format files. (For example, images are stored and transferred in GIF format, developed by CompuServe for the quick and efficient transfer of graphics.) Because of this, a browser can display any Web page on any type of computer, whether it be a Macintosh, PC, or UNIX machine, displaying the text first, then placing the remaining elements of the page as they are downloaded. With minor exception, a given Web page will look the same (for the most part) when the same company's browser is used on any of these platforms.

The major player in the "browser wars" is Netscape Navigator, which currently commands about 80% of the browser market. Netscape, developed by Marc Andreesen and colleagues, is the outgrowth of the first widely used Web browser, NCSA Telnet; most of the Netscape development team originally came from NCSA, having left NCSA when they recognized the commercial implications of developing Web technology. Netscape was able to capture its large market share by basically giving its browser away for years, relying for revenues on Web servers and other products. While Netscape can still be freely downloaded from the Netscape Web site, newly downloaded copies can be used free of charge only for the first 90 days, although the fee is waived for educational institutions. Netscape has some notable drawbacks, such as a clumsy bookmark system for storing the addresses of frequently visited sites, difficulty in displaying and navigating Web pages where the screens are split into separate frames, and a tendency to stall or crash frequently, but it does a more than adequate job in addressing most users' Web browser needs.

Netscape's main competition comes from Microsoft, whose Internet Explorer is aggressively seeking to displace Netscape as the market leader. Microsoft's strategy is to keep Internet Explorer a freeware product that can be downloaded directly from the Microsoft Web site. Internet Explorer will also gain ground when it replaces the current AOL proprietary browser, a program that has been roundly criticized for having few strengths and many flaws; rather than reinvent the wheel, AOL will simply give its users Internet Explorer, instantly picking up somewhere on the order of 10 million users. In addition, Internet Explorer is bundled with the Windows95 operating system, and future plans include integrating Internet Explorer into the operating system so that Windows95 users will actually be using the browser as their desktop. Internet Explorer has some key advantages over Netscape: pages tend to load faster, and the browser is more stable and handles frames much better than Netscape does. As the version numbers of both these browsers advance, users will find many of the same features in both programs, and the final decision will be based on cost and personal preference.

It is worth mentioning that while the Web is by definition a visually based medium, it is also possible to travel through Web space and view documents without the associated graphics. For users limited to line-by-line terminals, a browser called Lynx is available (Figure 1.6). Developed at the University of Kansas, Lynx allows users to highlight and select hyperlinks via their keyboard arrow keys, using the return key instead of a mouse, as required for Netscape and Internet Explorer. Lynx is available for both the DOS and UNIX platforms.

Internet vs. Intranet

The Web is normally thought of as a way to communicate with people at a distance, but the same infrastructure can be used to connect people within an organization. Such *intranets* provide an easily accessible repository of relevant information, capitalizing on the simplicity of the Web interface. They also provide another channel for broadcast or confidential communication within the organization. Having an intranet is of particular value when

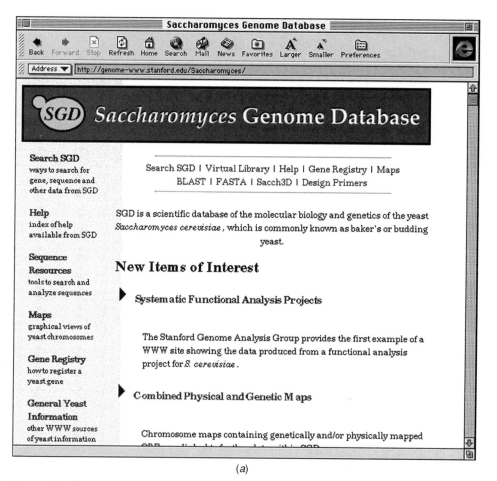

(a)

Figure 1.6 Comparison of (a) a Web browser with a graphical user interface (Microsoft Internet Explorer) with (b) a text-only Web browser (Lynx). Both browsers are pointing to the *Saccharomyces* Genome Database Home Page at Stanford University.

```
┌─────────────────────────────────────────────────────────────┐
│ ▣                       Lynx Session                       ⊟ │
│                        Saccharomyces Genome Database (p1 of 2) ⇧│
│                                                              │
│  [SGD Home] Search SGD                                       │
│  ways to search for gene, sequence and other data from SGD   │
│                                                              │
│                                                              │
│  Help                                                        │
│  index of help available from SGD                            │
│                                                              │
│                                                              │
│  Sequence Resources                                          │
│  tools to search and analyze sequences                       │
│                                                              │
│                                                              │
│  Maps                                                        │
│  graphical views of yeast chromosomes                        │
│                                                              │
│                                                              │
│  Gene Registry                                               │
│  how to register a yeast gene                                │
│                                                              │
│                                                              │
│  General Yeast Information                                   │
│  other WWW sources of yeast information                      │
│                                                              │
│                                                              │
│  News & Meetings                                             │
│  SGD news and yeast-related activities                       │
│                                                              │
│                                                              │
│  About SGD                                                   │
│  send suggestions or questions to SGD; information about SGD and staff │
│                                                              │
│                                                              │
│                                                              │
│  Search SGD | Virtual Library | Help | Gene Registry | Maps  │
│  BLAST | FASTA | Sacch3D | Design Primers                    │
│                                                              │
│                                                              │
│ ┌───────────────────────────┐                               │
│ -- press space for next page --                              │
│  Arrow keys: Up and Down to move. Right to follow a link; Left to go back. │
│  H)elp O)ptions P)rint G)o M)ain screen Q)uit /=search [delete]=history list │
│ ⇦                                                         ⇨ ▣ │
└─────────────────────────────────────────────────────────────┘
```

(b)

Figure 1.6 *(Continued).*

members of an organization are physically separated, whether in different buildings or different cities. Intranets are protected: that is, people who are not on the organization's network are prohibited from accessing the internal Web pages; additional protection through the use of passwords is also common.

Finding Information

Most people find information on the Web the old-fashioned way: by word of mouth, either using lists such as those preceding the References in the chapters of this book or by simply following hyperlinks put in place by Web authors. Continuously clicking from page to page can be a highly ineffective way of finding information, though, especially when the information sought is of a very focused nature. One way of finding interesting and relevant Web sites is to consult *virtual libraries,* which are curated lists of Web resources arranged by subject. Virtual libraries of special interest to biologists include the WWW Virtual Library, maintained by Keith Robison at Harvard; Pedro's Biomolecular Research

Tools, compiled by Pedro Coutinho at Iowa State; and the EBI BioCatalog, based at the European Bioinformatics Institute. The URLs for these sites can be found in the list at the end of this chapter.

It is also possible to directly search the Web by using *search engines.* A search engine is simply a specialized program that can perform full-text or keyword searches on databases that catalog Web content. The result of a search is a hyperlinked list of Web sites fitting the search criteria; the user can visit any or all of the sites identified directly from the search program. However, the search engines use slightly different methods in compiling their databases. Variations include attempting to either visit and read in data from all Web sites ("Web crawling"). Some search engines catalog only the titles of Web pages rather than the entire text of each one; some consider a phrase to be words that must appear next to each other, whereas others will pick out the words if they are only relatively close together. Because of these differences in search engine algorithms, the results returned by issuing the same query to a number of different search engines can vary greatly (Table 1.3); pay particular attention to the Yahoo results on querying `genetic mapping` as compared to the rest. The other important feature of Table 1.3 is that most of the numbers are exceedingly large, reflecting the overall size of the World Wide Web. Unless a particular search engine ranks its results by relevance (e.g., by scoring words in a title higher than words in the body of the Web page), the results obtained may not be particularly useful.

To address this point, a new class of search engines called *meta-search engines* have been developed. These programs, which take a more intelligent approach to Web discovery, act on the user's query by polling anywhere from five to ten of the "traditional" search engines. The meta-search engine then collects the results, filters out duplicates, and returns a single, annotated list to the user. One big advantage is that the meta-search engines take relevance statistics into account, returning much smaller lists of results (Table 1.3). Even though the hit list is substantially smaller, it is much more likely to contain sites that directly address the original query. Since the programs must poll a number of different search engines, searches conducted this way obviously take longer to perform, but the higher degree of confidence in the usefulness of the compiled results for a given query outweighs the extra few minutes (sometimes only seconds) of search time. Reliable and easy-to-use meta-search engines include SavvySearch and MetaCrawler.

A second solution to the overwhelming number of hits returned by search engines is to simply reduce the size of the search set. Several specialized search engines have emerged that cover Web sites in a particular area only. While no such engine has been introduced for the biological sciences as of this writing, examples of popular niche search engines include LookSmart, which is a service of the *Reader's Digest* and applies that organization's knack for condensation to defined interest areas on the Web.

TABLE 1.3 Number of Hits Returned for Four Defined Search Queries on Some of the More Popular Search and Meta-Search Engines

Search Term	Search Engine					Meta-Search Engine	
	Magellan	Excite	Yahoo	Infoseek	Lycos	MetaCrawler	SavvySearch
genetic mapping	40,934	16,396	1	6,307	24,515	40	22
human genome	9,678	26,364	31	11,484	48,146	44	40
positional cloning	4,886	955	808	550	9,385	38	88
prostate cancer	24,470	16,194	27	7,457	14,768	48	109

World Wide Web Sites for Topics in Chapter 1

ELECTRONIC MAIL

Eudora	*http://www.eudora.com*
Microsoft Exchange	*http://www.microsoft.com/exchange/eval.html*

FILE TRANSFER PROTOCOL

Fetch 3.0/Mac	*http://www.dartmouth.edu/pages/softdev/fetch.html*

GOPHER

Gopher User's Guide	*ftp://boombox.micro.umn.edu/pub/gopher/docs*
TurboGopher	*http://boombox.micro.umn.edu/hh/gopher/*

INTERNET ACCESS

America Online	*http://www.aol.com*
AT&T	*http://www.att.com/worldnet*
ClarkNet	*http://www.clark.net*
CompuServe	*http://www.compuserve.com*
MCI	*http://www.mci.com*
Prodigy	*http://www.prodigy.com*

VIRTUAL LIBRARIES

EBI BioCatalog	*http://www.ebi.ac.uk/biocat/biocat.html*
Molecular Biology E-mail servers	*ftp://expasy.hcuge.ch/databases/info/serv_ema.txt*
Molecular Biology FTP servers	*ftp://expasy.hcuge.ch/databases/info/serv_ftp.txt*
WWW Virtual Library	*http://www.golgi.harvard.edu/biopages/all.html*
Pedro's Biomolecular Research Tools	*http://www.public.iastate.edu/~pedro/*

WORLD WIDE WEB BROWSERS

Internet Explorer	*http://www.microsoft.com/ie*
Lynx	*ftp://ftp.cc.ukans.edu/pub/WWW*
Netscape Navigator	*http://home.netscape.com*

WORLD WIDE WEB SEARCH ENGINES

LookSmart	*http://www.looksmart.com*
Netscape Search Page	*http://home.netscape.com/home/internet-search.html*
MetaCrawler	*http://metacrawler.cs.washington.edu*
Savvy Search	*http://guaraldi.cs.colostate.edu:2000/form*

REFERENCES

Blundon, W. (1996). Off the charts: The internet 1996. *Internet World.*

Falk, B. (1994). *The Internet Roadmap* (San Francisco: Sybex).

Froehlich, F., and Kent, A. (1991). ARPANET, the Defense Data Network, and Internet. In *Encyclopedia of Communications* (New York: Marcel Dekker).

Krol, E. (1994). *The Whole Internet User's Guide and Catalog* (Sebastopol, CA: O'Reilly and Associates).

Lamb, L., and Peek, J. (1995). *Using E-Mail Effectively* (Sebastopol, CA: O'Reilly & Associates).

Quarterman, J. (1990). *The Matrix: Computer Networks and Conferencing Systems Worldwide* (Bedford, MA: Digital Press).

2

The GenBank Sequence Database

B. F. Francis Ouellette

National Center for Biotechnology Information
National Library of Medicine
National Institutes of Health
Bethesda, Maryland

INTRODUCTION

Primary protein and nucleic acids sequence databases are so pervasive to our way of thinking in molecular biology that few of us think of how these ubiquitous tools are built. Understanding how the products of these sequences are put together will allow us to move forward in our understanding of biology and to fully harvest the abstracted information present in these records.

GenBank® is the NIH genetic sequence database, an annotated collection of all publicly available nuclcotide and protein sequences. The unit records represent single, contiguous stretches of DNA or RNA with annotations. The files are grouped in divisions: some are phylogenetically derived, while others are based on the technical approach that was used to generate the sequence information. Presently all records in GenBank are generated from direct submissions to the DNA sequence databases from the original authors, who volunteer their records as part of their publication process or to make the data publicly available. GenBank, which is built by the National Center for Biotechnology Information at NIH in Bethesda, Maryland, is part of the International Nucleotide Sequence Database Collaboration, along with its two partners, the DNA Database of Japan (DDBJ, Mishima, Japan) and the European Molecular Biology Laboratory (EMBL) nucleotide database from the European Bioinformatics Institute (EBI, Hinxton, England). All three centers are separate points of data submission, but all are exchanging this information daily, and making the same

Bioinformatics: A Practical Guide to the Analysis of Genes and Proteins
Edited by A.D. Baxevanis and B.F.F. Ouellette
ISBN 0-471-19196-5, pages 16–45.   Copyright © 1998 Wiley-Liss, Inc.

database (albeit in slightly different format, and with different information systems) available to the community at large.

This chapter describes how the GenBank database is structured, how it fits into the realm of the protein databases, and how to fully interpret the various components. Numerous works have dealt with the topic of sequence databases (Schuler et al., 1996; Bairoch and Apweiller, 1997; Benson et al., 1997; George et al., 1997; Stoesser et al., 1997; Tateno et al., 1997). All these publications indicate the great rate at which the databases have grown and suggest various ways of using such biological resources. From a practical scientific point of view, as well as from a historical perspective, the sequence data has been separated into protein and nucleotide databases. The nucleotides are the primary entry points to the databases for both protein and nucleotide sequences, and there appears to be a migration toward having the nucleotide databases also involved in managing the protein data sets (as we will see below). This is not a surprising development, since clearly ongoing communication with submitters at a time of great receptiveness to the databases (since submitters want an accession number, and they want their new records in the databases) can help to ensure the validity and accuracy of the data. In many cases, such attention to the data means that the appropriate information will be present to annotate the CDS (coding sequences) feature, which tells how a translation product can be obtained. This trend of comanagement of protein and nucleotide sequences is apparent with NCBI's Entrez, and the management of GenBank and the formatting of records in the GenPept format, and also

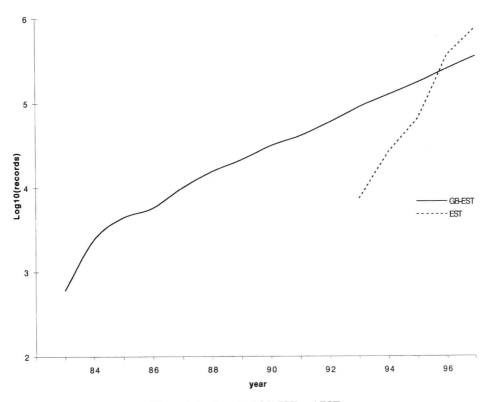

Figure 2.1   Growth of GB-EST and EST.

on the European side, where Swiss-Prot and TREMBL are being comanaged and created by the people at EBI, who also manage the EMBL nucleotide databases, and Amos Bairoch and his group at the University of Geneva (see end-of-chapter list). Nonetheless, the beginning of each database set is distinct. Implicit in the discussion of this chapter is also the underlying data model described in Chapter 6. This chapter is about the GenBank flatfile (GBFF) view of the sequence data, but it should be clear that the "flatfile view" (be it GenBank, EMBL, Swiss-Prot, or PIR) shows only one dimension, a report on a view of the ASN.1, which is the language in which the NCBI data model is represented. GenBank, a DNA-centric view of this information, represents the reference point for many resources in computational biology.

Historically, the protein databases preceded the nucleotide databases. In the early 1960s Dayhoff and colleagues collected all the known amino acid sequences which led to *the Atlas of Protein Sequences and Structures* (Dayhoff et al., 1965). This protein database eventually led to the PIR (George *et al.*, 1997). In this printed book lay the seed to the resources the entire bioinformatics community now depends on for day-to-day work in computational biology. A data set, which in 1965 could easily reside on a single floppy disk (although these did not then exist as we know them today), represented years of work from a small group of people. Today, this amount of data can be generated in a fraction of a day in any one of the DNA or protein sequence databases. The advent of the DNA sequence databases in 1982, initiated by the European Molecular Biology Laboratory (EMBL), led to the next phase, one of the database explosion (Figure 2.1). The history of this period has been described in detail in *Gene Wars* by R. Cook-Deegan (1993), a narrative on the history of the Human Genome Project. Soon thereafter joined by GenBank (then, through a contract from NIH to Los Alamos National Laboratory), both centers were contributing to the input activity, which consisted mainly of transcribing what was published in the printed journals to an electronic format more appropriate for use with computers. The DNA Data-Base of Japan (DDBJ) joined the collaboration in data collecting a few years later. In 1988, following a meeting of these three groups (now referred to as the "International Collaboration of DNA Sequence Databases"), there was an agreement to use a common format for data elements within a unit record and to have each database update only the records that were submitted to it. Now all three centers are collecting direct submissions and distributing them among themselves, so that any one center will have all the sequences, and can act as the primary distribution center for all sequences. In this way each record is owned by the database that created it. This means that an update can be done only by the database that created the record, preventing the "update clashes" that are bound to occur when any database can update any record, overwriting the work of the other databases. The arrangement that has been in place for the last few years ensures that no database will overwrite the updates performed by any other. All the sequence databases are also computational biology centers, and it has become clear that the sequence data cannot simply be generated by automated means. Each database has become a center where sequence data are generated and proofread by biologists, and where tools are developed to harness this information (*e.g.*, Entrez from NCBI, see Chapter 5 and SRS now developed at EBI). It has become critically clear that the user community is best served by stable agencies that are involved in gathering the data, providing tools for discoveries and retrieval, and serving as research institutes where new algorithms are studied, public databases are mined, and science is performed at the highest standard. In such environments knowledge is gained and shared with the highest efficiency, and new ways to study and understand this vast amount of data unfold.

Although this chapter is about the GenBank nucleotide database, GenBank is part of a community of databases that includes three important protein databases: Swiss-Prot, the Protein Information Resource (PIR) database, and the Protein DataBase (PDB). Each has, or has had, an important impact on the way databases have been used, and in the way they will be used in the years to come. PDB, the database of nucleic acid and protein structures is extensively described in Chapter 3. Swiss-Prot and PIR can be called secondary databases: databases which add value to what is already present in primary database. Both Swiss-Prot and PIR take the majority of their protein sequences from nucleotide databases. A small proportion of sequences is directly submitted to Swiss-Prot (when the protein is sequenced directly) or is processed via a journal scanning effort, where the sequence is taken directly from the published literature. Although these cases are not dealt with here, the reader is invited to learn about them elsewhere (Bairoch and Apweiller, 1997; George et al., 1997).

It is important to note that as in Chapters 6 and 14, "GenBank" as used here means DDBJ/EMBL/GenBank. The DDBJ and EMBL nucleic acid databases and GenBank work in close collaboration, exchanging data daily. They represent different distribution points for the same information, in different formats. They are also the product of institutions that provide other data, tools, and services, which are in theory unrelated activities, but in practice difficult to unweb from other projects. For example, Entrez (see Chapter 5) is an NCBI project that has GenBank data in it, but Entrez and GenBank (both NCBI products) are very different entities, the former being an information retrieval system and the latter a database on which Entrez draws.

PRIMARY AND SECONDARY DATABASES

An important distinction exists between primary (archival) and secondary (curated) databases. The most important contribution of the sequence databases to the scientific community is comprised of the sequences themselves. The primary databases represent experimental results with some interpretation but not a curated review, which is what may be found in the secondary databases. The primary database record is the sequence as it was experimentally derived, and this is what the nucleotide records represent. These records are the results of sequencing a biological molecule that exists in a test tube, somewhere in a lab. They do not represent consensus sequences (albeit from multiple reads of the same clone, or same genomic origin), nor do they represent some other computer-generated string of letters. This framework has consequences in the interpretation of sequence analysis. It also means that in most cases all a researcher needs is a given sequence. Each such DNA and RNA sequence will be annotated to describe the analysis from experimental results that indicate why a sequence was determined in the first place.

One common type of annotation on a DNA sequence record is the coding sequence (CDS). The great majority of the protein sequences are not experimentally determined, but rather inferred from a DNA sequence, presenting a great amount of scope with respect to experimental, computational, and similarity interpretations. This is in parallel to the assignment (via a subjective interpretation of a similarity analysis) of a product name or function qualifier, which can be very useful, but sometimes misleading. The DNA, RNA, or protein sequences are the items to be computed on and worked with. These are the valuable components of the primary databases.

Those who compute, analyze, or simply work with DNA sequence records generally assume that they are dealing with primary information. In many cases, however, amino acid sequences are the result of some level of interpretation; they are rarely sequenced themselves. Thus great care is needed in the use and interpretation of results derived from these sequences. The interpretation of a protein sequence is usually not too difficult from mRNA sequence data, but it is essential to choose the correct initiation codon. Interpretation is also relatively simple for prokaryotic sequences or those from lower eukaryotes, but again investigators must pay attention to avoid missing or overinterpreting the data (see Chapter 10 and Cannon et al., 1997). A CDS feature on a nucleotide sequence should always be made carefully, because this is the starting material for automated or semiautomated inclusion of these amino acid sequences in the protein databases.

FORMAT VS. CONTENT: COMPUTERS VS. HUMANS

Database records are used to hold the raw data, as well as an array of ancillary annotations. Different tools and programs use different parts of these information components. In a survey of the various formats, we can observe that different sets of rules are applied, making it possible in many cases to generate and interchange data among formats. The best format for a human to read may not be the most efficient for a computer program (e.g., the GenBank flatfile, see Appendix 2.1 vs. Appendix 2.2, a human-readable version of the ASN.1). There is also a binary version of these records, which is more compact and faster for computers to read. Unfortunately, history has taken its toll, and extensive use of a given format makes it difficult to introduce biologists to alternative views that offer greater informational content, more accurate, reproducible computations, extraction of information, and higher performance. (But we are trying: see Chapters 3, 6, and 14). The simplicity of the GBFF, which does lend itself to simple tools that are available to all, is in great part responsible for the popularity of the EMBL (Appendix 2.3) and GenBank (Appendix 2.1) flat file formats.

In its simplest form, a DNA sequence record can be represented as a string of nucleotides with some tag or identifier. Here is a nucleotide file as represented in a FASTA (or Pearson format) file:

```
>L04459
GCAGCGCACGACAGCTGTGCTATCCCGGCGAGCCCGTGGCAGAGGACCTCGCTTGCGAAAGCATCGAGTACC
GCTACAGAGCCAACCCGGTGGACAAACTCGAAGTCATTGTGGACCGAATGAGGCTCAATAACGAGATTAGCG
ACCTCGAAGGCCTGCGCAAATATTTCCACTCCTTCCCGGGTGCTCCTGAGTTGAACCCGCTTAGAGACTCCG
AAATCAACGACGACTTCCACCAGTGGGCCCAGTGTGACCGCCACACTGGACCCCATACCACTTCTTTTTGTT
ATTCTTAAATATGTTGTAACGCTATGTAATTCCACCCTTCATTACTAATAATTAGCCATTCACGTGATCTCA
GCCAGTTGTGGCGCCACACTTTTTTTTTCCATAAAAATCCTCGAGGAAAAGAAAAGAAAAAAATATTTCAGTT
ATTTAAAGCATAAGATGCCAGGTAGATGGAACTTGTGCCGTGCCAGATTGAATTTTGAAAGTACAATTGAGG
CCTATACACATAGACATTTGCACCTTATACATATAC
```

Or in a similar way for a protein record:

```
>P31373
MTLQESDKFATKAIHAGEHVDVHGSVIEPISLSTTFKQSSPANPIGTYEYSRSQNPNRENLERAVAALENAQ
YGLAFSSGSATTATILQSLPQGSHAVSIGDVYGGTHRYFTKVANAHGVETSFTNDLLNDLPQLIKENTKLVW
```

```
IETPTNPTLKVTDIQKVADLIKKHAAGQDVILVVDNTFLSPYISNPLNFGADIVVHSATKYINGHSDVVLGV
LATNNKPLYERLQFLQNAIGAIPSPFDAWLTHRGLKTLHLRVRQAALSANKIAEFLAADKENVVAVNYPGLK
THPNYDVVLKQHRDALGGGMISFRIKGGAEAASKFASSTRLFTLAESLGGIESLLEVPAVMTHGGIPKEARA
SGVFDDLVRISVGIEDTDDLLEDIKQALKQATN
```

The FASTA format is used in a variety of molecular biology software suites. In its simplest incarnation (as shown above) the "greater than" character (>) designates the beginning of a new file. An identifier—L04459 in the first of the preceding examples—is followed by the DNA sequence in lowercase or uppercase letters, usually with 60 characters per line (but this is not standard). Users and databases can then, if they wish, add complexity and structure to this format. For example, without breaking any of the rules just outlined, one could add more information to the FASTA definition line, making the simple format a little more informative, as follows:

```
>|171361|gb|L04459|YSCCYS3A Saccharomyces cerevisiae cystathionine
 gamma-lyase (CYS3) gene, complete cds.
GCAGCGCACGACAGCTGTGCTATCCCGGCGAGCCCGTGGCAGAGGACCTCGCTTGCGAAAGCATCGAGTACC
GCTACAGAGCCAACCCGGTGGACAAACTCGAAGTCATTGTGGACCGAATGAGGCTCAATAACGAGATTAGCG
ACCTCGAAGGCCTGCGCAAATATTTCCACTCCTTCCCGGGTGCTCCTGAGTTGAACCCGCTTAGAGACTCCG
AAATCAACGACGACTTCCACCAGTGGGCCCAGTGTGACCGCCACACTGGACCCCATACCACTTCTTTTTGTT
ATTCTTAAATATGTTGTAACGCTATGTAATTCCACCCTTCATTACTAATAATTAGCCATTCACGTGATCTCA
GCCAGTTGTGGCGCCACACTTTTTTTTTCCATAAAAATCCTCGAGGAAAAGAAAAGAAAAAAATATTTCAGTT
ATTTAAAGCATAAGATGCCAGGTAGATGGAACTTGTGCCGTGCCAGATTGAATTTTGAAAGTACAATTGAGG
CCTATACACATAGACATTTGCACCTTATACATATAC
```

This FASTA file now has the gi number (see below and Chapter 6), the GenBank accession number, the LOCUS name, and the DEFINITION line from the GenBank record. The record was passed from the ASN.1 record (see Appendix 2.2), which NCBI uses to store and maintain all its data. (Note that this data is stored on the computer in a single line that, if printed out, would be wider than the page of this book; hence the line break above.)

Over the years many formats have been in use; few have persisted. Tools exist to convert the sequence itself into the minimalist view of one format or another. NCBI's asn2ff will convert an ASN.1 file into a variety of flatfiles. The asn2ff (ASN.1 to Flat File) program will generate GenBank, EMBL, GenPept, Swiss-Prot, and FASTA formats and is available from the NCBI Toolkit (see Chapter 6). READSEQ from Don Gilbert (see the end-of-chapter list of Internet resources) is another tool that has been widely used and incorporated into many work environments. Users should be aware that the features from a Gen-Bank or EMBL format are lost when passed through such utilities. READSEQ works on the sequence itself, not the annotations. Programs that need only the sequence (e.g., BLAST, see Chapter 7) are best used with a FASTA format for the query sequence. Although less informative than other formats, the FASTA format offers a simple way of dealing with the primary data in a human- and computer-readable fashion.

THE DATABASE

As mentioned above, all sequences present in EMBL are also present in DDBJ and Gen-Bank, and this is true in all directions. GenBank is released on a bimonthly schedule with incremental (and nonincremental) daily updates available by anonymous FTP. The nucleotide databases also exchange new and updated record data daily and rely on a common data format of information described in the Feature table documentation (see below), which represents the *lingua franca* of the nucleotide sequence database annotations. Together the nucleotide sequence databases have developed the submission procedure (see Chapter 14), a series of guidelines for the content, and a format of records (see Internet resources at end of chapter).

The nucleotide records are the primary source of sequence and biological information. Most protein sequences in the protein databases are derived from nucleic acid database records. This has two important consequences:

1. If a coding sequence is not indicated on a nucleic acid record, it will not show in the protein databases. Thus, since querying the protein databases is the most sensitive way of doing similarity discoveries (Chapter 7), failure to indicate the CDS intervals on an mRNA or genomic sequence of interest (when one should be present) may cause important discoveries to be missed.

2. Unfortunately, the set of features usable in the nucleotide Feature table documentation that are specific to protein sequences is limited, as indicated in the list at the end of the chapter.

THE GENBANK FLATFILE: A DISSECTION

The GenBank flatfile (GBFF) is the unit of information in the GenBank database. It is one of the most commonly used formats in the representation of biological sequences. At the time of this writing, it is the format of exchange from GenBank to DDBJ and the EMBL databases and the way the EMBL or DDBJ exchange their flat files to other databases. The DDBJ flatfile format and the GBFF format are now identical (Appendix 2.1). The EMBL uses line type prefixes, which indicate the type of information present in the record (Appendix 2.3). The feature section (see below), prefixed with "FT," is identical in content to the other databases. All these formats are really reports from what is represented in a much more structured way in the ASN.1 (Appendix 2.2). Mainly for historical reasons, however, the GBFF (and EMBL flatfiles) are engraved in the way many users (expert and nonexpert) work.

The GBFF can be separated into three parts. The header contains the information (descriptors) that apply to the whole record. The second part comprises the features that describe the annotations on the record, and the third part is the nucleotide sequence itself. All nucleotide database records (DDBJ/EMBL/GenBank) end with // on the last line of the record.

The Header

The header is the most database-specific part of the record. The various databases are not obliged to carry the same information in this segment, and minor variations exist, but some effort is made to ensure that the same information is carried from one to the other.

All GenBank flatfiles start with a LOCUS line[1]:

[1] Note that all the items in the GBFF have specific positions. These are explained in excruciating detail in the GenBank release notes (see end-of-chapter Internet resources). The boxes and rulers shown in the illustrations in this section are not part of the record. A ruler indicates the position of the described items in the GBFF report.

```
1       10        20        30        40        50        60        70      79
--------+---------+---------+---------+---------+---------+---------+---------

LOCUS      |AF010325|   3291 bp    DNA            INV       08-JUL-1997
```

The first element on this line is the LOCUS name. This historically was a term representing the Locus that was the subject of the record, and submitters and database staff spent
considerable time in devising it. This element has to start with a letter, and its length cannot exceed 10 characters. Characters after the first can be numerical or alphabetic, and all
letters are uppercase. The LOCUS name was most useful back when most DNA sequence
records represented only one genetic locus, and it was simple to find in GenBank a unique
name that could represent the biology of the organism in a few letters and numbers. Classic examples include HUMHBB for the human β-globin locus, or SV40 for the Simian
virus (one of the copies anyway; there are many). To be usable, the LOCUS name needs
to be unique within the database, and since virtually all the meaningful designators have
been taken, the LOCUS name is past its time as a useful format element. Because so many
software packages rely on the presence of a unique LOCUS name, the databases have
been reluctant to remove it altogether, however. The preferred path has been to instead put
a unique word, and the simplest way to do this has been to use an accession number of
ensured uniqueness: AF010325 in the following example conforms to the Locus name
requirement.

```
1       10        20        30        40        50        60        70      79
--------+---------+---------+---------+---------+---------+---------+---------

LOCUS      AF010325   |3291 bp|    DNA            INV       08-JUL-1997
```

The next item on the LOCUS line is the length of the sequence: from 1 to 350,000 base
pairs. In practice GenBank and the other databases seldom accept records shorter than
50 bp. Therefore inclusion of PCR primers as sequences (i.e., submissions of 24 bp) is discouraged. The 350 kb limit is a practical one, and the various databases represent longer
contigs in a variety of ways (see Chapters 6 and 12 and Appendix 2.4).

```
1       10        20        30        40        50        60        70      79
--------+---------+---------+---------+---------+---------+---------+---------

LOCUS      AF010325   3291 bp    |DNA|            INV       08-JUL-1997
```

The next item on the LOCUS line indicates the molecule type. The "mol type" usually is
DNA or RNA, although a few variants are represented, and it also indicates the stranded-
ness (single or double: ss or ds), although these attributes are rarely used these days
(another historical leftover). The types are: DNA, RNA, tRNA, rRNA, mRNA, and uRNA,
representing the original biological molecule. For example, a cDNA that is sequenced
really represents an mRNA, and mRNA is the indicated mol type for such a sequence. If
the tRNA or rRNA has been sequenced directly or via some cDNA intermediate, then
tRNA or rRNA is the mol type. If the sequence was obtained via the polymerase chain
reaction from genomic data, then DNA is the mol type, even if the sequence encodes a
structural RNA.

```
1         10        20        30        40        50        60        70        79
---------+---------+---------+---------+---------+---------+---------+----------

LOCUS       AF010325    3291 bp    DNA              [INV]      08-JUL-1997
```

The next item is the GenBank division code: three letters, which have either taxonomic inferences or other classification purposes. Again these codes exist for historical reasons, recalling the time when the various GenBank divisions were used to break up the databases files into what was then a more manageable size. The GenBank divisions are slightly different from those of EMBL or DDBJ, as described elsewhere (Ouellette and Boguski, 1997). Again these divisions are very arbitrary, historical in purpose, and of much less use they used to be, since the taxonomic information is better represented in the Organism lines and the source features than in a three-letter division code. NCBI has not introduced additional organism-based divisions in quite a few years, but new, function-based divisions have been very useful because they represent functional and definable differences (Ouellette and Boguski, 1997). The Expressed Sequence Tags (EST) division was introduced in 1993 (Boguski et al., 1993), and soon followed by the division for Sequence Tagged Sites (STS). These, along with the Genome Survey Sequences (GSS) and the unfinished High Throughput Genome sequences (HTG), represent functional categories that need to be dealt with by the users and the database staff in very different ways. For example, a user can query within these data sets (e.g., via a BLASTN search against the EST or HTG division), and having one of these as an identified hit allows one to interpret the data accordingly. At this time, all databases interpret the various functional divisions in the same way, and all data sets are represented in the same division from one database to the next. The CON division, a new experimental division, being planned at the time of writing, will be for constructed (or contigged) records and will represent all segmented sets as well as all large assemblies, which may exceed (sometimes quite extensively) the 350,000 bp limit presently imposed on single records. Such records may take the form shown in Appendix 2.4. This record from the CON division gives the complete genomic sequence of *Escherichia coli,* which is more than 4.6 million base pairs in length. This CON record does not include sequences or annotations, but rather instructions on how to assemble pieces present in other divisions into larger or assembled pieces. Records within this experimental division will have accession and version numbers and will be exchanged, like all other records within the collaboration. All segmented sets will also be represented in this division.

```
1         10        20        30        40        50        60        70        79
---------+---------+---------+---------+---------+---------+---------+---------

LOCUS       AF010325    3291 bp    DNA              INV       [08-JUL-1997]
```

The date on the LOCUS line is the date the record was last made public. In many cases this is also the date it was first made public. Another date contained in the record is the date the record was submitted (see below) to the database. It should be noted that none of these dates are legally binding on the promulgating organization. The databases make no claim that the dates are error-free; they are included as guides to users and should not be submitted in any arbitration dispute. To the author's knowledge, they have never been used in establishing priority and publication dates for patent application.

```
1         10        20        30        40        50        60        70        79
---------+---------+---------+---------+---------+---------+---------+---------
```

```
DEFINITION  Drosophila melanogaster CHIP (Chip) gene, complete cds.
```

The DEFINITION line (also referred to as the "DEF line") is the line in the GenBank record that attempts to summarize the biology of the record. This is the line that will appear in the FASTA files that NCBI generates, and is therefore the information seen by anyone performing a BLAST similarity search (Chapter 7). Much care is taken in the generation of these lines, and while many of them can be partially automated, the database staff still checks to make sure that consistency and richness of information are maintained. Nonetheless, it is not always possible to capture all the biology in a single line of text, and various databases cope in a variety of ways. There are some agreements, and the various databases are aware of each other's guidelines and try to conform to them. Here is a summary of the standard DEFINITION lines construction scheme. For an mRNA we have:

```
Genus species product name (gene symbol) mRNA, complete cds.
```

or for a genomic record:

```
Genus species product name (gene symbol) gene, complete cds.
```

Of course records of many other types are accounted for by the guidelines used by the various databases. The following set of rules, however, applies to organelle sequences, and these rules are used to ensure that the biology and source of the DNA are clear to the user and to the database staff (assuming they are clear to the submitter):

```
DEFINITION  Genus species protein X (xxx) gene, [one choice from below],
complete cds.
        , nuclear gene encoding mitochondrial protein,
        , nuclear gene encoding chloroplast protein,
        , mitochondrial gene encoding mitochondrial protein,
        , chloroplast gene encoding chloroplast protein,        OR
```

```
DEFINITION  Genus species XXS ribosomal RNA gene, [one choice from below],
complete sequence.
        , mitochondrial gene for mitochondrial RNA,
        , chloroplast gene for chloroplast RNA,
```

In accordance with a recent agreement among the collaborative databases, the full genus–species names are given in the Definition lines; common names (e.g., human) or abbreviated genus names (e.g., H.sapiens for *Homo sapiens*) are no longer used. The many records in the database that precede this agreement will eventually be updated. One organism has escaped this agreement: the human immunodeficiency virus is to be represented in the DEFINITION line as HIV1 and HIV2.

```
1        10        20        30        40        50        60        70        79
---------+---------+---------+---------+---------+---------+---------+---------
```

```
ACCESSION    AF010325
```

The accession number, on the third line type of the record, represents the primary key to reference a given record in the database (see Chapter 6). This is the number that is cited in publications and will stay with this sequence; that is, if the sequence is updated (e.g., by changing a single nucleotide), the accession number will not change. At this time accession numbers exist in one of two formats: the 1 + 5 and 2 + 6 varieties, where 1 + 5 indicates one uppercase letter followed by five digits, while 2 + 6 is two letters plus six digits. Most of the new records now entering the databases are of the latter variety. All GenBank records have only a single line with the word ACCESSION on it, while there may be more than one accession number. The vast majority of records only have one accession number. This number is always referred to as the primary accession number; all others are secondary.

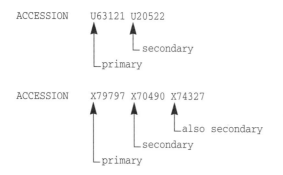

Unfortunately secondary accession numbers have meant a variety of things over the years, and no single definition applies. The secondary accession number may be related to the primary one, or the primary accession number may be a replacement for the secondary, which no longer exists. There is an ongoing effort within the Collaboration to make the latter the default for all cases, but since secondary accession numbers have been used for more than 15 years (a period during which the management of GenBank changed), all data needed to elucidate all cases is not available.

```
1        10        20        30        40        50        60        70        79
---------+---------+---------+---------+---------+---------+---------+---------
```

```
NID        g2245686
```

The NID line represents the gi (geninfo identifier) number for the nucleotide sequence (see Chapter 6). The prefix letter (d, e, or g) indicates which database issued the number, or the database from which it was used. Since NCBI was the first to use these numbers, DDBJ and EMBL primed their databases with numbers already assigned by NCBI (GenBank). Simply put, a gi number represents a unique identifier associated with a unique sequence, and in this case to a nucleotide sequence (protein sequences also have gi numbers: see below and Chapter 6). If the sequence changes, the gi will change, but the accession number will stay the same.

By the time this book is in print there will be a third type of identifier. The collaborative databases have agreed to issue version numbers associated with the version of the sequence (like the NID, or gi). The format will be: Accession.version. For example:

```
1        10        20        30        40        50        60        70        79
---------+---------+---------+---------+---------+---------+---------+---------


ACCESSION   AF010325
NID         g2245686
VERSION     AF010325.1   GI: 2245686
```

This represents version 1 of the sequence having accession number AF010325 and gi number 2245686. At the time of writing it had not been determined which line of type should carry this identifier, but it will positioned below the ACCESSION line and the NID line; the VERSION line (as shown above) is a likely candidate. Reference to the GenBank release notes will ensure the appraisal of the latest information of this new change. The version number of this new identifier will increment by one each time the sequence changes, the same way the gi changes (although not by one, but to the next available integer). The identifier-formatted Accession.number will assume the very same task presently performed by the accession number/gi number (on the NID line) pair. It should not be a surprise that this Accession.version will eventually replace the NID line in the GBFF. The Accession line will not be replaced (in the foreseeable future) because of its loaded historical values and because of all the secondary numbers also present, indicating some history.

```
1        10        20        30        40        50        60        70        79
---------+---------+---------+---------+---------+---------+---------+---------


KEYWORDS    .
```

The KEYWORDS is another interesting historical relic that is, in many cases, unfortunately misused. Adding keywords to one's records is often not very useful because over the years so many authors have selected words not on a list of controlled vocabulary and not uniformly applied to the whole database. Thus, NCBI discourages the use of keywords, but is happy to include them on request, especially if they include words not present elsewhere in the record or are used in a controlled fashion (e.g., for EST, STS, GSS, and HTG records). At this time, the resistance to adding keywords is a matter of policy at NCBI/GenBank only.

```
1        10        20        30        40        50        60        70        79
---------+---------+---------+---------+---------+---------+---------+---------


SOURCE      fruit fly.
ORGANISM    Drosophila melanogaster
            Eukaryotae; mitochondrial eukaryotes; Metazoa; Arthropoda;
            Tracheata; Hexapoda; Insecta; Pterygota; Diptera; Brachycera;
            Muscomorpha; Ephydroidea; Drosophilidae; Drosophila.
```

The SOURCE line will either have the common name for the organism or its scientific name. In some cases other source information (see below) also is present. A concerted effort is now under way to assure that all other information present in the source feature (as opposed to the SOURCE line), and all lines in the taxonomy block (SOURCE and ORGANISMS lines), can be derived from what is in the source feature and the taxonomy server at NCBI. Those interested in the lineage and other aspects of the taxonomy are encouraged to visit the Taxonomy home page at NCBI (see end-of-chapter list). This taxonomy is used by all nucleotide sequence databases, as well as Swiss-Prot, the protein database.

```
1        10       20        30        40        50        60        70        79
---------+---------+---------+---------+---------+---------+---------+---------+---------

REFERENCE   1  (bases 1 to 3291)
  AUTHORS   Morcillo, P., Rosen, C., Baylies, M.K. and Dorsett, D.
  TITLE     CHIP, a widely expressed chromosomal protein required for remote
            enhancer activity and segmentation in Drosophila
  JOURNAL   Unpublished
```

Each GenBank record must have a least one reference, or citation. In many cases it will have two, as shown in Appendix 2.1. The preceding sample indicates an unpublished paper (which could be "submitted") and is a placeholder for a publication, should there ever be one. It offers scientific credit and sets a context explaining why this particular sequence was determined. When a reference is published, usually a MEDLINE identifier will be present, as in the following example, providing the link to the MEDLINE/PubMed databases (see Chapter 5).

```
1        10       20        30        40        50        60        70        79
---------+---------+---------+---------+---------+---------+---------+---------+---------

REFERENCE   1  (bases 1 to 3240)
  AUTHORS   Manolson, M.F., Wu, B., Proteau, D., Taillon, B.E., Roberts, B.T.,
            Hoyt, M.A. and Jones, E.W.
  TITLE     STV1 gene encodes functional homologue of 95-kDa yeast vacuolar
            H(+)-ATPase subunit Vph1p
  JOURNAL   J. Biol. Chem. 269 (19), 14064-14074 (1994)
  MEDLINE   94245725
  PUBMED    7514599
```

In late 1998, a new line was introduced with its own identifier, PUBMED, allowing linkage to the PubMed database and publisher's version of the online full-text article. (see Chapter 5).

```
1        10       20        30        40        50        60        70        79
---------+---------+---------+---------+---------+---------+---------+---------+---------

REFERENCE   2  (bases 1 to 3291)
  AUTHORS   Morcillo, P., Rosen, C., Baylies, M.K. and Dorsett, D.
  TITLE     Direct Submission
  JOURNAL   Submitted (19-JUN-1997) Molecular Biology Program, Memorial
            Sloan-Kettering Cancer Center, 1275 York Avenue, New York, NY
            10021, USA
```

The last citation is present on most GenBank records and gives scientific credit to the people responsible for the work surrounding the submitted sequence. It usually includes the postal address of the first author, or the main lab where the work was done. The date represents the date the record was submitted to the database, but not the date on which the data were first made public, which is the date on the LOCUS line (see above) if the record was not updated.

The last part of the header section in the GBFF is the Comment. This section includes a great variety of notes and comments (also called "descriptors") that refer to the whole record. Genome centers like to include their coordinates in this segment, and give acknowledgments. This segment is missing from most records in GenBank, and is optional. They may also include e-mail addresses or URLs, but this practice is discouraged at NCBI (although certain exceptions have been made for genome centers as mentioned above). The simple reason is that e-mail addresses tend to change more than the postal addresses of buildings. DDBJ has been including e-mail addresses for some years, again representing a subtle difference in policy.

The Feature Table

The middle segment of the GBFF record, the Feature table, is the most important direct representation of the biological information in the record. One could argue that the biology is best represented in the bibliographic reference, cited by the record. Nonetheless, a full set of annotations within the record facilitates quick extraction of the relevant biological features and allows the submitter to indicate why this record was submitted to the database in the first place (see Chapter 14). What becomes relevant here is the choice of annotations presented in this section. The feature table documentation (see Chapter 14) describes in great detail the legal features (i.e., the ones that are allowed) and what qualifiers are permitted with them. This, unfortunately, has often invited an excess of invalid, speculative, or computed annotations. If an annotation is simply computed, its usefulness as a comment within the record is diminished.

General Consideration

This section describes some of the key GenBank features, telling why they are important and what information can be extracted from them. Since Chapter 14 contains extensive, up-to-date documentation on this segment of the GBFF, the discussion here is limited to the biology, and guidelines applied to this segment by the NCBI staff. This material will give the reader some insight on the data model (Chapter 6) and the important place the GBFF occupies in the analysis of sequences, serving also to introduce the concept of features and qualifiers in GenBank language. The features are slightly different from other features discussed in Chapters 6 and 14. In the GBFF records, any component of the feature section of the GBFF that is designated "feature." In the NCBI data model, "features" refers to annotations on parts of the sequences, whereas annotations that describe the whole sequence are called "descriptors." Thus in the GenBank vocabulary, the source feature is really a descriptor in the data model view (the BioSource, which refers to the whole sequence), not a feature as this term is used elsewhere. But since this is a chapter on the GenBank database, the former definition will be used. The readers should be aware of this subtle difference, especially when referring to other parts of this book.

The Source Feature

The source feature is the only feature that must be present on all GenBank records. All features have a series of legal qualifiers, some of which are mandatory (e.g., /organism for source). All DNA sequence records have some origin, even if synthetic in the extreme case. In most cases there will be a single source feature, and it will have the /organism. Here is what we have in the example from Appendix 2.1:

```
1        10        20        30        40        50        60        70        79
---------+---------+---------+---------+---------+---------+---------+---------


FEATURES                 Location/Qualifiers
     source              1..3291
                         /organism="Drosophila melanogaster"
                         /map="2-106.8 cM; 60B1-2"
                         /clone="P1 Phage DS00543"
                         /chromosome="2"
```

The organism qualifier is described by the scientific genus and species. In some cases, "organisms" can be described at the subspecies level. For the source feature, the series of qualifiers will contain all matters relating to the BioSource, and these may include mapping, chromosome or tissue assignment, clone identification, and other library information. For the source feature, as is true for all features in a GenBank record, care should be taken to avoid adding superfluous information to the record. For the reader of these records, anything that cannot be computationally validated should be taken with a grain of salt. Tissue source and library origin are only as good as the controls present in the associated publication (if any such publication exists) and only insofar as that type of information is applied uniformly across all records in GenBank. With sets of records in which the qualifiers are applied in a systematic way, as they are for many large EST sets, the taxonomy can be validated (i.e., the organism does exist in the database of all organisms that is maintained at the NCBI). If, in addition, the qualifier is applied uniformly across all records, it is of value to the researcher. Unfortunately, however, many qualifiers are derived without sufficient uniformity across the database and hence are of less value.

Implicit in the BioSource and the organism that is assigned to it is the genetic code used by the DNA/RNA that will be used to translate the nucleic acid to represent the protein sequence (if one is present in the record). This information is shown on the CDS feature.

The CDS Feature

As described in detail in Chapter 6, the CDS is an instruction to the reader on how to join two sequences together, or on how to make an amino acid sequence from the indicated coordinates and the inferred genetic code. The GBFF view, being as DNA-centric as it is, maps all features through a DNA sequence coordinate system, not that of amino acid reference points, as in the following example from GenBank accession Y11895 (contributed by a submission to EMBL).

```
FEATURES             Location/Qualifiers
     source          1..2242
                     /organism="Mus musculus"
                     /strain="C57B16 × DBA"
                     /dev_stage="7.5 days embryo"
                     /tissue_type="whole embryonic region"
     gene            140..1897
                     /gene="M-Delta-3"
     sig_peptide     140..235
                     /gene="M-Delta-3"
     CDS             140..1897
                     /gene="M-Delta-3"
                     /codon_start=1
                     /db_xref="PID:e322087"
                     /db_xref="PID:g2415691"
                     /translation="MVSLQVSPLSQTLILAFLLPQALPAGVFELQIHSFGPGPGLGTP
                     RSPCNARGPCRLFFRVCLKPGVSQEATESLCALGAALSTSVPVYTEHPGESAAALPLP
                     DGLVRVPFRDAWPGTFSLVIETWREQLGEHAGGPAWNLLARVVGRRRLAAGGPWARDV
                     QRTGTWELHFSYRARCEPPAVGAACARLCRSRSAPSRCGPGLRPCTPFPDECEAPSVC
                     RPGCSPEHGYCEEPDECRCLEGWTGPLCTVPVSTSSCLNSRVPGPASTGCLLPGPGPC
                     DGNPCANGGSCSETSGSFECACPRGFYGLRCEVSGVTCADGPCFNGGLCVGGEDPDSX
                     YVCHCPPGFQGSNCEKRVDRCSLQPCQNGGLCLDLGHAXXCRCRAGFAGPRCEHDLDD
                     CAGRACANAGTCVEGGGSRRCSCALGFGGRDCRERADPCASRPCAHGGRCYAHFSGLV
                     CACAPGYMGVRCEFAVRPDGADAVPAAPRGLRQADPQRFLLPPALGLLVAAGLAGAAL
                     LVIHVRRRGPGQDTGTRLLSGTREPSVHTLPDALNNLRLQDGAGDGPSSSADWNHPED
                     GDSRSIYVIPAPSIYAREA"
     misc_feature    661..778
                     /gene="M-Delta-3"
                     /note="DSL domain"
     misc_feature    1605..1678
                     /gene="M-Delta-3"
                     /note="transmembrane domain"
```

In reading this report we have to infer the amino acid position through those of the DNA coordinates, and we have to limit the description of what should really be protein features to miscellaneous DNA features, which point to features on the protein sequence. This is a limitation that Sequin overcomes (see Chapter 14). This example also illustrates the use of the database cross-reference (db_xref). This controlled qualifier allows the databases to cross-reference the sequence in question to an external database (the first identifier) with an identifier used in that database. The list of allowed db_xref databases is maintained by the collaborators (see end-of-chapter list).

As mentioned above, and in Chapter 6, NCBI assigns a gi (geninfo) identifier to all sequences. This means that translation products, which are sequences in their own right (not simply attachments to a DNA record, as they are shown in a GenBank record) also get a gi number, a unique identifier that will change if and only if the sequence changes. The protein gi numbers presently appear as a PID db_xref, or protein identifier. The present example shows two of these:

```
/db_xref="PID:e322087"
/db_xref="PID:g2415691"
```

The prefixes e and g stand for EMBL and GenBank, respectively. The integer with a "g" as a prefix is the NCBI-assigned gi (the gi does not have a letter component in it, only its PID representation). There can be two PIDs because each database maintain its own identifiers. In GenBank, only records that were created in EMBL have two PIDs, one with the e prefix, and one with a g prefix. This confusion will end soon, since in 1998 the use of gi numbers will be simplified. As for the nucleotide sequences, there will also be a sequence identifier, having a version number component, and a stable sequence identifier (or accession number) component.

```
CDS             140..1897
                /protein_id="AAA12345.1"
                /db_xref="GI:2415691"
                /db_xref="PID:e322087"
                /db_xref="PID:g2415691"
```

All sequence identifiers need to coexist for the transition period, but the PID eventually will be removed. The protein_id (or protein accession number issued by the nucleotide sequence databases) will consist of three letters plus five digits, followed by a period and another integer, referring to the version of that protein sequence. This number will increment, just as the gi would change, when the sequence changes. Thus the version number will present the user with an easy way to look up the previous version of the record, if one is present. Since amino acid sequences represent one of the most important by-products of the nucleotide sequence database, much attention is devoted to making sure they are valid. (If a translation is present in a GenBank record, there are valid coordinates, and these can direct the translation of presented sequence.) These sequences are the starting material for the protein databases and offer the most sensitive way of making new gene discoveries (Chapter 7). Because these annotations can be validated, they have added value, and having the correct identifiers also becomes important. The correct product name, or protein name, can be subjective and often is assigned via weak similarities to other poorly annotated sequences, which themselves have poor annotations. Thus users should be aware of potential circular amplification of paucity of information. A good rule is that more information is usually obtained from records describing single genes or full-length mRNA sequences with which a published paper is associated. These records usually describe the work from a group that has studied a gene of interest in some detail. Fortunately, quite a few records of these types are in the database, representing a foundation of knowledge used by many.

The Gene Feature

The recently added gene feature has nevertheless been implicitly in use since the beginning of the databases, as a gene qualifier on a number of other features. By making this a separate feature, the de facto status has been made explicit, greatly facilitating the generation and validation of components now annotated with this feature. The new feature has also made it clear in its short existence that biologists have very different definitions and uses for the gene feature in GenBank records. Although it is obvious that not all biologists will agree on a single definition of the gene feature, at its simplest interpretation, the gene feature represents a segment of DNA that can be identified with a name (*e.g.*, the CHIP gene in our example from Appendix 2.1) or some arbitrary number, as is often used in genome sequencing project (*e.g.,* T19D16.1 from GenBank accession number U95973). The gene feature will allows the user to see the gene area of interest, and in some cases to select it.

The RNA Features

The various structural RNA features can be used to annotate RNA on genomic sequences (e.g., mRNA, rRNA, tRNA). Although these are presently not instantiated into separate records as protein sequences are, these sequences (especially the mRNA) are essential to our understanding of how higher genomes are organized. RNAs deserve special mention because they represent biological entities that can be measured in the lab, and thus are pieces of information of great value for a genomic record and are often mRNA records on their own. This is in contrast to the promoter feature, which is poorly characterized, unevenly assigned in a great number of records, poorly defined from a biology point of view, and of lesser use in a GenBank record. The RNA feature on a genomic record should represent the experimental evidence of the presence of that biological molecule.

CONCLUSIONS

The DDBJ/EMBL/GenBank database is the most commonly used nucleotide and protein sequence database. It represents a public repository of molecular biology information. Knowing what the various fields mean, and how much biology can be obtained from these records, greatly advances our understanding of this file format. Although the database was never meant to be read from computers, an army of computer-happy biologists have nevertheless parsed, converted, and extracted these records by means of entire suites of programs. DDBJ/EMBL/GenBank remains the format of exchange between the international DNA sequence database collaborators, and this is unlikely to change for years to come, despite the availability of better, richer, alternatives, such as the data described in ASN.1. But therein lies the usefulness of the present arrangement: it is a readily available, simple format, which can represent some abstraction of the biology it wishes to depict.

Internet Resources Presented in Chapter 2

DB_XREF

http://www.ncbi.nlm.nih.gov/collab/db_xref.html

GENBANK RELEASE NOTES

ftp://ncbi.nlm.nih.gov/genbank/gbrel.txt

READSEQ SEQUENCE CONVERSION TOOL

http://magpie.bio.indiana.edu/Molecular-Biology/Molbio%20archive/readseq/

TAXONOMY BROWSER

http://www.ncbi.nlm.nih.gov/Taxonomy/tax.html

TREMBL AND SWISS-PROT RELEASE NOTES

http://www.ebi.ac.uk/ebi_docs/swissprot_db/documentation.html

REFERENCES

Bairoch, A., and Apweiler, R. (1997). The SWISS-PROT protein sequence data bank and its supplement TrEMBL. Nucl. Acids Res. *25*, 31–36.

Benson, D. A., Boguski, M. S., Lipman, D. J., and Ostell, J. (1997). GenBank. Nucl. Acids Res. *25*, 1–6.

Boguski, M. S., Lowe, T. M., Tolstoshev, C. M. (1993). dbEST—database for "expressed sequence tags" Nat. Genetics *4*: 332–333.

Cook-Deagan, R. (1993). *The Gene Wars. Science, Politics and the Human Genome* (New York and London: W. W. Norton & Company).

Dayhoff, M. O., Eck, R. V., Chang, M. A., Sochard, M. R. (1965). Atlas of Protein Sequence and Structure. National Biomedical Research Foundation, Silver Spring MD.

George, D. G., Dodson, R. J., Garavelli, J. S., Haft, D. H., Hunt, L. T., Marzec, C. R., Orcutt, B. C., Sidman, K. E., Srinivasarao, G. Y., Yeh, L. S. L., Arminski, L. M., Ledley, R. S., Tsugita, A., and Barker, W. C. (1997). The Protein Information Resource (PIR) and the PIR-International Protein Sequence Database. Nucl. Acids Res. *25*, 24–28.

Mewes, H. W., Albermann, K., Heumann, K., Liebl, S., and Pfeiffer, E. (1997). MIPS: A database for protein sequences, homology data and yeast genome information. Nucl. Acids Res. *25*, 28–30.

Ouellette, B. F. F., Boguski, M. S. (1997). Database Divisions and Homology Search Files: A Guide for the Perplexed. Genome Res. *7*, 952–955.

Schuler, G. D., Epstein, J. A., Ohkawa, H., Kans, J. A. (1996). Entrez: Molecular biology database and retrieval system. Methods Enzymol. *266*, 141–162.

Stoesser, G., Sterk, P., Tuli, M. A., Stoehr, P. J., and Cameron, G. N. (1997). The EMBL Nucleotide Sequence Database. Nucl. Acids Res. *25*, 7–14.

Tateno, Y., and Gojobori, T. (1997). DNA Data Bank of Japan in the age of information biology. Nucl. Acids Res. *25*, 14–17.

APPENDICES: DATABASE FILE FORMATS

Appendix 2.1   Example of a GenBank (or DDBJ) Record

```
LOCUS        AF010325 3291 bp DNA INV 08-JUL-1997
DEFINITION   Drosophila melanogaster CHIP (Chip) gene, complete cds.
ACCESSION    AF010325
NID          g2245686
KEYWORDS     .
SOURCE       fruit fly.
  ORGANISM   Drosophila melanogaster
             Eukaryotae; mitochondrial eukaryotes; Metazoa; Arthropoda;
             Tracheata; Hexapoda; Insecta; Pterygota; Diptera; Brachycera;
             Muscomorpha; Ephydroidea; Drosophilidae; Drosophila.
REFERENCE    1 (bases 1 to 3291)
  AUTHORS    Morcillo, P., Rosen, C., Baylies, M.K. and Dorsett, D.
  TITLE      CHIP, a widely expressed chromosomal protein required for remote
             enhancer activity and segmentation in Drosophila
  JOURNAL    Unpublished
REFERENCE    2 (bases 1 to 3291)
  AUTHORS    Morcillo, P., Rosen, C., Baylies, M.K. and Dorsett, D.
  TITLE      Direct Submission
  JOURNAL    Submitted (19-JUN-1997) Molecular Biology Program, Memorial
             Sloan-Kettering Cancer Center, 1275 York Avenue, New York, NY
             10021, USA
FEATURES             Location/Qualifiers
     source          1..3291
                     /organism="Drosophila melanogaster"
                     /map="2-106.8 cM; 60B1-2"
                     /clone="P1 Phage DS00543"
                     /chromosome="2"
     gene            604..2964
                     /gene="Chip"
                     /allele="wild type"
     mRNA            join(604..677,928..2964)
                     /gene="Chip"
                     /note="Allele: wild type"
```

```
                            /product="CHIP"
     intron                 678..927
                            /gene="Chip"
                            /note="Allele: wild type; P-lacW insertion occurs at
                            position 904 in the 1(2)k04405 allele"
     exon                   928..2964
                            /gene="Chip"
                            /note="Allele: wild type"
     CDS                    963..2696
                            /gene="Chip"
                            /note="Allele: wild type; GenBank Accession Numbers
                            AF010326, AF010327 and AF010328 encode short forms of the
                            CHIP protein"
                            /codon_start=1
                            /product="CHIP"
                            /db_xref="PID:g2245687"
                            /translation="MNRRGLNAGNTMTSQANIDDGSWKAVSEGGSMLPASNSAVLNPD
                            GSNQSGFAQGGLPYNSAGNPYPPAGQSSPAGNQSIVFQNSNQPGSNTPQYTSSPAPSG
                            SSTPGPVGAQNIPGNYPQSATAGNFNGPVGGPFGSPSSGLGQFSRPASSGTPFNSGQA
                            GHFSSPTVFSVGGQFNPMPPASPFGHGGNHPMMGGPQQMERIDQGFRRHNSYFSHTEH
                            RVFELNKRLQQRNEESDNCWWDSFTTEFFEDDARLTILFCLEDGPKRYTIGRTLIPRF
                            FRSIYEGGVSDLYFQLKHAKESFHNTSITLDCDQCTVITQHGKPFFTKVCADARLILE
                            FMYDDYMRIKSWHMTIKGHRELIPRSVIGTSLPPDPMLLDQITKNITRAGITNSTLNY
                            LRLCVILEPMQELMSRHKAYALSPRDCLKTTLFQKWQRMVAPPGKKDPQRPPNKRRKR
                            KGSNSGGGNNSNTPPVTNQKRSPSGPSFSLSSQDVMVVGEPTLMGGEFGEEDERLITR
                            LENTQYDGTNAVEHDNHTGFGHADSPISGSNPWSIDRAGAIPASPGNGAAPQNNANIS
                            DIDKKSPIVSQ"
     polyA_site             2964
                            /gene="Chip"
                            /note="Allele: wild type"
BASE COUNT        898 a     870 c     773 g     749 t      1 others
ORIGIN
        1 aaaatatgtt taccattcaa cgacactnga agatgtgcga aattaatgca gtttataaat

<< deleted to save space>>

3241 agctcctttg cgcatgcacg aatatctgcg ggatacagat acacagtttc g
//
```

Appendix 2.2   Example of an ASN.1 Record

```
Seq-entry ::= set {
  class nuc-prot ,
  descr {
    create-date
      std {
        year 1997 ,
        month 6 ,
```

```
          day 19 } ,
      source {
        genome genomic ,
        org {
          taxname "Drosophila melanogaster" ,
          common "fruit fly" ,
          db {
            {
              db "taxon" ,
              tag
                id 7227 } } ,
          orgname {
              lineage "Eukaryotae; mitochondrial eukaryotes; Metazoa; Arthropoda;
Tracheata; Hexapoda; Insecta; Pterygota; Diptera; Brachycera; Muscomorpha;
Ephydroidea; Drosophilidae; Drosophila" ,
              gcode 1 ,
              mgcode 5 ,
              div "INV" } } ,
        subtype {
          {
            subtype map ,
            name "2-106.8 cM; 60B1-2" } ,
          {
            subtype clone ,
            name "P1 Phage DS00543" } ,
          {
            subtype chromosome ,
            name "2" } } } ,
      title "Drosophila melanogaster CHIP (Chip) gene, complete cds." ,
      pub {
        pub {
          sub {
            authors {
              names
                std {
                  {
                    name
                      name {
                        last "Morcillo" ,
                        first "Patrick" ,
                        initials "P." } } ,
                  {
                    name
                      name {
                        last "Rosen" ,
                        first "Christina" ,
                        initials "C." } } ,
                  {
```

```
                name
                  name {
                    last "Baylies" ,
                    first "Mary" ,
                    initials "M.K." } } ,
                {
                  name
                    name {
                      last "Dorsett" ,
                      first "Dale" ,
                      initials "D." } } } ,
            affil
              std {
                affil "Memorial Sloan-Kettering Cancer Center" ,
                div "Molecular Biology Program" ,
                city "New York" ,
                sub "NY" ,
                country "USA" ,
                street "1275 York Avenue" ,
                postal-code "10021" } } ,
          medium other ,
          date
            std {
              year 1997 ,
              month 6 ,
              day 19 } } } } ,
      pub {
        pub {
          gen {
            cit "unpublished" ,
            authors {
              names
                std {
                  {
                    name
                      name {
                        last "Morcillo" ,
                        first "Patrick" ,
                        initials "P." } } ,
                  {
                    name
                      name {
                        last "Rosen" ,
                        first "Christina" ,
                        initials "C." } } ,
                  {
                    name
                      name {
```

```
                        last "Baylies" ,
                        first "Mary" ,
                        initials "M.K." } } ,
                 {
                   name
                     name {
                       last "Dorsett" ,
                       first "Dale" ,
                       initials "D." } } } ,
            affil
              std {
                affil "Memorial Sloan-Kettering Cancer Center" ,
                div "Molecular Biology Program" ,
                city "New York" ,
                sub "New York" ,
                country "USA" ,
                street "1275 York Avenue" ,
                postal-code "10021" } } ,
          title "CHIP, a widely-expressed chromosomal protein required for
remote enhancer activity and segmentation in Drosophila" } } } ,
    update-date
      std {
        year 1997 ,
        month 6 ,
        day 27 } } ,
  seq-set {
    seq {
      id {
        genbank {
          name "AF010325" ,
          accession "AF010325" } ,
        gi 2245686 } ,
      descr {
        molinfo {
          biomol genomic ,
          completeness complete } ,
        create-date
          std {
            year 1997 ,
            month 7 ,
            day 8 } } ,
      inst {
        repr raw ,
        mol dna ,
        length 3291 ,
        seq-data
          ncbi4na '1111818488812218821124121228F41141848424111881184214888818111
81121812281112124812828148181811111182411212888824218212122124442884214848212144
```

```
< < sequence deleted to save space > >

8188244188481182121484288142118218812228882248418888424114822142822888842421842
12411818284244418121418121214888240'H } ,
      annot {
        {
          data
            ftable {
              {
                data
                  rna {
                    type mRNA ,
                    ext
                      name "CHIP" } ,
                location
                  mix {
                    int {
                      from 603 ,
                      to 676 ,
                      strand plus ,
                      id
                        gi 2245686 } ,
                    int {
                      from 927 ,
                      to 2963 ,
                      strand plus ,
                      id
                        gi 2245686 } } } ,
              {
                data
                  cdregion {
                    code {
                      id 1 } } ,
                comment "GenBank Accession Numbers AF010326, AF010327 and
  AF010328 encode short forms of the CHIP protein" ,
                product
                  whole
                    gi 2245687 ,
                location
                  int {
                    from 962 ,
                    to 2695 ,
                    strand plus ,
                    id
                      gi 2245686 } } ,
              {
                data
                  imp {
```

```
                   key "intron" } ,
               comment "P-lacW insertion occurs at position 904 in the
1(2)k04405 allele" ,
               location
                 int {
                   from 677 ,
                   to 926 ,
                   strand plus ,
                   id
                     gi 2245686 } } ,
             {
               data
                 gene {
                   locus "Chip" ,
                   allele "wild type" } ,
               location
                 int {
                   from 603 ,
                   to 2963 ,
                   strand plus ,
                   id
                     gi 2245686 } } ,
             {
               data
                 imp {
                   key "polyA_site" } ,
               location
                 pnt {
                   point 2963 ,
                   strand plus ,
                   id
                     gi 2245686 } } ,
             {
               data
                 imp {
                   key "exon" } ,
               location
                 int {
                   from 927 ,
                   to 2963 ,
                   strand plus ,
                   id
                     gi 2245686 } } } } } } ,
     seq {
       id {
         gi 2245687 } ,
       descr {
         molinfo {
```

```
            biomol peptide ,
            tech concept-trans-a } } ,
        inst {
          repr raw ,
          mol aa ,
          length 577 ,
          seq-data
            ncbieaa "MNRRGLNAGNTMTSQANIDDGSWKAVSEGGSMLPASNSAVLNPDGSNQSGFAQGGLPYN
SAGNPYPPAGQSSPAGNQSIVFQNSNQPGSNTPQYTSSPAPSGSSTPGPVGAQNIPGNYPQSATAGNFNGPVGGPFGS
PSSGLGQFSRPASSGTPFNSGQAGHFSSPTVFSVGGQFNPMPPASPFGHGGNHPMMGGPQQMERIDQGFRRHNSYFSH
TEHRVFELNKRLQQRNEESDNCWWDSFTTEFFEDDARLTILFCLEDGPKRYTIGRTLIPRFFRSIYEGGVSDLYFQLK
HAKESFHNTSITLDCDQCTVITQHGKPFFTKVCADARLILEFMYDDYMRIKSWHMTIKGHRELIPRSVIGTSLPPDPM
LLDQITKNITRAGITNSTLNYLRLCVILEPMQELMSRHKAYALSPRDCLKTTLFQKWQRMVAPPGKKDPQRPPNKRRK
RKGSNSGGGNNSNTPPVTNQKRSPSGPSFSLSSQDVMVVGEPTLMGGEFGEEDERLITRLENTQYDGTNAVEHDNHTG
FGHADSPISGSNPWSIDRAGAIPASPGNGAAPQNNANISDIDKKSPIVSQ" } ,
        annot {
          {
            data
              ftable {
                {
                  data
                    prot {
                      name {
                        "CHIP" } } ,
                    location
                      int {
                        from 0 ,
                        to 576 ,
                        strand plus ,
                        id
                          gi 2245687 } } } } } } } }
```

Appendix 2.3   Example of an EMBL Record

```
ID    DMAF10325   standard; DNA; INV; 3291 BP.
XX
AC    AF010325;
XX
NI    g2245686
XX
DT    08-JUL-1997 (Rel. 52, Created)
DT    08-JUL-1997 (Rel. 52, Last updated, Version 1)
XX
DE    Drosophila melanogaster CHIP (Chip) gene, complete cds.
XX
KW
XX
OS    Drosophila melanogaster (fruit fly)
```

```
OC   Eukaryotae; mitochondrial eukaryotes; Metazoa; Arthropoda;
OC   Tracheata; Hexapoda; Insecta; Pterygota; Diptera; Brachycera;
OC   Muscomorpha; Ephydroidea; Drosophilidae; Drosophila.
XX
RN   [1]
RP   1-3291
RA   Morcillo P., Rosen C., Baylies M.K., Dorsett D.;
RT   "CHIP, a widely-expressed chromosomal protein required for remote
RT   enhancer activity and segmentation in Drosophila";
RL   Unpublished.
XX
RN   [2]
RP   1-3291
RA   Morcillo P., Rosen C., Baylies M.K., Dorsett D.;
RT   ;
RL   Submitted (19-JUN-1997) to the EMBL/GenBank/DDBJ databases.
RL   Molecular Biology Program, Memorial Sloan-Kettering Cancer Center,
RL   1275 York Avenue, New York, NY 10021, USA
XX
FH   Key             Location/Qualifiers
FH
FT   source          1. .3291
FT                   /organism="Drosophila melanogaster"
FT                   /map="2-106.8 cM; 60B1-2"
FT                   /clone="P1 Phage DS00543"
FT                   /chromosome="2"
FT   mRNA            join(604. .677,928. .2964)
FT                   /gene="Chip"
FT                   /note="Allele: wild type"
FT                   /product="CHIP"
FT   intron          678. .927
FT                   /gene="Chip"
FT                   /note="Allele: wild type; P-lacW insertion occurs at
FT                   position 904 in the 1(2)k04405 allele"
FT   exon            928. .2964
FT                   /gene="Chip"
FT                   /note="Allele: wild type"
FT   CDS             963. .2696
FT                   /gene="Chip"
FT                   /note="Allele: wild type; GenBank Accession Numbers
FT                   AF010326, AF010327 and AF010328 encode short forms of the
FT                   CHIP protein"
FT                   /codon_start=1
FT                   /product="CHIP"
FT                   /db_xref="PID:g2245687"
FT                   /translation="MNRRGLNAGNTMTSQANIDDGSWKAVSEGGSMLPASNSAVLNPDG
FT                   SNQSGFAQGGLPYNSAGNPYPPAGQSSPAGNQSIVFQNSNQPGSNTPQYTSSPAPSGSS
FT                   TPGPVGAQNIPGNYPQSATAGNFNGPVGGPFGSPSSGLGQFSRPASSGTPFNSGQAGHF
```

```
FT                      SSPTVFSVGGQFNPMPPASPFGHGGNHPMMGGPQQMERIDQGFRRHNSYFSHTEHRVFE
FT                      LNKRLQQRNEESDNCWWDSFTTEFFEDDARLTILFCLEDGPKRYTIGRTLIPRFFRSIY
FT                      EGGVSDLYFQLKHAKESFHNTSITLDCDQCTVITQHGKPFFTKVCADARLILEFMYDDY
FT                      MRIKSWHMTIKGHRELIPRSVIGTSLPPDPMLLDQITKNITRAGITNSTLNYLRLCVIL
FT                      EPMQELMSRHKAYALSPRDCLKTTLFQKWQRMVAPPGKKDPQRPPNKRRKRKGSNSGGG
FT                      NNSNTPPVTNQKRSPSGPSFSLSSQDVMVVGEPTLMGGEFGEEDERLITRLENTQYDGT
FT                      NAVEHDNHTGFGHADSPISGSNPWSIDRAGAIPASPGNGAAPQNNANISDIDKKSPIVS
FT                      Q"
FT     polyA_site       2964
FT                      /gene="Chip"
FT                      /note="Allele: wild type"
XX
SQ     Sequence 3291 BP; 898 A; 870 C; 773 G; 749 T; 1 other;
       AAAATATGTT TACCATTCAA CGACACTNGA AGATGTGCGA AATTAATGCA GTTTATAAAT        60

<< deleted to save space>>

       AGCTCCTTTG CGCATGCACG AATATCTGCG GGATACAGAT ACACAGTTTC G             3291
//
```

Appendix 2.4   Example of a GenBank Summary File

```
LOCUS       U00096     4639221 bp    DNA    circular  CON 12-SEP-1997
DEFINITION  Escherichia coli K-12 MG1655.
ACCESSION   U00096
KEYWORDS
SOURCE      Escherichia coli.
  ORGANISM  Escherichia coli
            Eubacteria; Proteobacteria; gamma subdivision; Enterobacteriaceae;
            Escherichia.
REFERENCE   1  (bases 1 to 4639221)
  AUTHORS   Blattner,F.R., Plunkett III,G., Bloch,C.A., Perna,N.T., Burland,V.,
            Riley,M., Collado-Vides,J., Glasner,J.D., Rode,C.K., Mayhew,G.F.,
            Gregor,J., Davis,N.W., Kirkpatrick,H.A., Goeden,M.A., Rose,D.J.,
            Mau,B. and Shao,Y.
  TITLE     The complete genome sequence of Escherichia coli K-12
  JOURNAL   Science 277 (5331), 1453-1462 (1997)
REFERENCE   2  (bases 1 to 4639221)
  AUTHORS   Blattner,F.R.
  TITLE     Direct Submission
  JOURNAL   Submitted (16-JAN-1997) Guy Plunkett III, Laboratory of Genetics,
            University of Wisconsin, 445 Henry Mall, Madison, WI 53706, USA.
            Email: ecoli@genetics.wisc.edu Phone: 608-262-2534 Fax:
            608-263-7459
REFERENCE   3  (bases 1 to 4639221)
  AUTHORS   Blattner,F.R.
  TITLE     Direct Submission
  JOURNAL   Submitted (02-SEP-1997) Guy Plunkett III, Laboratory of Genetics,
```

University of Wisconsin, 445 Henry Mall, Madison, WI 53706, USA.
Email: ecoli@genetics.wisc.edu Phone: 608-262-2534 Fax:
608-263-7459

COMMENT   The E. coli K-12 sequence and its annotations have been updated.
All of the ambiguous residues in our original submission have been
resolved, and mis-assemblies in two repetitive regions have been
realigned. The annotations have been improved and updated as well.
With this release we begin designating a version number for the
annotated sequence, to assist in keeping track of corrections,
updates, and other changes. This is version M52 (SEPT. 02, 1997).
In addition, a revised notation has been instituted which assigns
each gene (protein- or RNA-encoding) a unique numeric identifier
beginning with a lowercase 'b' (in the '/label' field); this will
remain constant through further updates, gene identifications, etc.
 This sequence was determined by the E. coli Genome Project at the
University of Wisconsin-Madison (Frederick R. Blattner, director).
Supported by NIH grants HG00301 and HG01428 (from the Human Genome
Project and NCHGR). The entire sequence was independently
determined from E. coli K-12 strain MG1655.
Predicted open reading frames were determined using GeneMark
software, kindly supplied by Mark Borodovsky, Georgia Institute of
Technology, Atlanta, GA, 30332.
e-mail: mark@amber.gatech.edu
Open reading frames that have been correlated with genetic loci are
being annotated with CG Site Nos., unique ID nos. for the genes in
the E. coli Genetic Stock Center (CGSC) database at Yale
University, kindly supplied by Mary Berlyn. A public version of the
database is accessible (http://cgsc.biology.yale.edu).
Annotation of the genome is an ongoing task whose goal is to make
the genome sequence more useful by correlating it with other data.
Comments to the authors are appreciated. Updated information will
be available at the E. coli Genome Project's World Wide Web site
(http://www.genetics.wisc.edu).
FEATURES   Location/Qualifiers
    source   1..4639221
                   /organism="Escherichia coli"
                   /strain="K-12"
                   /sub_strain="MG1655"
CONTIG   join(AE000111:1..10596,AE000112:59..10179,AE000113:59..13485,
           AE000114:59..13134,AE000115:59..10102,AE000116:59..13039,

< < total of 400 records referenced: deleted to save space > >

           AE000507:59..12359,AE000508:59..15518,AE000509:59..10589,
           AE000510:59..6309)
//

3

Structure Databases

Christopher W. V. Hogue

Samuel Lunenfeld Research Institute
Mount Sinai Hospital
Toronto, Ontario, Canada

Stephen H. Bryant

National Center for Biotechnology Information
National Library of Medicare
National Institutes of Health
Bethesda, Maryland

INTRODUCTION TO STRUCTURES

This chapter introduces the bioinformatics aspects of biomolecular structures, with special emphasis on the sequences that are contained in three-dimensional structures. It attempts to inform the reader about the contents of structure database records and how they are treated, and sometimes mistreated, by popular software programs. This chapter does not cover the computational processes used by structural scientists to obtain 3-D structures. Neither does it discuss the finer points of comparative protein architecture. Several excellent monographs regarding protein architecture and protein structure determination methods are listed following the chapter references.

The imagery of protein and nucleic acid structures has become a common feature of biochemistry textbooks and research articles. This imagery can be beautiful and intriguing enough to blind us to the experimental details an image represents—the underlying biophysical methods and the effort of hard-working X-ray crystallographers and NMR spectroscopists. The data stored in structure database records represents a practical summary of the experimental data. It is not the data gathered directly by instruments, nor is it a simple mathematical transform of that data. Each structure database record carries assumptions and biases that change as the state of the art in structure determination advances. Never-

Bioinformatics: A Practical Guide to the Analysis of Genes and Proteins
Edited by A.D. Baxevanis and B.F.F. Ouellette
ISBN 0-471-19196-5, pages 46–73. Copyright © 1998 Wiley-Liss, Inc.

theless, each **biomolecular structure is a hard-won piece of crucial information—the "missing" data of a sequence.**

The Notion of 3-D Molecular Structure Data

Let us begin with a mental exercise in recording the 3-D data of a biopolymer. Consider how we might record, on paper, all the details and dimensions of a three-dimensional ball-and-stick model of a protein like myoglobin. One way to begin is with the sequence, which can be obtained by tracing out the backbone of the 3-D model. Beginning from the N-terminus, we identify each amino acid side chain by comparing the atomic structure of each residue with the chemical structure of the 20 common amino acids, possibly guided by an illustration of amino acid structures from a textbook.

Once the sequence has been written down, we proceed with making a two-dimensional sketch of the biopolymer with all its atoms, element symbols, and bonds, possibly taking up several pieces of paper. The same must be done for the heme ligand. After drawing its chemical structure on paper, we might record the three-dimensional data by measuring the distance of each atom in the model starting from some origin point, along some orthogonal axis system. This would provide the x-, y-, and z-axis distances to each atomic "ball" in the ball-and-stick structure.

The next step is to come up with a bookkeeping scheme to keep all the (x, y, z) coordinate information connected to the identity of each atom. The easiest approach may be to write the (x, y, z) value as a coordinate triple on the same pieces of paper used for the 2-D sketch of the biopolymer, right next to each atom.

This mental exercise helps to conceptualize what a three-dimensional structure database record ought to contain. This is an adequate "human-readable" record of the structure, but one probably would not expect a computer to digest it. The computer needs clear, parsable encoding of the associations of atoms, bonds, coordinates, residues, and molecules. Here is where the real exercise in structural bioinformatics begins.

Coordinates, Sequences, and Chemical Graphs

The most obvious data in a typical 3-D structure record, irrespective of the file format in use, is the *coordinate data,* the locations in space of the atoms of a molecule, represented by (x, y, z) triples, distances along each axis to some arbitrary origin in space. The coordinate data for each atom is attached to a list of labeling information in the structure record: which element, residue, and molecule each point in space belongs to. For biopolymers this labeling information can be derived starting with the sequence. Implicit in each sequence is considerable chemical data. We can infer the complete chemical connectivity of the biopolymer molecule directly from a sequence, including all its atoms and bonds, and we could make a sketch, just like the one described earlier, from sequence information alone. We refer to this "sketch" of the molecule, as the *chemical graph* component of a 3D structure. **Sequence is an implicit notation for the complete chemical graph** of a biopolymer molecule.

When we sketch all the underlying atoms and bonds representing a sequence, we may defer to a textbook showing the chemical structures of each residue, lest we forget a methyl group or two. Likewise, computers could build up a sketchlike representation of the chemical graph of a structure in memory using a *residue dictionary,* which contains a table of the atom types and bond information for each of the common amino acid and nucleic acid building blocks.

Atoms, Bonds, and Completeness

Molecular graphics visualization software performs an elaborate "connect-the-dots" process to make the wonderful pictures of protein structure we see in textbooks of biomolecular structure, like the insulin structure 3INS (Isaacs and Agarwal, 1978) shown in Figure 3.1. The connections used are, of course, the chemical bonds between all the atoms. In current use, 3-D molecular structure database records employ two different "minimalist" approaches regarding the storage of bond data.

The legacy approach to recording atoms and bonds is something we shall call the *chemistry rules* approach. The rules are the observable physical rules of chemistry, such as "The average length of a stable C—C bond is about 1.5 angstroms." Applying these rules to derive the bonds means that any two coordinate locations in space that are 1.5 Å apart and are tagged as carbon atoms always form a single bond. With the chemistry rules approach, we can *simply disregard the bonds.* A perfect and complete structure can be recorded without any bond information, provided it does not break any of the rules of chemistry.

The chemistry rules approach is the basis for the original 3-D biomolecular structure file format, the PDB format from the Protein Data Bank at Brookhaven (Bernstein et al., 1977). These records, in general, lack complete bond information for biopolymers. There is no residue dictionary required to interpret data encoded by this approach, just a table of bond lengths and bond types for every conceivable pair of bonded atoms.

Every software package that reads in PDB datafiles must reconstruct the bonds based on these rules. Since the rules have never been explicitly codified for programmers interpret-

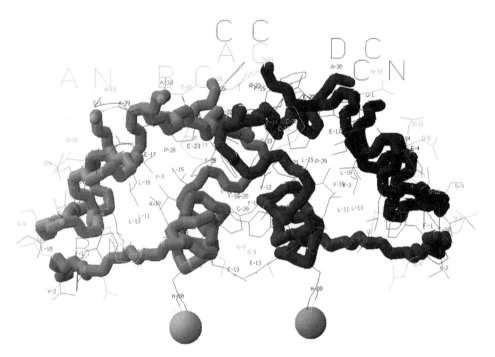

Figure 3.1   The insulin structure 3INS illustrated using Cn3D. Four chains are depicted in the crystallographic unit. This structure illustrates two of many bioinformatics bridges that must be spanned between sequence and structure databases, the lack of encoding of the active biological unit, and the lack of encoding of the relationship of the observed structure to the parent gene.

ing the bonding in PDB files, software can be inconsistent in the way it draws bonds, especially when different algorithms and distance tolerances are used. The PDB file approach is minimalist in terms of the data stored in a record, but the algorithms required to decipher this information properly are more sophisticated than would be needed if the bonding information and chemical graph were specified in the record. This forces the programmers to do much more work. Exceptions to the bonding rules need to be trapped by complicated logic statements programmed on a case-by-case basis.

The second approach is used in the database records of the Molecular Modeling Database (MMDB), which is derived from the data in PDB. MMDB uses a standard residue dictionary, a record of all the atoms and bonds in the polymer forms of amino acid and nucleic acid residues, plus end-terminal variants. Such data dictionaries are common in the specialized software used by structural scientists to solve structures. The software that reads in MMDB data can use the bonding information supplied in the dictionary to connect atoms together, without trying to enforce the rules of chemistry. As a result the 3-D coordinate data is consistently interpreted by software. This approach also lends itself to simpler software, because exceptions to bonding rules are recorded within the database file itself and read in without the need for another layer of exception-handling code.

Some scientists unfamiliar with structure data often expect all structures in the public databases to be of "textbook" quality. They are surprised when parts of a structure are missing. The availability of a 3-D database record for a particular molecule does not ever imply its *completeness*. Structural completeness is defined as follows: *At least one coordinate value for each and every atom in the chemical graph.*

Completeness is rare in structure database records. Most X-ray structures lack coordinates for hydrogen atoms because the locations of hydrogens in space are not resolved by the experimental method. However some modeling software can be used to algorithmically estimate the locations of hydrogens and reconstruct a structure record with model hydrogens added. It is easy to identify the products of molecular modeling in structure databases. These often have overly complete coordinate data, usually with all possible hydrogen atoms present that could not have been found using an experimental method.

PDB: PROTEIN DATA BANK AT BROOKHAVEN NATIONAL LABORATORIES

Overview

The use of computers in biology has its origins in biophysical methods, such as X-ray crystallography. Thus it is not surprising that the first "bioinformatics" database was built to store this complex 3-D data. The modern Protein Data Bank contains the core public collection of three-dimensional structures of proteins, as well as holding 3-D structures of nucleic acid, carbohydrates, and a variety of complexes experimentally determined by X-ray crystallographers and NMR spectroscopists. This section focuses briefly on the database/bioinformatics services offered by the Protein Data Bank.

PDB Database Services

The World Wide Web site of the Protein Data Bank at Brookhaven National Laboratories (see end-of-chapter list) offers a number of services for submitting and retrieving 3-D structure data.

Submitting Structures   For those who wish to submit 3-D structure information to PDB, there are now Web-based procedures for submitting structure data via the AutoDep service. Since this procedure is undergoing changes at the time of writing, the most up-to-date information must be found on PDB's Web site. Nucleic acid structures are now being accepted for deposition at NDB, the Nucleic Acids Database. The Biotech Validation Suite sites are mirrored sites that provides services that can be used to screen PDB files for stereochemical and geometrical inconsistencies prior to submitting a structure.

It has been the policy of PDB to reject 3-D structures that result from computational 3-D modeling procedures, rather than a physical experiment. Consult with PDB for the latest details on any exceptions that may have been declared. A separate database containing structure models may be forthcoming; look for information on the Web site for this book.

PDB-ID Codes   The structure record accessioning scheme of the Protein Data Bank is a unique four-character alphanumeric code called a PDB-ID or PDB code. This scheme uses the digits 0 to 9, and the uppercase letters A to Z. Thus there are over 1.3 million possible combinations. PDB-IDs are not assigned in any particular order. Rather, indexers at the Protein Data Bank try to devise mnemonics that make the structures easier to remember, such as 3INS, the record for insulin shown earlier (Figure 3.1).

Database Searching, PDB File Retrieval, and Links   PDB and several of its mirror sites offer a text search engine that uses an index of all the textual information in each PDB record, as well as some specialized fields (e.g., submission data, author names, structure resolution). PDB's latest search engine, the 3DB Atlas, can be used to retrieve PDB records, as shown in Figure 3.2. The 3DB Atlas is also the primary database of links to third-party annotation of PDB structure data. There are a number of maintained links in the 3DB Atlas to Internet-based 3-D structure services on other Web sites. These include such authored 2-D images and 3-D views as Kinemage (Richardson and Richardson, 1992, 1994) and RasMol (Sayle and Milner-White, 1995) scripts of many structures. Figure 3.2*b* shows some of the links connected to a 3DB record for the protein barnase, 1BNR (Bycroft et al., 1991). Authored images can be very helpful to see how to orient a 3-D structure for best viewing of certain features such as binding sites. The 3DB Atlas also maintains links to special project databases maintained by researchers interested in related topics such as structural evolution (FSSP: Holm and Sander, 1993), structure–structure similarity (DALI: Holm and Sander, 1996), and protein motions (Gerstein et al., 1994). 3DB contains reciprocal links to NCBI's MMDB service (Hogue et al., 1996), providing a gateway to the Entrez (Schuler et al., 1996), system with sequence, taxonomy, PubMed/MEDLINE services, and VAST (Gibrat et al., 1996) structure–structure similarities.

Sequences from PDB Structure Records

PDB-file-encoded sequences are notorious. Since completeness of a structure is not always guaranteed, PDB records contain two copies of the sequence information, an *explicit* sequence and an *implicit* sequence. Both are required to reconstruct the chemical graph of a biopolymer.

Explicit sequences in a PDB file are provided in lines starting with the keyword SEQRES. Unlike other sequence databases, PDB records use the three-letter amino acid code, and nonstandard amino acids are found in many PDB record sequence entries with arbitrarily chosen three-letter names. Some double-helical nucleic acid sequence entries in PDB are specified in 3′-to-5′ order in a entry above the complementary strand given in

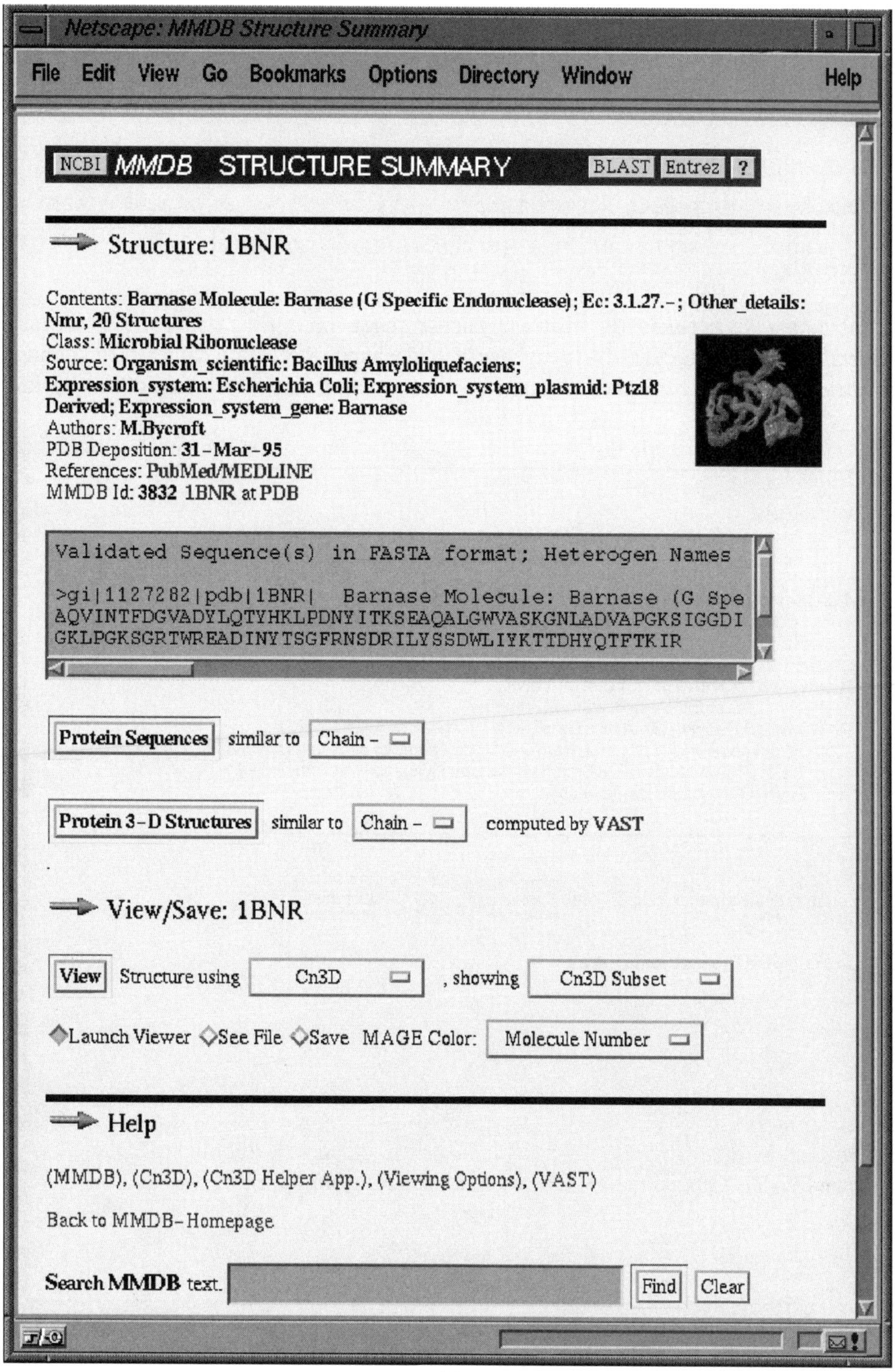

File   Edit   View   Go   Bookmarks   Options   Directory   Window   Help

NCBI *MMDB* STRUCTURE SUMMARY   BLAST Entrez ?

➡ Structure: 1BNR

Contents: Barnase Molecule: Barnase (G Specific Endonuclease); Ec: 3.1.27.−; Other_details:
Nmr, 20 Structures
Class: Microbial Ribonuclease
Source: Organism_scientific: Bacillus Amyloliquefaciens;
Expression_system: Escherichia Coli; Expression_system_plasmid: Ptzl8
Derived; Expression_system_gene: Barnase
Authors: M.Bycroft
PDB Deposition: 31−Mar−95
References: PubMed/MEDLINE
MMDB Id: 3832 1BNR at PDB

```
Validated Sequence(s) in FASTA format; Heterogen Names

>gi|1127282|pdb|1BNR|   Barnase Molecule: Barnase (G Spe
AQVINTFDGVADYLQTYHKLPDNYITKSEAQALGWVASKGNLADVAPGKSIGGDI
GKLPGKSGRTWREADINYTSGFRNSDRILYSSDWLIYKTTDHYQTFTKIR
```

Protein Sequences   similar to Chain − ▭

Protein 3−D Structures   similar to Chain − ▭   computed by VAST

➡ View/Save: 1BNR

View Structure using   Cn3D   ▭ , showing   Cn3D Subset   ▭

◆Launch Viewer ◇See File ◇Save MAGE Color: Molecule Number   ▭

➡ Help

(MMDB), (Cn3D), (Cn3D Helper App.), (Viewing Options), (VAST)

Back to MMDB−Homepage

Search MMDB text. [   ] Find Clear

(*a*)

Figure 3.2 Entry via (*a*) Entrez's Structure Division or (*b*) PDB's 3DB browser with the structure 1BNR (Bycroft et al., 1991) can link the user to a variety of other pages with information about this structure, including (*c*) VAST (Gibrat et al., 1996) structure–structure comparisons and the (*d*) SCOP (Murzin et al., 1995) database with information on protein family classification.

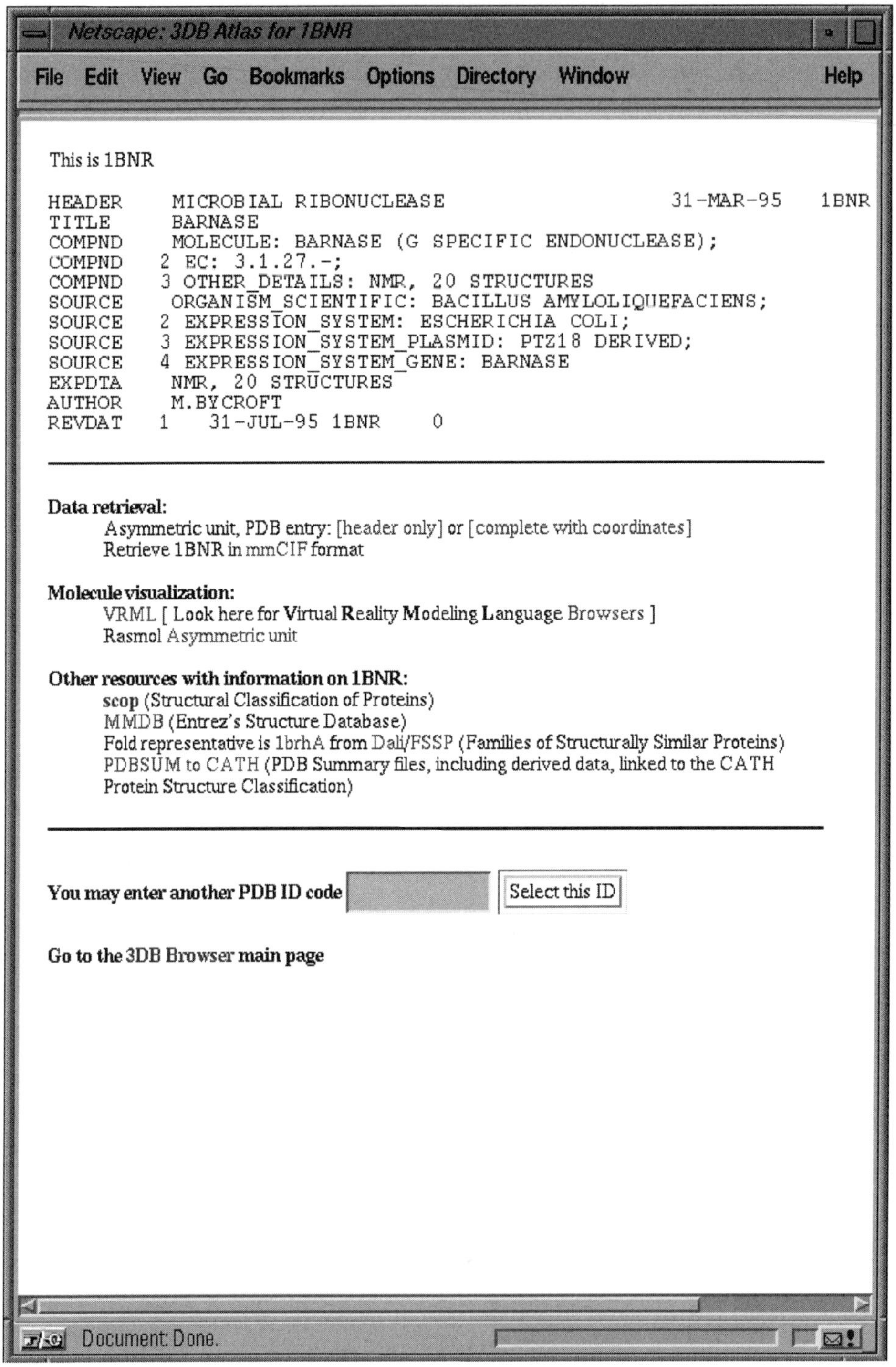

File   Edit   View   Go   Bookmarks   Options   Directory   Window   Help

This is 1BNR

```
HEADER      MICROBIAL RIBONUCLEASE                      31-MAR-95   1BNR
TITLE       BARNASE
COMPND      MOLECULE: BARNASE (G SPECIFIC ENDONUCLEASE);
COMPND      2 EC: 3.1.27.-;
COMPND      3 OTHER_DETAILS: NMR, 20 STRUCTURES
SOURCE      ORGANISM_SCIENTIFIC: BACILLUS AMYLOLIQUEFACIENS;
SOURCE      2 EXPRESSION_SYSTEM: ESCHERICHIA COLI;
SOURCE      3 EXPRESSION_SYSTEM_PLASMID: PTZ18 DERIVED;
SOURCE      4 EXPRESSION_SYSTEM_GENE: BARNASE
EXPDTA      NMR, 20 STRUCTURES
AUTHOR      M.BYCROFT
REVDAT      1    31-JUL-95 1BNR     0
```

Data retrieval:
  Asymmetric unit, PDB entry: [header only] or [complete with coordinates]
  Retrieve 1BNR in mmCIF format

Molecule visualization:
  VRML [Look here for Virtual Reality Modeling Language Browsers]
  Rasmol Asymmetric unit

Other resources with information on 1BNR:
  scop (Structural Classification of Proteins)
  MMDB (Entrez's Structure Database)
  Fold representative is 1brhA from Dali/FSSP (Families of Structurally Similar Proteins)
  PDBSUM to CATH (PDB Summary files, including derived data, linked to the CATH
  Protein Structure Classification)

You may enter another PDB ID code [   ]   [Select this ID]

Go to the 3DB Browser main page

Document: Done.

(b)

Figure 3.2   (Continued).

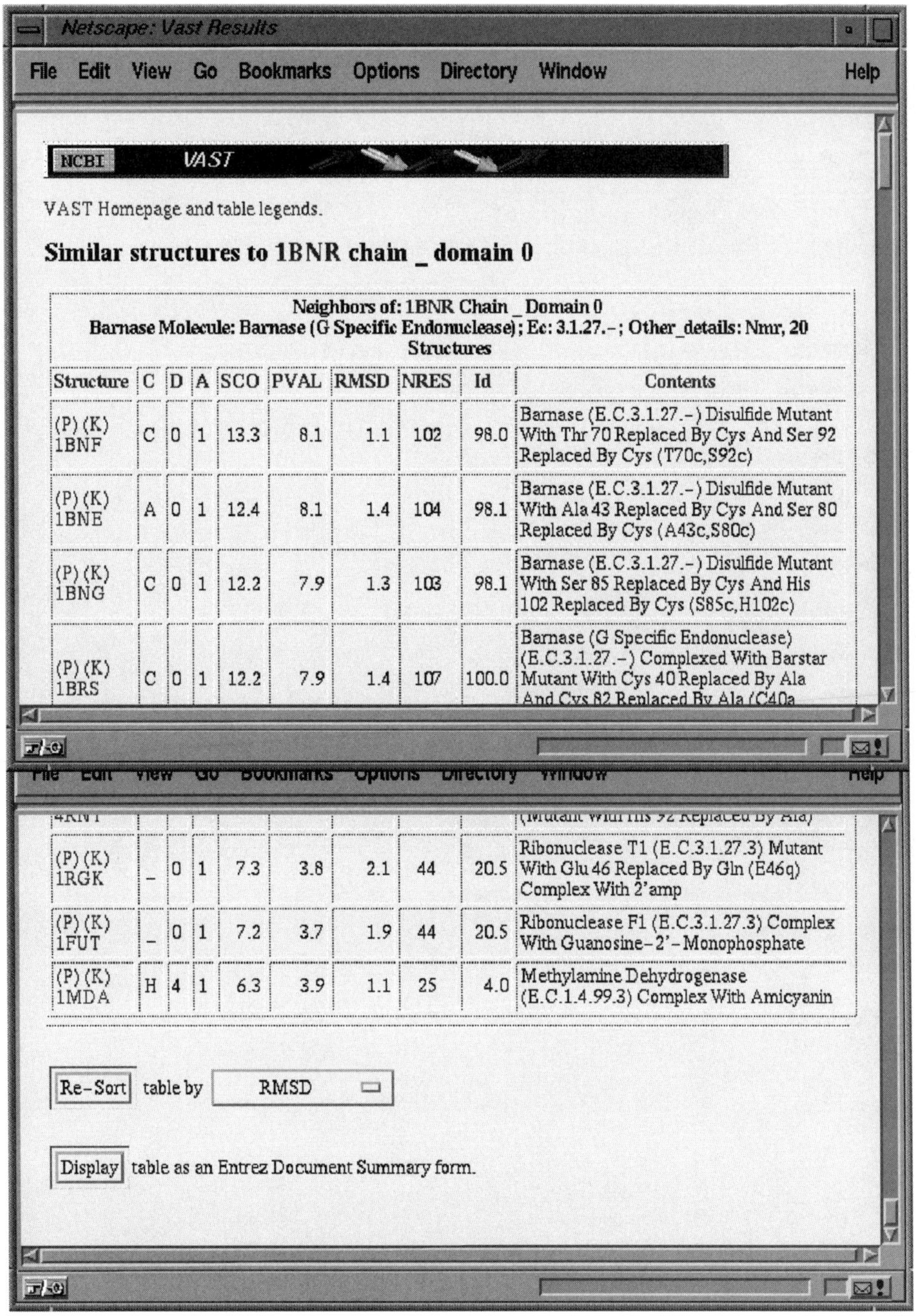

Netscape: Vast Results

File Edit View Go Bookmarks Options Directory Window   Help

NCBI   VAST

VAST Homepage and table legends.

Similar structures to 1BNR chain _ domain 0

Neighbors of: 1BNR Chain _ Domain 0
Barnase Molecule: Barnase (G Specific Endonuclease); Ec: 3.1.27.–; Other_details: Nmr, 20
Structures

Structure	C	D	A	SCO	PVAL	RMSD	NRES	Id	Contents
(P) (K) 1BNF	C	0	1	13.3	8.1	1.1	102	98.0	Barnase (E.C.3.1.27.–) Disulfide Mutant With Thr 70 Replaced By Cys And Ser 92 Replaced By Cys (T70c,S92c)
(P) (K) 1BNE	A	0	1	12.4	8.1	1.4	104	98.1	Barnase (E.C.3.1.27.–) Disulfide Mutant With Ala 43 Replaced By Cys And Ser 80 Replaced By Cys (A43c,S80c)
(P) (K) 1BNG	C	0	1	12.2	7.9	1.3	103	98.1	Barnase (E.C.3.1.27.–) Disulfide Mutant With Ser 85 Replaced By Cys And His 102 Replaced By Cys (S85c,H102c)
(P) (K) 1BRS	C	0	1	12.2	7.9	1.4	107	100.0	Barnase (G Specific Endonuclease) (E.C.3.1.27.–) Complexed With Barstar Mutant With Cys 40 Replaced By Ala And Cys 82 Replaced By Ala (C40a

File Edit View Go Bookmarks Options Directory Window   Help

4RNT								(Mutant With His 92 Replaced By Ala)
(P) (K) 1RGK	–	0	1	7.3	3.8	2.1	44	20.5 Ribonuclease T1 (E.C.3.1.27.3) Mutant With Glu 46 Replaced By Gln (E46q) Complex With 2'amp
(P) (K) 1FUT	–	0	1	7.2	3.7	1.9	44	20.5 Ribonuclease F1 (E.C.3.1.27.3) Complex With Guanosine-2'-Monophosphate
(P) (K) 1MDA	H	4	1	6.3	3.9	1.1	25	4.0 Methylamine Dehydrogenase (E.C.1.4.99.3) Complex With Amicyanin

Re–Sort table by   RMSD

Display table as an Entrez Document Summary form.

(c)

Figure 3.2 (Continued).

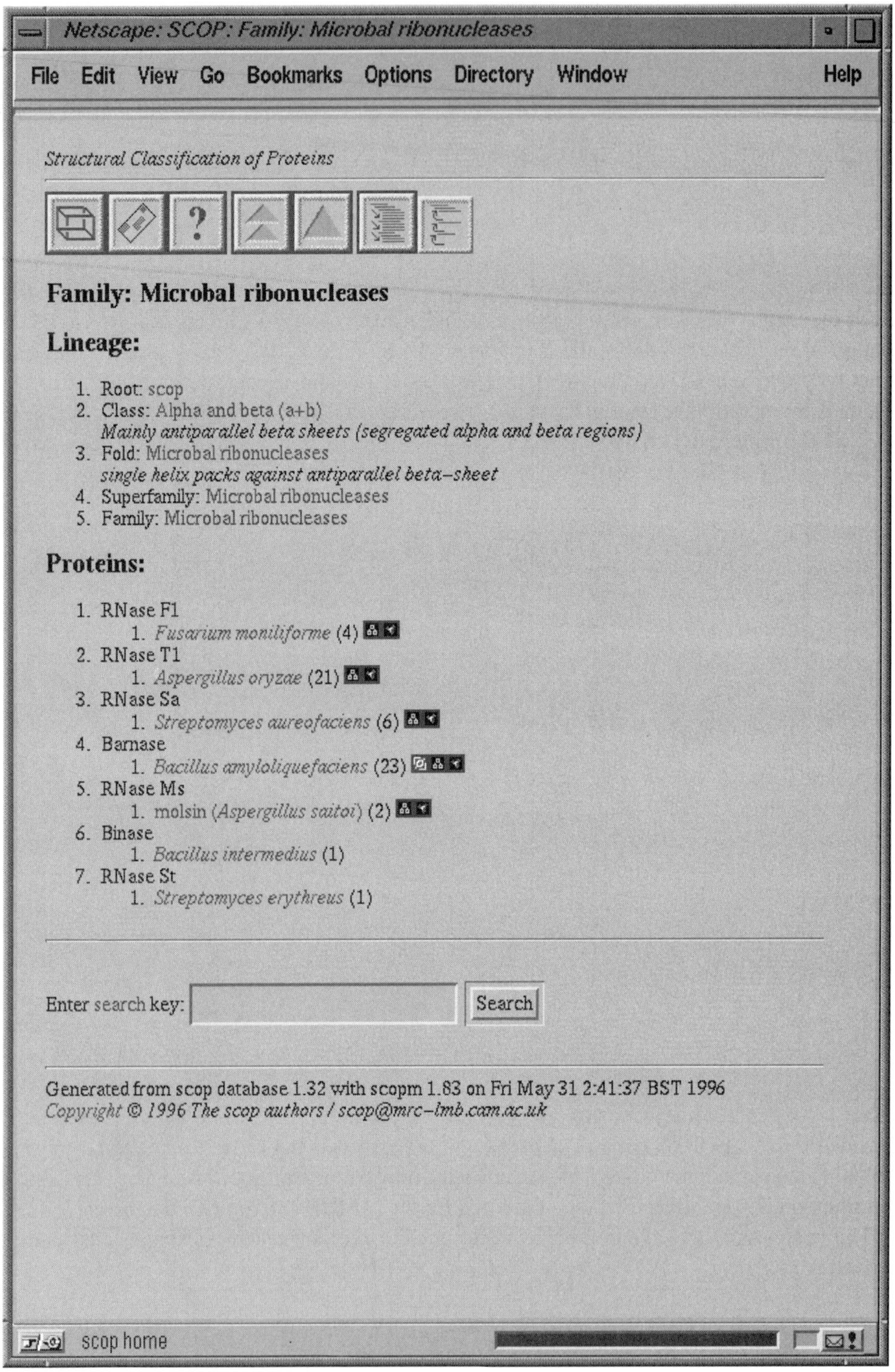
Netscape: SCOP: Family: Microbal ribonucleases
File Edit View Go Bookmarks Options Directory Window Help
Structural Classification of Proteins
Family: Microbal ribonucleases
Lineage:
1. Root: scop
2. Class: Alpha and beta (a+b)
Mainly antiparallel beta sheets (segregated alpha and beta regions)
3. Fold: Microbal ribonucleases
single helix packs against antiparallel beta-sheet
4. Superfamily: Microbal ribonucleases
5. Family: Microbal ribonucleases
Proteins:
1. RNase F1
1. Fusarium moniliforme (4)
2. RNase T1
1. Aspergillus oryzae (21)
3. RNase Sa
1. Streptomyces aureofaciens (6)
4. Barnase
1. Bacillus amyloliquefaciens (23)
5. RNase Ms
1. molsin (Aspergillus saitoi) (2)
6. Binase
1. Bacillus intermedius (1)
7. RNase St
1. Streptomyces erythreus (1)
Enter search key:
Search
Generated from scop database 1.32 with scopm 1.83 on Fri May 31 2:41:37 BST 1996
Copyright © 1996 The scop authors / scop@mrc-lmb.cam.ac.uk
scop home

(*d*)

Figure 3.2 *(Continued).*

5'- to 3'-order chain. While these sequences may be obvious to a human as a representation of a double helix, as read by a computer the 3'-to-5' explicit sequences are nonsense.

Since 3-D structures can have multiple biopolymer chains, to specify a sequence the user must provide the *PDB chain identifier.* SEQRES entries in PDB files have a chain identifier—*a single uppercase letter or blank space,* identifying each individual biopolymer chain in an entry. For the structure 3INS shown in Figure 3.1, there are two insulin molecules in the record. The 3INS record contains the sequences A, B, C, and D. Knowledge of the biochemistry of insulin is required to understand that protein chains A and B are in fact derived from the same gene, and that a post-translational modification cuts the proinsulin sequence into the A and B chains observed in the PDB record. This information is not recorded in a 3-D structure record. The one-letter chain-naming scheme has difficulties with enumerating large oligomeric 3-D structures, such as viral capsids, as one quickly runs out of single-letter chain identifiers.

The *implicit* sequences in PDB records are contained in the embedded stereochemistry of the (*x, y, z*) data and names of each ATOM record in the PDB file. The implicit sequences are useful in resolving explicit sequence ambiguities such as the backward encoding of nucleic acid sequences, or in verifying nonstandard amino acids. In practice many PDB file viewers, such as RasMol, reconstruct the chemical graph of a protein in a PDB record using only the *implicit* sequence, ignoring the *explicit* SEQRES information. If this software then is asked to print the sequence of certain incomplete molecules, it will produce a nonphysiological sequence. The *implicit sequence is not sufficient to reconstruct the complete chemical graph.*

For example, say the sequence ELVISISALIVES is represented in the SEQRES entry of a hypothetical PDB file, but the coordinate information is missing all (*x, y, z*) locations for the subsequence ISA. Software that reads the implicit sequence will often report the PDB sequence incorrectly from the chemical graph as ELVISLIVES. A test structure to determine whether software looks only at the implicit sequence is 3TS1 (Brick et al., 1989) as shown in the Java 3-D structure viewer WebMol in Figure 3.3.

Validating PDB Sequences

To properly validate a sequence from a PDB record, one must first derive the *implicit* sequence in the ATOM records. This is a nontrivial processing step. If the structure has gaps owing to lack of completeness, there may be a set of *implicit sequence fragments* for a given chain. Each of these fragments must be aligned to the *explicit* sequence of the same chain provided in the SEQRES entry. This treatment will produce the complete chemical graph, including the parts of the biological sequence that may be missing coordinate data. This kind of validation is done upon creation of records for the MMDB and mmCIF databases.

The best source of validated protein and nucleic acid sequences in single-letter code derived from PDB structure records is NCBI's MMDB service in the Entrez system. The sequence records for our insulin example have database accessions constructed systematically and can be retrieved from the protein sequence division of Entrez using the accessions: pdb|3INS|A, pdb|3INS|B, pdb|3INS|C, and pdb|3INS|D. PDB files also have references in DBXREF records to sequences in the Swiss-Prot protein database. Note that the Swiss-Prot sequences will not necessarily correspond to the structure, since the validation process described here is not carried out when these links are made! Also note that many PDB files currently have ambiguously indicated taxonomy, reflecting the presence in some in 3-D structures of complexes of molecules that come from different species.

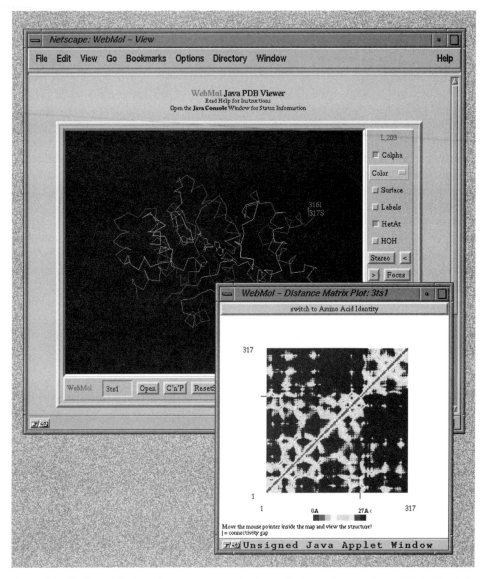

Figure 3.3 Testing a 3D viewer for sequence numbering artifacts with the structure 3TS1 (Brick et al., 1989). WebMol, a Java applet, follows the trend of not reconstructing the chemical graph of the molecule. This version of WebMol reassigns sequence numbering producing artifacts. Arg 317, Ile 318, and Ser 319 are off by two (i.e., WebMol reports Arg 315, Ile 316, and Ser 317). The actual sequence embedded in the PDB file is 419 residues long, but the C-terminal portion of the protein is lacking coordinates. (See color plate.)

MMDB: MOLECULAR MODELING DATABASE AT NCBI

Overview

NCBI's Molecular Modeling Database (MMDB: Hogue et al., 1996), is part of NCBI's Entrez (Schuler et al., 1996) system. It is a compilation of all the Brookhaven Protein Data-Bank (Bernstein et al., 1977) 3-D structures of biomolecules from crystallographic and

NMR studies. MMDB is a database of ASN.1-formatted records (Rose, 1990), not PDB-formatted records. Structures in MMDB have value-added information compared to the original PDB structures. These include the addition of the explicit chemical graph information following an extensive suite of validation procedures, the addition of uniformly derived secondary structure definitions, citation matching to MEDLINE, and the molecule-based assignment of taxonomy to each biologically derived protein or nucleic acid chain.

MMDB Database Services

A number of services including BLAST (Altschul et al., 1990) search sets of validated sequences, structure–sequence relationships, file format translation, and a programming interface are provided by NCBI's MMDB project.

Free Text Query of Structure Records   Like many other implementations of 3-D structure services, the MMDB database can be searched with free text using the World Wide Web Entrez or Network Entrez front end (Schuler et al., 1996). MMDB is also referred to as Entrez's Structure division. Search fields in MMDB include PDB and MMDB ID codes, free text from the original PDB Remark records, author name, and other bibliographic fields.

MMDB Structure Summary   MMDB's Web interface provides a Structure Summary page for each MMDB structure record, as shown in Figure 3.2*b*. MMDB Structure Summary pages provide the FASTA-formatted sequences for each chain in the structure, links to MEDLINE references, links to the 3DB Atlas record and the Brookhaven PDB site, links to protein or nucleic acid sequence neighbors for each chain in the structure, and links to the VAST structure–structure comparison for each domain on each chain in the structure.

BLAST Against PDB Sequences: New Sequence Similarities   When a researcher wishes to find a structure related to a new sequence, NCBI's BLAST (Altschul et al., 1990) service provides a copy of all the validated sequences from MMDB in "pdb" (a BLAST search database). The BLAST Web interface, can be used to paste a sequence in FASTA format into the sequence entry box and select the "pdb" sequence database to perform a search against all the validated sequences in the current public structure database.

Entrez Neighboring: Known Sequence Similarities   If one is starting with a sequence that is already in Entrez, BLAST has already been performed. Structures that are sequence similar to a given protein sequence can be found by means of Entrez's neighboring facilities.

To use Entrez's neighboring features to determine whether a sequence-similar 3-D structure exists for a known sequence, start with WWW Entrez's "Search the NCBI protein database" option and perform a query that retrieves the sequence of interest (e.g., query `oncomodulin`). Upon retrieving the summary of records in the query, select the Structure Links option on the pulldown list above the first hit and press the Display button to view two MMDB records, 1RRO (Ahmed et al., 1990) and 1OMD.

The query can be broadened to find remote similarities by performing protein neighboring first, then locating links from that list of protein neighbors to 3-D structures. Starting with the same example protein query, `oncomodulin`, will reveal that each protein record has a few hundred protein neighbors. Select the protein neighbor list first, then use the [Display] [structure links] commands at the top of the Summary page containing all the protein sequence neighbors. This will give a much longer list of 3-D structures, including all the other homologous calcium-binding proteins (e.g., parvalbumin) in the 3-D structure database.

VAST: Structure Similarity by 3-D Shape   VAST (Vector Analysis Search Tool: Gibrat et al., 1996) is a similarity measure of 3-D structure. It uses 3-D vector elements derived from secondary structure—no sequence information is used in the searching. VAST is capable of finding structural similarities when no sequence similarity is detected. VAST, like BLAST, is run on all entries in the database in an $N \times N$ manner, and the results are stored for fast retrieval using the Entrez interface. More than 10,000 domain substructures within the current 3-D structure database have been compared to one another using the VAST algorithm, and the structure–structure alignments (Figure 3.2c) and superpositions recorded. The VAST algorithm focuses on similarities that are surprising in the statistical sense. One does not waste time examining many similarities of small substructures that occur by chance in protein structure comparison. For example, very many small segments of β sheets have obvious, but not surprising, similarities. The similarities detected by VAST are often examples of remote homology, undetectable by sequence comparison. As such they may provide a broader view of the structure, function, and evolution of a protein family.

While a sequence–sequence similarity program provides an alignment of two sequences, a structure–structure similarity program provides a 3-D structural superposition. This is a set of 3-D rotation–translation matrix operations that superimpose the similar parts of the structure together. A conventional sequence alignment can be derived from the 3-D superposition by finding the α carbons in the protein backbone that are superimposed in space. In addition to a listing of similar structures, VAST-derived structure neighbors contain detailed residue-by-residue alignments and 3-D transformation matrices for structural superposition. In practice, refined alignments from VAST appear conservative, choosing a highly similar "core" substructure compared with DALI (Holm and Sander, 1996) superpositions. With the VAST superposition one easily identifies regions in which protein evolution has modified the structure, whereas DALI superpositions may be more useful for comparisons involved in making structural models. Both VAST and DALI superpositions are excellent tools to investigate relationships in protein structure, especially when used together with the SCOP (Murzin et al., 1995) database of protein families, shown in Figure 3.2d.

STRUCTURE FILE FORMATS

PDB

The PDB file format is column-oriented, like that of the punched cards used by early FORTRAN programmers. The file format specification is maintained at PDB's Web site. Most structural software developed by structural scientists is written in FORTRAN, while the rest of bioinformatics has adopted other languages, such as those based on C. PDB files are often a paradox: they look rather easy to parse, but they have a few nasty surprises, as already indicated in this chapter. To the uninitiated, the most obvious problem is that the information about biopolymer bonds is missing, obliging one to program in the rules of chemistry, clues to the identity of each atom given by the naming conventions of PDB, and robust exception handling. PDB parsing software often needs lists of synonyms and tables of exceptions to correctly interpret the information. However this chapter is not intended to be a manual of how to construct a PDB parser.

Two newer chemical-based formats have emerged: mmCIF (MacroMolecular Chemical Interchange Format) and MMDB (Molecular Modeling Database). Both these file formats are attempts to modernize PDB information. Both start by using data description languages, which are consistently machine parsable. The data description languages use "tag value" pairs, which are like variable names and values used in a programming language. In both cases the format specification is composed itself in a machine-readable form, and software uses this format specification document to validate incoming streams of data. Both file formats are populated from PDB file data using the strategy of alignment-based reconstruction of the implicit ATOM and HETATM chemical graphs with the explicit SEQRES chemical graphs, together with extensive validation, which is recorded in the file. As a result, both these file formats are superior for integrating with biomolecular sequence databases than PDB format data files, and their use in future software is encouraged.

mmCIF

The mmCIF (Bourne et al., 1995) file format was originally intended to be a biopolymer extension of the CIF (Chemical Interchange Format; Hall et al., 1991) familiar to small-molecule crystallographers, based on a subset of the STAR (Hall et al., 1991) syntax. CIF software for parsing and validating format specifications is not forward-compatible with mmCIF, since these have different implementations for the STAR syntax. The underlying data organization in an mmCIF record is a set of relational tables. The mmCIF project refers to their format specification as the *mmCIF dictionary,* kept on the World Wide Web at the Nucleic Acids Database site at Rutgers University. The mmCIF dictionary is a large document containing specifications for holding the information stored in PDB files as well as many other data items derivable from the primary coordinate data, such as bond angles. The mmCIF data specification gives this data a consistent interface, which has been used to implement the NDB Protein Finder, a WWW-based query format in a relational database style.

Validating an incoming stream of data against the large mmCIF dictionary entails a rather large overhead in the I/O of mmCIF data. Hence mmCIF is probably destined to be an archival and advanced query format. Software libraries for reading mmCIF tables into relational tables into memory in FORTRAN and C are available for a few UNIX platforms commonly used by crystallographers.

MMDB

The MMDB file format is specified by means of the ASN.1 (Rose, 1990) data description language, which is used in a variety of other settings, including telecommunications and automotive manufacturing. Since the U.S. National Library of Medicine also uses ASN.1 data specifications for sequence and bibliographic information, the MMDB format borrows certain elements from other data specifications, such as the parts used in describing bibliographic references cited in the data record. ASN.1 files can appear as human-readable text files or as a variety of binary and packed binary files that can be decoded by any hardware platform. The MMDB standard residue dictionary is a lookup table of information about the chemical graphs of standard biopolymer residue types. The MMDB format specification is kept at the MMDB FTP site at NCBI. The MMDB ASN.1 specification is much more compact and has fewer data items than the mmCIF dictionary, and avoids derivable data altogether.

In contrast to the relational table design of mmCIF, the MMDB data records are structured as hierarchical records. In terms of performance, ASN.1-formatted MMDB files are much faster I/O streams than mmCIF or PDB records. Their nested hierarchy requires fewer validation steps at load time than the relational scheme in mmCIF or in the PDB file format. Hence ASN.1 files are ideal for 3-D structure database browsing.

A complete application programming interface is available for MMDB as part of the NCBI toolkit containing a wide variety of C code libraries and applications. Both an ASN.1 I/O programming interface layer and a molecular computing layer (MMDB-API) are present in the NCBI toolkit. The NCBI toolkit supports x86 and Alpha-based Windows platforms, Macintosh 68K and PowerPC cpus, and a wide variety of UNIX platforms. The 3-D structure database viewer, Cn3D, is an MMDB-API–based application with source code included in the NCBI toolkit.

VISUALIZING STRUCTURAL INFORMATION

Multiple Representation Styles

We often use multiple styles of graphical representation to see different aspects of molecular structure. Typical images of a protein structure are shown in Figure 3.4 (see color plate). Here the enzyme barnase 1BN1 (Buckle et al., 1993) appears both in wireframe and space-filling model formats, as produced by RasMol (Sayle and Milner-White, 1995).

Since the protein structure record 1BN1 has three barnase molecules in the crystallographic unit, the PDB file has been hand-edited using a text editor to delete the superfluous chains. Editing datafiles is an accepted and widespread practice in 3-D molecular structure software to force the 3-D structure viewer to show what the user wants. In this case the crystallographic data recorded in the 3-D structure is not the *biological unit*. The biological unit, defined as the physiologically relevant form(s) of the 3-D structure, is one of the bioinformatics challenges facing the current implementation of the PDB database. In our example, the molecule barnase is a monomer, but we instead have three molecules in the crystallographic unit. In our other example, 3TS1 (Brick et al., 1989) (Figure 3.3) this molecule is a dimer, but only one of the symmetric subunits is recorded in the PDB file. A rotation–translation matrix is written into the remarks records of the file in a nonparsable manner. Rebuilding biological units from symmetry operations can be challenging, and typically requires specialized software.

The wireframe image in Figure 3.4*a* clearly shows the chemistry of the barnase structure, and we can easily trace of the sequence of barnase on the image of its biopolymer in an interactive computer display. The spacefilling model in Figure 3.4*b* gives a good indication of the size and surface of the biopolymer, yet it is difficult to follow the details of chemistry and bonding in this representation. The composite illustration in Figure 3.4*c* shows an α-carbon backbone is a typical pseudostructure representation. The lines drawn are not chemical bonds, but they guide us along the path made by the α carbons of the protein backbone. These are also called "virtual bonds." The purple tryptophan side chains have been selected and drawn together with a dot surface. This composite illustration highlights the volume taken up by the three tryptophan side chains in three hydrophobic core regions of barnase, while effectively hiding most of the structure's details.

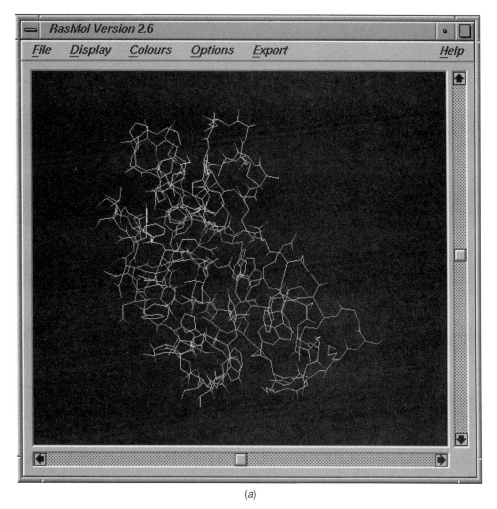

(a)

Figure 3.4 A constellation of viewing alternatives using RasMol with a portion of the barnase structure 1BN1 (Buckle et al., 1993). 1BN1 has three barnase molecules in the asymmetric unit. For this figure the author edited the PDB file to remove two extra barnase molecules to make the images. Like most crystal structures, 1BN1 has no hydrogen locations. (*a*) Barnase in CPK coloring (element-based coloring) in a wireframe representation. (*b*) Barnase in a spacefilling representation. (*c*) Barnase in an α-carbon backbone representation, colored by residue type. The command line was used to select all the tryptophan residues, render them with "sticks," color them purple, and show a dot surface representation. (*d*) Barnase in a cartoon format showing secondary structure, α helices in red; β strands in yellow. Note that in all cases the default atom or residue coloring schemes used are at the discretion of the author of the software. (See color plate.)

The ribbon model in Figure 3.4*d* shows the organization of the structural path of the secondary structure elements of the protein chain the α-helix and β-sheet regions. This representation is very often used, with the arrowheads indicating the N-to-C direction of the secondary structure elements, and is most effective for identifying secondary structure within complex topologies.

The variety of information conveyed by the different views in Figure 3.4 illustrates the need to visualize 3-D biopolymer structure data in unique ways that are not common to

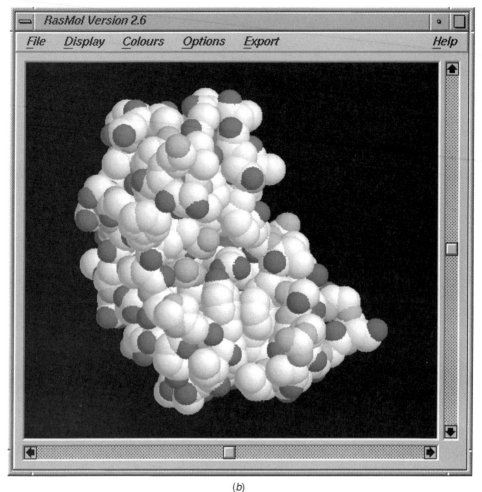

(b)

Figure 3.4 *(Continued).*

other 3-D graphics applications. This requirement often precludes the effective use of software from the "macroscopic world" such as computer-aided design (CAD) or Virtual Reality Modeling Language (VRML) packages.

Picture the Data: Populations, Degeneracy, and Dynamics

Both X-ray and NMR techniques infer 3-D structure from a *synchronized* population of molecules—synchronized in space as an ordered crystal lattice, or synchronized in behavior as nuclear spin states are organized by an external magnetic field. In both cases information is gathered from the population as a whole. The coordinate (x, y, z) locations of atoms in a structure are derived using numerical methods. These fit the expected chemical graph of the sample into the three-dimensional data derived from the experimental data. The expected chemical graph can include a mixture of biopolymer-sequence-derived information as well as the chemical graph of any other known small molecules present in the sample, such as substrates, prosthetic groups, and ions.

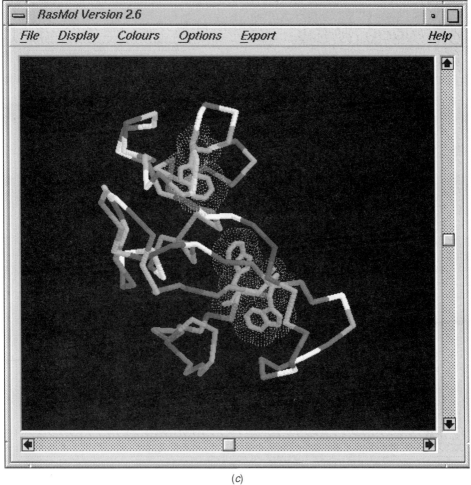

(c)

Figure 3.4   *(Continued).*

One somewhat unexpected result of the use of molecular populations is the assignment of degenerate coordinates in a database record, i.e. more than one coordinate location for a single atom in the chemical graph. This is recorded when the population of molecules has observable conformational heterogeneity.

NMR Models and Ensembles

Figure 3.5 (see color plate) presents four 3-D structures, on the left as determined using X-ray crystallography, and on the right as determined using NMR. The NMR structures on the left appear "fuzzy." In fact, there are several different, complete structures piled up one on top of another in these images. Each structure is referred to as a *model,* and the set of models is an *ensemble.* Each model in the ensemble is a chirally correct, plausible structure that fits the underlying NMR data as well as any other model in the ensemble.

The images from the ensemble of an NMR structure (Figure 3.5*b,d*) show the dynamic variation of a molecule in solution. This reflects the conditions of the experiment: mole-

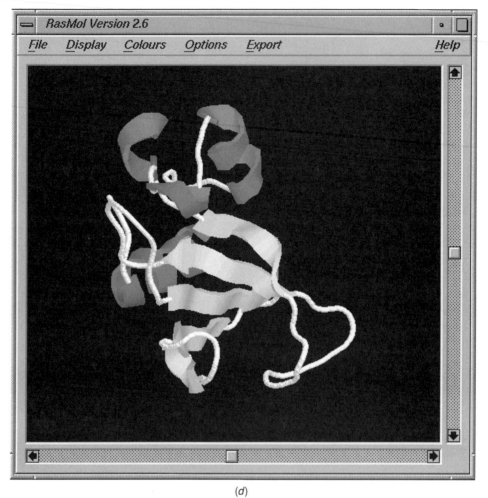

(d)

Figure 3.4   (Continued).

cules free in solution with freedom to pursue dynamic conformational changes. In contrast, the X-ray structures (Figure 3.5*a,c*) provide a very strong mental image of a static molecule. This also reflects the conditions of the experiment, an ordered crystal constrained in its freedom to explore its conformational dynamics. These mental images direct our interpretation of structure. If we measure distance between two atoms using an X-ray structure, we may get a single value. However we can get a range of values for the same distance in each model looking at an ensemble of an NMR structure. Clearly our interpretation of this distance can be dependent on the source of the 3-D structure data! Beware of any software that ignores or fails to show the population degeneracy present in structure database records, for absence of this information can further skew interpretations. Measuring the distance between two atoms in an NMR structure using software that hides the other members of the ensemble will give only one value, and not the true range of distance observed by the experimentalist.

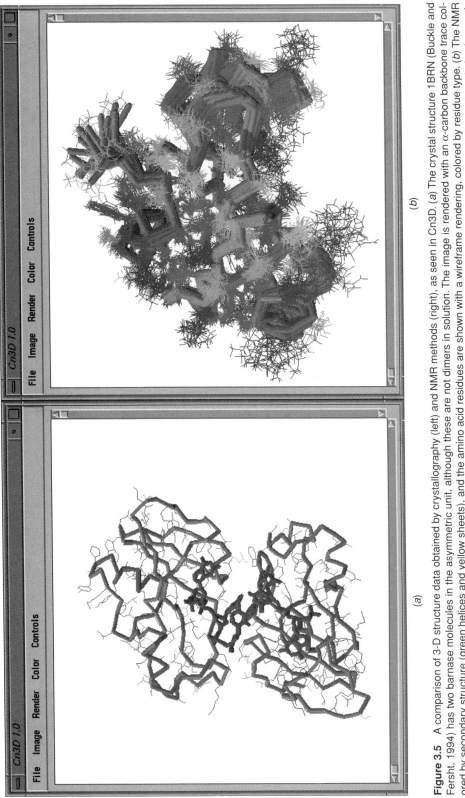

(a)

(b)

Figure 3.5 A comparison of 3-D structure data obtained by crystallography (left) and NMR methods (right), as seen in Cn3D. (*a*) The crystal structure 1BRN (Buckle and Fersht, 1994) has two barnase molecules in the asymmetric unit, although these are not dimers in solution. The image is rendered with an α-carbon backbone trace colored by secondary structure (green helices and yellow sheets), and the amino acid residues are shown with a wireframe rendering, colored by residue type. (*b*) The NMR structure 1BNR (Bycroft et al., 1991) showing barnase in solution. Here there are 20 different models in the ensemble of structures. The coloring and rendering is exactly as the crystal structure to its left. (*c*) The crystal structure 109D (Quintana et al., 1991) showing a complex between a minor-groove binding bisbenzimidazole drug and a DNA fragment. Note the phosphate ion in the lower left corner. (*d*) The NMR structure 107D showing four models of a complex between a different minor-groove binding compound (Duocarmycin A) and a different DNA fragment. It appears that the 3-D superposition of these ensembles is incorrectly shifted along the axis of the DNA, an error in PDB's processing of this particular file.

65

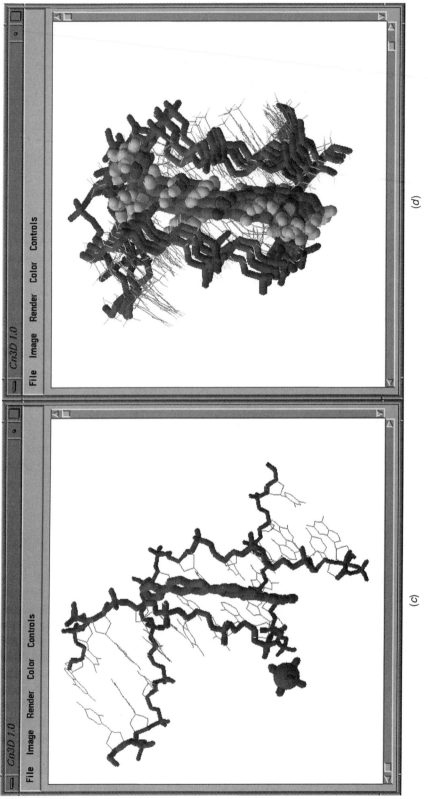

Figure 3.5 *(Continued).*

Correlated Disorder

Typically X-ray structures have only one model. Some subsets of atoms, however, may have degenerate coordinates, which we will refer to as *correlated disorder,* (Figure 3.6*a:* see color plate). Many X-ray structure database records have correlated disorder. Both correlated disorder and ensembles are often ignored by 3-D molecular graphics software. Some programs show only the first model in an ensemble, or the first location of a each atom in a correlated disorder set, ignoring the rest of the degenerate coordinate values. Worse still, sometimes erroneous bonds are drawn between the degenerate locations, making a mess of the structure, as seen in Figure 3.6*b.*

Local Dynamics

A single technique can be used to constrain the conformation of some atoms differently from others in the same structure. For example, an internal atom or a backbone atom that is locked in by a multitude of interactions may appear largely invariant in NMR or X-ray data, whereas an atom on the surface of the molecule may have much more conformational free-

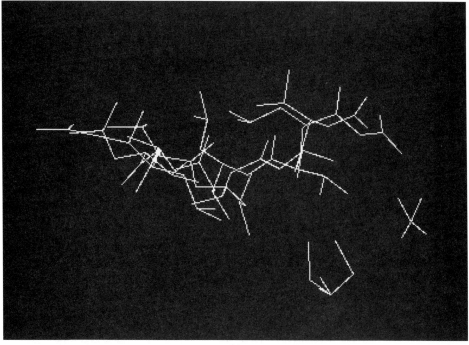

(*a*)

Figure 3.6 An example of crystallographic correlated disorder encoded in PDB files. This is chain C of the HIV protease structure 5HVP (Fitzgerald et al., 1990). This chain is in a symmetric binding site and can orient itself in two different directions. Therefore it has a single chemical graph, but each atom can be in one of two different locations. (*a*) The correct bonding is shown with an MMDB-generated Kinemage file, magenta and red are the correlated disorder ensembles as originally recorded by the depositor, bonding calculated using standard-residue dictionary matching. (*b*) Bonding of the same chain in RasMol, wherein the disorder ensemble information is ignored, and all coordinates are displayed and all possible bonds are bonded together.

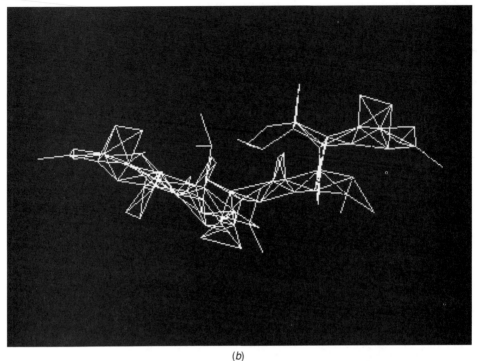

(b)

Figure 3.6   *(Continued).*

dom (look at the size of the smears of different residues in Figure 3.5*b*). Interior protein side chains typically show much less flexibility in ensembles, so it might be concluded that the interiors of proteins lack conformational dynamics altogether. However a more sensitive, biophysical method, time-resolved fluorescence spectroscopy of single tryptophan residues, has a unique ability to detect heterogeneity (but not the actual coordinates) of the tryptophan side chain conformation. Years of study with this method has shown that time and time again populations of interior tryptophans in pure proteins are more often in heterogeneous conformation than not (Beechen and Brand, 1985). Recently this method was shown to be able to detect rotamers of tryptophan within single crystals of erabutoxin, where X-ray crystallography could not (Dahms and Szabo, 1995). When interpreting 3-D structure data, remember that heterogeneity does persist in the data, and that the NMR and X-ray methods can be blind to all but the most populated conformations in the sample.

DATABASE STRUCTURE VIEWERS

RasMol and RasMol-Based Viewers

Several viewers for examining PDB files are available (Sanchez-Ferrer et al., 1995). The most popular one is Roger Sayle's RasMol (Sayle and Milner-White, 1995). RasMol represents a breakthrough in software-driven 3-D graphics, and its source code is recommended study material for anyone interested in high-performance 3-D graphics. RasMol treats PDB data with extreme caution and often recomputes information, making up for inconsistencies in the underlying database. It does not try to validate the chemical graph of sequences or structures encoded in PDB files. RasMol does not perform internally neither dictionary-based standard residue validations or alignment of explicit and implicit sequences. RasMol ignores information in correlated disorder ensembles and displays only one NMR model at a time. Other data elements encoded in PDB files, such as disulfide bonds, are recomputed based on rules of chemistry, rather than validated.

RasMol contains many excellent output formats and can be used with the Molscript (Kraulis, 1991) program to make wonderful PostScript™ ribbon diagrams for publication. For optimal use of RasMol, however, one must master its command line language, a familiar feature of many legacy 3-D structure programs. RasMol executables, a gallery of RasMol images, a RasMol tutorial, source code, and a user-based support mailing list are available from the RasMol home page maintained by Eric Martz at the University of Massachusetts.

Several new programs, free for academic users, are becoming available. Based on RasMol's software-driven 3D rendering algorithms and sparse PDB parser, these include Chime™, a Netscape™ plug-in provided by MDLI Inc. WebMol, a Java applet by Dirk Walther, is a Java-based 3D structure viewer apparently based on RasMol style rendering, as seen in Figure 3.3. WebMol has demonstrated that the Java bytecode interpreters in current use on most PCs and workstations are not sufficiently fast to perform RasMol-style software-based 3-D rendering for structures in excess of 200 residues. This limits WebMol's utility to the smaller structures, or to virtual bond representation of molecules.

MMDB Viewer: Cn3D

Cn3D is a new 3-D structure viewer, used for viewing MMDB data record. Because the chemical graph ambiguities in data in PDB entries have been removed to make MMDB data records and because all the bonding information is explicit, Cn3D has the luxury of being able to display 3D database structures consistently, without the parsing, validation, and exception-handling overhead required of programs that read PDB files. Cn3D's default image of a structure is more intelligently displayed because it works without fear of misrepresenting the data. However, because Cn3D is dependent on the complete chemical graph information in the ASN.1 records of MMDB, it does not currently read in PDB files.

Cn3D provides a set of control panels that can hide or appear at the side of the 3-D image. For example, the Viewer Control panel, which appears at the top of the 3-D image, has a set of animation controls that look like tape recorder controls and are used for displaying the multiple structure ensembles of NMR structures one after the other, or the multiple structures superimposed in a VAST similarity relationship image. The Go button makes the images animated, and the user can rotate or zoom the structure while it is playing the animation. Cn3D 2.0, which should be available by the time of publication, will have complete state-saving capabilities. This will make it possible to color and render a structure, and then save the information right into the ASN.1 structure record, a departure from hand-editing PDB files or writing scripts. This information can be shared with other Cn3D users on different platforms.

Other 3D Viewers: Mage, CAD, VRML

A variety of file formats have been used to present 3-D biomolecular structure data lacking in chemistry-specific data representations. These are viewed in generic 3-D data viewers such as those used for "macroscopic" data like engineering software or virtual reality browsers. The journal *Protein Science* published one such generic file format: the Kinemage (Richardson and Richardson, 1992, 1994) the first widely used molecular structure software made available to personal computer users prior to the emergence of the Internet and the World Wide Web. File formats like Kinemage and VRML contain 3-D graphical display information but little or no information about the underlying chemical graph of a molecule. Further, it is difficult to encode the variety of rendering styles in such a file; one needs a separate VRML file for a spacefilling model of a molecule, a wireframe model, a ball-and-stick model, and so on, since each explicit list of graphics objects (cylinders, lines, spheres) must be contained in the file.

Biomolecular 3-D structure database records are currently not compatible with "macroscopic" software tools such as those based on CAD software. Computer-aided design software is a mature, robust technology, generally superior to the available molecular structure software. But CAD software and file formats in general are ill-suited to examine the molecular world, owing to the lack of certain "specialty" views and analytical functions built in for the examination of details of protein structures.

CAN'T FIND A PUBLISHED STRUCTURE?

As the cornerstone of most all structure–function information, structures are indeed prized data. So prized, in fact, that a few structural scientists are reluctant to deposit their data into public databases. Historically, some journals have not required structures to be immediately submitted to the Brookhaven Protein Data Bank. This has led to a proliferation of structures that seem to be inaccessible because the authors never bothered or chose not to submit their data to a public database. Sometimes these decisions are made at variance with the very public nature of the funding used to determine the structure. With the emergence of new and successful fold-recognition techniques such as threading, the holding back of structures can lead to missed opportunities for discoveries. New computational methods are dependent on having complete 3-D structure databases.

It may be necessary to write to the authors of a structure to obtain 3-D structures published in the literature but not found in the databases listed here. Before doing so, as a courtesy to the structural scientist, find the original article describing the coordinates of interest. Next, do a thorough search using the Brookhaven Protein Data Bank's "Pending/Waiting List" to see whether the structure data is still in processing, or is "on hold." If these possibilities have been ruled out, write to the principal author of the article and request the coordinates directly. Usually the author will supply a crude PDB file, which may require some editing (usually renumbering) before it can be worked with it in another researcher's PDB browsing software. If it is necessary to edit a PDB file, first study the structure of other PDB format files and refer to the online PDB format document.

Internet Resources for Topics in Chapter 3

LARGE DATABASES

Brookhaven Protein Data Bank   *http://www.pdb.bnl.gov/*
   3DB Atlas   *http://www.pdb.bnl.gov/cgi-bin/pdbmain*
    Pending/Waiting list   *http://www.pdb.bnl.gov/cgi-bin/whsearch*
    Submitting, AutoDep   *http://www.pdb.bnl.gov/pdb-docs/submit_page.html*

National Center for Biotechnology Information (NCBI)   *http://www.ncbi.nlm.nih.gov/*
  BLAST   *http://www.ncbi.nlm.nih.gov/BLAST/*
  Cn3D Home page   *http://www.ncbi.nlm.nih.gov/Structure/Cn3D.html*
  db_xref   *http://www.ncbi.nlm.nih.gov/Structure/Cn3D.html*
  Entrez   *http://www.ncbi.nlm.nih.gov/Entrez/*
  MMDB ASN.1 specification   *http://www.ncbi.nlm.nih.gov/Toolbox/AsnBrowser*
  NCBI Structure   *http://www.ncbi.nlm.nih.gov/Structure*
  NCBI Toolkit   *http://www.ncbi.nlm.nih.gov/Toolbox*
  VAST   *http://www.ncbi.nlm.nih.gov/Structure/vast.html*

Nucleic Acids Database (NDB)   *http://ndbserver.rutgers.edu/*
  mmCif Project   *http://ndbserver.rutgers.edu/NDB/mmcif/index.html*
  NDB Structure Finder   *http://ndbserver.rutgers.edu/NDB/structure-finder*

ADDITIONAL TOOLS

Biotech Validation Suite for Protein Structures   *http://biotech.embl-heidelberg.de:8400/*
DALI   *http://croma.ebi.ac.uk/dali/*
FSSP   *http://ww2.embl-ebi.ac.uk/dali/fssp*
Protein Motions Database   *http://bioinfo.mbb.yale.edu/MolMovDB/*
SCOP   *http://scop.mrc-lmb.cam.ac.uk/scop/*

REFERENCES

Ahmed, F. R., Przybylska, M., Rose, D. R., Birnbaum, G. I., Pippy, M. E., and MacManus, J. P. (1990). Structure of oncomodulin refined at 1.85 angstroms resolution. An example of extensive molecular aggregation via Ca^{2+}. *J. Mol. Biol. 216,* 127–140.

Altschul, S. F., Gish, W., Miller, W., Myers, E. W., and Lipman, D. J. (1990). Basic local alignment search tool. *J. Mol. Biol. 215,* 403–410.

Beechem, J. M., and Brand, L. (1985). Time-resolved fluorescence of proteins. Annu. Rev. Biochem. *54,* 43–71.

Bernstein, F. C., Koetzle, T. F., Williams, G. J. B., Meyer, E. F., Jr., Brice, M. D., Rodgers, J. R., Kennard, O., Shimanouchi, T., and Tasumi, M. (1977). The Protein Data Bank. J. Mol. Biol. *112,* 535–542.

Bourne, P. E., Berman, H. M., McMahon, B., Watenpaugh, K. D., Westbrook, J., and Fitzgerald, P. M. D. (1995). The Macromolecular Crystallographic Information File (mmCIF). Methods in Enzymol. *277.*

Brick, P., Bhat, T. N., and Blow, D. M. (1989). Structure of tyrosyl–tRNA synthetase refined at 2.3 angstroms resolution. Interaction of the enzyme with the tyrosyl adenylate intermediate. J. Mol. Biol. *208,* 83–98.

Buckle, A. M., and Fersht, A. R. (1994). Subsite binding in an RNase: Structure of a barnase–tetranucleotide complex at 1.76-angstroms resolution. *Biochemistry 33,* 1644–1653.

Buckle, A. M., Henrick, K., and Fersht, A. R. (1993). Crystal structural analysis of mutations in the hydrophobic cores of barnase. J. Mol. Biol. *23,* 847–860.

Bycroft, M., Ludvigsen, S., Fersht, A. R., and Poulsen, F. M. (1991). Determination of the three-dimensional solution structure of barnase using nuclear magnetic resonance spectroscopy. Biochemistry *30,* 8697–8701.

Dahms, T., and Szabo, A. G. (1995). Conformational heterogeneity of tryptophan in a protein crystal. J. Am. Chem. Soc. *117,* 2321–2326.

Fitzgerald, P. M., McKeever, B. M., VanMiddlesworth, J. F., Springer, J. P., Heimbach, J. C., Leu, C.

T., Herber, W. K., Dixon, R. A., and Darke, P. L. (1990). Crystallographic analysis of a complex between human immunodeficiency virus type 1 protease and acetyl-pepstatin at 2.0-angstroms resolution. J. Biol. Chem. *265,* 14209–14219.

Gerstein, M., Lesk, A., and Chothia, C. (1994). Structural mechanisms for domain movements in proteins. Biochemistry *33,* 6739–6749.

Gibrat, J. F., Madej, T., and Bryant, S. H. (1996). Surprising similarities in structure comparison. Curr. Opin. Struct. Biol. *6,* 377–385.

Hall, S. R. (1991). The STAR file: A new format for electronic data transfer and archiving. J. Chem. Inf. Comput. Sci. *31,* 326–333.

Hall, S. R., Allen, A. H., and Brown, I. D. (1991). The crystallographic information file (CIF): A new standard archive file for crystallography. Acta Crystallogr. Sect. A *47,* 655–685.

Hogue, C. W. V., Ohkawa, H., and Bryant, S. H. (1996). A dynamic look at structures: WWW-Entrez and the Molecular Modeling Database. Trends Biochemical Sci. *21,* 226–229.

Holm, L., and Sander, C. (1993). Protein structure comparison by alignment of distance matrices. J. Mol. Biol. *233,* 123–138.

Holm, L., and Sander, C. (1996). The FSSP database: Fold classification based on structure–structure alignment of proteins. Nucl. Acids Res. *24,* 206–210.

Issacs, N. W., Agarwal, R. C. (1978). Experience with fast Fourier least squares in the refinement of the crystal structure of rhombohedral 2 zinc insulin at 1.5 angstroms resolution. Acta Crystallogr. Sect. A *34,* 782.

Kraulis, P. J. (1991). MOLSCRIPT: A program to produce both detailed and schematic plots of protein structures. J. Appl. Crystallogr. *24,* 946–950.

Murzin, A. G., Brenner, S. E., Hubbard, T., and Chothia, C. (1995). SCOP: A structural classification of proteins database for the investigation of sequences and structures. J. Mol. Biol. *24,* 536–540.

Quintana, J. R., Lipanov, A. A., and Dickerson, R. E. (1991). Low-temperature crystallographic analyses of the binding of Hoechst 33258 to the double-helical DNA dodecamer C-G-C-G-A-A-T-T-C-G-C-G. Biochemistry *30,* 10294–10306.

Richardson, D. C., and Richardson, J. S. (1992). The Kinemage: A tool for scientific communication. Protein Sci. *1,* 3–9.

Richardson, D. C., and Richardson, J. S. (1994). Kinemages—Simple macromolecular graphics for interactive teaching and publication. Trends Biochem. Sci. *19,* 135–138.

Rose, M. T. (1990). *The Open Book, A Practical Perspective on OSI* (Englewood Cliffs, NJ: Prentice-Hall), pp. 227–322.

Sanchez-Ferrer, A., Nunez-Delicado, E., and Bru, R. (1995). Software for viewing biomolecules in three dimensions on the Internet. Trends Biochem. Sci. *20,* 286–288.

Sayle, R. A., and Milner-White, E. J. (1995). RASMOL: Biomolecular graphics for all. Trends Biochem. Sci. *20,* 374–376.

Schuler, G. D., Epstein, J. A., Ohkawa, H., and Kans, J. A. (1996). Entrez: Molecular biology database and retrieval system. Methods Enzymol. *266,* 141–162.

MONOGRAPHS

Biomolecular Structural Methods

Drenth, J. (1994). *Principles of X-Ray Crystallography,* 2nd ed. (New York: Cambridge University Press).

Frank, J. (1996). *Three-Dimensional Electron Microscopy of Macromolecular Assemblies* (San Diego, CA: Academic Press).

Molecular Modeling and Visualization

Douchet, J.-P., and Weber, J. (1996). *Computer Aided Molecular Design* (San Diego, CA: Academic Press).

Leach, A. (1996). *Molecular Modeling: Principles and Applications* (London: Longmans).

Lesk, A. M. (1991). *Protein Architecture: A Practical Approach* (Oxford: IRL Press).

Protein Structure

Branden, C., and Tooze, J. (1991). *Introduction to Protein Structure* (New York: Garland Press).

4

Sequence Analysis Using GCG

Barbara A. Butler

Genetics Computer Group, Inc.
Oxford Molecular Group
Madison, Wisconsin

INTRODUCTION

The advent of rapid, economical nucleic acid sequencing methods revolutionized many scientific disciplines including molecular biology, genetics, and biochemistry (Gilbert, 1981; Sanger, 1981). This technology also established a need for public databases to house the enormous amount of sequence information that was soon being generated in laboratories worldwide (Benson et al., 1997; Stoesser et al., 1997). The fields of bioinformatics and computational biology came of age with the establishment of these databases, since sequences submitted to them required analysis and annotation. In addition, existing database entries needed to be identified and retrieved by researchers wishing to study them further.

Bioinformatics can be described as the acquisition, analysis, and storage of biological information, specifically nucleic acid and protein sequences. Computational biology is the development of algorithms and computer programs integral to these endeavors. Both fields have grown dramatically in the past decade, driven by the enormous amount of data accumulating from whole-genome sequencing projects. Programs for analyzing sequences and searching databases are available from a number of sources, both commercial and academic. Packages for personal computers and Macintoshes are often expensive, especially for multiple users, and can lack a comprehensive array of programs for analysis and editing. Publicly available stand-alone (i.e., not part of a package) programs are inexpensive, in contrast to commercial programs, but they have to be downloaded and sometimes compiled on the local machine, and users have to become familiar with the format for input sequences and learn how to run them effectively. Network access to selected programs has become available recently, but it is difficult to perform analyses requiring more than one of these programs. For example, depending on the software used, a researcher can run a data-

Bioinformatics: A Practical Guide to the Analysis of Genes and Proteins
Edited by A.D. Baxevanis and B.F.F. Ouellette
ISBN 0-471-19196-5, pages 74–97.   Copyright © 1998 Wiley-Liss, Inc.

base search but cannot then align the sequences found by that search. It is also difficult to create an alignment of sequences and then edit that alignment.

This chapter introduces and discusses an environment that provides interoperability among a large number of sequence analysis and database searching programs as well as access to sequence data from a variety of sources. The environment is SeqLab®, developed by the Genetics Computer Group (GCG), as part of the Wisconsin Package™. The Wisconsin Package, a comprehensive set of sequence analysis programs, is distributed with public nucleic acid and protein databases. SeqLab is a graphical user interface (GUI) that permits full access to Wisconsin Package programs and supported databases. In addition, it provides an environment for creating, displaying, editing, and annotating sequences. SeqLab can also be expanded to include other publicly and locally available programs and databases.

Many of the analyses performed by Wisconsin Package programs are discussed in detail in other chapters of this volume, as are the databases distributed with the Wisconsin Package and SeqLab. Therefore, this chapter emphasizes the environment within which database entries and local sequences can be accessed, the types of analysis that can be performed, and the means of editing and annotating these entries and sequences.

THE WISCONSIN PACKAGE

The Wisconsin Package is a comprehensive sequence analysis software package that consists of over 120 individual programs, each performing a single analytical task. Database entries from public and private databases as well as individual sequence files can be analyzed with Wisconsin Package programs because there is a uniform format for sequences used as input to all programs. In addition, the output files from some programs are in a format that permits them to be further analyzed with other programs. Because of this, and the modularity of the package as a whole, a user can analyze sequences in a number of different ways by using programs in different combinations. The appendix of this chapter lists and describes the most widely used programs. A complete listing and detailed description of all programs can be found in the Program Manual for the Wisconsin Package.

The Wisconsin Package supports a number of UNIX platforms as well as OpenVMS. General information about GCG, the Wisconsin Package, supported platforms, and hardware requirements can be found on the GCG home page, /www.gcg.com/, and in the Wisconsin Package User's Guide.

DATABASES THAT ACCOMPANY THE WISCONSIN PACKAGE

GCG supports and distributes five databases, two nucleic acid and three protein, for use with the Wisconsin Package. These databases are in both GCG format (for use with most Wisconsin Package programs), and BLAST format (for use with the BLAST database searching program). Indices for the LookUp program, for database reference searching, are also provided.

The two supported nucleic acid databases are the GenBank database (Benson et al., 1997), provided in its entirety, and an abridged version of the EMBL Nucleotide Sequence Database (Stoesser et al., 1997), consisting only of sequences not present in GenBank. These two databases have been combined for searching purposes into a single, comprehensive nucleotide database named GenEMBLPlus. This combined database includes the

GenBank and EMBL Nucleotide Sequence Database divisions for expressed sequence tag (EST), sequence tag site (STS), and genome sequence survey (GSS) entries. It is possible to search these three divisions separately with the specification TAGS or to search the Gen-EMBLPlus database without these divisions with the specification GenEMBL.

The three protein databases supported and distributed by GCG are the Protein Information Resource (PIR) International Protein Sequence Database (George et al., 1997), the SWISS-PROT Protein Sequence Databank (Bairoch and Apweiler, 1997), and SP-TrEMBL (Bairoch and Apweiler, 1997). SP-TrEMBL is a joint venture of the European Bioinformatics Institute and Dr. Amos Bairoch of the University of Geneva in Switzerland. It contains most of the predicted translated regions noted in EMBL database entries but does not contain any entries already present in SWISS-PROT. SP-TrEMBL entries are annotated using SWISS-PROT conventions, and as these entries appear in the SWISS-PROT database they will be removed from SP-TrEMBL. These two databases, SWISS-PROT and SP-TrEMBL, have been combined for searching purposes to create a comprehensive protein database named SWISS-PROTPlus.

New releases of the databases supported by GCG are available bimonthly (following the GenBank database release schedule) as part of the GCG Database Update Service. Alternatively, Wisconsin Package utility programs and scripts are available for downloading and formatting database releases on site. These programs can also be used to update databases between releases or to format private data into databases for use with the Wisconsin Package. A list and description of these utility programs can be found in the Wisconsin Package System Support Manual. Databases in FASTA format can be used directly, without further formatting, with all programs included in the Wisconsin Package except the BLAST and LookUp programs.

THE SEQLAB ENVIRONMENT

SeqLab is a graphical user interface to the Wisconsin Package based on OSF/Motif™. It allows access to most Wisconsin Package programs and all supported databases from a Windows-based environment. Use of SeqLab requires an X-terminal or X-server software running on a microcomputer. Recommendations for X-server software can be found on the GCG home page, *www.gcg.com.*

After the Wisconsin Package has been initialized, SeqLab is launched from the UNIX prompt with the command seqlab. A window appears entitled SeqLab Main Window (Figure 4.1). There are two modes in which this main window can appear: Main List mode and Editor mode (referred to here as the "SeqLab Editor"). In Main List mode the SeqLab Main Window displays a list file containing the names of single-sequence, list, multiple-sequence format (MSF), and rich-sequence format (RSF) files as well as database entries. In Editor mode the SeqLab Main Window displays the sequences listed in these files and database entries. Users can toggle between the two modes with the Mode: option button on the SeqLab Main Window (Figure 4.1). Both modes permit access to Wisconsin Package programs and supported databases, but from the SeqLab Editor a user can also edit and annotate sequences. This chapter concentrates on the SeqLab Editor.

Across the top of the SeqLab Main Window is a menu bar; the menu options can be summarized as follows:

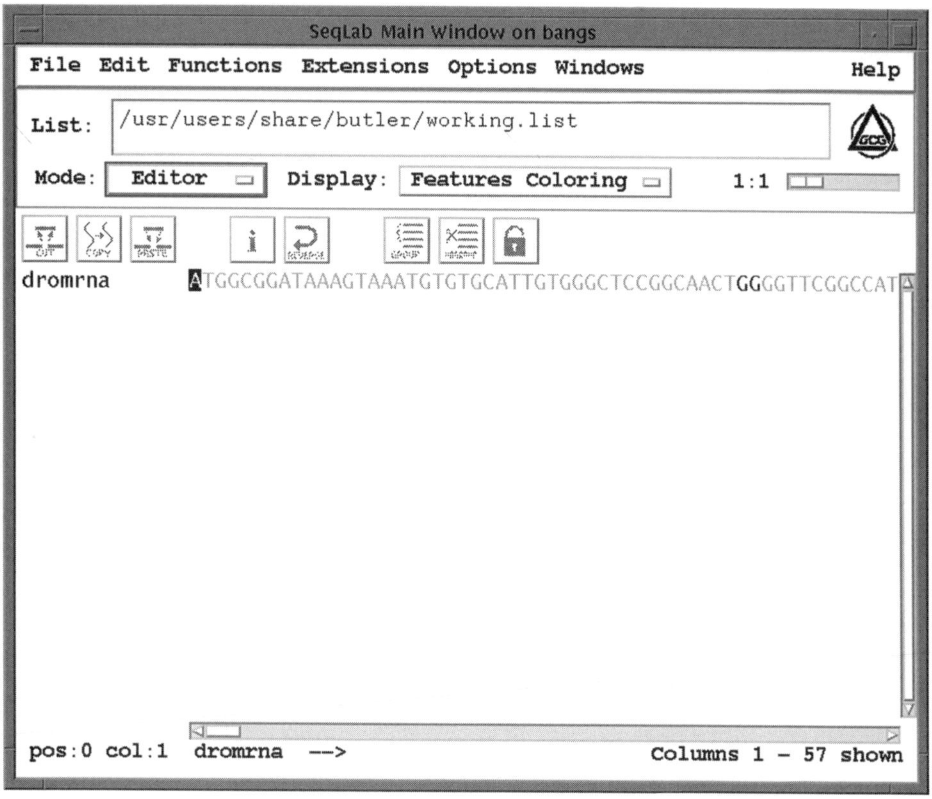

Figure 4.1   The SeqLab Main Window in Editor mode.

File: Options for adding sequences from databases or directory files or for creating sequences de novo.

Edit: Options for moving and editing sequences and performing simple operations.

Functions: Wisconsin Package programs organized by analysis topics.

Extensions: A list of additional programs, if any, that can be run from within SeqLab.

Options: Preferences for displaying sequences and output, file management, and printing.

Windows: A list of windows for output display, program monitoring, and features annotation.

Help: Online help for Wisconsin Package programs and the SeqLab interface.

In addition to the Mode option button, the SeqLab Main Window includes a Display option button for changing the color or shading of sequences displayed and a scale bar for changing their horizontal scale. A panel of icons offers an alternative method for selecting editing options, viewing sequence information, and setting protections. The majority of the space in this window, however, is reserved for displaying sequences (Figure 4.1).

Adding Entries from Databases and Sequence Files from Directories

A sequence must appear in the SeqLab Main Window before it can be edited or analyzed with Wisconsin Package programs. Database entries are added either by entry name or by accession number. Single-sequence files (in GCG format), list, MSF, and RSF files are added by file name. (See the SeqLab Guide for details on these file formats and how they are created.)

To add an entry from a database to the SeqLab Main Window, use the left mouse button to select File from the menu banner and then Add Sequences From from the pulldown menu. Next, select Databases from the extended menu that appears. A Database Browser window will appear (Figure 4.2). Type the entry name or accession number of the desired database entry in the Database Specification text box at the bottom of the window. Click the Add to Main Window button and the Close button. This procedure can be abbreviated as follows. (Similar abbreviations are used throughout the chapter to describe keyboard and mouse commands.)

To add an entry from a database to the SeqLab Main Window:

1. Select File; go to Add Sequences From, and click Databases.
2. Type the entry name or accession number in the Database Specification text box of the Database Browser (Figure 4.2).
3. Click Add to Main Window, then Close.

Users can also add GCG-formatted sequence files to the list displayed in the SeqLab Main Window.

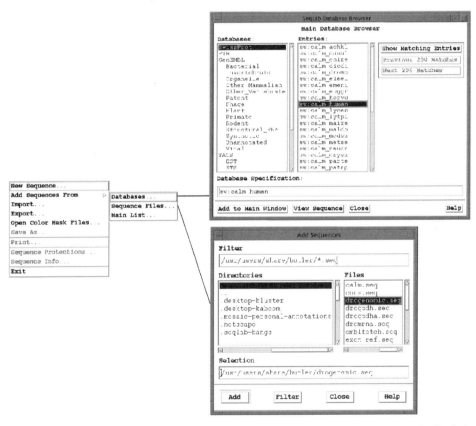

Figure 4.2 The Database Browser and Add Sequence windows for adding sequences to the SeqLab Editor.

To add a directory file to the SeqLab Main Window:

1. Select File; go to Add Sequences From, and click Sequence Files.
2. Select the appropriate filter in the Filter text box. (The default filter is *.seq, which will display all files in a directory ending in .seq. Replace *.seq with * to display all the files in a directory.)
3. Select the appropriate directory from the Directory area.
4. Click Filter.
5. Select the files by name from the Files area of the Add Sequences window.
6. Click Add, then Close.

Reference information for database entries and individual sequences can be viewed by double-clicking on the name of the entry or sequence. This action opens the Sequence Information window. Information in any of the text boxes on this window can be edited, as necessary. For example, it is often convenient to rename a database entry or add an ID/accession number to a sequence that is part of a large project.

Users can navigate within and among the sequences displayed in SeqLab with the arrow keys and horizontal and vertical scroll bars. Move to a residue within the sequence by typing the number of the residue and pressing the return key. Many other shortcuts for navigating within the SeqLab Editor, including moving relative to the current cursor position, are detailed in the SeqLab Guide.

Creating a New Sequence Entry

Users can also enter new protein or nucleic acid sequences into SeqLab.

To enter a new protein or nucleic acid sequence:

1. Select File and go to New Sequence.
2. Choose either DNA, RNA, or Protein from the New Sequence box.

When the listing appears, click at the beginning of the entry and either type in new sequence information or paste in sequence information from another window. Add reference information by double-clicking on the name of the new entry. This action opens the Sequence Information window. All the text boxes are editable, so in addition to renaming the entry, a description, author name, or ID/accession number can be included. General reference information can be added to the large text box at the bottom of the window.

Editing Existing Sequences

It is impossible to accidentally insert or delete residues because existing sequences displayed in the SeqLab Editor are protected. These protections can be changed, however, and when they have been removed, residues can be added and deleted, and it is possible to cut and paste sequences or regions of sequences between entries.

To change the protections on a sequence:

1. Select File and go to Sequence Protections.
2. Select all the buttons in the Sequence Protections window and click OK.

SeqLab is especially useful for editing multiple-sequence alignments. Useful features include the ability to move to absolute positions within either an individual sequence or an alignment, the ability to group and ungroup sequences so that a change in one sequence of the group also occurs in all other sequences of that group, and the ability to move "islands" of residues between gaps without changing the overall alignment. For example, a user can change an alignment that contains gq...psqalt.......asw to gq......psqalt....asw by sliding the psqalt island as if those six residues were beads on a string. The island over-writes one gap character to the right, as it moves in that direction, and a gap character appears to the left of the island such that the overall alignment is conserved. A complete list of editing operations is included in the Wisconsin Package SeqLab Guide.

ANALYZING SEQUENCES WITH OPERATIONS AND WISCONSIN PACKAGE PROGRAMS

Once sequences have been added and displayed in the SeqLab Main Window, they can be analyzed by running any Wisconsin Package program. The output files created by the programs are listed in the Output Manager window (see section entitled Viewing Output, below). Some of these files can be added back to the SeqLab Editor or SeqLab List mode for extended or related analysis. There are also a few simple operations that can be run directly from the SeqLab Editor.

Performing Simple Operations

The Edit menu in SeqLab Editor mode enables users to perform simple operations on displayed sequences without running programs. These operations include translating nucleic acid sequences, reversing and complementing nucleic acid sequences, calculating consensus sequences from aligned sequences, and finding short patterns. These operations have the advantage of running rapidly and displaying results automatically in the SeqLab Editor, where they can be edited, annotated, and, most importantly, used as input to Wisconsin Package programs selected from the Functions menu.

To select an operation:

1. Select a sequence by name or a range of a sequence.
2. Select Edit and go to the operation of choice.

Running Wisconsin Package Programs

Wisconsin Package programs are available for more extensive or robust analysis of sequences displayed in the SeqLab Editor. All the available programs are listed in the Functions menu and are divided by analysis topics. The Map program, from the Mapping functions topic, is used here as an example.

To run Map, a Wisconsin Package program:

1. Select a sequence by name or a region of a sequence with the cursor.
2. Select Functions and go to Mapping. Then select Map.

Selecting a program by name opens a Program window for that program. Every Program window has the same basic format, which includes the name of the selected sequence, the parameters required to run the program, a panel of buttons for selecting and saving optional parameters, and buttons for running the program, closing the window, and obtaining help. The Program window for the program Map is shown on the left in Figure 4.3.

Users can run a program with the default selections for required parameters or modify them with the buttons and text boxes on the Program window. In addition, each program has a unique set of optional parameters that will modify the analysis the program performs or change the way the output is displayed. These optional parameters are listed on the Program Options window, which is opened by selecting the Options button on the Program window. By selecting from required and optional parameters for the Map program, a user can select a subset of enzymes to include in a restriction map, opt for including only enzymes that produce a 5′ overhang on that map, or choose to omit the reverse complement strand normally included as part of a restriction map. The Map Options window is shown on the right in Figure 4.3.

Selecting the Run button on a Program window will run that program with the selected parameters and close the Program window. If a program is rerun during the same SeqLab session, the Program window will appear with all the previously selected parameters in place. Selected parameters can be saved between SeqLab sessions by selecting the Save Settings button. Selecting GCG Defaults from the Program window will reset the default parameter selections on both the Program and Program Options windows. All Program windows also include a Help button for accessing online help specific for that program.

VIEWING OUTPUT

Output files generated by programs run during a SeqLab session are listed in the Output Manager window (Figure 4.4).

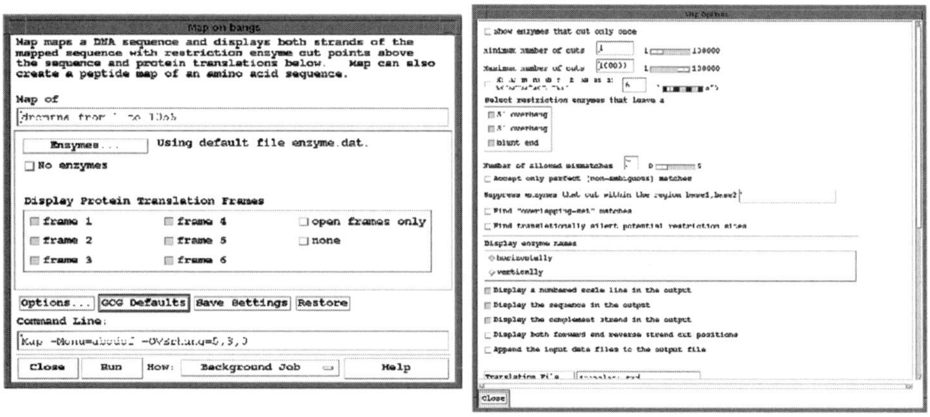

Figure 4.3 *Left:* Example of a Program window. For the Map program, this window is displayed by selecting Map from the Functions menu. *Right:* Example of a Program Options window. For the Map program, this window is displayed by selecting the Options button on the Map Program window.

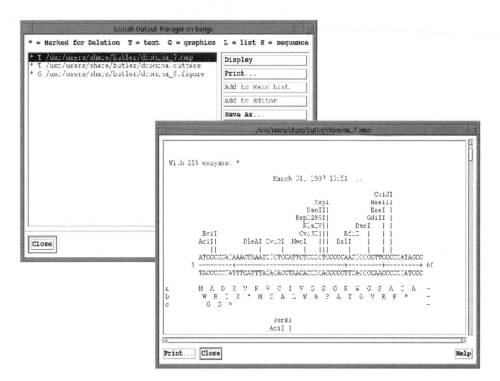

Figure 4.4 An output file created by the Map program displayed in an Output Display window (foreground). All output files created in SeqLab are displayed in the Output Manager window (background).

To open the Output Manager window:

1. Select Windows and go to Output Manager.

From this window output files can be displayed or printed. Click the Display button to display a highlighted file. An example of a displayed output file is shown in Figure 4.4. Click the Print button to send the selected file to a networked printer.

An output file generated in an earlier SeqLab session cannot be viewed or printed unless it is listed in the Output Manager window. Select the Add Text Files button, or Add Graphics Files, and select the file by name from the file browser that appears. Programs that produce graphics output create files with ".figure" extensions. When a file of this type is selected for display, it is translated for display in an X-window. When a file of this type is selected for printing, it is translated into either PostScript™ or HPGL™, depending on the printer selection and setup.

Some output files (sequence files, list files, and MSF files) can be added to the SeqLab Main List or Editor and used as input to Wisconsin Package programs. If such a file is selected in the Output Manager window, the Add to Main List and Add to Editor buttons will be active (Figure 4.4). If the selected output file cannot be added to these windows, the buttons will be inactive.

MONITORING PROGRAM PROGRESS AND TROUBLESHOOTING PROBLEMS

Every program run during a SeqLab session is recorded in the Job Manager window (Figure 4.5). This window can be accessed from the Windows menu bar on the SeqLab Main Window.

To open the Job Manager window:

1. Select Windows and go to Job Manager.

The top half of the Job Manager window is a log of all the programs that have been run during the current SeqLab session. The status of any program can be monitored by selecting the programs by name. If a program fails to run for any reason, a message will appear in this window and a log file for that program will appear in the Output Manager window. It is also possible to stop a running program from this window.

ANNOTATING SEQUENCES AND GRAPHICALLY DISPLAYING ANNOTATIONS IN THE SEQLAB EDITOR

A unique feature of SeqLab is its link to the Features table of database entries. For example, nucleic acid database entries often have features for the locations of coding regions,

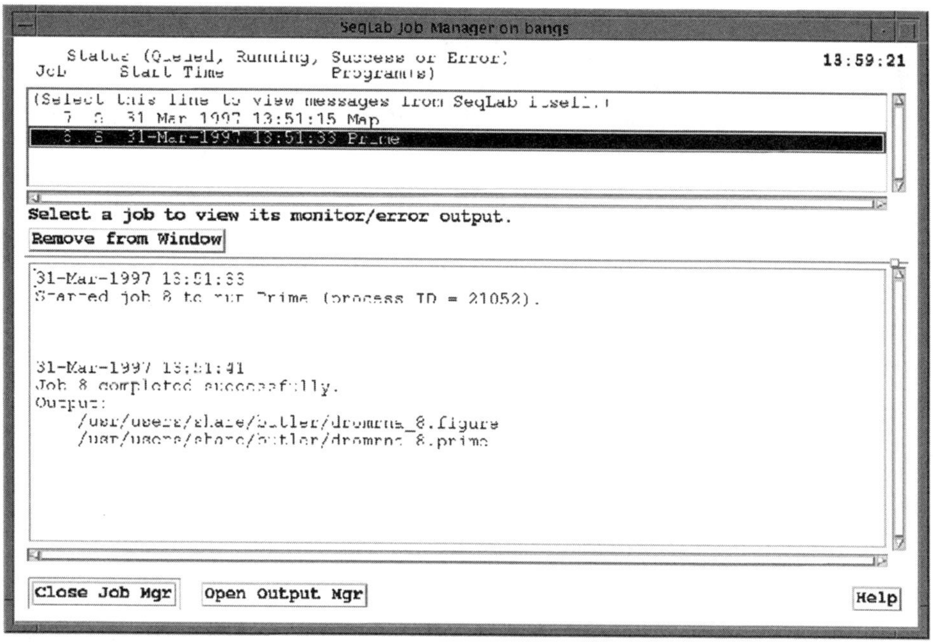

Figure 4.5   The Job Manager window. All programs run during a SeqLab session are listed in this window.

individual introns and exons, and polyadenlyation sites. SWISS-PROTPlus entries often have features for the locations of known protein pattern motifs, post-translational modification sites, and secondary structures. These features can be viewed in the SeqLab Editor with either colored residues (Features Coloring) or a schematic (Graphic Features).

To select features Display options:

1. Select the Display option button and then Features Coloring.
2. Select the Display option button and then Graphics Features.

An example of a Graphics Feature display for a set of aligned database entries is shown at the top of Figure 4.6. The 1:1 slide bar in the SeqLab Main Window (Figure 4.1) can be used to vary the horizontal scale of the schematic.

Database features can be displayed for an entry by selecting the Windows menu and then Features. This action opens a Sequence Features window (Figure 4.6). Users can opt to view all features for a sequence or just the selected feature. Selecting a feature in the upper area of the Sequence Features window displays detailed information about that feature in the lower area. This window can also be opened by double-clicking on a feature in an entry.

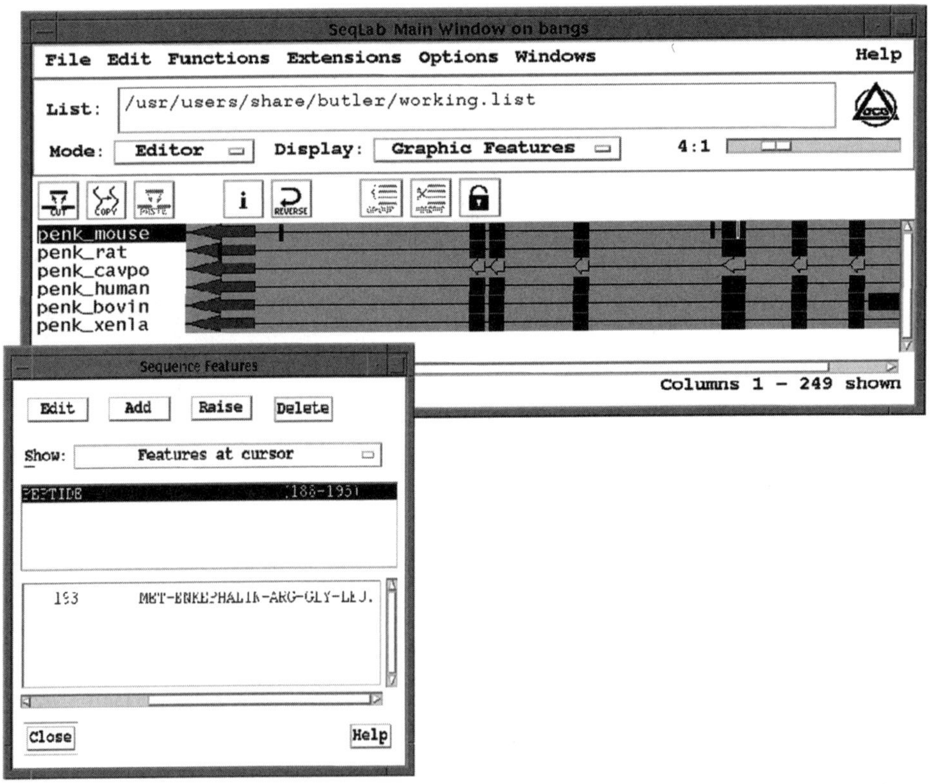

Figure 4.6 The SeqLab Editor displaying a multiple-sequence alignment in Graphics Display mode (*top*) and information about features are displayed in a Sequence Features window (*bottom*). Features can be added or edited by selecting option buttons at the top of this window.

Another unique and extremely useful feature of the SeqLab Editor is the ability to add features and edit existing ones. This is done from the Sequence Features and Feature Editor windows (Figure 4.6).

To add a feature:

1. Highlight a region with the cursor (or add ranges to the text boxes From and To, found in the Feature Editor).
2. Select Windows and then Features.
3. Select Add in the Sequence Features window.
4. Select Shape and Color in the Feature Editor window.
5. Type a name for the feature in the Keyword text box in the Feature Editor window.
6. Type a detailed comment in the Comments area of the Feature Editor window.
7. Click OK, then Close.

To edit a feature:

1. Select Windows and then Features.
2. Select the feature to edit in the Sequence Features window.
3. Select Edit in the Sequence Features window.
4. Modify Shape, Color, Range, Keyword, or Comments in the Feature Editor window.
5. Click OK, then Close.

SAVING SEQUENCES IN THE SEQLAB EDITOR

When a user exits SeqLab Editor mode, or saves editing work, the information is saved in a rich-sequence format (RSF) file. This is a new type of file that includes reference and features information as well as the sequence itself. The format of an RSF file enables features information to be displayed in the SeqLab Editor. RSF files can contain one or more sequence entries. If database entries are saved, copies of those entries (including all reference and features table information) are included in the RSF file. RSF files created in this way are automatically added to the current list file displayed in SeqLab List mode and are stored in the user's working directory.

EXAMPLES OF ANALYSES THAT CAN BE UNDERTAKEN IN SEQLAB

Having access to many sequence analysis programs confers the ability to use them sequentially to answer related questions or to repeat an analysis after the input sequences have been edited. The advantage of having access to both public databases and local sequences is the ability to use them both in a single analysis without first having to transfer or reformat them. This section describes six kinds of sequence analysis problems that can be solved with SeqLab.

Finding Open Reading Frames in Two mRNAs, Translating Them, and Aligning the RNAs and the Proteins

A user who has sequenced two related messenger RNAs may wish to find open reading frames, translate them, and create pairwise alignments of both the nucleic acid and amino acid sequences.

Add the sequences to the SeqLab Editor and run the Map program by selecting it from the Functions menu. The Map output file contains a restriction map and a display of open reading frames in any of the six possible translation frames. The begin and end positions of these open reading frames can be noted and selected as ranges in the sequences displayed in the SeqLab Editor where they can be translated with the Translate operation found in the Edit menu. These translations automatically appear in the SeqLab Editor.

Two related nucleic acid or protein sequences can be aligned to each other using either the Gap program (Needleman and Wunsch, 1970) or the BestFit (Smith and Waterman, 1981) program. Gap finds the best global alignment between the two sequences and is the program of choice if a user knows that the two sequences being compared are evolutionarily related. BestFit finds the best local alignment between two sequences and is the better program to use if the two sequences being compared are related not evolutionarily but, rather, functionally.

Finding Related Entries in Databases Through Reference Searching and Aligning Them

A user working with a member of a characterized sequence family may wish to find other members of that family and create a multiple sequence alignment of them all.

Select the LookUp program from the Functions menu. LookUp searches the reference sections of database entries for descriptive words and creates a list of the matching entries (Etzold and Argos, 1993; Etzold et al., 1996). Search for descriptive words in the Definition, Author, Keyword, and Organism fields of the reference sections and use the "and" (&), "or" (|), and "but not" (!) Boolean expressions between the words. For example, searching the Description field of SWISS-PROT entries for the words "lactate & dehydrogenase & h & chain" will create an output file listing lactate dehydrogenase H chain entries. This output file can be displayed from the Output Manager window and then added to the SeqLab Editor along with the user's sequence.

To create a multiple sequence alignment of all these sequences, select them by name and run the PileUp program from the Functions menu. The multiple-sequence file created by PileUp is also listed in the Output Manager window and can be added directly back to the SeqLab Editor. This step is recommended because Features table information from the database entries can be included with the alignment. The alignment can be edited if necessary, and similar features from the database entries can be added to the user's sequence, if present. The LookUp program window, the output file, and the alignment of the sequences within the output file are shown in Figure 4.7.

Searching a Database with a Query Sequence, Aligning the Found Entries and the Query Sequence, and Generating a Phylogenetic Tree

A user who has cloned and sequenced a gene of unknown function may wish to search a database for similar sequences. If any are found, the user may then wish to create a multiple-

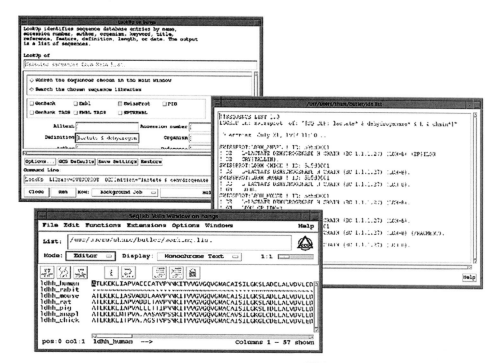

Figure 4.7 Windows showing a database reference search using the LookUp program, the output file from this search, and a multiple-sequence alignment of the entries that were found. The upper left-hand window is the LookUp program window. The middle window displays the results of this search, which were added to the SeqLab Editor and aligned using the PileUp program. The alignment is shown in the lower left-hand window.

sequence alignment of the sequences most similar to the query, and generate a phylogram of the data.

Add the query sequence to the SeqLab Editor and select the FASTA program from the Functions menu. FASTA (Pearson and Lipman, 1988) searches a database for sequences similar to a query sequence. The output file can be displayed from the Output Manager window and can be added directly to the SeqLab Editor. The best regions of local similarity between the database entries and the query sequence are noted in this output file, and only those regions of each database entry can be displayed in the SeqLab Editor, if a display is desired. Unwanted entries can be deleted from the SeqLab Editor altogether.

Select the PileUp program from the Functions menu to create a multiple-sequence alignment of these sequences. The output can be displayed from the Output Manager window and added to the SeqLab Editor, overwriting the existing, unaligned sequences. This alignment can be edited if necessary, and useful features table information from the database entries can be added to the query sequence.

Select the PaupSearch program from the Functions menu. This program provides a GCG interface with the tree-searching options in PAUP™ (Phylogenetic Analysis Using Parsimony) (Swofford, 1996). The PaupDisplay program provides a GCG interface to tree manipulation, diagnosis, and display options in PAUP. The output from the FASTA search, the alignment of the first six sequences, and the evolutionary tree generated from this alignment are shown in Figure 4.8.

Assembling Overlapping Sequence Fragments to Generate a Contiguous Sequence, Finding and Translating the Coding Regions of That Sequence, and Searching a Database for Similar Sequences

A user who has cloned a gene, subcloned it into a series of overlapping fragments, and sequenced those fragments may wish to reassemble the fragments into a contiguous

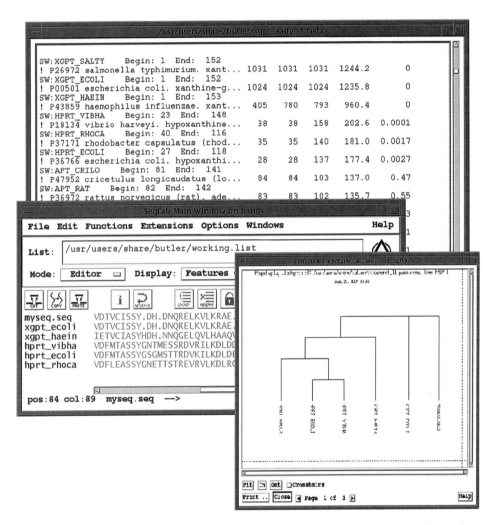

Figure 4.8 Windows showing a database search, an alignment of found database entries, and an evolutionary tree of this alignment. *Top:* Results of a FASTA search of the SWISS-PROT database. This file was added to the SeqLab Editor and the first six entries were aligned using the PileUp program. The alignment (*middle*) was used to create an evolutionary tree with the PaupSearch and PaupDisplay programs. The tree is shown in the lower window.

sequence. Once the contig has been assembled, the user may wish to find open reading frames within the sequence, translate them, and look for similar sequences in a database.

The programs of the Fragment Assembly System can be used to assemble overlapping sequence fragments. The GelStart program creates a project. The GelEnter program copies fragments into the project. The GelMerge program finds overlaps between the fragments and assembles them into contigs. The GelAssemble program is an editor for editing these contiguous units and resolving conflicts between the fragments. All these programs can be selected from the Functions menu. Once assembled, the consensus sequence for the final contig can be saved as a Sequence file and added to the SeqLab Editor.

Use the Map, Frames, TestCode (Fickett, 1982), or CodonPreference (Gribskov et al., 1983) programs to predict coding regions within the sequence. (All these programs can be selected from the Functions menu.) Use the Select Range function of the Edit menu to select the ranges predicted by these programs and the Translate operation of the Edit menu to translate them to protein. These proposed translated regions can also be added as features in the nucleic acid consensus sequence.

Select the protein sequence and then select BLAST (Altschul et al., 1990) from the Functions menu. BLAST searches databases for entries similar to a query sequence. Both remote and local searches are possible. The results can be displayed from the Output Manager window. If a local database is searched, the resulting file can be added to the SeqLab Editor or Main List window, allowing further analysis on the sequences found.

Aligning Related Protein Sequences, Calculating a Consensus Sequence for the Alignment, Identifying a Novel Pattern in the Sequences and Searching a Database for Sequences That Contain That Pattern, or Searching the Alignment Consensus for Known Protein Patterns

A user who has identified a group of related sequences may wish to align them and calculate a consensus sequence for the alignment. If a conserved pattern can be found in the alignment, the user may wish to search a database for other sequences that contain that pattern. The user may also wish to search the calculated consensus sequence for known protein patterns.

Select the sequences to align and select the PileUp program from the Functions menu to create a multiple sequence alignment. The PileUp output file can be displayed from the Output Manager window and added to the SeqLab Editor. It is possible for a user to realign a region of the alignment and place that region back into the original alignment. To do this, highlight the region and rerun PileUp. Select "realign a portion of an existing alignment" from the PileUp Options window. It might also be advantageous to select an alternate scoring matrix or different creation and extension penalties. The new output file will contain the original alignment, with the realigned region replacing the original alignment in that region.

Calculate a consensus sequence for the alignment with the Consensus operation in the Edit menu. If a conserved pattern can be identified, select the FindPatterns program from the Functions menu. Cut the pattern from the consensus sequence, paste it into the FindPatterns Pattern Chooser, and search a database for sequences containing that pattern.

Alternatively, search the consensus sequence for known protein pattern motifs by running the Motifs program. Motifs searches protein sequences for the known protein patterns listed in PROSITE, the PROSITE Dictionary of Protein Sites and Patterns (Bairoch et al., 1997). If a motif is identified, add a feature to all the sequences, noting its position. An alignment of protein sequences plus a consensus sequence is shown in Figure 4.9, along with the results of a Motifs search.

Using Profiles for Similarity Searches and Aligning Related Sequences

A new and expanding region of sequence analysis is profile technology. A profile is a position-specific scoring matrix that contains information about all the residues at each position in a sequence alignment. This is in contrast to a consensus sequence, which contains only information about the consensus residue at each position. Once made, a profile can be used to search a database, database division, or search set for sequences similar to the sequences in the original alignment. It can also be used to align a single sequence to the alignment.

Use the ProfileMake program (Gribskov et al., 1987, 1990) to create a profile of a sequence alignment. Use the ProfileSearch program to search a database with the profile and the ProfileSegments program to display the results (Gribskov et al., 1987, 1990). Use the ProfileGap program to align a sequence to the profile (Gribskov et al., 1987, 1990). ProfileMake, ProfileSearch, ProfileSegments, and ProfileGap are all available from the Functions menu.

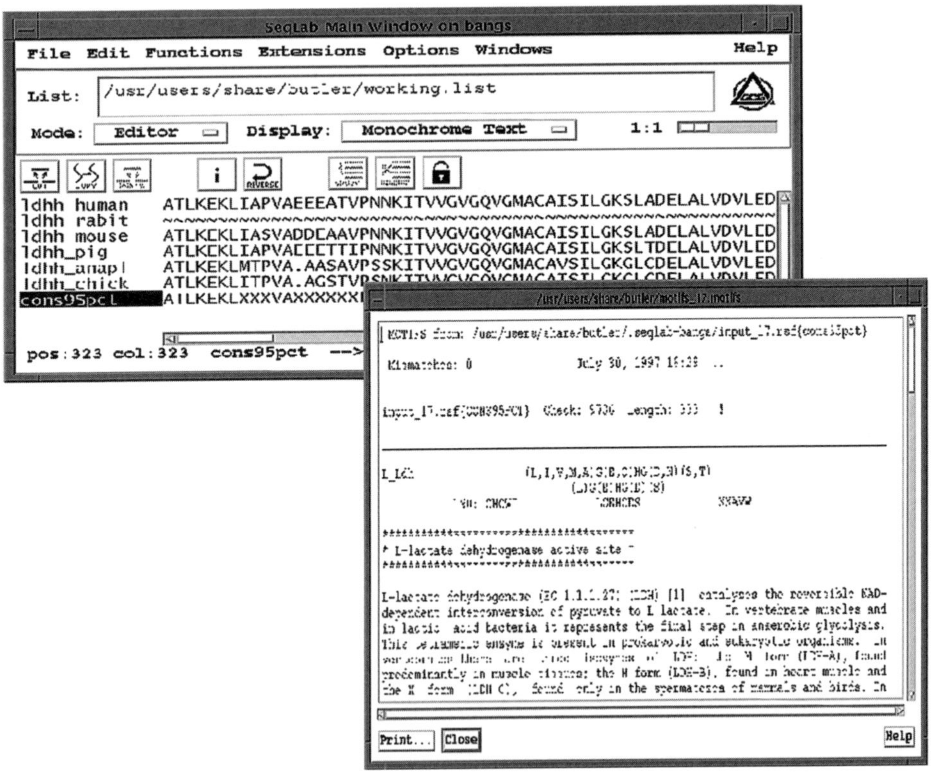

Figure 4.9 Windows showing a multiple-sequence alignment including a consensus sequence. The consensus was used to search PROSITE for known protein pattern motifs. An alignment of protein sequences in the SeqLab Editor, including a consensus sequence calculated at 95% identity, is shown in the upper window. This consensus sequence was used as input to the Motifs program to identify known protein pattern motifs common to the aligned sequences. The results from the Motifs program search are shown in the lower window.

EXTENDING SEQLAB BY INCLUDING PROGRAMS THAT ARE NOT PART OF THE WISCONSIN PACKAGE

Another key feature of SeqLab is the flexibility to insert additional programs in the environment. Briefly, the process entails obtaining an appropriate executable file for the program to be included and creating a configuration file that describes the required and optional parameters and formats the input and output files. Detailed instructions on how to create a configuration file can be found in the Wisconsin Package System Support Manual. It is not necessary to link these stand-alone program executables to any procedures in the Wisconsin Package. With this option, it is possible to run any program compiled to run under the operating system of the computer running the Wisconsin Package from within SeqLab and to view its output as easily as if it were part of the Wisconsin Package. ClustalW (Higgins et al., 1996) is the example extension program included with version 9.0 of the Wisconsin Package. Note that it is not a functional program unless the executable has been downloaded or built and the config file edited to point to the location of this file.

Programs added to the SeqLab environment can be selected from the Extensions menu of the SeqLab Main Window.

REFERENCES

Altschul, S. F., Gish, W., Miller, W., Myers, E. W., and Lipman, D. J. (1990). Basic local alignment search tool. J. Mol. Biol. *215*, 403–410.

Bairoch, A., and Apweiler, R. (1997). The SWISS-PROT protein data bank and its supplement TrEMBL. Nucl. Acids Res. *25*, 31–36.

Bairoch, A., Bucher, P., and Hofmann, K. (1997). The PROSITE Database: Its status in 1997. Nucl. Acids Res. *25*, 217–221.

Benson, D. A., Boguski, M. S., Lipman, D. J., and Ostell, J. (1997). GenBank. Nucl. Acids Res. *25*, 1–6.

Chou, P. Y., and Fasman, G. D. (1978). Prediction of the secondary structure of proteins from their amino acid sequence. Adv. Enzymol. *47*, 45–147.

Etzold, T., and Argos, P. (1993). SRS—An indexing and retrieval tool for flat file data libraries. Comput. Appl. Bioscie. *9*, 49–57.

Etzold, T., Ulyanov, A., and Argos, P. (1996). SRS: Information retrieval system for molecular biology data banks. Methods Enzymol. *266*, 114–128.

Fickett, J. (1982). Recognition of protein coding regions in DNA sequences. Nucl. Acids Res. *10*, 5303–5318.

George, D. G., Dodson, R. J., Garavelli, J. S., Haft, D. H., Hunt, L. T., Marzec, C. R., Orcutt, B. C., Sidman, K. E., Srinivasarao, G. Y., Yeh, L. L., Arminski, L. M., Ledley, R. S., Tsugita, A., and Barker, W. C. (1997). The Protein Information Resource (PIR) and the PIR–International Protein Sequence Database. Nucl. Acids Res. *25*, 24–27.

Gilbert, W. (1981). DNA sequencing and gene structure. Science *214*, 1305–1312.

Gribskov, M., Devereux, J. D., and Burgess, R. R. (1983). The codon preference plot: Graphic analysis of protein coding sequences and prediction of gene expression. Nucl. Acids Res. *12*, 539–549.

Gribskov, M., McLachlan, M., and Eisenberg, D. (1987). Profile analysis: Detection of distantly related proteins. Proc. Natl. Acad. Sci. U.S.A. *84*, 4355–4358.

Gribskov, M., Luthy, R., and Eisenberg, D. (1990). Profile analysis. Methods Enzymol. *183*, 146–159.

Higgins, D., Thompson, J. D., and Gibson, T. C. (1996). Using CLUSTAL for Multiple Sequence Alignments. Methods Enzymol. *183*, 383–402.

Li, W. H. (1993). Unbiased estimation of the rates of synonymous and nonsynonymous substitution. J. Mol. Evol. *36*, 96–99.

Needleman, S. B., and Wunsch, C. D. (1970). A general method applicable to the search for similarities in the amino acid sequences of two proteins. J. Mol. Biol. *48*, 443–453.

Pamilo, P., and Bianchi, N. O. (1993). Evolution of the *Zfx* and *Zfy* genes: Rates and interdependence between the genes. Mol. Biol. Evol. *10*, 271–281.

Pearson, W. R. (1990). Rapid and sensitive sequence comparison with FASTP and FASTA. Methods Enzymol. *183*, 63–98.

Pearson, W. R. (1996). Effective protein sequence comparison. Methods Enzymol. *266*, 227–258.

Pearson, W. R., and Lipman, D. J. (1988). Improved tools for biological sequence analysis. Proc. Natl. Acad. Sci. U.S.A. *85*, 2444–2448.

Sanger, F. (1981). Determination of nucleotide sequences in DNA. Science *214*, 1205–1210.

Smith, T. F., and Waterman, M. S. (1981). Comparison of bio-sequences. Adv. Appl. Math. *2*, 482–489.

Staden, R. (1980). A new computer method for the storage and manipulation of DNA gel reading data. Nucl. Acids Res. *8*, 3673–3694.

Stoesser, G., Sterk, P., Tuli, M. A., Stoehr, P. J., and Cameron, G. N. (1997). The EMBL Nucleotide Sequence Database. Nucl. Acids Res. *25*, 7–13.

Swofford, D. (1996). *PAUP*: Phylogenetic Analysis Using Parsimony (and Other Methods)*, version 4.0 (Sunderland, MA: Sinauer Associates).

Zuker, M. (1989). On finding all suboptimal foldings on an RNA molecule. Science *244*, 48–52.

APPENDIX

Wisconsin Package programs are organized into topics based on scientific application. The topics listed are present in the SeqLab Functions menu. Most, but not all, of the programs accessible through SeqLab are listed, along with a brief description. The GCG home page offers up-to-date information and a complete list of Wisconsin Package programs.

Pairwise Comparison

Gap: Uses the algorithm of Needleman and Wunsch (1970) to find the optimal global alignment of two sequences.

BestFit: Uses the algorithm of Smith and Waterman (1981) to find the optimal local alignment of two sequences.

FrameAlign: Creates an optimal local alignment between a protein sequence and the codons in the three forward reading frames of a nucleotide sequence, adding gaps as necessary to maintain the reading frame.

Compare/DotPlot: Compares two protein or nucleic acid sequences, creates a file that contains information about the regions of similarity between them, and displays these results graphically as a dot matrix of similarity.

ProfileMake/ProfileGap: Creates a position-specific scoring table, called a profile, that quantitatively represents the information from a group of aligned sequences. ProfileGap creates an optimal alignment between a profile and a sequence (Gribskov et al., 1990).

Multiple Comparison

PileUp: Creates a multiple sequence alignment from a group of sequences using progressive, pairwise alignments. It also creates a graphic file showing the clustering used to create the alignment.

PlotSimilarity: Graphs the running average of the similarity scores of the sequences in a multiple sequence alignment.

Database Reference Searching

LookUp: Finds database entries by searching indexed fields such as Name, Accession Number, Author, Organism, Keyword, Title, Reference, Feature, Definition, Length, or Date for descriptive terms (Etzold and Argos, 1993).

Database Sequence Searching

BLAST: Searches a database for sequences similar to a query sequence (Altschul et al., 1990). The query and the database searched can be either peptide or nucleic acid in any combination. The program can search databases on an individual user's computer or databases maintained at the National Center for Biotechnology Information (NCBI) in Bethesda, Maryland.

FASTA: Searches a database for sequences similar to a query sequence. It was written by William Pearson and David Lipman (Pearson and Lipman, 1988).

TFASTA: Searches a nucleotide database for sequences similar to a protein query sequence. It translates the database sequences in all six frames before performing the comparison (Pearson and Lipman, 1988).

FrameSearch: Searches a nucleotide database or list file for sequences similar to a protein query. It can also search a protein database or list file for sequences similar to a nucleotide query. For each sequence comparison, the program finds an optimal alignment between the protein sequence and all possible codons on each strand of the nucleotide sequence, adding gaps to maintain the reading frame.

ProfileMake/ProfileSearch/ProfileSegments: ProfileMake creates a position-specific scoring table, called a profile, that quantitatively represents the information from a group of aligned sequences. ProfileSearch uses this profile to search a database, database division, or list file for sequences similar to those that created the profile. ProfileSegments displays the local regions of similarity between the database entries and the profile (Gribskov et al., 1990).

FindPatterns: Identifies sequences containing short patterns. Patterns can be defined ambiguously at each position and/or overall mismatching can take place.

Editing and Publication

Pretty: Varies the display of multiple-sequence alignments. It can also calculate a consensus sequence for the alignment.

Publish: Varies the display of single or multiple sequences. A menu of options for display, translating, and noting identities is provided.

MapSort/PlasmidMap: MapSort with the Plasmid option creates a file containing the locations of restriction enzyme recognition sites. This file can be graphically displayed with the PlasmidMap program Only circular restriction maps are possible.

Evolution

Distances/GrowTree: Creates a distance matrix of the pairwise corrected distances within a group of aligned sequences, expressed as a number of nucleotide or amino acid substitutions per 100 residues and constructs a phylogram.

PaupSearch: Provides a GCG interface to the tree-searching options in PAUP (Phylogenetic Analysis Using Parsimony) (Swofford, 1996).

PaupDisplay: Provides a GCG interface to tree manipulation, diagnosis, and display options in PAUP (Phylogenetic Analysis Using Parsimony) (Swofford, 1996).

Diverge: Estimates the number of synonymous and nonsynonymous substitutions per site between two nucleic acid sequences that code for proteins. It uses a variant of the method published by Li (Li, 1993; Pamilo and Bianchi, 1993).

Fragment Assembly

GelStart/GelEnter/GelMerge/GelAssemble: GelStart creates a fragment assembly project or initialized an existing one. GelEnter copies or enters fragments into the project. GelMerge finds overlaps between the fragments and assembles them into contigs, or contiguous regions. GelAssemble is an editor that displays the contigs for the resolution of conflicts between the fragments.

GelView: Displays all the contigs of a project at a given time and the names of all the fragments contained in each contig.

Pattern Recognition and Gene Prediction

TestCode: Uses algorithms developed by Fickett (1982) to predict protein-coding regions based on the nonrandomness of the composition of a nucleic acid sequence at every third base.

CodonPreference: Predicts protein coding regions based on codon usage and third position GC bias. Codon frequency tables for several organisms are available (Gribskov et al., 1983).

Frames: Graphically displays open reading frames for the six translation frames of a nucleic acid sequence based on the position of start and stop codons.

FindPatterns: Identifies sequences containing short patterns. Patterns can be defined ambiguously at each position and/or overall mismatching can take place.

Motifs: Finds known protein pattern motifs by searching protein sequences for the patterns defined in the PROSITE Dictionary of Protein Sites and Patterns (Bairoch et al., 1997).

Composition: Determines the composition of nucleic acid or protein sequence(s). For nucleotide sequence(s), it also determines dinucleotide and trinucleotide content.

CodonFrequency: Creates a codon frequency table from coding regions of sequences or existing codon usage tables. The output can be used with many Wisconsin Package programs including CodonPreference.

Importing/Exporting

Reformat: Formats sequence files, symbol comparison tables, or enzyme data files for use with Wisconsin Package programs. It can also be used to modify the display of sequences.

FromStaden: Converts a sequence file in Staden format (Staden, 1980) to GCG format. If multiple sequences are present in the file, individual sequence files will be created.

FromGenBank: Converts to GCG format a sequence file in GenBank flatfile format (Benson et al., 1997). If multiple sequences are present in the file, individual sequence files will be created.

FromPIR: Converts a sequence file in PIR format (George et al., 1997) to GCG format. If multiple sequences are present in the file, individual sequence files will be created.

FromFASTA: Converts a sequence file in FASTA format (Pearson and Lipman, 1988) to GCG format. If multiple sequences are present in the file, individual sequence files will be created.

ToPIR: Converts a GCG-formatted sequence file or files to PIR format (George et al., 1997).

ToFASTA: Converts a GCG-formatted sequence file or files to FASTA format (Pearson and Lipman, 1988).

ToStaden: Converts a GCG-formatted sequence file or files to Staden format (Staden, 1980).

Mapping

Map: Displays both strands of a nucleic acid sequence with restriction enzyme cut points above the sequence and protein translations below. Map can also create a peptide map of an amino acid sequence.

MapPlot: Graphically displays restriction enzyme recognition sites, one enzyme per line.

MapSort: Predicts the putative size of fragments after digestion of a nucleic acid with one or more restriction enzymes.

PeptideSort: Predicts the peptide fragments from digest of an amino acid sequence. It sorts the predicted peptides by weight, position, and relative retention times determined by high-performance liquid chromatography (HPLC). It also includes the composition of each peptide as well as a summary of the composition of the whole protein.

Primer Selection

Prime: Selects oligonucleotide primers for polymerase chain reaction (PCR) reactions, primer sequencing, and primer extension experiments. PCR is covered by U.S. Patents 4,683,195 and 4,683,202, owned by Hoffmann–LaRoche.

Protein Analysis

CoilScan: Locates coiled-coil segments in protein sequences.

HTHScan: Scans protein sequences for the presence of helix–turn–helix motifs, indicative of sequence-specific DNA-binding structures often associated with gene regulation.

Isoelectric: Predicts and plots a titration curve for a protein sequence.

ProfileScan: Uses a database of profiles to find motifs in protein query sequences (Gribskov et al., 1990).

PeptideSort: Predicts the peptide fragments from digest of an amino acid sequence. It sorts the predicted peptides by weight, position, and relative HPLC retention times. It also includes the composition of each peptide as well as a summary of the composition of the whole protein.

PepPlot: Predicts secondary structure using the method of Chou and Fasman (Chou and Fasman, 1978). The predictions are in a series of parallel plots. Plots for hydropathy and hydrophobic moment are included.

PeptideStructure/PlotStructure: Predicts and displays secondary structure antigenicity, flexibility, hydrophobicity, and surface probability for a protein sequence.

SPScan: Scans protein sequences for the presence of secretory signal peptides (SPs).

RNA Secondary Structure

MFold/PlotFold: Predicts and displays optimal and suboptimal secondary structures for an RNA molecule using the energy minimization method of Zuker (1989).

StemLoop: Finds stems, or inverted repeats, within a sequence. The user specifies the minimum stem length, minimum and maximum loop sizes, and the minimum number of bonds per stem.

Translation

Translate: Translates nucleotide sequences into peptide sequences.

BackTranslate: Translates an amino acid sequence into a nucleotide sequence. The output display helps the user to recognize minimally ambiguous regions that may be good for constructing synthetic probes.

5

Information Retrieval from Biological Databases

Andreas D. Baxevanis

Genome Technology Branch
National Human Genome Research Institute
National Institutes of Health
Bethesda, Maryland

As discussed in Chapter 2, GenBank was created in response to the explosion in sequence information resulting from a panoply of scientific efforts, such as the Human Genome Project. To review, GenBank is an annotated collection of all publicly available DNA and protein sequences. As of this writing, GenBank contains 1.6 million sequence records covering over 1 billion nucleotide bases. Sequences find their way into GenBank in one of two ways: by direct submission through tools such as Sequin and BankIt or through a data-sharing agreement conducted between GenBank, EMBL, and DDBJ as part of the International Nucleotide Sequence Database Collaboration. More information on the submission tools and the nature of the Collaboration can be found in Chapter 14.

GenBank, or any other biological database for that matter, serves little purpose unless the database can be easily searched and entries retrieved in a usable, meaningful format. Otherwise, sequencing efforts serve no useful end, since the biological community as a whole cannot make use of the information hidden within these millions of bases and amino acids. Much effort has gone into making such data accessible to the average user, and the programs and interfaces resulting from these efforts are the focus of this chapter. The discussion centers on querying the NCBI databases, since these more "general" repositories are far and away the ones most often accessed by biologists, but attention also is given to a number of smaller, specialized databases that provide information not necessarily found in GenBank.

Bioinformatics: A Practical Guide to the Analysis of Genes and Proteins
Edited by A.D. Baxevanis and B.F.F. Ouellette
ISBN 0-471-19196-5, pages 98–120.   Copyright © 1998 Wiley-Liss, Inc.

RETRIEVING DATABASE ENTRIES: THE RETRIEVE SERVER

Perhaps the easiest way to retrieve entries from an NCBI database is by using an e-mail server called *Retrieve*. The Retrieve server retrieves records through a simple keyword search. Available databases can be searched one at a time, and searches may be simple (consisting of a single keyword) or complex (with multiple keywords strung together by Boolean operators). The address for the server is simply *retrieve@ncbi.nlm.nih.gov*. As with most e-mail servers, sending a mail message to the server with just the word `help` in the body of the message will return a detailed explanation of how to use the Retrieve service.

Recall from Chapter 1 that whenever an e-mail server is used, the message sent to the server needs to be precisely formatted so that the server can understand the instructions being conveyed by the user. Consider the following example:

```
To:      retrieve@ncbi.nlm.nih.gov
Subject: Complex Query

DATALIB swissprot
BEGIN
"histone H1" AND (Saccharomyces OR Schizosaccharomyces)
```

Here, the subject of the message is irrelevant to the server. However, since the subject is echoed back by the server when it returns the results, providing a descriptive subject allows the user to keep track of results when multiple messages are sent to Retrieve. The body of the message begins with a `DATALIB` search parameter, indicating which of the available databases should be searched (here, SWISS-PROT). The `BEGIN` flag indicates that there are no more search parameters, and the words that follow are all search terms. The Boolean operators AND, OR, and NOT can be used to join terms together; parentheses can be used to separate the terms into subsets; and quotation marks can be used to indicate a phrase that must be kept together. In the example, the server will return all entries containing the phrase `"histone H1"` and *either* the word `Saccharomyces` or `Schizosaccharomyces`. If no Boolean operators or delimiters were indicated (i.e., if the search terms read `histone H1 Saccharomyces Schizosaccharomyces`), a default OR would have been placed between terms, which is most likely *not* what the user intended the server to do. The results from this complex query are shown in Figure 5.1.

Often, when searches are submitted, the search is too general, returning many more entries than can be of use to the requester. For example, the foregoing search would have failed if the species names had been left out, because the phrase "histone H1" appears in many entries. Moreover, the phrase may appear in the entry even though it is not the actual subject of the entry: for example, although the phrase was part of the title of the paper, the sequence might be of something else. When an unmanageable number of entries is found, an error is generated to that effect. Limits are placed on the numbers of printed lines and entries that can be retrieved, primarily because many e-mail systems cannot handle inordinately large e-mail messages, and too many unfocused queries simply slow down the system. To help refine searches, users can specify additional search parameters, which can be used to change the number of lines or entries, or to return only the titles of the entries rather than the complete listings. Users can also restrict the fields that are actually searched. Returning to the example, if the search terms instead began as `"histone H1" [DEF]`, only

```
Database: Swiss-Prot Updates (33.0+, 4/19/96)
Query: "histone h1" AND (saccharomyces OR schizosaccharomyces)
Parse status: OK: 0 documents retrieved.

Database: Swiss-Prot (34.0, 10/96)
Query: "histone h1" AND (saccharomyces OR schizosaccharomyces)
Parse status: OK: 1 document retrieved.
Documents selected: 1-1  (up to 1000 lines)


>> Document 1 <<
[H1L_YEAST]    HISTONE H1-LIKE PROTEIN.

ID [LOC]
      H1L_YEAST        STANDARD;       PRT;     258 AA.

ACCESSION [ACC]
      P53551;

DATES [DAT]
      01-OCT-1996 (REL. 34, CREATED)
      01-OCT-1996 (REL. 34, LAST SEQUENCE UPDATE)
      01-OCT-1996 (REL. 34, LAST ANNOTATION UPDATE)

KEYWORDS [KEY]
      CHROMOSOMAL PROTEIN; NUCLEAR PROTEIN; DNA-BINDING.

GENE NAME[GEN]
      YPL127C OR LPI17C.

SOURCE [SRC]
      SACCHAROMYCES CEREVISIAE (BAKER'S YEAST).

ORGANISM CLASSIFICATION [CLS]
      EUKARYOTA; FUNGI; ASCOMYCOTINA; HEMIASCOMYCETES.

CROSS REFERENCE [DCR]
      EMBL; U43703; G1244786; -.

REFERENCE [REF]
      [1]
      SEQUENCE FROM N.A.
      HALL J., DEPAULO T., AHMED A., BUSSEY H., FORTIN N., FRIESEN J.D.,
      STORMS R.K., VO D.H., WANG Y., WINNETT E.;
      SUBMITTED (DEC-1995) TO EMBL/GENBANK/DDBJ DATA BANKS.
      [2]
      POSSIBLE FUNCTION.
      MEDLINE; 96368276.
      LANDSMAN D.;
      TRENDS BIOCHEM. SCI. 21:287-288(1996).

COMMENT [COM]
      -!- FUNCTION: COULD ACT AS AN H1-TYPE LINKER HISTONE. HAS BEEN SHOWN
          TO BIND DNA.
      -!- SUBCELLULAR LOCATION: NUCLEAR (POTENTIAL).
      -!- SIMILARITY: TO HISTONE H1.

FEATURES [FEA]
      DOMAIN        38     130       H1-LIKE, GLOBULAR.
      DOMAIN       148     258       H1-LIKE, GLOBULAR.

SEQUENCE DATA [BAS]
      SEQUENCE   258 AA;   27803 MW;   CE87A12B CRC32;

SEQUENCE
      MAPKKSTTKT TSKGKKPATS KGKEKSTSKA AIKKTTAKKE EASSKSYREL IIEGLTALKE
      RKGSSRPALK KFIKENYPIV GSASNFDLYF NNAIKKGVEA GDFEQPKGPA GAVKLAKKKS
      PEVKKEKEVS PKPKQAATSV SATASKAKAA STKLAPKKVV KKKSPTVTAK KASSPSSLTY
      KEMILKSMPQ LNDGKGSSRI VLKKYVKDTF SSKLKTSSNF DYLFNSAIKK CVENGELVQP
      KGPSGIIKLN KKKVKLST
```

Figure 5.1 Results of a complex query submitted to the Retrieve server. Note that the search was done against both SWISS-PROT and SWISS-PROT Updates (the latter contains new entries since the last major release of the database). Here, the submitted search returned one and only one entry.

the definition line of entries would be searched for the presence of the phrase. The complete list of search parameters and field restrictions, as well as a list of searchable databases, can be found in the Retrieve Help document.

INTEGRATED INFORMATION RETRIEVAL: THE ENTREZ SYSTEM

While the Retrieve server allows targeted retrieval of records, its main drawback is that records may be retrieved from only one database at a time; a user who wishes to poll a number of databases must send a separate request to the Retrieve server for each target database. It should be immediately apparent, though, that there are preexisting logical relationships between the individual entries in these numerous public databases. For example, a paper in MEDLINE may describe the sequencing of a gene whose sequence appears in GenBank. The nucleotide sequence, in turn, codes for a protein product whose sequence is stored in the protein databases. The three-dimensional structure of that protein may be known, and the coordinates for that structure may appear in the structural database. Finally, the gene may have been mapped to a specific region of a given chromosome, with that information being stored in a mapping database.

The existence of such natural connections, mostly biological in nature, argued for the development of a method through which all the information about a particular biological entity could be found without having to sequentially visit and query disparate databases. The answer to this need lies in a molecular retrieval system known as *Entrez*. Developed at and maintained by NCBI, Entrez software is freely available for all the major computer platforms and allows for integrated access to PubMed (MEDLINE) records, nucleotide and protein sequence data, three-dimensional structure information, and mapping information—all by issuing a single query. Entrez is able to offer integrated information retrieval through the use of two types of connection between database entries: *neighboring* and *hard links*.

Neighboring

Neighboring connects entries *within* a given database. A user who is looking at a MEDLINE entry can ask Entrez to "find all papers that are like this one." Similarly, a user who is looking at a sequence entry can ask Entrez to "find all sequences that are similar to this one." The establishment of neighboring relationships within a database is based on statistical measures of similarity:

BLAST   Sequence data are compared to one another using the Basic Local Alignment Search Tool, or BLAST (Altschul et al., 1990). This algorithm attempts to find "high-scoring segment pairs" (HSPs), which are pairs of sequences that can be aligned *without* gaps and meet certain scoring and statistical criteria. Chapter 7 discusses at length the family of BLAST algorithms and their application.

VAST   Sets of coordinate data are compared using a vector-based method known as VAST, for Vector Alignment Search Tool (Madej et al., 1995; Gibrat et al., 1996). There are three major steps in a VAST comparison:

- First, based on the coordinate data, all of the α helices and β sheets that comprise the core of the protein are identified. Straight-line vectors are then calculated based on the position of these secondary structure elements, and subsequent steps use these vectors rather than the entire coordinate set for comparison.

· Next, the algorithm attempts to optimally align these vectors, looking for pairs of structural elements that are of the same type and relative orientation, and have the same connectivity between elements. The object is to identify highly similar "core substructures," pairs that represent a statistically significant match above that which would be obtained by comparing randomly chosen proteins to one another.

· Finally, a refinement is done using Monte Carlo methods at each residue position in an attempt to optimize the structural alignment.

Through this method, it is possible to find structural (and, presumably, functional) relationships between proteins in cases that may lack overt sequence similarity. The resultant alignment need not be global; matches may be between individual domains of different proteins.

It is important to note here that VAST is *not* the best method for determining structural similarities. More robust methods, such as homology model building, provide much greater resolving power in determining such relationships, since the raw information within the three-dimensional coordinate file is used to perform more advanced calculations regarding the positions of side chains and the thermodynamic nature of the interactions between side chains. Reducing a structure to a series of vectors necessarily results in a loss of information. However, considering the *magnitude* of the problem here—that is, the *number* of pairwise comparisons to be made—and both the computing power and time needed to employ any of the more advanced methods, VAST provides a simple and fast first answer to the question of structural similarity. More information on other structure prediction methods based on X-ray or NMR coordinate data can be found in Chapter 11.

Weighted Key Terms   The problem of comparing sequence data somewhat pales next to that of comparing MEDLINE entries, free text whose rules of syntax are not necessarily fixed. Entrez employs a method known as the *relevance pairs model of retrieval* to make such comparisons, relying on what are known as weighted key terms (Wilbur and Coffee, 1994; Wilbur and Yang, 1996). This concept is best described by example. Consider two manuscripts with the following titles:

```
BRCA1 as a Genetic Marker for Breast Cancer
Genetic Factors in the Familial Transmission of the BRCA1 Gene
```

Both these titles contain the terms BRCA1, Breast, and Cancer, and the presence of these common terms may indicate that the manuscripts are similar in their subject matter. The proximity between the words is also taken into account, so that words common to two records that are closer together are scored higher than common words that are further apart. In the current example, the terms Breast and Cancer would score higher based on proximity than either of those words would against BRCA1, since the words are next to each other. Common words found in a title are scored higher than those found in an abstract, since title words are presumed to be "more important" than those found in the body of an abstract. Overall weighting depends on the frequency of a given word among all the entries in MEDLINE, with words that occur infrequently in the database as a whole carrying a higher weight.

Regardless of the method by which the neighboring relationships are established, the ability to actually code and maintain these relationships are based in the format underlying all of the constituent databases. This format, called *Abstract Syntax Notation* (ASN.1), provides a format in which all similar fields (e.g., those for a bibliographic citation) are all structured identically regardless of whether the entry is in a protein database, nucleotide database, and so forth. This NCBI data model is discussed in depth in Chapter 6.

Hard Links

The hard link concept is much easier conceptually than neighboring. Hard links are applied between entries in *different* databases and exist everywhere there is a logical connection between entries. For instance, if a MEDLINE entry talks about the sequencing of a cosmid, a hard link is established between the MEDLINE entry and the corresponding nucleotide entry. If an open reading frame in that cosmid codes for a known protein, a hard link is established between the nucleotide entry and the protein entry. If, by sheer luck, the protein entry has an experimentally deduced structure, a hard link would be placed between the protein entry and the structural entry.

The relationship between neighbors and hard links is best illustrated by Figure 5.2. Each of the constituent databases or divisions (MEDLINE, Protein, Nucleotide, Structure, and Genomes) is represented by a pentagon. The curved lines leading out of and back into any given pentagon represent the neighboring relationships, which allow related entries *within*

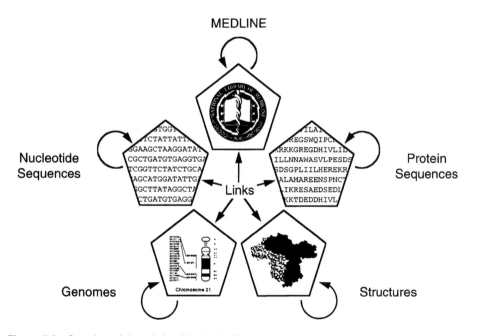

Figure 5.2 Overview of the relationships in the Entrez integrated information retrieval system. Each pentagon represents one of the component databases; the curved lines pointing back toward each pentagon represent neighboring relationships, and the straight lines in the center of the figure represent hard links.

the same database to be found. The straight-line connections at the center of the figure, going from pentagon to pentagon, represent the hard link relationships, which allow related entries *between* databases to be found. Wise use of both these types of relationship allow the user to amass an incredibly large amount of information based on just a single query, in much less time than queries of the individual databases would take.

Search Entry Points

As indicated by Figure 5.2, searches can, in essence, begin anywhere within Entrez—the user has no constraints with respect to where the foray into this information space must begin. However, depending on which database is used as the jumping-off point, different fields are available for searching. This stands to reason, inasmuch as the entries in databases of different types are necessarily organized differently, reflecting the biological nature of the entity they are trying to catalog. A list of searchable fields for each of the Entrez divisions is given in Table 5.1.

Implementations

Regardless of platform, Entrez searches can be performed using one of two interfaces. The first is a client–server implementation known as *Network Entrez*. This is the fastest of the Entrez programs in that it makes a direct connection to an NCBI "dispatcher." The graphical user interface features a series of windows, as illustrated shortly. Since the client software resides on the user's machine, it is up to the user to obtain, install, and maintain the software, downloading periodic updates as new features are introduced. The installation process is fairly trivial.

The second implementation is over the World Wide Web and is known as *WWW Entrez* or *Web Entrez*. This option makes use of available Web browsers, such as Internet Explorer or Netscape, to deliver search results to the desktop. The use of a Web browser relieves the user of having to make sure that the most current version of Entrez is installed—as long as the browser is of relatively recent vintage, results will always be received via the latest

TABLE 5.1 Searchable Fields for the Five Entrez Divisions

Category	MEDLINE	Nucleotide	Protein	Structure	Genome
Plain text	•	•	•	•	•
Author name	•	•	•	•	•
Journal title	•	•	•	•	•
Accession number	•	•	•	•	•
Date of publication	•	•	•	•	
Medical Subject Heading (Me SH)	•	•	•	•	
Organism name		•	•		•
Gene symbol or gene name	•	•	•		•
Protein name	•	•	•	•	•
EC number	•	•	•	•	•
Chemical substance name	•	•	•	•	
Sequence database keywords		•	•		
Feature key (*e.g.,* CDS)		•			
Properties (*e.g.,* partial)		•	•		•

Entrez release. The Web naturally lends itself to an application such as this, since all the neighboring and hard link relationships described above can easily be expressed as hypertext, allowing the user to navigate by clicking on selected words in an entry.

The advantage of the Web implementation over the Network version is that the Web allows for the ability to link to *external* data sources, such as full-text versions of papers maintained by a given journal or press, or specialized databases that are not part of Entrez proper. The speed advantage that is gained by the Network version causes its limitation in this respect; the direct connection to the NCBI dispatcher means that the user, once connected to NCBI, cannot travel anywhere else. The other main difference between the two methods lies simply in the presentation: the Network version uses a series of windows, while the Web version is formatted as sequential pages, following the standard Web paradigm. The final decision is one of personal preference, for both methods will produce the same results within the Entrez search space.

The Entrez Discovery Pathway: Examples

The best way to illustrate the integrated nature of the Entrez system and to drive home the power of neighboring is by considering a biological example, using the Web version of Entrez as the interface. Starting at the Entrez home page on the NCBI Web site, the user can select one of the five component Entrez databases as the initial point of entry for a query. In this case, the search will be performed against MEDLINE. The PubMed query page is shown in Figure 5.3, and the form on this page requires that two selections be made before

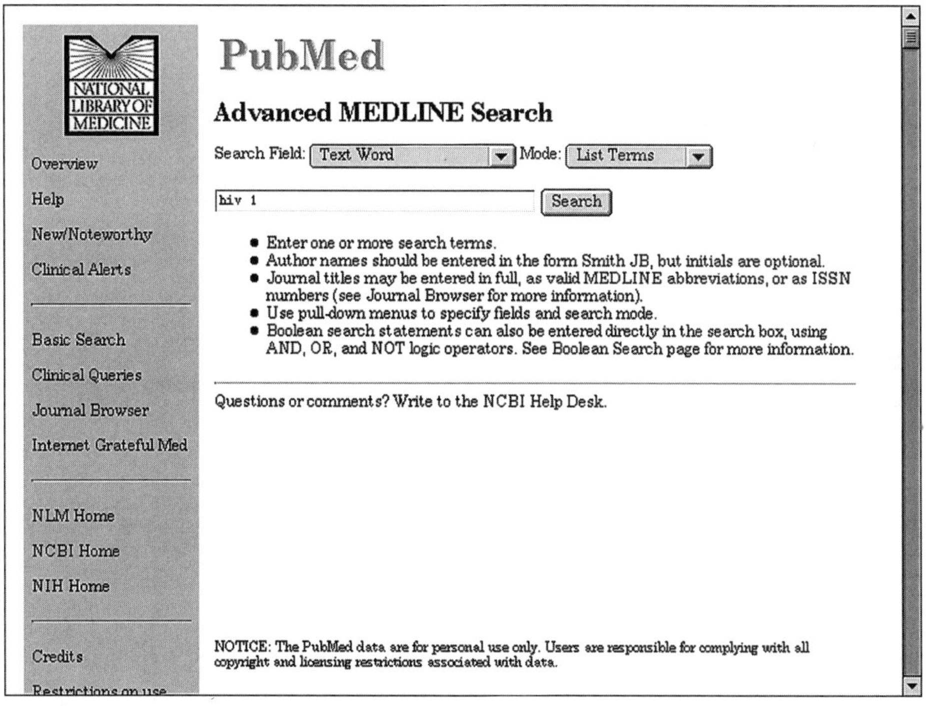

Figure 5.3 Starting an Entrez query against the MEDLINE database using the World Wide Web version of Entrez (*http://www.ncbi.nlm.nih.gov/Entrez*). See text for details.

a query is submitted. First, the user must select a Search field, which allows searches to be restricted to a particular field within a database entry (e.g., biological species or subject heading). Second, the user must select a search mode, which refers to the method of interaction between the user and the server. In Automatic mode, the server will look at the term that has been entered in the query box and look for the closest match that exists in the database. In List Terms mode, which provides finer control over the final search results, the user is returned a list of terms that most closely match the one the user requested. While Automatic and List Terms modes frequently return the same results, use of List Terms is highly recommended, since terms may be indexed in any one of a number of ways that may not be apparent to the user at the start of a search.

Suppose one wishes to retrieve abstracts on human immunodeficiency virus 1. Using the Entrez query window, one could enter hiv 1 in the query box, Text Word as the field (so that the titles and abstracts are searched for the occurrence of HIV 1), and List Terms as the mode. (Of course, Organism could have been used as the field; a good exercise would be to perform the search both ways to see how the output would differ.) Hitting the Search key then generates a new Web page (Figure 5.4). This page contains a term selection window that allows the user to browse the closest matches to the original query (HIV 1). Notice that the Select window shows a number of entries following HIV 1 that are catalogued slightly differently. If the user had chosen Automatic as the search mode, these extra entries would have been missed, and possibly important information as well. With List Terms, however, the user is guaranteed to see all variations of the original search term.

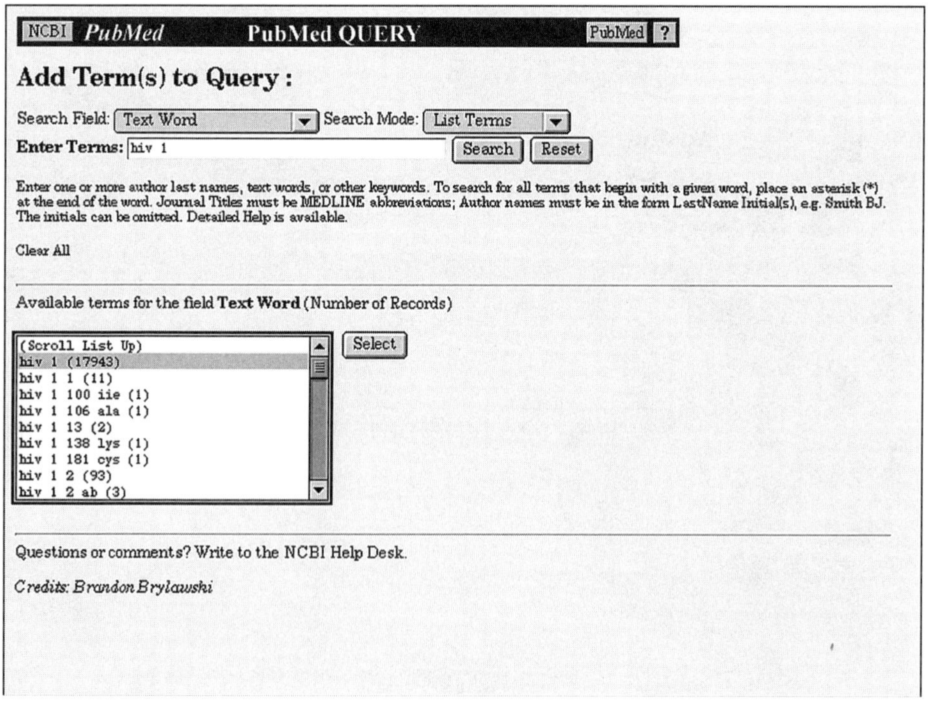

Figure 5.4 Terms retrieved as a result of an Entrez query against the MEDLINE database. See text for details.

To this point, no entries have actually been retrieved. To retrieve the entries, the user must highlight the desired term from the Term Selection box (here, `hiv 1`) and then click the Select button. Doing this produces the next Web page, which at the top shows the status of the current search and the number of entries found (Figure 5.5). Performing the search as described above returns 17,943 entries, far too many abstracts for anyone to sift through. Therefore, some refinement is necessary to narrow down the number of abstracts returned. If one is interested in the folding of HIV 1 heterodimers, the number of references returned could be lowered by repeating the steps above in turn, using `heterodimer` and `folding` as additional search terms. While each individual search returns thousands of entries, the union of these searches yields only six (Figure 5.6). In Entrez, the default Boolean operator is AND, as can be seen in the Query Refinement window beneath the individual search terms.

To actually view the results of the search, the user must click on the button labeled Retrieve 6 Documents; doing so spawns a new window (Figure 5.7). The individual entries in this window each have several elements: a checkbox, the name of the first author with the year of publication, and the title and citation information. Focusing on the Jacobo-Molina 1993 entry at the bottom of the window and clicking on the author's name brings up yet another window, this one containing the citation information, the name of the paper, a list of all the authors, their affiliation and the abstract (Figure 5.8) in standard citation format.

A number of alternate formats are available and can be selected using the pulldown menu next to the Display button on the page shown in Figure 5.7. Switching to Abstract

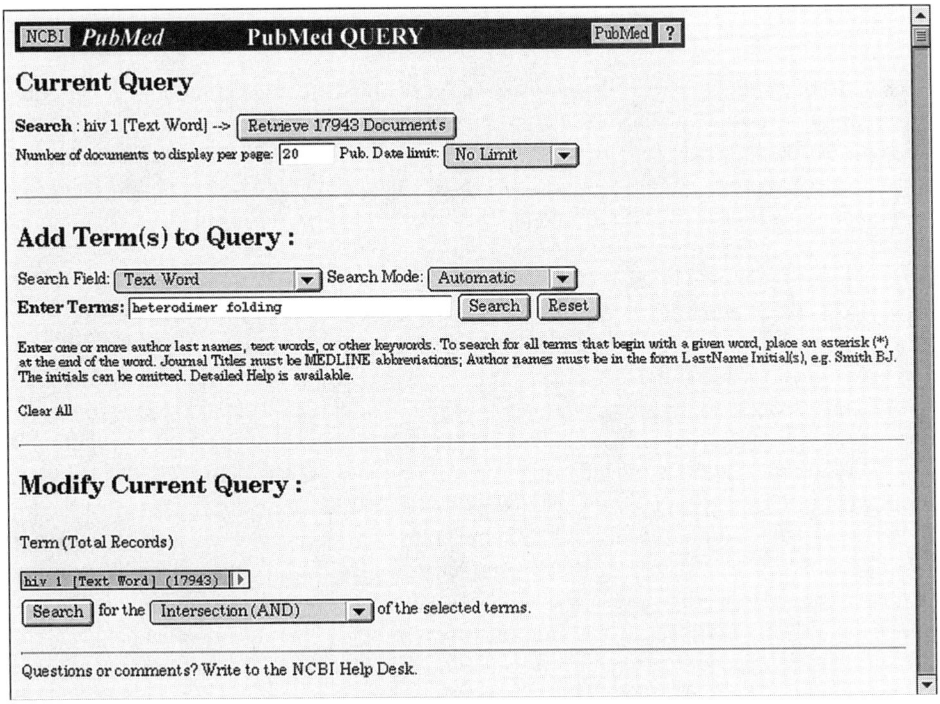

Figure 5.5 MEDLINE search page showing the progress of the current query at the top of the window and the addition of new terms to the search in the center of the window. See text for details.

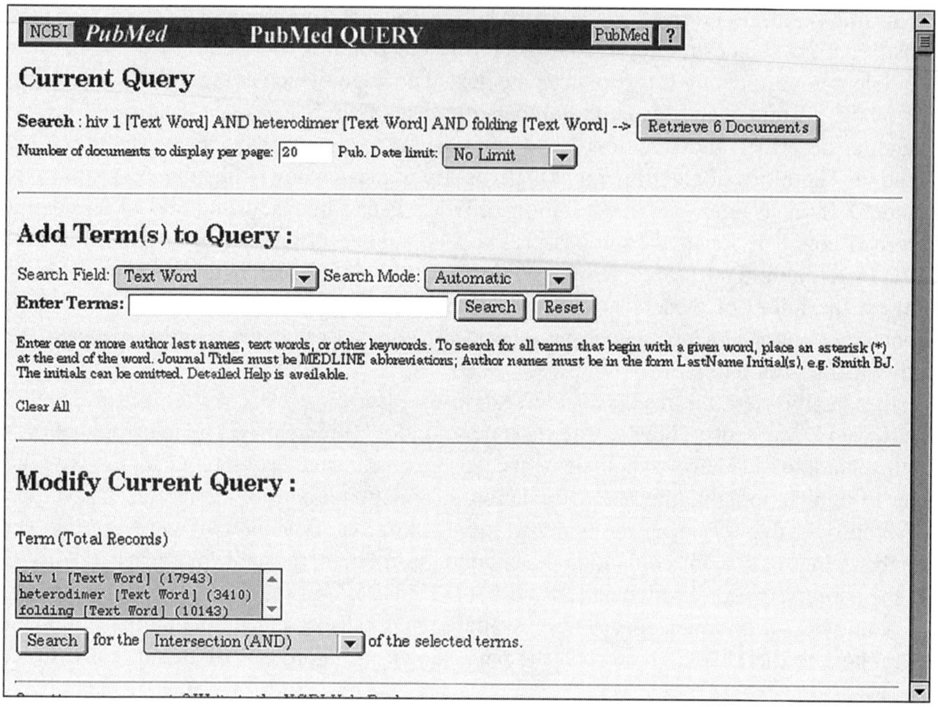

Figure 5.6 MEDLINE search page showing the result of adding terms to a search in progress. See text for details.

format would produce a very similar-looking entry, the difference being that cataloguing information such as MeSH terms and indexed substances relating to the entry are shown after the abstract. MEDLINE format produces the MEDLINE/MEDLARS layout, with two-letter codes corresponding to the contents of each field going down the left-hand side of the entry (e.g., the author field is denoted by the code AU). Entries in this format can be saved and easily imported into third-party bibliography management programs, such as EndNote and Reference Manager.

At the top of Figure 5.8 is a series of buttons labeled Links. This is one of the entry points from which the user can take advantage of the neighboring and hard link relationships described earlier. If the user clicks on Related Articles, Entrez will indicate that there are 133 neighbors associated with the Jacobo-Molina reference—that is, 133 references of similar subject matter—and the first of those papers are shown in a new list in Figure 5.9. The first reference in the list is the original paper on the crystal structure of HIV 1 reverse transcriptase. This is called *parents persist,* with the "parent" entry being shown at the top of the list and the neighbored entries following below it. The order in which the neighbored entries follows is from most statistically similar downward. Thus, the entry closest to the parent is deemed to be the closest in subject matter to the parent. By scanning the titles, the user can easily find related information on structural and functional studies having to do with HIV 1 proteins, which makes it possible to quickly amass a bibliography of relevant references. This is a particularly useful and time-saving functionality when one is writing grants or papers, since abstracts can be scanned and papers of real interest identified before one heads off for the library stacks.

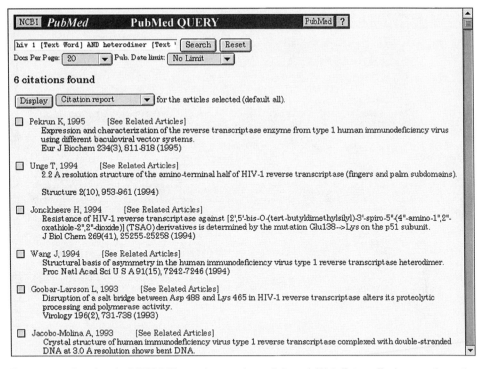

Figure 5.7   Results of a MEDLINE search as performed through Web Entrez. Each entry shows the name of the first author, the title of the paper, and the citation information. The actual record can be retrieved by clicking on the author's name.

From this new list of papers, one can summon up hard-linked entries using the check-boxes next to each entry in the list. Continuing with the example, changing the pulldown menu next to the Display button to Protein Links and then clicking the Display button, will produce a list of 19 entries from the protein databases associated with the MEDLINE entries on that page; six of these are shown in Figure 5.10. This page generally has the same format as those already seen for MEDLINE, except that a number of hyperlinks follow each entry, corresponding either to different available formats or providing paths to neighbors and hard-linked entries. One of the more useful formats is FASTA, which provides the format needed for import into most other sequence analysis programs. The output that would be produced by clicking on any of the Protein Neighbors hyperlinks would represent, in essence, the results of precomputed BLAST searches of that individual protein sequence. At this point, one could follow similar steps to get to the nucleotide databases.

In the list of protein entries obtained for this query were entries for 1HNV-A and 1HNV-B, an HIV-1 reverse transcriptase mutant with a point mutation (Cys 280 → Ser). Clicking on the Graphical View link produces a graphical view of all the information in that entry's Feature table (Figure 5.11). In this case, the protein has a large number of secondary structure elements, and this type of view makes it much easier to sort out exactly where those elements fall along the length of the protein. If the hyperlink labeled 1 structure link is clicked instead, a Structure Summary page will be produced (Figure 5.12). This page shows details from the header of the source PDB document, the primary structure in three-

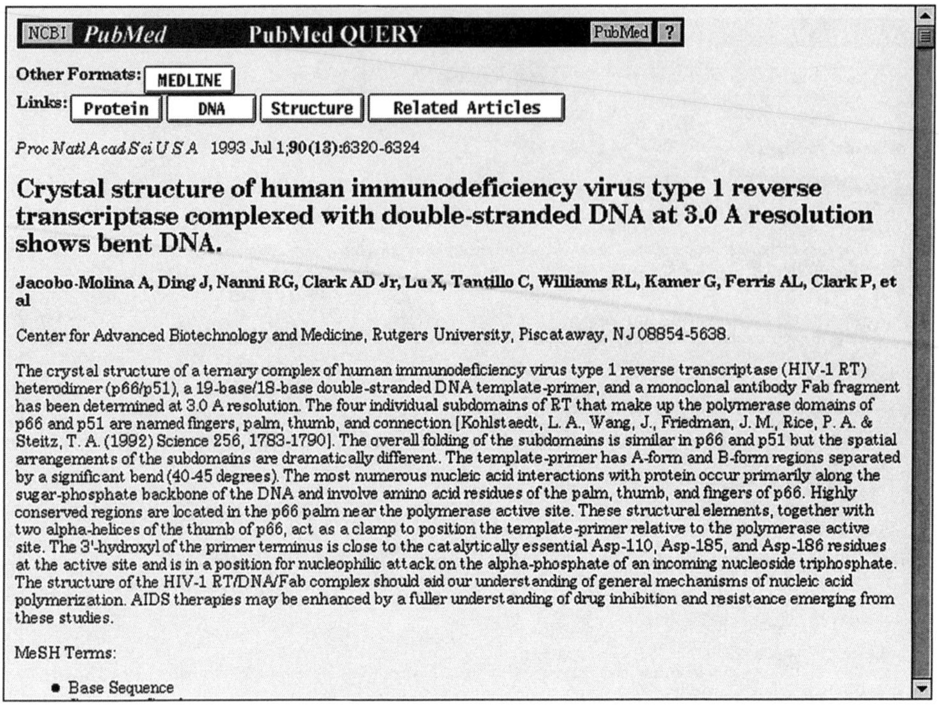

NCBI PubMed PubMed QUERY PubMed ?

Other Formats: MEDLINE

Links: Protein DNA Structure Related Articles

Proc Natl Acad Sci U S A 1993 Jul 1;**90(13)**:6320-6324

Crystal structure of human immunodeficiency virus type 1 reverse transcriptase complexed with double-stranded DNA at 3.0 A resolution shows bent DNA.

Jacobo-Molina A, Ding J, Nanni RG, Clark AD Jr, Lu X, Tantillo C, Williams RL, Kamer G, Ferris AL, Clark P, et al

Center for Advanced Biotechnology and Medicine, Rutgers University, Piscataway, NJ 08854-5638.

The crystal structure of a ternary complex of human immunodeficiency virus type 1 reverse transcriptase (HIV-1 RT) heterodimer (p66/p51), a 19-base/18-base double-stranded DNA template-primer, and a monoclonal antibody Fab fragment has been determined at 3.0 A resolution. The four individual subdomains of RT that make up the polymerase domains of p66 and p51 are named fingers, palm, thumb, and connection [Kohlstaedt, L. A., Wang, J., Friedman, J. M., Rice, P. A. & Steitz, T. A. (1992) Science 256, 1783-1790]. The overall folding of the subdomains is similar in p66 and p51 but the spatial arrangements of the subdomains are dramatically different. The template-primer has A-form and B-form regions separated by a significant bend (40-45 degrees). The most numerous nucleic acid interactions with protein occur primarily along the sugar-phosphate backbone of the DNA and involve amino acid residues of the palm, thumb, and fingers of p66. Highly conserved regions are located in the p66 palm near the polymerase active site. These structural elements, together with two alpha-helices of the thumb of p66, act as a clamp to position the template-primer relative to the polymerase active site. The 3'-hydroxyl of the primer terminus is close to the catalytically essential Asp-110, Asp-185, and Asp-186 residues at the active site and is in a position for nucleophilic attack on the alpha-phosphate of an incoming nucleoside triphosphate. The structure of the HIV-1 RT/DNA/Fab complex should aid our understanding of general mechanisms of nucleic acid polymerization. AIDS therapies may be enhanced by a fuller understanding of drug inhibition and resistance emerging from these studies.

MeSH Terms:

- Base Sequence

Figure 5.8 Example of a MEDLINE record in citation format as returned using Entrez. Links to neighbored and hard-linked entries, as well as other format options, are available through buttons at the top of the window.

letter format, and links to other information, such as a list of VAST neighbors. If the View button under "View/Save: 1HNV" is clicked, the Cn3D plug-in is invoked, producing a rendering of the structure in the new window (Figure 5.13). For a user interested in gleaning initial impressions about the shape of a protein, the Cn3D window provides a powerful interface, giving far more information than anyone could deduce from simply examining a string of letters (the sequence of the protein). The protein may be rotated along its axes by means of the scroll bars on the bottom and right-hand side of the window, or freely rotated by clicking and holding down the mouse key while the cursor is within the structure window, then dragging. Users are able to zoom in to particular parts of the structure and label the residues by number as needed; in this case, there is a point mutation, and its site can be identified. Users can also change the coloration of the figure, to determine specific structural features about the protein. In Figure 5.13, for instance, Spacefilling and Hydrophobicity were chosen as the Render and Color options, respectively. This combination of options can be used to envisage the distribution of surface charges on the protein, which may give an indication of the parts of the protein that are involved in protein–protein or protein–DNA interactions. More information on Cn3D is presented in Chapter 3, as well as in the online Cn3D documentation. In addition, users can save coordinate information to a file and view the data using third-party applications such as Kinemage (Richardson and Richardson, 1992) and Rasmol (Sayle and Milner-White, 1995).

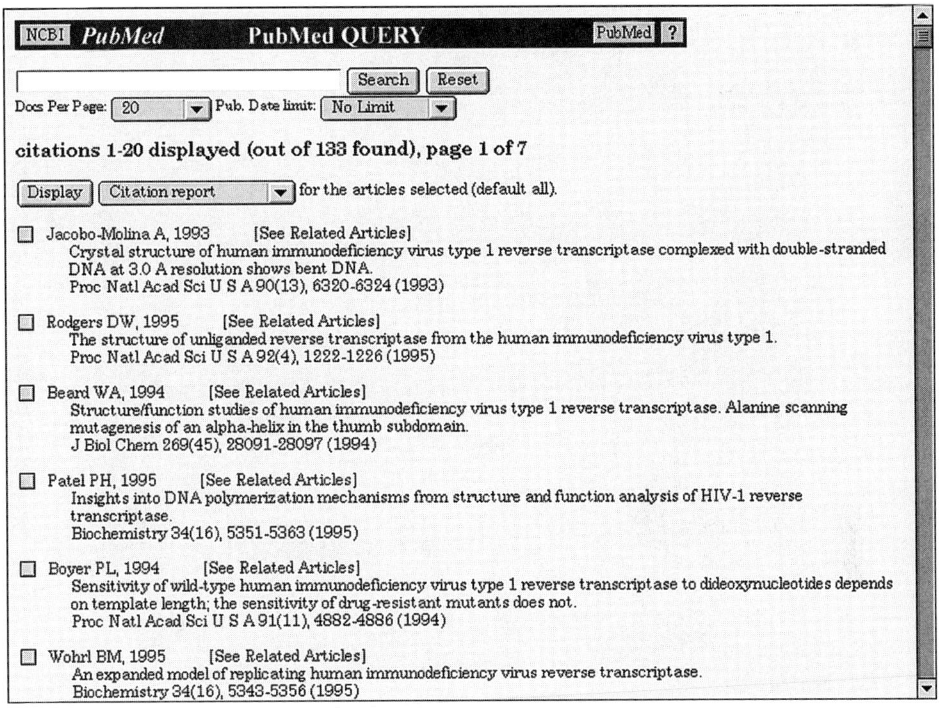

Figure 5.9 Neighbors to an entry found in MEDLINE from the original Entrez query. The original entry (Jacobo-Molina, 1993) is at the top of the list, indicating that this is the parent entry. See text for details.

INTEGRATED INFORMATION ACCESS: THE QUERY SERVER

When an Entrez platform is not available, as sometimes happens, a user will be restricted to performing searches via e-mail. Or, a user who can access Entrez from the lab through a T1 connection may not have a fast enough Internet connection at home to make using the World Wide Web practical. *Query,* the e-mail alternative to Entrez, fills the gap. The idea behind Query is very similar to that of Retrieve, but instead of querying just one database at a time, Query can search a given database domain (protein, nucleotide, structure, or MEDLINE) and is capable of returning both neighbors and hard-linked entries.

As with Retrieve, Query users must follow a defined format when sending a search request to the server. Figure 5.14 presents the format of a Query request in a generalized way, showing what flags and options can be thrown during any given search. (Query also supports the Retrieve syntax, so a search request that is sent to the Query server in Retrieve format can be properly interpreted.) The simplest type of search is done by search term. To perform such a search, the user merely specifies the target database and one or more search terms. As with Retrieve and Entrez, term-based searches can be restricted to particular fields in a database entry, which should yield more refined results. To show the differences between Query and Retrieve, we will begin with the same example considered in Figures 5.3 to 5.14, formulated for the Query server.

☐ 1HNV-A
  Chain A, Hiv-1 Reverse Transcriptase (Hiv-1 Rt) (E.C.2.7.7.49) Mutant With Cys 280 Replaced By Ser (C280s),
  Hiv-1 (Bh10 Isolate) Expressed In (Escherichia Coli)
  gi | 1065293 | pdb | 1HNV | A [1065293]
  *(View GenPept Report , FASTA report , ASN.1 report , Graphical view , 7 MEDLINE links , 1700 protein
  neighbors , or 1 structure link)*

☐ 1HNI-B
  Chain B, Human Immunodeficiency Virus Type 1 Reverse Transcriptase (Hiv-1rt) (E.C.2.7.7.49) Mutant With Cys
  280 Replaced By Ser (C280s), Hiv-1 (Bh10 Isolate) Expressed In (Escherichia Coli)
  gi | 1065288 | pdb | 1HNI | B [1065288]
  *(View GenPept Report , FASTA report , ASN.1 report , Graphical view , 9 MEDLINE links , 1683 protein
  neighbors , or 1 structure link)*

☐ 1HNI-A
  Chain A, Human Immunodeficiency Virus Type 1 Reverse Transcriptase (Hiv-1rt) (E.C.2.7.7.49) Mutant With Cys
  280 Replaced By Ser (C280s), Hiv-1 (Bh10 Isolate) Expressed In (Escherichia Coli)
  gi | 1065287 | pdb | 1HNI | A [1065287]
  *(View GenPept Report , FASTA report , ASN.1 report , Graphical view , 9 MEDLINE links , 1700 protein
  neighbors , or 1 structure link)*

☐ 3HVT-B
  Chain B, Reverse Transcriptase (E.C.2.7.7.49), Hiv-1 (Bh10 Isolate)
  gi | 640349 | pdb | 3HVT | B [640349]
  *(View GenPept Report , FASTA report , ASN.1 report , Graphical view , 4 MEDLINE links , 1678 protein
  neighbors , or 1 structure link)*

☐ 3HVT-A
  Chain A, Reverse Transcriptase (E.C.2.7.7.49), Hiv-1 (Bh10 Isolate)
  gi | 640348 | pdb | 3HVT | A [640348]
  *(View GenPept Report , FASTA report , ASN.1 report , Graphical view , 4 MEDLINE links , 1700 protein
  neighbors , or 1 structure link)*

☐ 1RDH-B
  Chain B, Hiv-1 Reverse Transcriptase (Ribonuclease H Domain) (E.C.2.7.7.49), Human Immunodeficiency Virus
  Type 1 Recombinant Form Expressed In (Escherichia Coli)
  gi | 576256 | pdb | 1RDH | B [576256]
  *(View GenPept Report , FASTA report , ASN.1 report , Graphical view , 2 MEDLINE links , 287 protein
  neighbors , or 1 structure link)*

Figure 5.10 Partial Entrez output produced by requesting protein neighbors from the previous screen. See text for details.

```
To:         query@ncbi.nlm.nih.gov
Subject:    Simple Query
DB p
TERM histone H1 [PROT]
     & (Saccharomyces [ORGN] | Schizosaccharomyces [ORGN])
```

The query begins with the line DB p, which signifies that the protein databases are to be searched. Recall that Retrieve allowed users to search only one database at a time; Query

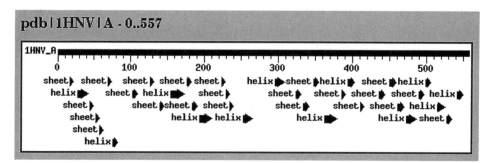

Figure 5.11 Graphical view of a protein entry, showing all the information available in that entry's Feature table. Any details known about this protein that can be attributed to particular locations along the primary sequence are shown in this view.

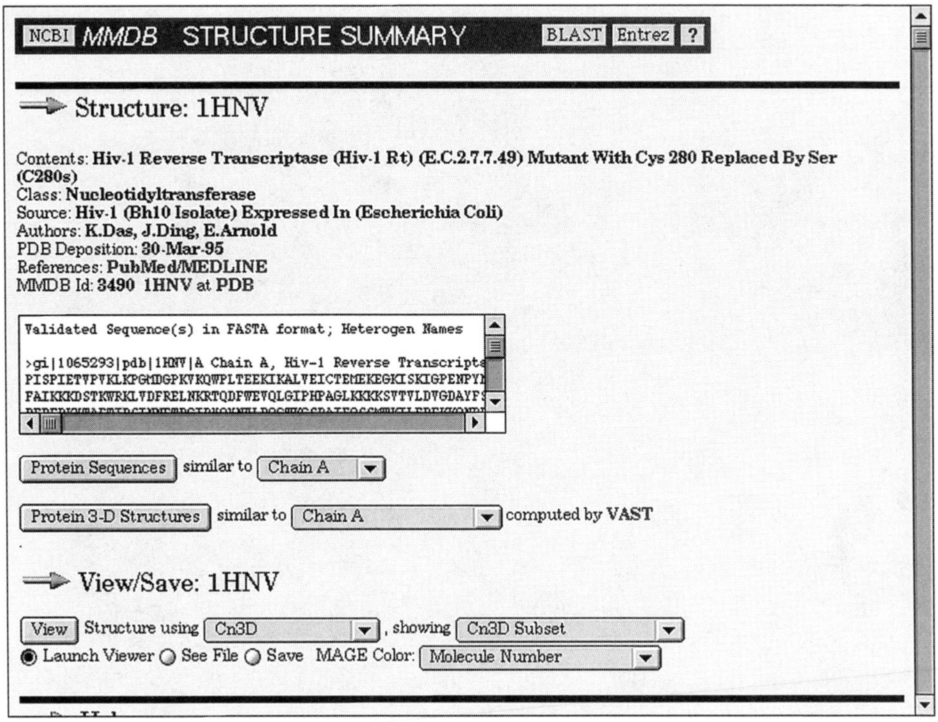

Figure 5.12 The Structure Summary for 1HNV, as displayed using Web Entrez. The entry shows header information from the corresponding MMDB entry, the primary sequence for the entry, and various display and analysis options.

allows searching of *all* like databases at once [here, the protein databases making up the nonredundant (*nr*) set]. Databases are specified by a single-letter code: p for protein, n for nucleotide, m for MEDLINE, t for structure, and s to search both protein and nucleotide databases at once. The search space, then, is the same as that used during an Entrez search.

Unlike the original Retrieve search, discrete fields have been specified to restrict the search: the histone H1 term will be looked for only in the Protein Name field ([PROT]), whereas the organism names will be looked for only in the Organism Name field ([ORGN]). Notice that the ampersand (&) has been used to specify the Boolean AND, while the vertical bar (|) has been used to specify the Boolean OR. The Boolean NOT is specified by a hyphen (-); since, however, a hyphen could be part of a search term as well, a hyphen representing a Boolean operator must have at least one space on either side of it, to separate it from the actual search terms.

Up to this point, Query does not seem to differ much from Retrieve. In fact, the foregoing search will produce the same results as Retrieve. However, use of the DOPT (**d**isplay **opt**ions) flag can drastically change the nature of the returned results, to the user's advantage. Continuing with the example, perhaps the user wants to have the results returned in FASTA format rather than the standard Entrez document summary format. Additionally, rather than seeing the protein entries themselves, the user wants the *nucleotide links* to those entries. To produce that result, the preceding search would be refined as follows:

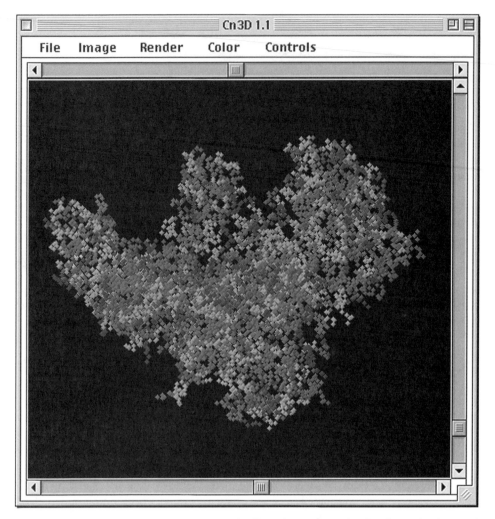

Figure 5.13 A structure entry rendered using Cn3D, an interactive molecular viewer that is part of Network Entrez. Cn3D can also be installed as a browser plug-in for use with Web Entrez. See text for details.

```
DB p
TERM histone H1 [PROT]
      & (Saccharomyces [ORGN] | Schizosaccharomyces [ORGN])
DOPT fn
```

The fn in the DOPT statement signifies that nucleotide records (n) linked to the protein records specified by the TERM command be displayed in FASTA format (f). The results of this particular search are shown in Figure 5.15. The versatility of the DOPT statement make Query very useful in amassing information that is to be handled off to other programs, such as sequence alignment editors or predictive tools, particularly when the results are obtained in FASTA format.

Database	**DB** [m|p|n|t|s]
Search type – *use one of:*	**UID** [MUID|gi|acc|FASTA-spec] or **TERM** term field_spec
Options – *use any or all:*	**DOPT** display_option **HTML** **DISPMAX** n **PATH** address

Figure 5.14 Generalized format for requests sent to the Query server. For bracketed items, users must select one of the variables in the brackets to execute the search. More detailed information on structuring Query searches can be found in the text and on the Query documentation Web page at NCBI.

Finally, three additional flags are available to Query users. HTML will return the results in HTML format, so that the results can be viewed using any Web browser. DISPMAX controls the number of entries returned; if DISPMAX is not invoked, the default is 200, but with an overriding e-mail line limit of 100,000. Finally, PATH can be used to return the results to an e-mail address different from the one that sent the request.

SEQUENCE DATABASES BEYOND NCBI

While it may appear from this discussion that NCBI is the center of the sequence universe, many specialized sequence databases throughout the world serve specific groups in the sci-

```
Requested WWW query:

http://www.ncbi.nlm.nih.gov/htbin-post/Entrez/query?db=p&form=4&term=

histone+H1+[PROT]++AND++(Saccharomyces+[ORGN]++OR++Schizosaccharomyces

+[ORGN])&dopt=fn&dispmax=200&html=no


Content-type: text/html


Entrez Reports
----------------
>gi|2131283|pir||S69056 histone H1 - yeast (Saccharomyces cerevisiae)

MAPKKSTTKTTSKGKKPATSKGKEKSTSKAAIKKTTAKKEEASSKSYRELIIEGLTALKERKGSSRPALK

KFIKENYPIVGSASNFDLYFNNAIKKGVEAGDFEQPKGPAGAVKLAKKKSPEVKKEKEVSPKPKQAATSV

SATASKAKAASTKLAPKKVVKKKSPTVTAKKASSPSSLTYKEMILKSMPQLNDGKGSSRIVLKKYVKDTF

SSKLKTSSNFDYLFNSAIKKCVENGELVQPKGPSGIIKLNKKKVKLST
```

Figure 5.15 Results of a complex query submitted to the Query server. Notice that the original request sent to the server has been reformatted as a URL that can be directly opened using a Web browser.

entific community. Often, these databases provide additional information such as phenotypes, experimental conditions, strain crosses, and map features. The data is of great importance to these subsets of the scientific community, inasmuch as they can influence rational experimental design, but such types of data do not fit neatly within the confines of the NCBI data model. Development of specialized databases necessarily ensued, but they are intended to be used as an adjunct to GenBank, not in place of it.

Two such specialized databases are the *Saccharomyces* Genome Database (SGD) and the *Arabidopsis thaliana* Database (AtDB), both housed at the Stanford Human Genome Center. Focusing on SGD because the entire *Saccharomyces* genome has been sequenced, the database provides a very simple search interface that allows text-based searches by gene name, gene information, clone, protein information, sequence name, author name, or full text. For example, using Gene Name as the search topic and hho1 as the name of the gene to be searched for produces a SacchDB information window showing all known information on locus HHO1 (Figure 5.16). The Locus window provides jumping-off points to other databases, such as MEDLINE and the Yeast Protein Database (YPD). Following the link to Sacch3D for this entry provides information on structural homologs of the HHO1 protein product found in PDB, links to secondary and tertiary structure prediction sites, and pre-

---

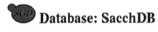 **Database: SacchDB**

[*Saccharomyces cerevisiae* | 14 Jul 1997]

Search SGD | Virtual Library | Help | Gene Registry | Maps | BLAST | FASTA | Sacch3D | Design Primers
Gene Names | Gene Info | Clones | Protein Info | Sequence Names | SGDID | Colleagues | Authors | Text

---

Locus : HHO1   ⬚ Help ⬚

[Seq & Display]

```
Locus_info: Other_name YPL127C
            Gene_class HHO
            Description Histone H1
            Gene_product histone H1
            Phenotype Null mutant is viable; other phenotype:
                      Increased basal expression of a
                      CYC1-lacz reporter gene; nuclear
                      localization of a Hho1-GFP fusion
                      protein
Position_info: Chromosome XVI
            ORF_name YPL127C
Sequence_info: ORF_sequence YPL127C [Seq & Display]
            Sequence YPL127C [Retrieve DNA]
Protein_info: YPD HHO1 [YPD]
            Sacch3D HHO1 [Sacch3D]
Reference Ushinsky, S.C., et al. (1996) Histone H1
            in Saccharomyces cerevisiae. Unpublished
Contact Bussey, Howard
Remark This gene name is reserved with SGD
            according to the Gene Naming Guidelines
            agreed upon by the yeast community.
Last_update 1996-08-29
SGDID L0003354
```

⬆ Return to Saccharomyces Genome Database   Send a Message to the SGD Curators ▦

Figure 5.16 A SacchDB Locus view resulting from a SGD query using HHO1 as the Locus name. Returned information includes locus, sequence, protein, and reference information. Hyperlinks provide access to graphical views and external database entries related to the current query.

computed BLAST reports against a number of query databases. Returning to the Locus window and clicking on the `Seq & Display` link, the user finds a graphical view of the area surrounding the locus in question. Available views include physical maps, genetic maps, and chromosomal features maps, among others. The physical map view for HHO1 is shown in Figure 5.17 (see color plate). Note the thick yellow bar at the top of the figure, which gives the position of the current view with respect to the centromere. Clicking on the yellow bar allows the user to move along the chromosome, and clicking on individual gene, clone, or sequence names gives more detailed information about that particular region.

Another example of an organism-specific database is FlyBase, whose goal is to maintain comprehensive information on the genetics and molecular biology of *Drosophila*. Access to FlyBase is available through the World Wide Web, Gopher, and FTP, and by e-mail. The information found in FlyBase includes an extensive *Drosophila* bibliography,

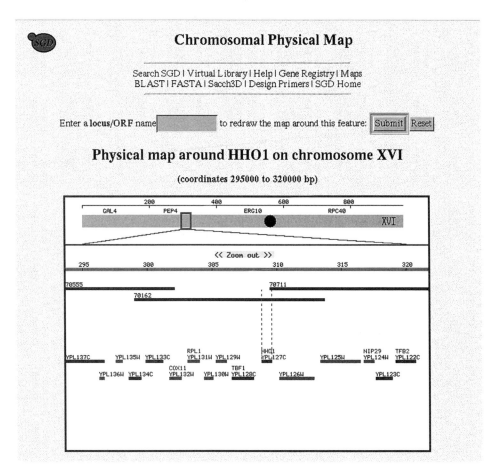

Figure 5.17 Physical map resulting from the query used to generate the Locus view shown in Figure 5.12. Chromosome XVI is shown at the top of the figure, with the exploded region highlighted by the red box. Watson-strand ORFs are shown in red, while Crick-strand ORFs are shown in blue. If an ORF has been defined, the gene name is shown in maroon, above the corresponding ORF name. Most items are clickable, returning detailed information about that particular entity.

addresses of researchers involved in *Drosophila* projects, a compilation of information on over 38,000 alleles of over 11,000 genes, descriptions of over 13,000 chromosomal aberrations, mapping information, functional information on gene products, lists of stock centers and genomic clones, and information from allied databases. Searches on any of these "fields" can be done through a simple search mechanism.

For example, searching by gene symbol using capu as the search term brings up a record for a gene named *cappuccino,* which is required for the proper polarity of the developing *Drosophila* oocyte (Emmons et al., 1995). Calling up the graphical view generates a map showing the gene and cytologic location of *cappuccino* and other genes in that immediate area, and users can click on any of the gene bars to bring up detailed information on that particular gene (Figure 5.18). Information on overlaps become obvious in this view; here, *cappuccino* is seen to overlap with *slp1* and *spl2,* which code for transcription factors. The view can be changed by selecting one of the Class buttons at the bottom of the window, so that a graphical view of clones, deficiencies, duplications, inversions, transpositions, translocations, or other aberrations can be examined instead.

MEDICAL DATABASES

While the focus of this chapter (and the book in general) is on sequences, databases cataloguing and organizing sequence information are not the only database types useful to the biologist. An example of such a non-sequence-based information resource is *Online Mendelian Inheritance in Man* (OMIM), the electronic version of the catalog of human genes and genetic disorders edited by Victor McKusick at The Johns Hopkins University. OMIM provides concise textual information from the literature published on most human

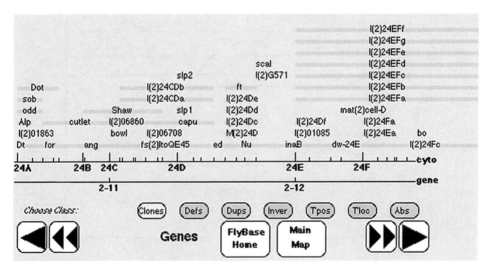

Figure 5.18   Genes view resulting from querying FlyBase for the *cappuccino* gene (*capu* in the figure, near position 24D on the cytologic map). The graphic view can be changed by clicking on any of the class buttons at the bottom of the figure, as described in the text. Information on any of the shown genes can be obtained by clicking on the appropriate bar.

conditions having a genetic basis, as well as pictures illustrating the condition or disorder where appropriate and full citation information. Since the online version of OMIM is housed at NCBI, links to Entrez are provided from all references cited within each OMIM entry.

OMIM has a defined numbering system in which each entry is assigned a unique number, similar to an accession number, but certain positions within that number indicate information about the genetic disorder itself. For example, the first digit represents the mode of inheritance of the disorder: 1 stands for autosomal dominant, 2 for autosomal recessive, 3 for X-linked locus or phenotype, 4 for Y-linked locus or phenotype, 5 for mitochondrial, and 6 for autosomal locus or phenotype. (The distinction between 1 or 2 and 6 is that entries catalogued before May 1994 were assigned either a 1 or 2, whereas entries after that date were assigned a 6 regardless of whether the mode of inheritance was dominant or recessive.) An asterisk preceding a number indicates that the *phenotype* caused by the gene at this locus is not influenced by genes at other loci; however, the disorder itself may be caused by mutations at multiple loci. Disorders for which no mode of inheritance has been determined do not carry asterisks. Finally, a pound sign (#) indicates that the phenotype is caused by two or more genetic mutations.

OMIM searches are very easy to perform. The search engine performs a simple query based on one or more words typed into a search window. A list of documents containing the query words is returned, and users can select one or more disorders from this list to look at the full text of the OMIM entry. The entries include information such as the gene symbol, alternate names for the disease, a description of the disease (including clinical, biochemical, and cytogenetic features), details on the mode of inheritance (including mapping information), a clinical synopsis, and references. While space precludes showing a full entry here, readers are encouraged to perform a sample search using the search term `Alzheimer` as the query input to see an example of an entry containing most of the features available through OMIM.

World Wide Web Sites for Topics in Chapter 5

AtDB	*http://genome-www.stanford.edu/Arabidopsis/*
BLAST	*http://www.ncbi.nlm.nih.gov/BLAST/*
Cn3D	*http://www.ncbi.nlm.nih.gov/Structure/cn3d.html*
EndNote	*http://www.niles.com/*
Entrez	*http://www.ncbi.nlm.nih.gov/Entrez/*
FlyBase	*http://flybase.bio.indiana.edu*
Kinemage	*http://www.umass.edu/microbio/rasmol/mage.htm*
MIPS	*http://speedy.mips.biochem.mpg.de/mips/yeast/*
OMIM	*http://www.ncbi.nlm.nih.gov/Omim*
Query	*http://www.ncbi.nlm.nih.gov/Web/Search/query.txt*
PDB	*http://www.pdb.bnl.org*
RasMol	*http://www.umass.edu/microbio/rasmol/*
Reference Manager	*http://www.risinc.com/*
Retrieve	*http://www.ncbi.nlm.nih.gov/Web/Search/retrieve.txt*
Sacch3D	*http://www-genome.stanford.edu/Sacch3D/*
SGD	*http://genome-www.stanford.edu/Saccharomyces/*
VAST	*http://www.ncbi.nlm.nih.gov/Structure/vast.html*
YPD	*http://quest7.protease.com/YPDhome.html*

REFERENCES

Altschul, S., Gish, W., Miller, W., Myers, E., and Lipman, D. (1990). Basic local alignment search tool. J. Mol. Biol. *215,* 403–410.

Emmons, S., Phan, H., Calley, J., Chen, W., James, B., and Manseau, L. (1995). *Cappuccino, a Drosophila* maternal effect gene required for polarity of the egg and embryo, is related to the vertebrate limb deformity locus. Genes Dev. *9,* 2484–2494.

Gibrat, J.-F., Madej, T., and Bryant, S. (1996). Surprising similarities in structure comparison. Curr. Opin. Struct. Biol. *6,* 377–385.

Madej, T., Gibrat, J.-F., and Bryant, S. (1995). Threading a database of protein cores. Proteins. *23,* 356–369.

Richardson, D., and Richardson, J. (1992). The kinemage: A tool for scientific communication. Protein Sci. *1,* 3–9.

Sayle, R., and Milner-White, E. (1995). RasMol: Biomolecular graphics for all. Trends Biochem. Sci. *20,* 374.

Wilbur, W., and Coffee, L. (1994). The effectiveness of document neighboring in search enhancement. Process Manage. *30,* 253–266.

Wilbur, W., and Yang, Y. (1996). An analysis of statistical term strength and its use in the indexing and retrieval of molecular biology texts. Comput. Biol. Med. *26,* 209–222.

6

The NCBI Data Model

James M. Ostell and Jonathan A. Kans

National Center for Biotechnology Information
National Library of Medicine
National Institutes of Health
Bethesda, Maryland

INTRODUCTION

What Is a Data Model?

Most biologists are familiar with the use of animal models to study human diseases. Although a disease that occurs in humans may not be found in exactly the same form in animals, often an animal disease shares enough attributes with a human counterpart to allow data gathered on the animal disease to be used to make inferences about the process in humans. Mathematical models describing the forces involved in musculoskeletal motions can be built by imagining that muscles are combinations of springs and hydraulic pistons and bones are lever arms; such models allow meaningful predictions to be made and tested about the much more complex biological system. Obviously the more closely and elegantly a model follows a real phenomenon, the more useful it is in predicting or understanding the natural phenomenon it mimics.

Some eight years ago NCBI introduced a new model of sequence-related information. This new and more powerful model made possible the rapid development of the software and integrated databases that underlie the popular Entrez retrieval system and on which the GenBank database is now built. The advantages of the model (e.g., the ability to move effortlessly from the published literature to DNA sequences to the proteins they encode, to chromosome maps of the genes, and to the 3-D structures of the proteins: see Chapter 5), have been apparent for years to biologists using Entrez, but very few biologists understand the foundation on which the model is built. As genome information becomes richer and more complex, more of the real data model is appearing in common representations such

Bioinformatics: A Practical Guide to the Analysis of Genes and Proteins
Edited by A.D. Baxevanis and B.F.F. Ouellette
ISBN 0-471-19196-5, pages 121–144.   Copyright © 1998 Wiley-Liss, Inc.

as GenBank files, and a better understanding the model itself is becoming more valuable in understanding what is going on. Without going into great detail, this chapter attempts to present a practical guide to the principles and effects of the NCBI data model.

Some Examples of the Model

The GenBank flatfile is a "DNA-centered" report (see Chapter 2). That is, the assertion that a region of DNA codes for a protein is represented by a CDS feature on the DNA. A qualifier, /translation="MLLYY", describes a sequence of amino acids produced by translating the CDS. A limited set of additional features on the DNA, such as mat_peptide, occasionally are used in GenBank flatfiles to describe cleavage products of the (unnamed) protein partially described by /translation, but clearly this is not a satisfactory solution. Conversely, most protein sequence databases present a "protein-centered" view in which the connection to the encoding gene may be completely lost, or may be only indirectly referenced by an accession number (which does not, for example, provide the exact codon-to-amino acid correspondence important for mutation analysis).

The NCBI data model directly models the two sequences involved, one DNA, one protein. The translation process is represented as a link between the two sequences, rather than an annotation on one or the other. Protein-related annotations, such as peptide cleavage products, are represented as features annotated directly on the protein sequence. In this form, it becomes very natural to analyze the protein sequences derived from translations of CDS features by BLAST or any other sequence search tool, and yet still not lose the precise linkage back to the gene. A collection of a DNA sequence and its translated proteins is called a Nuc-prot set and is the internal representation in use at NCBI for this data. The GenBank flatfile format is simply a particular style of human-readable report of the data, which flattens this connected collection of sequences back into the familiar one-sequence, DNA-centered view. The navigation provided by Entrez much more directly reflects the underlying structure of the data. The protein sequences derived from GenBank translations that are returned by BLAST searches are, in fact, the protein sequences from the Nuc-prot sets.

The GenBank format can also hide the multiple-sequence nature of some DNA sequences. In one common case, for example, the three genomic exons of a gene are sequenced, and maybe a bit of the flanking noncoding or intron DNA surrounding each exon as well, but the full length of the introns is not sequenced. There would be three GenBank flatfiles in this case, one for each exon. There is no explicit representation of the complete set of sequences over that genomic region; these three exons come in order and are separated by a certain length of unsequenced DNA. In GenBank format there is a Segment line of the form (in this case) of SEGMENT 1 of 3 in the first record, SEGMENT 2 of 3 in the second, and SEGMENT 3 of 3 in the third, but this tells the user only that the lines are part of some undefined ordered series (Figure 6.1A). Out of the whole GenBank release, one locates the correct Segment records to place together by an algorithm involving the LOCUS name. All segments that go together use the same first combination of letters, ending with the numbers appropriate to the segment, e.g., RNKOR1, RNKOR2, RNKOR3. Obviously this complicated arrangement can result in problems when LOCUS names include numbers that inadvertently interfere with such series. In addition, there is no one sequence record that describes the whole assembled series, nor is there any way to describe the distance between the pieces. There is no segmenting convention in the EMBL sequence database at all, so

Part A:

```
LOCUS        RNKOR1        1757 bp    DNA             ROD       25-MAR-1995
DEFINITION   Rattus norvegicus kappa opioid receptor gene, exons 1 and 2.
ACCESSION    U17993
NID          g727256
KEYWORDS     .
SEGMENT      1 of 3
....
LOCUS        RNKOR2         658 bp    DNA             ROD       25-MAR-1995
DEFINITION   Rattus norvegicus kappa opioid receptor gene, exon 3.
ACCESSION    U17994
NID          g727257
KEYWORDS     .
SEGMENT      2 of 3
....
LOCUS        RNKOR3        4048 bp    DNA             ROD       25-MAR-1995
DEFINITION   Rattus norvegicus kappa opioid receptor gene, exon 4 and complete
             cds.
ACCESSION    U17995
NID          g727258
KEYWORDS     .
SEGMENT      3 of 3
```

Part B:

```
LOCUS        RNKOR         6463 bp    DNA             CON       25-MAR-1995
DEFINITION   Rattus norvegicus kappa opioid receptor gene.
ACCESSION    ZZ123456
NID          g2182225
KEYWORDS     .
SOURCE       Norway rat.
  ORGANISM   Rattus norvegicus
             Eukaryotae; mitochondrial eukaryotes; Metazoa; Chordata;
             Vertebrata; Eutheria; Rodentia; Sciurognathi; Myomorpha; Muridae;
             Murinae; Rattus.
REFERENCE    1  (bases 1 to 1757)
  AUTHORS    Yakovlev,A.G., Krueger,K.E. and Faden,A.I.
  TITLE      Structure and expression of a rat kappa opioid receptor gene
  JOURNAL    J. Biol. Chem. 270, 6421-6424 (1995)
  MEDLINE    95204422
   PUBMED    7896774
REFERENCE    2  (bases 1 to 1757)
  AUTHORS    Yakovlev,A.G.
  TITLE      Direct Submission
  JOURNAL    Submitted (02-DEC-1994) Alexander G. Yakovlev, Georgetown
             University School of Medicine, Neurology, 3900 Reservoir Rd.,
             Washington, DC 20007, USA
FEATURES             Location/Qualifiers
     source          1..1757
                     /organism="Rattus norvegicus"
                     /strain="Sprague-Dawley"
                     /sex="male"
CONTIG       join(U17993:1..1757,gap(200),U17994:1..658,gap(),U17995:1..4048)
```

Figure 6.1 (*A*) Parts from a GenBank format of individual records in a segmented sequence. GenBank format historically indicates merely that records are part of some ordered series; it offers no information on what the other components are or how they are connected. To see the complete view of these records, see *http://www.ncbi.nlm.nih.gov/htbin-post/Entrez/query?uid=2182225&form=6&db=n&Dopt=g* (*B*) Representation of segmented sequences in the new CON division. A new extension of GenBank format will allow the details of construction of segmented records to be presented. The Contig line can include individual accessions, gaps of known length, and gaps of unknown length. The individual components can still be displayed in the traditional form, although no features or sequences are present in this format.

records derived from that source or distributed in that format lack even this imperfect information.

The NCBI data model defines a sequence type that directly represents such a segmented series, called a "segmented sequence." Rather than containing the letters A, G, C, and T, the segmented sequence contains instructions on how it is to be built from other sequences. So, for the example above, the segmented sequence would contain the instructions "take all of RNKOR1, then a gap of 200 bp, then all of RNKOR2, then a gap of unknown length, then all of RNKOR3". The segmented sequence itself can have a name (say RNKOR), an accession number, features, citations, and comments, like any other record. We commonly store this type of data in a so-called Seg set, containing the sequences RNKOR, RNKOR1, RNKOR2, RNKOR3, and all of their connections and features. When the GenBank release is made, as in the case of Nucprot sets, the Seg sets are broken up into multiple records and the segmented sequence itself is not visible. In the Entrez graphical views of segmented sequences, however, the segmented sequence is visible as a line connecting all its component sequences. DDBJ/EMBL/GenBank have recently agreed on a way to represent these constructed assemblies. They will be placed in the new CON division (Figure 6.1*B*).

An NCBI segmented sequence has no requirement that there be gaps between the pieces, and in fact the pieces can overlap, unlike the case of segmented series in a GenBank format. This makes the segmented sequence ideal for representing large sequences such as bacterial genomes, which may be megabases long. This is exactly what is done in the Entrez Genomes division for the bacterial genomes and also for other complete chromosomes such as for yeast. The NCBI Software Toolkit (Ostell, 1996; also see the list of Internet resources at the end of the chapter) contains functions that can gather the data a segmented sequence points to "on the fly," including sequence and features, automatically remapped from the coordinates of the small individual record to that of the complete chromosome. This makes it possible to provide graphical views, GenBank flatfile views, or FASTA views, or perform analyses on the whole chromosome easily even though the data itself exists only in the pieces. This ability to readily assemble on demand any region of a very large chromosome from smaller pieces is already valuable for bacterial genomes. Assembly on demand will only become more important as larger and larger regions are sequenced, perhaps by many different groups, and the notion that an investigator will be working on one huge single record becomes completely impractical.

What Does ASN.1 Have to Do with It?

The NCBI data model is often referred to, and confused with, the "NCBI ASN.1" or "ASN.1 Data Model." *Abstract Syntax Notation 1* (ASN.1) is an International Standards Organization (ISO) standard for describing structured data and reliably encoding data according to that description in a way that permits computers and software systems of all types to reliably exchange both the structure and the content. Saying a data model is written in ASN.1 is like saying a computer program is written in C or Fortran. The statement identifies the language; it does not say what the program does. The familiar GenBank flatfile was really designed for humans to read, from a particular DNA-centered viewpoint. ASN.1 is designed for a computer to read and is amenable to describing complicated data relationships in a very specific way. NCBI describes and processes data using the ASN.1 form. From that single common form, we produce a number of human-readable formats and tools such as Entrez, GenBank, and the BLAST databases. Without the existence of a common form such as this, for example, the neighboring and hard link relationships present in Entrez (see Chapter 5) would not be possible. This chapter is about the structure and content of the NCBI data model and its implications for biomedical databases and tools. Discussion about the choice of ASN.1 for this task and its form can be found elsewhere (Ostell, 1995).

What to Define?

We have given a few examples of how the NCBI data model defines sequences in a way that supports a richer and more explicit description of the experimental data than can be obtained with the GenBank format. The details of the model are important, and we expanded on them below. At this point, we briefly describe the reasoning and general principles behind the model as a whole.

There are two main reasons for putting data on a computer: retrieval and discovery. Retrieval is basically being able to get back out what was put in. While this is important, it is even more valuable to be able to get back from the system *more* knowledge than was put in—that is, to be able to use the information to make discoveries. Scientists can make discoveries by discerning connections between two pieces of information that were not known when the pieces were entered separately into the database, or by performing computations on the data that offer new insight into the records. The emphasis in the NCBI data model is on facilitating discovery, and that means defining and developing data useful for linking information and data that is amenable to computation.

A second type of general consideration for the model is stability. NCBI is a U.S. government agency, not a group supported year to year by grants. Thus the staff takes a very long view of its role in supporting bioinformatics efforts. NCBI provides large-scale information systems that support scientific inquiry over the time span of at least decades. As anyone involved in biomedicine knows, many major conceptual and technical revolutions can happen over decades. Somehow NCBI must serve those changing views and needs with software and data that may have been created years earlier. For that reason we have tried to choose as central data elements basic observations or data points, and to place outside that core the interpretation and nomenclature of those elements (i.e., the part most likely to change).

Taking all factors into account, NCBI has four core data elements: bibliographic citations, DNA sequences, protein sequences, and 3-D structures. In addition, two projects (taxonomy and genome maps) are more interpretive, but nonetheless are so important as organizing and linking resources that NCBI has built a considerable base in these areas as well.

PUBS: PUBLICATIONS OR PERISH

Publication is at the core of every scientific endeavor. It is the process whereby scientific information is reviewed, evaluated, distributed, and entered into the permanent record of scientific progress. Publications can serve as vital links between factual databases of different structures or content domains (e.g., a record in a sequence database and a record in a genetic database may cite the same article). They serve as valuable entry points into factual databases ("I read an article about this, now I want to see the data").

Publications also act as essential annotation of function and context to records in factual databases, perhaps the best annotation. One reason for this is that factual databases have a structure that is essential for efficient use of the database but may not have the representational capacity to set forward the full biological, experimental, or historical context of a particular record. On the other hand, the published paper is limited only by language, and contains much fuller and more detailed explanatory information than will ever be in the record in the factual database. Perhaps even more important, authors are evaluated by their scientific peers based on the content of their published papers, not by the content of database records. Even with the best of intentions, scientists move on, and database records become static, even though the knowledge about them has expanded, and there is very little incentive for the busy scientist to learn a database system and keep personal records up to date.

NCBI has a number of ongoing projects to ensure the highest possible quality of GenBank records at the time of submission, to provide convenient and powerful tools to encourage record updates, and to make the data so useful that the data records will become more visible within scientists' daily work habits (and thus more important to keep reflecting well on the submitter). Nevertheless, reliable linkage to the published literature will continue to provide the richest and most up-to-date annotation for database records for a long time to come.

Generally form and content of citations have not been given careful thought by the factual databases, and the quality, form, and content of citations can vary widely from one database to the next. Being aware of the importance of the link to the published literature, realizing that bibliographic citations are much less volatile than scientific knowledge, and being advantageously positioned (since NCBI is part of the National Library of Medicine at the National Institutes of Health), we felt that a careful and complete job of defining citations was a worthwhile endeavor. However, as any professional librarian could have told us, it was a nontrivial task. Some components of the publication specification described below may be of particular interest to scientists or users of the NCBI databases, but a full discussion of all the issues would require another chapter in itself.

Authors

Author names are represented in many formats by various databases: last name only, last name and initials, last name-comma-initials, last name/first name, all authors with initials and the last with a full first name, with and without honorifics (Ph.D.) or suffixes (Jr., III), to name a few. Some bibliographic databases (such as MEDLINE) might represent only a fixed number of authors. While this is merely ugly to a human reader, it poses *severe* problems for database systems incorporating names from many sources and providing functions as simple as looking up citations by author last name, such as Entrez does. For this reason, the specification provides two alternative forms of author name representation, one a simple string, the other a structured form with fields for last name, first name, and so on. When data is submitted directly to NCBI or where there is a consistent format of author names from a particular source (such as MEDLINE), the structured form is used. When the form cannot be deciphered, author name remains as a string, which limits its use for retrieval, but at least one can view the data when the record is retrieved by other means.

Even the structured form of author names must support diversity, since some sources give only initials, while other sources provide a first and middle name. This is mentioned to emphasize two points. First, the NCBI data model is designed both to direct our view of the data to a more useful form and to be able to accommodate the available existing data. (This pair of functions can be confusing to people reading the specification and seeing alternate forms of the same data defined.) The second point is that software developers must be aware of the range of representations and accommodate whatever form had to be used when a particular source was being converted. In general, NCBI tries to get as much of the data into a uniform, structured form as possible, but carries the rest in a less optimal way rather than lose it.

Author affiliations (i.e., authors' institutional addresses) are even more complicated. As with author names there is the problem of supporting both structured forms and unparsed strings. However, even sources with reasonably consistent author name conventions often produce affiliation information that cannot be parsed from text into a structured format. In addition, there may be an affiliation associated with the whole author list, or there may be different affiliations associated with each author. The NCBI data model supports both types. Although at the time of this writing, only the first form is supported in either MEDLINE or GenBank, both types may appear in published articles.

Articles

The most commonly cited bibliographic entity in biological science is an article in a journal, so the citation formats of most biological databases are defined with that type in mind. However, "articles" can also appear in books, manuscripts, theses, and now in electronic journals as well. The data model defines the fields necessary to cite a book, a journal, or a manuscript. An article citation occupies one field; other fields display additional information necessary to uniquely identify the article in the book, journal, or manuscript—the author(s) of the article (as opposed to the author or editor of the book), the title of the article, page numbers, and so on.

There is an important distinction between the fields necessary to uniquely identify a published article from a citation and those necessary to describe the same article meaningfully to a database user. The NCBI Citation Matching Service (see end-of-chapter list) takes fields from a citation and attempts to locate the article to which they refer. In this process a good match would involve only correctly matching the journal title, the year, and the first page of the article, and the last name of an author of article. Other information (e.g., article title, volume, issue, full pages, author list) is useful to look at but very often not available or incorrect from input sources. Once again, the data model must allow the minimum information set to come in as a citation, be matched against MEDLINE, and then be replaced by a citation having the full set of desired fields obtained from MEDLINE to produce accurate, useful data for consumption by the scientific public.

Patents

With the advent of patented sequences, it became necessary to cite a patent as a bibliographic entity instead of an article. The data model supports a very complete patent citation developed in cooperation with the U.S. Patent Office. In practice, however, patented sequences tend to have limited value to the scientific public. The reasons are as follows.

A patent is a *legal* document, not a scientific one. Its purpose is to present and support the claims of the patent, not to fully describe the biology of the sequence. It is often prepared in a lawyer's office, not by the scientist who did the research. So the sequences presented may function only to illustrate some aspect of the patent, rather than being the focus of the document. Organism information, location of biological features, and so on may not appear at all if they are not germane to the patent. Finally, thus far the vast majority of sequences appearing in patents also appear in a more useful form (to scientists) in the public databases anyway.

In NCBI's view, the main purpose of listing patented sequences in GenBank is to be able to retrieve sequences (by similarity search) that may serve to locate patents related to a given sequence. To make a legal determination in the case, however, one would still have to examine the full text of the patent. To evaluate the biology of the sequence, one generally must locate information other than that contained in the patent. Thus the critical linkage is between sequence and patent number. Additional fields in the patent citation itself may be of some interest, such as the title of the patent and the names of the inventors.

Citing Electronic Data Submission

A relatively new class of citation comprises the act of data submission to a database, such as GenBank. This is an act of publication, similar but not identical to the publication of an article in a journal. In some cases data submission precedes article publication by a considerable time; or there may never be a publication beyond the deposition of the sequence in the database. Thus there is a separate citation for deposition. The submission citation, since it is an act of publication, may have an author list including the names of scientists who worked on the record. This may or may not be the same as the author list on a published paper also cited in the record. In most cases the scientist who submitted the data to the database is an author on the submission citation, but not always, especially in the case of large sequencing centers. Finally, NCBI has begun the practice of citing the update of a record with a submission citation as well. A comment can be included with the update briefly describing the changes made in the record. All the submission citations can be retained in the record, providing an editing history for the record over time.

MEDLINE and PubMed UIDs

Once an article citation has been matched to MEDLINE, the simplest and most reliable key to point to the article is the MEDLINE unique identifier (MUID). This is simply an integer number. NCBI provides many services that use the MUID to retrieve the citation and abstract from MEDLINE, to link together data citing the same article, or to provide WWW hot links.

Recently, in concert with MEDLINE and a large number of publishers, NCBI has introduced *PubMed*. PubMed contains *all* of MEDLINE, as well as citations provided directly by the publishers. As such, PubMed contains more recent articles than MEDLINE, as well as articles that may never appear in MEDLINE because of their subject matter. Thus NCBI had to introduce a new article identifier called a PubMed identifier (PMID). Articles appearing in MEDLINE will have *both* a PMID and a MUID. Articles appearing only in PubMed will have only a PMID. The PMID serves the same purpose as the MUID in providing a simple, reliable link to the citation, a means of linking records together, and a means of setting up hotlinks. NCBI is currently moving most of its services over to use PMIDs.

The NCBI data model stores most citations as a collection called a Pub-equiv, a set of equivalent citations that includes a reliable pointer (PMID or MUID) and the citation itself. The presence of the citation form allows a useful display without an extra retrieval from the database, while the pointer provides a reliable key for linking or indexing the same citation in the record.

SEQIDS: WHAT'S IN A NAME?

The NCBI data model defines a whole class of objects called Sequence Identifiers (SeqId). There has to be a whole class because NCBI integrates sequence data from many sources that name sequence records in different ways and where the names mean different things. In one simple case, PIR, SWISS-PROT, and the nucleotide sequence databases all use a string called an accession number, with a similar format. Just saying "A10234" is not enough to uniquely identify a sequence record from the collection of all these databases. One must distinguish "A10234" from SWISS-PROT and "A10234" from PIR. (The DDBJ/EMBL/GenBank nucleotide databases share a common set of accession numbers, so "A12345" from EMBL is the same as "A12345" from GenBank.) The forms may also be different. So while the sequence databases consider a record to contain a single sequence, PDB records contain a single structure, which may contain more than one sequence. Thus a PDB SeqId contains a molecule name and a chain ID to identify a single unique sequence. The subsections that follow describe the form and use of a few types of SeqId in common use.

Locus Name

The Locus appears on the LOCUS line in GenBank and DDBJ records (ID line in EMBL records) and was originally the only identifier of a GenBank record. Like a genetic locus name, it was intended to act both as a unique identifier for the record and as a mnemonic for the function and source organism of the sequence. Since the LOCUS line is in a fixed format, the LOCUS name is restricted to 10 or fewer numbers and uppercase letters. For many years in GenBank, the first three letters of the name were an organism code, and the remaining letters a code for the gene (e.g., HUMHBB = human β-globin region). However, as with genetic locus names, LOCUS names were changed when the function of a region was discovered to be different than what was originally thought. This instability is obviously a problem for an identifier for retrieval. Another was that as the number of sequences and organisms represented in GenBank increased geometrically over the years, it became impossible to invent and update such mnemonic names. At this point the LOCUS name is dying out as a useful name in GenBank, although it continues to appear prominently on the first line of the flatfile to avoid breaking the established format.

Accession Number

Because of the difficulties in using the LOCUS (or ID) name as the unique identifier for a nucleotide sequence record, the International Nucleotide Sequence Database Collaborators (DDBJ/EMBL/GenBank) introduced the accession number. It intentionally carries no biological meaning, to ensure that it will remain relatively stable. It consisted of one uppercase letter followed by five digits. (New accessions consist of two uppercase letters followed by six digits.) The first letters were allocated to the different databases so that accession numbers would be unique across the Collaboration.

The accession number was an improvement over the LOCUS/ID name, but with use, problems and deficiencies became apparent. For example, while the accession is stable over time, many users noticed that the sequence retrieved by a particular accession was not always the same. This is because the accession identifies the whole database record. If the sequence in a record was updated (say by the insertion of 1000 bp at the beginning), the accession number did not change (it is an updated version of the same record). If one had analyzed the original sequence and recorded that at position 100 of accession U00001 was a putative protein-binding site, after the update a completely different sequence would be found at position 100!

The accession number appears on the ACCESSION line of the GenBank record. The first accession on the line, called the "primary" accession, is the key for retrieving this record. Most records have only this accession. However, other accessions may follow the primary accession on the ACCESSION line. These "secondary" accessions are intended to give some notion of the history of the record. For example, if U00001 and U00002 were merged into a single updated record, then U00002 would be the primary accession on the new record, and U00001 would appear as a secondary accession. In standard practice, the U00001 record would be removed from GenBank, since the older record had become obsolete, and the secondary accessions would allow users to retrieve whatever records superseded the old one. It should also be noted that historically, secondary accession numbers do not always mean the same thing, and so users should exercise care in their interpretations. (Database policies differed, and even shifted over time in a given database.) The use of secondary accession numbers caused its own problems in that there was still not enough information to determine exactly what happened and why. Nonetheless, the accession number remains the most controlled and reliable way to point in a general way to a record in DDBJ/EMBL/GenBank.

gi Number

In 1992 NCBI began assigning genInfo identifiers (gi) to all sequences processed into Entrez, including nucleotide sequences from DDBJ/EMBL/GenBank, the protein sequences from the translated CDS features, protein sequences from SWISS-PROT, PIR, PRF, PDB, patents, and others. The gi is assigned in addition to the SeqId provided by the source database. While the form and meaning of the source SeqId varied depending on the source, the meaning and form of the gi is the same for all sequences regardless of source.

In form, it is simply an integer number (and is sometimes called a "GI number"). It is an identifier for a particular sequence only. Suppose a sequence enters GenBank and is given an accession number U00001. When the sequence is processed internally at NCBI, it enters a database called ID. ID determines that it has not seen U00001 before and assigns it a gi number, let's say 54. Then the submitter updates the record by changing the citation. U00001 enters ID again. ID, recognizing the record, retrieves the first U00001 and compares its sequence to the new one. If the two are completely identical, ID reassigns gi 54 to the record. If the sequence differs in any way, even a single base pair, it is given a new gi number, say 88. However, the new sequence retains accession number U00001, because of the semantics of the source database. At this time, ID marks the old record (gi 54) with the date it was replaced and adds a "history" indicating that it was replaced by gi 88. ID also adds a history to gi 88 indicating that it replaced gi 54.

The gi number serves three major purposes:

1. It provides a single identifier across sequences from many sources.
2. It provides an identifier that specifies an exact sequence. Anyone who analyzes gi 54 and stores the analysis can be sure that it will be valid as long as U00001 has gi 54 attached to it.

3. It is stable and retrievable. NCBI keeps the last version of every gi number. Since the history is included in the record, anyone who discovers that gi 54 is no longer part of the GenBank release can still retrieve it from ID through NCBI, and examine the history to see that it was replaced by gi 88. Upon aligning gi 54 to gi 88 to determine their relationship, a researcher may decide to remap the former analysis to gi 88, or perhaps to reanalyze the data. This can be done at any time, not just at GenBank release time, since gi 54 will always be available from ID.

For the foregoing reasons, all internal processing of sequences at NCBI, from computing Entrez sequence neighbors to determining when new sequence should be processed or producing the BLAST databases, is based on gi numbers.

NID/PIDs

The NID and PID lines in the GenBank flatfile show the gi numbers for the nucleotide and protein sequences in a record. These were added to permit scientists who wish to compute on sequences in the flatfile release to take advantage of the stable gi numbers assigned to track sequences. As mentioned earlier, an analysis that cites a gi, rather than an accession number, will remain valid even if the sequence in the record is later changed (e.g., by 5′ extension).

At the time of this writing, an improved SeqId is being developed (ACCESSION.VERSION, see below), which is expected to become the sequence identifier of choice. Once this transition has been made, it is likely that the NID and PID numbers will no longer be presented in the flatfile format, although analyses using these gi numbers will of course remain valid. In addition, the original numbers will still be present in the ASN.1 files that NCBI prepares in parallel to the GenBank flatfiles.

Accession.Version Combined Identifier

Recently, the members of the International Nucleotide Sequence Database Collaboration (DDBJ, EMBL, and GenBank) have agreed to introduce a better sequence identifier, one that combines an accession (which identifies a particular sequence record) with a version number (which tracks changes to the sequence itself). It is expected that this kind of SeqId will become the preferred method of citing sequences.

Users will still be able to retrieve a record based on just the accession number, without having to specify a particular version. In this case, the latest version of the record will be obtained, which is the current behavior for queries with Entrez and other retrieval programs.

Scientists who are analyzing sequences in the database (e.g., aligning all alcohol dehydrogenase sequences from a particular taxonomic group) and wish to have their conclusions remain valid over time will want to reference sequences by accession and the given version number. Subsequent modification of one of the sequences by its owner (e.g., 5′ extension during a study of the gene's regulation) will result in incrementation of the version number. The analysis that cited accession and version remains valid, because a query will return the previous record.

Combining accession and version makes it clear to the casual user that a sequence has changed since an analysis was done. Also, telling how many times a sequence has changed is trivial with a version number. Because of the superiority of the Accession.version identifier, it is expected that NIDs and PIDs (which are simply gi numbers) will be removed from the flatfile presentation in the future.

Accession Numbers on Protein Sequences

The Collaborators have also agreed to assign Accession.version numbers to protein sequences within the records. Previously, it was difficult to reliably cite the translated product of a given coding region feature, except by its gi number. This limited the usefulness of translated products in BLAST results, for example. These sequences will now have the same status as protein sequences submitted directly to the protein databases, and they have the benefit of direct linkage to the nucleotide sequence in which they are encoded.

General SeqId

The General SeqId is meant to be used by genome centers and other groups as a way of identifying their sequences. Some of these sequences may never appear in the public databases, and others may be preliminary data that eventually will be submitted. For example, records of human chromosomes in the Entrez Genomes division contain multiple physical and genetic maps, in addition to sequence components. The physical maps are generated by various groups, and they use General SeqIds to identify the group.

Local SeqId

The Local sequence identifier is most prominently used in the data submission tool Sequin (see Chapter 14). Each sequence will eventually get an accession number and a gi number, but only when the completed submission has been processed by a public database. During the submission process, Sequin assigns a Local identifier to each sequence. As many of the software tools made by NCBI require a sequence identifier, having a local ID allows the use of these tools without having to submit data first to a public database.

BIOSEQ: SEQUENCES

The Bioseq, or biological sequence, is a central element in the NCBI data model. It comprises a single, continuous molecule of nucleic acid or protein, and it defines a linear, integer coordinate system for the sequence. A bioseq must have at least one sequence identifier (SeqId). It has information on the physical type of molecule (DNA, RNA, or protein). It may also have annotations (information, such as biological features, that refer to specific locations on specific bioseqs). And it may have descriptors (information, such as the organism from which the molecule was obtained, that describes the entire bioseq).

However, the bioseq isn't necessarily a fully sequenced molecule. It may be a segmented sequence in which, for example, exons are sequenced but not all the intron sequences have been determined. Or it may be a genetic or physical map, where only a few landmarks have been positioned.

Sequences Are the Same

All bioseqs have an integer coordinate system, with an integer length value, even if the actual sequence isn't completely determined. Thus, for physical maps, or for exons in highly spliced genes, the spacing between markers or exons may be known only from a band on a gel. So while the coordinates of a fully sequenced chromosome are known exactly, those in a genetic or physical map are a best guess, with the possibility of significant error from the "real" coordinates.

Nevertheless, any kind of bioseq can be annotated with the same kinds of information. For example, a gene feature can be placed on a region of sequenced DNA, or at a location on a physical map. The map and the sequence can then be aligned based on the common gene feature. This greatly simplifies the task of writing software that can display these seemingly disparate kinds of data.

Sequences Are Different

In spite of the benefits derived from having a common coordinate system, the different bioseq classes do differ in the way they are represented. The most common classes (see Figure 6.2) are described briefly as follows.

Virtual Bioseq   In the virtual bioseq we know the molecule type, and possibly its length and topology (e.g., linear, circular), but not the actual sequence. This can represent an intron in a genomic molecule in which only the exon sequences have been determined. The length may be known only by the size of a band on an agarose gel.

Raw Bioseq   This is what most people would think of as a sequence, a single contiguous string of bases or residues, in which the actual sequence is known. The length is therefore known exactly, and it should match the number of bases or residues in the sequence.

Segmented Bioseq   A segmented bioseq does not contain raw sequences, but rather the identifiers of other bioseqs from which it is made. This can be used to represent a genomic sequence in which only the exons are known. The "parts" in the segmented bioseq would be raw bioseqs representing the exons and virtual bioseqs representing the introns.

Segmented bioseqs are also used by NCBI to represent entire chromosomes. This is how the Entrez Genomes division is built (see Figure 6.3). In this case, all the parts may be raw bioseqs (in many cases records that were already in GenBank), and there may be overlap between adjoining parts.

Delta Bioseq   Delta bioseqs are used to represent the unfinished high-throughput genome sequences (HTGS) from the various genome sequencing centers. Using delta bioseqs instead of segmented bioseqs means that only one SeqId is needed for the entire sequence, even though subregions of the bioseq are not known at the sequence level. Implicitly, then, even at the early stages of their presence in the databases, delta bioseqs maintain the same accession number (see end-of-chapter list).

Map Bioseq   Used to represent genetic and physical maps, a map bioseq is similar to a virtual bioseq in that it has a molecule type, perhaps a topology, and a length that may be a very rough estimate of the molecule's actual length. This information merely supplies the coordinate system, a property of every bioseq. Given this coordinate system for a genetic map, we estimate the positions of genes on it based on genetic evidence. The table of the

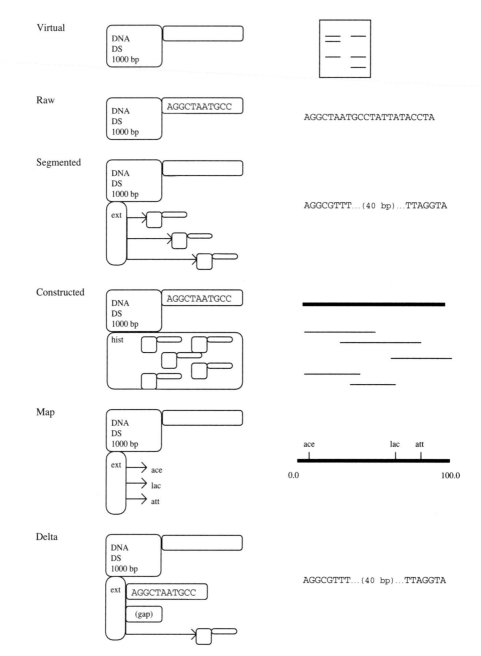

Figure 6.2 Classes of Bioseqs. All bioseqs represent a single, continuous molecule of nucleic acid or protein, although the complete sequence may not be known. In a **virtual bioseq** the type of molecule is known, but the sequence is not known, and the precise length may not be known (e.g., from the size of a band on an electrophoresis gel). A **raw bioseq** contains a single contiguous string of bases or residues. A **segmented bioseq** points to its components, which are other raw or virtual bioseqs (e.g., sequenced exons and undetermined introns). A **constructed** sequence takes its original components and subsumes them, resulting in a bioseq that contains the string of bases or residues and a "history" of how it was built. A **map bioseq** places genes or physical markers, rather than sequence, on its coordinates. A **delta bioseq** can represent a segmented sequence, but without the requirement of assigning identifiers to each component (including gaps of known length), although separate raw sequences can still be referenced as components. The delta sequence is used for unfinished high-throughput genome sequences (HTGS) from genome centers.

134

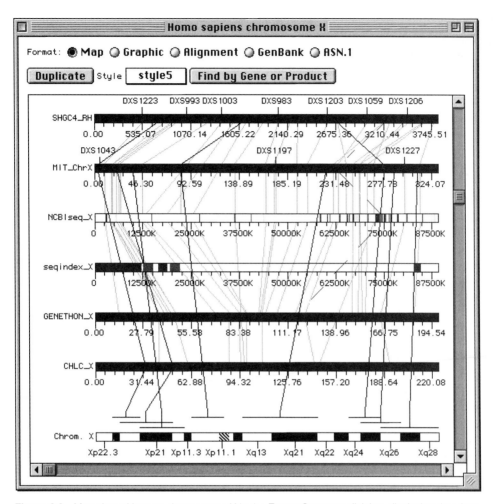

Figure 6.3 Map view of human chromosome X in the Entrez Genomes division, displaying data from the Stanford radiation hybrid map, the MIT physical map, NCBI sequence records, Genethon (as derived from MIT), the CHLC framework map, and the GDB cytogenetic map. These groups use different approaches to make genetic and physical maps of human chromosomes. NCBI maps them onto a common coordinate system, aligns any markers they share, and attempts to place existing sequence records onto integrated map. See *http://www.ncbi.nlm.nih.gov/cgi-bin/Entrez/framik?db=Genome&gi=23*. (Buttons on the web page link to the source database home pages.)

resulting gene features is the essential data of the map bioseq, just as bases or residues constitute the raw bioseq's data.

BIOSEQSETS: COLLECTIONS OF SEQUENCES

A biological sequence is often most appropriately stored in the context of other, related sequences. For example, a nucleotide sequence and the sequences of the protein products it encodes naturally belong in a set. The NCBI data model provides the BioseqSet for this purpose.

A BioseqSet can have a list of descriptors. When packaged on a bioseq, a descriptor applies to the entirety of that bioseq. When packaged on a BioseqSet, the descriptor applies to every bioseq in the set. This arrangement is convenient for attaching publications and biological source information, which are expected on all sequences but frequently are identical within sets of sequences. For example, both the DNA and protein sequences are from the same organism, and so this descriptor information can be applied to the set. The same logic may apply to a publication.

The most common BioseqSets are described in the subsections that follow.

Nucleotide/Protein Sets

The Nuc-prot set, containing a nucleotide and one or more protein products, is the set most frequently produced by a Sequin data submission. The component bioseqs are connected by coding region (CDS) features that describe how translation from nucleotide to protein sequence is to proceed. In a traditional nucleotide or protein sequence database, these records might have cross-references to each other to indicate this relationship. The Nuc-prot set makes this explicit by packaging them together. It also allows descriptive information that applies to all sequences (e.g., the organism, or publication citation) to be entered once (see Seq-descr, below).

Population and Phylogenetic Studies

A major class of sequence submissions is in the form of population or phylogenetic studies. Such research involves sequencing the same gene from a number of individuals in the same species (population study) or in different species (phylogenetic study). An alignment between the sequences may also be submitted (see Seq-align, below). If the gene encodes a protein, the components of the Population or Phylogenetic BioseqSet may themselves be Nuc-prot sets.

Other BioseqSets

A Seg set contains a segmented bioseq and a Parts BioseqSet, which in turn contains the raw bioseqs that are referenced by the segmented bioseq. (This may constitute the nucleotide component of a Nuc-prot set.)

An Equiv BioseqSet is used in the Entrez Genomes division to hold multiple equivalent bioseqs. For example, human chromosomes have one or more genetic maps, physical maps of several different kinds, and a segmented bioseq on which "islands" of sequenced regions are placed. An alignment between the various bioseqs is made based on references to common markers (see Chapter 12 and Figure 12.4).

SEQ-ANNOT: ANNOTATING THE SEQUENCE

A Seq-annot is a self-contained package of sequence annotations, or information that refers to specific locations on specific bioseqs. It may contain a feature table, a set of sequence alignments, or a set of graphs of attributes along the sequence.

Multiple Seq-annots can be placed on a bioseq, or on a Bioseq Set. Each Seq-annot can have specific attribution. For example, PowerBLAST (Zhang and Madden, 1997) produces a Seq-annot containing sequence alignments, and each Seq-annot is named based on the BLAST program used (e.g., BLASTN, BLASTX). The individual blocks of alignments are visible in the Entrez and Sequin viewers.

Because the components of a Seq-annot have specific references to locations on Bioseqs, the Seq-annot can stand alone or be exchanged with other scientists; it need not reside in a sequence record. (The scope of descriptors, on the other hand, does depend on where they are packaged.) Thus, information ABOUT bioseqs can be created, exchanged, and compared independently from the bioseq itself. This is an important attribute of the Seq-annot and of the NCBI data model.

Seq-feat: Features

A sequence feature (Seq-feat) is a block of structured data explicitly attached to a region of a Bioseq through one or two sequence locations (Seq-locs). The Seq-feat itself can carry information common to all features. For example, there are flags to indicate whether a feature is partial (i.e., goes beyond the end of the sequence of the Bioseq), whether there is a biological exception (e.g., RNA editing that explains why a codon on the genomic sequence does not translate to the expected amino acid), and whether the feature was experimentally determined (e.g., an mRNA was isolated from a proposed coding region).

A feature must always have a location. This is the Seq-loc that states where on the sequence the feature resides. A coding region's location usually starts at the ATG and ends at the terminator codon. The location can have more than one interval if it is on a genomic sequence and mRNA splicing occurs. (In cases of alternative splicing, separate coding region features are created, with one multi-interval Seq-loc for each isolated molecular species.)

A feature may optionally have a product. For a coding region, the product Seq-loc points to the resulting protein sequence. This is the link that allows the data model to separately maintain the nucleotide and protein sequences, with annotation on each sequence appropriate to that molecule. An mRNA feature on a genomic sequence could have as its product an mRNA bioseq whose sequence reflects the results of post-transcriptional RNA editing. Features also have information unique to the kind of feature. For example, the CDS feature has fields for the genetic code and reading frame, while the tRNA feature has information on the amino acid transferred.

This design completely modularizes the components required by each feature type. If a particular feature type calls for a new field, no other field is affected. A new feature type, even a very complex one, can be added without changing the existing features. And software to display feature locations on a sequence need consider only the location field common to all features.

While the DDBJ/EMBL/GenBank Feature table allows numerous features (see Chapter 2), the NCBI data model treats some features as more equal than others. Specifically, certain features directly model the central dogma of molecular biology and are most likely to be used in making connections between records and in discovering new information by computation. These features are discussed next.

Genes   A gene is a feature in its own right. In the past, it was merely a qualifier on other features. The Gene feature indicates the location of a gene, a heritable region of nucleic acid sequence that confers a measurable phenotype. That phenotype may be achieved by many components of the gene being studied, including, but not limited to, coding regions, promoters, enhancers, and terminators. The Gene feature is meant to approximately cover the region of nucleic acid considered by workers in the field to be the gene. This admittedly fuzzy concept has an appealing simplicity, and it fits in well with higher level views of genes such as genetic maps. It has practical utility in the era of large genomic sequencing when a biologist may wish to see just the "xyz gene" and not a whole chromosome. The Gene feature may also contain cross-references to genetic databases, where more detailed information on the gene may be found.

RNAs An RNA feature can describe both coding intermediates (e.g., mRNAs) and structural RNAs (e.g., tRNAs, rRNAs). The locations of an mRNA and the corresponding coding region (CDS) completely determine the locations of 5′ and 3′ untranslated regions (UTRs), exons, and introns.

Coding Regions A Coding Region (CDS) feature in the NCBI data model can be thought of as "instructions to translate" a nucleic acid into its protein product, via a genetic code (see Figure 6.4). A coding region serves as a link between the two sequences.

Several situations can provide exceptions to the classical colinearity of gene and protein. Translational stuttering (ribosomal slippage), for example, merely results in the presence of overlapping intervals in the feature's location Seq-loc.

The genetic code is assumed to be universal unless explicitly given in the Coding Region feature. When the genetic code is not followed at specific positions in the sequence—for example, when alternative initiation codons are used in the first position, when suppressor

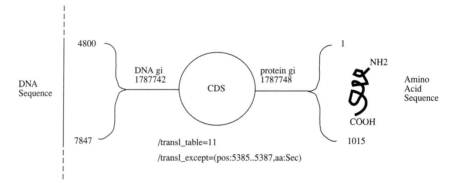

Figure 6.4 The Coding Region (CDS) feature links specific regions on a nucleotide sequence with its encoded protein product. All features in the NCBI data model have a "location" field, which is usually one or more intervals on a sequence. (Multiple intervals on a CDS feature would correspond to individual exons.) Features may optionally have a "product" field, which for a CDS feature is the entirety of the resulting protein sequence. The CDS feature also contains a field for the genetic code. This appears in the GenBank flatfile as a /transl_table qualifier. In this example, the Bacterial genetic code (code 11) is indicated. A CDS may also have translation exceptions indicating that a particular residue is not what is expected given the codon and the genetic code. In this example, residue 196 in the protein is selenocysteine, indicated by the /transl_except qualifier. NBCI software includes functions for converting between codon locations and residue locations, using the CDS as its guide. This capability is used to support the historical conventions of GenBank format, allowing a signal peptide, annotated on the protein sequence, to appear in the GenBank flatfile with a location on the nucleotide sequence.

tRNAs bypass a terminator, or when selenocysteine is added—the Coding Region feature allows these anomalies to be indicated.

Proteins   A Protein feature names (or at least describes) a protein or proteolytic product of a protein. A single protein bioseq may have many Protein features on it. It may have one over its full length describing a pro-peptide, the primary product of translation. (The name in this feature is used for the `/product` qualifier in the CDS feature that produces the protein.) It may have a shorter protein feature describing the mature peptide, or, in the case of viral polyproteins, several mature peptide features. Signal peptides that guide a protein through a membrane may also be indicated.

Others   Several other features are less commonly used. A Region feature provides a simple way to name a region of a chromosome (e.g., "major histocompatibility complex") or a domain on a polypeptide. A Bond feature annotates a bond between two residues in a protein (e.g., disulfide). A Site feature annotates a known site (e.g., active, binding, glycosylation, methylation).

Finally, numerous features exist in the table of legal features, covering many aspects of biology. However, they are less likely than the above-mentioned features to be used for making connections between records or for making discoveries based on computation.

Seq-align: Alignments

A sequence alignment is a mapping of the coordinates of one bioseq onto the coordinates of one or more other bioseqs. For example, the same gene from two organisms may have diverged since the organisms evolved from their common ancestor, and individual bases (or full triplet codons) may have been added or lost in one sequence. In an alignment, gaps are introduced at appropriate places in one or both sequences to restore the "original" coordinate system.

An alignment can be generated algorithmically by software (e.g., BLAST produces a Seq-annot containing one or more Seq-aligns) or manually by a scientist (e.g., one who is submitting an aligned population study using a favorite submission program). The Seq-align is desired to capture the final result of the process, not the process itself.

All forms of Seq-align are composed of segments. Each segment is an aligned region that contains only sequence or only a gap for any sequence in the alignment (not a mixture of sequence and gap). The following three-dimensional alignment (a multiple alignment between three sequences) results in five segments:

```
GATATAATCAGTTTATGGGATCAAAGCCTAAAGCCATGTGTAAAATTA
GATATAATCAGTTTA--------------AAGCCATGTGTAAAATTA
GATATAATCAGTTTATGGGATCAA-----------TGTGTAAAATTA
|            |       |    |     |            |
```

The Sequence Is Not the Alignment

Note that the actual sequences in the three bioseqs just displayed do NOT contain dashes. A fundamental property of the genetic code is that it is "commaless" (Crick et al., 1961). That is, there is no "punctuation" to distinguish one codon from the next or to keep translation in the right frame. The gene is a contiguous string of nucleotides. We remind the reader that sequences are also "gapless." Gaps are shown only in the alignment report, generated from the alignment data; they are used only for comparison.

Sets of Diagonals

In the Seq-align of type "diags" each segment is independent of the next, and no claims are made about the reasonableness of connecting one segment to another. This is the kind of relationship shown by a "dot matrix" display (see Chapter 7 and Figure 7.4). A series of diagonal lines in a square matrix indicates unbroken regions of similarity between the sequences. However, diagonals may overlap multiple times (e.g., indicating repeated regions in a sequence), or regions of the matrix may have no diagonals at all.

Classes of Alignments

A "partial," or local, alignment defines a relationship between sequences for only the lengths actually included in the alignment. However, it does imply an ordered relationship between one segment and the next. This kind of alignment is useful for general searches with proteins, where several domains, each with a different function, may occur in a single polypeptide.

A "discontinuous" alignment is one in which an algorithm declines to align certain blocks, being unable to detect a significant similarity. It is usually a list of partial alignments.

A "global" alignment aligns sequences over their entire length. It is typically used in studies of homology between closely related proteins or genomes, where there is reason to believe they share a common origin over their complete lengths. The segments making up a global alignment are also assumed to be connected in the order in which they appear in the data.

Seq-graph: Graphs

Graphs are the third kind of annotation that can go in Seq-annots. A Seq-graph defines some continuous set of values over a defined interval on a bioseq. It can be used to show properties like G+C content, surface potential, hydrophobicity, or base accuracy over the length of the sequence (see Figure 6.5).

SEQ-DESCR: DESCRIBING THE SEQUENCE

A Seq-descr is meant to describe a bioseq (or BioseqSet) and place it in its biological and/or bibliographic context. Seq-descrs apply to the whole bioseq, or to the whole of each bioseq in the BioseqSet to which the Seq-descr is attached.

Descriptors were introduced in the NCBI data model to reduce redundant information in records. For example, the protein products of a nucleotide sequence should always be from the same biological source (organism, tissue) as the nucleotide itself. And the publication that describes the sequencing of the DNA in many cases also discusses the translated pro-

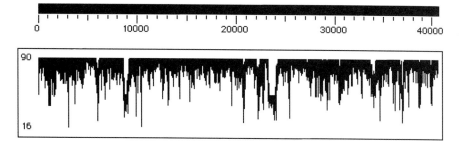

Figure 6.5 Seq-graph of base assignment confidence. Like features and alignments, graphs can be used to annotate a sequence. In this example, the confidence of correct base assignment on the vertical axis is plotted as solid shading against each position in a sequence on the horizontal axis.

teins. By placing these items as descriptors at the Nuc-prot set level, only one copy of each item is needed to properly describe all the sequences.

BioSource: The Biological Source

The BioSource includes information on the source organism (scientific name and common name), its lineage in the NCBI integrated taxonomy, and its nuclear and (if appropriate) mitochondrial genetic code. It also includes information on the location of the sequence in the cell (e.g., nuclear genome or mitochondrion) and additional modifiers (e.g., strain, clone, isolate, chromosomal map location).

A sequence record for a gene and its protein product will typically have a single BioSource descriptor at the Nuc-prot set level. A population or phylogenetic study, however, will have BioSource descriptors for each component. (The components can be nucleotide bioseqs, or they can themselves be Nuc-prot sets.) The BioSources in a population study will have the same organism name, and usually will be distinguished from each other by modifier information, such as strain or clone name.

MolInfo: Molecule Information

The MolInfo descriptor indicates the type of molecule [e.g., genomic, mRNA (usually isolated as cDNA), rRNA, tRNA, or peptide], the technique with which it was sequenced (e.g., standard, EST, conceptual translation with partial peptide sequencing for confirmation), and the completedness of the sequence [e.g., complete, missing the left (5′ or amino) end, missing both ends]. Each nucleotide and each protein should get its own MolInfo descriptor. Normally, then, this descriptor will not appear attached at the Nuc-prot set level. (It may go on a Seg set, since all parts of a segmented bioseq should be of the same type.)

USING THE MODEL

There are a number of consequences of using the NCBI data model for building databases and generating reports. Some of these are discussed in the remainder of this section.

GenBank Format

GenBank format presents a "DNA-centered" view of a sequence record. (GenPept view presents the equivalent "protein-centered" view.) To maintain compatibility with these historical views, some mappings are performed between features on different sequences, or between overlapping features on the same sequence.

In GenBank format, the protein product of a coding region feature is displayed as a /translation qualifier, not as a sequence that can have its own features. The largest protein feature on the product bioseq is used as the /product qualifier. Some of the features that are actually annotated on the protein bioseq in the NCBI data model, such as mature peptide or signal peptide, are mapped onto the DNA coordinate system (through the CDS intervals) in GenBank format.

The Gene feature names a region on a sequence, typically covering anything known to affect that gene's phenotype. Other features contained in this region will pick up a /gene qualifier from the Gene feature. Thus, there is no need to separately annotate the /gene qualifier on the other features.

FASTA Format

FASTA format contains a definition line and sequence characters, and may be used as input to a variety of analysis programs (see Chapter 2). The definition line starts with a right angle bracket (>) and is usually followed by the sequence identifiers in a parsable form. For example:

```
>gi|1322283|gb|U54469|DMU54469
```

The remainder of the definition line, a title for the sequence, can be generated by software from features and other information in a Nuc-prot set.

For a segmented bioseq, each raw bioseq part can be separately presented, with a dash separating the segments. (The regular BLAST search service uses this method for producing search databases, so that the resulting "hits" will map to individual GenBank records.) But the segmented bioseq can also be treated as a single sequence, in which case the raw components will be catenated. (This form is used for generating the BLAST neighbors in Entrez. See Chapter 5.)

BLAST

The Basic Local Alignment Search Tool (BLAST, Altschul et al., 1990) is a popular method of ascertaining sequence similarity. The BLAST program takes a query sequence supplied by the user and searches it against the entire database of sequences maintained at NCBI. The output for each "hit" is a Seq-align, and these are combined into a Seq-annot. (Details on performing BLAST searches can be found in Chapter 7.)

The resulting Seq-annot can be used to generated the traditional BLAST printed report, but it is much more useful when viewed with software tools such as Entrez and Sequin. The viewer in these programs is now designed to display alignment information in useful forms. For example, Graphical view shows only insertions and deletions relative to the query sequence, while Alignment view fetches the individual sequences and displays mismatches between bases or residues in aligned regions. And Sequence view shows the alignment details at the level of individual bases or residues. This ability to zoom in from overview to fine details makes it much easier to see the relationships between sequences than with a single report.

Finally, the Seq-annot, or any of its Seq-aligns, can be passed to other tools (such as banded or gapped alignment programs) for refinement. The results then may be sent back into a display program.

Entrez

The Entrez sequence retrieval program (Schuler et al., 1996, and Chapter 5) was designed to take advantage of connections that are captured by the NCBI data model. For example, the publication in a sequence record may contain a MEDLINE UID or PubMed UID. These are direct links to the PubMed article, which Entrez can retrieve. And the product Seq-loc of a Coding Region feature points to the protein product, which Entrez can also retrieve. The links in the data model allow retrieval of linked records at the touch of a button. The Genomes division in Entrez takes further advantage of the data model in providing "on the fly" display of certain regions of large genomes, as is the case when one hits the ProtTable button.

Sequin

Sequin is a submission tool that takes raw sequence data and other biological information and assembles a record (usually a BioseqSet) for submission to one of the DDBJ/EMBL/Gen-Bank databases (see Chapter 14). It makes full use of the NCBI data model and takes advantage of redundant information to validate entries. For example, since the user supplies both the nucleotide and protein sequences, Sequin can determine the coding region location (one or more intervals on the nucleotide that, through the genetic code, produce the protein product). It compares the translation of the coding region to the supplied protein, and reports any discrepancy. It also makes sure that each bioseq has BioSource information applied to it. This requirement can be satisfied for a nucleotide and its protein products by placing a single BioSource descriptor on the Nuc-prot set.

Sequin's viewers are all active, in that double-clicking on an existing item (shown as a GenBank flatfile paragraph or a line in the graphical display of features on a sequence) will launch an editor for that item (e.g., feature, descriptor, or sequence data).

CONCLUSIONS

The NCBI data model is a natural mapping of how biologists think of sequence relationships and how they annotate these sequences. The data that results can be saved, passed to other analysis programs, modified, and then displayed, all without having to go through multiple format conversions. The model definition concentrates on fundamental data elements that can be measured in a laboratory, such as the sequence of an isolated molecule. As new biological concepts are defined and understood, the specification for data can be easily expanded without the need to change existing data. Software tools are stable over time, and only incremental changes are needed for a program to take advantage of new data fields. Separating the specification into domains (e.g., citations, sequences, structures, maps) reduces the complexity of the data model. Providing neighbors and links between individual records increases the richness of the data and enhances the likelihood of making discoveries from the databases.

Internet Resources for Topics in Chapter 6

NCBI Software Toolkit	*ftp://ncbi.nlm.nih.gov/toolbox/*
NCBI Citation Matching Service	*http://www.ncbi.nlm.nih.gov/PubMed/citmatch.html*
High-Throughput Genome Sequences	*http://www.ncbi.nlm.nih.gov/HTGS/*

REFERENCES

Altschul, S. F., Gish, W., Miller, W., Meyers, E. W., and Lipman, D. J. (1990). Basic Local Alignment Search Tool. J. Mol. Biol. *215*, 403–410.

Crick, F. H. C., Barnett, L., Brenner, S., and Watts-Tobin, R. J. (1961). General nature of the genetic code for proteins. Nature *192*, 1227–1232.

Ostell, J. M. (1995). Integrated access to heterogeneous biomedical data from NCBI. IEEE Eng. Med. Biol. *14*, 730–736.

Ostell, J. M. (1996). The NCBI software tools. In *Nucleic Acid and Protein Analysis: A Practical Approach,* M. Bishop and C. Rawlings, Eds. (IRL Press, Oxford), pp. 31–43.

Schuler, G. D., Epstein, J. A., Ohkawa, H., and Kans, J. A. (1996). Entrez: Molecular biology database and retrieval system. Methods Enzymol. *266*, 141–162.

Zhang, J., and Madden, T.L. (1997). Power BLAST: A new network BLAST application for interactive or automated sequence analysis and annotation. Genome Res. *7*, 649–656.

7

Sequence Alignment and Database Searching

Gregory D. Schuler

National Center for Biotechnology Information
National Library of Medicine, National Institutes of Health
Bethesda, Maryland

INTRODUCTION

Biology has a long tradition of comparative analysis leading to discovery. For instance, Darwin's comparison of morphological features of the Galapagos finches and other species ultimately led him to postulate the theory of natural selection. In essence, we are performing the same type of analysis today, but in much greater detail, when we compare the sequences of genes and proteins. In this activity, we analyze the similarities and differences—at the level of individual bases or amino acids—with the aim of inferring structural, functional, and evolutionary relationships among the sequences under study. The most common comparative method is *sequence alignment,* which provides an explicit mapping between the residues of two or more sequences. In this chapter we discuss only *pairwise alignments,* in which only two sequences are compared; the process of constructing *multiple alignments,* which involves more than two sequences, is discussed in Chapter 8.

The number of sequences available for comparison has grown explosively since the 1970s, when development of rapid DNA sequencing methodology sparked the "big bang" of sequence information expansion. Comparison of one sequence to the entire database of known sequences is an important discovery technique that should be at the disposal of all molecular biologists. Over the last 30 years, improvements in the speed and sophistication of sequence alignment algorithms, not to mention performance of computers, has more than kept pace with the growth in the size of the sequence databases. Today, with the complete sequences of several small genomes and a large sampling of human gene sequences,

Bioinformatics: A Practical Guide to the Analysis of Genes and Proteins
Edited by A.D. Baxevanis and B.F.F. Ouellette
ISBN 0-471-19196-5, pages 145–171.   Copyright © 1998 Wiley-Liss, Inc.

we are in the era of "comparative genomics" in which the full gene complements of two organisms can be compared to each other.

THE EVOLUTIONARY BASIS OF SEQUENCE ALIGNMENT

One goal of sequence alignment is to enable the researcher to determine whether two sequences display sufficient similarity to justify the inference of homology. Although these two terms are often interchanged in popular usage, let us distinguish them to avoid confusion. *Similarity* is an observable quantity that might be expressed as, say, percent identity or some other suitable measure. *Homology,* on the other hand, refers to a conclusion drawn from these data that two genes share a common evolutionary history. Genes either are or are not homologous—there are not degrees of homology as there are of similarity. For example, Figure 7.1 shows an alignment between the homologous trypsin proteins from *Mus musculus* (house mouse) and *Astracus astracus* (broad-fingered crayfish), from which it can be calculated that these two sequences have 41% identity.

Bearing in mind the goal of inferring evolutionary relationships, it is fitting that most alignment methods try, at least to some extent, to model the molecular mechanisms by which sequences evolve. While it is presumed that homologous sequences have diverged from a common ancestral sequence through iterative molecular changes, we do not actually know what the ancestral sequence was (barring the possibility that DNA could be recovered from a fossil); all we have to observe are the sequences from extant organisms. The changes that occur during divergence from the common ancestor can be categorized as substitutions, insertions, and deletions. In the ideal case that a sequence alignment genuinely reflects the evolutionary history of two genes or proteins, residues that have been aligned, yet are not identical, would represent substitutions. Regions in which the residues of one sequence correspond to nothing in the other would be interpreted as either an insertion into one sequence or a deletion from the other. These *gaps* are usually represented in the alignment as consecutive dashes (or other punctuation character) aligned with letters. For example, the alignment in Figure 7.1 contains five gaps.

```
                                            ┌────────S-S──────┐
                                                             *
Mouse      IVGGYNCEENSVPYQVSLNS-----GYHFCGGSLINEQWVVSAGHCYK-------SRIQV
Crayfish   IVGGTDAVLGEFPYQLSFQETFLGFSFHFCGASIYNENYAITAGHCVYGDDYENPSGLQI

                                                   *
Mouse      RLGEHNIEVLEGNEQFINAAKIIRHPQYDRKTLNNDIMLIKLSSRAVINARVSTISLPTA
Crayfish   VAGELDMSVNEGSEQTITVSKIILHENFDYDLLDNDISLLKLSGSLTFNNNVAPIALPAQ

                                                       ┌───S-S───┐
Mouse      PPATGTKCLISGWGNTASSGADYPDELQCLDAPVLSQAKCEASYPG-KITSNMFCVGFLE
Crayfish   GHTATGNVIVTGWG-TTSEGGNTPDVLQKVTVPLVSDAECRDDYGADEIFDSMICAGVPE

              ◊* ┌───────────S-S───────────┐
Mouse      GGKDSCQGDSGGPVVCNG----QLQGVVSWGDGCAQKNKPGVYTKVYNYVKWIKNTIAAN
Crayfish   GGKDSCQGDSGGPLAASDTGSTYLAGIVSWGYGCARPGYPGVYTEVSYHVDWIKANAV--
```

Figure 7.1 Conserved positions are often of functional importance. Alignment of trypsin proteins of mouse (Swiss-Prot P07146) and crayfish (Swiss-Prot P00765). Identical residues are underlined. Indicated above the alignment are three disulfide bonds (—S—S—) whose participating cysteine residues are conserved, amino acids whose side chains are involved in the charge relay system (asterisk), and the active site residue that governs substrate specificity (diamond).

In a residue-by-residue alignment it is often apparent that certain regions of a protein, or perhaps specific amino acids, are more highly conserved than others. This information may be suggestive of which residues are most crucial for a maintaining a protein's structure or function. In the trypsin alignment of Figure 7.1, the active site residues, which determine substrate specificity and provide the "charge relay system" of serine proteases, correspond to conserved positions, as do the cysteines residues, which form several disulfide bonds important for maintaining the enzyme's structure. On the other hand, there may be other positions that do not play a significant functional role yet happen to be identical for historical reasons. There is reason for particular caution when the sequences are taken from very closely related species, since similarities may be more reflective of history than of function. For example, regions of high sequence similarity between mouse and rat homologs may simply be those that have not had sufficient time to diverge. Nevertheless, sequence alignments provide a useful way to gain new insights by leveraging existing knowledge, for example, by deducing structural and functional properties of a novel protein from comparison to those that have been well studied. It must be emphasized, however, that these inferences should not be assumed to be correct based on computational analysis alone; they must always be tested experimentally.

Upon observing a surprisingly high degree of sequence similarity between two genes or proteins, we might infer that they share a common evolutionary history, and from this we might anticipate that they will have similar biological functions. But again, this prediction should be treated as hypothetical until tested experimentally. ζ-Crystallin, for instance, is a component of the transparent lens matrix of the vertebrate eye. However, based on extended sequence similarity, it can be inferred that its homolog in *E. coli* is the metabolic enzyme quinone oxidoreducatse (Figure 7.2). Despite the common ancestry, the function has changed during the course of evolution (Gonzalez et al., 1994). This is analogous to a railroad car that has been converted into a diner—inspection of the exterior structure reveals the structure's history, but relying exclusively on perceptions based on this information may lead to an erroneous conclusion about current function. When a gene adapts to a new niche, a change in the pattern of conserved positions might also be anticipated. For

```
Human-ZCr   MATGQKLMRAVRVFEFGGPEVLKLRSDIAVPIPKDHQVLIKVHACGVNPVETYIRSGTYS
Ecoli-QOR   ------MATRIEFHKHGGPEVLQA-VEFTPADPAENEIQVENKAIGINFIDTYIRSGLYP
                     ******   . .  *  .... .* *.* ..****** *

Human-ZCr   RKPLLPYTPGSDVAGVIEAVGDNASAFKKGDRVFTSSTISGGYAEYALAADHTVYKLPEK
Ecoli-QOR   -PPSLPSGLGTEAAGIVSKVGSGVKHIKAGDRVVYAQSALGAYSSVHNIIADKAAILPAA
             * **   *.. **..  **.   * ****  . * *.         **

Human-ZCr   LDFKQGAAIGIPYFTAYRALIHSACVKAGESVLVHGASGGVGLAACQIARAYGLKILGTA
Ecoli-QOR   ISFEQAAASFLKGLTVYYLLRKTYEIKPDEQFLFHAAAGGVGLIACQWAKALGAKLIGTV
             . * * **    * * *  *  ..* *  * * *.***** *** *.* * *,.**

Human-ZCr   GTEEGQKIVLQNGAHEVFNHREVNYIDKIKKYVGEKGIDIIIEMLANVNLSKDLSLLSHG
Ecoli-QOR   GTAQKAQSALKAGAWQVINYREEDLVERLKEITGGKKVRVVYDSVGRDTWERSLDCLQRR
             **  .  *. ** .* * **   ....*   * *......*         *  * .

Human-ZCr   GRVIVVG-SRGTIEINPRDTMAKES----SIIGVTLFSSTKEEFQQYAAALQAGMEIGWL
Ecoli-QOR   GLMVSFGNSSGAVTGVNLGILNQKGSLYVTRPSLQGYITTREELTEASNELFSLIASGVI
             * ..   * * *..            .*.**  . *  . .  * .

Human-ZCr   KPVIGSQ--YPLEKVAEAHENIIHGSGATGKMILLL
Ecoli-QOR   KVDVAEQQKYPLKDAQRAHE-ILESRATQGSSLLIP
             *  .  *  ***   *** *.    .  *  .*.
```

Figure 7.2 Optimal global sequence alignment. Alignment of the amino acid sequences of human ζ-crystallin (Swiss-Prot Q08257) and *E. coli* quinone oxidoreductase (Swiss-Prot P28304). It is an optimal global alignment produced by the CLUSTAL W program (Higgins et al., 1996). Identical residues are marked by asterisks below the alignment, while dots indicate conserved residues.

example, active site residues should be conserved as long as the protein plays a role in catalysis but could drift when the protein takes on a different function.

The earliest sequence alignment methods were applicable to a simple type of relationship in which the sequences show easily detectable similarity along their entire lengths. An alignment that spans essentially the full extents of the input sequences is called a *global alignment*. The trypsin and quinone oxidoreductase/ζ-crystallin alignments discussed above are examples of global alignments. Proteins consisting of a single globular domain can often be aligned by means of a global strategy, as can any homologous sequences that have not diverged substantially.

THE MODULAR NATURE OF PROTEINS

Many proteins do not display global patterns of similarity but instead appear to be mosaics of modular domains (Baron et al., 1991; Patthy, 1991; Doolittle and Bork, 1993). One example of this is illustrated in Figure 7.3, which shows the modular structure of two proteins involved in blood clotting: coagulation factor XII (F12) and tissue-type plasminogen activator (PLAT). Besides the catalytic domain, which provides the serine protease activity, these proteins have different numbers of other structural modules: two types of fibronectin repeat, a domain with similarity to epidermal growth factor, and a module that is called a "kringle" domain. These modules can be repeated, and they can appear in different orders. Patterns of modularity often arises by in-frame exchange of whole exons (Patthy, 1991). Global alignment methods do not take this phenomenon into account, which is understandable considering that they were developed before the exon/intron structure of genes had been discovered. In most cases it is advisable to instead use a sequence comparison method that can produce a *local alignment*. Such an alignment consists of paired subsequences, which may be surrounded by residues that are completely unrelated. Consequently, users should bear in mind that some local similarities may be missed if a global alignment strategy is applied inappropriately. Another obvious case in which local alignments are desired is the alignment of the nucleotide sequence of a spliced mRNA to its genomic sequence, where each exon would be in a distinct local alignment.

Dot matrix representations have enjoyed widespread popularity, in part because of their ability to reveal complex relationships involving multiple regions of local similarity (Fitch, 1969; Gibbs and McIntyre, 1970). An example of this approach is shown in Figure 7.4, in which the F12 and PLAT protein sequences were compared using the DOTTER program (Sonnhammer and Durban, 1996) (for software availability, see the list at the end of the chapter). The basic idea is to use the sequences as the coordinates of a two-dimensional

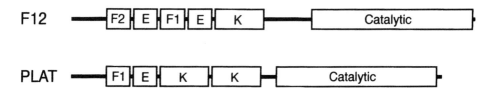

Figure 7.3 Modular structure of two proteins involved in blood clotting. Schematic representation of the modular structure of human tissue plasminogen activator and coagulation factor XII. The module labeled Catalytic are shared by several proteins involved in blood clotting. **F1** and **F2** are frequently repeated units that were first seen in fibronectin. **E** is a module resembling epidermal growth factor. A module known as a "kringle domain" is denoted **K**.

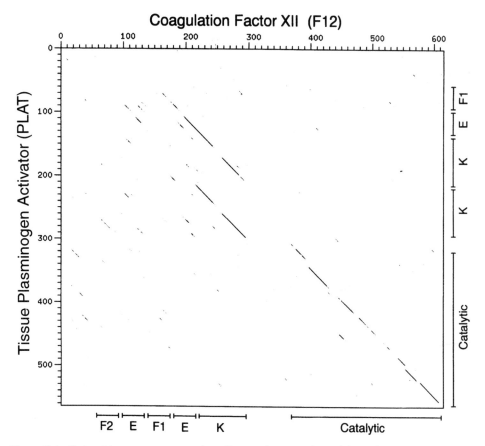

Figure 7.4 Dot matrix sequence comparison. Dot matrix comparison of the amino acid sequences of human coagulation factor XII (F12; Swiss-Prot P00748) and tissue plasminogen activator (PLAT; Swiss-Prot P00750) and proteins. The figure was generated using the DOTTER program (Sonnhammer and Durban, 1996).

graph and then plot points of correspondence within its interior. Each dot usually indicates that within some small window, the sequence similarity is above some cutoff (or a range of cutoffs in the case of DOTTER, each plotted using a different shade of grey). When two sequences are consistently matching over an extended region, the dots will merge to form a diagonal line segment. It is instructive to compare the positions of the diagonals in dot matrix of Figure 7.3 with the known modular structure of the two proteins. In particular, note the way in which repeated domains appear: starting with the kringle domain in the PLAT and scanning horizontally, two diagonal segments may be seen, corresponding to the two kringle domains present in the F12 sequence. Although more sophisticated methods for finding local similarities are now available (discussed below), dot matrix representations have remained popular as illustrative tools.

In a dot matrix representation, certain patterns of dots may appear to sketch out a "path," but it is up to the viewer to deduce the alignment from this information. Another graphical representation known as a *path graph* provides an explicit representation of an alignment. Figure 7.5 illustrates the relationship between the dot matrix, path graph, and alignment representations for the EGF similarity domain present in both the tissue-type plasminogen activator (PLAT) and the urokinase-type plasminogen activator (PLAU) proteins.

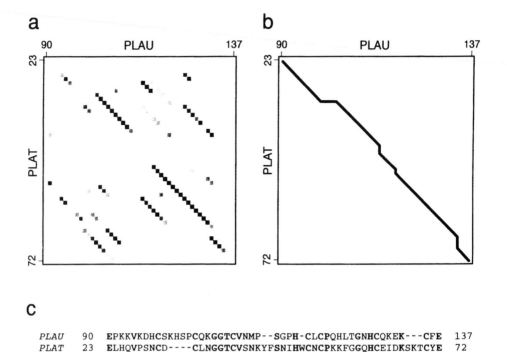

a

b

c

| PLAU | 90 | EPKKVKDHCSKHSPCQKGGTCVNMP--SGPH-CLCPQHLTGNHCQKEK---CFE | 137 |
| PLAT | 23 | ELHQVPSNCD----CLNGGTCVSNKYFSNIHWCNCPKKFGGQHCEIDKSKTCYE | 72 |

Figure 7.5 Dot matrix, path graph, and alignment. All three views represent the alignment of the EGF similarity domains in the human urokinase plasminogen activator (PLAU; Swiss-Prot P00749) and tissue plasminogen activator (PLAT; Swiss-Prot P00750) proteins. (*a*) The entire proteins were compared with DOTTER: an enlargement of the small region corresponding to the EGF domain is shown here. (*b*) The path graph representation of the alignment found by BLASTP. (*c*) the BLASTP gap alignment represented in the familiar text form.

To understand a path graph, imagine a two-dimensional lattice in which the vertices represent points between the sequence residues (as opposed to the residues themselves as in the case of the dot matrix). An edge that connects two vertices along a diagonal corresponds to the pairing of one residue from each sequence. Horizontal and vertical edges pair a residue from one sequence with nothing in the other; in other words, these edges constitute a gap in the alignment. The entire graph corresponds to the *search space* that must be examined for potential alignments. Each possible path through this space corresponds to exactly one alignment.

OPTIMAL ALIGNMENT METHODS

For any but the most trivial problems, the total number of distinct alignments is extraordinarily large, so it is usually of interest to identify the "best" one among them (or the several best ones). This is where the concept of representing an alignment as a path pays off. Many problems in computer science can be reduced to the task of finding the optimal path through a graph (e.g., the problem of finding the most efficient way to route a telephone call from New York to San Francisco), and efficient algorithms have been developed for this purpose. One requirement is a means of assigning a quality score to each possible path (alignment). Normally this is accomplished by summing the incremental contributions of each step along its route. More sophisticated scoring schemes are discussed later, but for now let us assume that some positive incremental scores will be used for aligning identical residues, with negative scores used for substitutions and gaps. According to this definition of alignment quality, finding the path whose total score is maximal will give us the best sequence alignment.

What is today known as the Needleman–Wunsch algorithm is an application of a best-path strategy called *dynamic programming* to the problem of finding optimal sequence alignments (Needleman and Wunsch, 1970). The idea behind dynamic programming comes from the observation that any partial subpath that ends at a point along the true optimal path must itself be the optimal path leading up to that point. Thus, the optimal path can be found by incremental extension of optimal subpaths. In the basic Needleman–Wunsch formulation, the optimal alignment must extend from beginning to end in both sequences, that is, from the top-left corner in the search space to bottom right (as it is typically drawn). In other words, it seeks global alignments.

But a simple modification to the basic strategy allows the optimal local alignment to be found (Smith and Waterman, 1981). The path for this alignment need not reach the edges of the search graph, but may begin and end internally. Such an alignment would be locally optimal if its score could not be improved by either increasing or decreasing the extent of the alignment. This procedure relies on a property of the scoring system, namely, that the cumulative score for a path will decrease in regions of poorly matching sequence (the scoring systems described below satisfy this criterion). When the score drops to zero, extension of path is terminated and a new one can begin. There can be many individual paths bounded by regions of poorly matching sequence instead of by the ends of the sequences, as is the case for global alignments. Of these paths, the single one with the highest score is reported as the optimal local alignment.

It is important to bear in mind that optimal methods always report the best alignment that can be achieved, even if it has no biological meaning. On the other hand, a search for local alignments may reveal several significant alignments, so it is a mistake to look only at the optimal one. Refinements to the Smith–Waterman algorithm were proposed for detecting the k best nonintersecting local alignments (Altschul and Erickson, 1986; Waterman and Eggert, 1987). These ideas were later extended in the development of the SIM algorithm (Huang et al., 1990). A program called LALIGN (distributed with the FASTA package) provides a useful implementation of SIM (Pearson, 1996). Looking for suboptimal alignments is especially important when multimodule proteins are compared, as illustrated in Figure 7.6, in which the LALIGN program was used to find the three best local alignments of the human coagulation factor IX and factor XII proteins. The second and third alignments represent functional modules that would have been missed by a standard Smith–Waterman search, which would have reported only the first (optimal) alignment.

SUBSTITUTION SCORES AND GAP PENALTIES

The scoring system just described made use of a simple match/mismatch scheme, but in comparisons of proteins, we can increase sensitivity to weak alignments through the use of a *substitution matrix*. It is well known that certain amino acids can substitute easily for one another in related proteins, presumably owing to their similar physicochemical properties. Examples of these "conservative substitutions" include isoleucine for valine (both small

```
     Comparison of:
     (A) f9-human.aa >F9   gi|119772|sp|P00740|FA9_HUMAN COAGULATION FA  - 461 aa
     (B) f12-hum.aa >F12   gi|119763|sp|P00748|FA12_HUMAN COAGULATION    - 615 aa
     using protein matrix
```

①   35.4% identity in 254 aa overlap; score: 358

```
          220       230       240       250       260       270
   F9   QSFNDFTRVVGGEDAKPGQFPWQVVLNGKVDAFCGGSIVNEKWIVTAAHCVE---TGVKI
        .:.....::::::  :  :. .. ::   ...:.::....  :..::::..    .  .
   F12  KSLSSMTRVVGGLVALRGAHPYIAALY-WGHSFCAGSLIAPCWVLTAAHCLQDRPAPEDL
          370       380       390       400       410       420

          280       290       300       310       320       330
   F9   TVVAGEHNIEETEHTEQKRNVIRIIPHHNYNAAINKYNHDIALLELDEPL-----VLNSY
        :::  :...  ...  .. :. .:  .  :.......  .:.::.::: :.:    .:..:
   F12  TVVLGQERRNHSCEPCQTLAVRSYRLHEAFSPV--SYQHDLALLRLQEDADGSCALLSPY
          430       440       450       460       470       480

          340       350       360       370       380
   F9   VTPICIADKEYTNIFLKFGSGYVSGWGRVFHKGRS-ALVLQYLRVPLVDRATCLRSTKF-
        : :.:...  .         ..     :.::::. :. . . :  ::   .::...  .  ..
   F12  VQPVCLPSGAARPSETTLCQ--VAGWGHQFEGAEEYASFLQEAQVPFLSLERCSAPDVHG
          490       500       510       520       530

          390       400       410       420       430       440
   F9   -TIYNNMFCAGFHEGGRDSCQGDSGGPHVTEVEGTS---FLTGIISWGEECAMKGKYGIY
        .:  .:.::::: :::  :.:::::::  : :  ....   :  :::::::..  ...:  :.:
   F12  SSILPGMLCAGFLEGGTDACQGDSGGPLVCEDQAAERRLTLQGIISWGSGCGDRNKPGVY
          540       550       560       570       580       590

          450
   F9   TKVSRYVNWIKEKT
        :.:.  :..::.:.:
   F12  TDVAYYLAWIREHT
          600       610
```

\- - - - - - - - - -

②   34.7% identity in 49 aa overlap; score: 120

```
            100       110       120       130       140
   F9   VDGDQCESNPCLNGGSCKDDINSYECWCPFGFEGKNCELDVTCNIKNGR
        .....:  .:::::.::.:    .   :  ::  :..:  :...:.   ..::
   F12  LASQACRTNPCLHGGRCLEVEGHRLCHCPVGYTGPFCDVDTKASCYDGR
            180       190       200       210       220
```

\- - - - - - - - - -

③   33.3% identity in 36 aa overlap; score: 87

```
            100       110       120
   F9   DQCESN-PCLNGGSCKDDINSYECWCPFGFEGKNCE
        :.:....  ::  .::.:  .    .:  ::   ...:...:.
   F12  DHCSKHSPCQKGGTCVNMPSGPHCLCPQHLTGNHCQ
            100       110       120      130
```

\- - - - - - - - - -

Figure 7.6 Optimal and suboptimal local alignments. The best three alignments found when using LALIGN to align the sequences of human coagulation factor IX (F9; Swiss-Prot 900740) and coagulation factor XII (F12; Swiss-Prot P00748).

and hydrophobic) and serine for threonine (both polar). When calculating alignment scores, identical amino acids should be given greater value than substitutions, but conservative substitutions should also be greater than nonconservative changes. In other words, a range of values is desired. Furthermore, different sets of values may be desired for comparing very similar sequences (e.g., a mouse gene and its rat homolog) as opposed to highly divergent sequences (e.g., mouse and yeast genes). These considerations can be dealt with in a flexible manner through the use of a substitution matrix, in which the score for any pair of amino acids can be obtained with a simple lookup.

The first substitution matrices to gain widespread usage were those based on the point-accepted-mutation (*PAM*) model of evolution (Dayhoff et al., 1978). One PAM is a unit of evolutionary divergence in which 1% of the amino acids have been changed. This does not imply that after 100 PAMs every amino acid will be different; some positions may change several times, perhaps even reverting to the original amino acid, while others may not change at all. If these changes were purely random, the frequencies of each possible substitution would be determined simply by the overall frequencies of the different amino acids (called the *background frequencies*). However, in related proteins, the observed substitution frequencies (called the *target frequencies*) are biased toward those that do not seriously disrupt the protein's function. In other words, these are point mutations that have been "accepted" during evolution. Dayhoff and coworkers were the first to explicitly use a *log-odds* approach, in which the substitution scores in the matrix are proportional to the natural log of the ratio of target frequencies to background frequencies. To estimate the target frequencies, pairs of very closely related sequences (which could be aligned unambiguously without the aid of a substitution matrix) were used to collect mutation frequencies corresponding to 1 PAM, followed by extrapolation of the data to a distance of 250 PAMs. The resulting PAM250 matrix is shown in Figure 7.7. Although PAM250 was

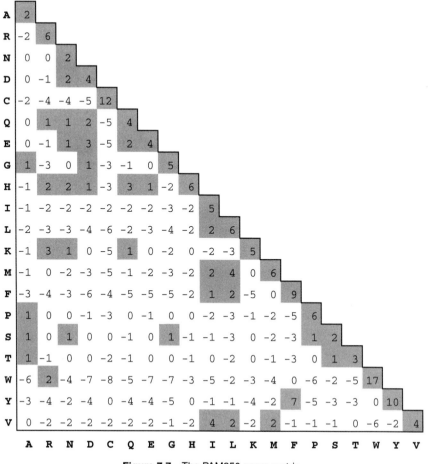

Figure 7.7 The PAM250 score matrix.

the only matrix published by Dayhoff et al., the underlying mutation data can be extrapolated to other PAM distances to produce a family of matrices. In the alignment of sequences that are highly divergent, best results are obtained at higher PAM values, such as PAM200 or PAM250. Matrices constructed from lower PAM values can be used if the sequences have a greater degree of similarity. (Altschul, 1991).

The BLOSUM substitution matrices have been constructed in a similar fashion, but making use of a different strategy for estimating the target frequencies (Henikoff and Henikoff, 1992). The underlying set of data was derived from the BLOCKS database (Henikoff and Henikoff, 1991), which contains local multiple alignments ("blocks") involving distantly related sequences (as opposed to the closely related sequences used for PAM). Although there is no evolutionary model in this case, it is advantageous to have data generated by direct observation rather than extrapolation. As with the PAM model, there is a numbered series of BLOSUM matrices, but the number in this case refers to the maximum level of identity that sequences may have and still contribute independently to the model. For example, with the BLOSUM62 matrix (Figure 7.8), sequences having at least 62% identity are merged into a single sequence, so that the substitution frequencies are more heavily influenced by sequences that are more divergent than this cutoff. Substitution matrices have been

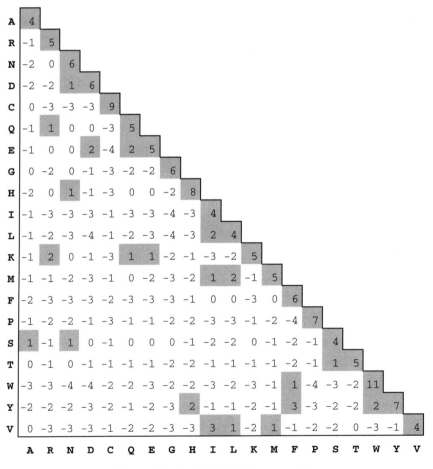

Figure 7.8   The BLOSUM62 score matrix.

constructed using higher cutoffs (up to BLOSUM90) for comparing very similar sequences and lower cutoffs (down to BLOSUM30) for highly divergent sequences.

To compensate for insertions and deletions, it is desirable to allow some gaps to be introduced into an alignment but not so many that the alignment asserts an implausible series of molecular alterations. This is accomplished by deducting some amount from the alignment score for each gap introduced. Although a number of strategies have been proposed for penalizing gaps, the most common formulation involves a fixed deduction for introducing a gap plus an additional deduction proportional to the length of the gap. This is governed by two parameters: G (sometimes called the gap opening penalty) and L (the gap extension penalty). For a gap of length n, the total deduction would be $G + Ln$. Unfortunately, the selection of gap parameters is highly empirical; there is little theory to support the choice of any particular set of values. However, it is common to use a high value for G (around 10–15, in the context of BLOSUM62) and a low value for L (around 1–2). The rationale for this range of choices is that insertion and mutation events are rare, but when they do occur, several adjacent residues may be involved.

STATISTICAL SIGNIFICANCE OF ALIGNMENTS

For any given alignment we can calculate a score, but it is important to determine whether this score is high enough to provide evidence of homology. In addressing this matter, it is helpful to have some notion of the highest score that can be expected due to chance alone. Unfortunately, there is no mathematical theory to describe the expected distribution of scores for global alignments. One of the few methods available for assessing their significance is comparison of the observed alignment score to those of many alignments made from random sequences of the same length and composition as those under study (Fitch, 1983).

However, for local alignments the situation is much better. As an initial simplification of the problem, attention has been focused on local alignments that do not contain any gaps (Karlin and Altschul, 1990). This type of alignment is called a high-scoring segment pair (*HSP*). HSPs may be found using a modification of the Smith–Waterman algorithm or by simply imposing huge penalties for gaps. Karlin–Altschul statistics provides a mathematical theory to describe the expected distribution of random HSP scores. The form of the probability density function is known as the *extreme value distribution*. This is worth noting because application of the more familiar normal distribution can result in greatly exaggerated claims of significance. By relating an observed alignment score S to the expected distribution, it is possible to calculate a *p value*, which gives the probability that an alignment with that score or better could be due simply to chance. Highly significant scores would therefore be those with p values very close to zero.

A related quantity is E, the expected number of chance alignments with scores at least equal to S. The extreme value distribution is characterized by two parameters, K and λ, which can be calculated analytically and are constant for any particular scoring system and set of background frequencies. The significance of an alignment also depends on the size of the search space that was examined (just as one's chances of finding a needle in a haystack depend on the size of the haystack). The size of the search space has typically been calculated as the product of the sequence lengths; but for correct statistics, these lengths must be reduced by the expected length of a local alignment to avoid an "edge effect" (Altschul and Gish, 1996). This reduction is required because an alignment that begins near the edge of the search space will run out of sequence before it can achieve a significant score.

The restriction that alignments cannot contain gaps is a useful simplification but represents a departure from biological reality, since in fact gaps are needed to accurately model insertions and deletions. However, provided the gaps are relatively few in number, it may still be possible to find high-scoring ungapped regions between them. Typically, several HSPs occurring in close proximity will be observed. In this case it is desirable to evaluate their significance as an ensemble rather than individually. Perhaps, for example, no segment is significant in its own right, but the appearance of several together is very unlikely to have occurred by chance. Karlin–Altschul *sum statistics* allows the significance of the N best HSPs to be calculated (Karlin and Altschul, 1993). The essence of this method is to sum the scores of the N best segments and then attempt to determine the probability that this value could be due to chance. Typically, some additional heuristics are applied to ensure that scores are summed only if the segments are compatible with an alignment (i.e., ascending coordinates in both sequences with little or no overlap). Although the distribution of summed scores will differ from that of maximal HSP scores, it may still be calculated analytically.

Finally, it is desirable to have the ability to evaluate the significance of local alignments in which gaps are explicitly modeled, such as the traditional Smith–Waterman alignments. Although no formal proof exists, it is believed that scores for these alignments will also follow the extreme value distribution (Smith et al., 1985; Waterman and Vingron, 1994; Altschul and Gish, 1996). However, the values of K and λ needed to parameterize this distribution cannot be directly calculated. Instead, methods for estimating these values through simulations have been developed (Waterman and Vingron, 1994; Altschul and Gish, 1996).

DATABASE SIMILARITY SEARCHING

The discussion above focuses on the alignment of specific pairs of sequences, but for a newly determined sequence we generally have no way of knowing the appropriate sequence(s) to use in such a comparison. Database similarity searching allows us to determine which of the hundreds of thousands of sequences present in the database are potentially related to a particular sequence of interest. This process sometimes leads to unexpected discoveries. The first "eureka moment" with this strategy came when the viral oncogene v-*sis* was found to be a modified form of the normal cellular gene that encodes platelet-derived growth factor (Doolittle et al., 1983; Waterfield et al., 1983). At the time of this discovery, sequence databases were small enough that such a finding might have been considered surprising. But today it would be much more surprising to perform a database search and *not* get a hit. The genome of the yeast *Saccharomyces cerevisiae* has been completely sequenced, as have several smaller genomes. Among the vertebrates, large numbers of partial sequences representing novel human and mouse genes have been deposited in GenBank as the result of a number of expressed sequence tag (EST) projects. The chief utility of observing EST matches in a database search is that the cDNA clones from which they were derived are freely available and can provide the critical reagents for isolating genes of interest, including their homologs in other model organisms. For example, the recently reported gene for multiple endocrine neoplasia (*MEN1*) matches shows matches to several ESTs from both human and mouse, one of which had been deposited more than a year before the *MEN1* gene was published (Chandrasekharappa et al., 1997).

In database searching, the basic operation is to sequentially align a *query sequence* to each *subject sequence* in the database. The results are reported as a ranked *hit list* followed by a series of individual sequence alignments, plus various scores and statistics (e.g., Figure 7.9). As discussed in more detail later, choices of search program, sequence database, and various optional parameters can have impact on the effectiveness of a search. Furthermore, there are various interfaces to these facilities such as console-style commands, WWW forms, and e-mail. Figure 7.10 shows an example of performing a database search using the Web interface. One advantage of this approach is that for any interesting alignment observed, complete annotation and literature citations can be obtained simply by following hypertext links to the original sequences entries and related online literature.

Current sequence databases are already immense and have continued to increase at an exponential rate, making straightforward application of dynamic programming methods impractical for database searching. One solution is to use massively parallel computers and other specialized hardware, but for the purposes of this discussion we consider only what

a

```
     The best scores are:                          initn initl opt   z-sc E(59248)
     gi|1706794|sp|P49789|FHIT_HUMAN FRAGILE HISTIDINE  996  996  996 1350.4       0
     gi|1703339|sp|P49776|APH1_SCHPO BIS(5'-NUCLEOSYL)  431  395  395 536.2 2.8e-23
     gi|1723425|sp|P49775|YD15_YEAST HYPOTHETICAL 24.8  290  171  316 428.1 2.9e-17
     gi|1724021|sp|Q11066|YHIT_MYCTU HYPOTHETICAL 20.0  178  178  184 250.7 2.2e-07
     gi|417124|sp|Q04344|HIT_YEAST HIT1 PROTEIN (ORF U   159  104  157 216.2 1.8e-05
     gi|418447|sp|P32084|YHIT_SYNP7 HYPOTHETICAL 12.4    139  139  140 195.0 0.00028
     gi|1351828|sp|P47378|YHIT_MYCGE HYPOTHETICAL 15.6   132  132  133 183.9 0.0012
  →  gi|1169826|sp|P43424|GAL7_RAT GALACTOSE-1-PHOSPHA    97   97  128 169.7 0.0072
     gi|418446|sp|P32083|YHIT_MYCHR HYPOTHETICAL 13.1    102  102  119 166.8   0.01
     gi|1708543|sp|P49773|IPK1_HUMAN PROTEIN KINASE C     87   87  118 164.5  0.014
     gi|1724020|sp|P49774|YHIT_MYCLE HYPOTHETICAL 17.0   131   82  117 161.6   0.02
     gi|1724019|sp|P53795|YHIT_CAEEL HYPOTHETICAL HIT-    98   98  116 161.5   0.02
     gi|1170581|sp|P16436|IPK1_BOVIN PROTEIN KINASE C     86   86  115 160.4  0.023
     gi|1730188|sp|Q03249|GAL7_MOUSE GALACTOSE-1-PHOSP    87   87  120 159.3  0.027
     gi|1177047|sp|P42856|ZB14_MAIZE 14 KD ZINC-BINDIN   132   79  112 156.3   0.04
     gi|120908|sp|P07902|GAL7_HUMAN GALACTOSE-1-PHOSPH    78   78  117 154.8  0.048
     gi|1177046|sp|P42855|ZB14_BRAJU 14 KD ZINC-BINDIN   115   76  110 154.5   0.05
     gi|140775|sp|P26724|YHIT_AZOBR HYPOTHETICAL 12.2    115   65  109 152.6  0.064
     gi|1169825|sp|P31764|GAL7_HAEIN GALACTOSE-1-PHOSP    62   62  104 137.9   0.42
     gi|113999|sp|P16550|APA1_YEAST 5',5'''-P-1,P-4-TE   108   66  103 137.1   0.47
```

b

```
     >>gi|1169826|sp|P43424|GAL7_RAT GALACTOSE-1-PHOSPHATE UR (379 aa)
     initn:   97 initl:   97 opt:   128 z-score: 169.7 E(): 0.0072
     Smith-Waterman score: 128;    30.8% identity in 107 aa overlap

                                         10        20        30
     FHIT                           MSFRFG-QHLIKPSVVFLKTELSFALVNRKPV
                                    ...: X.:..   .: :.. ..::     :
     GAL7    VWASNFLPDIAQREERSQQTYHNQHGKPLLLEYGHQELLRKERLVLTSEYWIVLVPFWAV
             190       200       210       220       230       240

                 40        50        60        70        80
     FHIT    VPGHVLVCPLRPVERFHDLRPDEVADLFQTTQRVGTVVEKHFHGTSLTFSM--QDGP---
             : .::.  : :  .: : :.  : ... :  .. X. ::.  ::. :
     GAL7    WPFQTLLLPRRHVQRLPELTPAERDDLASTMKKLLTKYDNLFE-TSFPYSMGWHGAPMGL
             250       260       270       280       290       300

                 90       100       110       120       130       140
     FHIT    EAGQTVKH--VHVHVLPRKAGDFHRNDSIYEELQKHDKEDFPASWRSEEEMAAEAAALRV
             ..: :  :  .::.:   :
     GAL7    KTGATCDHWQLHAHYYPPLLRSATVRKFMVGYEMLAQAQRDLTPEQAAERLRVLPEVHYC
             310       320       330       340       350       360
```

Figure 7.9 Output of a FASTA search. (*a*) Hit list from a FASTA search with human histidine triad (HIT) protein (Swiss-Prot P49789) as the query against the *swissprot* database. The search was performed using *ktup*=1. (*b*) Optimal local alignment of the query to one of the database entries (marked by arrow in hit list) containing the sequence of rat galactose-1-phosphate uridylyltransferase. Although the sequence similarity is weak, these proteins have been shown to share structural similarity.

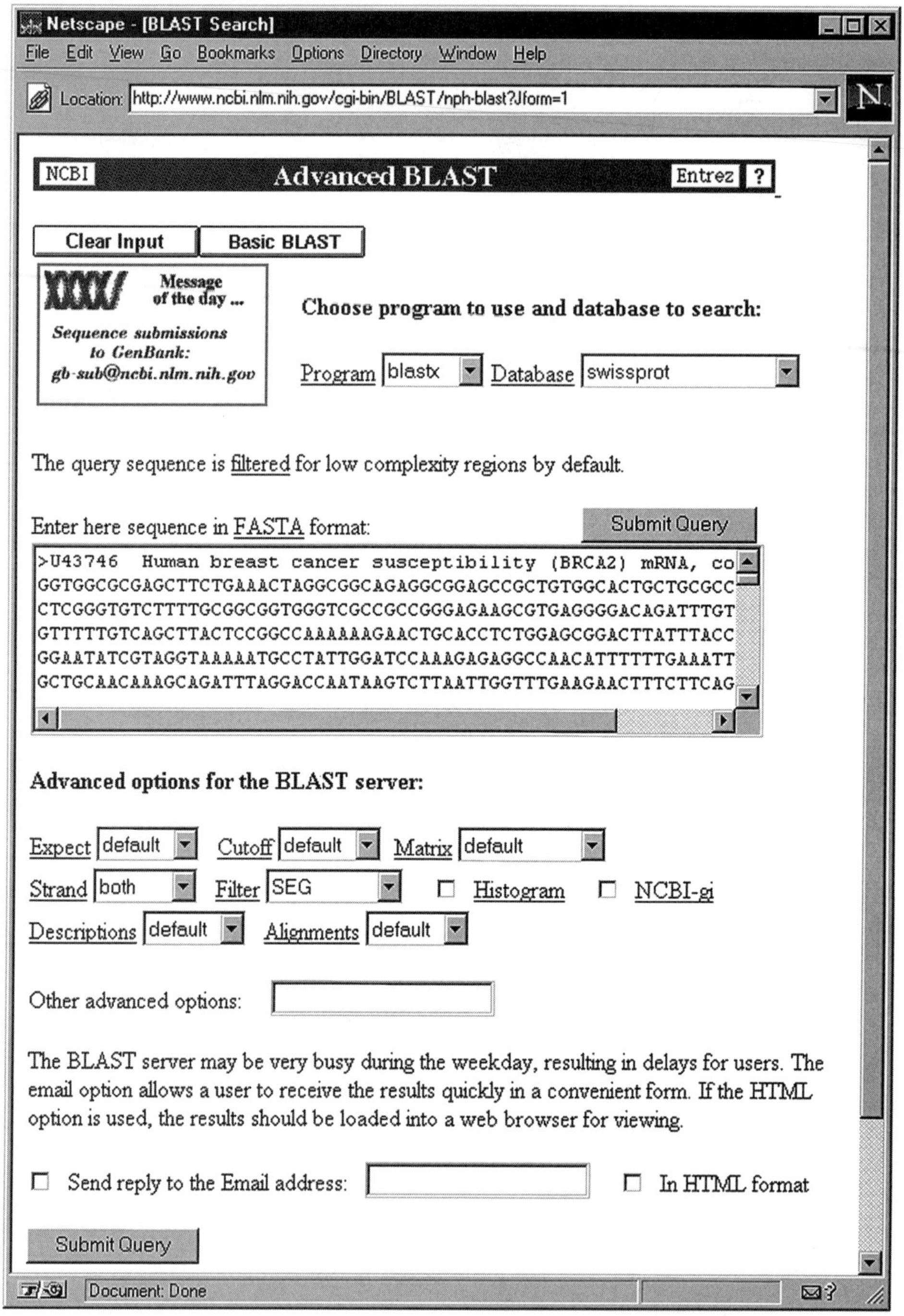

Figure 7.10 Database similarity search on the World Wide Web. The Advanced BLAST form of the NCBI's database searching facility on the Web. The query sequence should be pasted from the clipboard into the large text field (where the sequence of U43746 is shown in this figure). Other essential elements of the search are the name of the search program and the database, both of which may be selected from drop down lists. Additional optional parameters may be set if desired. There is also a Basic BLAST form in which the advanced options are hidden. In either case, simply click on the Submit Query button to begin the search.

can be done via general-purpose computers. When optimal methods are impractical, it is necessary to resort to heuristic methods, which make use of approximations to significantly speed up sequence comparisons, but with a small risk of missing true alignments.

One heuristic method is based on the strategy of breaking a sequence up into short runs of consecutive letters called *words*. Word-based methods, introduced in the early 1980s by Wilbur and Lipman, are used by virtually all today's popular search programs (Wilbur and Lipman, 1983). The basic idea is that an alignment representing a true sequence relationship will contain at least one word that is common to both sequences. These *word hits* can be identified extremely rapidly by preindexing all words from the query and then consulting the index as the database is scanned. (The precise implementation details may vary.)

FASTA

The FASTA program was the first widely used program for database similarity searching (Lipman and Pearson, 1985; Pearson and Lipman, 1988). To achieve a high degree of sensitivity, this program performs optimized searches for local alignments using a substitution matrix. As noted, however, it would take a substantial amount of time to apply this strategy exhaustively. To improve speed, the program uses the observed pattern of word hits to identify potential matches before the more time-consuming optimized search is attempted. The trade-off between speed and sensitivity is controlled by the *ktup* parameter, which specifies the size of a word. Increasing the value of *ktup* decreases the number of background word hits (i.e., those that do not mark the position of an optimal alignment). This in turn decreases the amount of optimized searching required and improves overall search speed. The default *ktup* value for comparing proteins is 2, but for finding very distant relationships, reduction to 1 is recommended.

The FASTA program does not investigate every word hit encountered, but instead looks initially for segments containing several nearby hits. Using a heuristic method, these segments are assigned scores, and the score of the best segment found appears in the output as the *init1* score (Figure 7.9a). Several segments may then be combined and a new *initn* score is calculated from the ensemble. Most potential matches are then further evaluated by performing a search for a gapped local alignment that is constrained to a diagonal band centered around the best initial segment. The score of this optimized alignment is shown in the output as the *opt* score. For alignments finally reported (a user-specified number from the top of the hit list), a full Smith–Waterman alignment search (i.e., without the constraining band) is performed. An example of such an alignment is shown in Figure 7.9b. Only the single optimal alignment is produced for each database sequence. Since, however, meaningful alignments can be missed by this approach if the proteins contain multiple modules, matching sequences should be further analyzed with the LALIGN program.

Beginning with version 2.0, FASTA provides an estimate of the statistical significance of each alignment found. The program assumes an extreme value distribution for random scores, but uses a rewritten form of the probability density function in which the expected score is a linear function of the natural log of the length of the database sequence. Simple linear regression can then be used to calculate a normalized *z score* for each alignment. Finally, an expectation E is calculated, which gives the expected number of random alignment with z scores greater than or equal to the value observed.

BLAST

The BLAST programs introduced a number of refinements to database searching that improved overall search speed and put database searching on a firm statistical foundation (Altschul et al., 1990). However, one trade-off was made to achieve this goal, namely, the constraint that local alignments produced by the program may not contain gaps (i.e., the local alignments are HSPs). This constraint has the chief advantage of allowing the application of Karlin–Altschul statistics. On the other hand, since gaps are not explicitly modeled, the results will not be as close to the desired type of alignment as one might like. This is not to say that insertions or deletions will prevent a match from being found. In most cases, the alignment simply will be broken into several distinct HSPs. In any event, these limitations of "old" BLAST programs (versions 1.4 and earlier) have been eliminated in the most recent version (2.0) of the BLAST programs, which provides explicit treatment of gaps (discussed below).

For an alignment to be reported by BLAST, there must be an HSP whose score is at least equal to the score cutoff S. This cutoff may be altered by the user, but it can be difficult to know the appropriate value to use. Because it is based on Karlin–Altschul statistics, one can instead specify an expectation cutoff E. The software can then calculate the correct value for S, taking into account properties of the search context (e.g., size of the database, properties of the substitution matrix employed). One innovation introduced in BLAST is the idea of *neighborhood words*. Instead of requiring words to match exactly, this convention declares that a word hit has been made if the word taken from the subject sequence has a score of at least T when a substitution matrix is used to compare the word from the query. This strategy allows the word size (W) to be kept high (for speed), without sacrificing sensitivity. Thus, T becomes the critical parameter determining speed and sensitivity, and W is rarely varied. If the value of T is increased; the number of background word hits will go down and the program will run faster. Reducing T allows more distant relationships to be found.

The occurrence of a word hit is followed by an attempt to find a locally optimal, but ungapped, alignment whose score is at least S. This is accomplished by accumulating the score as the alignment is extended both to the left and to the right. When a run of mostly negative scores is encountered, the cumulative score will drop substantially. When this happens, it is unlikely that the score will rebound and ultimately reach S. This observation provides the basis for an additional heuristic whereby the extension of a hit is terminated when the reduction in score (relative to the maximum value encountered) exceeds the score dropoff threshold X. Thus by reducing the time spent with unpromising hit extensions, the system just described improves performance.

Using BLAST

The functionality of BLAST may be accessed using e-mail, the World Wide Web, or console-style commands. In each case, a database search consists of four basic elements: the name of a BLAST program, the name of a database, the query sequence, and various optional parameters. Naturally, the details of performing a search differ among these variants. To avoid confusion, we describe the BLAST functionality in general terms and avoid referring specifically to any particular implementation. The reader may consult documentation for the specific implementation being employed. To obtain instructions for performing BLAST searches by e-mail version, send a message containing the word "HELP" to *blast@ncbi.nlm.nih.gov.* In the WWW implementation, help is available online. When a Unix system is used, complete usage details may be obtained by typing `man blast`.

The several variants of BLAST can be distinguished by the type of sequence (DNA or protein) of the query and database sequences (see Table 7.1). blastp compares a protein query to a protein database. The corresponding program for nucleotide sequences is blastn. If the sequence types differ, the DNA sequence can be translated by the program (in all six reading frames) and compared to the protein sequence. blastx compares a DNA query sequence to the protein database, which gives results that are useful for analyzing new sequence data and ESTs. For a protein query against a nucleotide database, the tblastn program is useful for finding unannotated coding regions in database sequences. A final variant, used only in specialized situations, is mentioned for the sake of completeness: tblastx takes DNA query and database sequences, translates them both, and compares them as protein sequences. This program is mainly useful for comparisons of ESTs when it is suspected that sequences have coding potential even though the exact coding region has not been determined.

All these programs make use of sequence databases located on server machines, which obviates the need for any local database maintenance. The protein and nucleotide sequences databases currently available for BLAST searching are listed in Tables 7.2 and 7.3, respectively. For routine searches, the nr database provides comprehensive collections of both amino acid and nucleotide sequence data, with redundancy reduced by merging sequences that are completely identical. To examine all sequences submitted or updated within the last 30 days, a database called month is provided. Both nr and month are updated daily. Several other databases listed in Tables 7.2 and 7.3 are useful in more specialized situations, such as comparing against the complete genomes of model organisms (ecoli or yeast), searching specific classes of sequences (dbest or dbsts), or testing for the presence of contaminating or otherwise problematic sequences (vector, alu, or mito).

An example of a BLAST search will serve to introduce various elements of a search output. For the example of Figure 7.11, the amino acid sequence of one of the Alzheimer's disease susceptibility proteins (conceptual translation of GenBank L43964) was used as the query in a tblastn search of the dbest database. One goal of such a search would be to identify cDNA clones for potential homologs in model organisms, thereby opening the door for experimental studies that would not be practical in humans (the clones corresponding to EST sequences are readily available). Each of the EST sequences in the database is translated in all reading frames before being compared to the Alzheimer's protein sequence. Figure 7.11a shows part of the hit list produced by this search. The first two columns give

TABLE 7.1   BLAST Programs

Program	Database	Query	Comments
blastp	Protein	Protein	Uses substitution matrix for finding distant relationships; SEG filtering available
blastn	Nucleotide	Nucleotide	Tuned for very-high-scoring matches, not distant relationships
blastx	Nucleotide (translated)	Protein	Useful for analysis of new DNA sequences and ESTs
tblastn	Protein	Nucleotide (translated)	Useful for finding unannotated coding regions in database sequences
tblastx	Nucleotide (translated)	Nucleotide (translated)	Useful for EST analysis

TABLE 7.2 Protein Sequence Databases for Use with BLAST

Database	Description
nr	Nonredundant merge of Swiss-Prot, PIR, PRF, and proteins derived from GenBank coding sequences and PDB atomic coordinates
month	Subset of *nr* that is new or modified within the last 30 days
swissprot	The Swiss-Prot database
pdb	Amino acid sequences parsed from atomic coordinates of three-dimensional structures
yeast	Complete set of proteins encoded by the *S. cerevisiae* genome
ecoli	Complete set of proteins encoded by the *E. coli* genome

the identifiers and descriptions for each sequence having a significant match. Even though the definitions are truncated in this overview, it may be seen that sequences from both mouse and *Drosophila* are represented. The next column gives the reading frame that produced the best HSP (although there may be hits to translations from other frames as well). The next three columns provide the score of the best HSP, the sum *p* value, and the number of HSPs that were used in the *p*-value calculation.

The alignment involving one of the *Drosophila* ESTs (marked by the arrow) is shown in Figure 7.11*b*. There are actually two HSPs involved, and scores are provided for each. In each case, the conceptual translation of the EST is shown aligned with the query sequence. Identical amino acids are echoed to the text line between the sequences, and plus symbols (+) are used to indicate nonidentical residues that have positive substitution scores (i.e., conservative substitutions). It is noteworthy that the two HSPs arise from different reading frames and are adjacent to each other, as can be seen from the sequence coordinates. This pattern is indicative of a reading frame error in the EST sequence. It is extremely useful to have relatively error-tolerant tools for the analysis of sequence single-pass data.

Recent Improvements to BLAST

Recently released revisions of the BLAST programs have resulted in improved speed, sensitivity, and utility (Altschul et al., 1997). This completely rewritten software package has

TABLE 7.3 Nucleotide Sequence Databases for Use with BLAST

Database	Description
nr	Nonredundant GenBank, excluding the EST, STS, and GSS divisions
month	Subset of nr that is new or modified within the last 30 days
est	GenBank EST division (expressed sequence tags)
sts	GenBank STS division (sequence tagged sites)
htgs	GenBank HTG division (high throughput genomic sequences)
gss	GenBank GSS division (genome survey sequences)
yeast	Complete genomic sequence of *S. cerevisiae*
ecoli	Complete genomic sequence of *E. coli*
mito	Complete genomic sequences of vertebrate mitochondria
alu	Collection of primate Alu repeat sequences
vector	Collection of popular cloning vectors

```
                                              Reading  High  Sum
                                                             Probability
     Sequences producing High-scoring Segment Pairs:   Frame Score  P(N)       N

     gb|AA056325|AA056325  zf53a03.s1 Soares retina N2b4HR H...  +3  724  3.4e-102   2
     gb|T03796|T03796      IB913 Infant brain, Bento Soares ...  +3  567  2.6e-78    2
     gb|AA260597|AA260597  mx76g09.r1 Soares mouse NML Mus m...  +2  239  4.9e-53    4
     gb|H86456|H86456      yt01b06.s1 Homo sapiens cDNA clon...  +2  323  4.3e-52    4
     gb|N24576|N24576      yx72a04.s1 Homo sapiens cDNA clon...  +1  365  5.5e-47    2
     gb|AA265273|AA265273  mx91c12.r1 Soares mouse NML Mus m...  +2  239  6.4e-41    2
     gb|AA237206|AA237206  mx18e01.r1 Soares mouse NML Mus m...  +3  159  1.5e-40    3
     gb|R14600|R14600      yf34b10.r1 Homo sapiens cDNA clon...  +1  278  1.5e-40    2
     gb|AA200706|AA200706  mu03f12.r1 Soares mouse 3NbMS Mus...  +1  343  1.9e-40    1
     gb|AA045064|AA045064  zk77f12.s1 Soares pregnant uterus...  -3  269  2.3e-37    1
     gb|AA087434|AA087434  mm28a04.r1 Stratagene mouse skin ...  +3  322  3.6e-37    1
     gb|R05907|R05907      ye93h02.r1 Homo sapiens cDNA clon...  +3  252  7.7e-37    2
     gb|AA268820|AA268820  vb01c10.r1 Soares mouse NML Mus m...  +2  234  7.7e-35    2
     gb|AA162310|AA162310  mn44a07.r1 Beddington mouse embry...  +1  134  8.3e-34    3
     gb|N27820|N27820      yx54h10.r1 Homo sapiens cDNA clon...  +3  154  7.8e-29    2
     gb|AA234907|AA234907  zs38f03.r1 Soares NhHMPu S1 Homo ...  +2  155  1.8e-28    2
     gb|AA231081|AA231081  mw11d11.r1 Soares mouse 3NME12 5 ...  +3  134  8.8e-23    2
     gb|H91652|H91652      ys80c04.s1 Homo sapiens cDNA clon...  -3  215  3.7e-22    1
     gb|H50532|H50532      yo30h08.s1 Homo sapiens cDNA clon...  -2  211  1.2e-21    1
     gb|AA150236|AA150236  z103c01.r1 Soares pregnant uterus...  +1  159  5.0e-21    2
     gb|AA144382|AA144382  mr15d12.r1 Soares mouse 3NbMS Mus...  +3  159  7.6e-21    2
  -> gb|AA390557|AA390557  LD09473.5prime LD Drosophila Embr...  +3  130  1.6e-20    2
     gb|AA210480|AA210480  mo86b03.r1 Beddington mouse embry...  +2  128  2.0e-20    3
     gb|H19012|H19012      ym44b02.r1 Homo sapiens cDNA clon...  +2  134  5.9e-20    2
     gb|AA283084|AA283084  zt14g09.s1 Soares NbHTGBC Homo sa...  -3  175  2.3e-19    2
     gb|H25759|H25759      y149d01.s1 Homo sapiens cDNA clon...  -2  185  5.0e-18    1
     gb|H33787|H33787      EST110123 Rattus sp. cDNA 5' end ...  +1  137  6.7e-17    2
     gb|AA201988|AA201988  LD05058.5prime LD Drosophila Embr...  +3  175  5.5e-15    1
     gb|AA263526|AA263526  LD06652.5prime LD Drosophila Embr...  +1  167  7.0e-14    1
     gb|R46340|R46340      yj52c04.s1 Homo sapiens cDNA clon...  -1  151  5.6e-13    1
     gb|AA246675|AA246675  LD05588.5prime LD Drosophila Embr...  +2  117  2.8e-10    2
     gb|AA282899|AA282899  zt14g09.r1 Soares NbHTGBC Homo sa...  +3  118  6.1e-07    1
     gb|AA247705|AA247705  csh0941.seq.F Human fetal heart, ...  +3   56  0.0039     2
```

b

```
     gb|AA390557|AA390557 LD09473.5prime LD Drosophila Embryo Drosophila
                 melanogaster cDNA clone LD09473 5'
                 Length = 659

     Score = 130 (60.4 bits), Expect = 1.6e-20, Sum P(2) = 1.6e-20
     Identities = 25/60 (41%), Positives = 40/60 (66%), Frame = +3

     Query:   105 TIKSVRFYTEKNGQLIYTTFTEDTPSVGQRLLNSVLNTLIMISVIVVMTIFLVVLYKYRC 164
                  +I S+ FY   + L+YT F E +P   + +++LI++SV+VVMT  L+VLYK RC
     Sbjct:   480 SINSISFYNSTDVYLLYTPFHEQSPEPSVKFWSALGSSLILMSVVVVMTFLLIVLYKKRC 659

     Score = 117 (54.3 bits), Expect = 1.6e-20, Sum P(2) = 1.6e-20
     Identities = 23/30 (76%), Positives = 27/30 (90%), Frame = +1

     Query:    75 LEEELTLKYGAKHVIMLFVPVTLCMIVVVA 104
                  +EEE  LKYGA+HVI LFVPV+LCM+VVVA
     Sbjct:   391 MEEEQGLKYGAQHVIKLFVPVSLCMLVVVA 480
```

Figure 7.11 Output of a TBLASTN search. The protein product of the Alzheimer's disease susceptibility gene (GenBank accession number L43964) was used as the query in a TBLASTN search against
the dbest database. The goal was to identify cDNA clones from other organisms that may represent
homologs of the human gene. (*a*) Portion of the hit list showing the 25 best hits. Each sequence is identified by GenBank accession number and a portion of the definition line. The reading frame and score
of the best HSP are shown, together with the sum probability of a chance occurrence. The value in the
last column gives the number of HSP that were used in the sum probability calculation. At least 10
sequences from mouse and one from *Drosophila* may be seen on the hit list. (*b*) Match to the conceptual translation of the *Drosophila* EST sequence (GenBank AA390557). Two HSPs were found, each in
a different reading frame. Identical residues are echoed to the central line and plus (+) symbols indicate
pairs of nonidentical amino acids with positive substitution scores.

been designated version 2.0 (which should not be confused with WU-BLAST, developed at Washington University and sometimes called BLAST2). It should be noted, however, that the set of command line parameters has changed in the 2.0 release. Several of the most frequently used parameters are summarized in Table 7.4.

One improvement comes from a change in the criterion for triggering extension of a word hit. Now, two word hits must be found within a window of A residues in order to be considered. Use of this strategy increases search speed because many random word hits can be ignored and those that are processed are more likely to lead to a significant alignment. A second improvement is the ability to treat gaps explicitly rather than implicitly. In addition to producing alignments that are easier for users to comprehend, the new variants improve sensitivity toward distant relationships, which may have accumulated many insertions and deletions. Comparisons begin with the standard strategy of finding ungapped HSPs. Next, the column that is central to the highest scoring region of this alignment is identified. The search for a local gapped alignment proceeds by evaluating paths that extend forward and backward from this point. As with the initial HSP search, a score dropoff threshold X is used to abandon paths in which many negative substitution scores are encountered. Repeating this process for the remaining HSPs may uncover additional gapped alignments, provided they do not intersect those already reported. This system differs from the strategy employed by FASTA, which produces only the one best alignment.

One way to make database searches highly sensitive toward weak, yet significant, alignments is to use a data structure known as a *profile* (Gonzalez et al., 1994). This strategy might once have been considered an advanced topic for database searching (and it is discussed further in Chapter 8), but a new feature of BLAST simplifies profile-based searches. A profile can be understood as a table that lists the frequencies of finding each of the 20 amino acids at each position in conserved protein domain. Building a profile can be tedious; the information is derived from a multiple alignment of sequences containing the domain of interest, which must be constructed in advance. Moreover, there are a variety technical issues that are not discussed in detail here.

Position-specific iterative BLAST (PSI-BLAST) refers to a feature of the BLAST 2.0 programs in which a profile is constructed on the fly and iteratively refined. The process

TABLE 7.4 Some Useful BLAST Parameters

Parameter	BLAST 1.4	BLAST 2.0
Database	first parameter	`-d` database
Query sequence file	second parameter	`-i` filename
Expectation cutoff (E)	`E` = number	`-e` number
HSP score cutoff (S)	`S` = number	`-s` number
Word score cutoff (T)	`T` = number	`-f` number
Multihit window (A)	n/a	`-A` number
Score matrix	`-matrix` matrix	`-M` matrix
Low-complexity filtering	`-filter` seg	`-F`
Gap opening penalty	n/a	`-G` number
Gap extension penalty	n/a	`-E` number
PSI-BLAST iterations	n/a	`-j` number

begins with a standard database search using a single query sequence. A profile is constructed from highly significant alignments in this initial search result. The profile is then used in a second-pass search of the database. The process may be repeated if desired, with additional sequences found in each cycle being used to refine the profile.

To demonstrate the improved sensitivity of the PSI-BLAST approach, the sequence of histidine triad protein (HIT) was used as a database search query. Similarity between HIT and galactose-1-phosphate uridylyltransferase (GalT) based on superimposition of their three-dimensional structures was recently described (Holm and Sander, 1997). However, sequence similarity between these two proteins is extremely weak. With a standard (single-pass) BLASTP search, no significant hits to GalT sequences are observed. But with a multi pass search, new relationships are discovered at each iteration, as shown in Figure 7.12. The rat GalT protein is found in the second iteration and, after information from this alignment has been incorporated into the profile, several additional homologs from other organisms are also identified.

```
                                                            High    E
Sequences producing significant alignments:                Score  Value

Pass 1:

sp|P49789|FHIT_HUMAN FRAGILE HISTIDINE TRIAD PROTEIN         290   7e-79
sp|P49776|APH1_SCHPO BIS(5'-NUCLEOSYL)-TETRAPHOSPHATASE (ASYMME...  117   8e-27
sp|P49775|YD15_YEAST HYPOTHETICAL 24.8 KD HIT-LIKE PROTEIN   88.0   6e-18
sp|Q11066|YHIT_MYCTU HYPOTHETICAL 20.0 KD HIT-LIKE PROTEIN   52.7   3e-07
sp|Q04344|HIT_YEAST HIT1 PROTEIN (ORF U)                     45.3   4e-05

Pass 2:

sp|P47378|YHIT_MYCGE HYPOTHETICAL 15.6 KD HIT-LIKE PROTEIN   70.5   1e-12
sp|P32083|YHIT_MYCHR HYPOTHETICAL 13.1 KD HIT-LIKE PROTEIN IN P...  59.0   3e-09
sp|P26724|YHIT_AZOBR HYPOTHETICAL 13.2 KD HIT-LIKE PROTEIN IN H...  57.6   9e-09
sp|P32084|YHIT_SYNP7 HYPOTHETICAL 12.4 KD HIT-LIKE PROTEIN IN P...  55.7   3e-08
sp|P53795|YHIT_CAEEL HYPOTHETICAL HIT-LIKE PROTEIN F21C3.3   54.3   9e-08
sp|P42856|ZB14_MAIZE 14 KD ZINC-BINDING PROTEIN (PROTEIN KINASE...  52.8   2e-07
sp|P42855|ZB14_BRAJU 14 KD ZINC-BINDING PROTEIN (PROTEIN KINASE...  50.2   1e-06
sp|P49774|YHIT_MYCLE HYPOTHETICAL 17.0 KD PROTEIN HIT-LIKE PROT...  49.5   2e-06
sp|P49773|IPK1_HUMAN PROTEIN KINASE C INHIBITOR 1 (PKCI-1)   49.1   3e-06
sp|P16436|IPK1_BOVIN PROTEIN KINASE C INHIBITOR 1 (PKCI-1) (17 ...  48.7   4e-06
sp|P44956|YCFF_HAEIN HYPOTHETICAL HIT-LIKE PROTEIN HI0961    47.3   1e-05
sp|P43424|GAL7_RAT GALACTOSE-1-PHOSPHATE URIDYLYLTRANSFERASE 41.0   8e-04

Pass 3:

sp|Q03249|GAL7_MOUSE GALACTOSE-1-PHOSPHATE URIDYLYLTRANSFERASE 87.2   1e-17
sp|P07902|GAL7_HUMAN GALACTOSE-1-PHOSPHATE URIDYLYLTRANSFERASE 79.8   2e-15
sp|P31764|GAL7_HAEIN GALACTOSE-1-PHOSPHATE URIDYLYLTRANSFERASE 64.7   6e-11
sp|P09148|GAL7_ECOLI GALACTOSE-1-PHOSPHATE URIDYLYLTRANSFERASE 62.5   3e-10
sp|P22714|GAL7_SALTY GALACTOSE-1-PHOSPHATE URIDYLYLTRANSFERASE 58.1   6e-09
sp|P09580|GAL7_KLULA GALACTOSE-1-PHOSPHATE URIDYLYLTRANSFERASE 48.5   4e-06
sp|P08431|GAL7_YEAST GALACTOSE-1-PHOSPHATE URIDYLYLTRANSFERASE 40.8   0.001

Pass 4:

sp|P40908|GAL7_CRYNE GALACTOSE-1-PHOSPHATE URIDYLYLTRANSFERASE 71.0   8e-13
sp|P13212|GAL7_STRLI GALACTOSE-1-PHOSPHATE URIDYLYLTRANSFERASE 57.0   1e-08
```

Figure 7.12 Increased sensitivity using PSI-BLAST. The human histidine triad (HIT) protein (Swiss-Prot P49789) was used as the query in a BLASTP search with the PSI-BLAST functionality enabled. Definition lines, scores, and *E* values are shown for all statistically significant matches newly identified in each iteration.

LOW-COMPLEXITY REGIONS

Both proteins and nucleic acids contain regions of biased composition, which can lead to confusing results during the performance of sequence database searches. These *low-complexity regions* (LCRs) range from the obvious homopolymeric runs and short-period repeats to the more subtle cases in which one or a few different residues may be overrepresented. A program called SEG was developed to optimally partition a protein sequence into segments of low and high compositional complexity (Wootton and Federhen, 1993, 1996). Results from this program showed that more than half of the proteins in the database contain at least one LCR (Wootton and Federhen, 1993; Wootton, 1994). The evolutionary, functional, and structural properties of LCRs are not well understood. In DNA, there are many classes of simple repeats, some of which are known to be highly polymorphic (e.g., CA repeats) and are often exploited in genetic mapping. Perhaps they arise by such mechanisms as polymerase slippage, biased nucleotide substitution, or unequal crossing over. In proteins, LCRs are likely to exist structurally as nonglobular regions. Regions that have been defined physicochemically as nonglobular are usually identified correctly by means of SEG (Wootton, 1994).

Alignment of LCR-containing sequences is problematic because these sequences do not fit the model of residue-by-residue sequence conservation. In some cases, the functionally relevant attributes may be only the periodicity or composition, not any specific sequence. Furthermore, methods for assessing the statistical significance of alignments are based on certain notions of randomness which LCRs do not obey. Consequently, many false positives may be observed in the output of a database search with an LCR-containing query sequence because the significance of matches can be overestimated (Altschul et al., 1994). This problem can be substantially reduced through the practice of *filtering* (also known as masking), in which problematic subsequences are converted to ambiguity characters (X for proteins, N for nucleotide sequences) that do not make a positive contribution to the alignment score.

The human homolog of the *Drosophila* achaete–scute gene product provides a good example of an LCR-containing protein. When analyzed with SEG, two regions of low compositional complexity were identified. Figure 7.13*a* shows the default "tree" output, in which the low-complexity sequences are shown in lowercase letters on the left and the high-complexity sequences in uppercase on the right. The first region is a 61-residue segment containing homopolymeric tracts of glutamine and alanine. The second is a 14-residue segment with a bias toward arginine. Without filtering, many database sequences with biased regions involving these amino acids would be reported. Using a command-line option, SEG can generate the filtered version of the sequence for use as a search query (Figure 7.13*b*). Alternatively, filtering can be performed automatically by the BLAST programs through the use of optional parameters. Note that in some implementations of BLAST, filtering may be enabled by default (e.g., in the WWW version). This explains why runs of ambiguity characters within the query sequence that were not present in the original sequence are occasionally observed in alignments (Figure 7.13*c*).

REPETITIVE ELEMENTS

If the query contains the sequence of a repetitive element—an Alu repeat, for instance—many false and confusing hits are likely to result. Although this would not generally be a

a

```
>gi|1703441|sp|P50553|ASH1_HUMAN ACHAETE-SCUTE HOMOLOG 1

                                   1-11    MESSAKMESGG
     agqqpqpqpqqpflppaacffataaaaaaa  12-72
     aaaaaaqsaqqqqqqqqqqqqqqqapqlrpa
                                 a
                                  73-119  DGQPSGGGHKSAPKQVKRQRSSSPELMRCK
                                          RRLNFSGFGYSLPQQQP
              aavarrnerernrv      120-133
                                 134-238  KLVNLGFATLREHVPNGAANKKMSKVETLR
                                          SAVEYIRALQQLLDEHDAVSAAFQAGVLSP
                                          TISPNYSNDLNSMAGSPVSSYSSDEGSYDP
                                          LSPEEQELLDFTNWF
```

b

```
>gi|1703441|sp|P50553|ASH1_HUMAN ACHAETE-SCUTE HOMOLOG 1
MESSAKMESGGxxxxxxxxxxxxxxxxxxxxxxxxxxxxxxxxxxxxxxxxxxxxxxxxxxx
xxxxxxxxxxxxxDGQPSGGGHKSAPKQVKRQRSSSPELMRCKRRLNFSGFGYSLPQQQPx
xxxxxxxxxxxxxKLVNLGFATLREHVPNGAANKKMSKVETLRSAVEYIRALQQLLDEHD
AVSAAFQAGVLSPTISPNYSNDLNSMAGSPVSSYSSDEGSYDPLSPEEQELLDFTNWF
```

c

```
>gi|540240 (U14590) achaete-scute homolog b [Danio rerio]
          Length = 195

Score =  193 bits (512), Expect = 7e-49
Identities = 107/155 (69%), Positives = 118/155 (76%)
Gaps = 8/155 (5%)

QUERY     86   KQVKRQRSSSPELMRCKRRLNFSGFGYSLPQQQPXxxxxxxxxxxxxxxxKLVNLGFATLRE 145
               K +KRQRSSSPEL+RCKRRL F+G GY++PQQQP          K VN+GF TLR+
540240    32   KVLKRQRSSSPELLRCKRRLTFNGLGYTIPQQQPMAVARRNERERNRVKQVNMGFQTLRQ 91

QUERY     146  HVPNGAANKKMSKVETLRSAVEYIRALQQLLDEHDAVSAAFQAGVLSPTISPNYSNDLNS 205
               HVPNGAANKKMSKVETLRSAVEYIRALQQLLDEHDAVSA  Q GV SP++S  YS
540240    92   HVPNGAANKKMSKVETLRSAVEYIRALQQLLDEHDAVSAVLQCGVPSPSVSNAYS----- 146

QUERY     206  MAG--SPVSSYSSDEGSYDPLSPEEQELLDFTNWF 238
               AG   SP S+YSSDEGSY+ LS EEQELLDFT WF
540240    147  -AGPESPHSAYSSDEGSYEHLSSEEQELLDFTTWF 180
```

Figure 7.13 Identifying low-complexity regions with SEG. Analysis of the human achaete–scute protein (Swiss-Prot P50553) using SEG reveals two regions of low compositional complexity. (*a*) Program output in the default "tree" format shows the low-complexity sequences in lowercase letters on the left and high-complexity in uppercase on the right. (*b*) Using the -x command line switch, the SEG program will generate a version of the sequence in which the low-complexity sequences have been masked. (*c*) For convenience, the BLAST programs can be instructed to perform the masking for the user. When a masked query sequence is used in a database search, some of the alignments may contain masked segments as shown in this BLASTP output.

problem with protein–protein searches, it is an important consideration for any comparison involving DNA sequences. Genomic sequences are likely to contain many dispersed repeats, typically involving multiple families (e.g., Alus, LINEs, and MERs in human sequences). Even mRNA sequences can contain repeats, almost always falling within the untranslated regions of the message. Consequently, repetitive elements are quite commonplace among database sequences, and if the query also contains them, many false positives will result. Although repetitive elements display a fair amount of heterogeneity, the similarity will still be high enough to cause the alignments to be rated highly significant. Although the alignments will span the repeats only and not the flanking unique sequences, this will not be easily apparent from inspection of the database search output alone.

a

```
                                                                 Smallest
                                                                   Sum
                                                           High  Probability
Sequences producing High-scoring Segment Pairs:           Score   P(N)      N

gb|L20298|HUMCBFB          Homo sapiens transcription factor ...  8691  0.0       2
dbj|D14571|MUSPEBP2B2      Mouse mRNA for PEBP2b2 protein, co...   2574  0.0      25
gb|L03279|MUSP215CBF       Mus musculus core-binding factor m...   2574  0.0      25
dbj|D14572|MUSPEBP2B1      Mouse mRNA for PEBP2b1 protein, co...   2130  0.0      26
dbj|D14570|MUSPEBP2B3      Mouse mRNA for PEBP2b3 protein, co...   1701  0.0      26
gb|L03305|MUSCBFAA         Mus musculus core-binding factor m...    942  0.0      27
gb|L03306|MUSCBFAB         Mus musculus core-binding factor m...   2130  1.6e-282 10
gb|U22177|DMU22177         Drosophila melanogaster Big brothe...    382  1.5e-37   2
emb|Y10196|HSPEX           H.sapiens PEX gene                       400  4.4e-22   1
gb|L77570|HUMDGCRCEN       Homo sapiens DiGeorge syndrome cri...    409  6.7e-22   2
gb|AD000671|1010603        Homo sapiens DNA from chromosome 1...    392  2.0e-21   1
emb|Z83822|HS306D1         Human DNA sequence from PAC 306D1 ...    392  2.0e-21   1
emb|Z82097|HSF77D12        Human DNA sequence from fosmid F77...    391  2.5e-21   1
dbj|D42052|HUMKIAA000      Human cosmid Q7A10 (D21S246) inser...    391  2.5e-21   1
gb|U83511|HSU83511         Human Xp22 cosmids U177G4, U152H5,...    386  6.5e-21   1
gb|U52112|HSU52112         Human Xq28 genomic DNA in the regi...    386  6.5e-21   1
gb|S83170|S83170           tissue-type plasminogen activator ...    382  1.1e-20   1
emb|X96421|HSCAMF3X1       H.sapiens Y chromosome cosmid cAMF...    383  1.1e-20   1
gb|U95739|HSU95739         Human chromosome 16p11.2-p12 BAC c...    383  1.1e-20   1
gb|U95743|HSU95743         Human chromosome 16p13.1 BAC clone...    383  1.1e-20   1
gb|U91322|HSU91322         Human chromosome 16p13 BAC clone C...    383  1.1e-20   1
gb|U82609|HSU82609         Human centromere-specific histone ...    382  1.3e-20   1
gb|AC001061|HSAC001061     Homo sapiens (subclone 2_g6 from P...    382  1.3e-20   1
emb|Z46940|HSPRMTNP2       H.sapiens PRM1 gene, PRM2 gene and...    382  1.4e-20   1
gb|K03021|HUMTPA           Human tissue plasminogen activator...    382  1.4e-20   1
gb|U15422|HSU15422         Human protamine 1 (PRM1), protamin...    382  1.4e-20   1
gb|U91323|HSU91323         Human chromosome 16p13 BAC clone C...    382  1.4e-20   1
emb|Z54147|HSL129H7A       Human DNA sequence from cosmid L12...    381  1.7e-20   1
emb|Z82194|HSJ272J12       Human DNA sequence from clone J272J12   374  1.7e-20   2
dbj|D00835|HIV2CAM2        Human immunodeficiency virus type-...    380  2.0e-20   1
gb|U14567|HSU14567         ***ALU WARNING: Human Alu-J subfam...    373  2.4e-20   1
gb|L81578|HSL81578         Homo sapiens (subclone 2_b2 from P...    386  3.0e-20   2
gb|L81854|HSL81854         Homo sapiens (subclone 2_b8 from P...    377  3.4e-20   1
```

b

```
                                                                 Smallest
                                                                   Sum
                                                           High  Probability
Sequences producing High-scoring Segment Pairs:           Score   P(N)      N

lcl|HSU14567      ***ALU WARNING: Human Alu-J subfamil...   373  4.1e-24  1
lcl|unknown       gb|M94643_HSAL001949 (Alu-J)             349  1.4e-22  1
lcl|HSU14574      ***ALU WARNING: Human Alu-Sx subfami...   347  7.0e-22  1
lcl|HSU14573      ***ALU WARNING: Human Alu-Sq subfami...   347  7.0e-22  1
lcl|unknown       gb|Z15026_HSAL001005 (Alu-J)             324  1.4e-21  1
lcl|unknown       gb|M15657_HSAL001243 (Alu-J)             337  6.3e-21  1
lcl|unknown       gb|M61839_HSAL002304 (Alu-J)             314  6.6e-21  1
lcl|unknown       gb|X17354_HSAL000525 (Alu-J)             314  6.6e-21  1
lcl|HSU14572      ***ALU WARNING: Human Alu-Sp subfami...   329  2.4e-20  1
lcl|unknown       gb|J03619_HSAL001939 (Alu-Sx)            329  2.8e-20  1
lcl|unknown       gb|L11910_HSAL002838 (Alu-J)             307  2.8e-20  1
lcl|unknown       gb|M11228_HSAL002744 (Alu-Sp)            329  2.8e-20  1
lcl|unknown       gb|L18035_HSAL004322 (Alu-J)             318  9.3e-20  1
lcl|unknown       gb|L05367_HSAL002551 (Alu-J)             318  1.0e-19  1
lcl|unknown       gb|M58600_HSAL002004 (Alu-J)             322  1.2e-19  1
lcl|unknown       gb|Z23796_HSAL005276 (Alu-J)             306  1.7e-19  1
lcl|unknown       gb|M90058_HSAL002955 (Alu-J)             294  2.5e-19  2
lcl|unknown       gb|D13642_HSAL003786 (Alu-J)             315  4.0e-19  1
lcl|unknown       gb|M29038_HSAL002942 (Alu-J)             314  5.5e-19  1
lcl|unknown       gb|M92357_HSAL001387 (Alu-J)             310  9.8e-19  1
```

Figure 7.14 Repetitive elements can lead to confusing results. The query sequence used for blastn searching was the cDNA sequence of human transcription factor CBFB (GenBank L20298). (*a*) When the *nr* database is used, the first few matches have true relationships to the query, but many false hits to genomic regions on different human chromosomes are also reported. The consensus Alu-J sequence included as a warning sequence is at position 31 on the hit list (arrow). (*b*) When the *alu* database is used, the Alu-J warning sequence is the best match.

Both the GenBank and Swiss-Prot databases include "warning sequences," which indicate to the user that the query contains repetitive sequences. In the case of GenBank, these entries represent the consensus sequences of different subfamilies of human Alu repeats (Claverie and Makalowski, 1993). The analogous entries in Swiss-Prot are six-frame translations of consensus Alu sequences (one frame after the other, separated by several X characters). In both cases, the word "WARNING" is quite prominent in the definition lines. The warning sequences will not necessarily appear at the top of the hit list, however; there may be many database sequences containing Alu repeats that are more similar to the query than the query is to the consensus sequence of the warning entry. This is illustrated in Figure 7.14a, which shows a portion of the hit list from a blastn search of human transcription factor CBFB (which contains an Alu in its 3′ UTR) against the nr database. The warning sequence (marked by arrow) is at position 31 on the hit list. Although a few of the matches at the top of the list represent true relationships (the very first one is a self-hit), most are false positives only because of the presence of the Alu repeat.

A more direct way to test for presence of Alu repeats in the query is to perform a preliminary search against the *alu* database. As shown in Figure 7.14b, when this is done, the Alu-J consensus (warning) sequence is now the highest scoring match reported. When the query is found to contain a repetitive element, one course of action is to edit the sequence such that the repeat is either removed or masked. One tool that may be helpful in this regard is CENSOR (Jurka et al., 1996), which automatically detects and eliminates repetitive elements.

To identify potential search artifacts, it is important learn to critically evaluate search results. The strategies described above apply only to Alu repeats, which are the most highly represented family in humans and other primates, but repeats of other types also exist at lower abundance. Furthermore, other organisms exhibit entirely different classes of repetitive elements. There are additional properties of a database search output that may be indicative of repetitive elements. For example, it is instructive to look at the positions of the alignments with respect to coding regions of DNA sequences. If noncoding sequences match, but coding sequences do not, a repetitive element (or other artifact) should be suspected. If there are matches to a large number of sequences that seem to have nothing to do with one another, yet have alignments with very similar scores, the results should similarly be regarded with suspicion. In Figure 7.14a, for example, many of the matches have nearly identical similarity scores yet involve cosmids from several different human chromosomes. Although there are multiple explanations for this observation (e.g., a dispersed gene family; multiple pseudogenes), it is wise to at least consider the possibility that an artifact, such as presence of a repetitive element, is responsible.

CONCLUSIONS

Sequence alignment and database searching are performed tens of thousands of times per day by scientists around the world, and all molecular biologists should be familiar with these critical techniques. These methods will surely continue to evolve to meet the challenges of ever-increasing database size. In particular, as the amount of available information increases, it becomes more difficult for the user to interpret the results. Database-searching "workbenches" attempt to address this problem by postprocessing search results and displaying them graphically. Examples of these strategies include PowerBLAST (Zhang and Madden, 1997), BLIXEM (Sonnhammer and Durban, 1994), and BEAUTY (Worley et al., 1995).

This chapter has described some of the fundamental concepts of sequence comparison, but it is useful to consult the documentation of the various programs for more detailed information. Researchers should have a basic understanding of how the programs work so that parameters can be intelligently selected. In addition, they should be aware of potential artifacts and know how to avoid them. Above all, it is important to apply the same powers of observation and critical evaluation that are used with any experimental method.

Internet Availability of Software Mentioned in Chapter 7

CLUSTAL W	*ftp://ftp.ebi.ac.uk/pub/software/*
DOTTER	*ftp://ftp.sanger.ac.uk/pub/dotter/*
LALIGN, FASTA	*ftp://ftp.virginia.edu/pub/fasta/*
BLAST	*ftp://ncbi.nlm.nih.gov/blast/*
SEG	*ftp://ncbi.nlm.nih.gov/pub/seg/*

REFERENCES

Altschul, S. F. (1991). Amino acid substitution matrices from an information theoretic perspective. J. Mol. Biol. *219*, 555–565.

Altschul, S. F., and Erickson, B. W. (1985). Significance of nucleotide sequence alignments: A method for random sequence permutation that preserves dinucleotide and codon usage. Mol. Biol. Evol. *2*, 526–538.

Altschul, S. F., and Erickson, B. W. (1986). Locally optimal subalignments using nonlinear similarity functions. Bull. Math. Biol. *48*, 633–660.

Altschul, S. F., and Gish, W. (1996). Local alignment statistics. Methods Enzymol. *266*, 460–480.

Altschul, S. F., Gish, W., Miller, W., Myers, E. W., and Lipman, D. J. (1990). Basic local alignment search tool. J. Mol. Biol. *215*, 403–410.

Altschul, S. F., Boguski, M. S., Gish, W., and Wootton, J. C. (1994). Issues in searching molecular sequence databases. Nature Genet. *6*, 119–129.

Altschul, S. F., Madden, T. L., Schaffer, A. A., Zhang, J., Zhang, Z., Miller, W., and Lipman, D. J. (1997). Gapped BLAST and PSI-BLAST: A new generation of protein database search programs. Nucl. Acids Res. *25*, 3389–3402.

Baron, M., Norman, D. G., and Campbell, I. D. (1991). Protein modules. Trends Biochem. Sci. *16*, 13–17.

Chandrasekharappa, S. C., Guru, S. C., Manickam, P., Olufemi, S. E., Collins, F. S., Emmert-Buck, M. R., Debelenko, L. V., Zhuang, Z., Lubensky, I. A., Liotta, L. A., Crabtree, J. S., Wang, Y., Roe, B. A., Weisemann, J., Boguski, M. S., Agarwal, S. K., Kester, M. B., Kim, Y. S., Heppner, C., Dong, Q., Spiegel, A. M., Burns, A. L., and Marx, S. J. (1997). Positional cloning of the gene for multiple endocrine neoplasia—Type 1. Science *276*, 404–407.

Claverie, J.-M., and Makalowski, W. (1993). Alu alert. Nature *371*, 752.

Dayhoff, M. O., Schwartz, R. M., and Orcutt, B. C. (1978). A model of evolutionary change in proteins. In *Atlas of Protein Sequence and Structure*, M. O. Dayhoff, ed. (Washington, DC: National Biomedical Research Foundation), pp. 345–352.

Doolittle, R. J., and Bork, P. (1993). Evolutionarily mobile modules in proteins. Sci Am. *269*, 50–56.

Doolittle, R. F., Hunkapiller, M. W., Hood, L. E., Devare, S. G., Robbins, K. C., Aaronson, S. A., and Antoniades, H. N. (1983). Simian sarcoma virus *onc* gene, v-*sis,* is derived from the gene (or genes) encoding a platelet-derived growth factor. Science *221*, 275–277.

Fitch, W. M. (1969). Locating gaps in amino acid sequences to optimize the homology between two proteins. Biochem. Genet. *3*, 99–108.

Fitch, W. M. (1983). Random sequences. J. Mol. Biol. *163*, 171–176.

Gibbs, A. J., and McIntyre, G. A. (1970). The diagram: A method for comparing sequences. Its use with amino acid and nucleotide sequences. Eur. J. Biochem. *16*, 1–11.

Gonzalez, P., Hernandez-Calzadilla, C., Rao, P. V., Rodriguez, I. R., Zigler, J. S., Jr., and Borras, T. (1994). Comparative analysis of the zeta-crystallin/quinone reductase gene in guinea pig and mouse. Mol. Biol. Evol. *11*, 305–315.

Henikoff, S., and Henikoff, J. G. (1991). Automated assembly of protein blocks for database searching. Nucl. Acids Res. *19*, 6565–6572.

Henikoff, S., and Henikoff, J. G. (1992). Amino acid substitution matrices from protein blocks. Proc. Natl. Acad. Sci. U.S.A. *89*, 10915–10919.

Higgins, D. G., Thompson, J. D., and Gibson, T. J. (1996). Using CLUSTAL for multiple sequence alignments. Methods Enzymol. *266*, 383–402.

Holm, L., and Sander, C. (1997). Enzyme HIT. Trends Biochem. Sci. *22*, 16–117.

Huang, X., Hardison, R. C., and Miller, W. (1990). A space-efficient algorithm for local similarities. Comput. Appli. Biosci. *6*, 373–381.

Jurka, J., Klonowski, P., Dagman, V., and Pelton, P. (1996). CENSOR: A program for identification and elimination of repetitive elements from DNA sequences. Comput. Chem. *20*, 119–122.

Karlin, S., and Altschul, S. F. (1990). Methods for assessing the statistical significance of molecular sequence features by using general scoring schemes. Proc. Natl. Acad. Sci. U.S.A. *87*, 2264–2268.

Karlin, S., and Altschul, S. F. (1993). Applications and statistics for multiple high-scoring segments in molecular sequences. Proc. Natl. Acad. Sci. U.S.A. *90*, 5873–5877.

Lipman, D. J., and Pearson, W. R. (1985). Rapid and sensitive protein similarity searches. Science *227*, 1435–1441.

Needleman, S. B., and Wunsch, C. (1970). A general method applicable to the search for similarities in the amino acid sequence of two proteins. J. Mol. Biol. *48*, 443–453.

Patthy, L. (1991). Modular exchange principles in proteins. Curr. Opin. Struct. Biol. *1*, 351–361.

Pearson, W. R. (1996). Effective protein sequence comparison. Methods Enzymol. *266*, 227–258.

Pearson, W. R., and Lipman, D. J. (1988). Improved tools for biological sequence comparison. Proc. Natl. Acad. Sci. U.S.A. *85*, 2444–2448.

Smith, T. F., and Waterman, M. S. (1981). Identification of common molecular subsequences. J. Mol. Biol. *147*, 195–197.

Smith, T. F., Waterman, M. S., and Burks, C. (1985). The statistical distribution of nucleic acid similarities. Nucl. Acids Res. *13*, 645–656.

Sonnhammer, E. L. L., and Durban, R. (1994). A workbench for large scale sequence homology analysis. Comput. Appl. Biosci. *10*, 301–307.

Sonnhammer, E. L. L., and Durban, R. (1996). A dot-matrix program with dynamic threshold control suited for genomic DNA and protein sequence analysis. Gene *167*, GC1–10.

Waterfield, M. D., Scrace, G. T., Whittle, N., Stroobant, P., Johnsson, A., Wasteson, A., Westermark, B., Heldin, C. H., Huang, J. S., and Deuel, T. F. (1983). Platelet-derived growth factor is structurally related to the putative transforming protein p28sis of simian sarcoma virus. Nature *304*, 35–39.

Waterman, M. S., and Eggert, M. (1987). A new algorithm for best subsequence alignments with applications to tRNA–rRNA comparisons. J. Mol. Biol. *197*, 723–728.

Waterman, M. S., and Vingron, M. (1994). Rapid and accurate estimates of statistical significance for sequence database searches. Proc. Natl. Acad. Sci. U.S.A. *91*, 4625–4628.

Wilbur, W. J., and Lipman, D. J. (1983). Rapid similarity searches of nucleic acid and protein data banks. Proc. Natl. Acad. Sci. U.S.A. *80*, 726–730.

Wootton, J. C. (1994). Non-globular domains in protein sequences: Automated segmentation using complexity measures. Comput. Chem. *18*, 269–285.

Wootton, J. C., and Federhen, S. (1993). Statistics of local complexity in amino acid sequences and sequence databases. Comput. Chem. *17*, 149–163.

Wootton, J. C., and Federhen, S. (1996). Analysis of compositionally biased regions in sequence databases. Methods Enzymol. *266*, 554–571.

Worley, K. C., Wiese, B. A., and Smith, R. F. (1995). BEAUTY: An enhanced BLAST-based search tool that integrates multiple biological information resources into sequence similarity search results. Genome Res. *5*, 173–184.

Zhang, J., and Madden, T. L. (1997). PowerBLAST: A new network BLAST application for interactive or automated sequence analysis and annotation. Genome Res. *7*, 649–656.

8

Practical Aspects of Multiple Sequence Alignment

Andreas D. Baxevanis

Genome Technology Branch
National Human Genome Research Institute
National Institutes of Health
Bethesda, Maryland

During the course of gene hunting and other efforts that result in the discovery of new proteins, it is customary to align the new sequence with the sequences of proteins of known function. While such an alignment is usually aimed at deducing the function of the new protein, these alignments, whether they are pairwise or involve multiple sequences, can serve to answer numerous other biological questions. For instance, by considering a collection of aligned sequences, one can study the underlying phylogenetic relationships between the proteins to better understand the evolution of the protein. Instead of examining a single protein, one can look at a family of related proteins to see how evolutionary pressures and biological economy have combined to produce new proteins having slightly different yet related functions. After considering highly conserved regions within a multiple alignment, one can make educated guesses regarding the overall structure of the protein and the importance of certain regions in maintaining three-dimensional shape.

Obviously, understanding the proper construction of an alignment becomes critical in the analysis of a group of related sequences. The development of programs with which to perform multiple sequence alignments is a very active area of research, and most of the methods are based on a concept called *progressive alignment* (Sankoff, 1975). The idea of progressive alignment depends on the existence of a biological or, more properly, a phylogenetic relationship between the proteins the user is attempting to align. Different algorithms tackle this problem in different ways, but suffice it to say that when the number of sequences to be aligned is greater than two (i.e., a pairwise alignment), the computational challenge becomes somewhat daunting. In practice, then, the algorithms attempt to find

Bioinformatics: A Practical Guide to the Analysis of Genes and Proteins
Edited by A.D. Baxevanis and B.F.F. Ouellette
ISBN 0-471-19196-5, pages 172–188.   Copyright © 1998 Wiley-Liss, Inc.

trade-offs between the speed of computation and arriving at the optimum alignment, often settling for alignments that are "close enough." Regardless of the method ultimately used, the user *must* examine the resultant alignment, for it will almost surely be necessary to manually make changes that account for factors such as conserved regions.

Since this book focuses on methods rather than theory, only a small subset of the available programs is discussed here. We begin with two methods that perform multiple sequence alignments, followed by a series of methods that capitalize on the presence of motifs or patterns within protein families. Finally, two presentation methods are discussed, since most of the alignment algorithms that are publicly available often are not capable of producing publication-quality output. A more complete list of multiple sequence alignment algorithms is presented at the end of the chapter.

PROGRESSIVE ALIGNMENT METHODS

CLUSTAL W

The CLUSTAL W algorithm is one of the most widely used multiple sequence alignment programs and is freely available for use on all major computer platforms (Higgins et al., 1996). Based on the idea of progressive alignment, this program takes an input set of sequences and calculates a series of pairwise alignments, comparing each sequence to every other sequence, one at a time. Based on these comparisons, a distance matrix is calculated, reflecting the relatedness of each pair of sequences. The distance matrix, in turn, serves in the calculation of a phylogenetic guide tree, based on the neighbor-joining method (see Chapter 9). The guide tree, which can be weighted to favor closely related sequences, then provides the basis for constructing the alignment, starting with a pairwise alignment of the most closely related sequences, then realigning with the addition of the next sequence, and so on. As more sequences are added, it will undoubtedly be necessary to introduce gaps to accommodate divergent sequences, and their addition is controlled by both a gap opening penalty and gap extension penalty. In most cases, users will not have structural information on which to base their alignments, but gap opening compensates by taking advantage of the probability that a particular residue can occur at either end of an α-helix or β-sheet, with gap opening favored for residues that, based on known cases, are most likely to exhibit this anomaly. The extension of an existing gap is controlled simply by trying to extend gaps only in places most likely to represent loops in the structure, and this gap extension penalty is calculated position by position.

To illustrate the use of CLUSTAL W on the UNIX platform, consider the protein U1A from four different organisms (human, mouse, *Xenopus laevis,* and *Drosophila melanogaster*). The four input sequences are placed in a single file in one of six acceptable formats, and then CLUSTAL W is launched by simply typing `clustalw` at the UNIX prompt. To see the main menu, the user issues the command:

```
*****************************************************************
******** CLUSTAL W(1.60) Multiple Sequence Alignments  ********
*****************************************************************

1. Sequence Input From Disc
2. Multiple Alignments
```

```
3. Profile / Structure Alignments
4. Phylogenetic trees

S. Execute a system command
H. HELP
X. EXIT (leave program)
```

```
Your choice: 1
```

The sequences that are to be aligned can be pulled in by picking 1 from the menu. The choice of Sequence Input From Disc then advances the user to the sequence input menu:

```
Sequences should all be in 1 file.

6 formats accepted:
NBRF/PIR, EMBL/SwissProt, Pearson (Fasta), GDE, Clustal, GCG/MSF.

Enter the name of the sequence file: U1A.seqs
```

The user is reminded of the acceptable input formats and asked for the name of the input sequence file. The sequences that are to be aligned in this case are in a file named U1A.seqs. Once the proper file has been specified, progress of the read is shown on the screen, and the user is returned to the main menu to select 2, for Multiple Alignments.

```
****** MULTIPLE ALIGNMENT MENU ******

1. Do complete multiple alignment now (Slow/Accurate)
2. Produce guide tree file only
3. Do alignment using old guide tree file

4. Toggle Slow/Fast pairwise alignments = SLOW

5. Pairwise alignment parameters
6. Multiple alignment parameters

7. Reset gaps between alignments? = ON
8. Toggle screen display = ON
9. Output format options

S. Execute a system command
H. HELP
    or press [RETURN] to go back to main menu
```

```
Your choice: 1
```

From this point, the user has a number of options for influencing the performance of the multiple sequence alignment. For example, under Multiple Alignment Parameters, the user can designate the gap opening and extension penalties, indicate what degree of divergence justifies temporarily skipping over a sequence when constructing the guide tree, select a scoring matrix (BLOSUM or PAM), and choose whether special penalties for the presence (or absence) of a hydrophilic residue at a specific position are to be instituted and, if so, for which ones. Under Pairwise Alignment Parameters, the user can adjust the penalties and window sizes used for both slow and fast alignments. Since in this example we have no information to lead us to change any of these parameters going into the first alignment attempt, option 1 ("Do complete multiple alignment now") has been chosen.

Upon selection of option 1, the program will indicate the progress of the construction of the guide tree on the screen, and then begin the actual multiple alignment.

When CLUSTAL W has finished, the resultant alignment is displayed, and the results of the current example can be found in Figure 8.1. Under the alignment, some positions are denoted by asterisks or dots, which signify absolute conservation or a high degree of conservation across the sequences, respectively. If the returned alignment had too many gaps or did not take into account any known information about this protein, the user could adjust the alignment parameters and then rerun the program to see how they affect the final alignment.

MultAlin

The MultAlin method (Corpet, 1988) is also based on the idea of starting with a series of pairwise alignments. Then, a hierarchical clustering of the sequences is undertaken, based

```
CLUSTAL W(1.60) multiple sequence alignment


hum-U1A    ------MAVPETRPNHTIYINNLNEKIKKDELKKSLYAIFSQFGQILDILVSRSLKMRGQ
mse-U1A    MATIATMPVPETRANHTIYINNLNEKIKKDELKKSLYAIFSQFGQILDILVSRIMKMRGQ
xla-U1A    ------MSIQEVRPNNTIYINNLNEKIKKDELKKSLYAIFSQFGQILDILVSRNLKMRGQ
dme-U1A    ---------MEMLPNQTIYINNLNEKIKKEELKKSLYAIFSQFGQILDIVALKTLKMRGQ
                *    * ************* ******************* .  . .*****

hum-U1A    AFVIFKEVSSATNALRSMQGFPFYDKPMRIQYAKTDSDIIAKMKGTFVERDRKR-EKRKP
mse-U1A    AFVIFKEVTSATNALRSMQGFPFYDKPMRIQYAKTDSDIIAKMKGTYVERDRKR-EKRKP
xla-U1A    AFVIFKETSSATNALRSMQGFPFYDKPMRIQYSKTDSDIIAKMKGTFVERDRKRQEKRKV
dme-U1A    AFVIFKEIGSASNALRTMQGFPFYDKPMQIAYSKSDSDIVAKIKGTFKERPKKVKPPKPA
           ******* **.****.**********.* *.*.**** **.***. **  .*      .

hum-U1A    KSQETPATKKAVQGGGATPVVGAVQGPVPGMPPMTQAPRIMHHMPGQPPYMPPPGMIPPP
mse-U1A    KSQETPAAKKAVQGGAAAPVVGAVQ-PVPGMPPMPQAPRIMHHMPGQPPYMPPPGMIPPP
xla-U1A    KVPEVQGVKNAMPGAALLPGVPGQMAAMQDMPGMTQAPRMMH-MAGQAPYMHHPGMMPPP
dme-U1A    PGTDEKKDKKKK------------------------------------------------P
            .         *                                                *

hum-U1A    GLAPGQIPPGAMPPQQLMPGQMPPAQPLSENPPNHILFLTNLPEETNELMLSMLFNQFPG
mse-U1A    GLAPGQIPPGAMPPQQLMPGQMPPAQPLSENPPNHILFLTNLPEETNELMLSMLFNQFPG
xla-U1A    GMAPGQMPPGGMPHGQLMPGQMAPMQPISENPPNHILFLTNLPEETNELMLSMLFNQFPG
dme-U1A    SSAENSNP---------------NAQTEQPPNQILFLTNLPEETNEMMLSMLFNQFPG
            * .  *             .  .*.***.************ .**********

hum-U1A    FKEVRLVPGRHDIAFVEFDNEVQAGAARDALQGFKITQNNAMKISFAKK
mse-U1A    FKEVRLVPGRHDIAFVEFDNEVQAGAARDALQGFKITQNNAMKISFAKK
xla-U1A    FKEVRLVPGRHDIAFVEFDNEVQAGARESLQGFKITQSNSMKISFAKK
dme-U1A    FKEVRLVPNRHDIAFVEFTTELQSNAAKEALQGFKITPTHAMKITFAKK
           ******** ********* .*.*..**...******  ..***.****
```

Figure 8.1 Results of a CLUSTAL W multiple sequence alignment, using four U1A sequences as the input set. Positions with absolute conservation are noted with an asterisk, while relatively conserved positions are indicated with a dot.

on the scores calculated during the pairwise alignments. As sequences are clustered together and the multiple sequence alignment built, a new score is calculated, representing the pairwise alignments *within* the multiple sequence alignment. Based on these new scores, the tree is rebuilt. The process continues until the score can no longer be improved, whereupon the multiple sequence alignment is deemed final.

MultAlin can very easily be executed through a Web site at the INRA Toulouse. The sequences to be aligned, expressed in FASTA format, are pasted into a sequence input box. Then, from a series of pulldown menus, the user can specify optional parameters, such as the output format, alternate input formats, the scoring matrix to employ, and the values of gap opening and gap extension penalties. Most users will change only the scoring matrix, depending on how closely or distantly related the input sequences are. Then the sequences are submitted to the server, and when the multiple sequence alignment is returned, a consensus sequence is calculated and displayed at the bottom of the alignment. For example, the same sequences aligned using CLUSTAL W in Figure 8.1 were submitted to the MultAlin server, accepting the default values for the alignment; the resulting multiple sequence alignment is shown in Figure 8.2. In the Consensus lines, an absolute match across all sequences is indicated by an uppercase letter, and majority-rule matches are shown by a lowercase letter. Also, the symbols !, $, %, and # are employed to indicate conservative substitutions, as indicated at the top of Figure 8.2.

Obviously, the alignments obtained by the two methods are not the same. The major difference is that CLUSTAL W opened two gaps in excess of 10 residues in the *Drosophila* U1A sequence (dme-U1A), whereas MultAlin opened only one long gap. Also, MultAlin was able to line up with absolute identity over 20 more positions than were aligned by CLUSTAL W. Of course, this is not to imply that one method is better than the other—the recurring theme in this book is now revisited, in that different methods will work with different degrees of success depending on the nature of the input sequences. The careful user will opt for more than one technique, making the final adjustments to the alignment by hand.

MOTIFS AND PATTERNS

The methods presented in the preceding section are extremely useful in constructing multiple sequence alignments, but the user must collect the actual input sequences independently, either through a series of BLAST or other database searches or through direct determination in the laboratory. However, numerous methods can take a single sequence and, based on any motifs or patterns present in that sequence, return entire protein families, complete with what that particular method considers to be the "best alignment." Many times, these methods reveal distant relationships that were not inherently obvious from passing the sequence through the standard set of database search routines. In this section, we consider two methods that search specialized databases for the presence of a motif or sequence pattern in a query sequence, as well as two methods that are of great use in building protein families from a minimum of sequence information.

ProfileScan

Based on the classic Gribskov method of profile analysis (Gribskov et al., 1987, 1988), ProfileScan uses a method called *pfscan* to find similarities between a protein or nucleic acid query sequence and a profile library (Lüthy et al., 1994). In this case, two profile

```
Symbol comparison table: blosum62
Gap weight: 12
Gap length weight: 2
Consensus levels: high=90% low=50%
Consensus symbols:
 ! is anyone of IV
 $ is anyone of LM
 % is anyone of FY
 # is anyone of NDQEBZ

MSF:    289   Check:    0       ..
Name: hum-U1A       Len:    289  Check: 9991  Weight:   0.56
Name: mse-U1A       Len:    289  Check: 9174  Weight:   0.56
Name: xla-U1A       Len:    289  Check: 7674  Weight:   1.08
Name: dme-U1A       Len:    289  Check: 3145  Weight:   1.81
Name: Consensus     Len:    289  Check:  255  Weight:   4.00

//


                 1                                                  50
     hum-U1A    ......MAVP ETRPNHTIYI NNLNEKIKKD ELKKSLYAIF SQFGQILDIL
     mse-U1A    MATIATMPVP ETRANHTIYI NNLNEKIKKD ELKKSLYAIF SQFGQILDIL
     xla-U1A    ......MSIQ EVRPNNTIYI NNLNEKIKKD ELKKSLYAIF SQFGQILDIL
     dme-U1A    .........M EMLPNQTIYI NNLNEKIKKE ELKKSLYAIF SQFGQILDIV
   Consensus    ......m... E.rpN.TIYI NNLNEKIKK# ELKKSLYAIF SQFGQILDIl

                 51                                                 100
     hum-U1A    VSRSLKMRGQ AFVIFKEVSS ATNALRSMQG FPFYDKPMRI QYAKTDSDII
     mse-U1A    VSRIMKMRGQ AFVIFKEVTS ATNALRSMQG FPFYDKPMRI QYAKTDSDII
     xla-U1A    VSRNLKMRGQ AFVIFKETSS ATNALRSMQG FPFYDKPMRI QYSKTDSDII
     dme-U1A    ALKTLKMRGQ AFVIFKEIGS ASNALRTMQG FPFYDKPMQI AYSKSDSDIV
   Consensus    vsr.$KMRGQ AFVIFKE..S AtNALRsMQG FPFYDKPMrI qYsKtDSDI!

                 101                                                150
     hum-U1A    AKMKGTFVER DRKR.EKRKP KSQETPATKK AVQGGGATPV VGAVQGPVPG
     mse-U1A    AKMKGTYVER DRKR.EKRKP KSQETPAAKK AVQGGAAAPV VGAVQ.PVPG
     xla-U1A    AKMKGTFVER DRKRQEKRKV KVPEVQGVKN AMPGAALLPG VPGQMAAMQD
     dme-U1A    AKIKGTFKER PKK....... .......... .......... ..........
   Consensus    AKmKGT%vER drKr.ekrk. k..e....k. a..g....p. v.........

                 151                                                200
     hum-U1A    MPPMTQAPRI MHHMPGQPPY MPPPGMIPPP GLAPGQIPPG AMPPQQLMPG
     mse-U1A    MPPMPQAPRI MHHMPGQPPY MPPPGMIPPP GLAPGQIPPG AMPPQQLMPG
     xla-U1A    MPGMTQAPRM MH.MAGQAPY MHHPGMMPPP GMAPGQMPPG GMPHGQLMPG
     dme-U1A    .......... .......... ......VKPP KPAPGTDEKK DKKKKPSSAE
   Consensus    mp.m.qapr. mh.m.gq.py m..pgm.pPP g.APGq.ppg .mp..qlmpg

                 201                                                250
     hum-U1A    QMPPAQPLSE NPPNHILFLT NLPEETNELM LSMLFNQFPG FKEVRLVPGR
     mse-U1A    QMPPAQPLSE NPPNHILFLT NLPEETNELM LSMLFNQFPG FKEVRLVPGR
     xla-U1A    QMAPMQPISE NPPNHILFLT NLPEETNELM LSMLFNQFPG FKEVRLVPGR
     dme-U1A    NSNP.NAQTE QPPNQILFLT NLPEETNEMM LSMLFNQFPG FKEVRLVPNR
   Consensus    #m.P.#p.sE #PPNhILFLT NLPEETNE$M LSMLFNQFPG FKEVRLVPgR

                 251                                     289
     hum-U1A    HDIAFVEFDN EVQAGAARDA LQGFKITQNN AMKISFAKK
     mse-U1A    HDIAFVEFDN EVQAGAARDA LQGFKITQNN AMKISFAKK
     xla-U1A    HDIAFVEFDN EVQAGAARES LQGFKITQSN SMKISFAKK
     dme-U1A    HDIAFVEFTT ELQSNAAKEA LQGFKITPTH AMKITFAKK
   Consensus    HDIAFVEFdn EvQagAAr#a LQGFKITq.n aMKIsFAKK
```

Figure 8.2 Results of a MultAlin multiple sequence alignment, using four U1A sequences as the input set. On the Consensus lines, positions with absolute conservation are indicated by an uppercase letter and majority-rule matches are shown by a lowercase letter. The symbols employed to indicate conservative substitutions are indicated at the top of the figure.

libraries are available for searching. First is PROSITE, an ExPASy database that catalogs biologically significant sites through the use of motif and sequence patterns known as fingerprints (Bairoch, 1997). Second is Pfam, which is a collection of protein domain families that differ from most such collections in one important aspect: the initial alignment of the protein domains is done by hand, rather than by depending on automated methods. As such, Pfam contains slightly over 500 entries, but the entries are potentially of higher quality.

Searches against both PROSITE and Pfam can be done through the ProfileScan Web page, which simply requires either an input sequence in plaintext format, or an identifier such as a SWISS-PROT ID. The user can select the sensitivity of the search, returning either significant matches only or all matches, including borderline cases. To illustrate the output format, the sequence of a human heat-shock-induced protein was submitted to the server for searching against PROSITE.

```
normalized raw        from -   to Profile | Description
355.9801 41556 pos.      6 -  612 PF00012 | HSP70  Heat shock hsp70 proteins
```

While the actual PROSITE entry returned is no great surprise, the output contains scores that are worth understanding. The raw score is the actual score calculated from the scoring matrix used in the course of the search. The more informative number is the normalized, or N score. The N score formally represents the number of matches one would expect in a database of given size. Basically, the larger the N score, the lower the probability that the hit occurred by chance. In the example, the N score of 355 translates to a 1.94×10^{-349} expected chance matches when normalized against SWISS-PROT. The from and to numbers simply show the positions of the overlap between the query and the matching profile.

BLOCKS

The BLOCKS database utilizes the concept of *blocks* to identify a family of proteins, rather than relying on the individual sequences themselves (Henikoff and Henikoff, 1996). The idea of a block is derived from the more familiar notion of a *motif,* which usually refers to a conserved stretch of amino acids that confer a specific function or structure to a protein. When these individual motifs from proteins in the same family are aligned without introducing gaps, the result is a block, with the term "block" referring to the *alignment,* not the individual sequences themselves. Obviously, an individual protein can contain one or more blocks, corresponding to each of its functional or structural motifs.

The BLOCKS database itself is derived from the entries in PROSITE. When a BLOCKS search is performed using a sequence of interest, the query sequence is aligned against all the blocks in the database at all possible positions. For each alignment, a score is calculated using a position-specific scoring matrix, or PSSM. The important difference between a PSSM and the matrices discussed earlier in this book (e.g., BLOSUM62) is that the scoring takes into account both whether there is or is not a match at a given position *and* the probability that a given amino acid occupies that position in the block. At the heart of all such pattern-based methods is the idea of seeing how often residues occur at a specific position in a block of aligned proteins, as will become obvious by the end of this section.

BLOCKS searches can be performed using the BLOCKS Web site at the Fred Hutchinson Cancer Research Center in Seattle. The Web site is straightforward, allowing both sequence-based and keyword-based searches to be performed. If a DNA sequence is used as the input, users can specify which genetic code to use and which strand to search.

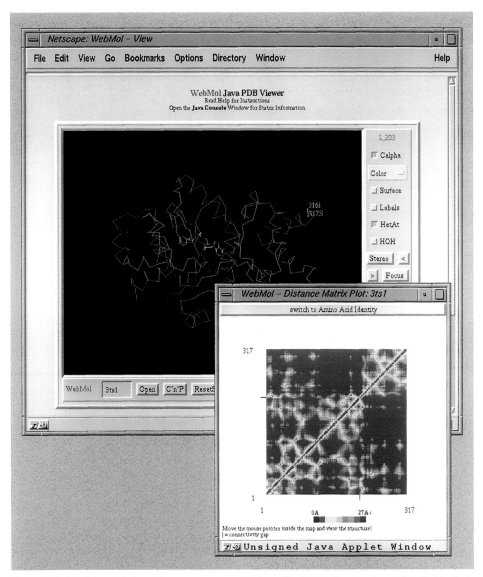

Figure 3.3 Testing a 3D viewer for sequence numbering artifacts with the structure 3TS1 (Brick et al., 1989). WebMol, a Java applet, follows the trend of not reconstructing the chemical graph of the molecule. This version of WebMol reassigns sequence numbering producing artifacts. Arg 317, Ile 318, and Ser 319 are off by two (i.e., WebMol reports Arg 315, Ile 316, and Ser 317). The actual sequence embedded in the PDB file is 419 residues long, but the C-terminal portion of the protein is lacking coordinates.

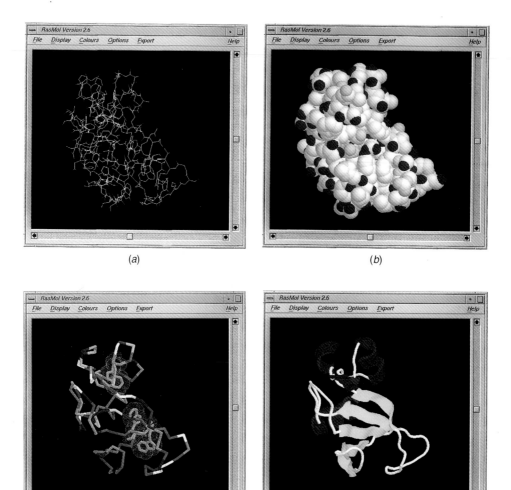

(a)   (b)

(c)   (d)

Figure 3.4 A constellation of viewing alternatives using RasMol with a portion of the barnase structure 1BN1 (Buckle et al., 1993). 1BN1 has three barnase molecules in the asymmetric unit. For this figure the author edited the PDB file to remove two extra barnase molecules to make the images. Like most crystal structures, 1BN1 has no hydrogen locations. (a) Barnase in CPK coloring (element-based coloring) in a wireframe representation. (b) Barnase in a spacefilling representation. (c) Barnase in an α-carbon backbone representation, colored by residue type. The command line was used to select all the tryptophan residues, render them with "sticks," color them purple, and show a dot surface representation. (d) Barnase in a cartoon format showing secondary structure, α helices in red; β strands in yellow. Note that in all cases the default atom or residue coloring schemes used are at the discretion of the author of the software.

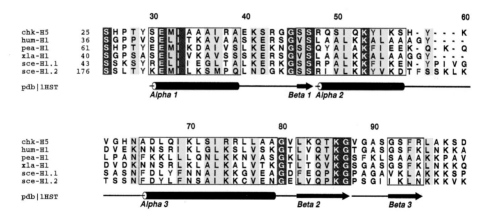

```
                              PICT output
chk-H5     25  SHPTYSEMIAAAIRAEKSRGGSSRQSIQKYIKSH-Y----KVGHNADLQIK
hum-H1     36  SGPPVSELITKAVAASKERSGVSLAALKKALAAAGY-----DVEKNNSRIK
pea-H1     61  SHPTYEEMIKDAIYSLKEKNGSSQYAIAKFIEEK-Q-K-QLPANFKKLLL
xla-H1     40  SGPSASELIYKAVSSSKERSGVSLAALKKALAAGGY-----DVDKNNSRLK
sce-H1.1   43  SSKSYRELIIEGLTALKERKGSSRPALKKFIKEN-YPIVGSASNFDLYFN
sce-H1.2  176  SSLTYKEMILKSMPQLNDGKGSSRIVLKKYVKDTFSSKLKTSSNFDYLFN
consensus   1  S ptysEmIvkai alker GsSr alkKyike   y       nfd  ik

chk-H5     71  LSIRRLLAAGVLKQTKGYGASGSFRLAKSD
hum-H1     82  LGLKSLVSKGTLVQTKGTGASGSFKLNKKA
pea-H1    108  QNLKKNVASGKLIKYKGSFKLSAAAKKPAV
xla-H1     86  LALKALVTKGTLTQVKGSGASGSFKLNKKQ
sce-H1.1   92  NAIKKGVEAGDFEQPKGPAGAVKLAKKKSP
sce-H1.2  226  SAIKKCVENGELYQPKGPSGIIKLNKKKVK
consensus  51  laikklv  G lvq KGtqasgsfr kk
```

Figure 8.7 PICT output from MacBoxShade. The derived consensus is shown at the bottom of the figure. In the consensus, positions with absolute conservation are shown as uppercase letters, positions deemed as being "similar" are shown in lowercase, and unconserved positions have no representation in the consensus. Within the alignment, all positions identical to the consensus are shown in white against a blue background. All positions similar to the consensus are shown in black against a purple background.

```
                30              40              50                  60
chk-H5     25  S H P T Y S E M I A A A I R A E K S R G G S S R Q S I Q K Y I K S H - Y - - - K
hum-H1     36  S G P P V S E L I T K A V A A S K E R S G V S L A A L K K A L A A A G Y - - - -
pea-H1     61  S H P T Y E E M I K D A I V S L K E K N G S S Q Y A I A K F I E E K - Q - K - Q
xla-H1     40  S G P S A S E L I V K A V S S S K E R S G V S L A A L K K A L A A G G Y - - - -
sce-H1.1   43  S S K S Y R E L I I E G L T A L K E R K G S S R P A L K K F I K E N - Y P I V G
sce-H1.2  176  S S L T Y K E M I L K S M P Q L N D G K G S S R I V L K K Y V K D T F S S K L K

pdb|1HST
               Alpha 1                       Beta 1 Alpha 2

                70              80              90
chk-H5         V G H N A D L Q I K L S I R R L L A A G V L K Q T K G V G A S G S F R L A K S D
hum-H1         D V E K N N S R I K L G L K S L V S K G T L V Q T K G T G A S G S F K L N K K A
pea-H1         L P A N F K K L L L Q N L K K N V A S G K L I K V K G S F K L S A A A K K P A V
xla-H1         D V D K N N S R L K L A L K A L V T K G T L T Q V K G S G A S G S F K L N K K Q
sce-H1.1       S A S N F D L Y F N N A I K K G V E A G D F E Q P K G P A G A V K L A K K K S P
sce-H1.2       T S S N F D Y L F N S A I K K C V E N G E L V Q P K G P S G I I K L N K K K V K

pdb|1HST
               Alpha 3                       Beta 2              Beta 3
```

Figure 8.9 Output from the ALSCRIPT command file shown in Figure 8.8. The input data is the same as for the MacBoxShade alignment shown in Figure 8.7; note the differences between the two outputs, which primarily reflect the difference between speed and control.

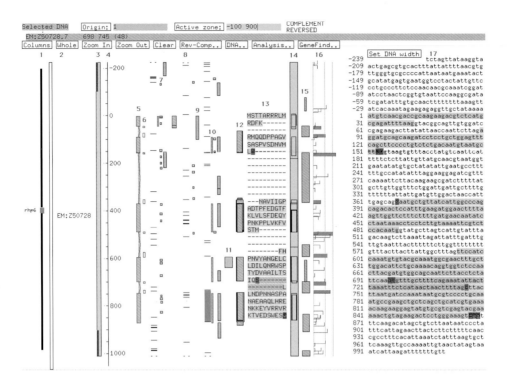

Figure 13.4 Fmap display of *rhp6* from *S. pombe*. Details can be found in the text.

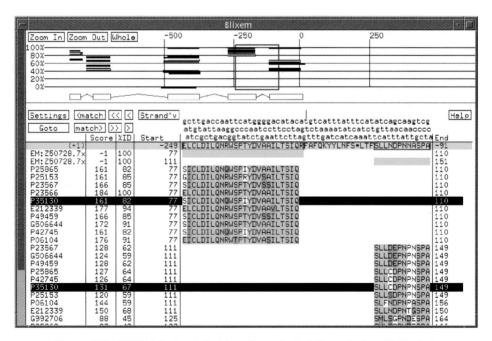

Figure 13.5 BLIXEM display of *rhp6* from *S. pombe*. Details can be found in the text.

Regardless of whether the query is performed via a sequence or via keywords, a successful search will return the relevant block. An example is shown in Figure 8.3. In this entry (for a nuclear hormone receptor called a steroid finger), the header lines marked ID, AC, and DE give, in order, a short description of the family represented by this block, the BLOCKS database accession number, and a longer description of the family. The BL line gives information regarding the original sequence motif that was used to construct this particular block. The `width` and `seqs` parameters show how wide the block is, in residues, and how many sequences are in the block, respectively. Then follows some information on the statistical validity and the strength of the construct. Finally, a list of sequences is presented, showing only the part of the sequence corresponding to this particular motif. Each line begins with the SWISS-PROT accession number for the sequence, the number of the first residue shown based on the entire sequence, the sequence itself, and a position-based sequence weight. These values are scaled, with 100 representing the sequence that is most distant from the group. Notice that there are blank lines between some of the sequences; parts of the overall alignment are clustered, and in each cluster, 80% of the sequence residues are identical.

MoST

The Motif Search Tool, or MoST, is a UNIX program that can be used to search databases for the presence of conserved motifs (Tatusov et al., 1994). This method uses a block of aligned sequences (the *alignment block*), having any number of sequences N, each of length L; all the sequences must be of the same length, and gaps are not tolerated in the present implementation. This alignment block is used to generate a protein weight matrix. The searches are then performed by sliding this weight matrix along all the sequences in the target protein database. A score is computed for every segment of length L by summing

```
ID   STEROID_FINGER; BLOCK
AC   BL00031; distance from previous block=(4,603)
DE   Nuclear hormones receptors DNA-binding region proteins.
BL   CCR motif; width=37; seqs=120; 99.5%=1711; strength=1689
 ECR_DROME  ( 264) CLVCGDRASGYHYNALTCEGCKGFFRRSVTKSAVYCC   16

ODR7_CAEEL  ( 331) QVCLSTHANGLHFGARTCAACAAFFRRTISDDKRYVC  100

 TLL_DROME  (  34) CKVCRDHSSGKHYGIYACDGCAGFFKRSIRRSRQYVC   34

YKC8_CAEEL  (  18) CLVCSDISTGYHYGVPSCNGCKTFFRRTIMKNQTFSC   31

7UP1_DROME  ( 200) CVVCGDKSSGKHYGQFTCEGCKSFFKRSVRRNLTYSC    7
7UP2_DROME  ( 200) CVVCGDKSSGKHYGQFTCEGCKSFFKRSVRRNLTYSC    7
ARP1_HUMAN  (  79) CVVCGDKSSGKHYGQFTCEGCKSFFKRSVRRNLSYTC    8
ARP1_MOUSE  (  79) CVVCGDKSSGKHYGQFTCEGCKSFFKRSVRRNLSYTC    8
COTF_HUMAN  (  86) CVVCGDKSSGKHYGQFTCEGCKSFFKRSVRRNLTYTC    7
EAR2_HUMAN  (  56) CVVCGDKSSGKHYGVFTCEGCKSFFKRTIRRNLSYTC    7
EAR2_MOUSE  (  57) CVVCGDKSSGKHYGVFTCEGCKSFFKRTIRRNLSYTC    7
 TR2_HUMAN  ( 113) CVVCGDKASGRHYGAVTCEGCKGFFKRSIRKNLVYSC   10
```

Figure 8.3 Structure of a typical BLOCKS entry. This entry is for the steroid finger block. The structure of the entry is discussed in the text.

up the appropriate weight matrix elements. As statistically significant matches to the alignment block are found, they are in turn added to the alignment block. At the end of a round of database searches, the weight matrix is recalculated and the database searches repeated. This iterative process continues until no new statistically significant segments are found. The process, therefore, capitalizes on *new* information obtained in the course of the database searches.

One of the parameters that can be set in the course of a MoST run is a ratio R, which represents the expected number of false positives divided by the predicted number of true positives. As MoST searches are expected to converge (i.e., the iterative process eventually stops, since no new sequences are found), the selection of the R value is important. If R is set too high, the searches diverge rather than converge, eventually bringing in every last sequence of the target database. One approach that can be used to avoid spurious matches is to gradually increase the value of R, observing the number and quality of the matches, and backing off when divergence becomes a problem.

The MoST command line takes the form

```
most database block [method] [seg] [cutoff] [i#%] > outfile
```

where `database` specifies which database should be searched against (e.g., nr) and `block` specifies the name of the file containing the input alignment block, in FASTA format. The optional `method` parameter specifies how the position-dependent weight matrix will be calculated. The default value, invoked if nothing is specified, is based on Dirichlet distributions of the probability of the occurrence of a particular residue. Option 1 would invoke weighted averaging (the Gribskov method), 2 would invoke a Bayesian pseudocount method, and 3 would invoke a data-dependent pseudocount model. Specifics on how each of these methods performs are outlined in the original reference for MoST (Tatusov et al., 1994); new users should accept the default and examine the quality of their results before changing this parameter. The `seg` parameter specifies whether the seg filtering algorithm should be applied during the course of the search, with `seg` (the default) turning it on and `-seg` turning it off. The cutoff score can be used to specify the ratio R described above, with recommended starting values ranging from `r.01` to `r.05`. Finally, the input block can be collapsed through the use of the `i#%` parameter. For example, when `i80%` is specified, only one member of the group that is 80% or more identical will be used; this option is useful to prevent the skewing of data sets in favor of multiple occurrences of the same sequence from different organisms.

A portion of the MoST output is shown in Figure 8.4. The output file conveniently echoes the starting command, allowing multiple MoST runs to be discerned one from another. Following is the actual block, with an extra sequence at the top and the bottom. The sequence labeled `max` can be thought of as the de facto consensus, the sequence that would score highest based on the calculated matrix; here, this sequence would score 609, shown at the end of the line. In the same way, the line labeled `min` would be the anticonsensus, the sequence that would score the worst against the calculated matrix. The actual sequences from the alignment block appear between these two lines, ranked from highest to lowest score, with a numerical identifier to the left of the sequence and the sequence's score to the right.

The output is continued in Figure 8.5; as a result of the first iteration with this input block, five new sequences were found (top of the alignment). To the left of the new sequences are the first several characters from the Def line for that entry, the number of the

```
Searching command: moss nr <block> r.001 one
Method: Simple Bayesian prediction
Block (18x64)
max   TKPAIRRLARRGGVKRISGLIYEETRGVLKIFLENVIRDAVTYTEHAKRKTVTAMDVVYALKRQ     609
  4   TKPAIRRLARRGGVKRISGLIYEETRGVLKVFLENVIRDAVTYTEHAKRKTVTAMDVVYALKRQ     608
  3   TKPAIRRLARRGGVKRISGLIYEETRGVLKIFLENVIRDAVTYTEHARRKTVTAMDVVYALKRQ     607
  5   TKPAIRRLARRGGVKRISGLIYEETRGVLKVFLENVIRDAVTYCEHAKRKTVTAMDVVYALKRQ     606
 16   TKPAIRRLARRGGVKRISGLIYEETRGVLKIFLENVIRDSVTYTEHARRKTVTAMDVVYALKRQ     605
 13   TKPAIRRLARRGGVKRISGLIYEETRGVLKVFLENVIRDAVTYCEHAKRKTVTSMDVVYALKRQ     603
 15   TKPAIRRLARRGGVKRISGLIYEETRGVLKVFLENVIRDAVTYTEHAKRKTVTALDVVYALKRQ     602
 11   TKPAIRRLARRGGVKRISGLIYEETRGVLKIFLENVIRDAVTYTEHAXRKTVTAMDVVYALKRQ     595
  9   TKPAIRRLARRGGVKRISNTIYEETRGVLKTFLENVIRDAVTYTEHARRKTVTAMDVVYALKRQ     593
 18   TKPAIRRLARRGGVKRISGLIYEETRTVLKNFLENVIRDSVTYTEHARRKTVTAMDVVYALKRQ     593
 10   TKPAIRRLARRGGVKRISKTIYEETRGVLKTFLENVIRDAVTYTEHARRKTVTAMDVVYALKRQ     592
  8   TKPAIRRLARRGGVKRISGLIYEETRGVLKIFLENVIRDSVTYTEHAKRKTVTALDVVYALKRS     590
  2   TKPAIRRLARRGGVKRISAMIYEETRGVLKSFLESVIRDAVTYTEHAKRKTVTSLDVVYALKRQ     583
  1   TKPAIRRLARRGGVKRISAMIYEETRGVLKTFLEGVIRDAVTYTEHAKRKTVTSLDVVYALKRQ     580
  7   TKPAIRRLARRGGVKRISSLIYEETRNVLRSFLENVIRDSVTYTEHAKRKTVTALDVVYALKRQ     579
 12   TKPAIRRLARRGGVKRISGLIYEEVRAVLKSFLESVIRDSVTYTEHAKRKTVTSLDVVYALKRQ     573
 14   TKPAIRRLARRGGVKRISALVYEETRAVLKLFLENVIRDAVTYTEHAKRKTVTSLDVVYSLKRQ     564
 17   TKPAIRRLARRGGVKRISSFIYDDSRQVLKSFLENVVRDAVTYTEHARRKTVTAMDVVYALKRQ     552
  6   TKPAIRRLARRGGVKRINGAVYDETRNVLKQFLEQVIRDSVTYTEHARRKTVTAMDVVYALKRQ     548
min   AAARAAAARAAAAAAAAARRAAAAAARAAAAAAAAAAAARAAAAAARAAAAAARAAAAARAAAA    -384
Database:   Non-redundant PDB+SwissProt+SPupdate+PIR+GenPept+GPupdate, 4:58 AM
            EST Nov 28, 1994
            132,570 sequences; 37,990,230 total letters.
```

Figure 8.4 Processed alignment block from a MoST run. Details on the structure of the output can be found in the text.

first residue shown, the sequence, and the statistics for that sequence. Further down, the original sequences (those from the alignment block) are repeated, and these can be related back to the alignment block using the numerical identifier following the Def line. The figure is truncated, but the output file continues, showing the results of every round of calculations until the search converges. One of the nice features of the output is that residues not matching the block can easily be spotted, since they are in lowercase, and the alignment is already done for the user.

PROBE

Among the newest of the programs that can generate an alignment model is PROBE (Neuwald et al., 1997). In certain respects, PROBE is similar to MoST in that it employs an iterative strategy to detect distantly related sequences. However, the algorithm is substantially different in its mechanics, so some further discussion of the method is warranted.

PROBE performs a transitive search in determining which sequences are interrelated. If a pairwise search finds that sequences A and B are related, and a second search finds that sequences B and C are related, then sequences A and C must be related, even if a pairwise search between A and C failed to reveal a direct relationship. Through a series of BLAST searches, all such relationships are deduced iteratively until no new sequences are found. Upon assembly of this collection of related sequences, a series of alignments and realignments is performed until the alignment can no longer be improved. At this point, another round of database searches begins, using the best alignment, to find related sequences that were missed during the first pass. PROBE keeps performing these steps until the method converges.

One of the significant differences between PROBE and MoST is that PROBE requires only a single sequence to "seed" the search, although a family of sequences can be used. In

```
1 iteration
Block of 18 items resulted in 48 matches - 5 new
                                             ....:....|....:....|....:....|....:....|....:....|....:....|..   Score  Expected  Ratio
>gi|571471|gp|U16724|          31:  TKPAIRRLARRGGVKRISGLIYEETRTVLKTFLENVIRDSVTYTEHARRKTVTAMDVVYALKRQ   595,      0    5.29e-70
>gi|32097|gp|X00038|H          31:  TKPAIRRxARRGGVKRISGLIYEETRGVLKVFLENVIRDAVTYTEHAKRKTVTAMDVVYALKRQ   594,      0    8.39e-70
>pir|S03427|S03427 hi          31:  TKPAIRRLARRGGVKRISGLIYEETRGVLKVFLENVIRDAVTYTEHAKRKTVTAMDVVYrLKRQ   593,      0    1.22e-69
>gi|404467|gp|S64499|          31:  TKPAtRRLARRGGVKRISGLIYEETRGVLKVFLENVIRDAVTYTEHAKRKTVTALDVVYALKRQ   586,      0    2.56e-68
>pir|C47036|C47036 HM           4:  piapIgRiiknaGaeivSddarEalaKVLeakgEeiaenAVklakHagRKTVkAsDielAvKRm   -59,  0.017    0.000263
>sp P35059 H4_ACRFO H     4    30:  TKPAIRRLARRGGVKRISGLIYEETRGVLKVFLENVIRDAVTYTEHAKRKTVTAMDVVYALKRQ   608,      0    3.32e-72
>sp P02308 H4_WHEAT H     3    30:  TKPAIRRLARRGGVKRISGLIYEETRGVLKIFLENVIRDAVTYTEHARRKTVTAMDVVYALKRQ   607,      0    4.45e-72
>sp P02306 H4_CAEEL H     5    30:  TKPAIRRLARRGGVKRISGLIYEETRGVLKVFLENVIRDAVTYCEHAKRKTVTAMDVVYALKRQ   606,      0    6.53e-72
>sp P35057 H4_LYCES H    16    30:  TKPAIRRLARRGGVKRISGLIYEETRGVLKIFLENVIRDSVTYTEHARRKTVTAMDVVYALKRQ   605,      0    8.89e-72
>sp|P27996|H4_SOLST H    13    30:  TKPAIRRLARRGGVKRISGLIYEETRGVLKVFLENVIRDAVTYCEHAKRKTVTSMDVVYALKRQ   603,      0    1.9e-71
>pir|JN0688|JN0688 hi    15    31:  TKPAIRRLARRGGVKRISGLIYEETRGVLKVFLENVIRDAVTYTEHAKRKTVTALDVVYALKRQ   602,      0    2.79e-71

...

2 iteration
Block of 23 items resulted in 53 matches - 4 new

...
```

Figure 8.5   Sequences found by querying the alignment block in Figure 8.4 against the nonredundant sequence database (nr) using MoST. Details on the structure of the output can be found in the text.

MoST, a predetermined, ungapped alignment must be used as the input. While there is no guarantee that a machine-generated alignment is better than a user-determined manual alignment (more often, the opposite is true), any positional bias introduced by the hand-calculated alignment will be carried through the MoST search. MoST and PROBE handle the input set differently in that MoST does one alignment block at a time, whereas PROBE will split the input into multiple blocks, based on what is found during the iterative searches. Here, the user needs to decide whether the integrity of the block needs to be preserved, versus whether the block can be broken down into smaller component units, a decision that is probably best made by considering biological function. Finally, MoST is a "greedy" algorithm, in that sequences added in subsequent rounds of a search are never removed. Thus false positives will be propagated through a search, possibly introducing more false positives. PROBE eliminates unrelated sequences by means of a "jackknife" procedure: that is, putative false positives are removed from the data set, the databases are re-searched, and if the sequence is a true positive, the sequence is reintroduced into the data set.

PROBE commands are issued from the UNIX command line and take the following form:

```
probe fastafile database -s<int> [options] > outfile
```

where `fastafile` is the file containing the sequence that will seed the search, in FASTA format; `database` is the target database to be searched against; and the number following the `-s` flag is the random seed for the search, followed by any one of a number of options pertaining to score cutoffs, the maximum number of returned sequences, and the like. Runs take a substantial amount of time to complete, but the resulting output is well worth the investment. In one output file produced by PROBE (Figure 8.6), the sequence of amphoterin, a DNA-binding protein related to the high mobility group protein HMG-1, was used as the seed; two blocks were found, covering a total of 50 residues. Each block is optimally aligned

```
//
ID   XXX
AC   A00000
DE   amph.seq3
CC   log(prob_ratio) = 838.955
CC   comments
NU   2 blocks; 50 columns.
AL   ****************
     DPNTPKRNMSAFMFFS 12-27 gi|2058376|gnl|PID|e314000 10.16
     DPNAPKRALSSYMFFA 19-34 gi|155890 10.13
     DSNAPKRAMTSFMFFS 202-217 gi|162109 9.62
     STPKIPRPKNAFILFR 6-21 gi|805045 8.29
     DPNAPKRAKSAYMFWL 11-26 gi|455103 9.62
     ...

AL   ********************************
     QLGSLLGKRWKELTSTEREPYEEKARQDKERYER 45-78 gi|2058376|gnl|PID|e314000 15.91
     AIGKMIGAAWNALSDEEKKPYERMSDEDRVRYER 54-87 gi|155890 17.45
     EMSKAAGAAWKELGPEERKVYEEMAEKDKERYKR 231-264 gi|162109 17.11
     NISKIIGTKWKGLQPEDKAHWENLAEKEKLEHER 44-77 gi|805045 16.62
     VIDVSKAAGVEWGKVKDKSKYEKMASQDKQRYEA 40-73 gi|455103 3.64
     ...
```

Figure 8.6 Conserved blocks found by running PROBE using the sequence for human amphoterin as the search seed. The two alignment blocks produced when performing the search against GenPept are shown in this `.mtf` file generated by PROBE. Details on the structure of the output can be found in the text.

based on the statistics calculated during the PROBE run. For each sequence, the residue numbers of the sequence that are part of the block are shown, followed by a gi identifier and the calculated statistics for that entry. Output files produced by PROBE contain information on residue frequencies, as well as information content, statistical information, and lists of sequences rejected as a result of the jackknife procedure.

PRESENTATION METHODS

While the alignment methods presented above are quite rigorous in their determination of optimal alignments, their output often is not of publication quality. It is possible, though, to take the output from these programs and import the information into software whose job it is to make multiple sequence alignments more readable. The features built into these presentation methods often allow for much easier recognition of subtle sequence patterns present among all the sequences in the set, going further than the usual proclamation of a "consensus sequence."

MacBoxShade

MacBoxShade, or MacBox for short, is a Macintosh version of the VMS/UNIX utility BoxShade that provides a very simple mechanism for producing formatted outputs of multiple alignments. MacBox can read alignment files in GCG MSF format only, relying on other programs (such as ReadSeq) to do the conversion into the accepted style. While only one input format is supported, a number of output options are available; these include PostScript, for printing on a PostScript printer or viewing using a PostScript viewer, and PICT, the default Macintosh format for importing into wordprocessing or graphics applications. Through a number of simple dialog boxes, users can specify color schemes, the way in which residues are numbered, and options related to the calculation of a consensus sequence.

Two important dialogs are Sims and Groups, which control how a consensus sequence is calculated; the difference between the two is subtle but important. The Sims dialog defines what residues are considered to be similar to one another, and the relationships are not necessarily reciprocal. The Groups dialog allows the identification of discrete groups in which all the residues in the same group are considered to be the same; that is, if a group is defined as having lysine, arginine, and histidine, the occurrence of any one of those residues at a given position in an alignment is considered to be an exact match. It is important to check these two dialog boxes, since the user wants the consensus sequence calculated according to the default values.

To illustrate the use of MacBox, a number of histone H1 sequences and the sequence of a putative H1 from yeast were aligned and converted into MSF format. The MSF sequence file was opened from within MacBox, and the program was instructed to print a consensus sequence through the General dialog box. Within the same dialog box, the method by which a consensus sequence is displayed was changed to BLU, meaning that at a given position, nonconserved positions should be represented by a blank (B), conserved residues as a lowercase character (L), and identical residues should be shown as an uppercase character (U). To actually run the alignment, Display PICT was selected from the Do it! pulldown menu, generating the window shown in Figure 8.7. The consensus notation can be altered in the General dialog box as desired. Instead of shading according to similarity across all sequences, as was done here, the user can specify a single sequence in the alignment, in which case shading will be based on similarity to that one sequence alone.

For those without a Macintosh or UNIX-based machine, the original BoxShade program can be accessed over the Web, with pulldown menus taking the place of the dialogs described above. However, there is no ability to choose color schemes or to designate how a consensus should be represented, other than to specify that the consensus should be letter-based or symbol-based.

ALSCRIPT

ALSCRIPT is a UNIX- and PC-based program that allows users to neatly format multiple sequence alignments output in PostScript format; the alignments can then be printed to a PostScript printer or viewed using a PostScript viewer (Barton, 1993). Input to ALSCRIPT must be in one of three formats: as a block file, in CLUSTAL W format, or in GCG format. Conversion of file formats to one that can be read by ALSCRIPT is accomplished through the use of CLUS2BLC and MSF2BLC, programs which are part of the ALSCRIPT package. ALSCRIPT offers great flexibility in rendering an alignment: the user can specify fonts, the boxing of parts of the alignment, selective shading, the addition of text identifiers, the addition of symbols and lines, and the use of color. While ALSCRIPT itself cannot be used to generate or edit an alignment, it can calculate a consensus sequence and display residues matching the consensus appropriately. Judicious use of these and other features can reveal special features present in the sequences, such as charge distributions or sequence signatures.

An example of the ALSCRIPT command file format is shown in Figure 8.8. The command file is broken up into two logical parts, called Step 1 and Step 2. Step 1 commands control the overall appearance of the alignment: font faces, font sizes, page orientation, color definitions, and the like. Step 1 also gives the location of the input file (BLOCK_FILE)

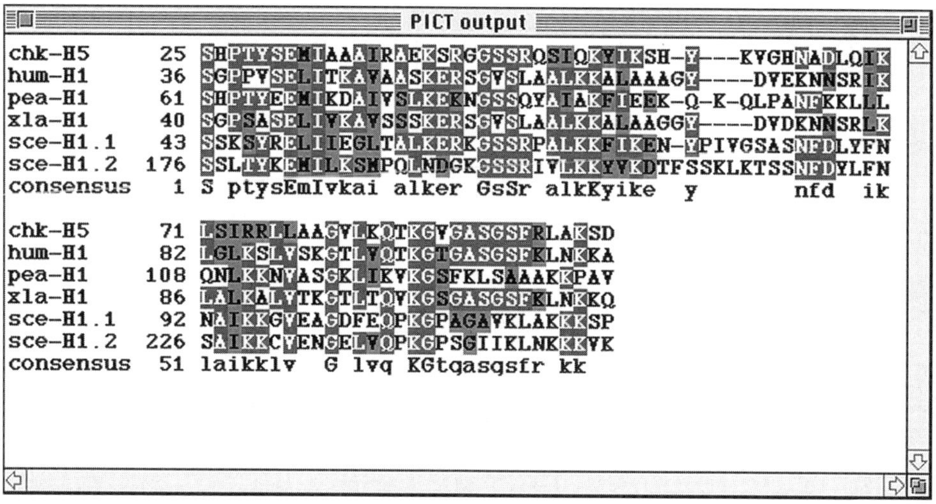

Figure 8.7 PICT output from MacBoxShade. The derived consensus is shown at the bottom of the figure. In the consensus, positions with absolute conservation are shown as uppercase letters, positions deemed as being "similar" are shown in lowercase, and unconserved positions have no representation in the consensus. Within the alignment, all positions identical to the consensus are shown in white against a blue background. All positions similar to the consensus are shown in black against a purple background. (See color plate.)

Step 1 Commands

```
# Input and output files
BLOCK_FILE      H1.blc
OUTPUT_FILE     H1.ps
# Page orientation, default font size
LANDSCAPE
POINTSIZE       10
MAX_SIDE        8.2
MIN_SIDE        6
# Give each font a number for reference
DEFINE_FONT 0   Helvetica-Bold DEFAULT
DEFINE_FONT 1   Helvetica-BoldOblique DEFAULT
DEFINE_FONT 4   Courier-Bold DEFAULT
# Define three colors in terms of RGB
DEFINE_COLOUR 3 1 0 0   # Red
DEFINE_COLOUR 2 1 1 0   # Yellow
DEFINE_COLOUR 1 0 0 1   # Blue
# Add sequences, two at the top, four after
# sequence 6.
ADD_SEQ         0 2
ADD_SEQ         6 4
# Don't use automatic numbering. The
# numbering scheme will follow in Step 2
NO_NUMBERS
# Signify end of Step 1 and beginning of Step 2
SETUP
```

Step 2 Commands

```
# Define fonts to be used in left-hand column
ID_FONT         ALL  4
# Alternate sequence labels
# Syntax: SUB_ID <seqnum> <newlabel>
SUB_ID      3   "chk-H5"     25"
SUB_ID      4   "hum-H1"     36"
    ...
# Box for each core region
# Syntax: BOX_REGION <res1> <seq1> <res2> <seq2>
BOX_REGION  6   3   15  8
BOX_REGION  22  3   23  8
# Color all Phe and Tyr residues blue
# Syntax: CCOL_CHARS <characters> <location> <color>
CCOL_CHARS  FY  ALL  3
# Make PDB box below sequence
# Make HELIX/COIL/STRAND followed by <res1> <seq> <res2>
FONT_REGION 1   10  79  11  1
HELIX       6   10  15
COIL        16  10  21
STRAND      22  10  23
    ...
TEXT        6   11  "Alpha 1"
TEXT        21  11  "Beta 1"
    ...
# Mask sequences to match first
# CALCONS calculates the consensus for the region
# CONSERVATION specifies "how conserved?"
# MASK commands do the coloring
CALCONS     1   3   79  8
mask SETUP
mask CONSERVATION ALL 5
mask SCOL   1   3   79  8   2
mask RESET
mask CONSERVATION ALL 10
mask SCOL   1   3   79  8   1
mask CCOL   1   3   79  8   99
mask RESET
# Place numbers at top of alignment, based on seq 1
# Syntax: TEXT <position> <seq> <text>
TEXT        6   1   "30"
TEXT        16  1   "40"
    ...
```

Figure 8.8 ALSCRIPT command file used to generate the multiple sequence alignment output shown in Figure 8.9. The command file is divided into Step 1 and Step 2 commands, with Step 1 commands controlling overall appearance of the alignment and Step 2 commands controlling specific residues or regions within the alignment. Comments (preceded by #) are included to show the purpose and syntax of each block of text. An ellipsis in a line indicates code removed for brevity.

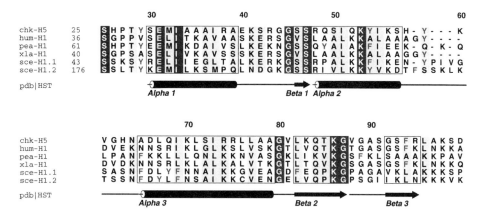

Figure 8.9 Output from the ALSCRIPT command file shown in Figure 8.8. The input data is the same as for the MacBoxShade alignment shown in Figure 8.7; note the differences between the two outputs, which primarily reflect the difference between speed and control. (See color plate.)

and the file to which the alignment should be written (OUTPUT_FILE). Step 2 deals with specific parts of the alignment, such as changing the identifiers that appear next to each sequence, boxing or shading particular residues or regions, annotating the alignment, and calculating consensus sequences. Examples of all of these are shown in Figure 8.8. Note the comment lines (beginning with #), which briefly explain the purpose of each block of code, along with the general syntax for most of the commands used here. The four numbers following the BOX_REGION command show how areas of the alignment are called; here, the first BOX_REGION command is followed by 6 3 15 8, meaning "box the region starting at residue 6 of sequence 3, all the way through to residue 15 of sequence 8." Well-written documentation is available for ALSCRIPT and can be obtained either over the Web or as part of the UNIX distribution of the program.

The sequences used for both the ALSCRIPT and MacBoxShade examples are the same, but the programs differ substantially in how the sequences can be rendered, as should be obvious from Figures 8.7 and 8.9. The trade-off here is ease of use: MacBoxShade is by far the easier program to use, since everything is dialog driven, but options are limited. ALSCRIPT provides much more in the way of output options, but as the format of the command file clearly shows, learning to format an output calls for a substantial time investment. In practice, ALSCRIPT command files can be developed as "modules" that are ported from alignment to alignment, with the user making the necessary adjustments to the numbering; a very professional-looking product results. The choice of alignment formatting tool will depend on the ultimate need of the user—whether for a quick representation or a publication-quality image.

World Wide Web Sites for Topics Presented in Chapter 8

ALIGNMENT METHODS

Clustal W	*http://www2.ebi.ac.uk/clustalw/*
MSA	*http://www.ibc.wustl.edu/ibc/msa.html*
MultAlin	*http://www.toulouse.inra.fr/cgi-bin/multalin.pl*

MOTIFS AND PATTERNS

BLOCKS	*http://blocks.fhcrc.org*
MoST	*ftp://ncbi.nlm.nih.gov/pub/koonin/most/*
Pfam	*http://www.sanger.ac.uk/Software/Pfam*
PROSITE	*http://expasy.hcuge.ch/sprot/prosite.html*
PROBE	*ftp://ncbi.nlm.nih.gov/pub/neuwald/probe1.0/*

PRESENTATION METHODS

ALSCRIPT	*http://geoff.biop.ox.ac.uk/manuals/alscript/alscript.html*
BoxShade	*http://ulrec3.unil.ch/software/BOX_form.html*
MacBoxShade	*ftp://ulrec3.unil.ch/pub/boxshade/MacBoxshade*

CONVERSION UTILITIES

ReadSeq	*http://dot.imgen.bcm.tmc.edu:9331/seq-util/Options/readseq.html*

REFERENCES

Bairoch, A. (1997). The PROSITE database: Its staus in 1997. Nucl. Acids Res. *25*, 217–221.

Barton, G. (1993). ALSCRIPT, a tool to format multiple sequence alignment. Protein Eng. *6*, 37–40.

Corpet, F. (1988). Multiple sequence alignment with hierarchical clustering. Nucl. Acids Res. *16*, 10881–10890.

Gribskov, M., McLachlan, A., and Eisenberg, D. (1987). Profile analysis: Detection of distantly-related proteins. Proc. Natl. Acad. Sci. U.S.A. *84*, 4355–4358.

Gribskov, M., Homyak, M., Edenfield, J., and Eisenberg, D. (1988). Profile scanning for three-dimensional structural patterns in protein sequences. Comput. Appl. Biosci. *4*, 61–66.

Henikoff, J. G., and Henikoff, S. (1996). BLOCKS database and its applications. Methods Enzymol. *266*, 88–105.

Higgins, D. G., Thompson, J. D., and Gibson, T. J. (1996). Using CLUSTAL for multiple sequence alignments. Methods Enzymol. *266*, 383–402.

Lüthy, R., Xenarios, I., and Bucher, P. (1994). Improving the sensitivity of the sequence profile method. Protein Sci. *3*, 139–146.

Neuwald, A. F., Liu, J. S., Lipman, D. J., and Lawrence, C. E. (1997). Extracting protein alignment models from the sequence database. Nucl. Acids Res. *25*, 1665–1677.

Sankoff, D. (1975). SIAM J. Appl. Math. *78*, 35.

Tatusov, R., Altschul, S., and Koonin, E. (1994). Detection of conserved segments in proteins: Iterative scanning of sequence databases with alignment blocks. Proc. Natl. Acad. Sci. U.S.A. *91*, 12091–12095.

## 9

Phylogenetic Analysis

Mark A. Hershkovitz and Detlef D. Leipe

National Center for Biotechnology Information
National Library of Medicine
National Institutes of Health
Bethesda, Maryland

Phylogenetics is the study of evolutionary relationships. Phylogenetic analysis is the means of inferring or estimating these relationships. The evolutionary history inferred from phylogenetic analysis is usually depicted as branching (treelike) diagrams, which represent a sort of pedigree of the inherited relationships among molecules ("gene trees"), organisms, or both. Phylogenetics is sometimes called cladistics, because the word "clade," a set of descendants from a single ancestor, is derived from the Greek word for branch. Macromolecules, especially sequences, have surpassed morphological and other organismal characters as the most popular form of data for phylogenetic analysis.

The objective of this volume notwithstanding, the expectation that an all-purpose phylogenetic analytical recipe can be delineated is unrealistic, if not naive (Hillis et al., 1993). Although numerous phylogenetic algorithms, procedures, and computer programs have been devised, their reliability and practicality are in all cases dependent on the structure and size of the data. The merits and pitfalls of various methods are the subject of often acrimonious debates in taxonomic/phylogenetic journals. Some of these debates are summarized in useful reviews of phylogenetics (Avise, 1994; Saitou, 1996; Li, 1997; Swofford et al., 1996a). An especially concise introduction to molecular phylogenetics is provided by Hillis et al. (1993).

The danger of generating incorrect results is inherently greater in computational phylogenetics than in many other fields of science. While other scientific analyses generally have empirical bases, phylogenetic analyses do not, except perhaps in the case of simulations and virions (Hillis et al., 1994). The physical events yielding a phylogeny happened in the past, and can only be inferred or estimated. Despite the well-documented limitations of available phylogenetics procedures, current biological literature is replete with examples of conclusions derived from the results of analyses in which data had been simply submitted

Bioinformatics: A Practical Guide to the Analysis of Genes and Proteins
Edited by A.D. Baxevanis and B.F.F. Ouellette
ISBN 0-471-19196-5, pages 189–230.   Copyright © 1998 Wiley-Liss, Inc.

to one or another phylogenetics program. Occasionally, the limiting factor in phylogenetic analysis is not so much in the facility of software application as in conceptual understanding of what the software is doing with the data.

This guide to phylogenetic analysis has several objectives. First, we attempt to introduce a conceptual approach that describes some of the most important principles underlying the most widely and easily applied methods of phylogenetic analysis of biological sequences. This approach recognizes that all phylogenetics methods assume that the observed differences between the sequences are the result of specific evolutionary processes that are modeled in the method. A model consists of the assumptions inherent in the method. Practical phylogenetic analysis should be conceived as search for a correct model, as much as a correct tree. In this context, we consider some of the particular models assumed by various popular methods and how these models might affect analysis of particular data sets. Finally, we provide some examples of the application of particular methods to the derivation of phylogenetic models and inferences of evolutionary history.

ELEMENTS OF PHYLOGENETIC MODELS

Phylogenetic tree-building methods presume particular evolutionary models (Penny et al., 1994). For example, all the widely used methods assume that evolutionary divergences are strictly bifurcating, so that the observed data can be represented by a treelike phylogeny. In a given data set, this model can be violated because of organismal hybridization, the transfer of genetic material between organisms. Thus, to the degree that the observed sequences were not strictly inherited, most phylogenetic methods will fail to give correct results.

Models inherent in phylogenetics methods make additional "default" assumptions:

1. The sequence is correct and originates from the specified source (Helbig and Seibold, 1996; Hershkovitz and Lewis, 1996; Soltis et al., 1997).
2. The sequences are homologous (i.e., are all descended from a shared ancestral sequence); they are not a mixture of different paralogs (diverged infragenomic forms of a sequence that descended from an ancestral gene duplication).
3. Each position in a sequence alignment is homologous with every other in that alignment.
4. Each of multiple sequences included in a common analysis has a common phylogenetic history with the others (e.g., there are no mixtures of nuclear and organellar sequences).
5. The sampling of taxa is adequate to resolve the problem of interest.
6. Sequence variation among the samples is representative of the broader group of interest.
7. The sequence variability in the sample contains phylogenetic signal adequate to resolve the problem of interest.

There are additional assumptions that are default in some methods but can be at least partially corrected for in others:

8. The sequences in the sample evolved according to a single stochastic process.
9. All positions in the sequence evolved according to the same stochastic process.
10. Each position in the sequence evolved independently.

Errors in published phylogenetic analyses can often be attributed to violations of one of the foregoing assumptions, especially inasmuch as the popular methods have not been able to detect such violations. Every sequence data set must be evaluated in view of these assumptions in conjunction with the analytical process, as that described next.

PHYLOGENETIC DATA ANALYSIS: ALIGNMENT, SUBSTITUTION MODEL BUILDING, TREE BUILDING, AND TREE EVALUATION

The four steps in phylogenetic analysis of DNA sequences are alignment, determining the substitution model, tree building, and tree evaluation. The computational procedures for executing these steps have commonly been undertaken independently, but they all are integral parts of phylogenetic analysis.

The present discussion emphasizes methods for analysis of DNA sequences that have diverged primarily (although not necessarily completely) by means of base and codon substitutions. The principles apply to protein sequences, but the greater biochemical diversity of amino acids requires more mathematical parameters. Thus, references to nucleotide bases in the following discussion generally apply to amino acids and codons. Protein-specific problems and procedures are reviewed elsewhere (Felsenstein, 1996).

Because the tree-building criterion has some bearing on the alignment and substitution model, it is necessary to introduce these methods at the outset. The three major tree-building criteria are distance, maximum parsimony (MP), and maximum likelihood (ML). Distance trees use pairwise divergence estimates of all sequences in the data to determine tree topology and branch lengths. Maximum parsimony finds the tree that explains with the fewest number of discrete steps all the base differences in a multiple sequence alignment. Maximum likelihood finds the topology and branch lengths that have the highest probability of producing the observed multiple sequence alignment. These methods are discussed in greater detail later.

BUILDING THE DATA MODEL (ALIGNMENT)

Phylogenetic sequence data usually consists of a multiple sequence alignment, that is, the individual, aligned-base positions, commonly referred to in phylogenetics literature as "sites." These sites are equivalent to "characters" in theoretical phylogenetic discussions, and the actual base (or gap) occupying a site is the "character state." An exception to this generalization is the STATALIGN program (Thorne and Kishino, 1992), which estimates phylogeny using raw, unaligned sequences and produces no multiple alignment.

Multiple alignment methods are reviewed in Chapter 7. This discussion reviews alignment methods in the context of phylogenetic analysis. Aligned sequence positions subjected to phylogenetic analysis represent a priori phylogenetic conclusions because the sites themselves (not the actual bases) are effectively assumed to be genealogically homologous (Mindell, 1991; Wheeler, 1994). Thus, for phylogenetic purposes, the alignment procedure is part and parcel of the phylogenetic analysis.

Steps in building the alignment include selection of the alignment procedure(s) and extracting a phylogenetic data set from the alignment. The latter procedure requires determination of how ambiguously aligned regions and insertion/deletions (indels, or gaps) will be treated in the tree-building procedure.

Multiple Alignment Procedures

Multiple alignment procedures and computational subroutines can be characterized by the following attributes and options:

Computer dependence: none; partial; complete

Phylogeny invocation: none; a priori; recursive

Alignment parameter estimation: a priori; dynamic; recursive

Aligned features: primary structure (i.e., sequence); higher order structures

Mathematical optimization: statistical; nonstatistical

A typical alignment procedure applied in phylogenetics studies involves the application of CLUSTAL W followed by manual alignment editing and submission to a tree-building program. This procedure can be characterized by the following attributes: (1) partial computational dependence (i.e., manually edited), (2) phylogeny criteria invoked a priori (i.e., the "guide tree"), (3) alignment parameter estimation either a priori or dynamically (optional), (4) alignment of primary structure (partial secondary structural basis optional in the case of hydrophilic amino acids), and (5) mathematical optimization nonstatistical. These options bear on phylogenetic analysis as described in the subsections that follow.

Computer Dependence Fully computational multiple alignment is sometimes advocated on the grounds that manual editing is inexplicit and/or unobjective (Gatesy et al., 1993). The MALIGN (Wheeler and Gladstein, 1994) and TreeAlign (Hein, 1990, 1994) programs attempt to implement fully computational procedures that optimize alignment according to a phylogenetic function, specifically an MP tree determined from preliminary multiple alignment. Usually, however, a fully computational approach is adopted under the assumption that the program will produce the "correct" alignment. Manual alignment editing has been advocated (e.g., Thompson et al., 1994) because alignment algorithms and programs are not optimally adapted for phylogenetic alignment.

Phylogenetic Criteria Many computational multiple alignment methods (e.g., CLUSTAL, PileUp, ALIGN in ProPack) align according to an explicitly phylogenetic criterion (a "guide tree"), which is generated on the basis of pairwise sequence alignability. SAM (Hughey et al., 1996) and MACAW (Lawrence et al., 1993) are examples of multiple alignment programs that do not explicitly invoke phylogenetic criteria, although it is possible to manipulate parameters in these programs to mimic phylogenetic processes.

If a tree is used to generate the alignment for phylogenetic analysis, then the tree inferred from the alignment logically should have the same topology. The guide tree (Figure 9.1) from CLUSTAL is formatted as a PHYLIP tree file and can be imported in tree-drawing programs like TreeTool (Xwindows), TreeDraw (Macintosh), PHYLODENDRON (Macintosh), TREEVIEW (Macintosh, Microsoft Windows) or the tree-drawing tool in PAUP (Figure 9.1; Macintosh, Microsoft Windows). One could work backward and specify a guide tree for the CLUSTAL alignment, but this approach does not appear to be used in practice. Some programs are designed to simultaneously (recursively) optimize an alignment and a phylogenetic tree (e.g., TreeAlign and MALIGN). In theory, an optimal simultaneous solution or set of solutions to an alignment/phylogeny problem exists, but the hazard of the recursive approach lies in the possibility of canalizing the result toward a wrong or incomplete solution (Thorne and Kishino, 1992). Thus, following the tree-building analysis based on the alignment, one should consider whether slightly suboptimal alternative trees would be favored using an alternative alignment.

Alignment Parameter Estimation   The most important parameters in an alignment method are those that determine the placement of indels in an alignment of length-variable sequences. The placement of indels will depend on all elements of the evolutionary model (including, e.g., nucleotide transition/transversion rates). As with the guide tree, these parameters should be consistent with those observed in the tree inferred from the alignment. Alignment parameters should also vary dynamically with evolutionary divergence (Thompson et al., 1994), such that base mismatches are more likely as the sequences become more divergent. Alignment parameters should also be adjusted to prevent closely related overrepresented sequences from entraining alignment of underrepresented sequences (Thompson et al., 1994, Hughey et al., 1996). This is accomplished by downweighting the alignment score contribution of the closely related sequences. Both these dynamic parameter adjustments are implemented in CLUSTAL, and sequence weighting is implemented in SAM.

Alignment of Primary Versus Higher Order Sequence Structure   Aligning according to secondary or tertiary sequence structure is considered phylogenetically more reliable than sequence-based alignment because confidence in homology assessment is greater in comparisons of complex (structures) than of simple (nucleotides, amino acids) characters. In addition, structural approaches permit recognition of functional, hence evolutionary, nonindependence of particular sites. There does not appear to be any computational facilitation of phylogeny-based structural multiple alignment (i.e., sequence alignment forced to conform to the evolution of structure consistent with phylogeny). A heuristic, manual approach to structural alignment of ribosomal DNA involves examining patterns of correlated substitutions (Figure 9.2) (Gutell et al., 1994), but this "correlation" must be inferred on the basis of multiple independent compensatory mutations on a phylogenetic tree (cf. Harvey and Pagel, 1991).

Mathematical Optimization   Some alignment programs (e.g., MACAW, SAM) optimize according to a statistical model, but the relationship of these statistics to phylogenetic models is not clear. No methods are available for determining whether one multiple alignment is significantly better than another according to a phylogenetic model.

Summary: Which Alignment Procedure Is Best for Phylogenetic Analysis?
Unless phylogenetic relations are known beforehand, there is no clear way to determine which alignment procedure is best for a given phylogenetic analysis (cf. Morrison and Ellis, 1997). In general, however, it is inadvisable to simply subject a computer-generated alignment to a tree-building procedure because the latter is blind to errors in the former. This caution applies especially to tree-building programs included in alignment packages (e.g., CLUSTAL and TREE in ProPack) (Feng and Doolittle, 1996), since the tree-building methods in these programs are not rigorous. The entire alignment should be scrutinized in

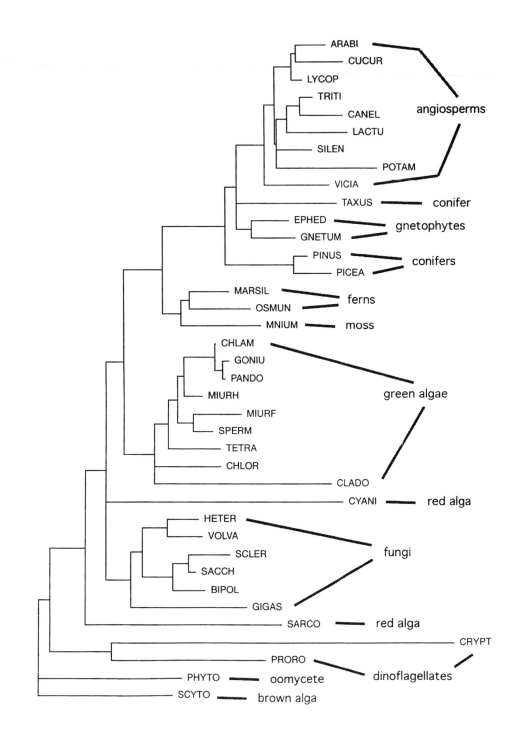

Figure 9.1 CLUSTAL guide tree for 5.8S rDNA sequences of selected plants, fungi, and protists. The taxa and sequences corresponding to the acronyms are described elsewhere (Hershkovitz and Lewis, 1996). The tree is a neighbor-joining (distance) resolution of pairwise sequence similarities determined by pairwise alignment according to specified (in this case, default) gap penalties in CLUSTAL. Similarity is calculated as the proportion of pairwise shared bases, ignoring gap positions in either sequence. The tree can be generated as an end product or as a preliminary step in a multiple-alignment procedure. Either way, it is saved to a PHYLIP-formatted treefile. For the multiple-alignment procedure, the guide tree topology determines the sequence input order (outermost clusters are aligned first) and the branch lengths determine the sequence weights. This tree includes (see Hershkovitz and Lewis, 1996) several groupings that contradict broader evidence (e.g., polyphyly of conifers and red algae; monophyly of ferns plus moss). Such inaccuracies potentially mislead the multiple alignment. This tree was drawn and printed using the tree-drawing feature in the Macintosh version of PAUP, followed by aesthetic modification in Macintosh graphics programs. The general tree-viewing and -drawing protocol for PAUP is as follows: (1) execute a PAUP file containing the same taxon names as the tree; (2) import the treefile using the `GETTREES` command, specifying the option to retain the branch lengths in the treefile; (3) draw the tree using the `PRINT TREES` command, again specifying use of input branch lengths; and (4) save the tree to a PICT file using the Preview option in the pop-up Print Trees menu. Note that for using the PAUP tree-drawing tool, the content of the executed datafile (sequences and alignment) is not important, as long as the taxon names are the same. There may even be additional taxa in the datafile, as long as these are ignored using the `DELETE TAXA` command.

view of independent phylogenetic evidence and assumptions that can be made concerning molecular structure–function and base substitution processes.

Extraction of a Phylogenetic Data Set from an Alignment

In alignments that include length variation, the phylogenetic data set usually is not identical to the alignment. Even in alignments of length-invariable sequences, the data set can be different—for example, when only first and second codon positions are to be analyzed. This topic is referred to again in the section on the substitution model.

In the case of length-variable sequences, the degree of difference between an alignment and the phylogenetic data set is determined mainly by the extent of alignment ambiguities and the treatment of indels. The treatment of indels will depend both on the perceived phylogenetic information they contain and on the tree-building method. The most extreme way to treat indels is to remove from the analysis all sites that include gaps (cf. Swofford et al., 1996a). This approach has the advantage of permitting all the variation in the sequences to be described in terms of the substitution model, without the need for an ad hoc model to account for indels. In addition, a gap-free data set requires no consideration of gap interpretations specific to particular tree-building methods. The disadvantage of this approach is that phylogenetic signal contained in the indel regions is discarded.

Including indel regions in the data but treating all gap scores as missing offers the advantage of extracting from base variation information that occurs at sites also including gaps. Some of the length-variable regions may, however, be poorly alignable in some or all sequences. In this case, the actual bases that cannot be confidently aligned should also be rescored as missing. The disadvantage of this approach is that the MP and ML tree-building methods will interpret missing data scores as essentially zero divergence, whereas the actual data underlying the missing data scores, whether gaps or unalignable bases, generally reflects high divergence. The distance tree-building methods in PAUP 4.0 (see below) permit distances for gap regions to be extrapolated from nongapped regions.

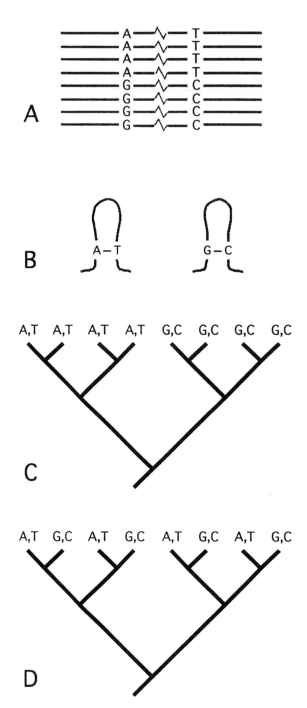

Figure 9.2 Phylogenetic evidence in structural RNA sequence alignment. (*A*) Hypothesized alignment of eight sequences showing alignment of bases putatively paired in secondary structure, separated by a length-variable (indicated by zigzag) loop region. (*B*) Illustration of putative secondary structural pairing relationship. (*C, D*) Alternative phylogenetic relationships among sequences with A and T versus those with G and C. The alignment in (*C*) is consistent with the phylogeny, but not correlated with it, because the substitution between A-T and G-C takes place only once. Thus, support for the alignment must come from biochemical or statistical evidence. In (*D*) there are multiple independent substitutions between A-T and G-C; hence the alignment is supported by phylogenetic evidence.

Maximum parsimony (MP; see below) is the only method that permits incorporation of alignable gaps as characters. These can be included in either of two ways: as an additional character state (a "fifth" nucleotide base or "twenty-first" amino acid), or as a set of characters independent of base substitutions. The first approach is not tenable for gaps occupying more than one site, for these will be counted as independent character state changes at each site so occupied. The latter approach is useful for analyzing an alignment in which subsets of sequences contain perfectly aligned gaps. A set of gap characters can be appended to the aligned sequence data set, or the gaps can be scored "in place" by using the extra base approach but scoring only one of the gap positions in a sequence as a gap and the remainder as missing. These approaches can be implemented using PAUP.

For some alignments, procedures that ignore all gap scores or all sites including gap scores are less than ideal. However, there is not yet any program that allows one to ignore individual sites in individual sequences. When alignment might be unambiguous within groups of sequences but ambiguous among them, alignment "surgery" is warranted, to ensure that unambiguous information relevant to groups of sequences can be retained and ambiguous information removed.

An example of alignment surgery is given in Figure 9.3. In gapped regions, one should determine whether alternative alignments seem reasonably plausible and, just as important, whether they might bias the tree-building analysis. When alignment ambiguities are resolved manually, phylogenetic relations, substitution processes (e.g., transitions vs. transversions), and base composition should be considered. It is perfectly reasonable at this stage to resolve ambiguities in favor of phylogenetic evidence. In a sequence region prone to length variability, the alignment of very distantly related sequences or groups sequences can be spread out laterally (i.e., with artificial gaps introduced and scored as missing), with the result that only the regions of the closely related sequences are juxtaposed. Ambiguously aligned sites in particular sequences can be rescored as missing. The advantage of this approach is that unambiguous information relevant to particular sequences can be retained. The disadvantage is that parsimony and likelihood tree-building methods can interpret "missing" scores only as zero divergence.

Alignments derived using MALIGN (Wheeler and Gladstein, 1994) and TreeAlign do not require postalignment data modification for analyses using the tree-building methods built into these programs, although the alignments may still include ambiguities of the very same sort that would require editing for analysis by another program. As mentioned earlier, these programs allow recursive optimization of alignment parameters according to the best MP phylogenetic tree generated by the alignment. MALIGN also permits tree building based on concatenated alternative alignments optimized using a range of gap costs. In this method, termed the "elision" procedure, alignment features that occur in the most alternative alignments are effectively weighted. This provides a means of capturing the quantum of sequence divergence that is ignored when ambiguously aligned regions are scored as missing, since all possible alignments of such regions will tend to show maximal sequence divergence in these regions. The sites in ambiguously aligned regions probably are not homologous, however, hence will likely introduce noise or bias in the tree.

DETERMINING THE SUBSTITUTION MODEL

The substitution model should be given the same emphasis as alignment and tree building. As implied in the preceding section, the substitution model influences both alignment and

B

```
        116    122-144                    155          [   122'-141'        ]
 1 ARABI GCGCCC ???CAAGCCTTCT?GGCCG????  AGGGCACGTCT  ??????????????????
 2 LYCOP GCGCCC ???GAAGCCATTT?GGCCG????  AGGGCACGTCT  ???????????????????
 3 triti GCGCCC ???GAGGCCACTC?GGCCG????  AGGGCACGCCT  ???????????????????
 4 LACTU GCGCCC ???GAAGCCATCC?GGCTG????  AGGGCACGCCT  ???????????????????
 5 SILEN GCGCCC ???GAAGC?-TTC?GGCTG????  AGGGCACGTCT  ???????????????????
 6 vicia GCGCCC ???GATGCCATTA?GGTTG????  AGGGCACGTCT  ???????????????????
 7 CANEL GCGCCC ???GAGGCCACTA?GGCTG????  AGGGCTCGCCT  ???????????????????
 8 potam GCGCCC ???TAAGCTTCCG?GGCCG????  AGGGCAAGCCT  ???????????????????
 9 ephed G-GCCC ???GAAGC?-TC?CGCCA???    G-GCCCCACGTCT ???????????????????
10 gnetu G-GCCC TCCG?GC?-TA?GGCCG????   AGGGCACGTCT  ???????????????????
11 PINUS GCGCCC ???GAGGC?-TC?GGTCG????   AGGGCACGTCT  ???????????????????
12 PICEA GCGCCC ???GAG?C?-TC?GGTCG????   AGGGCACGTCT  ???????????????????
13 TAXUS GGCCCG ???GAG-C?-TC?GGCCG????   AGGGCACGTCT  ???????????????????
14 marsi G-GCCC ???GAGGC?-TC?GTCCG????   AGGGCACGTCT  ???????????????????
15 osmun G-GCCC ???GCGGC?-TC?GTCCA????   AGGGCATGTCC  ???????????????????
16 mnium GCGCCC ???GAGGC?-TC?GTCCG????   AGGGCATTTCC  ???????????????????
17 CHLAM GCGCTC ???GAGGC?-TTC?GGCCA????  AGAGCATGTCT  ???????????????????
18 SPERM GCGCTC ???GAGGC?-TTC?GGCCG????  AGAGCATGTTT  ???????????????????
19 TETRA GCGCTC ???GAGGC?-CTC?GGCCA????  AGAGCACGCCT  ???????????????????
20 CHLOR GCGCTC ???GAGAC?-CTC?GGTCA????  AGAGCATGTCT  ???????????????????
21 CLADO GCGCTC ??AAGTC?-TAC?GGACT????   TGAGCATGTCT  ??????????????????
22 HETER GCGCCC ??T?????????????????     AGG-CACGCCT  TTT?GGT-ATT???CCGA
23 VOLVA GCGCTC ?????????????????????    AGAGCATGCCT  TTT?GGCCATT???CCGA
24 SCLER GCGCCC ?????????????????????    GGGGCATGCCT  CTT?GGT-ATT???CCGG
25 sacch GCGCCC ?????????????????????    GGGGCATGCCT  CTT?GGT-ATT???CCAG
26 BIPOL GCGCCC ?????????????????????    AGGGCATGCCT  TTT?GGT-ATT???CCAA
27 GLOMU GCACTC ?????????????????????    GGAGTATGCCT  CCT?GGT-ATT???CCGG
28 CYANI GCGCTT ?????????????????????    GGAGCACGTCT  ???????????????????
29 SARCO GCGCTC ?????????????????????    GCAG-?TGTCT  ???????????????????
30 PHYTO GCGCTC ?????????????????????    GGAGTATGCCT  ???????????????????
31 SCYTO GCG-TT ?????????????????????    GGAGCATGCTT  ???????????????????
32 crypt G??-CT ?????????????????????    ?????TGTCA   ???????????????????
33 PRORO GCGCTT ?????????????????????    AAGGCATGCCT  ???????????????????
```

A

```
        116    122-144                    155
 1 ARABI GCGCCC ---CAAGCCTTCT-GGCCG----  AGGGCACGTCT
 2 LYCOP .....C ---GAAGCCATTT-GGCCG----  A..........
 3 triti .....C ---GAGGCCACTC-GGCCG----  A.........C.
 4 LACTU .....C ---GAAGCCATCC-GGCTG----  A.........C.
 5 SILEN .....C ---GAAGC--TTC-GGCTG----  A..........
 6 vicia .....C ---GATGCCATTA-GGTTG----  A..........
 7 CANEL .....C ---GAGGCCACTA-GGCTG----  A.....T..C.
 8 potam .....C ---TAAGCTTCCG-GGCCG----  A.....A.C.
 9 ephed .-...C ---GAAGCC--TC-CGCCA----  A..........
10 gnetu .-...C TCCG-AGCC--TA-GGCCG----  A..........
11 PINUS ....TC ---GAGGC--TC-GGTCG----   A..........
12 PICEA ....TC ---GAGNCC--TC-GGTCG----  A..........
13 TAXUS .GC.G  ---GAG-C--TC-GGCCG----   A..........
14 marsi ....TC ---GAGGC--TC-GTCCG----   A..........
15 osmun .-...C ---GCGGC---TC-GTCCA----  A.....T.C..
16 mnium ....TC ---GAGGC---TC-GTCCG----  A.....TT..C
17 CHLAM ...TC  ---GAGGC--TTC-GGCCA----  A.A...T..T.
18 SPERM ...TC  ---GAGGC--TTC-GGCCG----  A.A...T..T.
19 TETRA ...TC  ---GAGGC--CTC-GGCCA----  A.A.....C.
20 CHLOR ...TC  ---GAGAC--CTC-GGTCA----  A.A...T....
21 CLADO ...TC  ---AAGTC--TAC-GGACT----  T.A...T....
22 HETER ....C  TTT--GGT-ATT----CCGA---- A.-...C...
23 VOLVA ...TC  TTT--GGCCATT----CCGA---- A.A...T.C.
24 SCLER ...C   CTT--GGT-ATT----CCGG---- G.....T.C.
25 sacch ....C  CTT--GGT-ATT----CCAG---- G.....T.C.
26 BIPOL ...C   TTT--GGT-ATT----CCAA---- C.....T.C.
27 GLOMU ...TC  CCT--GGT-ATT----CCGG---- G.A..T.C.
28 CYANI ...TT  TC--AGGAGAATTTATTTTCCT   G.A........
29 SARCO ...TC  GC---GGTAA-TC------CT    GCA...-T...
30 PHYTO .A.TT  CCG--GGTTAGTC----CTG---- G.A.T.T.C.
31 SCYTO ...-TT CCG--GGATATGC----CTG---- G.A..T.CT.
32 crypt .---CT CC---AGC--TGA------CT---- .....T...A
33 PRORO ...TT  TCG--GGATATCC----CTG---- AA....T.C.
```

198

Figure 9.3   Alignment modification for phylogenetic analysis. (*A*) Alignment showing a length-variable region (boxed) of 5.8S rDNA for the taxa in the guide tree of Figure 9.1. Taxa 1–8 are angiosperms; 9 and 10, gnetophytes; 11–13, conifers; 14 and 15, ferns; 16, moss; 17–21, green algae; 22–27, fungi; and 28–33, protists. The alignment positions correspond to those published elsewhere (Hershkovitz and Lewis, 1996). Each sequence is unique in the shaded region. Taxa represented in the Figure 9.1 tree having the same sequence as any shown here were omitted for brevity. Note that taxa grouped in the guide tree (based on the entire sequence) appear to form alignment groups in the length-variable region. On a pairwise basis, alternative alignments of some of the distantly related taxa seem plausible. For example, if moved two spaces to the left, the TAC in the center of the CLADO sequence might appear to align better with YAY in several angiosperms than the YYC in other green algae. Sufficient sampling, however, shows that YAY is not universal in the angiosperms, and the guide tree supports the present alignment, which allows no length variability in green algae. In the absence of sufficient sampling, a guide tree, or other prior phylogenetic evidence, no such conclusion could be drawn. Note also that the taxa of the green plant lineage (1–21) do not align well with the fungi and protists. The variability in the shaded region and the divergences indicated in the guide tree suggest that there is no true alignment between these distantly related groups, that the alignment indicated is arbitrary, and that the actual bases are not likely homologous. (*B*) The same alignment, modified as follows for phylogenetic analysis: (1) the fungi and protists are rescored as "missing" for all positions in the shaded region, where alignment with the green plant lineage is ambiguous; (2) the length-variable regions of the fungi were appended to the end of the alignment, because these sequences are alignable among fungi and include phylogenetically useful variation; and (3) multiple-position gaps were rescored as one gap position and the rest missing, so that in MP analysis, multiposition gaps are not counted as several independent deletions. The length-variable region of protists was not appended to the end of the alignment because both the alignment and the guide tree indicate that the original alignment is arbitrary.

tree building; hence a recursive approach is warranted. At the present time, two elements of the substitution model can be computationally assessed for nucleotide data (Swofford, 1997), but not for amino acid or codon data (Felsenstein, 1996). One element is the model of substitution between particular bases; the other is the relative rate of overall substitution among different sites in the sequence. Simple computational procedures have not been developed for assessing more complex variables (e.g., site- or lineage-specific substitution models). Likewise, such complex variables cannot yet be interpreted by existing tree-building software.

Models of Substitution Rates Between Bases

In general, substitutions are more frequent between bases that are biochemically more similar. In the case of DNA, the four types of transition (A $\to$ G, G $\to$ A, C $\to$ T, T $\to$ C) are usually more frequent than the eight types of transversion (A $\to$ C, A $\to$ T, C $\to$ G, G $\to$ T, and the reverse). Such biases will affect the estimated divergence between two sequences.

Specification of relative rates of substitution among particular residues usually takes the form of a square matrix; the number of rows/columns is 4 in the case of bases, 20 in the case of amino acids (e.g., PAM matrices), and 61 in the case of codons (excluding stop codons). The off-diagonal elements of the matrix correspond to the relative costs of going from one base to another. The diagonal elements represent the cost of having the same base in different sequences.

The cost schedule can be fixed a priori, to ensure that the tree-building method will tally an exact cost for each substitution incurred. Fixed-cost matrices are character state weight matrices and are applied in MP tree building (Figure 9.4). When such weights are applied, the method is referred to as "weighted parsimony." For distance and ML tree building, the costs can be derived from instantaneous rate matrices representing ML estimators of the

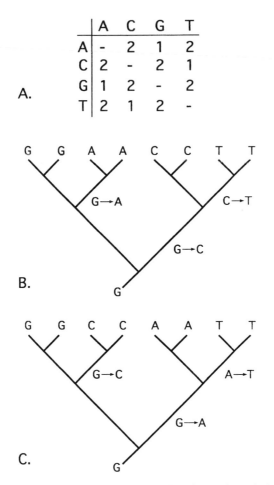

Figure 9.4 Character weight matrix and application in MP phylogenetic analysis. (A) Matrix indicating that a transversion substitution costs twice that of a transition. Since according to MP bases shared between two sequences cannot ever have changed, diagonal elements of the matrix are ignored. (B, C) Two phylogenetic resolutions and reconstructions of the evolution of a hypothetical pattern of aligned bases at a particular site in eight sequences. With unweighted MP, both reconstructions (among several others) have the same cost (three steps), hence they are equally acceptable. With the weight matrix in (A), the reconstruction of (B) requires four steps, and the reconstruction of (C) requires five. Thus, the first reconstruction (B) and others requiring four steps are preferred.

probability that a particular type of substitution will occur (Figure 9.5). While the MP weight matrix is simple arithmetic, application of the distance and ML rate matrices can involve complex algebra. To avoid blind application of possibly inappropriate methods, practitioners are well advised to familiarize themselves with the underlying theory (see Li, 1997, and/or Swofford et al., 1996a).

In practice, the "forward" and "reverse" substitution rates are presumed to be the same. This substitution model is said to be "time reversible"; it has the quality of being "stationary" in that there is no predicted change in overall base frequencies. In a particular phylogenetic history, the forward and reverse rates might actually differ, which would be

$$
\begin{array}{cccc}
 & \text{A} & \text{C} & \text{G} & \text{T} \\
\begin{array}{c} \text{A} \\ \text{C} \\ \text{G} \\ \text{T} \end{array} &
\left[\begin{array}{cccc}
-(a_1+a_2+a_3) & a_1 & a_2 & a_3 \\
a_4 & -(a_4+a_5+a_6) & a_5 & a_6 \\
a_7 & a_8 & -(a_7+a_8+a_9) & a_9 \\
a_{10} & a_{11} & a_{12} & -(a_{10}+a_{11}+a_{12})
\end{array} \right]
\end{array}
$$

Figure 9.5 Simplified substitution rate matrix used in ML and distance phylogenetic analysis. The matrix is analogous to the weight matrix in Figure 9.4, but the actual computation of divergence involves more complex algebra and cannot be determined by simply counting steps between bases. The off-diagonal values a_n represent a product of an instantaneous rate of change, a relative rate between the different substitutions, and the frequency of the target base. In practice, the forward rates (upper triangular values) are presumed to equal the reverse rates (corresponding lower triangular values). The diagonal elements are nonzero, which effectively accounts for the possibility that more divergent sequences are more likely to share the same base by chance. In the simplest model of sequence evolution (the Jukes–Cantor model), all values of a are the same: all substitution types and base frequencies are presumed equal.

manifest in different base frequencies in different sequences. This "nonstationary" condition cannot be accommodated in conventional substitution weight or rate matrices. An alternative computational means of tree building under a nonstationary substitution model ("log-det") is discussed at the end of this section.

Character state weight matrices have usually been estimated more or less by eye, but they can also be derived from a rate matrix. For example, if it is presumed that each of the two transitions occurs at double the frequency of each transversion, a weight matrix can simply specify, for example, that the cost of A-G is 1 and the cost of A-T is 2 (Figure 9.4). (The parsimony method dictates that the diagonal elements of the matrix, or the cost of having the same base in different sequences, be zero. This proves to be a shortcoming of parsimony—see below.) In the subsequent tree-building step, this set of assumptions will minimize the overall number of transversions and tend to cluster sequences differing mainly by transitions.

Any type of time-reversible nucleotide substitution model can be envisioned with Figure 9.5, merely by differentiating between any one rate and any other, in any combination, up to the maximum of six parameters, in which each rate is unique (Swofford et al., 1996a; Li, 1997). Additional parameters are needed if the equilibrium base frequencies are unequal. If the substitution model presumes that equilibrium base frequencies are equal when they are not, the resulting phylogenetic trees may be distorted (Li, 1997).

The paralinear (Lake, 1994) or "log-det" (Lockhart et al., 1994) transformation corrects for nonstationarity (see Swofford et al., 1996a). In this method, which is applicable only to distance tree building, the numbers of raw substitutions of each type and in each direction are tallied for each sequence pair in a 4×4 matrix like Figure 9.6. Each matrix has an algebraic determinant, the log of which becomes a factor in estimating sequence divergence, hence the name "log-det." Pairwise comparisons of sequences having various and assorted patterns of base frequencies will yield a variety of matrix patterns, hence a variety of determinant values. Thus, each estimated pairwise distance will be affected by the determinant peculiar to each pair, which effectively allows the substitution model to be different for each, hence to vary along different branches of a phylogenetic tree. Log-det is especially sensitive to among-site rate heterogeneity (see below), since base frequency bias can exist only in sites that are subject to variation.

Sclerotinium sclerotiorum

		A	C	G	T	total
	A	340	6	13	4	363
Spinacia	C	10	229	6	36	281
oleracea	G	25	8	229	12	372
	T	5	22	6	312	345
	total	380	265	352	364	1361

Figure 9.6   Pairwise sequence comparison. The table compares 1361 sites of 18S rDNA aligned between spinach (*Spinacia oleracea*) and a rust fungus (*Sclerotinium sclerotiorum*). The rows indicate the distribution of bases in the fungus aligned to particular bases in spinach. The columns indicate the reverse. The diagonal values are the number of sitewise identities between the sequences. Note the AT bias in the fungus: 83 (10 + 36 + 25 + 12) sites that are G or C in spinach are A or T in the fungus. In contrast, only 47 sites (6 + 22 + 13 + 6) that are G or C in the fungus are A or T in spinach. This bias is muted in simple comparison of base frequencies in the two sequences (the totals) because most sites are the same in both sequences and are probably mutationally constrained. Note also the obviously larger number of transition (13 + 36 + 25 + 22 = 96) versus transversion (6 + 4 + 10 + 6 + 8 + 12 + 5 + 6 = 57) substitutions, and that C-T transitions account for 58/153 total differences. The data shown can be generated using the PAUP or MEGA programs.

Models of Among-Site Substitution Rate Heterogeneity

In addition to variation in substitution patterns, variation in substitution rates among different sites in a sequence has been shown to profoundly affect the results of tree building (Swofford et al., 1996a). The most obvious example of among-site rate variation, or heterogeneity, is that evident among the three codon positions in a coding sequence. The third codon position tends to be much more variable than the first two. For this reason, many phylogenetic analyses of coding sequences exclude the third codon position. In some cases, however, rate variation patterns are more subtle (e.g., those corresponding to conserved regions of proteins or rRNA).

Approaches to the estimation of substitution rate heterogeneity are the nonparametric models (W. M. Yang et al., 1996), the invariants model, and the gamma distribution models (Swofford et al., 1996a). The nonparametric approach derives categories of relative rates for particular sites. This approach can be used with MP tree building simply by weighting particular sites according to relative mutation frequency, although such weighting tends to require prior knowledge of the true tree. The approach is also applicable to ML tree building, but it is considered computationally impractical (W. M. Yang et al., 1996). The invariants approach estimates a proportion of sites that are not free to vary. The remaining sites are presumed to vary equiprobably. The gamma approach assigns a substitution probability to sites by assuming that for a given sequence, the probabilities vary according to a gamma distribution. The shape of the gamma distribution, as described by the shape parameter α, describes the distribution of substitution probabilities among sites in a sequence (Swofford et al., 1996a, p. 444, Figure 13; cf. Li, 1997, p. 76, Figure 3.10; note that the scales differ). In a combined approach, it can be presumed that a proportion of sites are invariant and that the remainder vary according to a gamma distribution.

In practice, gamma correction can be continuous, discrete, or "autodiscrete" (W. M. Yang et al., 1996). "Continuous gamma" means that sites are assigned to a change probability along a continuous curve. At present, this approach is computationally impractical in most cases. The discrete gamma approximation assigns sites to a specified number of categories that approximate the shape of the gamma curve. The autodiscrete model assumes that adjacent sites have correlated rates of change. Groups of sites are assigned to categories, and sites within a category can be assumed to have either constant or heterogeneous rates.

Various rate heterogeneity corrections are implemented in several tree-building programs. For nucleotide data, PAUP 4.0 implements both invariants and discrete gamma models for separate or combined use with time-reversible distance and likelihood tree-building methods, and invariants in conjunction with the log-det distance method (see below). For nucleotide, amino acid, and codon data, PAML implements continuous, discrete, and autodiscrete models. For nucleotide and amino acid data, PHYLIP implements a discrete gamma model.

Which Substitution Model to Use?

Although any of the parameters in a substitution model might prove critical in a given data set, the best model is not always the one with the most parameters. To the contrary, the fewer the parameters, the better. This is because every parameter estimate has an associated variance. As additional parametric dimensions are introduced, the overall variance increases, sometimes prohibitively (see Li, 1997: p. 84, Table 4.1). For a given sequence comparison, a two-parameter model will require that the summed base differences be sorted into two categories, and for a six-parameter model, six. Obviously, the number of sites sampled in each of the six categories would be much smaller, and perhaps too small to give a reliable estimate.

A good strategy for substitution model specification for DNA sequences is the "describe tree" feature in PAUP, which uses likelihood to simultaneously estimate the six reversible substitution rates, the α shape parameter of the gamma distribution, and the proportion of invariant sites (Figure 9.7). These parameters can be estimated by means of equal or specified base frequencies. Usually, any reasonable phylogenetic tree (e.g., an easily generated neighbor-joining tree) is suitable for this procedure because parameter estimates are apparently influenced predominantly by the character pattern rather than by the tree topology (Swofford et al., 1996b). This estimation procedure is not overly time-consuming for up to 50 sequences. If there will be more sequences or less time, the test tree can be selectively pruned to reduce the number of taxa while retaining the overall phylogenetic range and structure. From the estimated substitution parameters, one can determine whether a simpler model is justified (e.g., whether the six substitution categories can be reduced to two) by comparing likelihood scores estimated for this tree using more or fewer parameters. Parameters for α and the proportion of invariant sites sometimes can substitute for each other, so one should compare likelihoods with each estimated alone versus both together. Note that unlike MP and ME, the ML scores derived using different parameter values are directly comparable (Swofford et al., 1996b).

In the case of protein-coding DNA sequences, it is sometimes obvious that depending on the divergence of the samples, the useful variation is essentially either in the first and second codon positions, with the third positions randomized across the data set, or in the third position, with the first and second positions invariant. The procedure above will correct for this rate heterogeneity, although removing the "useless" sites may permit a more precise estimate of rate heterogeneity in the remaining sites. For parsimony tree building, one sometimes removes randomized third position data from the analysis, since it contributes only noise and may introduce errors if there are unequal base frequencies.

```
P A U P *
Version 4.0.0d55 for Macintosh
Wednesday, June 25, 1997  10:59 PM
```

[paup> exe 18s.paup]

```
Processing of file "18s.paup" begins...

Data matrix has 33 taxa, 1813 characters
Data read in DNA format
Valid character-state symbols: ACGT
Missing data identified by '?'
Gaps identified by '-', treated as "missing"

Processing of file "18s.paup" completed.
```

[paup> hs]

```
Heuristic search settings:
    Optimality criterion = maximum parsimony
[stuff deleted]

Heuristic search completed
    Total number of rearrangements tried = 427548
    Score of best tree(s) found = 2315
    Number of trees retained = 36
    Time used = 00:02:28.2
```

[paup> set cri=l]

```
Optimality criterion set to maximum likelihood
```

[paup> lse nst=6 rma=est ra=ga sha=est pi=est]
[paup> lse ?]

```
Usage: LSet [options] ;

Available options:
Keyword ---- Option type ----------------------- Current default setting --
NST          1|2|6                                6
TRatio       <real-value>|Estimate|Previous       2
RMatrix      (<rAC><rAG><rAT><rCG><rCT>)|
             Estimate|Previous                     Estimate
Variant      HKY|F84                              HKY
BaseFreq     Empirical|Equal|(<frqA><frqC><frqG>) Empirical
Rates        Equal|Gamma|SiteSpec                 Gamma
Shape        <real-value>|Estimate|Previous       Estimate
NCat         <integer-value>                      4
[stuff deleted]
PInvar       <real-value>|Estimate                Estimate
[stuff deleted]
```

[paup>set tcom]
[paup>desc 16 /pl=ph]

(a)

Figure 9.7 Strategy for estimating a nucleotide substitution model using PAUP. A PAUP output is shown, with some output deleted for brevity. Commands are indicated in brackets in bold face type. The commands are required for command line versions of the program, but the same commands can be issued using the menu interface. After the program has been opened and the datafile executed [paup> exe 18s.paup], a tree is built using a relatively rapid procedure—in this case, an MP search (the default optimality criterion in PAUP) using the program defaults. The complete search settings (here truncated) are output. In this case, 36 equally parsimonious trees are found. The optimality criterion is changed to likelihood [paup> set cri=1] and settings changed to use six substitution types and the combined gamma and invariants corrections for among-site rate heterogeneity, with the substitution rate matrix,

```
Tree description:

    Optimality criterion = maximum likelihood
    MLE settings:
      Assumed nucleotide frequencies (estimated from data):
        A = 0.25995
        C = 0.20897
        G = 0.27252
        T = 0.25856
      Number of substitution types = 6
      Some sites assumed to be invariable with proportion estimated via maximum likelihood
  (observed proportion of constant sites = 0.523442)
      Rates (for variable sites) assumed to follow a gamma distribution with shape
        parameter estimated via maximum likelihood
      Settings for discrete gamma approximation:
        Number of rate categories = 4
      Substitution rate-matrix parameters estimated via maximum likelihood
  [stuff deleted]

  Tree number 16 (rooted using user-specified outgroup)

  -Ln likelihood = 13373.63356
    Estimated R-matrix:
        -4.3494440    0.80390972     2.5700133    0.97552098
         0.80390972  -6.7773472      1.0326461    4.9407914
         2.5700133    1.0326461     -4.6026594            1
         0.97552098   4.9407914             1    -6.9163123
  [stuff deleted]
    Estimated value of proportion of invariable sites = 0.229703
    Estimated value of gamma shape parameter = 0.495257
```

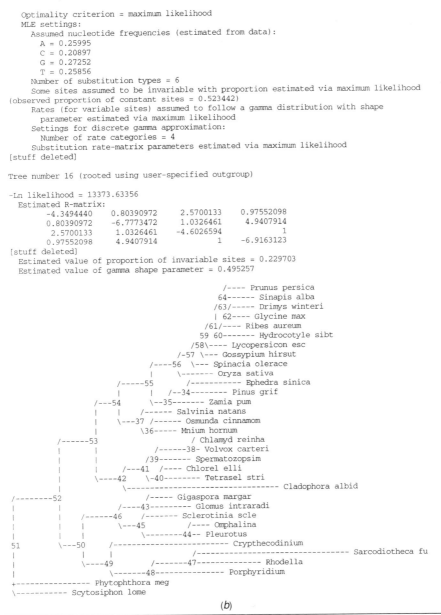

(b)

gamma shape parameter, and invariant proportion estimated from the data and tree [paup> lse nst=6 rma=est ra=ga sha=est pi=est]. The command lse ? shows the current likelihood settings (here truncated). The command set tcom compresses the output trees, which saves space. The values of the likelihood parameters are estimated by describing a tree in memory, in this case tree number 16 (the same topology shown in Hershkovitz and Lewis, 1996). An option directs the tree output to be a phylogram, which shows the branch lengths [paup>desc 16 /pl=ph]. Alternatively, the tree output can be suppressed [paup>desc 16 /pl=no]. The output indicates the values of the likelihood parameters, the score of the tree, and other information not shown. The *R* matrix is a factor of the generalized matrix shown in Figure 9.5; it includes the relative rate parameters that are used in the likelihood settings. The parameter estimates can be activated by issuing the command to change the likelihood settings to the earlier values, which sets them to the values for the tree just described [paup> lse rma=pre sha=pre pi=pre]. The values are thus set for an ML tree-building search. Alternatively, the values can be plugged into the analogous set of distance parameter settings for a distance tree-building search.

Perhaps the easiest way to determine whether nonstationarity is a problem in the data set is to simply compare thorough tree building and tree evaluation results generated using time-reversible versus log-det distances in PAUP. These procedures are described in the following sections.

Computational means for assessing nonstationarity directly from the sequence data are not well developed. PAUP includes a command for listing base frequencies in all sequences. For this procedure, the Exclude Constant Sites option should be used. Base frequencies in the sequences can be compared visually. The datafile should specify `gap-mode=missing`, or PAUP will count a gap character as a base variation. The base frequency command also performs a chi-square test on the data, but the test is unrealistic in that it presumes that the sequences are drawn from a random sample, with the result that observed inequalities are presumed to be independent rather than the result of phylogenetic structure. An insignificant chi-square score does not rule out nonstationarity, and a significant score may not confirm it. The base composition command in PAUP has been used to demonstrate that base bias in 5.8S rDNA sequences of angiosperms versus green algae was concentrated at sites that vary between the two groups but are not subject to vary within either one (Hershkovitz and Lewis, 1996).

TREE-BUILDING METHODS

Tree-building methods implemented in available software are discussed in detail in the literature (Saitou, 1996; Swofford et al., 1996a; Li, 1997). This section briefly describes the most popular methods. Tree-building methods can be sorted into two categories two different ways:

1. Algorithm-based vs. criterion-based. Algorithm-based methods generate a tree according to a series of steps. The criterion-based approach is a means of evaluating alternative trees according to some optimizable function. An example of a purely algorithmic method is neighbor joining (NJ), which derives a single tree having the desirable property of being nearly or quite optimally distance-additive (see below). A criterion-based distance approach evaluates the universe of possible trees (however they are generated) according to the criterion that tree additivity be optimized.

2. Distance-based vs. character-based. Much of the historical and current discussion in molecular phylogenetics dwells on the utility of various distance- and character-based methods (e.g., Saitou, 1996; Li, 1997). Distance methods compute pairwise distances according to some measure, then discard the actual data, using only the fixed distances to derive trees. Character-based methods derive trees that optimize the distribution of the actual data patterns for each character. Pairwise distances are thus not fixed, as they are determined by the tree topology. The most commonly applied character-based methods include MP and ML.

Distance-Based Methods

Distance methods use the amount of dissimilarity (the distance) between two aligned sequences to derive trees. A distance method would reconstruct the true tree if all genetic divergence events were accurately recorded in the sequence (Swofford et al., 1996a). However, divergence encounters an upper bound as sequences become mutationally saturated.

After one sequence of a diverging pair has mutated at a particular site, subsequent mutations in either sequence cannot render the sites any more "different." In fact, subsequent mutations can make them again equal, thereby masking prior mutations; therefore, most distance-based methods correct for such "unseen" substitutions. In practice, application of the rate matrix effectively presumes that some proportion of observed pairwise base identities actually represents multiple mutations, and that this proportion increases with increasing overall sequence divergence. Some programs implement, at least optionally, calculation of uncorrected distances while, for example, the MEGA program (Kumar et al., 1994) implements only uncorrected distances for codon and amino acid data. Unless overall divergences are very low, the latter approach is virtually guaranteed to give inaccurate results.

Pairwise distance is calculated using maximum-likelihood estimators of substitution rates. The most popular distance tree-building programs have been limited to time-reversible models using only a limited number of substitution models, but PAUP 4.0 implements essentially any variation of the time-reversible model, including the actual model estimated from the data using maximum likelihood, as well as the log-det distance method for nonstationary data.

Distance methods are much less computationally intensive than maximum likelihood but can employ the same models of sequence evolution. This is their biggest advantage. The disadvantage is that the actual character data is discarded. The most commonly applied distance-based methods are the unweighted pair group method with arithmetic mean (UPGMA), neighbor joining (NJ), and methods that optimize the additivity of a distance tree, including the minimum evolution (ME) method. Several methods are available in more than one phylogenetics software package, but not all implementations allow the same parameter specifications and/or tree optimization features (e.g., branch swapping—see below).

Unweighted Pair Group Method with Arithmetic Mean (UPGMA) UPGMA is a clustering or phenetic algorithm—it joins tree branches on the criterion of greatest similarity among pairs and averages of joined pairs. It is not strictly an evolutionary distance method (Li, 1997). UPGMA is expected to generate an accurate topology with true branch lengths only when the divergence is according to a molecular clock (ultrametric; Swofford et al., 1996a) or approximately equal to raw sequence dissimilarity. As discussed earlier, these conditions are rarely met in practice.

Neighbor Joining (NJ) The neighbor-joining algorithm is commonly applied with distance tree building, regardless of the optimization criterion. The fully resolved tree is "decomposed" from a fully unresolved "star" tree by successively inserting branches between a pair of closest (actually, most isolated) neighbors and the remaining terminals in the tree (Fig. 9.8). The closest neighbor pair is then consolidated, effectively reforming a star tree, and the process is repeated. The method is comparatively rapid, i.e., requiring only a few seconds or less for a 50-sequence tree.

Fitch–Margoliash (FM) The Fitch–Margoliash (FM) method seeks to maximize the fit of the observed pairwise distances to a tree by minimizing the squared deviation of all possible observed distances relative to all possible path lengths on the tree (Felsenstein, 1997). There are several variations that differ in how the error is weighted. The variance estimates are not completely independent, because errors in all the internal tree branches are counted at least twice (Rzhetsky and Nei, 1992).

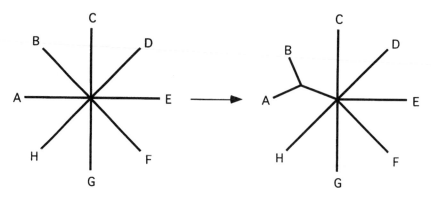

Figure 9.8 Star decomposition. This is how tree-building algorithms such as neighbor-joining work. The most similar terminals are joined and a branch inserted between them and the remainder of the star. Subsequently, the new branch is consolidated, so that its value is a mean of the two original values, yielding a star tree with *n* – 1 terminals. The process is repeated until only one terminal remains.

Minimum Evolution (ME) Minimum evolution seeks to find the shortest tree that is consistent with the path lengths measured in a manner similar to FM; that is, it works by minimizing the squared deviation of observed to tree-based distances (Rzhetsky and Nei, 1992; Swofford et al., 1996a; Felsenstein, 1997). Unlike FM, ME does not use all possible pairwise distances and all possible associated tree path lengths. Rather, it fixes the location of internal tree nodes based on the distance to external nodes, and then optimizes the internal branch length according to the minimum measured error between these "observed" points. It thus purports to eliminate the nonindependence of FM measurements.

Which Distance-Based Tree-Building Procedure Is Best? ME and FM appear to be the best procedures, and they perform nearly identically in simulation studies (Huelsenbeck, 1995). ME is becoming more widely implemented in computer programs, including METREE (Rzhetsky and Nei, 1994) and PAUP. For protein data, the FM procedure in PHYLIP offers the greatest range of time-reversible substitution models, but no correction for among-site rate heterogeneity. The MEGA (Kumar et al., 1994) plus METREE package includes a gamma correction for protein, but only in conjunction with a raw ("*p*-distance") divergence model (no distance or bias correction), which is unreliable except for small divergences (Rzhetsky and Nei, 1994). MEGA also computes separate distances for synonymous and nonsynonymous sites, but this method is valid only in the absence of substitution or base frequency bias, and when there is no correction for among-site rate heterogeneity. Thus for most data sets, using the nucleotide data under a more realistic model might be preferable to MEGA's methods.

Simulation studies indicate that UPGMA performs poorly over a broad range of tree shape space (Huelsenbeck, 1995). The use of this method is not recommended; it is mentioned here only because its application seems to persist, as evidenced by UPGMA "gene trees" appearing in current publications (Huelsenbeck, 1995).

NJ is clearly the fastest procedure and generally yields a tree close to, if not the actual, ME tree (Rzhetsky and Nei, 1992; Li, 1997). However, it yields only one tree. Depending on the structure of the data, numerous different trees might be as good or significantly better than the NJ tree (Swofford et al., 1996a). One of us (MAH) and D. Hillis (personal communication) have independently come across some (albeit few) data sets in which NJ gives a relative poor tree; and a better distance tree is found using stepwise addition with the "closest" option in PAUP (Swofford, 1997).

Character-Based Methods

The character-based methods have little in common besides the use of the character data at all steps in the analysis. This allows the assessment of the reliability of each base position in an alignment on the basis of all other base positions. The most widely used character-based methods are maximum parsimony and maximum likelihood.

Maximum Parsimony (MP) Maximum parsimony is an optimality criterion that appeals to the principle of "Occam's razor": the best explanation of the data is the simplest, which in turn is the one requiring the fewest ad hoc assumptions. In practical terms, the MP tree is the shortest—the one with the fewest changes, which, by definition, is also the one with the fewest parallel changes, or least homoplasy. There are several variants of MP that differ with regard to the permitted directionality of character state change (Swofford et al., 1996a).

To accommodate substitution bias, MP is amenable to weighting; for example, the transformation of a transversion can be weighted relative to a transition (see above). The easiest way to do this is to create a weighting step matrix in which the weights are the reciprocal of the rates estimated using ML as described above. Step-matrix weighting can greatly slow MP computation.

The MP method performs poorly when there is substantial among-site rate heterogeneity (Huelsenbeck, 1995). There are few good fixes for this problem. One approach is to modify the data set to include only sites that exhibit little or no heterogeneity as determined by likelihood estimation (see above). More often, MP analyses simply remove sites suspected of exhibiting high homoplasy (e.g., third codon positions in some sequence alignments). Another approach is to recursively reweight positions according to their propensity to change as observed in preliminary trees. This "successive approximations" approach is automatically facilitated in PAUP, but it is prone to error to the degree that the preliminary trees are incorrect.

MP analyses tend to yield numerous (sometimes many thousands of) trees that have the same score. Because each is held to be as optimal as any other, only groupings present in the strict consensus of all trees are considered to be supported by the data. The reason that distance and ML tree methods tend to arrive a single best tree is that their calculation involves division and decimals, whereas MP merely counts discrete steps. For a given data set, a strict consensus of all ME or ML trees that are not significantly worse than optimal probably would yield resolution more or less comparable to the MP consensus. Unfortunately, while MP users conventionally present strict consensus (and sometimes consensus of trees one or two steps worse), ME and ML users typically do not.

Numerous tree statistics have been developed to describe an MP tree. Besides its length, these include various ratios that describe the amount of homoplasy, such as the consistency index, or the average number of times a character changes state in a tree (Swofford, 1990). Although still typically reported in MP analyses, these indices have proven to be subject to numerous artifacts, such as the number of taxa being analyzed.

Simulation studies (Huelsenbeck, 1995) have shown that MP performs no better than ME and worse than ML when the amount of sequence evolution since lineages diverged is much greater than the amount of divergence that occurred between lineage splits (i.e., in a tree with very long terminal branches and short internal internodes). This condition produces "long branch attraction"—the long branches become artificially connected because the number of nonhomologous similarities the sequences have accumulated exceeds the number of homologous similarities they have retained with their true closest relatives (Swofford et al., 1996a). Character weighting improves the performance of MP under these conditions (Huelsenbeck, 1995).

Maximum Likelihood (ML) ML turns the phylogenetic problem inside out. ML searches for the evolutionary model, including the tree itself, that has the highest likelihood of producing the observed data.

In practice, ML is derived for each base position in an alignment. The likelihood is calculated in terms of the probability that the pattern of variation at a site would be produced by a particular substitution process, given a particular tree and the overall observed base frequencies. The likelihood becomes the sum of the probabilities of each possible reconstruction of substitutions under a particular substitution process. The likelihoods for all the sites are multiplied to give an overall "likelihood of the tree" (i.e., the probability of the data given the tree and the substitution process). As one can imagine, for one particular tree, the likelihood of the data is low at some sites and high at others. For a "good" tree, many sites will have higher likelihood, so the product of likelihoods is high. For a "poor" tree, the reverse will be true. If there is no phylogenetic signal in the data, all random trees will be comparable in likelihood.

The substitution model should be optimized to fit the observed data. For example, if there is a transition bias, evident by an inordinate number of sites that include only purines or pyrimidines, the likelihood of the data under a model that assumes no bias will never be as good as one that does. Likewise, if a substantial proportion of the sites are occupied by a single base, and another substantial proportion have equal base frequencies, the likelihood of the data under a model that assumes that all sites evolve equally will be less than that of a model that allows rate heterogeneity. Modifying the substitution parameters, however, modifies the likelihood of the data associated with particular trees. Thus the tree yielding the highest likelihood under one substitution model might yield much lower likelihood under another.

Because ML uses great amounts of computation time, it is usually impractical to perform a complete search that simultaneously optimizes the substitution model and the tree for a given data set. An economical, heuristic approach is recommended (Adachi and Hasegawa, 1996; Swofford et al., 1996a). Perhaps the best time-saver in this regard is preliminary ML estimation of the substitution model (Figure 9.7). This procedure can be applied iteratively, searching for better ML trees, then reestimating the parameters, then searching for better trees.

As algorithms, computers, and phylogenetic understanding have improved, the ML criterion has become more popular for molecular phylogenetic analysis. In simulation studies, ML has consistently outperformed ME and MP when the data analysis proceeds according to the same model that generates the data (Huelsenbeck, 1995). ML will always be the most computationally intensive method of all, however, so there will always be situations in which it is not practical. Moreover, the same simulation studies indicate that under many conditions, ME and MP will perform as well (or as poorly) as ML.

DISTANCE, PARSIMONY, AND MAXIMUM LIKELIHOOD: WHAT IS THE DIFFERENCE?

Distance matrix methods simply count the number of differences between two sequences. This number is referred to as the evolutionary distance, and its exact size depends on the evolutionary model used. The actual tree is then computed from the matrix of distance values by running a clustering algorithm that starts with the most similar sequences (i.e., those that have the shortest distance between them) or by trying to minimize the total branch length of the tree.

The principle of maximum parsimony searches for a tree that requires the smallest number of changes to explain the differences observed among the taxa under study.

A maximum-likelihood approach to phylogenetic inference evaluates the probability that the chosen evolutionary model has generated the observed data. The evolutionary model could simply mean that one assumes that changes between all nucleotides (or amino acids) are equally probable. The program will then assign all possible nucleotides to the internal nodes of the tree in turn and calculate the probability that each such sequence would have generated the data (if two sister taxa have the nucleotide "A," a reconstruction that assumes derivation from a "C" would be assigned a low probability compared to a derivation that assumes there already was a "A"). The probabilities for all possible reconstructions (not just the more probable one) are summed up to yield the likelihood for one particular site. The likelihood for the tree is the product of the likelihoods for all alignment positions in the data set.

SEARCHING FOR TREES

The number of unique phylogenetic trees increases exponentially with the number of taxa, becoming astronomical even for, say, 50 sequences (Swofford et al., 1996a; Li, 1997). In most cases, computational limitations permit exploration of only a small fraction of possible trees. The exact number will depend mainly on the number of taxa, the optimality criterion (e.g., MP is much faster than ML), the parameters (e.g., unweighted MP is much faster than weighted; ML with fewer preset parameters is much faster than with more and/or simultaneously optimized parameters), computer hardware, and, to a lesser degree, computer software (some algorithms are faster than others; some software allows multiprocessing; some software limits the number and kind of trees that can be stored in memory). The search procedure is also affected by data structure: poorly resolvable data produces more "nearly optimal" trees that must be evaluated to find the most optimal.

Branch-swapping algorithms successively modify existing trees built by an initial step (Swofford et al., 1996a). The algorithms range from those that generate all possible unique trees (exhaustive algorithms) to those that evaluate only minor modifications.

Two search methods are guaranteed to find the most optimal tree: exhaustive and branch-and-bound (BB) (Swofford et al., 1996a). For larger data sets, these methods usually are not practical. The practical limit for the number of taxa depends on the structure of the data and computer speed, but the BB method has rarely been applied for data sets of more than 20 taxa. The exhaustive method requires that each tree be evaluated according to the optimality criterion. The BB method provides a logical means of deciding which trees are worth evaluating and which can simply be discarded. It is therefore much faster than exhaustive.

Most analyses employ "heuristic" searches (Swofford et al., 1996a). Heuristic algorithms search for families ("islands") of related suboptimal trees for optimal solutions ("peaks"). Different algorithms search for islands and peaks with varying degrees of rigor. The most thorough, and slowest, procedure (tree bisection–reconnection, TBR), splits the tree at each internal branch and reattaches the pieces in every possible way (Swofford et al., 1996a). The fastest algorithms merely examine trivial rearrangements of adjacent terminals, hence are prone to find only the peak of the nearest island.

There are different software implementations of tree-searching algorithms. PAUP permits a full spectrum of search options, from the most superficial to the most exhaustive. Moreover, in a single customized search it permits the use of any combination of algorithms, each with multiple user-definable parameters, as well as providing a means of interactively evaluating the progress of the search and modifying its course midsearch. PAUP can also keep track of tree islands and how many times they are "hit."

Numerous strategies can be tried for improving search efficiency and tree optimization. For example, some analysts prefer to spend more time and effort looking for islands. This is accomplished by generating a wide variety of "starting" trees that fulfill an initial criterion, and then allowing PAUP to sort these into islands for more thorough algorithmic evaluation.

One of the best ways to economize search effort is to prune the data set. For example, it might be apparent from the data alone or from preliminary searching that a particular cluster of five terminals is unresolvable, that the arrangement of these terminals does not impact the remainder of the topology, and/or that resolution of these terminals is not the objective of the analysis. Removing four of the terminals from the analysis simplifies the search by several orders of magnitude.

Every analysis is unique. The elements that influence the choice of optimal search strategy (amount of data, structure of data, amount of time, hardware, objective of analysis) are too variable to suggest a foolproof recipe. Thus researchers must be familiar with their data; they must also have specific objectives in mind, understanding the various search procedures as well as the capabilities of their hardware and software, and they must be able to develop their own protocols.

Other Methods for Building and Searching for Trees

The methods described above are currently the most widely applied. Numerous other methods for building and searching trees are reviewed elsewhere (Swofford et al., 1996a; Li, 1997). These include the distance Wagner and neighborliness methods (distance transformations); Lake's method of invariants (a character-based method that selects a topology having a significantly positive number of supporting transversions); the Hadamard conjugation (an elaborate matrix algebraic means of correcting observed character or distance data); and split decomposition (a method for determining support in the data for alternative distance-based topologies). Quartet puzzling is a relatively rapid tree-searching algorithm available for ML tree building (Strimmer and von Haeseler, 1996).

ROOTING TREES

The methods described here produce unrooted trees (i.e., trees having no evolutionary polarity). To evaluate evolutionary hypotheses, it is often necessary to locate the root. Rooting phylogenetic trees is not a trivial problem (Nixon and Carpenter, 1993).

In the case of sequence data, if one accepts a molecular clock, then the root will always be at the midpoint of the longest span across the tree (Weston, 1994). Whether molecular evolution is indeed clocklike generally remains a contentious issue (Li, 1997), but most gene trees exhibit unclocklike behavior regardless of where the root is placed. Thus, rooting is generally evaluated by extrinsic evidence, that is, by means of determining where the tree would attach to an "outgroup," which can be any organism/sequence not descended from the nearest common ancestor of the organisms/sequences analyzed. Outgroup rooting, however, creates a dilemma: an outgroup that is closely related to the ingroup might be simply an erroneously excluded member of the ingroup. A clearly distant outgroup (e.g., a fungus for an analysis of plants) will probably have a sequence so diverged that its attachment to the ingroup is subject to the long branch attraction (see above).

A clever means of rooting involves analysis of a duplicated gene (Baldauf et al., 1996; Lawson et al., 1996). If all the paralogs from most or all of the organisms are included in the analysis, then one can logically root the tree exactly where the paralog gene trees converge, assuming that there are not long branch problems in all trees.

EVALUATING TREES AND DATA

Several procedures are available that evaluate the phylogenetic signal in the data and the robustness of trees (Swofford et al., 1996a; Li, 1997). The most popular of the former class are tests of data signal versus randomized data (skewness and permutation tests). The latter class includes tests of tree support from resampling of observed data (nonparametric bootstrap and jackknife). The likelihood ratio test provides a means of evaluating both the substitution model and the tree.

Randomized Trees (Skewness Test)

Simulation studies indicate that the distribution of random MP tree lengths generated using random data sets will be symmetrical, while that using data sets with phylogenetic signal will be skewed (Figure 9.9; Hillis and Huelsenbeck, 1992). The critical value of the g_1 statistic of skewness will vary with the number of taxa and variable sites in the sequence. The test does not estimate the reliability of a particular topology, and it is sensitive to even very small amounts of signal present in an otherwise random data set. If taxa from groups that are obviously well supported by the data are selectively deleted, the test can be used to determine whether phylogenetic signal remains, provided at least 10 variable characters and 5 taxa are examined. The procedure is implemented in PAUP.

Randomized Character Data (Permutation Tests)

The randomized data approach determines whether an MP tree or portion thereof derived from the actual data could have arisen by chance. The data is not truly randomized, but permuted within each aligned column, so that covariation in the initial data is removed. The result is an alignment of sequences that are not random sequences; rather, the base at each site in these sequences is randomly drawn from the population of bases occupying that site in the overall alignment. The permutation tail probability test (PTP) compares the score for the MP tree with trees generated by numerous permutations of the data at each site, determining only whether there is phylogenetic signal in the original data. A topology-dependent

```
[paup> exc uninf]
[stuff deleted]
   Number of included characters = 535

[paup>  rand nrep=5000  fdt=hist]
[stuff deleted]

Frequency distribution of lengths of 5000 random trees:

          mean=3244.498600 sd=80.237273 g1=-0.507536 g2=0.281260
2874.000 /-----------------------------------------------------------------------
2901.900 | (3)
2929.800 | (0)
2957.700 | (4)
2985.600 |# (6)
3013.500 |## (22)
3041.400 |### (25)
3069.300 |####### (73)
3097.200 |########### (107)
3125.100 |################# (159)
3153.000 |########################## (249)
3180.900 |################################### (358)
3208.800 |################################################# (513)
3236.700 |################################################################### (642)
3264.600 |#################################################################### (660)
3292.500 |#################################################################### (661)
3320.400 |#################################################################### (661)
3348.300 |############################################### (442)
3376.200 |########################### (257)
3404.100 |############## (130)
3432.000 |### (28)
         \-----------------------------------------------------------------------

[paup>del  11-33]

[stuff deleted]
   Number of undeleted taxa = 10

[paup>  rand nrep=5000  fdt=hist]
[stuff deleted]

Frequency distribution of lengths of 5000 random trees:

          mean=331.129600 sd=5.027724 g1=0.005071 g2=-0.103043
315.00000 /-----------------------------------------------------------------------
316.65000 |# (7)
318.30000 |## (26)
319.95000 |## (22)
321.60000 |####### (87)
323.25000 |############## (163)
324.90000 |############## (159)
326.55000 |#################################### (422)
328.20000 |##################################################### (618)
329.85000 |################################## (392)
331.50000 |################################################################### (777)
333.15000 |############################################################### (728)
334.80000 |############################### (334)
336.45000 |############################################# (537)
338.10000 |################################ (376)
339.75000 |######### (109)
341.40000 |############ (142)
343.05000 |####### (77)
344.70000 |# (13)
346.35000 |# (7)
348.00000 | (4)
```

214

Figure 9.9 Skewness test for phylogenetic signal in data: a PAUP output (commands in brackets in bold face type). The commands are required for command line versions of the program, but the same commands can be issued using the menu interface. This test uses the same 18S rDNA set as in Figure 9.7 and presumes that the optimality criterion is MP. The MP uninformative characters have been deleted because having a high proportion of these in the data biases the result. A complete output of all tree scores can be very lengthy; hence the test command is issued with the option to output a histogram with 20 categories (the default). The default number of replications is 1000 and has been here increased. The g_1 statistic for 33 taxa is highly significant: it is much more negative than the critical value (-0.09; $p = 0.01$) for 25 taxa and 500 characters (Hillis and Huelsenbeck, 1992); the critical value for more taxa and characters is not available but would be even less negative. The score of the MP trees was 2315 (cf. Figure 9.7), which is much less than any of the 500 random trees. A second test was performed after all but the angiosperms in the 18S data set had been deleted. Taxa can be temporarily deleted by name or by number, and the angiosperms happened to be the first 10 taxa in the data file. In this case, the g statistic is much more positive than the critical value for 500 characters and 10 taxa (-0.16; $p = 0.5$), suggesting that 18S sequences have no phylogenetic signal for resolving relationships among this sample. The MP score using the 18S data and the 10 angiosperms is 312, which is only slightly better than the best random tree scores.

test (T-PTP) compares the scores for specific trees to determine whether the difference can be attributed to chance. This method does not evaluate whether the tree or any portion thereof is correct (Faith and Trueman, 1996; Swofford et al., 1996b). In particular, the T-PTP test will appear to corroborate groups that are in trees close to the MP tree but not in it. This is because the method is detecting the collective signal that places a taxon even approximately, if not actually, in its correct position. The results can be fine-tuned, however, by additional applications using relevant subsets of the data (Faith and Trueman, 1996). The procedure is implemented in PAUP.

Bootstrap

Bootstrapping is a resampling tree evaluation method that works with distance, parsimony, likelihood, and just about any other tree derivation method. It was invented in 1979 (Efron, 1979) and introduced as a tree evaluation method in phylogenetic analysis by Joe Felsenstein (Felsenstein, 1985). The result of bootstrap analysis is typically a number associated with a particular branch in the phylogenetic tree that gives the proportion of bootstrap replicates that support the monophyly of the clade.

How is it done practically? Bootstrapping can be considered a two-step process comprising the generation of (many) new data sets from the original set and the computation of a number that gives the proportion of times that a particular branch (e.g., a taxon) appeared in the tree. That number is commonly referred to as the bootstrap value. New data sets are created from the original data set by sampling columns of characters at random from the original data set with replacement. "With replacement" means that each site can be sampled again with the same probability as any of the other sites. As a consequence, each of the newly created data sets has the same number of total positions as the original data set, but some positions are duplicated or triplicated and others are missing. It is therefore possible that some of the newly created data sets are completely identical to the original set—or, on the other extreme, that only one of the sites is replicated, say, 500 times, while the remaining 499 positions in the original data set are dropped.

While it has become common practice to include bootstrapping as part of a thorough phylogenetic analysis, there is some discussion on what exactly is measured by the method. It was originally suggested that the bootstrap value is a measure of repeatability (Felsenstein, 1985). In more recent interpretations, it has been considered to be a measure of accuracy—a biologically more relevant parameter that gives the probability that the true phylogeny has been recovered (Felsenstein and Kishino 1993). Based on simulation studies, it has been suggested that under favorable conditions (roughly equal rates of change, symmetric branches), bootstrap values greater than 70% correspond to a probability of greater than 95% that the true phylogeny has been found (Hillis and Bull, 1993). By the same token, under less favorable conditions, bootstrap values greater than 50% will be overestimates of accuracy (Hillis and Bull, 1993). Simply put, under certain conditions, high bootstrap values can make the wrong phylogeny look good.

Practical Considerations   The technique is not recommended when the sample size is small. If it is not possible to place confidence in a particular group, bootstrapping can be used to assess whether the group can be confidently placed within a larger monophyletic group (Sanderson, 1989). Also, bootstrapping can be used in experiments that recompute trees with internal branches deleted one at a time, in order to gather information on branching orders that are ambiguous in the full data set (see example in Leipe et al., 1994).

Jackknife

The jackknife is a resampling technique like the bootstrap. However, instead of generating new data sets with replacement, the jackknife resamples the original data set by dropping one or more alignment positions in each replicate. As a consequence, each jackknife replicate is smaller than the original data set and cannot contain duplicated data points. Although most treatises assume that variability estimated by one technique should be very similar to that estimated by the other (Swofford and Olsen, 1990; Swofford et al., 1996a), in practice the jackknife is used much less frequently than the bootstrap approach. Nevertheless, the jackknife is included as an option in programs like PAUP and PHYLIP.

Parametric Bootstrap

The parametric bootstrap differs from the nonparametric in that it uses simulated, nonetheless actual, replicates, rather than pseudoreplicates. In the case of phylogenetic sequence analysis, replicate data sets of the same size as the original data set are generated according to a specified model of sequence evolution, including the optimal tree topology according to that model (Huelsenbeck et al., 1996a). Each data set is then analyzed according to the method of interest. Support for the branches in the test tree can be determined in much the same way as in the nonparametric bootstrap.

The parametric bootstrap is not so much an alternative to the nonparametric as a means of testing hypotheses untestable by other means, such as the monophyly of any group of taxa represented in the tree (Huelsenbeck et al., 1996a, 1996b). In each of the replicate analyses, the "true" tree (the tree that was assumed for generating the simulated data) may have a score that is more or less than that of the best tree in each replicate. The plot of the differences in score represents a true normal distribution of the sampling error. The significance of the score difference of any desired alternative tree topology can be determined by means of this normalized plot. The parametric bootstrap can be used in conjunction with any tree-building method. The limiting factor at the present time is the availability of programs for generating simulated data. A program that simulates sequence data under a model of two substitution types (transitions, transversions), unequal base frequencies, with or without a gamma correction for among-site rate heterogeneity, is available from the authors' Web site, maintained at Berkeley (see list of Internet resources at the end of the chapter).

Likelihood Ratio Tests

As the name implies, likelihood ratio tests are applicable to ML analyses. A suboptimal likelihood value is evaluated for significance against a normal distribution of the error in the optimal model. In ideal applications, the error curve is presumed to be a chi-square distribution. Thus the test statistic is twice the difference between the optimal and test values, and the degrees of freedom is the number of parameter differences.

Application of the chi-square test to alternative phylogenetic trees is problematic, especially because of the "irregularity of [the] parameter space" (Z. Yang et al., 1995), but its use has been advocated for evaluating optimality of the substitution model when the number of parameters between models is known. Once a substitution model and tree have been estimated using the maximum likelihood procedures described above, the same tree can be evaluated using fewer parameters (e.g., by setting among-sites rate to equality: Figure 9.7).

Kishino–Hasegawa Test

Given the uncertainty that accompanies determinations of the errors of trees, another approach is to determine the sampling error associated with each site in the alignment (Kishino and Hasegawa, 1989). This procedure, implemented in PAUP, can be used to test whether a particular suboptimal ML or MP topology is significantly different from the optimal, assuming that the model used to generate the optimal tree is correct. The method cannot be used to evaluate the difference between arbitrarily selected topologies: since different topologies may have different likelihood functions, a statistically worse tree under one model may be statistically better under another. This problem can be circumvented by using the test in conjunction with the parametric bootstrap, where the model and tree have been optimized a priori (see Sullivan et al., in press).

Constraint Tree Searches

One of the most useful ways to evaluate a tree is to compare unconstrained searches with those constrained to find optimal trees consistent with a specified topology. Besides a simple score comparison, constraint trees can be used in conjunction with permutation, likelihood ratio, Kishino–Hasegawa, and parametric bootstrap evaluation methods.

PHYLOGENETICS SOFTWARE

PHYLIP

PHYLIP is a package now comprising about 30 programs that cover almost any aspect of phylogenetic analysis. PHYLIP is free, available for a wide variety of platforms (Mac, DOS, Unix, VAX/VMS, and others). According to its author, Joe Felsenstein from the University of Washington, PHYLIP is currently the most widely used phylogeny program.

PHYLIP is a command line program and does not have a point-and-click interface, as programs like PAUP or MACCLADE do. The documentation is well written and very comprehensive, however, and the interface is straightforward. A program is invoked by typing its name, which automatically causes the data to be read from a file called "infile". The user can then choose from an option menu or accepted the default value, and the program will write its output to a file called "outfile" (and "treefile" where applicable). If the output is to be read by another program, "outfile" must be renamed (to "infile"). The steps involved in building a bootstrapped neighbor-joining tree for protein sequences are outlined in Figure 9.10. Particulars of some of the PHYLIP tree inference programs are discussed in the following subsections.

Programs for Protein Data   PROTDIST is a program that computes a distance matrix for an alignment of protein sequences. It allows the user to choose between one of three evolutionary models of amino acid replacements. The simplest, fastest (and least realistic) model assumes that each amino acid has an equal chance of turning into one of the other 19 amino acids. The second is a category model in which the amino acids are distributed among different groups, and transitions are evaluated differently depending on whether the change would result in an amino acid in the same or in a different group. The third (default) method, which is recommended, uses a table of empirically observed transitions between amino acids, the Dayhoff PAM 001 matrix (Dayhoff, 1979). More details can be found in the PHYLIP documentation and a recent publication (Felsenstein, 1996).

PROTPARS is a parsimony program for protein sequences. The evolutionary model is different from the ones used in the PROTDIST program in that it considers the underlying changes in the nucleotide sequence to evaluate the probabilities of the observed amino acid changes. Specifically, it makes the (biologically meaningful) assumption that synonymous changes [e.g., GCA (alanine) → GCC (alanine)] occur more often than nonsynonymous changes. As a consequence, a transition between two amino acids that would require, for example, three nonsynonymous changes in the underlying nucleotide sequences, is assigned a lower probability than an amino acid change calling for two nonsynonymous changes and one synonymous change. PROTPARS does not have an option that uses empirical values for amino acid changes (e.g., PAM matrices).

Programs for Nucleotide Data   DNADIST computes a distance matrix from nucleotide sequences. Trees are generated by running the output through NEIGHBOR or other distance matrix programs in the PHYLIP package. DNADIST allows the user to choose between three models of nucleotide substitution. The older (1969) Jukes and Cantor model is similar to the simple model in the PROTDIST program in that it assumes equal probabilities for all changes. The more recent (1980) Kimura two-parameter model is very similar but allows the user to weigh transversion more heavily than transitions. PHYLIP also comprises DNAML, a maximum-likelihood program for nucleotide data. Since the program is fairly slow, the use of its faster "sibling," Gary Olsen's fastDNAml program (Olsen et al., 1994) described below, is recommended.

PAUP

The objective of the development of PAUP (Swofford, 1997) is to provide a phylogenetics program that includes as many functions (including tree graphics) as possible in a single, platform-independent program with a menu interface. The menu interface is familiar to users of PAUP version 3 for Macintosh, which is no longer distributed. Version 3 performed only MP-associated tree-building and analytical functions. PAUP version 4 includes distance and ML functions for nucleotide data and other new features.

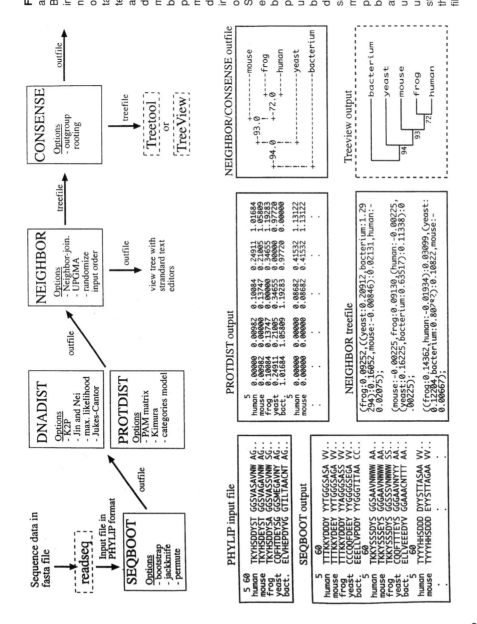

Figure 9.10 Workflow for bootstrap analysis with the PHYLIP program. SEQBOOT accepts a file in PHYLIP format as input and multiplies it a user-specified number of times (e.g., 1000). The resulting outfile can be used to calculate 1000 distance matrices for DNA (DNADIST) or protein (PROTDIST) data. In this step, the actual data (nucleotides, amino acids) are discarded and replaced by a figure that is a measure for the amount of divergence between two sequences. The NEIGHBOR program will create 1000 trees from these matrices. The CONSENSE program reduces the 1000 trees to a single one and indicates the bootstrap values as numbers on the branches. The topology of the CONSENSE tree can be viewed with any text editor in the "outfile" while the "treefile" can be further processed for publication purposes. Treetool and TREEVIEW allow the user to manipulate the tree (rerooting, branch rearrangements, conversions from dendrograms to phylograms, etc.) and to save the file in commonly used graphic formats (like PICT). Although these are not part of the PHYLIP package (indicated by boxes with dashed lines), they are freely available (see end-of-chapter list). The figure also shows the different file formats used during date processing through the stages of a bootstrap analysis. Periods to the right and at the bottom of a box indicate files that were truncated to save space.

219

Program Availability and Compilations Dozens of analyses employing test versions of PAUP 4 (distributed by the author via *blue@onyx.si.edu*) were published prior to the commercial release. Menu interface test versions have been compiled for Macintosh 68k and PPC computers and Microsoft Windows. Command line versions have been compiled for Sun Sparc and Supersparc, DEC Alpha (OSF1 and OPENVMS), SGI (32 and 64 bit), and Linux.

A novice user should explore one of the menu versions. The command line is also available in these versions, which facilitates command tutorial. In general, commands can be abbreviated. For example, the command for heuristic tree search can be entered as `hs[earch]` (case insensitive; characters in brackets are optional). Also, because the files are fully portable among platforms, the menu version can be used to test datafiles. This protocol is especially useful when it is desirable to actually run the analysis on a faster Unix computer. A menu version will not only report errors in the file format, it will open the datafile and highlight errors.

Data Format PAUP uses a data format called NEXUS, which is also used by the MACCLADE program, but it will also import PHYLIP, GCG-MSF, NBRF-PIR, HENNIG86, and text alignments (a list of `{name}<tab or space>{same-length sequences}<ret>`, ending with `;<ret>end;`). The Sequencher (Genecodes, Inc.) and Sequin programs can output NEXUS format. Aligned sequences from other formats (CLUSTAL, FASTA, GDE, etc.) can be converted to NEXUS using the ReadSeq program. If ReadSeq is used, it is necessary to devise unique sequence (taxon) names with no more than eight characters, because longer names are truncated. Sequence names can be any length in PAUP, but they all must be unique. Alignment blocks (e.g., as in MSF files) can be separated by spaces to better track sequence positions. Alignments can be continuous or interleaved. Comments and notes (e.g., base position numbering in an alignment) can be included in PAUP files within square brackets. PAUP recognizes IUPAC nucleotide ambiguity codes, but these are treated as missing data in distance and ML analyses.

The data block in PAUP files can include additional optional information, such as character and sequence labels, definition for missing data, and definitions of character sets and character weight sets. The syntax is the same as in PAUP version 3 and is available in the interactive help documentation. A PAUP file can also include assumptions and trees blocks. The format of these blocks is generally the same as in the MACCLADE program, with several exceptions (Maddison and Maddison, 1992); for example, MACCLADE does not recognize Gap mode, which permits gaps to be treated as additional character states in MP analysis (`FORMAT<space>GAP={character}<space> GAPMODE=newstate<space>{other format options};`). Some MACCLADE data options likewise are ignored by PAUP.

In case of difficulty formatting data manually, it is also possible to output correctly formatted files using the menu interface and or the interactive MACCLADE program. For example, "assumption sets" can be created using the PAUP menu interface. The assumptions can include specification of an outgroup, exclusion of particular taxa and characters, and, for MP analysis, specifications of character weights and character types. The assumptions can be saved to a properly formatted file. The file can be loaded while a datafile is open, or the contents can be pasted into a file created earlier, to avoid the need for loading in subsequent sessions.

PAUP also reads PHYLIP tree descriptions (output from PHYLIP or CLUSTAL), provided data is pasted into a PAUP-formatted trees block (`begin trees; <ret>utree={tree name}<space>{tree description};<ret>end;` in a NEXUS file. However, a PAUP datafile must be active and must include exactly the taxa in the PHYLIP tree. PAUP will import the topology and, optionally, the PHYLIP- or CLUSTAL-derived branch lengths (command: `gett[trees] /file={treefile} st[oredbrlens]`).

Tree Building Current tree-building functions in PAUP include MP, and, for nucleotide data, distance and ML using the fastDNAml algorithm (Olsen et al., 1994). In addition, PAUP performs Lake's method of invariants (Swofford et al., 1996a; Li, 1997). Each tree-building program permits a variety of options. The MP options include specification of any character-weighting scheme. Distance options include choice of NJ, ME, FM (see PAUP release notes re: PHYLIP), and UPGMA procedures. The full range of options and their current values can be examined using the menu and/or by typing `pse[ttings] ? dse[ttings] ?` and `lse[ttings] ?` for parsimony, distance, and likelihood, respectively. Both distance and ML allow detailed specification of the substitution model (values of substitution, gamma, and invariant-sites parameters, assuming equal, specified, or empirical base frequencies), and these can be estimated for any tree by setting the parameter values to `est[imate]` and applying the `des[cribe tree]` command with a desired tree in memory (Figure 9.7).

According to the release notes accompanying PAUP test version 4, "PAUP* *usually* finds trees with likelihoods as high or higher [i.e., better] than PHYLIP" (both because PAUP*'s tree rearrangements are more extensive and because its convergence criterion for branch length iteration is stricter).

With any tree-building method, PAUP allows a variety of tree search options. These include algorithm specification for generating the initial tree (starting tree): NJ, stepwise addition, or input tree(s). The stepwise-addition algorithm allows numerous options, including addition of taxa "asis" (taxa added in file order): closest, furthest, or random with any number of replicates. All the stepwise options allow for any maximal number of partial trees to be retained and built on during taxon addition. Increasing this number to, say, 100, is another means of increasing the diversity of starting topologies, although these are not random.

A random addition strategy provides a useful complement to the default search strategy (closest addition, TBR swapping, saving all best trees). In the random search, a large number of replicates can be combined with the faster NNI swapping algorithm. For MP analysis, in which a large number of equal-length trees might exist, the search should specify saving from each replicate only a few trees that match or better the score of the slower search. In addition, the number of suboptimal trees (the trees that will be swapped on to find better trees) should be limited by setting MAXTREES to a low number (e.g., 10). By using this strategy to explore areas of "tree space" possibly missed in the slow search, one sometimes finds better trees and/or additional unique optimal trees. The seed for random addition can be specified, but the default is always the same. Thus replications of a random addition search will be identical unless the seed is changed.

Tree Evaluation PAUP performs the nonparametric bootstrap and jackknife for distance, MP, and ML, using all options available for tree building with these methods. Unless otherwise specified, all bootstraps start with the same seed (i.e., replicates of the same bootstrap analysis are identical). Bootstrap values of $50^+\%$ are plotted on a tree, while all values less than 50% down to any specified cutoff can be determined from the tabular output.

When a bootstrap or jackknife with MP is under way, MAXTREES should be set between 10 and no more than 100. This is because poorly resolvable portions of an MP tree will usually be even less resolvable with resampled data; hence a replicate could find astronomical numbers of equal-length trees. Because tree branches weakly supported by the full data set will not have high bootstrap or jackknife values, limiting MAXTREES will have little, if any, bearing on the results, especially if the number of replicates is increased to, say, 1000.

In addition, PAUP performs the Kishino–Hasegawa test to compare MP or ML trees (see release notes re: PHYLIP), computes four types of consensus of multiple trees (usually used for multiple equal-length MP trees), computes stepwise differences between MP trees, and evaluates signal conflict between specified partitions of sites (e.g., nuclear and organellar sequence data in a combined analysis).

There are different ways to specify a constraint tree in PAUP, but the easiest is use the `loa[d constraints]` command to import one or more tree definitions from any tree file or trees block in any datafile into the constraint tree buffer. The constraint tree is selected by qualifying the `hs[earch]` command. This procedure is simple when the menu is used, and the command line syntax is available via the `help loa[dconstr]` and `help hs[earch]` commands.

Other Features   Many, but not all, PAUP command options are toggles, so that a set option remains active during the session. Before implementing a new command or procedure, especially in a complex session when many different procedures and/or data sets are involved, it is useful to examine the current settings, either with the menu or by typing `{command-name}<space>?` in the appropriate field.

PAUP includes a wide array of additional features, only a few of which we mention here: (1) basic graphics features for drawing, printing, or exporting PICT files trees (including PHYLIP or CLUSTAL trees; Figure 9.1) in several formats (but, unfortunately, not as radial trees as in TreeDraw, PHYLODENDRON, and TREEVIEW); (2) a text editor to edit data and log files, which can be split into up to four panels for examining different parts of long alignments or logs; (3) logging of output to a new log file or appending it to an existing file; (4) rooting of trees using the outgroup, specified ancestor, specified ancestral states, or midpoint method; and (5) computation of character state reconstructions for MP and ML (the procedure is probably more accurate using ML, but it is much slower, and possibly impractical for more than 100 variable sites and 50 taxa; the output can be used to manually label changes on a tree); and (6) a summary of pairwise base differences between sequences (currently called "dinucleotide frequencies," although future releases may use a different term).

Other Programs

In addition to PAUP and PHYLIP, there are phylogenetics programs that have some unique capabilities but are generally more limited in their procedures and portability. These include FastDNAml, MACCLADE, MEGA plus METREE, MOLPHY, and PAML.

FastDNAml   FastDNAml (Olsen et al., 1994) is a freestanding maximum-likelihood, tree-building program. Although it is currently not part of the PHYLIP package, it uses largely the same input and output conventions, and the results of fastDNAml and PHYLIP's DNAML should be very similar or identical. FastDNAml can be run on parallel processors, and it comes with a number of useful scripts (in particular for bootstrapping and jumbling the sequence input order). To take full advantage of the program, Unix knowledge is beneficial. The source code for Unix and VAX/VMS systems is publicly available from the RDP Web site and a Power Macintosh version is available by FTP (see end-of-chapter list).

MACCLADE MACCLADE (Maddison and Maddison, 1992) is an interactive Macintosh program for manipulating trees and data and studying the phylogenetic behavior of characters. It uses the NEXUS format and will read PAUP data and treefiles. Some information in PAUP files will be ignored in MACCLADE (e.g., gapmode), but information in a PAUP "assumptions" block will be imported, including character weightings and character and taxon sets. Several subtle differences exist between PAUP and MACCLADE files. Thus, PAUP files edited with MACCLADE and vice versa should be saved under new names and the unedited file maintained. PHYLIP, NBRF-PIR, and text files (see above) are also readable by MACCLADE. Any method can be used to generate the trees, but MACCLADE's functions are based strictly on parsimony. For example, the program allows one to trace the evolution of each individual character on any tree. The MP and ML reconstruction functions differ, however, and the ML function is considered more realistic (Swofford et al., 1996a). Tree topologies can be manipulated by dragging branches, and flipping branches can produce aesthetic modifications in tree symmetry.

MACCLADE includes the following additional features relevant to sequence analysis:

1. a data editor that facilitates editing ambiguous regions because blocks of sequence can be converted to missing data symbols
2. RNA or DNA translation to amino acid data
3. recognition of IUPAC nucleotide ambiguity codes
4. a chart of character number versus number of changes in a tree, which is useful for visualizing among-site rate heterogeneity
5. a chart of the overall numbers of changes from one base to another over an MP tree ("state changes and stasis" chart: the values are sometimes erroneously reported in the literature as substitution "rates," but there is no correction for branch lengths or among-site rate heterogeneity)
6. automatic transformation of state changes and stasis values into a weight matrix according to four different formulas
7. calculation of codon position
8. selection of codon positions for charting functions and for position removal from the data set
9. a basic alignment editor that allows dragging of selected sequence blocks
10. ability to output a format similar to PRETTY with sequence blocks separated by spaces and bases matching the first sequence denoted by "."
11. a tree graphics editor similar to that in PAUP, which also permits labeling of character changes on each branch
12. an easy means of defining constraint trees for PAUP analysis (simply collapse the nodes that are not constrained and save the tree to a file)

MEGA plus METREE MEGA (Kumar et al., 1994) is a package of DOS programs for sequence analysis and comparative statistics. Distance and MP tree-building methods are included. For MP, branch-and-bound and heuristic algorithms are implemented. For distance, MEGA provides a subset of the substitution models in PAUP and the NJ tree-building algorithm. An ME search is provided in the companion program, METREE (Rzhetsky and Nei, 1994). Comparisons of the efficiency and reliability of the tree-searching algorithms in MEGA versus PAUP or PHYLIP are not available. For tree building with nucleotide data, MEGA is less well suited than PAUP (Lewis and Lewis, 1995) or PHYLIP. For example: the format does not allow assumptions to be stored in the datafile, so these must be manually specified during each session; the ranges of substitution models and treatments of gaps and missing data are limited, and parameter values cannot be evaluated by the program; weighted parsimony is not allowed; IUPAC nucleotide ambiguity codes are not recognized; bootstrapping is not allowed for MP; the tree graphics are simple, and trees cannot be saved. Although MEGA can build distance trees from codon and amino acid data, the substitution models are too simplified to yield reliable trees for most data sets. MEGA does include, however, some useful features that are not yet available in other programs (Lewis and Lewis, 1995): gap and gap size frequencies, codon usage, and amino acid frequencies.

MOLPHY MOLPHY (Adachi and Hasegawa, 1996) is a shareware package (see end-of-chapter list) of programs and utilities for ML analysis and statistics of nucleotide or amino acid sequences. It has been tested on Sun OS and HP9000/700 systems. Practical application requires some knowledge of Unix file management. The utilities include datafile file conversions to and from NEXUS, MEGA, and PHYLIP formats, as well as two that extract coding regions from EMBL or GenBank nucleotide sequence documents. The ML procedures are similar to those in PHYLIP, but there is a wider range of amino acid substitution models and options for faster, heuristic searches, including an option to use "local bootstrap" analyses (i.e., a bootstrap on subtrees under the assumption that the remainder of the tree is correct) to search for better ML trees. The output includes branch length estimates and standard error. Analysis of separate codon positions is possible. MOLPHY uses a subset of the nucleotide substitution models available in PAUP, although it allows user-specified parameter values. The current MOLPHY lacks a bootstrap option and also has no accommodation for among-site rate heterogeneity.

PAML PAML (Yang et al., 1996) is a shareware package (see end-of-chapter list) of programs and utilities for ML model- and tree building, Bayesian tree building, simulations, parsimony-based tree analysis, tree evaluation, and data and tree statistics. It has been compiled for Macintosh 68k and PowerPC computers and is available in uncompiled form for Unix (GNU gcc or Sun ANSI C). This program includes the most detailed and flexible parameter specification/estimation available for codon and amino acid data. For nucleotide data (BASEML and BASEMLG), the range of substitution models is nearly as broad as in PAUP and probably includes all models worth considering. PAML implements additional models: the correlation of rates at adjacent sites (the `autodiscrete-gamma` model) and a multigene model that allows specification of the substitution model for each gene. The latter is useful for analyses combining data from different genes evolving under different constraints. It may be useful to use PAUP for ML tree building, and then move to PAML to evaluate whether adding these parameters improves the likelihood. In addition, PAML gives standard errors for branch lengths. PAML also includes a likelihood approach to tree building under nonstationary conditions (base frequencies variable among the sequences), but it is considered impractical for more than four sequences. The CODONML program is useful for estimating codon frequencies, base frequencies per codon position, and the number of (non)synonymous substitutions per (non)synonymous site. A limiting feature of PAML is the exclusion from the data set of all sites that contain a gap or missing data score (IUPAC ambiguity codes are not permitted). As the number of taxa increases, the likelihood that at least one such score will occur at a given site increases; hence this limitation risks discarding much useful data. Also, the tree-searching algorithm in PAML is limited to the nonrigorous star decomposition method implemented in MOLPHY. Thus, multiple searches must be undertaken.

SOME SIMPLE PRACTICAL CONSIDERATIONS

1. Paradoxical as it may sound, by far the most important factor in inferring phylogenies is not the method of phylogenetic inference but the quality of the input data. The importance of data selection and in particular of the alignment process cannot be overestimated. Even the most sophisticated phylogenetic inference methods are not able to correct for erroneous input data.

2. Look at the data from as many angles as possible. Use each of the three main methods (distance, maximum parsimony, maximum likelihood), and compare the resulting trees for consistency. At the same time, be aware that one cannot rely on having arrived at a good estimate for the true phylogeny just because all three methods produce the same tree. Unfortunately, consistency among results obtained by different methods does not necessarily mean that the result is statistically significant (or represents the true phylogeny), since there can be several reasons for such correspondence.

3. The choice of outgroup taxa can have as much influence on the analysis as the choice of ingroup taxa. Complication will occur in particular when the outgroup shares an unusual property (e.g., composition bias or clock rate) with one or several ingroup taxa (Leipe et al., 1993). It is therefore advisable to compute every analysis with several outgroups and check for congruency of the ingroup topologies.

4. Be aware that programs can give different answers (trees) depending on the order in which the sequences appear in the input file. PHYLIP, PAUP and other phylogenetic software provide a "jumble" option that reruns the analysis with different (jumbled) input orders. If for whatever reason the tree must be computed in a single run, sequences that are suspected of being "problematic" should be placed toward the end of the input file, to lower the probability that tree rearrangement methods will be negatively influenced by a poor initial topology stemming from any problematic sequences.

Internet Resources for Topics in Chapter 9

PHYLOGENETIC RESOURCES

This extremely well-organized Web site at the Museum of Paleontology, of the University of California at Berkeley should be bookmarked by anybody interested in the field. The selection of phylogenetic software programs is not as large as that at some sites, but there are links covering many other aspects of phylogenetics, including publications, introductory texts, newsgroups, societies, meeting announcements, and a range of molecular and taxonomy databases.

http://www.ucmp.berkeley.edu/subway/phylogen.html

PHYLOGENY PROGRAMS

This part of the PHYLIP Web site is an excellent choice for browsing the available phylogeny software. The site offers one-paragraph descriptions for almost a hundred phylogeny programs arranged by methods (distance, likelihood, parsimony, etc.) and the computer platform they run on (Unix, Mac, PC, etc.). In addition, there are the links to the Web sites from which these programs can be downloaded or the addresses of publishers of the commercial programs.
http://evolution.genetics.washington.edu/phylip/software.html

PHYLOGENETIC ANALYSIS COMPUTER PROGRAMS

This is part of the Tree-of-Life Web pages. There are not as many programs available as from the Phylogeny Programs pages, but the program descriptions are quite good, and links to sequence editors and molecular biology tools are provided in addition to tree inference programs.
http://phylogeny.arizona.edu/tree/programs/programs.html

PARSIMONY ANALYSIS SOFTWARE

A site maintained by the International Willi Hennig Society and dedicated to parsimony methods. Many of the programs here are built to interact with PAUP or Hennig86.
http://www.vims.edu/~mes/hennig/software.html

BIOCATALOG MOLECULAR EVOLUTION

The European Bioinformatics Institute offers links to a number of phylogeny programs. The Web site holds a link to the STATALIGN program that seems to be missing from other sites.
http://www.ebi.ac.uk:/biocat/Phylogeny.html

ROD PAGE'S HOME PAGE

Contains a small number of programs for phylogenetic analysis for Macintosh or Windows, including the TreeView program mentioned below.
http://taxonomy.zoology.gla.ac.uk/rod/rod.html

READSEQ

A file conversion program that converts one sequence file format into another. The Web site has a copy-and-paste window and a pulldown menu that allows the user to choose one of 14 commonly encountered sequence file formats as output.
http://dot.imgen.bcm.tmc.edu:9331/seq-util/Options/readseq.html

SEQIO

A software package that contains an implementation of the READSEQ program in addition to many other tools for database searches and other computational tasks that molecular biologists might want to perform. It is more complex than the ReadSeq program and must be downloaded and installed— for a simple file conversion problem, ReadSeq is faster.
http://wwwcsif.cs.ucdavis.edu/~knight/seqio.html

PHYLIP

A free package of programs for inferring phylogenies. Short descriptions of the programs on the package are available online. The complete documentation and the programs must be downloaded.
http://evolution.genetics.washington.edu/phylip.html

TREEVIEW

Tree-drawing software for Apple Macintosh and Windows computers that reads standard NEXUS and PHYLIP format treefiles. The program allows the user to reroot trees and a number of other simple manipulation. The trees can be printed or saved to a file (PICT on Macintosh, Windows Metafile on Windows) for further fine-tuning. This program can be very helpful in preparing trees for a publication.

http://taxonomy.zoology.gla.ac.uk/rod/treeview.html

SUGGESTING A PHYLOGENETIC PLACEMENT ON THE RDP TREE

This service uses the fastDNAml tree-building procedure to place a small subunit RNA sequence, input by the user, on a preexisting tree maintained by the Ribosomal Database Project (RDP). This surprisingly fast service can return a 20-organism tree in less than a minute, but it does not replace a thorough analysis.

http://rdp.life.uiuc.edu/RDP/commands/sgtree.html

ACKNOWLEDGMENTS

The authors gratefully acknowledge Dave Swofford for access to pre-release test versions of PAUP 4.0, and Dave Swofford and Jack Sullivan for helpful discussion. M.A.H. was supported as an IRTA Postdoctoral Fellow, National Center for Biotechnology Information, NIH, Bethesda, Maryland, and, in part as a Research Associate, Laboratory of Molecular Systematics, Smithsonian Institution, Washington, D.C.

REFERENCES

Adachi, J., and Hasegawa, M. (1996). *MOLPHY Version 2.3. Programs for Molecular phylogenetics based on maximum likelihood* (Tokyo: Institute of Statistical Mathematics).

Avise, J. C. (1994). *Molecular Markers, Natural History and Evolution* (New York: Chapman & Hall).

Baldauf, S. L., Palmer, J. D., and Doolittle, W. F. (1996). The root of the universal tree and the origin of eukaryotes based on elongation factor phylogeny. Proc. Natl. Acad. Sci. U.S.A. *93*, 7749–7754.

Efron, B. (1979). Bootstrapping methods: Another look at the jackknife. Ann. Stat. *7*, 1–26.

Dayhoff, M. O., Schwartz, R. M., and Orcutt, B.C. (1978). A model of evolutionary change in proteins. In *Atlas of Protein Sequence and Structure* M. O. Dayhoff, ed. (Washington, DC., National Biomedical Research Foundation), pp 345–362.

Faith, D. P., and Trueman, J. W. H. (1996). When the topology-dependent permutation test (T-PTP) for monophyly returns significant support for monophyly, should that be equated with (a) rejecting the null hypothesis of nonmonophyly, (b) rejecting the null hypothesis of "no structure," (c) failing to falsify a hypothesis of monophyly, or (d) none of the above? Syst. Biol. *45*, 580–586.

Felsenstein, J. (1985). Confidence intervals on phylogenies: An approach using the bootstrap. Evolution *39*, 783–791.

Felsenstein, J. (1996). Inferring phylogenies from protein sequences by parsimony, distance, and likelihood methods. Methods Enzymol. *266*, 418–427.

Felsenstein, J. (1997). An alternative least-squares approach to inferring phylogenies from pairwise distances. Syst. Biol. *46*, 101–111.

Felsenstein, J., and Kishino, H. (1993) Is there something wrong with the bootstrap on phylogenies. A reply to Hillis and Bull. Systematic biology *42*, 193–200.

Feng, D. F., and Doolittle, R. F. (1996). Progressive alignment of amino acid sequences and construction of phylogenetic trees from them. Methods Enzymol. *266*, 368–382.

Gatesy, J., DeSalle, R., and Wheeler, W. (1993). Alignment-ambiguous nucleotide sites and the exclusion of systematic data. Mol. Phylogenet. Evol. *2*, 152–157.

Gutell, R. R., Larsen, N., and Woese, C. R. (1994). Lessons from an evolving rRNA: 16S and 23S rRNA structures from a comparative perspective. Microbiol. Rev. *58*, 10–26.

Harvey, P. H., and Pagel, M. D. (1991). *The Comparative Method in Evolutionary Biology* (Oxford: Oxford University Press).

Hein, J. (1990). Unified approach to alignment and phylogenies. Methods Enzymol. *183*, 626–645.

Hein, J. (1994). TreeAlign. Methods Mol. Biol. *25*, 349–364.

Helbig, A. J., and Seibold, I. (1996). Are storks and New World vultures paraphyletic? Mol. Phylogenet. Evol. *6*, 315–319.

Hershkovitz, M. A., and Lewis, L. A. (1996). Deep-level diagnostic value of the rDNA-ITS region. Mol. Biol. Evol. *13*, 1276–1295.

Hillis, D. M., and Bull, J. J. (1993). An empirical test of bootstrapping as a method for assessing confidence in phylogenetic analysis. Syst. Biol. *42*, 182–192.

Hillis, D. M., and Huelsenbeck, J. P. (1992).

Hillis, D. M., Allard, M. W., and Miyamoto, M. M. (1993). Analysis of DNA sequence data: Phylogenetic inference. Methods Enzymol. *224*, 456–487.

Hillis, D. M., Huelsenbeck, J. P., and Cunningham, C. W. (1994). Application and accuracy of molecular phylogenies. Science *264*, 671–677.

Huelsenbeck, J. P. (1995). Performance of phylogenetic methods in simulation. Syst. Biol. *44*, 17–48.

Huelsenbeck, J. P., Hillis, D. M., and Jones, R. (1996a). Parametric bootstrapping in molecular phylogenetics. In *Molecular Zoology: Advances, Strategies, and Protocols*, J. D. Ferraris and S. R. Palumbi, Eds. (New York: Wiley-Liss), pp. 19–45.

Huelsenbeck, J. P., Hillis, D. M., and Nielsen, R. (1996b). A likelihood-ratio test of monophyly. Syst. Biol. *45*, 546–558.

Hughey, R., Krogh, A., Barrett, C., and Grate, L. (1996). SAM: Sequence alignment and modelling software: University of California, Baskin Center for Computer Engineering and Information Sciences.

http://www.cse.ucsc.edu/research/compbio/papers/sam_doc/sam_doc.html)

Kishino, H., and Hasegawa, M. (1989). Evaluation of the maximum likelihood estimate of the evolutionary tree topologies from DNA sequence data, and the branching order in Hominoidea. J. Mol. Evol. *29*, 170–179.

Kumar, S., Tamura, K., and Nei, M. (1994). MEGA: Molecular Evolutionary Genetics Analysis software for microcomputers. Comput. Appl. Biosci. *10*, 189–191.

Lake, J. A. (1994). Reconstructing evolutionary trees from DNA and protein sequences: Paralinear distances. Proc. Natl. Acad. Sci. U.S.A. *91*, 1455–1459.

Lawrence, C. E., Altschul, S. F., Boguski, M. S., Liu, J. S., Neuwald, A. F., and Wootton, J. C. (1993). Detecting subtle sequence signals: A Gibbs sampling strategy for multiple alignments. Science *262*, 208–214.

Lawson, F. S., Charlebois, R. L., and Dillon, J. A. (1996). Phylogenetic analysis of carbamoylphosphate synthetase genes: Complex evolutionary history includes an internal duplication within a gene which can root the tree of life. Mol. Biol. Evol. *13*, 970–977.

Leipe, D. D., Gunderson, J. H., Nerad, T. A., and Sogin, M. L. (1993). Small subunit ribosomal RNA of *Hexamita inflata* and the quest for the first branch in the eukaryotic tree. Mol. Biochem. Parasitol. *59*, 41–48.

Leipe, D. D., Wainright, P. O., Gunderson, J. H., Porter, D., Patterson, D. J., Valois, F., Himmerich, S., and Sogin, M. L. (1994). The Stramenopiles from a molecular perspective: 16S-like rRNA sequences from *Labyrinthuloides minutum* and *Cafeteria roenbergensis.* Phycologia *33,* 369–377.

Lewis, P., and Lewis, L. A. (1995). MEGA: Molecular Evolutionary Genetics Analysis, Version 1.02, by S. Kumar, K. Tamura, and M. Nei. Syst. Biol. *44,* 576–577.

Li, W.-H. (1997). *Molecular Evolution* (Sunderland, MA: Sinauer Associates).

Lockhart, P. J., Steel, M. A., Hendy, M. D., and Penny, D. (1994). Recovering evolutionary trees under a more realistic model of sequence evolution. Mol. Biol. Evol. *11,* 605–612.

Maddison, W. P., and Maddison, D. R. (1992). *MacClade: Analysis of Phylogeny and Character Evolution. Version 3.0* (Sunderland, MA: Sinauer Associates).

Mindell, D. P. (1991). Aligning DNA sequences: Homology and phylogenetic weighting. In *Phylogenetic Analysis of DNA Sequences,* M. M. Miyamoto and J. Cracraft, Eds. (New York: Oxford University Press), pp. 73–89.

Morrison, D. A., and Ellis, J. T. (1997). Effects of nucleotide sequence alignment on phylogeny estimation: A case study of 18S rDNAs of Apicomplexa. Mol. Biol. Evol. *14,* 428–441.

Nixon, K. C., and Carpenter, J. M. (1993). On outgroups. Cladistics *9,* 413–426.

Olsen, G. J., Matsuda, H., Hagstrom, R., and Overbeek, R. (1994). fastDNAml: A tool for construction of phylogenetic trees of DNA sequences using maximum likelihood. Comput. Appl. Biosci. *10,* 41.

Penny, D., Lockhart, P. J., Steel, M. A., and Hendy, M. D. (1994). The role of models in reconstructing evolutionary trees. In *Models in Phylogeny Reconstruction, Systematics Association* Special Volume No. 52, R. W. Scotland, D. J. Siebert and D. M. Williams, Eds. (Oxford: Clarendon Press), pp. 211–230.

Rzhetsky, A., and Nei, M. (1992). A simple method for estimating and testing minimum evolution trees. Mol. Biol. Evol. *9,* 945–967.

Rzhetsky, A., and Nei, M. (1994). METREE: A program package for inferring and testing minimum-evolution trees. Comput. Appl. Biosci. *10,* 409–412.

Saitou, N. (1996). Reconstruction of gene trees from sequence data. Methods Enzymol. *266,* 427–449.

Sanderson, M. J. (1989). Confidence limits on phylogenies: the bootstrap revisited. Cladistics *5,* 113–129.

Soltis, D. E., Soltis, P. S., Nickrent, D. L., Johnson, L. A., Hahn, W. A., Hoot, S. B., Sweere, J. A., Kuzoff, R. K., Kron, K. A., Chase, M. W., Swenson, S. M., Zimmer, A. A., Chaw, S.-M., Gillespie, L. J., Kress, W. J., and Sytsma, K. J. (1997). Angiosperm phylogeny inferred from 18S ribosomal DNA sequences. Ann. Missouri Bot. Garden *84,* 1–49.

Strimmer, K., and von Haeseler, A. (1996). Quartet puzzling: A quartet maximum likelihood method for reconstructing tree topologies. Mol. Biol. Evol. *13,* 964–969.

Sullivan, M. J., and Swofford, D. L. (1997) Are guinea pigs rodents? The importance of adequate models in molecular phylogenetics. J. Mammal. Evol. *4,* 77–86.

Swofford, D. L. (1990). PAUP. Phylogenetic Analysis Using Parsimony, Version 3.0. Computer program distributed by the Illinois Natural History Survey, Champaign, IL.

Swofford, D. L. (1997).

Swofford, D. L., and Olsen, G. J. (1990).

Swofford, D. L., Olsen, G. J., Waddell, P. J., and Hillis, D. M. (1996a). Phylogenetic inference. In *Molecular Systematics,* D. M. Hillis, C. Moritz, and B. K. Mable, Eds. (Sunderland, MA: Sinauer Associates), pp. 407–514.

Swofford, D. L., Thorne, J. L., Felsenstein, J., and Wiegmann, B. M. (1996b). The topology-dependent permutation test for monophyly does not test for monophyly. Syst. Biol. *45,* 575–579.

Thompson, J. D., Higgins, D. G., and Gibson, T. J. (1994). Clustal W: Improving the sensitivity of progressive multiple alignment through sequence weighting. Nucl. Acids Res *22,* 4673–4680.

Thorne, J. L., and Kishino, H. (1992). Freeing phylogenies from artifacts of alignment. Mol. Biol. Evol. *9,* 1148–1162.

Weston, P. H. (1994). Methods for rooting cladistic trees. In *Models in Phylogeny Reconstruction,* R. W. Scotland, D. J. Siebert, and D. M. Williams, Eds. (Oxford: Systematics Association), pp. 125–155.

Wheeler, W. C. (1994). Sources of ambiguity in nucleic acid sequence alignment. Exs *69,* 323–352.

Wheeler, W. C., and Gladstein, D. (1994). MALIGN: A multiple sequence alignment program. J. Hered. *85,* 417.

Yang, W. M., Inouye, C. J., Zeng, Y., Bearss, D., and Seto, E. (1996). Transcriptional repression by YY1 is mediated by interaction with mammalian homolog of the yeast global regulator RPD3. Proc. Natl. Acad. Sci. U.S.A. *93,* 12845–12850.

Yang, Z., Goldman, N., and Friday, A. (1995). Maximum likelihood trees from DNA sequences: A peculiar statistical problem. Syst. Biol. *44,* 384–399.

10

Predictive Methods Using Nucleotide Sequences

James W. Fickett

SmithKline Beecham Pharmaceuticals
King of Prussia, Pennsylvania

This chapter discusses DNA sequence interpretation methods that rely primarily on detection of functional patterns rather than on comparison with other individual sequences. For the most part, such methods are intended to first find/mask repeats and other low-complexity sequences, and then find the genes and their associated regulatory regions. These methods play a major role both in intensive investigation of individual sequences and in rapid scanning, for the preliminary inventorying of possible genes, of whole genomes, or of large regions thereof. As a result of rapid progress in algorithm development, there is no single tool that can perform all the relevant sequence analysis. Thus, to make use of the best computational techniques, it is necessary to submit one's sequence to the analysis of several different software packages. To make the process as efficient as possible, this chapter provides a concise guide to current tools. Useful materials available elsewhere include the online bibliography compiled by Wentian Li (see "Bibliography . . ." in the list at the end of the chapter for the URL for this resource) and related reviews, listed in the References: Gelfand (1995), Claverie (1996), Fickett and Guigó (1996), Snyder and Stormo (1996), and Guigó (1997).

The chapter is organized as follows: first, a description of a conceptual framework, to help put the different tools in context; next, a review of the main types of computer tool and, for each, a discussion of the underlying logic and use of example programs. Current tools are useful, but by no means infallible. One limitation of current development, for example, is that many descriptions of prototype functional domains are derived, by software developers, from the domains annotated in the DDBJ/EMBL/GenBank international sequence database. However the annotation in that database can itself be derived in part

Bioinformatics: A Practical Guide to the Analysis of Genes and Proteins
Edited by A.D. Baxevanis and B.F.F. Ouellette
ISBN 0-471-19196-5, pages 231–245.   Copyright © 1998 Wiley-Liss, Inc.

from sequence analysis, leading to circularity. The strengths and limitations of individual analysis methods receive special attention in what follows. Some of the most commonly used, network-available tools are listed in tables below.

FRAMEWORK

Whether an overall gene-finding protocol is carried out by one integrated program or by a person using several specialized programs, the basic information flow is the same. First, evidence is gathered from several sources:

- A map of repeat locations shows where regulatory and protein-coding regions are *unlikely* to occur.
- Sequence similarity to other genes or gene products provides strong positive evidence for exons.
- Statistical regularity evincing apparent "codon bias" over a region is one of the clearest indicators of protein-coding regions.
- Matches to template patterns may indicate the locations of functional sites on the DNA. Such analysis can be based on very simple patterns (e.g., the well-known consensus sequences for the TATA box and splice junctions) or on much more complex reasoning (e.g., in promoter-finding algorithms described below).

Next, all the information so gathered is integrated to make as coherent a picture as possible of the overall situation. The rules applied at the integration stage are basically common sense: for example, an exon boundary found by a codon bias analysis may be adjusted slightly to take advantage of a better splice site; and codon bias is to be taken more seriously if there is also similarity to a known protein sequence.

For any particular inquiry, only a few of the many programs for gene identification are relevant. In setting up a protocol, certain main points need to be considered: (1) for eukaryotic sequences, screening for repeats should precede all other analysis; (2) most programs are organism specific; (3) many programs are specific for either genomic or cDNA data; and (4) the length of the sequence is a major factor. For example, single reads from shotgun sequencing seldom can be analyzed by the more sophisticated programs designed to find whole genes in the sequence.

MASKING REPETITIVE DNA

It is best to locate and remove interspersed and simple repeats from eukaryotic sequences as the first step in any gene identification analysis. Although such repeats may well overlap regions transcribed by RNA polymerase II, they rarely overlap promoters or the coding portions of exons. Thus their locations can provide important negative information on the location of gene features. Also, repeats can often confuse other analysis, especially database searches.

For occasional analyses of single sequences, an e-mail or Web-based server is adequate. CENSOR (Jurka et al., 1996) and RepeatMasker (Smit, 1996) are such servers, which provide annotation and masking of both interspersed and simple repeats, through either an e-mail or a World Wide Web interface (see end-of-chapter list). Figure 10.1 shows an example of repeat analysis and masking by CENSOR.

For high-volume analysis, installation of software locally may be necessary for efficiency. Of course privacy is also enhanced by carrying out the analysis locally. The source code for XBLAST (Claverie, 1996) (not to be confused with BLASTX) is available on the Internet. Several collections of repeats are provided by J. Jurka in the Repbase collection. J.-M. Claverie also provides a curated Alu collection in association with the XBLAST software. For local installation it may also be useful to add cloning vector sequences to these sequence collections, to allow vectors to be masked out in the same step with repeat masking.

```
(a)
;           HUMCKMM1
HUMCKMM1
ggatccttcctccttggcctcccaaagtgctgggattacaggtgtgagccactgcacctg
gcctattacccttctcaggctctggagtccatccttctgctctgtctccctcagttcaat
tgtttttttgtttttttgttttttttttttagacacagtctcgctctgtcaccaaggctggagt
gcagcagtgcgatcacagctcaccgcagcctcacctcccaggctcaagtgatcctcccat
ctcggcctctgagtagctgagactataggtgtgtccacatgtccggctaatttttgtatt
tttagtagagacagggtttcaccgcgttggccagggtggtcttgaactcctgagctcaag
caatcctcctgcctcagcctccttgttttgattttttagatcccacaaataacttgtgatg
tttgtctttctataccctggttcatttaacattttcttttttcttttctttttctttttttt
ttttttgtgagactgagtcttgctctgtcactcaggctggagggcaatggtgcatctcag
ctcactgcaacctccacctcctaggttcaagcaattcttatgcctcagcctcctggctag
ctgggattacaggcgtgtgtcaccatgccaggctaattttttgtactttttagtagagatgg
ggtttcaccatgttggccaggctggtcttgaactcctggcctcaagtgatccaccgcct
ccgcctctgcctcccaaagtgctgggattacgggcctgagccactgtgcccggcccatct
aacattttcactgtcaatcacaatgggattaaaactcctcccacagcccctagggaccal
(b)
humckmm1          2         63    Alu-Jb         1        62  c
humckmm1         67        119    L1MA2        697       751  c
humckmm1        138        382    Alu-Jb        42       290  c
humckmm1        383        449    L1MA2        623       696  c
humckmm1        451        480    (TTTTC)        5        33  d
humckmm1        481        775    Alu-Sz         1       290  c
(c)
;           humckmm1
;humckmm1
humckmm1
GXXXXXXXXXXXXXXXXXXXXXXXXXXXXXXXXXXXXXXXXXXXXXXXXXXXXXXXXXXXXTATXXXX
XXXXXXXXXXXXXXXXXXXXXXXXXXXXXXXXXXXXXXXXXXXXXXXXXXTTGTTTTTTGTTTTTTGTXXX
XXXXXXXXXXXXXXXXXXXXXXXXXXXXXXXXXXXXXXXXXXXXXXXXXXXXXXXXXXXXXXXXXX
XXXXXXXXXXXXXXXXXXXXXXXXXXXXXXXXXXXXXXXXXXXXXXXXXXXXXXXXXXXXXXXXXX
XXXXXXXXXXXXXXXXXXXXXXXXXXXXXXXXXXXXXXXXXXXXXXXXXXXXXXXXXXXXXXXXXX
XXXXXXXXXXXXXXXXXXXXXXXXXXXXXXXXXXXXXXXXXXXXXXXXXXXXXXXXXXXXXXXXXX
XXXXXXXXXXXXXXXXXXXXXXXXXXXXXAXXXXXXXXXXXXXXXXXXXXXXXXXXXXXXXXXXXX
XXXXXXXXXXXXXXXXXXXXXXXXXXXXXXXXXXXXXXXXXXXXXXXXXXXXXXXXXXXXXXXXXX
XXXXXXXXXXXXXXXXXXXXXXXXXXXXXXXXXXXXXXXXXXXXXXXXXXXXXXXXXXXXXXXXXX
XXXXXXXXXXXXXXXXXXXXXXXXXXXXXXXXXXXXXXXXXXXXXXXXXXXXXXXXXXXXXXXXXX
XXXXXXXXXXXXXXXXXXXXXXXXXXXXXXXXXXXXXXXXXXXXXXXXXXXXXXXXXXXXXXXXXX
XXXXXCATCTAACATTTTCACTGTCAATCACAATGGGATTAAAACTCCTCCCACAGCCCCTAGGGACCA1
```

Figure 10.1 Repeat analysis by CENSOR: *(a)* the input sequence, *(b)* the Feature table produced by CENSOR, and *(c)* the output sequence, with the repeats masked.

DATABASE SEARCHES

Searching for a known homolog is perhaps the oldest and most widely understood means of identifying new protein-coding genes (e.g., Doolittle, 1986; Gish and States, 1993; Robison et al., 1994; Claverie, 1996; Gelfand et al., 1996), as well as snRNA and rRNA genes. Such searches depend only on evolutionary relatedness, and so are widely applicable. Database searching techniques are treated in detail in Chapter 7. This section comments only on their specific application to finding genes.

Integrated gene-finding services are beginning to include database searches as part of the analysis. However, in some cases, the database search step still needs to be done separately by the user. For protein-coding genes, translating the sequence in all six possible reading frames and using the result as a query against databases of amino acid sequences and functional motifs is usually the best first step for finding important matches. Once a homolog has been found, Procrustes (Gelfand et al., 1996) may be used to make an optimal alignment between the known gene product and the new gene.

A major advantage of finding a homologous product is of course that some of the biology of the gene may be already elucidated. But there are two caveats. First, annotation by similarity may merely propagate errors (Bork, 1996). Second, only about half the new proteins being discovered have a homolog already in the databases, and this fraction seems to be increasing rather slowly. Green et al. (1993) found that (1) most ancient conserved regions (or ACRs, roughly defined as regions of protein sequences showing highly significant homologies across phyla) of the protein universe are already known and may be found in current databases, (2) roughly 20–50% of newly found genes contain an ACR that is represented in the databases, and (3) rarely expressed genes are less likely to contain an ACR than moderately or highly expressed ones.

A direct search of nucleotide sequence databases will also be valuable. The EST (partial cDNA sequence) databases probably contain fragments of a majority of all genes (Aaronson et al., 1996; Hillier et al., 1996). Thus they are an important resource for locating some part of most genes. However it is not yet clear to what extent they are useful for delimiting gene structure. It is well known that nucleotide database searches are a valuable means of locating rRNA and snRNA genes (though of course pseudogenes remain a problem). Such searches may also be useful for locating regulatory regions (Duret and Bucher, 1997).

CODON BIAS DETECTION

Most computational identification of protein-coding genes relies heavily on recognizing the somewhat diffuse regularities in protein-coding regions that are due to bias in codon usage. Simply tabulating codon frequencies is one example of a *coding measure,* that is, a rule for calculating a number, or table of numbers, meant to summarize such regularities. Many coding measures have been suggested; probably the most informative are dicodon counts (i.e., frequency counts for the occurrence of successive codon pairs), some direct measure of periodicity (in this context, "periodicity" means the tendency of multiple occurrences of the same nucleotide to be found at distances of 3, 6, 9, . . . , bp), a measure of homogeneity versus complexity (such as counting long homopolymer runs), and open reading frame occurrence (Fickett and Tung, 1992).

Many coding region detection programs are primarily the result of combining the numbers from one or more coding measures (using, e.g., probability theory, discriminant analysis techniques from multivariate statistics, or neural net methods from the field of artificial intelligence) to form a single number called a discriminant. Such a combination forms, for example, the primary basis for the well-known GRAIL program (Xu et al., 1994). Typically, then, the discriminant is calculated in a "sliding window" (i.e., for successive subsequences of fixed length) and the result plotted (Figure 10.2).

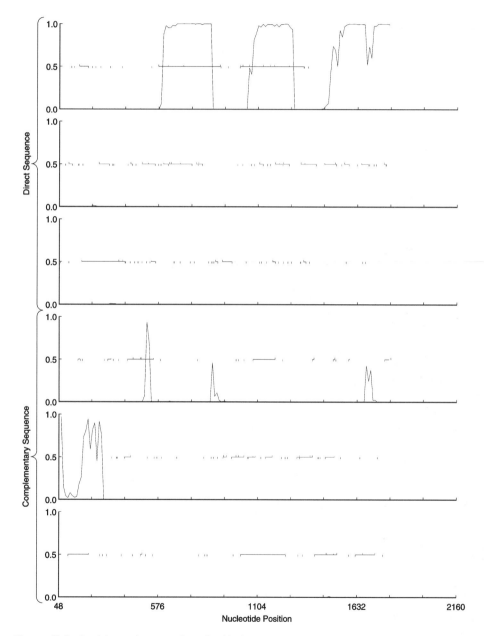

Figure 10.2 Partial sample output from GenMark, an e-mail service for coding region identification. GenMark has seven probabilistic models of DNA, based on counts of hexamers in noncoding regions and in each of the six possible reading frames of coding regions. The program calculates the probability that windows of DNA are noncoding, or should be read in one of the six reading frames.

Something on the order of a hundred bases is required to gain significant information from a coding measure discriminant. More concretely, the following benchmark was carried out by Fickett and Tung (1992): (1) GenBank was divided into successive 108 bp windows; (2) only those fully coding or fully noncoding were saved; (3) half the windows were used to set the parameters in a linear discriminant combination of four measures, as described above; and (4) the other half were used to measure the accuracy of prediction of the resulting discriminant. A correct prediction rate of 88% was found. Thus coding measures give a rather low-resolution picture of coding region boundaries. However, coding measures may reasonably be applied to fragmentary sequences (e.g., single reads of a few hundred base pairs from shotgun sequencing projects), and this is a major advantage.

Many coding measures are quite organism specific, and one must look closely to determine the subset of the taxonomic universe in which a particular service was developed and tested.

DETECTING FUNCTIONAL SITES IN THE DNA

Coding measures probably have little in common with the way a cell recognizes and expresses genes (though see Knudsen and Brunak, 1997). It will be more enlightening (and accuracy probably will improve) when we are able to recognize those locations, such as transcription factor binding sites and exon/intron junctions, where the gene expression machinery interacts with the nucleic acid.

One way to summarize the essential information content of these locations (typically called "signals" by those who develop gene identification algorithms) is to give the *consensus sequence,* consisting of the most common base at each position of an alignment of specific binding sites. Consensus sequences are very useful as mnemonic devices but are typically not very reliable for discriminating true sites from pseudosites, in part because they contain no information on how often the other three bases can occur at each position. Many algorithms using more sophisticated techniques can give better discrimination. One technique with a basis in physical chemistry is that of the position weight matrix (PWM). A score is assigned to each possible nucleotide at each possible position of the signal. For any particular sequence, considered as a possible occurrence of the signal, the appropriate scores are summed to give a score to a potential site. Under some circumstances this score may be approximately proportional to the energy of binding for a control (ribonucleo)protein (see Stormo, 1990, and von Hippel, 1994, for an overview).

There have been a few studies (e.g., Barrick et al., 1994) showing that a PWM works well to evaluate individual binding sites of a particular kind. Unfortunately, however, using PWMs in isolation for recognizing complex elements of general eukaryotic gene expression (e.g., splice sites and promoter sequences) has had relatively limited success. Major reasons probably include context-specific expression mechanisms and cooperativity among multiple binding molecules.

Promoters

Only recently has it become common to determine eukaryotic genomic sequences large enough to contain several genes. With the data comes a new problem for gene finding programs: to partition a set of exons correctly among multiple genes. The promoter is an information-rich signal that performs this function biologically. Computer recognition of promoters (recently reviewed in Fickett and Hatzigeorgiou, 1997) is important partly for the advance it may provide in gene identification. A number of sophisticated programs depend on libraries describing transcription factor binding specificities, together with some description of promoter structure. But these descriptions seem not to capture some important aspects of transcription initiation and, perhaps surprisingly, programs depending primarily on simple oligonucleotide frequency counts perform about as well. Promoter recognition still represents a significant challenge: in the review just cited, currently available programs were tested on 18 sequences containing 24 recently determined transcription start sites. The programs found at best about half of the promoters, with a false positive rate on the order of one per kilobase.

Intron Splice Sites

PWMs have been compiled for splice sites in a number of different taxonomic groups (Senapathy et al., 1990), and these may be the best resource available for analysis in many organisms. Unfortunately, PWM analysis of the splice junction provides rather low specificity, perhaps because of the existence of multiple splicing mechanisms (for a brief overview of some recent discoveries, see Nilsen, 1996) and regulated alternative splicing (McKeown, 1992). (In fact, because most alternative splicing is not documented in the databases, it is difficult even to fully assess the accuracy of current algorithms.) As part of the integrated gene-finding program GENSCAN, Burge and Karlin (1997) cluster splice sites into different categories and use a decision tree (e.g., Breiman et al., 1984) with a PWM applied at each leaf of the tree. This measure seems to improve accuracy significantly. Many of the integrated gene identification services (see below) provide separate splice site predictions (e.g., the H/D/N/ASPL components of the FGENEH/D/N/A program of Solovyev and Salamov, 1997). In addition, Brunak et al. (1991) provide a standalone splice site prediction program NetGene (see list at the end of the chapter) that combines information on the splice site per se with an estimate of coding potential on either side.

Translation Initiation Site

In eukaryotes, if the transcription start site is known, and there is no intron interrupting the 5′ untranslated region, Kozak's rules (Kozak, 1996) probably will locate the correct initiation codon in most cases. Splicing is normally absent in prokaryotes, but finding the correct initiation codon within an open reading frame is still difficult. In this case because of the existence of multicistronic operons, promoter location, though useful, is not the key information it is for eukaryotes. Rather, for prokaryotes, the key is reliable localization of the ribosome binding site. A number of programs are available for this purpose; see Gelfand (1995) for a review.

Termination Signals

The polyadenylation and translation termination signals seem to be much less informative than the signals at the beginnings of genes, but these can nevertheless also help to demarcate the extent of a gene. See, for example, Kondrakhin, et al. (1994), Wahle and Keller (1996), Dalphin et al. (1997), and Solovyev and Salamov (1997) for the state of the art.

INTEGRATED GENE PARSING

The first generation of computational aids for gene identification treated mainly the recognition of isolated aspects of genes—for example, splice sites alone, or the regularities of coding regions without reference to signals. But if, for example, a splice site interrupts a coding region, it will help in detection to look for coding region on one side and noncoding on the other. It has been shown that taking into account the overall consistency of putative features significantly increases prediction accuracy. For example, 60% of exons under 50 bp missed by the original GRAIL e-mail program may be detected when a simple logical analysis of splicing and frame is added (Einstein et al., 1992).

Integrated gene-finding programs begin by searching for signals and performing a coding region analysis (and sometimes doing homology searches as well). Then, by optimizing some scoring function, they attempt to define exons and to give one or more tentative gene structures that seem most consistent with all the data at hand. Increased accuracy and user convenience are the primary forces behind the development of these programs.

Several such integrated algorithms are now available (Table 10.1), and at least in some circumstances can give a good idea of gene structure. The results of analyzing the human enolase gene sequence (HSENO3; accession X56832) with GENSCAN (after masking repeats) are shown in Figure 10.3.

The results of analyzing this same sequence with most of the other programs can be found in Fickett and Guigó (1996). For comparison, the GenBank annotation reads:

```
CDS join (1579..1663, 2540..2635, 2796..2854, 3016..3085, 3455..3588,
4820..5042, 5153..5350, 5688..5889, 6318..6426, 6576..6634, 6723..6792)
```

Table 10.2 lists these results in more human-readable form.

The main limitations of the programs (in this first generation of a new technology) are these: (1) integrated algorithms are currently available for only a few organisms; (2) for all but one (GENSCAN) of these programs, if the input includes multiple genes or partial genes, the predicted exons may still make sense, but predicted gene structures may not; (3) for reasons that are not altogether clear, accuracy may be considerably lower than originally thought, particularly on genes recently discovered (when Burset and Guigó, 1996, benchmarked available programs on a few hundred simple cases, no program succeeded in correctly predicting more than about half the exons); (4) most integrated algorithms are apparently quite sensitive to sequencing errors (Burset and Guigó, 1996), and (5) such facets of gene syntax as alternative splicing, overlapping genes, and promoter structure remain beyond the reach of current programs.

Since none of the integrated gene identification programs is perfect, all embody somewhat different algorithms, and all are rapidly evolving, analysis of each sequence with, say, three or four programs and carefully comparing the results is very strongly suggested. If the tools are to be used often, it may be worthwhile to analyze a number of test sequences, where the answer is already known, to get a feeling for algorithm capabilities.

FINDING tRNA GENES

Recognition of tRNA genes is easier than recognition of protein coding genes, in part because of the simpler structure of pol III promoters and the conserved secondary structure of

TABLE 10.1 Internet Tools for Identification of Protein-Coding Genes

Service	Ref.	Organism(s)	E-Mail Address and/or Web Site
EcoParse	Krogh et al. (1994)	*Escherichia coli*	e-mail: *ecoparse@cse.ucsc.edu*
FGENEH/D/N/Y/A	Solovyev and Salamov (1997)	Mammalian, *Drosophila*, nematode, yeast, plant, and bacteria	e-mail: *analysis@theory.bchs.uh.edu*
CDSB			*http://defrag.bcm.tmc.edu:9503/ltp.html*
GeneID	Guigó et al. (1992)	Vertebrate	e-mail: *geneid@darwin.bu.edu*
GeneMark	Borodovsky and McIninch (1993)	Many individual species	e-mail: *genemark@ford.gatech.edu* *http://intron.biology.gatech.edu/~genmark*
GeneParser	Snyder and Stormo (1995)	Human	*http://beagle.colorado.edu/~eesnyder/GeneParser.html*
Genie	Kulp et al. (1996)	Human	*http://www-hgc.lbl.gov/inf/genie.html*
GenLang	Dong and Searls (1994)	Dicotyledons, *Drosophila*, vertebrates	e-mail: *genlang@cbil.humgen.upenn.edu* *http://cbil.humgen.upenn.edu/~sdong/genlang_home.html*
GENSCAN	Burge and Karlin (1997)	Vertebrate, *Caenorhabditis*, maize, *Arabidopsis*	e-mail: *genscan@gnomic.stanford.edu* *http://gnomic.stanford.edu/~chris/GENSCANW.html*
GenView	Milanesi et al. (1993)	Human, mouse, Diptera	*http://www.itba.mi.cnr.it/webgene*
GRAIL/GAP/ XGRAIL	Xu et al. (1994)	Human	e-mail: *grail@ornl.gov* *http://avalon.epm.ornl.gov/gallery.html*
MZEF	Zhang (1997)	Human, mouse, *Arabidopsis*, fission yeast	*http://www.cshl.org/genefinder*
Procrustes	Gelfand et al. (1996)	Any	*http://www-hto.usc.edu/software/procrustes*

```
Predicted genes/exons:
Gn.Ex Type -S .Begin ...End .Len Fr Ph I/Ac Do/T CodRg P.... Tscr..
----- ---- -- ------ ------ ---- -- -- ---- ---- ----- ----- ------
1.01 Init +    1579   1663    85  0  1  114   54   131 0.741 13.24
1.02 Intr +    2540   2635    96  0  0    1  100   134 0.698  6.38
1.03 Intr +    3455   3588   134  0  2  101   81   136 0.999 15.07
1.04 Intr +    4820   5042   223  1  1   85   56   432 0.998 37.93
1.05 Intr +    5153   5350   198  0  0   73   81   371 0.999 34.74
1.06 Intr +    5688   5889   202  1  1   53   69   378 0.979 31.27
1.07 Intr +    6318   6426   109  0  1   62   80    20 0.843 -0.61
1.08 Intr +    6576   6634    59  2  2  105   77    51 0.888  3.87
1.09 Term +    6723   6792    70  0  1   63   54    98 0.785  1.61
1.10 PlyA +    6853   6858     6                            1.05
Predicted peptide sequence(s):
>gi|GENSCAN_predicted_peptide_1|391_aa
MAMQKIFAREILDSRGNPTVEVDLHTAKGRFRAAVPSGASTGIYEALELRDGDKGRYLGK
AKFGANAILGVSLAVCKAGAAEKGVPLYRHIADLAGNPDLILPVPAFNVINGGSHAGNKL
AMQEFMILPVGASSFKEAMRIGAEVYHHLKGVIKAKYGKDATNVGDEGGFAPNILENNEA
LELLKTAIQAAGYPDKVVIGMDVAASEFYRNGKYDLDFKSPDDPARHITGEKLGELYKSF
IKNYPVVSIEDPFDQDDWATWTSFLSGVNIQIVGDDLTVTNPKRIAQAVEKKACNCLLLK
VNQIGSVTESIQACKLAQSNGWGVMVSHRSGETEDTFIADLVVGLCTGQIKTGAPCRSER
LAKYNQLMRIEEALGDKAIFAGRKFRNPKAK
```

```
Column  Description
------  ------------------------------------------------------------------
Gn.Ex   gene number, exon number (for reference)
Type    Init = Initial exonIntr = Internal exon
        Term = Terminal exonSngl = Single-exon gene
        Prom = PromoterPlyA = poly-A signal
S       DNA strand (+ = input strand; - = opposite strand)
Begin   beginning of exon or signal (numbered on input strand)
End     end point of exon or signal (numbered on input strand)
Len     length of exon or signal (bp)
Fr      reading frame (a codon ending at x is in frame f = x modulo 3)
Ph      net phase of exon (exon length modulo 3)
I/Ac    initiation signal or acceptor splice site score (x 10)
Do/T    donor splice site or termination signal score (x 10)
CodRg   coding region score (x 10)
P       probability of exon (sum over all parses containing exon)
Tscr    exon score (depends on length, B/Ac, Do/T and CodRg scores)
```

Figure 10.3 Sample output from GENSCAN; see text for details.

tRNAs. The tRNA gene recognition problem has apparently been solved in tRNAscan-SE (Lowe and Eddy, 1997), which combines elements of several earlier programs. Lowe and Eddy found that over 99% of true tRNA genes could be identified by taking the union of the predictions of tRNAscan (Fichant and Burks, 1991), which relies on a secondary structure check and PWM detection of two conserved promoter elements, with those of the algorithm of Pavesi et al. (1994), which relies on an analysis of transcription control elements. This merged prediction list contains over 50% false positives. A very selective algorithm, COVELS (Eddy and Durbin, 1994), was found to remove essentially all false positives from this list. The overall result is a method that reportedly identifies over 99% of true tRNA genes with less than one false positive expected per genome. Both a server and

TABLE 10.2 Comparison of Predicted and Annotated Gene

Predicted Exons	Annotated Exons
1579 1663	1579 1663
2540 2635	2540 2635
	2796 2854
	3016 3085
3455 3588	3455 3588
4820 5042	4820 5042
5153 5350	5153 5350
5688 5889	5688 5889
6318 6426	6318 6426
6576 6634	6576 6634
6723 6792	6723 6792

the tRNAscan-SE software are available (see end-of-chapter list). Sample output is shown in Figure 10.4.

FUTURE PROSPECTS

In the recent past the best techniques often were not easily accessible to the average user. The situation is getting better, with a number of Internet services easily available and a WWW page that is continually providing more of these services through a single interface (Smith et al., 1996). Even so, a user wanting access to a suite of state-of-the-art algorithms still must be willing to submit the data to a number of programs and, furthermore, to either send data over the Internet (a difficulty if privacy is essential) or hire a programmer to import and install various programs. In the case of large-scale sequencing, one must further devise a means to automatically submit the sequence to all the programs and distill all the results in a way that makes sense to the end user. A very valuable development would be a framework for tool integration allowing every member of the community to continue independent development, and also allowing workers with relatively little training in program-

```
Sequence          tRNA Bounds    tRNA   Anti    Intron Bounds   Cove
Name       tRNA #  Begin   End    Type   Codon   Begin  End      Score
--------   ------  -----   ---    ----   -----   -----  -----    -----
Your-seq   1       2348    2420   Val    TAC     0      0        76.52
Your-seq   2       2440    2512   Thr    TGT     0      0        77.70
Your-seq   3       2522    2594   Lys    TTT     0      0        84.24
Your-seq   4       2627    2698   Gly    GCC     0      0        75.46
Your-seq   5       2709    2794   Leu    TAA     0      0        62.99
Your-seq   6       2803    2876   Arg    ACG     0      0        71.02
Your-seq   7       2900    2973   Pro    TGG     0      0        79.67
Your-seq   8       2997    3069   Ala    TGC     0      0        71.25
Your-seq   9       4841    4914   Ile    GAT     0      0        84.04
```

Figure 10.4 Sample output from tRNAscan-SE. The sequence analyzed was SA5SRR, accession L36472, from *Staphylococcus aureus*. The tRNA genes predicted coincide exactly with those annotated in DDBJ/EMBL/GenBank.

ming to integrate any set of such programs into a protocol appropriate for a particular laboratory. Such a framework might be based on e-mail and the World Wide Web.

A new and very exciting development is the attempt to capture current understanding of transcriptional regulatory mechanisms in software, so as to provide, by computational analysis, some idea of the context under which a gene is expressed. Methods for identifying putative protein binding sites have been reviewed in Frech et al. (1997). The specification of transcriptional context seems usually to depend on more complex patterns than the binding of a single factor. Early attempts to define the functional implication of such patterns in the DNA include Claverie and Sauvaget (1985), Fondrat and Kalogeropoulos (1994), Fickett (1996), Pedersen et al. (1996), Rosenblueth et al. (1996), and Tronche et al. (1997). While practical tools do not yet exist for the prediction of gene expression patterns from DNA sequence, it is not unreasonable to hope that such tools will be available in the next few years.

Internet Resources for Repeat Analysis and Other Topics Presented in Chapter 10

SERVICE	ORGANISM(S)	ADDRESS
Repeat Analysis		
CENSOR: annotates repeats in sequence and masks them out	Human or rodent	e-mail: *censor@sharon.lpi.org* see also *http://www.girinst.org*
Repbase: repeat collections	Human and several other collections	*ftp ncbi.nlm.nih.gov; repository/repbase/REF;* also *http://www.girinst.org*
Repeat Masker: annotates repeats in sequence and masks them out	Several sub-groups of vertebrates	*http://ftp.genome.washington.edu/index.html*
XBLAST: tools to mask repeat occurrences	Any	*ftp ncbi.nlm.nih.gov; pub/jmc*
Other Topics		
BCM Search Launcher (interface to multiple analysis tools)	Any	*http://gc.bcm.tmc.edu:8088/search-launcher/launcher.html*
Bibliography for computational gene identification	All	*http://linkage.rockefeller.edu/wli/gene/list.html*
Netgene (splice site identification)	Human	e-mail: *netgene@cbs.dtu.dk*
Procrustes (gene delineation by alignment)	Any	*http://www-hto.usc.edu/software/procrustes*
tRNAscan-SE (tRNA gene identification)	Any	*http://genome.wustl.edu/eddy/*

ACKNOWLEDGMENTS

This work was supported by SmithKline Beecham Pharmaceuticals and Public Health Service grant HG00981-01A1 from the National Human Genome Research Institute.

REFERENCES

Aaronson, J., Eckman, B., Blevins, R. A., Borkowski, J. A., Myerson, J., Imran, S., and Elliston, K. O. (1996). Toward the development of a gene index to the human genome: An assessment of the nature of high-throughput EST sequence data. Genome Res. *6,* 829–845.

Barrick, D., Villaneuba, K., Childs, J., Kalil, R., Schneider, T. D., Lawrence, C. E., Gold, L., and Stormo, D. (1994). Quantitative analysis of ribosome binding sites in *E. coli.* Nucl. Acids Res. *22,* 1287–1295.

Bork, P. (1996). Go hunting in sequence databases but watch out for the traps. Trends Genet. *12,* 425–427.

Borodovsky, M., and McIninch, J. (1993). Genmark: Parallel gene recognition for both DNA strands. Compu. Chem. *17,* 123–134.

Breiman, L., Friedman, J. H., Olshen, R. A., and Stone, C. J. (1984). *Classification and Regression Trees* (Pacific Grove, CA: Wadsworth and Brooks/Cole).

Brunak, S., Engelbrecht, J., and Knudsen, S. (1991). Prediction of human mRNA donor and acceptor sites from the DNA sequence. J. Mol. Biol. *220,* 49–65.

Burge, C., and Karlin, S. (1997). Prediction of complete gene structures in human genomic DNA. J. Mol. Biol. *268,* 78–94.

Burset, M., and Guigó, R. (1996). Evaluation of gene structure prediction programs. Genomics *34,* 353–367.

Claverie, J.-M. (1996). Effective large-scale sequence similarity searches. Methods Enzymol. *266,* 212–227.

Claverie, J.-M., and Sauvaget, I. (1985). Assessing the biological significance of primary structure consensus patterns using sequence databanks. I. Heat-shock and glucocorticoid control elements in eukaryotic promoters. Comput. Appl. Biosci. *1,* 95–104.

Dalphin, M. E., Brown, C. M., Stockwell, P. A., and Tate, W. P. (1997). The translational signal database, TransTerm: More organisms, complete genomes. Nucl. Acids Res. *25,* 246–247.

Dong, S., and Searls, D. B. (1994). Gene structure prediction by linguistic methods. Genomics *23,* 540–551.

Doolittle, R. F. (1986). *Of URFs and ORFs* (Mill Valley, CA: University Science Books).

Duret, L., and Bucher, P. (1997). Searching for regulatory elements in human noncoding sequences. Curr. Opin. Struct. Biol. *7,* 399–406.

Eddy, S. R., and Durbin, R. (1994). RNA sequence analysis using covariance models. Nucl. Acids Res. *22,* 2079–2088.

Einstein, J. R., Mural, R. J., Guan, X., and Uberbacher, E. C. (1992). Computer-Based Construction of Gene Models Using the GRAIL Gene Assembly Program. Oak Ridge National Laboratory Report TM-12174 (Oak Ridge, TN-ORNL).

Fichant, G., and Burks, C. (1991). Identifying potential tRNA genes in genomic DNA sequences. J. Mol. Biol. *220,* 659–671.

Fickett, J. W. (1996). Coordinate positioning of MEF2 and myogenin binding sites. Gene *172,* GC19–GC32.

Fickett, J. W., and Guigó, R. (1996). Computational gene identification. In *Internet for the Molecular Biologist,* S. R. Swindell, R. R. Miller, and G. Myers, Eds. (Washington, DC: Horizon Scientific Press), pp. 73–100.

Fickett, J. W., and Hatzigeorgiou, A. G. (1997). Eukaryotic promoter recognition. Genome Res. *7,* 861–878.

Fickett, J. W., and Tung, C.-S. (1992). Assessment of protein coding measures. Nucl. Acids Res. *20*, 6441–6450.

Fondrat, C., and Kalogeropoulos, A. (1994). Approaching the function of new genes by the detection of their potential upstream activation sequences in *Saccharomyces cerevisiae:* Application to chromosome III. Curr. Genet. *25*, 396–406.

Frech, K., Quandt, K., and Werner, T. (1997). Finding protein-binding sites in DNA sequences: The next generation. Trends Biochem. Sci. *22*, 103–104.

Gelfand, M. S. (1995). Prediction of function in DNA sequence analysis. J. Comput. Biol. *2*, 87–115.

Gelfand, M. S., Mironov, A. A., and Pevzner, P. A. (1996). Gene recognition via spliced alignment. Proc. Natl. Acad. Sci. U.S.A. *93*, 9061 9066.

Gish, W., and States, D. J. (1993). Identification of protein coding regions by database similarity search. Nature Genet. *3*, 266–272.

Green, P., Lipman, D., Hillier, L., Waterston, R., States, D., and Claverie, J.-M. (1993). Ancient conserved regions in new gene sequences and the protein databases. Science *259*, 1711–1716.

Guigó, R. (1997). Computational gene identification. J. Mol. Med. *75*, 389–393.

Guigó, R., Knudsen, S., Drake, N., and Smith, T. (1992). Prediction of gene structure. J. Mol. Biol. *226*, 141–157.

Hillier, L., Lennon, G., Becker, M., Bonaldo, M. F., Chiapelli, B., Chissoe, S., Dietrich, N., DuBuque, T., Favello, A., Gish, W., Hawkins, M., Hultman, M., Kucaba, T., Lacy, M., Le, M., Le, N., Mardis, E., Moore, B., Morris, M., Parsons, J., Prange, C., Rifkin, L., Rohlfing, T., Schellenberg, K., Soares, M. B., Tan, F., Thierry-Meg, J., Trevaskis, E., Underwood, K., Wohldman, P., Waterston, R., Wilson, R., and Marra, M. (1996). Generation and analysis of 280,000 human expressed sequence tags. Genome Res. *6*, 807–828.

Jurka, J., Klonowski, P., Dagman, V., and Pelton, P. (1996). CENSOR—A program for identification and elimination of repetitive elements from DNA sequences. Comput. Chem. *20*, 119–122.

Knudsen, S., and Brunak, S. (1997). Kissing loops hide premature termination codons in pre-mRNA of selenoprotein genes and in genes containing programmed ribosomal frameshifts. RNA *3*, 697–701.

Kondrakhin, Y., Shamir, V., and Kolchanov, N. (1994). Construction of a generalized consensus matrix for recognition of vertebrate pre-mRNA 3′ terminal processing sites. Comput. Appl. Biosci. *10*, 597–603.

Kozak, M. (1996) Interpreting cDNA sequences: Some insights from studies on translation. Mamm. Genome *7*, 563–574.

Krogh, A., Mian, I. S., and Haussler, D. (1994). A hidden Markov model that finds genes in *E. coli* DNA. Nucl. Acids Res. *11*, 4768–4778.

Kulp, D., Haussler, D., Reese, M. G., and Eckman, F. H. (1996). A generalized hidden Markov model for the recognition of human genes in DNA, In *Proceedings of the Fourth International Conference on Intelligent Systems in Molecular Biology,* D. J. States, P. Agarwal, T. Gaasterland, L. Hunter, and R. Smith, Eds. (Menlo Park, CA: AAAI Press), pp. 134–142.

Lowe, T. M. and Eddy, S. R. (1997). tRNAscan-SE: A program for improved detection of transfer RNA genes in genomic sequence. Nucl. Acids Res. *25*, 955–964.

McKeown, M. (1992). Alternative mRNA splicing. Annu. Rev. Cell Biol. *8*, 133–155.

Milanesi, L., Kolchanov, N. A., Rogozin, I. B., Ischenko, I. V., Kel, A. E., Orlov, Yu. L., Ponomarenko, M. P., and Vezzoni, P. (1993). GenView: A computing tool for protein-coding regions prediction in nucleotide sequences. In *Proceedings of the Second International Conference on Bioinformatics, Supercomputing and Complex Genome Analysis,* H. A. Lim, J. W. Fickett, C. R. Cantor, and R. J. Robbins, Eds. (Singapore: World Scientific Publishing), pp. 573–588.

Nilsen, T. W. (1996). A parallel spliceosome Science *273*, 1813.

Pavesi, A., Conterio, F., Boichi, A., Dieci, G., and Ottonello, S. (1994). Identification of new eukaryotic tRNA genes in genomic DNA databases by a multistep weight matrix analysis of transcriptional control regions. Nucl. Acids Res. *22*, 1247–1256.

Pedersen, A. G., Baldi, P., Brunak, S. and Chauvin, Y. (1996). Characterization of prokaryotic and eukaryotic promoters using hidden Markov models. In *Fourth International Conference on Intel-*

ligent Systems in Molecular Biology, D. J. States, P. Agarwal, T. Gaasterland, L. Hunter, and R. Smith, eds. (Menlo Park, CA: AAAI Press), pp. 182–191.

Robison, K., Gilbert, W. and Church, G. M. (1994). Large scale bacterial gene discovery by similarity search. Nature Genet. *7,* 205–214.

Rosenblueth, D. A., Thieffry, D., Huerta, A. M., Salgado, H., and Collado-Vides, J. (1996). Syntactic recognition of regulatory regions in *Escherichia coli.* Comput. Appl. Biosci. *12,* 415–422.

Senapathy, P., Shapiro, M. B., and Harris, N. L. (1990). Splice junctions, branch point sites, and exons: Sequence statistics, identification, and applications to genome project. Methods Enzymol. *183,* 252–278.

Smit, A. F. A. (1996). Origin of interspersed repeats in the human genome. Curr. Opin. Genet. Devl. *6,* 743–749.

Smith, R. F., Wiese, B. A., Wojzynski, M. K., Davison, D. B., and Worley, K. C. (1996). BCM search launcher—An integrated interface to molecular biology data base search and analysis services available on the World Wide Web. Genome Res. *6,* 454–462.

Snyder, E. E., and Stormo, G. D. (1995). Identification of coding regions in genomic DNA. J. Mol. Biol. *248,* 1–18.

Snyder, E. E., and Stormo, G. D. (1996). Identifying genes in genomic DNA sequences. In *DNA and Protein Sequence Analysis: A Practical Approach,* M. J. Bishop and C. J. Rawlings, Eds. (Oxford: IRL Press), pp. 209–224.

Solovyev, V., and Salamov, A. (1997). The Gene-Finder computer tools for analysis of human and model organism genome sequences. In *Proceedings of the Fifth International Conference on Intelligent Systems for Molecular Biology,* T. Gaasterland, P. Karp, K. Karplus, C. Ousounis, C. Sander, and A. Valencia, Eds. (Menlo Park, CA: AAAI Press), pp. 294–302.

Stormo, G. D. (1990). Finding protein coding regions in genomic sequences. Methods Enzymol. *183,* 211–220.

Tronche, F., Ringeisen, F., Blumenfeld, M., Yaniv, M., and Pontoglio, M. (1997). Analysis of the distribution of binding sites for a tissue-specific transcription factor in the vertebrate genome. J. Mol. Biol. *266,* 231–245.

von Hippel, P. H. (1994). Protein–DNA recognition: New perspectives and underlying themes. Science *263,* 769–770.

Wahle, E., and Keller, W. (1996). The biochemistry of polyadenylation. Trends Biochem. Sci. *21,* 247–250.

Xu, Y., Einstein, J. R., Mural, R. J., Shah, M., and Uberbacher, E. C. (1994). An improved system for exon recognition and gene modeling in human DNA sequences. In *Proceedings of the Second International Conference on Intelligent Systems for Molecular Biology,* R. Altman, D. Brutlag, P. Karp, R. Lathrop, and D. Searls, Eds. (Menlo Park, CA: AAAI Press), pp. 376–383.

Zhang, M. Q. (1997). Identification of protein coding regions in the human genome based on quadratic discriminant analysis. Proc. Natl. Acad. Sci. U.S.A. *94,* 565–568.

## 11

Predictive Methods Using Protein Sequences

Andreas D. Baxevanis

Genome Technology Branch
National Human Genome Research Institute
National Institutes of Health
Bethesda, Maryland

David Landsman

National Center for Biotechnology Information
Computational Biology Branch
National Library of Medicine
National Institutes of Health
Bethesda, Maryland

The discussions of databases and information retrieval in earlier chapters of this book document the tremendous explosion in the amount of sequence information available in a variety of public databases. As we have already seen with nucleotide sequences, all protein sequences, whether determined directly or through the translation of an open reading frame in a nucleotide sequence, contain intrinsic information of value in determining their structure or function. Unfortunately, experiments aimed at extracting such information cannot keep pace with the rate at which raw sequence data is being produced. Techniques such as circular dichroism spectroscopy, optical rotatory dispersion, X-ray crystallography, and nuclear magnetic resonance are extremely powerful in determining structural features, but their execution requires many hours of highly skilled, technically demanding work. The gap in information becomes obvious in comparisons of the size of the protein sequence and structure databases; as of this writing, there were 428,814 entries in the nonredundant protein sequence database (nr), but only 5017 protein entries in PDB.[1] Attempts to close the

Bioinformatics: A Practical Guide to the Analysis of Genes and Proteins
Edited by A.D. Baxevanis and B.F.F. Ouellette
ISBN 0-471-19196-5, pages 246–267.   Copyright © 1998 Wiley-Liss, Inc.

[1] GenBank release 100.0, April 15, 1997. PDB holdings as of March 13, 1997.

gap center around *predictive methods.* These entries can provide insights as to the properties of a protein in the absence of biochemical data.

This chapter focuses on computational techniques that allow for biological discovery based on the protein sequence *itself;* most of these techniques do not rely on pairwise or multiple sequence alignments in the sense used in earlier chapters. Unlike nucleotide sequences, which are composed of four bases that are chemically rather similar (yet distinct), the alphabet of 20 amino acids found in proteins allows for much greater diversity of structure and function, primarily because the differences in the chemical makeup of these residues are more pronounced. Each residue can influence the overall physical properties of the protein because these amino acids are basic or acidic, hydrophobic or hydrophilic, have straight chains, branched chains, or are aromatic. Thus each residue has certain propensities to form structures of different types in the context of a protein domain. These properties, of course, are the basis for one of the central tenets of biochemistry: that *sequence specifies conformation* (Anfinsen et al., 1961).

The major precaution with respect to these or any other predictive techniques is that regardless of the method, the results are *predictions.* Different methods, using different algorithms, may or may not produce different results, and it is important to understand *how* a particular predictive method works rather than just approaching the algorithm as a "black box": one method may be appropriate in a particular case but totally inappropriate in another. Even so, the potential for a powerful synergy exists: proper use of these techniques along with primary biochemical data can provide valuable insights into protein structure and function.

PROTEIN IDENTITY BASED ON COMPOSITION

The physical and chemical properties of each of the 20 amino acids are fairly well understood, and a number of useful computational tools have been developed for making predictions regarding the identification of unknown proteins based on these properties (and vice versa). Many of these tools are available through the ExPASy server at the Geneva University Hospital and the University of Geneva (Appel et al., 1994). The focus of the ExPASy tools is twofold: to assist in the analysis and identification of unknown proteins isolated through two-dimensional gel electrophoresis, as well as to predict basic physical properties of a known protein. These tools capitalize on the curated annotations in the SWISS-PROT database in making their predictions. While calculations such as these are useful in electrophoretic analysis, they can be very valuable in any number of experimental areas, particularly in chromatographic and sedimentation studies. In this and the following section, tools in the ExPASy suite are identified, but the ensuing discussion also includes a number of useful programs made available by other groups. Internet resources related to these and other tools discussed in this chapter are listed at the end of the chapter.

AAComp Ident and AACompSim (ExPASy)

Rather than using an amino acid sequence to search SWISS-PROT, AACompIdent uses the amino acid composition of an unknown protein to identify known proteins of the same composition (Wilkins et al., 1996). As inputs, the program requires the desired amino acid composition, the pI and molecular weight of the protein (if known), the appropriate taxonomic class, and any special keywords. In addition, the user must select from one of six amino acid "constellations," which influence how the analysis is performed; for example, certain constellations may combine residues like Asp/Asn (D/N) and Gln/Glu (Q/E) into Asx (B) and Glx (Z), or certain residues may be eliminated from the analysis altogether.

For each sequence in the database, the algorithm computes a score based on the difference in compositions between the sequence and the query composition. The results, returned by e-mail, are organized as three ranked lists: first, a list based on all proteins from the specified taxonomic class without taking pI or molecular weight into account; second, a list based on all proteins regardless of taxonomic class without taking pI or molecular weight into account; and finally, a list, based on the specified taxonomic class, that does take pI and molecular weight into account. Since the computed scores are a difference measure, a score of zero implies that there is exact correspondence between the query composition and that sequence entry.

A variant of AACompIdent, AACompSim performs a similar type of analysis, but rather than using an experimentally derived amino acid composition as the basis for searches, the sequence of a Swiss-Prot protein is used instead (Wilkins et al., 1996). A theoretical pI and molecular weight are computed prior to computing the difference scores using Compute pI/MW (see below). It has been documented that amino acid composition across species boundaries is well conserved (Cordwell et al., 1995) and that by considering amino acid composition, investigators can detect weak similarities between proteins whose sequence identity falls below 25% (Hobohm and Sander, 1995). Thus consideration of composition in addition to performing "traditional" database searches may provide additional insight into the relationships between proteins.

PROPSEARCH

Along the same lines as AACompSim, PROPSEARCH uses the amino acid composition of a protein to detect weak relationships between proteins, and the authors have demonstrated that this technique can be used to easily discern members of the same protein family (Hobohm and Sander, 1995). However, this technique is more robust than AACompSim in that 144 different physical properties are used in performing the analysis, among which are molecular weight, the content of bulky residues, average hydrophobicity, and average charge. This collection of physical properties is called the query vector, and it is compared against the same type of vector precomputed for every sequence in the target databases (SWISS-PROT and PIR). Having this "database of vectors" calculated in advance vastly improves processing time for a query.

The input to the PROPSEARCH Web server is just the query sequence, and an example of the program output is shown in Figure 11.1. Here, the sequence of human autoantigen NOR-90 was used as the input query. The results are ranked by a distance score, and this score represents the likelihood that the query sequence and new sequences found through PROPSEARCH belong to the same family, thereby implying common function in most cases. A distance score of 10 or below indicates that there is a better than 87% chance that there is similarity between the two proteins. A score below 8.7 increases the reliability to 94%, and a score below 7.5 increases the reliability to 99.6%. Examination of the results showed NOR-90 to be similar to a number of nucleolar transcription factors, protein kinases, a retinoblastoma-binding protein, the actin-binding protein radixin, and RalBP1, a putative GTPase target. None of these hits would necessarily be expected, since the functions of these proteins are dissimilar; however, a good number of these are DNA-binding proteins, opening the possibility that a very similar domain is being used in alternative

Fragment search: OFF (POS1 and POS2 are begin and end of sequence)

Rank	ID	DIST	LEN2	POS1	POS2	pI	DE
1	>p1;s18193	0.00	727	1	727	5.33	autoantigen NOR-90 - human
2	ubf1_human	1.36	764	1	764	5.62	NUCLEOLAR TRANSCRIPTION FACTOR 1 (UPSTREAM BINDING FACTOR 1) (UBF-1) .
3	ubf1_mouse	1.40	765	1	765	5.55	NUCLEOLAR TRANSCRIPTION FACTOR 1 (UPSTREAM BINDING FACTOR 1) (UBF-1) .
4	ubf1_rat	1.57	764	1	764	5.61	NUCLEOLAR TRANSCRIPTION FACTOR 1 (UPSTREAM BINDING FACTOR 1) (UBF-1) .
5	ubf1_xenla	3.95	677	1	677	5.79	NUCLEOLAR TRANSCRIPTION FACTOR 1 (UPSTREAM BINDING FACTOR-1) (UBF-1) .
6	ubf2_xenla	4.18	701	1	701	6.05	NUCLEOLAR TRANSCRIPTION FACTOR 2 (UPSTREAM BINDING FACTOR-2) (UBF-2) .
7	>p1;s57552	7.72	606	1	606	6.63	hypothetical protein YPR018w - yeast (Saccharomyces cerevisiae)
8	>p1;i50463	8.49	772	1	772	5.71	protein kinase - chicken
9	>p1;h54024	8.83	768	1	768	5.27	protein kinase (EC 2.7.1.37) cdc2-related PITSLRE alpha 2-3 - human
10	>p1;b54024	8.87	777	1	777	5.27	protein kinase (EC 2.7.1.37) cdc2-related PITSLRE alpha 2-2 - human
11	>p1;g54024	8.90	766	1	766	5.21	protein kinase (EC 2.7.1.37) cdc2-related PITSLRE beta 2-2 - human
12	>p1;a55817	9.00	783	1	783	5.19	cyclin-dependent kinase p130-PITSLRE - mouse
13	>p1;f54024	9.11	777	1	777	5.30	protein kinase (EC 2.7.1.37) cdc2-related PITSLRE beta 2-1 - human
14	>p1;e54024	9.11	779	1	779	5.42	protein kinase (EC 2.7.1.37) cdc2-related PITSLRE alpha 2-1 - human
15	yaa5_schpo	9.45	598	1	598	4.78	HYPOTHETICAL 69.5 KD PROTEIN C22G7.05 IN CHROMOSOME I.
16	>p1;s62449	9.45	598	1	598	4.78	hypothetical protein SPAC22G7.05 - fission yeast (Schizosaccharomyces pombe)
17	>f1;i58390	9.45	920	1	920	5.00	retinoblastoma binding protein 1 isoform I - human (fragment)
18	>p1;s63193	9.58	590	1	590	6.15	hypothetical protein YNL227c - yeast (Saccharomyces cerevisiae)
19	ynw7_yeast	9.58	590	1	590	6.15	HYPOTHETICAL 68.8 KD PROTEIN IN URE2-SSU72 INTERGENIC REGION.
20	>p1;s49634	9.74	899	1	899	4.79	hypothetical protein YML093w - yeast (Saccharomyces cerevisiae)
21	ymj3_yeast	9.74	899	1	899	4.79	HYPOTHETICAL 103.0 KD PROTEIN IN RAD10-PRS4 INTERGENIC REGION.
22	radi_human	9.76	583	1	583	6.33	RADIXIN.
23	radi_pig	9.81	583	1	583	6.21	RADIXIN (MOESIN B).
24	>f1;i78883	9.83	866	1	866	4.77	retinoblastoma binding protein 1 isoform II - human (fragment)
25	>p1;b42997	9.87	754	1	754	5.17	retinoblastoma-associated protein 2 - human
26	>p1;a57467	9.91	647	1	647	5.74	RalBP1 - rat

Figure 11.1 Results of a PROPSEARCH database query based on amino acid composition. The input sequence used was that of the human autoantigen NOR-90. Explanatory material and a histogram of distance scores against the entire target database have been removed for brevity. The columns in the table give the rank of the hit based on the distance score, the SWISS-PROT or PIR identifier, the distance score, the length of the overlap between the query and subject, the positions of the overlap (from POS1 to POS2), the calculated pI, and the definition line for the found sequence.

functional contexts. At the very least, a BLASTP search would be necessary to both verify the results and identify critical residues.

MOWSE

The Molecular Weight Search algorithm (MOWSE) capitalizes on information obtained through mass spectrometric (MS) techniques (Pappin et al., 1993). Using both the molecular weights of intact proteins and those resulting from digestion of the same proteins with specific proteases, an unknown protein can be unambiguously identified given the results of several experimental determinations. This approach substantially cuts down on experimental time, since the unknown protein does not have to be sequenced in whole or in part.

MOWSE input is a simple text file, containing a list of experimentally determined peptide masses in the range of 0.7 to 4.0 kDa. Calculations are based on information contained in the OWL nonredundant protein sequence database (Akrigg et al., 1988). Scoring is based on the how often a fragment molecular weight occurs in proteins within a given range of molecular weights, and the output is returned as a ranked list of the top 30 scores, with the OWL entry name, matching peptide sequences, and other statistical information. Simulation studies produced an accuracy rate of 99% using five or fewer input peptide weights. Searches are performed by sending an e-mail message to *mowse@daresbury.ac.uk*. Detailed information on formatting a query can be obtained by sending a message to the same address, with the word help in the body of the message.

PHYSICAL PROPERTIES BASED ON SEQUENCE

Compute pI/MW (ExPASy)

Compute pI/MW is a tool that calculates the isoelectric point and molecular weight of an input sequence. Determination of pI is based on pK values found in an earlier study on protein migration in denaturing conditions at neutral to acidic pH (Bjellqvist et al., 1993). Because of this, the authors caution that pI values determined for *basic* proteins may not be accurate. Molecular weights are calculated by the addition of the average isotopic mass of each amino acid in the sequence plus that of one water molecule. The sequence can be furnished by the user in FASTA format, or a Swiss-Prot identifier or accession number can be specified. If a sequence is furnished, the tool automatically computes the pI and molecular weight for the entire length of the sequence. If a Swiss-Prot identifier is given, the definition and organism lines of the entry are shown, and the user may specify a range of amino acids so that the computation is done on a fragment rather than on the entire protein.

PeptideMass (ExPASy)

Designed for use in peptide mapping experiments, PeptideMass determines the cleavage products of a protein after exposure to a given protease or chemical reagent (Wilkins et al., 1997). The enzymes and reagents available for cleavage through PeptideMass are trypsin, chymotrypsin, Lys C, cyanogen bromide, Arg C, Asp N, and Glu C (bicarbonate or phosphate). Cysteines and methionines can be modified prior to the calculation of the molecular weight of the resultant peptides. By furnishing a Swiss-Prot identifier rather than pasting in a raw sequence, PeptideMass is able to use information within the SWISS-PROT annotation to improve the calculations, such as by removing signal sequences or including known post-translational modifications prior to cleavage. The results are returned in tabular format, giving a theoretical pI and molecular weight for the starting protein, and then the mass, position, modified masses, information on variants from SWISS-PROT, and the sequence of the peptide fragments.

TGREASE

TGREASE calculates the hydrophobicity of a protein along its length (Kyte and Doolittle, 1982). Inherent in each of the 20 amino acids is its hydrophobicity: the relative propensity the acid to bury itself in the core of a protein and away from surrounding water molecules. This tendency, coupled with steric and other considerations, influence how a protein ultimately folds into its final three-dimensional conformation. As such, TGREASE finds application in the determination of putative transmembrane sequences as well as the prediction of buried regions of globular proteins. TGREASE is part of the FASTA suite of programs available from the University of Virginia and runs as a stand-alone application that can be downloaded and run on either Macintosh or DOS-based computers.

The method relies on a hydropathy scale, where each amino acid is assigned a score reflecting its relative hydrophobicity based on a number of physical characteristics (e.g., solubility, the free energy of transfer through a water–vapor phase transition). Amino acids with higher, positive scores are more hydrophobic; those with more negative scores are more hydrophilic. A moving average, or hydropathic index, is then calculated across the protein. The window length is adjustable, with a span of 7 to 11 residues recommended to minimize noise and maximize information content. The results are then plotted as hydropathic index versus residue number. The sequence for the human interleukin 8 receptor B was used to generate a TGREASE plot, as shown in Figure 11.2. Correspondence between the peaks and the actual location of the transmembrane segments, while not exact, is fairly good; keep in mind that the method is predicting *all* hydrophobic regions, not just those located in transmembrane regions. The specific detection of transmembrane regions is discussed further below.

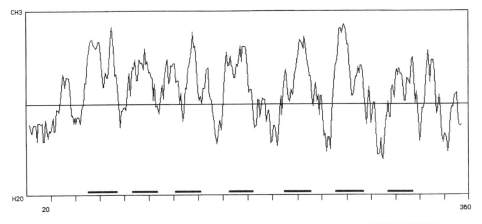

Figure 11.2 Results of a Kyte–Doolittle hydropathy determination using TGREASE. The input sequence was of the high affinity interleukin 8 receptor B from human. Default window lengths were used. The thick, horizontal bars across the bottom of the figure were added manually and represent the positions of the seven transmembrane regions of IL-8R-B, as given in the SWISS-PROT entry for this protein (P25025).

SAPS

The Statistical Analysis of Protein Sequences algorithm provides extensive statistical information for any given query sequence (Brendel et al., 1992). When a protein sequence is submitted via the SAPS Web interface, the server returns a large amount of physical and chemical information on the protein, based solely what can be inferred from its sequence. The output begins with a compositional analysis, with counts of amino acids by type. This is followed by a charge distribution analysis, including the locations of positively or negatively charged clusters, high-scoring charged and uncharged segments, and charge runs and patterns. The final sections present information on high-scoring hydrophobic and transmembrane segments, repetitive structures, and multiplets, as well as a periodicity analysis.

SECONDARY STRUCTURE AND FOLDING CLASSES

The first step in the analysis of a newly discovered protein or gene product of unknown function is to perform a BLAST or other similar search against the public databases. However, such a search might not produce a match against a known protein; if there is a statistically significant hit, there may not be any information in the sequence record regarding the secondary structure of the protein, information that is very important in the rational design of biochemical experiments. In the absence of "known" information, there are methods available for predicting the ability of a sequence to form α helices and β strands. These methods rely on observations made from groups of proteins whose three-dimensional structure has been experimentally determined.

A brief review of secondary structure and folding classes is warranted before the techniques themselves are discussed. As already alluded to, a significant number of amino acids have hydrophobic side chains, while the main chain, or backbone, is hydrophilic. The required balance between these two seemingly opposing forces is accomplished through the formation of discrete secondary structural elements, first described by Linus Pauling and colleagues in 1951 (Pauling and Corey, 1951). An α helix is a corkscrew-type structure with the main chain forming the backbone and the side chains of the amino acids projecting outward from the helix. The backbone is stabilized by the formation of hydrogen bonds between the CO group of each amino acid and the NH group of the residue four positions C-terminal ($n + 4$), creating a tight, rodlike structure. Some residues form α helices better than others: alanine, glutamine, leucine, and methionine are commonly found in α helices, whereas proline, glycine, tyrosine, and serine usually are not. Proline is commonly thought of as a helix-breaker, since its bulky ring structure disrupts the formation of $n + 4$ hydrogen bonds.

In contrast, the β *strand* is a much more extended structure. Rather than having hydrogen bonds form within the secondary structural unit itself, stabilization occurs through bonding with one or more *adjacent* β strands. The overall structure formed through the interaction of these individual β strands is known as a β-*pleated sheet*. These sheets can be parallel or antiparallel, depending on the orientation of the N- and C-terminal ends of each component β strand. A variant of the β sheet is the β *turn,* where the polypeptide chain makes a sharp, hairpin bend, producing an antiparallel β sheet in the process.

In 1976 Levitt and Chothia proposed a classification system based on the order of secondary structural elements within a protein (Levitt and Chothia, 1976). Quite simply, an α structure is made up primarily from α helices, and a β structure is made up of primarily β strands. Myoglobin is the classic example of a protein comprised entirely of α helices, falling into the α class of structures (Takano, 1977). Plastocyanin is a good example of the β class, where the hydrogen-bonding pattern between eight β strands form a compact, barrel-like structure (Guss and Freeman, 1983). The combination class, α/β, is comprised primarily of β strands alternating with α helices. Flavodoxin is a good example of an α/β protein; its β strands form a central β sheet, which is surrounded by α helices (Burnett et al., 1974).

An important term that appears repeatedly below is *neural network*. Basically, a neural network gives computational processes the ability to "learn" in an attempt to approximate human learning, whereas most computer programs execute their instructions blindly in a sequential manner. The use of neural networks has found extensive application for problems that require analysis of patterns and trends, such as secondary structure prediction. Every neural network has an *input layer* and an *output layer*. In the case of secondary structure prediction, the input layer would be information from the sequence itself, and the output layer would be the probabilities of whether a particular residue could form a particular structure. Between the input and output layers would be one or more *hidden layers* in which the actual "learning" takes place. This is accomplished by providing a training data set for the network. Here, an appropriate training set would be all sequences for which three-dimensional structures have been deduced. The network can process this information to look for what are possibly weak relationships between an amino acid sequence and the structures they can form in a particular context. A more complete discussion of neural networks as applied to secondary structure prediction can be found in Kneller et al. (1990).

nnpredict

The nnpredict algorithm uses a two-layer, feed-forward neural network to assign the predicted type for each residue (Kneller et al., 1990). In making the predictions, the server uses a FASTA format file with the sequence in either one-letter or three-letter code, as well as the folding class of the protein (α, β, or α/β). Residues are classified as being within an α helix (H), a β strand (E), or neither (–). If no prediction can be made for a given residue, a question mark (?) is returned to indicate that an assignment cannot be made with confidence. If no information is available regarding the folding class, the prediction can be made without a folding class being specified; this is the default. For the best-case prediction, the accuracy rate of nnpredict is reported at over 65%.

Sequences are submitted to nnpredict by sending an e-mail message to *nnpredict @celeste.ucsf.edu*. Using flavodoxin as an example, the format of the e-mail message would be as follows:

```
option: a/b
>flavodoxin - Anacystis nidulans
AKIGLFYGTQTGVTQTIAESIQQEFGGESIVDLNDIANADASDLNAYDYLIIGCPTWNVGELQSDWEGIY
DDLDSVNFQGKKVAYFGAGDQVGYSDNFQDAMGILEEKISSLGSQTVGYWPIEGYDFNESKAVRNNQFVG
LAIDEDNQPDLTKNRIKTWVSQLKSEFGL
```

The Option line specifies the folding class of the protein: n uses no folding class for the prediction, a specifies α, b specifies β, and a/b specifies α/β. Only one sequence may be submitted per e-mail message. The results returned by the server are shown in modified form in Figure 11.3.

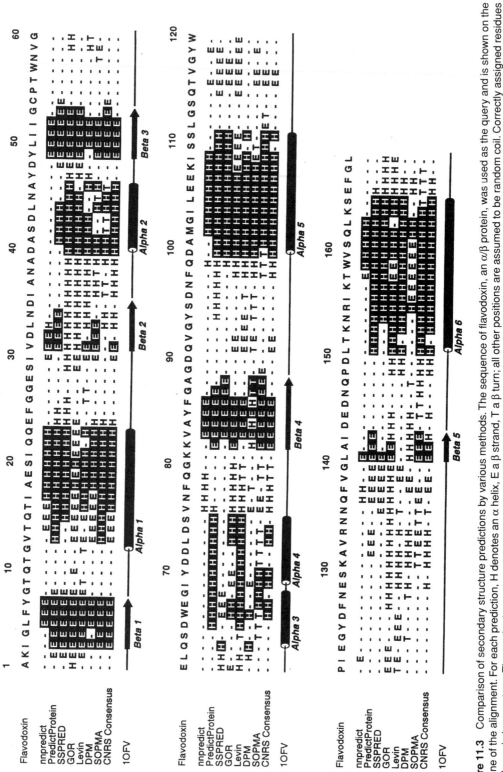

Figure 11.3 Comparison of secondary structure predictions by various methods. The sequence of flavodoxin, an α/β protein, was used as the query and is shown on the first line of the alignment. For each prediction, H denotes an α helix, E a β strand, T a β turn; all other positions are assumed to be random coil. Correctly assigned residues are shown in inverse type. The methods used are listed along the left side of the alignment and are described in the text. At the bottom of the figure is the secondary structure assignment given in the PDB file for flavodoxin (1OFV, Smith et al., 1983).

PredictProtein

PredictProtein (Rost et al., 1994) uses a slightly different approach in making its predictions. First, the protein sequence is used as a query against Swiss-Prot to find similar sequences. When similar sequences are found, an algorithm called MaxHom is used to generate a profile-based multiple sequence alignment (Sander and Schneider, 1991). MaxHom uses an iterative method to construct the alignment: After the first search of SWISS-PROT, all found sequences are aligned against the query sequence and a profile is calculated for the alignment. The profile is then used to search SWISS-PROT again to search for new, matching sequences. The multiple alignment generated by MaxHom is subsequently fed into a neural network for prediction by one of a suite of methods collectively known as PHD (Rost, 1996). PHDsec, the method in this suite used for secondary structure prediction, not only assigns each residue to a secondary structure type, it provides statistics indicating the confidence of the prediction at each position in the sequence. The method produces an average accuracy of better than 72%; the best-case residue predictions have an accuracy rate of over 90%.

The input message, sent to *predictprotein@embl-heidelberg.de,* takes the following form:

```
Joe Buzzcut
National Human Genome Research Institute, NIH
buzzcut@baldguys.org
# flavodoxin - Anacystis nidulans
AKIGLFYGTQTGVTQTIAESIQQEFGGESIVDLNDIANADASDLNAYDYLIIGCPTWNVGELQSDWEGIY
DDLDSVNFQGKKVAYFGAGDQVGYSDNFQDAMGILEEKISSLGSQTVGYWPIEGYDFNESKAVRNNQFVG
LAIDEDNQPDLTKNRIKTWVSQLKSEFGL
```

After the Name, Affiliation, and Address lines, the # signals to the server that a sequence in one-letter code follows. The sequence format is essentially FASTA, except that blanks are not allowed, and the standard > symbol is replaced by #. Nothing is allowed to follow the sequence.

The output from such a search is quite copious but contains a large amount of pertinent information. The results of the MaxHom search are returned, complete with a multiple alignment that may be of use in further study, such as profile searches or phylogenetic studies. If the submitted sequence has a known homolog in PDB, the PDB identifiers are furnished. Information follows on the method itself, finally followed by the actual prediction. Unlike nnpredict, PredictProtein returns a "reliability index of prediction" for each position ranging from 0 to 9, with 9 being the maximum confidence that a secondary structure assignment has been made correctly. The results returned by the server for this particular sequence, as compared to those obtained by other methods, are shown in modified form in Figure 11.3.

SSPRED

Like PredictProtein, the EMBL method for secondary structure prediction (Mehta et al., 1995) performs a search of the protein sequence databases for similar proteins, constructs a multiple sequence alignment, and then performs the prediction. The method uses the alignment, paying particular attention to the nature of substitutions at nonconserved positions, to make an initial prediction. The initial prediction is then filtered to remove structural elements that are simply not plausible, either because of their length or because one structural type is interrupting a stretch of another (e.g., a prediction of HHHEHH would become HHHHHH). All α helices must be at least four residues long, while all β strands must be at least three residues long.

Again using flavodoxin as the example, the following is the format for an SSPRED search, submitted to *sspred@embl-heidelberg.de:*

```
SEQUENCE
TITLE flavodoxin - Anacystis nidulans
BLOSUM 62
ALIGN 50
INDEL 10
Z_SCORE 7.0
SEQ
AKIGLFYGTQTGVTQTIAESIQQEFGGESIVDLNDIANADASDLNAYDYLIIGCPTWNVGELQSDWEGIY
DDLDSVNFQGKKVAYFGAGDQVGYSDNFQDAMGILEEKISSLGSQTVGYWPIEGYDFNESKAVRNNQFVG
LAIDEDNQPDLTKNRIKTWVSQLKSEFGL
END
```

The keyword SEQUENCE alerts the server that a single sequence is being submitted. The line TITLE allows a comment regarding the sequence to be entered and will appear in the results when returned. The command BLOSUM 62 instructs SSPRED to use that matrix when scoring alignments generated during the search. Both PAM and BLOSUM matrices are available, with the default being PAM 120. INDEL 10 is the value of the gap penalty. Users can leave this line out and allow SSPRED to predict a suitable default based on the scoring matrix used. Decreasing the value of INDEL makes the insertion of gaps more favorable. ALIGN 50 instructs the server to use the 50 best alignments in making the secondary structure predictions. The line Z_SCORE 7.0 allows users to increase or decrease the sensitivity of the BLITZ searches. Finally, the sequence is specified by a beginning keyword of SEQ and a termination keyword of END.

Upon completion of the analysis, a series of output files is returned to the user via e-mail. These include a message containing the multiple sequence alignment generated by BLITZ that was used in the prediction and a message containing the final results. The e-mail message containing the prediction shows both the first prediction result and the final, filtered result. The final results of SSPRED on the query above are shown in relation to the outputs from the other algorithms in Figure 11.3.

SOPMA

The Protein Sequence Analysis server at the Centre National de la Recherche Scientifique (CNRS) in Lyons, France, takes a unique approach in making secondary structure predictions: rather than using a single method, it uses *five,* the predictions from which are subsequently used to come up with a "consensus prediction." The methods used are the Garnier–Gibrat–Robson (GOR) method (Garnier et al., 1996), the Levin homolog method (Levin et al., 1986), the double-prediction method (Deléage and Roux, 1987), the PHD method described above as part of PredictProtein, and the method of CNRS itself, called

SOPMA (Geourjon and Déleage, 1995). Briefly, this self-optimized prediction method builds sub-databases of protein sequences with known secondary structures; each of the proteins in a sub-database is then subjected to secondary structure prediction based on sequence similarity. Then the information from the sub-databases is used to generate a prediction on the query sequence.

The method can be run by submitting just the sequence itself in single-letter format to *deleage@ibcp.fr*, using SOPMA as the subject of the mail message, or by using the SOPMA Web interface. The output from each of the component predictions, as well as the consensus, is shown in Figure 11.3.

Comparison of Methods

Based on Figure 11.3, it is immediately apparent that all the methods described above do a relatively good, but not perfect, job of predicting secondary structure. Flavodoxin was selected as the input query because it has a relatively intricate structure, falling into the α/β folding class with its six α helices and five β sheets. Some assignments were consistently made by all methods; for example, all the methods detected $\beta1$, $\beta3$, $\beta4$, and $\alpha5$ fairly well. However, some methods missed some elements altogether (e.g., nnpredict with $\alpha2$, $\alpha3$, and $\alpha4$), and some predictions made no biological sense (e.g., the double-prediction method and $\beta4$, where helices, sheets, and turns alternate, residue by residue). PredictProtein, which correctly found all the secondary structure elements and, in several places, identified structures of the correct length, appears to have made the best overall prediction. This is *not* to say that the other methods are not useful or not as good; undoubtedly in some cases another method would have emerged as having made a better prediction. Where no other information is known, the best approach is to submit a query sequence to a number of these servers, compile the results, and then *manually* judge the validity of the predictions in comparison to one another. (While the CNRS consensus sequence shown in Figure 11.3 attempts to do this, the consensus in this case is not completely correct either.) This approach does not provide a fail-safe method of prediction, but it does reinforce the level of confidence resulting from these predictions.

SPECIALIZED STRUCTURES OR FEATURES

Just as the position of α helices and β sheets can be predicted with a relatively high degree of confidence, the presence of certain specialized structures or features, such as coiled coils and transmembrane regions, can be predicted. There are not as many methods for making such predictions as there are for secondary structure, primarily because the rules of folding that induce these structures are not completely understood. Despite this, when query sequences are searched against databases of known structure, the accuracy of prediction can be quite high.

Coiled Coils

The COILS algorithm runs a query sequence against a database of proteins known to have a coiled-coil structure (Lupas et al., 1991). The program also compares query sequences to a PDB subset containing globular sequences, and based on the differences in scoring between the PDB subset and the coiled coils database, determines the probability with which the input sequence can form a coiled coil. COILS can be downloaded for use with VAX/VMS, or may more easily be used through a simple Web interface.

The program takes sequence data in GCG or FASTA format; one or more sequences can be submitted at once. In addition to the sequences, users may select one of two scoring matrices: MTK, based on the sequences of myosin, tropomyosin, and keratin, or MTIDK, based on myosin, tropomyosin, intermediate filaments types I–V, desmosomal proteins, and kinesins. The authors cite a trade-off between the scoring matrices, with MTK being better for detecting two-stranded structures and MTIDK being better for all other cases. Users may invoke an option giving the same weight to the residues at the *a* and *d* positions of each coil (normally hydrophobic) as that given to the residues at the *b, c, e, f,* and *g* positions (normally hydrophilic). If the results of running COILS both weighted and unweighted are substantially different, it is likely that a false positive has been found. The authors caution that COILS is designed to detect solvent-exposed, left-handed coiled coils, and that buried or right-handed coiled coils may not be detected. When a query is submitted to the Web server, a prediction graph showing the propensity toward the formation of a coiled coil along the length of the sequence is generated.

A slightly easier to interpret output comes from MacStripe, a Macintosh-based application that uses the Lupas COILS method to make its predictions (Knight, 1994). MacStripe takes an input file in FASTA, PIR, and other common file formats and, like COILS, produces a plot file containing a histogram of the probability of forming a coiled coil, along with bars showing the continuity of the heptad repeat pattern. The following portion of the statistics file generated by MacStripe uses the complete sequence of GCN4 as an example.

```
 89    89 L 5 a 0.760448 0.000047
 90    90 D 5 b 0.760448 0.000047
 91    91 D 5 c 0.760448 0.000047
 92    92 A 5 d 0.760448 0.000047
 93    93 V 5 e 0.760448 0.000047
 94    94 V 5 f 0.760448 0.000047
 95    95 E 5 g 0.760448 0.000047
 96    96 S 5 a 0.760448 0.000047
 97    97 F 5 b 0.760448 0.000047
 98    98 F 5 c 0.774300 0.000058
 99    99 S 5 d 0.812161 0.000101
100   100 S 5 e 0.812161 0.000101
101   101 S 5 f 0.812161 0.000101
102   102 T 5 g 0.812161 0.000101
```

The columns, from left to right, represent the residue number (shown twice), the amino acid, the heptad frame, the position of the residue within the heptad (*a-b-c-d-e-f-g*), the Lupas score, and the Lupas probability. In this case, focusing on the fifth column, we can easily discern heptad repeat pattern. Examination of the results for the entire GCN4 sequence shows that the heptad pattern is fairly well maintained but falls apart in certain areas. While the statistics should not be ignored, the results are easier to interpret if the heptad pattern information is clearly presented. It is possible to get a similar type of output from COILS, but not through the COILS Web server; instead, a C-based program must be installed on an appropriate Unix machine, a step that may be untenable for many users.

Transmembrane Regions

The Kyte–Doolittle TGREASE algorithm discussed above is very useful in detecting regions of high hydrophobicity, but as such it does not exclusively predict transmembrane regions, since buried domains in soluble, globular proteins can also be primarily hydrophobic. We consider first a predictive method specifically for the prediction of transmembrane regions. This method, TMpred, relies on a database of transmembrane proteins called TMbase (Hofmann and Stoffel, 1993). TMbase, which is derived from Swiss-Prot, contains additional information on each sequence regarding the number of transmembrane domains they possess, the location of these domains, and the nature of the flanking sequences. TMpred uses this information in conjunction with several weight matrices in making its predictions.

The TMpred Web interface is very simple. The sequence, in one-letter code, is pasted into the query sequence box, and the user can specify the minimum and maximum lengths of the hydrophobic part of the transmembrane helix to be used in the analysis. The output has four sections: a list of possible transmembrane helices, a table of correspondences, suggested models for transmembrane topology, and a graphic representation of the same results. When the sequence of the G-protein-coupled receptor (P51684) served as the query, the following models were generated:

```
2 possible models considered, only significant TM-segments used


-----> STRONGLY prefered model: N-terminus outside
7 strong transmembrane helices, total score :      14196
# from   to length score orientation
1   55   74 (20)    2707 o-i
2   83  104 (22)    1914 i-o
3  120  141 (22)    1451 o-i
4  166  184 (19)    2155 i-o
5  212  235 (24)    2530 o-i
6  255  276 (22)    2140 i-o
7  299  319 (21)    1299 o-i


------> alternative model
7 strong transmembrane helices, total score :      11974
# from   to length score orientation
1   47   69 (23)    2494 i-o
2   84  104 (21)    1470 o-i
3  123  141 (19)    1352 i-o
4  166  185 (20)    1904 o-i
5  219  236 (18)    2453 i-o
6  252  274 (23)    1386 o-i
7  300  319 (20)     915 i-o
```

Each of the proposed models indicates the starting and ending position of each segment, along with the relative orientation (inside-to-outside or outside-to-inside) of each segment. The authors appropriately caution that the models are based on the assumption that all transmembrane regions were found in the course of the prediction. These models, then, should be considered in light of the raw data also generated by this method.

The second predictive method, TMAP, takes an approach similar to that used by SSPRED in that it utilizes a multiple sequence alignment to improve its accuracy of prediction (Persson and Argos, 1994). Considering again the G-protein-coupled receptor as the input sequence, a query would be formatted as follows and submitted to *tmap@embl-heidelberg.de:*

```
SEQUENCE
TITLE G protein-coupled receptor
BLOSUM 62
INDEL 10
ALIGN 50
Z_SCORE 4
SEQ
MSGESMNFSDVFDSSEDYFVSVNTSYYSVDSEMLLCSLQEVRQFSRLFVPIAYSLICVFGLLGNILVVIT
FAFYKKARSMTLVYLLNMAIADLLFVLTLPFWAVSHATGAWVFSNATCKLLKGIYAINFNCGMLLLTCIS
       .
       .
       .

END
```

The line TITLE allows the sequence to be easily identified on output sent back to the user. The BLOSUM 62 command indicates the scoring matrix to be used in the performance of a BLITZ search against Swiss-Prot, and any valid BLOSUM or PAM matrix may be specified here; INDEL, ALIGN, and Z_SCORE all have the same meaning as with the SSPRED server described above. The sequence is preceded by a beginning SEQ keyword, and the end of the query is signaled by the END keyword. Regardless of whether the e-mail server or Web interface is used, the results are returned by e-mail. The messages returned include a multiple sequence alignment as generated by BLITZ for the query sequence, a prediction regarding the position of all the transmembrane regions, and a PostScript file providing a graphical overview of the results. The prediction made on the G-coupled-protein receptor by TMAP is as follows:

```
PREDICTED TRANSMEMBRANE SEGMENTS FOR PROTEIN G protein-coupled receptor
    TM   1:    46 -    74 (29)
    TM   2:    82 -   108 (27)
    TM   3:   117 -   145 (29)
    TM   4:   159 -   187 (29)
    TM   5:   212 -   240 (29)
    TM   6:   251 -   276 (26)
```

The output format is quite simple, giving the number of the transmembrane segment, the start and end points of each segment, and the length of the segment in parentheses. It is apparent that for the same protein, these two methods have produced significantly different results; TMpred predicts seven transmembrane regions and TMAP predicts six, with marginal overlap between the two sets. The Swiss-Prot entry for this sequence indicates seven transmembrane regions (43–69, 79–99, 115–136, 155–175, 206–233, 250–274, and 299–316), and the results from TMpred compare favorably to these positions: in most cases,

TMpred predictions are either slightly longer than or slightly offset from the actual locations. The same is true for TMAP, except that TMAP failed to detect the final transmembrane region altogether. One can envision TMAP performing better than TMpred, however, again reinforcing the general strategy of using several algorithms to make predictions and then manually inspecting the results.

Signal Peptides

The Center for Biological Sequence Analysis at the Technical University of Denmark has developed SignalP, a powerful tool for the detection of signal peptides and their cleavage sites (Nielsen et al., 1997). The algorithm is neural-network based, using separate sets of Gram-negative prokaryotic, Gram-positive prokaryotic, and eukaryotic sequences with known signal sequences as the training sets. SignalP predicts secretory signal peptides and not those that are involved in intracellular signal transduction.

Using the Web interface, the sequence of the human insulin-like growth factor IB precursor (somatomedin C, P05019), whose cleavage site is known, was submitted to SignalP for analysis. The eukaryotic training set was used in the prediction, and the results of the analysis are as follows:

```
*************************** SignalP predictions ************************
Using networks trained on euk data

>IGF-IB        length = 195

# pos  aa    C       S       Y
           .
           .
           .
    46   A   0.365   0.823   0.495
    47   T   0.450   0.654   0.577
    48   A   0.176   0.564   0.369
    49   G   0.925   0.205   0.855
    50   P   0.185   0.163   0.376
           .
           .
           .

< Is the sequence a signal peptide?
# Measure  Position  Value  Cutoff  Conclusion
  max. C     49        0.925  0.37    YES
  max. Y     49        0.855  0.34    YES
  max. S     37        0.973  0.88    YES
  mean S    1-48       0.550  0.48    YES
# Most likely cleavage site between pos. 48 and 49: ATA-GP
```

In the first part of the output, the column labeled C is a raw cleavage site score. The value of C is highest at the position C-terminal to the cleavage site. The column labeled S contains the signal peptide scores, which are high at all positions before the cleavage site and very low after the cleavage site. S is also low in the N-termini of nonsecretory proteins. Finally, the Y column gives the combined cleavage site score, a geometric average indicating when the C score is high and the point at which the S score shifts from high to low. The end of the output file asks the question, "Is the sequence a signal peptide?" Based on the statistics, the most likely cleavage site is deduced. Based on the Swiss-Prot entry for this protein, the mature chain begins at position 49, the same position predicted to be the most likely cleavage site by SignalP.

Nonglobular Regions

The use of the program SEG in the masking of low-complexity segments prior to database searches was discussed in Chapter 7. The same algorithm can also be used to detect putative nonglobular regions of protein sequences by altering the trigger window length W, the trigger complexity K_1, and extension complexity K_2. Upon receiving the command `seg sequence.txt 45 3.4 3.75`, SEG will use a longer window length than the default of 12, thereby detecting long nonglobular domains. An example of using SEG to detect nonglobular regions is shown in Figure 11.4.

TERTIARY STRUCTURE

By far the most complex and technically demanding predictive method based on protein sequence data has to do with structure prediction. The importance of being able to ade-

```
                                        1-307   MAGAIASRMSFSSLKRKQPKTFTVRIVTMD
                                                AEMEFNCEMKWKGKDLFDLVCRTLGLRETW
                                                FFGLQYTIKDTVAWLKMDKKVLDHDVSKEE
                                                PVTFHFLAKFYPENAEEELVQEITQHLFFL
                                                QVKKQILDEKIYCPPEASVLLASYAVQAKY
                                                GDYDPSVHKRGFLAQEELLPKRVINLYQMT
                                                PEMWEERITAWYAEHRGRARDEAEMEYLKI
                                                AQDLEMYGVNYFAIRNKKGTELLLGVDALG
                                                LHIYDPENRLTPKISFPWNEIRNISYSDKE
                                                FTIKPLDKKIDVFKFNSSKLRVNKLILQLC
                                                IGNHDLF
mrrrkadslevqqmkaqareekarkqmerq          308-478
rlarekqmreeaertrdelerrllqmkeea
tmanealmrseetadllaekaqiteeeakl
laqkaaeaeqemqrikatairteeekrlme
qkvleaevlalkmaeeserrakeadqlkqd
        lqeareaerrakqklleiatk
                                        479-496  PTYPPMNPIPAPLPPDIP
sfnligdslsfdfkdtdmkrlsmeiekekv          497-587
eymekskhlqeqlnelkteiealklkeret
aldilhnensdrggsskhntikkltlqsak
                s
                                        588-595  RVAFFEEL
```

Figure 11.4 Predicted nonglobular regions for the protein product of the neurofibromatosis type 2 gene (L11353) as deduced by SEG. The nonglobular regions are shown in the left-hand column in lowercase. Numbers denote residue positions for each block.

quately and accurately predict structure based on sequence is rooted in the knowledge that while sequence may specify conformation, the same conformation may be specified by multiple sequences. The ideas that structure is conserved to a much greater extent than sequence and that there is a limited number of backbone motifs (Chothia and Lesk, 1986; Chothia, 1992) indicate that similarities between proteins may not necessarily be detected through traditional, sequence-based methods only. Deducing the relationship between sequence and structure is at the root of the "protein-folding problem," and current research on the problem has been the focus of a number of recent reviews (Bryant and Altschul, 1995; Eisenhaber et al., 1995; Lemer et al., 1995).

The most robust of the structure prediction techniques is homology model building, or "threading" (Bryant and Lawrence, 1993; Fetrow and Bryant, 1993; Jones and Thornton, 1996). This method takes a query sequence whose structure is not known and threads it through the coordinates of a target protein whose structure has been solved, either by X-ray crystallography or NMR imaging. The sequence is moved position by position through the structure, subject to some predetermined physical constraints; for example, the lengths of secondary structure elements and loop regions may either be fixed or varying within a given range. For each placement of sequence against structure, pairwise and hydrophobic interactions between nonlocal residues are determined. These thermodynamic calculations are used to determine the most energetically favorable and conformationally stable alignment of the query sequence against the target structure. Programs such as this are computationally intensive, requiring, at a minimum, a powerful UNIX workstation; they also require knowledge of specialized computer languages.

While techniques such as threading are obviously very powerful, their current requirements in terms of both hardware and expertise may prove to be obstacles to most biologists. In an attempt to lower the height of the barrier, easy-to-use programs have been developed to give the average biologist a good first approximation for comparative protein modeling. (Numerous commercial protein structure analysis tools, such as WHAT-IF and LOOK, provide advanced capabilities, but this discussion is limited to Web-based freeware.)

The use of SWISS-MODEL, a program that performs automated sequence–structure comparisons (Peitsch, 1996), is a two-step process. The First Approach mode is used to determine whether a sequence can be modeled at all: when a sequence is submitted, SWISS-MODEL compares it to the crystallographic database (ExPdb), and modeling is attempted only if there is a homolog in ExPdb with sufficient sequence identity to the query protein. If the first approach finds one or more appropriate entries in ExPdb, an atomic model is built, and the results are returned by e-mail. Those results can be resubmitted to SWISS-MODEL using its Optimize mode, which allows for alteration of the proposed structure based on other knowledge, such as biochemical information.

The second method compares structures to structures, in the same light as does the vector alignment search tool (VAST) discussed in Chapter 7. The DALI algorithm looks for similar contact patterns between two proteins and performs an optimization to return the best set of structure alignment solutions for those proteins (Holm and Sander, 1993). The method is flexible in that gaps may be of any length, and it allows for alternate connectivities between aligned segments, thereby facilitating identification of specific domains that are similar in two different proteins, even if the proteins as a whole are dissimilar. The DALI Web interface will perform the analysis on either two sets of coordinates already in PDB, or by using a set of coordinates in PDB format submitted by the user. Alternatively, if both proteins of interest are present in PDB, their precomputed structural neighbors can be found by accessing the FSSP database of structurally aligned protein fold families (Holm and Sander, 1994), an "all-against-all" comparison of PDB entries.

The final method to be discussed here expands on the PHD secondary structure method discussed above. In the TOPITS method (Rost, 1995), a searchable database is created by translating the three-dimensional structure of proteins in PDB into one-dimensional "strings" of secondary structure. Then, the secondary structure and solvent accessibility of the query sequence is determined by the PHD method, with the results of this computation also being stored as a one-dimensional string. The query and target strings are then aligned by dynamic programming, to make the structure prediction. The results are returned as a ranked list, indicating the optimal alignment of the query sequence against the target structure, along with a probability estimate (Z score) of the accuracy of the prediction.

The three methods discussed here are fairly elementary, hence their speed in returning results and their ability to be adapted to a Web-style interface. Yet their level of performance is impressive in that they often can detect weak structural similarities between proteins. The ultimate potential of threading techniques in general was illustrated at a recent Asilomar conference, where a number of groups were invited to participate in a "structure prediction contest" (Lemer et al., 1995). This proving ground for the more complex techniques alluded to above showed that while the protein-folding problem is nowhere near being solved, numerous protein folds can reliably be identified. Since different methods proved to have different strengths in the contest, the sponsors suggested using a "consensus approach," similar to the approach used in the secondary structure prediction examples given earlier. The timing of these developments is quite exciting, inasmuch as concurrence with the Human Genome Project will give investigators a powerful handle for predicting structure–function relationships as putative gene products are identified.

Internet Resources for Topics Presented in Chapter 11

PREDICTION OF PHYSICAL PROPERTIES

Compute pI/MW	*http://expasy.hcuge.ch/ch2d/pi_tool.html*
PeptideMass	*http://expasy.hcuge.ch/sprot/peptide-mass.html*
TGREASE	*ftp://ftp.virginia.edu/pub/fasta/*
SAPS	*http://ulrec3.unil.ch/software/SAPS_form.html*

PREDICTION OF PROTEIN IDENTITY BASED ON COMPOSITION

AACompIdent	*http://expasy.hcuge.ch/ch2d/aacompi.html*
AACompSim	*http://expasy.hcuge.ch/ch2d/aacsim.html*
PROPSEARCH	*http://www.embl-heidelberg.de/prs.html*

PREDICTION OF SECONDARY STRUCTURE AND FOLDING CLASSES

nnpredict	*http://www.cmpharm.ucsf.edu/~nomi/nnpredict.html*
PredictProtein	*http://www.embl-heidelberg.de/predictprotein/*
SOPMA	*http://www.ibcp.fr/predict.html*
SSPRED	*http://www.embl-heidelberg.de/sspred/sspred_info.html*

PREDICTION OF SPECIALIZED STRUCTURES OR FEATURES

COILS	*http://ulrec3.unil.ch/software/COILS_form.html*
MacStripe	*http://www.wi.mit.edu/matsudaira/macstripe.html*

SignalP	*http://www.cbs.dtu.dk/services/SignalP/*
TMAP	*http://www.embl-heidelberg.de/tmap/tmap_sin.html*
TMpred	*http://ulrec3.unil.ch/software/TMPRED_form.htm*

STRUCTURE PREDICTION

Bryant–Lawrence	*ftp://ncbi.nlm.nih.gov/pub/pkb*
DALI	*http://www.embl-heidelberg.de/dali/dali.html*
FSSP	*http://www.embl-heidelberg.de/dali/fssp/fssp.html*
SWISS-MODEL	*http://expasy.hcuge.ch/swissmod/SWISS-MODEL.html*
TOPITS	*http://www.embl-heidelberg.de/predictprotein/phd_help.html*

REFERENCES

Akrigg, D., Bleasby, A. J., Dix, N. I. M., Findlay, J. B. C., North, A. C. T., Parry-Smith, D., Wootton, J. C., Blundell, T. I., Gardner, S. P., Hayes, F., Sternberg, M. J. E., Thornton, J. M., Tickle, I. J., and Murray-Rust, P. (1988). A protein sequence/structure database. Nature *335*, 745–746.

Anfinsen, C. B., Haber, E., Sela, M., and White, F. H. (1961). The kinetics of the formation of native ribonuclease during oxidation of the reduced polypeptide chain. Proc. Natl. Acad. Sci. U.S.A. *47*, 1309–1314.

Appel, R. D., Bairoch, A., and Hochstrasser, D. F. (1994). A new generation of information retrieval tools for biologists: The example of the ExPASy WWW server. Trends Biochem. Sci. *19*, 258–260.

Bjellqvist, B., Hughes, G., Pasquali, C., Paquet, N., Ravier, F., Sanchez, J.-C., Frutiger, S., and Hochstrasser, D. F. (1993). The focusing positions of polypeptides in immobilized pH gradients can be predicted from their amino acid sequence. Electrophoresis *14*, 1023–1031.

Brendel, V., Bucher, P., Nourbakhsh, I., Blasidell, B. E., and Karlin, S. (1992). Methods and algorithms for statistical analysis of protein sequences. Proc. Natl. Acad. Sci. U.S.A. *89*, 2002–2006.

Bryant, S. H., and Altschul, S. F. (1995). Statistics of sequence-structure threading. Curr. Opin. Struct. Biol. *5*, 236–244.

Bryant, S. H., and Lawrence, C. E. (1993). An empirical energy function for threading protein sequence through the folding motif. Proteins *16*, 92–112.

Burnett, R. M., Darling, G. D., Kendall, D. S., LeQuesne, M. E., Mayhew, S. G., Smith, W. W., and Ludwig, M. L. (1974). The structure of the oxidized form of clostridial flavodoxin at 1.9 Å resolution. J. Biol. Chem. *249*, 4383–4392.

Chothia, C. (1992). One thousand families for the molecular biologist. Nature *357*, 543–544.

Chothia, C., and Lesk, A. M. (1986). The relation between the divergence of sequence and structure in proteins. EMBO J. *5*, 823–826.

Cordwell, S. J., Wilkins, M. R., Cerpa-Poljak, A., Gooley, A. A., Duncan, M., Williams, K. L., and Humphery-Smith, I. (1995). Cross-species identification of proteins separated by two-dimensional electrophoresis using matrix-assisted laser desorption ionization/time-of-flight mass spectrometry and amino acid composition. Electrophoresis *16*, 438–443.

Deléage, G., and Roux, B. (1987). An algorithm for protein secondary structure based on class prediction. Protein Eng. *1*, 289–294.

Eisenhaber, F., Persson, B., and Argos, P. (1995). Protein structure prediction: Recognition of primary, secondary, and tertiary structural features from amino acid sequence. Crit. Rev. Biochem. Mol. Biol. *30*, 1–94.

Fetrow, J. S., and Bryant, S. H. (1993). New programs for protein tertiary structure prediction. Bio/Technology *11*, 479–484.

Garnier, J., Gibrat, J.-F., and Robson, B. (1996). GOR method for predicting protein secondary structure from amino acid sequence. Methods Enzymol. *266*, 540–553.

Geourjon, C., and Déleage, G. (1995). SOPMA: Significant improvements in protein secondary structure prediction by consensus prediction from multiple alignments. CABIOS *11*, 681–684.

Guss, J. M., and Freeman, H. C. (1983). Structure of oxidized poplar plastocyanin at 1.6 Å resolution. J. Mol. Biol. *169*, 521–563.

Hobohm, U., and Sander, C. (1995). A sequence property approach to searching protein databases. J. Mol. Biol. *251*, 390–399.

Hofmann, K., and Stoffel, W. (1993). TMbase: A database of membrane-spanning protein segments. Biol. Chem. Hoppe-Seyler *347*, 166.

Holm, L., and Sander, C. (1993). Protein structure comparison by alignment of distance matrices. J. Mol. Biol. *233*, 123–138.

Holm, L., and Sander, C. (1994). The FSSP database of structurally-aligned protein fold families. Nucl. Acids Res. *22*, 3600–3609.

Jones, D. T., and Thornton, J. M. (1996). Potential energy functions for threading. Curr. Opin. Struct. Biol. *6*, 210–216.

Kneller, D. G., Cohen, F. E., and Langridge, R. (1990). Improvements in protein secondary structure prediction by an enhanced neural network. J. Mol. Biol. *214*, 171–182.

Knight, A. E. (1994). *The Diversity of Myosin-like Proteins* (Cambridge: Cambridge University Press).

Kyte, J., and Doolittle, R. F. (1982). A simple method for displaying the hydropathic character of a protein. J. Mol. Biol. *157*, 105–132.

Lemer, C. M., Rooman, M. J., and Wodak, S. J. (1995). Protein structure prediction by threading methods: Evaluation of current techniques. Proteins *23*, 337–355.

Levin, J. M., Robson, B., and Garnier, J. (1986). An algorithm for secondary structure determination in proteins based on sequence similarity. FEBS Lett. *205*, 303–308.

Levitt, M., and Chothia, C. (1976). Structural patterns in globular proteins. Nature *261*, 552–558.

Lupas, A., Van Dyke, M., and Stock, J. (1991). Predicting coiled coils from protein sequences. Science *252*, 1162–1164.

Mehta, P. K., Heringa, J., and Argos, P. (1995). A simple and fast approach to prediction of protein secondary structure from multiply aligned sequences with accuracy above 70%. Protein Sci. *4*, 2517–2525.

Nielsen, H., Engelbrecht, J., Brunak, S., and von Heijne, G. (1997). Identification of prokaryotic and eukaryotic signal peptides and prediction of their cleavage sites. Protein Eng. *10*, 1–6.

Pappin, D. J. C., Hojrup, P., and Bleasby, A. J. (1993). Rapid identification of proteins by peptide-mass fingerprinting. Curr. Biol. *3*, 327–332.

Pauling, L., and Corey, R. B. (1951). The structure of proteins: Two hydrogen-bonded helical configurations of the polypeptide chain. Proc. Natl. Acad. Sci. U.S.A. *37*, 205–211.

Peitsch, M. C. (1996). ProMod and SWISS-MODEL: Internet-based tools for automated comparative protein modelling. Biochem. Soc. Trans. *24*, 274–279.

Persson, B., and Argos, P. (1994). Prediction of transmembrane segments in proteins utilising multiple sequence alignments. J. Mol. Biol. *237*, 182–192.

Rost, B. (1995). TOPITS: Threading one-dimensional predictions into three-dimensional structures. In *Third International Conference on Intelligent Systems for Molecular Biology,* C. Rawlings, D. Clark, R. Altman, L. Hunter, T. Lengauer, and S. Wodak, Eds. (Cambridge: AAAI Press), pp. 314–321.

Rost, B. (1996). PHD: Predicting one-dimensional protein structure by profile-based neural networks. Methods Enzymol. *266*, 525–539.

Rost, B., Sander, C., and Schneider, R. (1994). PHD: A mail server for protein secondary structure prediction. CABIOS *10*, 53–60.

Sander, C., and Schneider, R. (1991). Proteins *9*, 56–68.

Smith, W. W., Pattridge, K. A., Ludwig, M. L., Petsko, G. A., Tsernoglou, D., Tanaka, M., and Yasunobu, K. T. (1983). Structure of oxidized flavodoxin from *Anacystis nidulans*. J. Mol. Biol. *165*, 737–755.

Takano, T. (1977). Structure of myoglobin refined at 2.0 Å. J. Mol. Biol. *110,* 537–584.

Wilkins, M. R., Pasquali, C., Appel, R. D., Ou, K., Golaz, O., Sanchez, J.-C., Yan, J. X., Gooley, A. A., Hughes, G., Humphery-Smith, I., Williams, K. L., and Hochstrasser, D. F. (1996). From proteins to proteomes: Large-scale protein identification by two-dimensional electrophoresis and amino acid analysis. Bio/Techniques *14,* 61–65.

Wilkins, M. R., Lindskog, I., Gasteiger, E., Bairoch, A., Sanchez, J.-C., Hochstrasser, D. F., and Appel, R. D. (1997). Detailed peptide characterization using PeptideMass, a World Wide Web-accessible tool. Electrophoresis *18,* 403–408.

12

Of Mice and Men: Navigating Public Physical Mapping Databases

Lincoln D. Stein

Cold Spring Harbor Laboratory
Cold Spring Harbor, New York

Only a few years ago, just a handful of ready-made maps of the human genome existed, and these were low-resolution maps of small areas. Biomedical researchers wishing to localize and clone a disease gene were forced, by and large, to map their region of interest, a time-consuming and painstaking process. This situation has changed dramatically in recent years. There are now high-quality genetic maps of the human genome based on simple sequence repeat polymorphisms (Murray et al., 1994; Dib et al., 1996) that provide mapping information at resolutions of at 1–5 megabases (Mb). In addition, there exist a variety of physical maps that provide mapping resolutions in the sub-megabase range (see Hudson et al., 1995; O'Connell et al., 1996, among others); a map of ~16,000 expressed sequences (ESTs; Schuler et al., 1996) is also available. By taking advantage of these maps, a researcher can, in many cases, focus in on a candidate region by searching public mapping databases in a matter of hours rather than by performing laboratory experiments over a course of months.

Ironically, the researcher's burden has now shifted from mapping the genome to navigating a vast terra incognita of World Wide Web sites, FTP servers, and databases. There are large databases such as NCBI Entrez and GDB, smaller databases serving the primary maps published by genome centers, sites sponsored by individual chromosome committees, and sites used by smaller laboratories to publish highly detailed maps of specific

This chapter was adapted from *Current Protocols in Human Genetics,* edited by N. Dracopoli, J. Haines, B. Korf, D. Moir, C. Morton, J. Seidman, C. Seidman, and D. Smith (John Wiley & Sons, New York, 1997).

Bioinformatics: A Practical Guide to the Analysis of Genes and Proteins
Edited by A.D. Baxevanis and B.F.F. Ouellette
ISBN 0-471-19196-5, pages 268–298.   Copyright © 1998 Wiley-Liss, Inc.

regions. Each type of resource contains information that is valuable in its own right even when it overlaps with the information found at others. Finding one's way around this web of information is not easy. A recent search for the word "genome" in the AltaVista Web search engine turned up over 80,000 potentially relevant documents. This chapter is intended as a map of the maps, to guide readers through the physical mapping database maze.

After a brief overview of physical mapping methods, the chapter discusses the large community databases NCBI Entrez and GDB, which provide easy access to maps from many different sources and allow one to make comparisons between them. It then examines the resources published by individual mapping laboratories, starting with the centers involved in genome-wide mapping efforts and moving to individual chromosome-mapping efforts. Because of the author's field of expertise, this chapter focuses on the available human and mouse maps.

The full URLs of all Web pages referred to here can be found in the list at the end of the chapter.

TYPES OF PHYSICAL MAP

Physical maps come in many shapes and forms. At one end of the spectrum are restriction maps, useful for fine-structure mapping of small regions measured in kilobases; at the other end are cytogenetic maps suitable for mapping loci relative to regions that are tens of megabases in size. However, the two most widely used types are STS content maps and radiation hybrid maps, both of which can resolve regions much larger than 1 Mb and have the advantage of using convenient PCR-based positional markers.

In STS content maps (Figure 12.1), STS markers are assayed by the polymerase chain reaction against a library of large-insert clones such as yeast artificial chromosomes (YACs), bacterial artificial chromosomes (BACs), and cosmids. If two or more STSs are found to be contained in the same clone, chances are high that those markers are located close together (that they are not close 100% of the time is a reflection of various artifacts in the mapping procedure, such as the presence of chimeric clones). Over a period of time the STS content mapping technique builds a series of contigs (i.e., overlapping clusters of clones held together by shared STSs). The resolution and coverage of such a map is determined by a number of factors, including the density of STSs, the size of the clones, and the depth of the clone library. Typical STS content maps that are based on 1 Mb insert YAC libraries have a resolving power of several hundred base pairs. Maps that use a cloning vector with a smaller insert size have a higher theoretical resolution but require far more STSs to achieve coverage of the same area of the genome. Although it is generally possible to deduce the relative order of markers on STS content maps, the distances between adjacent markers cannot be measured with accuracy. However STS content maps have the advantage of being associated with a clone resource that can be used for further studies, such as subcloning or DNA sequencing. To date, the single most widely used resource for STS content mapping is the YAC library of the Centre d'Études du Polymorphisme Humain (CEPH), in Paris (Cohen et al., 1993). This is a 10× coverage library with an average insert size of ~1 Mb.

Radiation hybrid maps (Figure 12.2; Cox, 1992) are based on the ability to map breakpoints in fragmented DNA. In this technique, a human cell line is lethally irradiated with gamma radiation, fragmenting its chromosomal DNA. The cell line is then rescued by

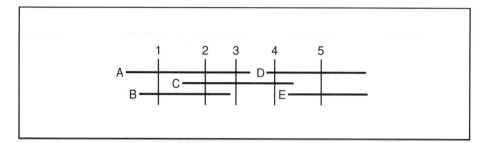

Figure 12.1 STS content mapping. STSs (vertical lines 1 to 5) are screened against a large insert clone library (horizontal lines A–E). If STSs are detected within the same clone, there is presumptive evidence that they are close together. Mutually linked STSs are clustered together into contigs.

fusion with a hamster cell line and passaged for several generations, during which time the human/hamster hybrid loses its human chromosomal fragments in a random manner. A hundred or more clones from the hybrid cell line, each with a different population of chromosomal fragments, are now picked and grown up, forming a hybrid panel to use for subsequent mapping experiments.

To map an STS on a radiation hybrid panel, one performs PCR of the STS against DNA from each of the hybrid panel cell lines. Cell lines that have retained a chromosomal fragment in which the STS is present will give a positive PCR signal. STSs that are very close together in the genome will have similar retention patterns because the chance of a radiation-induced breakpoint falling between them is low. STSs that are further apart will have less similar retention patterns, and those that are located very far apart will

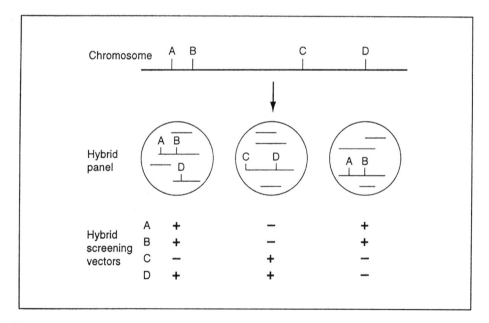

Figure 12.2 Radiation hybrid mapping. In this technique, a parental cell line's DNA is fragmented and distributed among multiple subclones that retain chromosomal fragments randomly. The subclones are screened with STSs to detect cell lines carrying fragments that contain the STSs. If two STSs show similar patterns of fragment retention, they are likely to be located close together on the chromosome.

show completely dissimilar retention patterns. Software based on algorithms similar to those used for genetic mapping can deduce a relative ordering of STSs on the radiation hybrid map, as well as distances between adjacent markers, by means of a distance system based on the probability that a breakpoint will fall between the markers. Radiation hybrid mapping is also capable of providing likelihood estimates (lod scores) for the assignment of a marker to a particular position. The resolution of a radiation hybrid map depends on the size of the chromosomal fragments contained in the hybrids, which in turn is the consequence of the amount of irradiation the human cell line was given. The radiation hybrid cell lines typically used for genome wide mapping have resolutions of ~1 Mb.

Several techniques in addition to STS content and radiation hybrid mapping have been used to produce human physical maps. Clone maps rely on techniques other than STS content to determine the adjacency of clones. For example, the CEPH YAC map (Chumakov et al., 1995) used a combination of fingerprinting, inter-Alu product hybridization, and STS content to create a map of overlapping YAC clones. Deletion and somatic cell hybrid maps rely on large genomic reorganizations (induced deliberately or occurring as an experiment of nature) to place markers into bins defined by chromosomal breakpoints (Vollrath et al., 1992). FISH maps (Lichter et al., 1990), which use a fluorescent signal to detect the hybridization of clone DNA-to-metaphase spreads, typically give the location of clones in terms of a cytogenetic band location.

Of particular interest to researchers chasing disease genes are maps of transcribed sequences. These maps consist of expressed sequences and sequences derived from known genes that have been converted into STSs and placed on conventional physical maps. Recent projects for creating large numbers of ESTs (Adams et al., 1991; Houlgatte et al., 1995; Hillier et al., 1996) have made tens of thousands of unique expressed sequences available to the mapping laboratories. Transcribed sequence maps can significantly speed the search for candidate genes once a disease locus has been identified.

YAC libraries work well for ordering STSs, but the high rate of chimerism and deletion in these clones makes them unsuitable for DNA sequencing. The last year has seen a push for high-resolution, sequence-ready maps based on cosmids or BACs, which are thought to have a lower level of cloning artifacts. With a few notable exceptions, such as the Lawrence Livermore Laboratory cosmid map of chromosome 19, these maps are still in their nascent stages.

GENOME-WIDE MAPS FROM LARGE COMMUNITY DATABASES

The mainstays for retrieval of human genome physical mapping information are the large community databases maintained by the National Center for Biotechnology Information (NCBI) and the Genome Data Base (GDB).[1] By providing access to maps produced by multiple groups, these databases allow the researcher to make comparisons between maps using a uniform user interface and query system. To some extent, these databases also provide map integration and analysis as well. NCBI Entrez and GDB are discussed in this section. Databases maintained by individual centers, where more detailed information is often available, are surveyed in the section entitled "Genome-Wide Maps from Individual Sources."

---

[1] Note added in proof: In January 1998, the GDB announced its termination due to discontinued funding. As of July 31, 1998, the GDB will no longer update its content, although the current database will continue to be available for some period of time.

Navigating Chromosome Maps in NCBI Entrez

Among the most accessible of the resources for physical mapping information is the Genomes division of Entrez, a service provided by the National Center for Biotechnology Information. Entrez attempts to integrate, in a browsable manner, several genetic and physical maps with DNA and protein-sequencing information, a bibliographic citation database, and three-dimensional crystallographic structure information. Entrez is recommended as a starting point for map searches because of its rich interconnectedness and simple interface. The Entrez information retrieval system is discussed in more detail in Chapter 5.

Any computer system that supports a Web browser such as Netscape, Mosaic, or Microsoft Internet Explorer may be used to navigate in Entrez. An Internet connection that supports TCP/IP is required; this can be a dedicated network connection or a dialup connection via an Internet service provider. Because the information is rich in graphics, a connection of 28,800 bps or better is recommended.

To begin, point the browser to the URL at Entrez's home page.[2] This will load a page with a series of links to Entrez's nucleotide, protein, bibliographic, genomic, and three-dimensional structures databases, as well as to documentation and help pages. Select the link marked Search the Genomes Database. This will display a page that contains a search field in one frame (Figure 12.3) and a series of species names in another. Each organism has a number next to it that indicates the number of maps in the database. The easiest way to retrieve the list of human maps is to click on the link labeled Homo sapiens. This will retrieve a list of 25 chromosome maps (chromosomes 1 through X plus two entries for the mitochondrial genome; no Y map is currently available).

Now select the link labeled Graphical View under the chromosome of interest. This will retrieve and display a graphic similar to that shown in Figure 12.4. The graphical view is a composite comprising several maps. The particular maps displayed vary from chromosome to chromosome, but at a minimum all chromosomes will display the Genethon and CHLC (Cooperative Human Linkage Center) genetic maps (Murray et al., 1994; Dib et al., 1996), the Whitehead Institute radiation hybrid and STS content maps (Hudson et al., 1995), the Stanford University radiation hybrid map, the cytogenetic map, and a sequence map that is essentially a placeholder for the mapped DNA sequence contigs that sequencing centers are expected to produce over the next decade. Markers present in more than one of the maps are connected by green diagonal lines, allowing the investigator to compare the maps and to remain oriented when moving from one to the next. For purposes of comparison and display, each map has been adapted to use a common coordinate system based on an estimate of physical distance (in DNA base pairs). However a glance at the maps shows that they are only roughly collinear and contain many contradictions in marker order, shown as crossing diagonal lines.

These maps can be navigated with a mouse. The pair of radio buttons labeled Action and Zoom control what happens when the graphic is clicked. To view a region of the map with greater detail, select the Zoom button and press in the region to be magnified. By default, when Zoom is selected, clicking on a region of the map will increase the magnification by 10%. It is possible to change the amount of magnification using the pop-up menu above the graphic. At higher magnifications, such features as individual marker names, mapped genes, YAC contigs, and mapped clones are easily distinguished. It is possible to zoom in

---

[2] See the end-of-chapter list for URLs of the WWW home pages and overview pages for databases, genome centers, and mapping projects mentioned in the text.

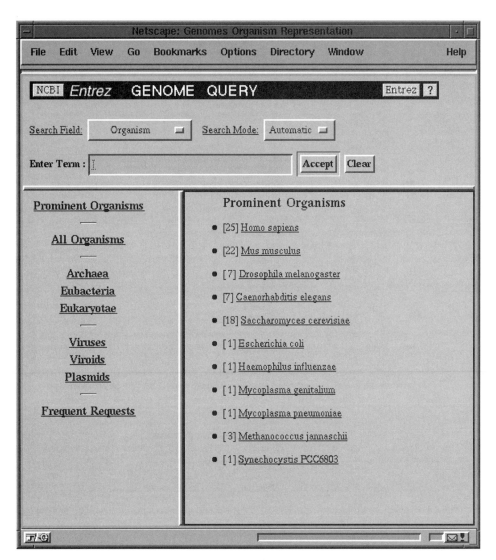

Figure 12.3 Entrez query window. To view the complete list of human chromosome maps on file in Entrez, use Homo sapiens as the search term.

even further or to select the Left, Right, and Align buttons to adjust the graphic to individual tastes (the Left and Right buttons appear after one round of zooming). The Overview command returns the display to its initial bird's-eye view.

To retrieve information about a particular labeled map element, select the radio button labeled Action and click on the element. Note that this button does not appear until zooming has been performed at least once. For example, clicking on an STS name will display its GenBank entry, which in turn will contain links to other entries in the Entrez bibliographic, nucleic acid, protein, and three-dimensional structure databases.

Web Entrez also provides a crude way to locate a particular marker on the map. Type the marker's name or GenBank accession number in one of the two text boxes labeled Search

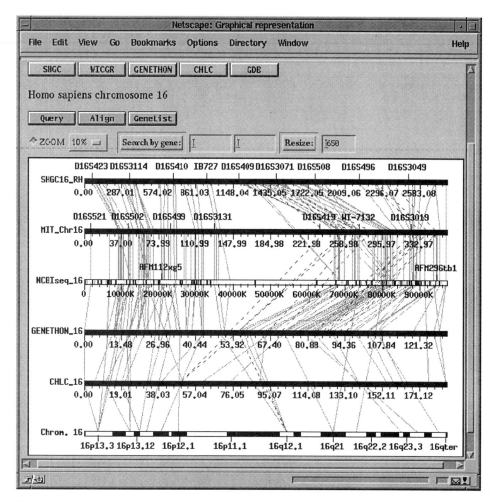

Figure 12.4 Entrez map overview: screen shows multiple maps with lines connecting the common landmarks. The user clicks on a region of interest to zoom in on it.

by Gene; then press the adjacent button. This will regenerate the map, with the marker highlighted in yellow. Typing two names will highlight the region between them. Despite the name of this function, few of the elements on the physical maps actually correspond to genes. Most markers are anonymous sequences or genetically polymorphic simple sequence repeats (STSs in many cases).

To save an Entrez map to a local disk, press the right mouse button (or Shift-Click on the Macintosh) with the cursor over the graphic, which will cause a pop-up menu to appear. Select Save Image As and type in a name for the saved graphics file. The image will be saved as a graphics file in GIF format, which can be displayed, printed, and manipulated by many different graphics programs. This procedure varies slightly between Web browsers: some require selection of a menu item labeled Save Next Link to Disk from the File menu before clicking on the graphic.

In addition to maps of the human genome, Entrez provides access to maps of the mouse, the fruit fly, *C. elegans,* and yeast, as well as a number of prokaryotes. Although comparative (synteny) maps are not yet available, this database currently represents the largest and most complete set of mapping information for multiple organisms.

Although the Web-based version of Entrez is sufficient for occasional use, heavy users of this resource may want to install Network Entrez, the NCBI's stand-alone client–server version of the software. This system provides the same features as the Web version but has substantially better performance and a somewhat more intuitive interface. It is available in Windows, Macintosh, and Unix versions and can be downloaded from the Entrez overview page.

Entrez has a number of limitations. The most severe is that maps constructed by quite different methodologies are forced to use the same coordinate system. This simplification, which was necessary to allow all maps to be presented in the same graphic, sometimes hide ambiguities and contradictions in the mapping information, creating an illusion of certainty where there is none. In particular, the integration between the cytogenetic map and the physical and genetic maps is loose at best and must be used with caution. However, Entrez has links to the Web sites maintained by each of the laboratories contributing the source maps; here it will be possible to find the most up-to-date versions of the maps in the representation that the contributing laboratory prefers. These individual center maps are described in more detail below.

Navigating Chromosome Maps in GDB

Another general source of human physical mapping data is the Genome Data Base (GDB). Although its original organization was geared toward the preponderance of genetic maps available at the time of its creation, GDB has undergone extensive revision in recent years and is now a repository of physical mapping data as well. Unlike NCBI, GDB is limited to human mapping data. It contains no sequence data, nor does it have information from other species.

Like NCBI, GDB is available on the World Wide Web. GDB provides a full-featured query interface to its database, which, although powerful, can be intimidating to novice users. More limited query interfaces, including a Search Maps by Location feature, provide a more intuitive entry into GDB. In particular, GDB's Mapview 2 program, introduced in December 1996, provides a graphical interface to the genetic and physical maps available at GDB using the new Java applet technology, which allows Web pages to incorporate active content (Anuff, 1995). A Web browser that can handle Java applets is required for the following protocol. Such browsers include Microsoft Internet Explorer (version 3.0 or higher) and Netscape Navigator (version 2.0 or higher).

To start access GDB, point the browser at the GDB home page. From this Web site, find and select the link labeled Advanced Search to retrieve a page containing links to several query forms.

The simplest query form is named Search Maps by Location. Select this link to display the form shown in Figure 12.5. To use this form, it is necessary to choose the chromosome or subchromosomal region to be displayed. To view an entire chromosome, simply select it from the pop-up menu. To view a chromosomal region, type in the names of two cytogenetic bands or genetic markers into the text fields labeled From and To.

Two scrolling lists at the bottom of the search page allow the user to restrict the search to maps and markers of certain types. For example, it is possible to limit the search to STSs (amplimers, in GDB parlance) that have been placed on radiation hybrid maps.

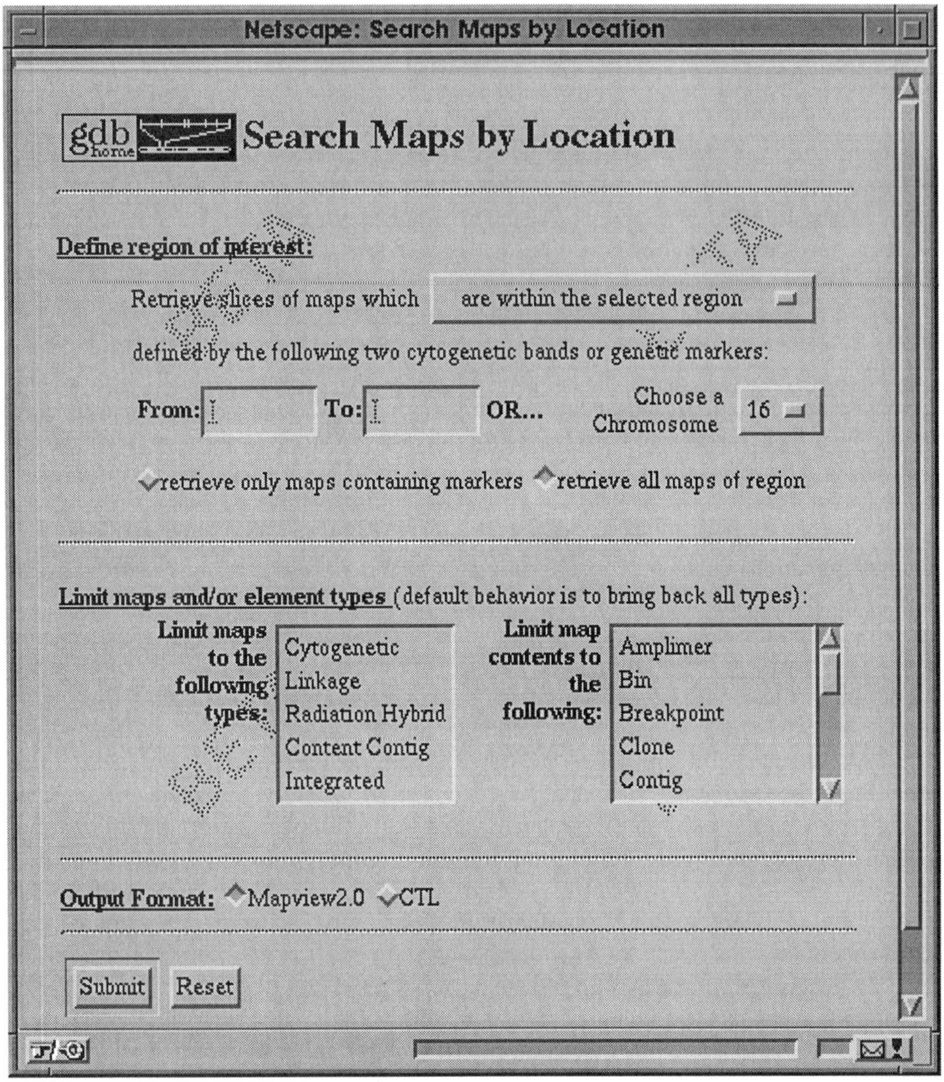

Figure 12.5   GDB map query window. This allows the user to select the region of interest on the basis of cytogenetic band. The user can type the band designations for the desired region into the From and To fields or select an entire chromosome from the pop-up menu.

To start the search, press the button labeled Submit. After a brief pause, a scrolling list will appear, containing all the maps that satisfied the request. Typically there will be a mixture of genetic, cytogenetic, and physical maps.

Select the map(s) of interest and press Submit again. Because each map takes a significant time to fetch and display, it is a good idea to limit retrieval to no more than three simultaneous maps, unless a fast network connection is being used.

When the maps have been computed, a new window will open, displaying the selected maps in side-by-side fashion (Figure 12.6). Markers that are shared among two or more maps are connected by lines, highlighting any contradictions that may be present.

To retrieve additional information on a marker that is shown, double-click on its name. The browser window will come to the foreground and display the GDB entry for the selected marker. This entry will contain hyperlinks to other information in GDB (such as bibliographic entries) and to other biological databases.

To retrieve information on the mapping methodologies and other information on a specific map, double-click on the map's vertical backbone to retrieve a Web page that describes the map and gives contact information. (**Important note:** Do not close the browser window behind Mapview. Because of an idiosyncrasy of Java's security specification, the applet cannot display information about selected markers unless the browser window remains open.)

Mapview's display can be customized by selecting either Marker Names or Display Options from the View menu. These options allow the user to turn the display of particular maps on and off, change the relative ordering of the maps, and customize the choice of marker names. By default, markers are displayed using their locus D-segment names. However it is sometimes more informative to display markers using the names assigned to them by their originating laboratories, which often give clues to the nature of an individual marker (e.g., whether it is a microsatellite repeat or an expressed sequence).

To search for a particular marker in the map, select Find from the Edit menu. Type in the name(s) of one or more markers and press the OK button. Any of a marker's aliases is accepted, as well as a single wild-card character (*). The selected markers will be highlighted and scrolled into view.

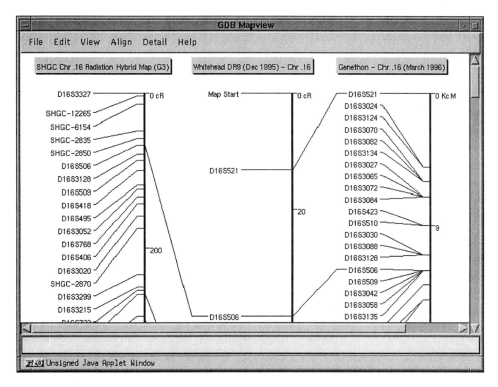

Figure 12.6 GDB's Mapview applet, showing the selected maps side by side. Common landmarks are connected by diagonal lines. The user can click on a map element, such as a marker name, to retrieve more information about it.

GENOME-WIDE MAPS FROM INDIVIDUAL SOURCES

Although one-stop databases such as Entrez and GDB are invaluable sources of published maps, they are no substitute for the primary data. The laboratories responsible for creating each of the physical maps invariably maintain Web sites of their own, often with a connection to their mapping database. By retrieving this material directly from the source, one can view maps in the form preferred by the originating laboratory, download the raw data, and review the laboratory protocols used for map construction. In addition, it often happens that maps are released by the primary laboratory before they appear in Entrez and GDB. The presentation style chosen by the Entrez and GDB databases, however, provides minimal aid to researchers who wish to assign new markers to existing physical maps.

Genetic Maps of the Genome

Although this chapter is concerned with resources for physical mapping, the discussion would not be complete without reference to the genetic maps, which form the backbone of many physical mapping efforts and are the starting point for many gene-mapping projects. Two genome-wide genetic maps are available. The Genethon map (Dib et al., 1996) consists of 5264 polymorphic microsatellite repeats that have been placed in 1.6 cM intervals. The complete datafiles, along with graphical representations of the map in PostScript format, are available at Genethon's FTP site. These maps are also available in browsable form through GDB.

The second large genetic map is produced by the Cooperative Human Linkage Center (Murray et al., 1994). The CHLC map consists of 10,775 markers, mostly microsatellite repeats, placed in 3.7 cM intervals.

Transcript Map of the Human Genome

In October 1996, a whole-genome transcript map of *Homo sapiens* was published in *Science* by an international consortium of research laboratories (Schuler et al., 1996). This map consists of ~15,000 unique expressed sequences localized by radiation hybrid mapping relative to a framework derived from the Genethon genetic map. An additional 1000 expressed sequences were mapped by STS content on yeast artificial chromosomes. Approximately one-fifth of the markers in this map have a known or putative function, whereas the rest represent transcribed sequences of unknown function. The mapped sequences were primarily derived from the UniGene set, a publicly available database of overlapping ESTs curated by NCBI (Boguski et al., 1994).

The transcript map was created by combining mapping data from eight different laboratories. To accommodate slightly different mapping methodologies, expressed sequences were placed relative to a framework constructed from the Genethon genetic map. As a consequence, the maximum resolution of this map is ~2 cM. In many cases, however, finer mapping information for a portion of the data set is available from the databases maintained by the individual contributors, specifically the Whitehead Institute and Stanford University.

Browsing the NCBI Transcript Map

The transcript map is available to the public at two Web sites. The parent site for the data is at NCBI. Here the full text of the *Science* article containing the whole-genome transcript map of *Homo sapiens* will be found, along with images of the colorful, but essentially decorative, wall chart that accompanied it. In addition, there are search pages that allow the investigator to query the map for particular genes of interest or to search through the map for expressed sequences that do not have a known function but whose open reading frames are highly similar to proteins of known function.

A limitation of the NCBI Web site is its failure to provide a graphical view of the transcript map beyond low-resolution histograms of marker distributions. However a graphical representation of the map is available at GDB via the Mapview applet. From GDB's welcome page, follow the links to What's New and then scroll down to Whole Genome Transcript Maps (the link organization may be slightly different by the time this book is published). It is also expected that the transcript map will be made part of the next release of Web Entrez.

Any computer system that supports a Web browser can be used to browse the NCBI transcript map. A connection to the Internet that supports TCP/IP is required; this can be a dedicated network connection or a dialup connection via an Internet service provider. Because this site is not graphically intensive, a fast connection is not a requirement.

To start, point the browser at the *Science* transcript map page. This will pull up the transcript map's home page, easily recognizable by its pleasant peach-colored background. Now find and click on the link labeled Research Tools Page. Currently this link is very inconspicuous (it is on the right of the page, underneath the graphic). This link will lead to a page with links to a number of different types of search. It is possible to search the map by position, by putative function, or by sequence similarity.

To search the map for potential candidate genes in a particular region of the genome, choose the link labeled Map Search to bring up a second page that presents a list of chromosomes. Choose the link for the chromosome of interest, which will call up a page similar to the one shown in Figure 12.7. Now, in the text field labeled Interval, enter two Genethon genetic markers that define the region of interest.

The Genethon map can be obtained from GDB, or directly from Genethon at the URL given above. For example, as shown in Figure 12.7, to search for expressed sequences located in the interval between 32 and 34 cM on the Genethon map of chromosome 18, enter `D18S464-D18S1153` and press the Select Markers button to start the search. The page that appears will list the expressed sequences in the region of interest (Figure 12.7); with each EST on a separate line, accompanied by a short description. The phrase "Highly similar to" or "Similar to" will precede sequences that do not correspond to known genes but have a sequence similarity to something in Swiss-Prot.

Each transcript's name is a hypertext link. Selecting the link generates a page giving details on the transcript. Among the available information is the listing of overlapping genes and ESTs that formed the cluster from which this transcript was selected, the source tissue from which the cDNA clone was prepared, the transcript's clone ID (clones for most of the ESTs are available through the I.M.A.G.E. Consortium's web pages), the results of Swiss-Prot similarity searches, and links into Entrez for sequence and bibliographic information.

To search for a mapped transcript by name or by putative function, return to the search page and select Text Search. This will lead to a page that prompts for one or more search terms. Search terms of any of the following types are allowed: a GenBank accession number, a marker or locus name, a descriptive term found in the description field of the transcript's GenBank entry, or a descriptive term found in the description field of a Swiss-Prot entry to which the transcript is similar. It is possible to use multiple search terms, in which case the search system retrieves entries containing all the terms.

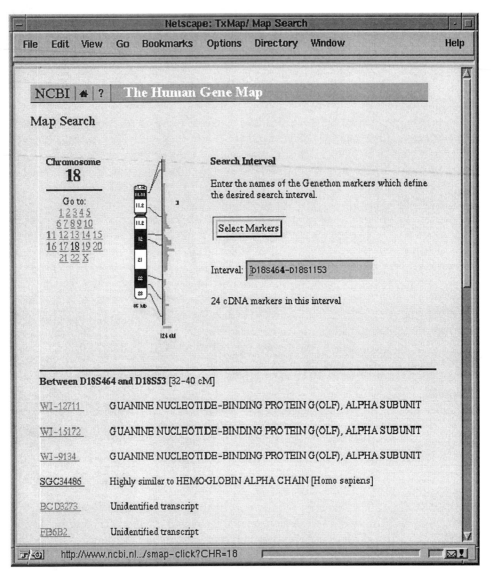

Figure 12.7 The Human Gene Map. The map can be searched by position by typing in a region defined by two genetically mapped markers. This screen shot shows the results of searching for the region between chromosome 18 markers D18S464 and D18S1153.

Press the Enter key to submit the search. A list of matching transcripts will be returned in a format similar to that described for the map search. For example, a search for keratin currently retrieves 17 keratins and keratin-like transcripts and indicates their map positions.

The final type of search is based on BLAST similarity. To search the map for transcripts that are similar to a DNA sequence, choose Sequence Search from the search page, which will lead to a page with a large text field. Cut and paste the sequence of interest into the text field using FASTA format, consisting of the right angle (>) characters followed by the name of the sequence (any arbitrary label will do), followed by the sequence itself on a new line, for example:

```
>blunderglobin 3' end
CTTGCATGCCTGCAGGTCGACTCTAGAGGATCCCCCTGTGCAGCATTCCATAAT
GTGAATATATAACACTTTATTCAAAATTTGGGGAAATAGTACCTTGTACATACA
TAATTTCACATGTTTGCCAGTGTGTGTTTTAGATACATGCCTGGA
```

If the sequence already has a GenBank entry, it is possible to simply enter its accession number instead. Press the Submit Query button. After performing a BLAST search of the query sequence against the transcript sequences, the NCBI server will present a page summarizing the identity and map positions of all similar transcripts.

Human Physical Maps Available at the Whitehead Institute

The Whitehead Institute/MIT Center for Genome Research is the primary source of two genome-wide physical maps. The maps maintained here are an STS content map of more than 10,000 markers assigned to YACs and a radiation hybrid map of some 12,000 markers. The Genebridge 4 radiation hybrid panel used at the Whitehead provides a resolution of ~1 Mbp, whereas the YAC-based map provides a resolution of roughly 200 kbp. These maps have been combined with the Genethon genetic map to create an integrated map of 20,000 STSs at an average spacing of 150 kb. Approximately half the markers on the Whitehead maps are expressed sequences that appear on the human transcript map as well.

The Whitehead Institute's maps are available via the Web at the Whitehead Center for Genome Research home page. Follow the links to Human Physical Mapping Project, and from there to the map of interest. The maps are browsable in a number of ways. A series of pop-up menus allows maps of selected chromosomes to be generated, and radio buttons allow views of the radiation hybrid, STS content, and genetic maps to be combined. As with Entrez, the maps are live. Clicking on an STS or contig will display a page with more information about the map element. The graphical maps can be downloaded from this site in either GIF or Macintosh native (PICT) format. A recently introduced multiple map viewer with the unimaginative name "Multimap" provides a detailed view of the maps for Java-capable browsers (Fig. 12.8). PostScript representations of the maps are available at Whitehead's FTP site. Be warned, however, that the PostScript maps are wall-size monstrosities many feet in length. A laser printer or plotter with ample memory (at least 8 megabytes) is necessary for producing hard copy.

The Whitehead Web site provides a number of search pages for querying the map database. There are links for searching the database by marker name, GenBank accession number, STS type, and chromosomal assignment. In addition, the Whitehead Web pages allow searching mapped transcribed sequences by functional keyword and provide links to the master transcript map maintained at NCBI.

Whitehead provides mapping services for researchers who wish to create their own STSs and place them on one or more of the maps. The services provided include:

an on-line primer-picking program, Primer3
a service for placing an STS on the STS/YAC content map
a service for placing an STS on the radiation hybrid map

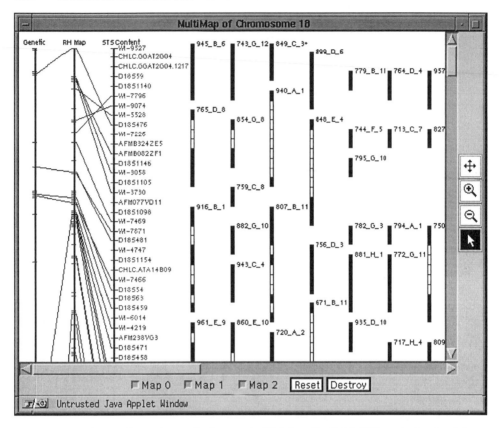

Figure 12.8   A Java applet can be used to browse the Whitehead Institute's STS content and radiation hybrid maps. It is possible to change the magnification by selecting the magnifying lens buttons on the right or to click on a map element (e.g., an STS or YAC) to retrieve raw mapping data.

The Whitehead maps are far from perfect. Even a cursory examination of the integrated maps shows contradictions between the positions of STSs on the genetic, radiation hybrid, and STS/YAC maps. These conflicts appear as crossing lines on the integrated maps. An important key to interpreting these maps is an understanding of the maps' differing levels of reliability and resolution. The genetic map backbone has the ability to link markers reliably across tens of megabases but cannot reliably resolve the order of two STSs below ~2 Mb. The radiation hybrid map can detect linkage across ~10 Mb and has an effective resolution of ~1 Mb (smaller intervals can be ordered, but with progressively increasing uncertainty). The STS/YAC map can detect linkage between two STSs within 1 Mb of each other and has an estimated resolving power of 100–300 kb. These differences in scale should be borne in mind when the maps are interpreted. Below the 1 Mb range, the STS/YAC map is generally the most reliable indication of order.

There are also regional variations in the reliability of the STS content map that result from the uneven distribution of STSs and YACs. In areas where YACs are dense (five or more YAC hits per STS), the map is relatively reliable as a result of the preponderance of ordering information. In areas of lower density, there may be several alternative STS orders that are equally likely, given the data at hand. Putative false negatives, indicated by empty boxes in the display shown in Figure 12.8, also significantly degrade the accuracy of the map. Finally, because of the problem of chimerism in all YAC libraries, double linkage (i.e., a pair of STSs linked by two or more shared YACs) is a far more reliable indication of adjacency than single linkage (STSs linked by only one YAC). Although the maps have been constructed to use single-linkage information only when there is supporting data from the genetic or radiation hybrid maps, a connection between two singly linked STSs should still be regarded with some skepticism. These factors should all be taken into account whenever mapped regions are examined in detail.

The following sections show how to use the Whitehead Web site to place new STSs on the Whitehead maps, beginning with STS design and proceeding to mapping relative to the Whitehead YAC and radiation hybrid maps.

Designing an STS for Placement on the Whitehead Maps

The design of an STS calls for a high-quality DNA sequence at least as long as the desired PCR product. For best results, sequences must be free of repetitive elements and vector sequence, and must be of relatively high quality. Any computer system that supports a World Wide Web browser may be used in this procedure; an Internet connection that supports TCP/IP is required.

To start, point the browser to the Whitehead Genome Center's home page. Find and follow the link to WWW Primer Picking. The page that appears will contain a large text field at the top. Cut and paste the source sequence into this field: paste just the source sequence, not names or other identifiers. Bases may be upper- or lowercase, and white space is ignored.

Now scroll the window downward and adjust the PCR conditions to the desired preferences. The default conditions of salt concentration, temperature, and product size range happen to be those preferred by the Whitehead Institute. When any changes deemed to be necessary have been properly entered, press the button labeled Pick Primers to return a set of primers meeting the specifications. These primers may now be used in a screening experiment for the sequence of interest. It is necessary to characterize the primer pairs empirically for their ability to amplify a unique band in genomic DNA. Primer failures are often associated with repetitive elements in the area spanned by the primers, and it is wise to screen input sequences against repetitive sequences by running a BLAST or FASTA search prior to choosing primer pairs. If the STS successfully amplifies a unique band, it can now be mapped relative to the Whitehead STS/YAC content or radiation hybrid maps.

Mapping an STS Relative to the Whitehead STS/YAC Content Map

Once created, an STS can be placed on the STS/YAC content map by screening it against the CEPH mega-YAC library. Screening the YAC library, which contains over 30,000 clones distributed among some 1200 row, plate, and column pools, is something of an undertaking. Fortunately several biotechnology companies offer replicas of the CEPH YAC library and/or screening services, including the Research Genetics Corporation. The Whitehead map was constructed from the latter part of the YAC library only. This means that only library plates in the range 709–972 need be screened. The STSs can then be placed on the map by using the following procedure.

Point the browser to the Whitehead home page and follow the link labeled Human Physical Mapping Project to jump to the institute's physical mapping page. From here, find and select "Search for a YAC to its address." The page that appears has a series of pop-up menus that can be used to enter the address of a single YAC, a small text field in which to type in the name of a single YAC, and a large text area in which to paste a list of YAC addresses. The latter is preferred if there is more than one YAC hit to investigate. Enter the list of YAC addresses in this field. Use the form plate_row_column, where underscores separate the plate, row, and column dimensions, (e.g., 709_A_1). Multiple YAC addresses can be entered, separated by spaces or carriage returns. The search is not case sensitive, and multiple YAC formats are recognized (including 709_a_1 and 709a1).

When the list of YACs is satisfactory, press the Search button to bring up a table listing each of the YACs, its contig position and chromosomal assignments, and the positions of nearby STSs that are on the radiation hybrid and/or genetic maps (see Example 1, below).

To interpret the results of this search, it should be understood that a significant percentage (40–50%) of the clones in the CEPH YAC library are chimeric. This means that a single YAC may be present in contigs located in several different parts of the genome. For this reason, it is important to find multiple YACs that confirm the assignment of an STS to a particular contig, or to confirm the assignment by other means (e.g., FISH, somatic cell hybrid mapping, radiation hybrid mapping data).

Example 1: Assigning an STS to the Whitehead STS/YAC Content Map

As a concrete example, consider an STS that is found by YAC library screen to be contained within three YACs: 945_B_6, 743_G_12, and 765_D_8. After their addresses have been typed into the Web page, pressing Search will return the following tables (abbreviated slightly here for clarity):

945_B_6

			Map Position		Contig	
	STS	Chrom	Genetic	RH	Single	Double
1	D18S59	Chr18	-	-	WC18.0	WC-1465
2	D18S1140	Chr18	-	-	WC18.0	WC-1465
3	CHLC.GGAT2G04.1217	Chr18	-	-	WC18.0	WC-1465
4	CHLC.GGAT2G04	Chr18	-	-	WC18.0	WC-1465
5	WI-9527	Chr18	-	-	WC18.0	WC-1465
6	WI-7796	Chr18	-	15cR	WC18.0	-

743_G_12

			Map Position		Contig	
	STS	Chrom	Genetic	RH	Single	Double
1	D18S1140	Chr18	-	-	WC18.0	WC-1465
2	CHLC.GGAT2G04	Chr18	-	-	WC18.0	WC-1465
3	WI-9527	Chr18	-	-	WC18.0	WC-1465
4	D18S59	Chr18	-	-	WC18.0	WC-1465
5	CHLC.GGAT2G04.1217	Chr18	-	-	WC18.0	WC-1465
6	WI-7796	Chr18	-	15 cR	WC18.0	-
8	D6S1634	Chr6	96 cM	-	WC6.12	WC-1197
9	WI-3308	Chr6	-	584 cR	WC6.12	WC-1197

```
10  FB10A2              Chr17    -     424 cR WC17.8 WC-1673
11  AFM198YB2           Chr5     -      32 cR WC5.0  WC-596
12  CHLC.GATA82H02      Chr5     -       -     WC5.0  WC-596
13  D5S406              Chr5    12 cM   -     WC5.0  WC-596
```

765_D_8

	STS	Chrom	Map Position		Contig	
			Genetic	RH	Single	Double
1	D14S69	Chr14	39 cM	-	WC14.0	WC-1651
2	AFMA133WF1	Chr14	-	-	WC14.0	WC-1651
3	D18S1105	Chr18	1 cM	-	WC18.0	WC-909
4	WI-5528	Chr18	-	7 cR	WC18.0	-
5	WI-3058	Chr18	-	5 cR	WC18.0	WC-909
6	WI-5872	Chr11	-	145 cR	WC11.4	-
7	WI-6096	Chr11	-	143 cR	WC11.4	-

Each table corresponds to one of the entered YAC addresses. Each table contains the list of STSs known to be contained in the YAC, along with STS mapping information. For each STS, the chromosomal assignment, genetic map position, and radiation hybrid map position are given when known. In addition, the named contig to which the STS belongs is listed. Most of the elements in these tables are hypertext links. It is possible to obtain more information about an STS or a contig by selecting the appropriate link. For historical reasons, many STSs have two contig assignments. Doubly linked contig (i.e., contigs held together by pairs of YACs) are shorter, more reliable contigs that were created during the initial phases of map building; they can safely be ignored. Single contigs are longer and have been validated by a variety of means.

In this example, two of the three YACs appear to be chimeric, since they appear in contigs that are scattered among several different chromosomes; it is apparent that all three YACs share contig WC18.0 in common. This makes it possible to tentatively assign the STS to this contig, and we know from the genetic and radiation hybrid positions of other STSs in the contig that WC18.0 is located close to the p terminus of chromosome 18.

Whitehead Radiation Hybrid Map

STSs can also be placed on the Whitehead radiation hybrid map. This is a much simpler proposition than STS/YAC content mapping, since screening an STS on radiation hybrids involves 93 PCRs rather than a thousand. The Whitehead radiation hybrid map uses the Genebridge 4 radiation hybrid panel. As with the CEPH YAC library, DNAs from these cell lines are available from a number of biotechnology companies, and some companies also offer screening services. For best results, the PCRs must be performed under the same conditions used to create the Whitehead maps (see Hudson et al., 1995) and should be performed in duplicate. Results that indicate discrepancies between duplicate PCRs should be repeated or treated as unknown.

To start, reformat the hybrid panel screening results in "radiation hybrid vector" format, which will look something like this:

```
sts_name1  0010010110000010000000110100011011100111001010012110011101010101000101000
sts_name2  0000011110000010000000110100000011100111001010012110011101010101000100000
...
```

Each digit is the result of the PCR on one of the radiation hybrid cell lines: "0" indicates that the PCR was negative (no reaction product), "1" indicates that it was positive, and "2" is used for "unknown" or "not done." The order of digits in the vector is important and must correspond to the official order of the Genebridge 4 radiation hybrid panel. To find this order, follow the link labeled "How the radiation hybrid maps were constructed" from the Whitehead physical mapping page, and then follow the link labeled "GeneBridge 4 order." The order is identical to the order in which the DNAs are packaged when they are shipped by Research Genetics, so this will ordinarily not be an issue. To increase readability, place spaces in the vector. The STS name should be separated from the screening data with one or more spaces or tabs.

From the Whitehead physical mapping page, follow the link labeled "Place your own STSs on the genome framework map." Enter the appropriate e-mail address where indicated, and paste the PCR scores into the large text field at the top of the page. It is very important to enter the correct e-mail address; otherwise the mapping results will be misdirected.

By default, the mapping data is returned in text form. To generate graphical pictures of the STSs placed on the Whitehead map, select one of the radio buttons marked Mac PICT (for a Macintosh system) or GIF (for Windows and Unix systems).

When the settings are satisfactory, press the Submit button. A confirmation that the data has been submitted for mapping will be generated, and the results will be returned via e-mail within an hour.

For large amounts of screening data, it may be inconvenient to use cut-and-paste to submit these files to the server. An alternative is to save the data to the local disk in text-only format. Then use the Browse button located in the RH mapping page to locate and upload this file to the Whitehead server. The e-mail address must still be entered manually.

The Whitehead radiation hybrid mapping server finds unique placements for ~98% of the markers that are submitted to it. If successful, the software returns the marker's chromosomal assignment and position within the chromosomal linkage group, a tabular representation of the marker, and its data in the context of flanking markers on the Whitehead radiation hybrid map. A picture of the map in Macintosh or GIF format is available on request. These maps consist of the Whitehead framework maps with the positions of the submitted STSs indicated in red.

Mapping runs may fail, either because the marker is found to link to more than one chromosome or because no linkage is found at all. In the former case it may be possible to map the marker by resubmitting it using a higher setting for the lod score at which the server will declare linkage to a chromosome. In the latter case, one might try reducing the threshold, via a pop-up menu located on the radiation hybrid mapping page. If a marker stubbornly insists on linking to multiple chromosomes, it is possible that the STS detects a repetitive sequence.

Stanford University Radiation Hybrid Map

The Stanford Human Genome Center has developed a radiation hybrid map of the genome that uses the G3 mapping panel. Created with a higher radiation dosage than the Genebridge 4 panel, the G3 panel has greater order resolving power, but at the cost of more limited ability to detect linkage across long distances. The Stanford map currently consists of ~8000 STSs at an average spacing of 375 kb. Some 3700 of these markers are expressed sequences that were contributed to the NCBI transcription map. As before, in some parts of the genome, expressed sequences on Stanford's map will be ordered with greater accuracy than those found on the all-inclusive NCBI map.

Stanford's map can be accessed via the World Wide Web. Follow the home page links to Mapping and then to RH Mapping, which leads to the genomic radiation hybrid map. From here, the link labeled Maps leads to a page that prompts the user to select a chromosome to display. The site then displays an ideogram of the selected chromosome, a density graph indicating the location of each mapped marker, and a list of the Genethon genetic markers used as a framework for building the map (Figure 12.9). Clicking on the name of one of the genetic framework markers retrieves a detailed list of the markers in this region. Selecting one of the marker names leads to further pages presenting detailed information about the marker and its mapping data. Locations of specific markers can be retrieved from a search page. Valid search terms include marker names, GenBank accession numbers, GDB locus identifiers, and dbSTS numbers.

Stanford provides a radiation hybrid mapping server. Like the Whitehead service, this server allows one to enter data from screening an STS against the G3 panel readily available from Research Genetics and other vendors. The server will attempt to link the STS to the Stanford map, and will return the results by e-mail. Because the G3 panel cannot detect linkage across large distances, the Stanford server is able to assign an STS to a chromosome map only 75% of the time in the absence of other mapping information. If a chromosomal assignment is provided for the marker in an optional field, however, the server will be able to run the analysis with a lower lod score for linkage, allowing it to make a map assignment in 90% of cases.

When PCR is used, the STS must be screened against the 83 G3 panel DNAs. For best results, follow the PCR protocol given at Stanford's RH Protocol home page. Each assay should be performed in duplicate, and assays that disagree between replicates should be repeated or marked as unknown.

The Stanford server returns the mapping results as a series of placements relative to genetic markers. For each STS, the server reports the closest genetic marker, its chromosome, and the distance, in centirays (cR), from the marker to the STS. Although no graphical display is provided for the mapping results, the mapping information can be used in conjunction with the browsable maps described above to infer the location of the submitted STS relative to other STSs on the Stanford map.

Start by reformatting the screening results in "radiation hybrid vector" format:

```
sts_name1 10000000000000001000000000000100000001001100100000011000000100000R1100000
sts_name2 000000000000000R00000111100000000000100110010000001100000100000R1100000
...
```

Each digit is the result of the PCR on one of the radiation hybrid cell lines; "0" indicates that the PCR was negative (no reaction product), "1" indicates that it was positive, and "R" is used for "unknown" or "ambiguous" (this is different from the Whitehead format, although the Whitehead will also recognize "R"). The order of digits in the vector is important and must correspond to the official order of the G3 radiation hybrid panel. This is the

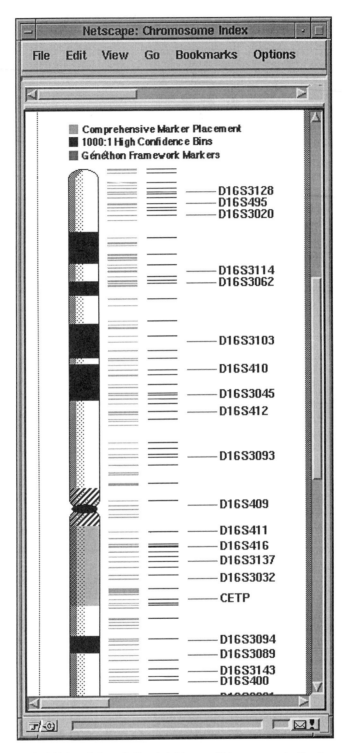

Figure 12.9 Stanford University's radiation hybrid map. This appears in the form of a clickable ideogram. The user can click on the names of one of the genetically mapped markers to obtain the list of STSs mapped to that interval.

same order in which the panel DNAs are shipped by Research Genetics. Separate the STS name from the screening data with a single tab (not spaces). White space is not allowed in the vector (another difference from the Whitehead format).

To submit this data, connect to Stanford's home page and follow the links to RH Server and then to RH Server Web Submission. Fields in which to enter an e-mail address and a reference number are indicated. The e-mail address is vital to ensure receipt of the mapping results. The reference number is an optional field that will be returned to the user with the results and is intended to help workers keep the results organized. If the STS's chromosomal assignment is known, it too should be entered into the field labeled Chromosome Number. This information increases the ability of the mapping software to detect a valid linkage.

Now paste the screening results into the large text field and press the Submit button. Mapping results are typically returned via e-mail within a few minutes. The Stanford server returns the mapping results as a series of placements relative to genetic markers. For each STS, the server reports the closest genetic marker, its chromosome, and the distance, in centirays, from the marker to the STS. Although no graphical display is provided for the mapping results, the mapping information can be used in conjunction with the browsable maps described above to infer the location of the user's STS relative to other STSs on the Stanford map.

CEPH YAC Map

In 1993 the Centre d'Études du Polymorphisme Humain (CEPH) in Paris, in collaboration with Genethon, published the first physical map of the human genome (Cohen et al., 1993; Chumakov et al., 1995). This map consists of sets of overlapping YACs that form paths connecting adjacent genetic markers. YAC overlaps were determined by a variety of techniques, including YAC fingerprinting, hybridization to inter-Alu PCR products, fluorescence in situ hybridization (FISH), and STS content. Although the YAC clone map has largely been superseded by more convenient STS-based maps, it is still useful for mapping projects that involve the CEPH YAC library or that require clone-based reagents.

Because of the high rate of chimerism in YAC libraries, each step between two YACs thought to overlap by fingerprinting or inter-Alu PCR hybridization carries with it a significant chance of stepping into a physically distant part of the genome. For this reason, short paths are more reliable than long ones. This concept is embodied in the CEPH term "level." A level 1 path consists of two genetically anchored STSs that are directly connected by at least one YAC. This type of path, which is equivalent to the double or single linkage used to establish adjacency in plain STS content mapping, allows the investigator to walk from one STS to the next without hopping across any YAC/YAC junctions. A level 2 path, in contrast, consists of two anchored STSs which, although not directly connected by any single YAC, are connected via inter-Alu PCR or fingerprinting data that establishes an overlap between two or more of the YACs that contain them. Thus a level 2 path calls for a hop across a single YAC/YAC junction. A level 3 path requires two hops across YAC overlaps, a level 4 path requires three hops, and so forth. Although reliability for each level has not been empirically determined, an analysis of the CEPH data set (J. Orlin, personal communication) suggests that paths of level 4 and higher are likely to be inaccurate. Fortunately nearly 90% of the genetic intervals covered by CEPH paths are level 3 and below.

Retrieving YAC Overlap from the CEPH Server   The CEPH map is available online at the organization's Web site. Here, links can be found to information on the YAC library as well as to a series of PostScript files of the map, the QuickMap software used to generate the maps, and files containing the raw mapping data. The best way to interactively browse the CEPH map is to download the QuickMap software, install it, then use it to view the datafiles. Since, however, QuickMap works only with Sun workstations, this will not always be possible. CEPH offers an online interface to QuickMap, available through the link labeled Infoclone, which leads to a page prompting for the name of an STS, a genetic marker, or a YAC. Submitting the name returns all raw mapping data concerning it. The text is hyperlinked, allowing one to follow a single inter-Alu PCR hybridization from one YAC to the next.

To access the data, point the browser to the CEPH Web site. This will lead to the CEPH Genethon Web pages. Now locate and select the Infoclone link. The page that appears will show a prompts to type the name of either a YAC or an STS into a small text field. YACs follow the conventional plate_row_column format, as in `923_f_6`. For STSs, either the GDB-assigned D-segment name (if available) or the laboratory-assigned assay name can be used. The software is case sensitive, so `AFM220ZE3` will not correctly retrieve the STS named `AFM220ze3`. Also note that the row name in YAC addresses must be in lowercase.

Press the Query button. If the name is known to the CEPH database, a page containing information similar to that shown in shortly Example 2 will appear. The first section contains general information about the STS including the primer sequences and genetic mapping information. The second section gives YAC screening data for the STSs. All the YACs listed in this section have been found to contain the STS by direct PCR screening. The notation `Alu-PCR probe` indicates that this YAC was selected for use as a probe in an inter-Alu PCR hybridization experiment. The third section contains information on YACs that are thought to be adjacent to the STS. They are all one inter-Alu-PCR hop away from the STS.

To retrieve mapping information on a YAC, enter its name in the text field and press Query. The retrieved page will give sizing information for the YAC, FISH, and STS content data, as well as overlap information derived from inter-Alu PCR and fingerprinting experiments.

Example 2: Genethon Genotyping Information

```
Genotyping information from Genethon 1994 genetic map:
    Number of alleles: 7
    Heterozygosity: 0.78
    Reference alleles: 1-4
    Size range: 204,206,208,210,212,214,218
    Primer sequences:
    (ca) TGTACCTAAGCCCACCCTTTAGAGC
    (gt) TGGCCTCCAGAAACCTCCAA


YACs specific for STS AFM220ze3:
678_g_3   CE                    (1730 kb)
746_e_4   CE                    (1080 kb,1350 kb,1500 kb)
756_e_8   IE   Alu-PCR probe    (1380 kb)
765_d_4   IE                    (1060 kb)
765_e_4   IE   Alu-PCR probe    (880 kb)
826_e_6   IE   Alu-PCR probe    (820 kb)
```

```
YACs neighbouring STS AFM220ze3:
56_c_5      a  Alu-PCR probe (no size)
154_d_3     a  Alu-PCR probe (no size)
261_c_12    a  Alu-PCR probe (no size)
309_c_11    a  Alu-PCR probe (no size)
340_g_10    a  Alu-PCR probe (no size)
366_f_1     a  Alu-PCR probe (no size)
682_a_11    f                (no size)
```

Several codes are associated with each YAC entry. For example, in the table of direct PCR screening, a C indicates an unambiguous result from an experiment performed at CEPH, an I indicates a YAC hit that has been individually verified, and an E indicates individually verified YAC hits performed at external (non-CEPH) laboratories. In the table of YAC/YAC overlaps, an a indicates an Alu-PCR relationship, whereas an f indicates a fingerprinting relationship. Complete tables of codes can be found by selecting various Help links located on this page.

A subset of the CEPH YAC library has been sized by pulsed-field gel electrophoresis. When available, YAC sizes are given. In some cases, multiple bands were found, either as the result of contamination or because of spontaneous deletions of DNA from within the YAC insert during clone growth. In this case, multiple YAC sizes may be displayed.

CHROMOSOME-SPECIFIC HUMAN MAPS

In addition to the genome-wide maps, physical maps of many individual chromosomes have been built by research laboratories and genome centers. In many cases, these maps provide greater detail than the corresponding whole-genome maps do. Table 12.1 lists the maps and where to find them on the Web. In addition to the URLs shown here, an up-to-date list can always be found at GDB's resource page. Another listing is maintained at the Web site of the National Human Genome Research Institute (NHGRI). The URLs for all the sites discussed below are listed in Table 12.1.

Chromosome 3 maps are available at two centers. The University of Texas Health Center at San Antonio offers an STS content map based on YACs, as well as a radiation hybrid map (O'Connell et al., 1996). This Web site provides a graphical clickable interface to the mapping data, as well as a query-based mechanism. The University of Texas also maintains a radiation hybrid map of chromosome 8, available from the same Web site.

An STS content map of chromosome 4, containing 1280 STSs and 3300 YACs, is available at the Stanford Human Genome Center's site. The map is distributed as a series of PostScript files only. Raw screening data is not yet available online.

A set of Web pages devoted to chromosome 6 is available at the Sanger Centre, where the progress of that group's radiation hybrid and sequencing projects can be followed. Mapping data is available as clickable images, and sequencing data can be downloaded in the form of Unix tape archives (tar files).

The primary site for chromosome 7 mapping data is in Eric Green's laboratory at the NHGRI. The main map is an STS/YAC content map, supplemented with EST, BAC, and cosmid contig data. The data is cross-linked to the Chromosome 7 Sequencing Project at Washington University. A number of physical maps of chromosome 7 are also available at the Department of Genetics at The Hospital for Sick Children, in Toronto. The main map

TABLE 12.1 Chromosome-Specific Physical Maps[a]

Chromosome	Laboratory	Map Type	URL
3	University of Texas Health Science Center	STS/YAC + RH	*http://mars.uthscsa.edu/*
	Eleanor Roosevelt Institute	STS/YAC	*http://www-eri.uchsc.edu/*
4	Stanford Human Genome Center	STS/YAC	*http://shgc.stanford.edu/*
6	Sanger Centre	RH	*http://www.sanger.ac.uk/chr6/chr6.html*
7	The Hospital for Sick Children, Toronto	YAC	*http://www.genet.sickkids.on.ca/*
7	National Human Genome Research Institute	STS/YAC, BAC, cosmid, EST	*http://www.nhgri.nih.gov/DIR/GTB/CHR7/*
8	University of Texas Health Science Center	RH	*http://www-eri.uchsc.edu/*
10	Genome Therapeutics Corporation	STS/YAC	*http://www.cric.com/*
11	University of Texas Southwestern Medical Center	STS/YAC, RH, cosmid	*http://mcdermott.swmed.edu/datapage/*
12	Yale/Albert Einstein	STS/YAC	*http://paella.med.yale.edu/chr-12/Home.html*
13	Columbia University	STS/YAC	*http://genome1.ccc.columbia.edu/~genome/*
16	Los Alamos National Laboratories	RH + STS/cosmid	*http://www-ls.lanl.gov/masterhgp.html*
19	Lawrence Livermore National Laboratories	Cosmid	*http://www-bio.llnl.gov/bbrp/genome/genome.html*
22	Sanger Centre	YAC, BAC, PAC	*http://www.sanger.ac.uk/hum22/*
	University of Pennsylvania	STS/YAC	*http://www.cbil.upenn.edu/HGC22.html*
X	Baylor College of Medicine	STS/YAC	*http://gc.bcm.tmc.edu:8088/chrx/home.html*
Mito	Emory University	Sequence	*http://infinity.gen.emory.edu/mitomap.html*

[a] Abbreviations: Mito, mitochondrial genome; PAC, P1 artificial chromosome; RH, radiation hybrid; STS, sequence-tagged site; YAC, yeast artificial chromosome.

was assembled from overlapping chromosome-7-specific YACs; overlaps were determined by a combination of inter-Alu PCR hybridization, fingerprinting, and STS content mapping. Approximately 90% of 7q is thought to be covered by contigs.

The Genome Therapeutics Corporation of Waltham, Massachusetts, has produced STS content maps covering several portions of chromosome 10. Abstracts and lists of references for the maps are available at the company's Web site, but the maps themselves are available through GDB only.

Chromosome 11 maps are available at the University of Texas/Southwestern Medical Center's Genome Center. The largest is an STS content map containing ~1200 STSs mapped against the CEPH YAC library and the Roswell Park chromosome-11-specific YAC library. The data is available as a flatfile or as GIF images. FISH mapping results and the results of hybridizing YACs to a chromosome-specific cosmid library can also be found at this Web site.

Yale University and the Albert Einstein Medical Center have published an STS content map of chromosome 12 (Marynen and Kucherlapati, 1995). The map is based largely on the CEPH YAC library, but includes cosmids and other types of clones as well.

A set of chromosome 13 maps is available at Columbia University. These maps consist of CEPH YAC clones that have been probed against a chromosome-13-specific cosmid library using inter-Alu PCR product hybridization. On top of these clone-based maps have been placed genes, STSs, and cDNAs. The maps and raw data are available at Columbia's Web site as a series of hyperlinked tables and flatfiles.

Los Alamos National Laboratory's map of chromosome 16 (Doggett et al., 1995) is an STS content map consisting of over 500 STSs mapped relative to the CEPH YAC library and a series of cosmids and other clones. The Los Alamos Web site features a fully queryable database of the chromosome 16 mapping data, as well as a series of pictures of the maps and flatfiles containing the mapping data. The popular Sigma map construction program was developed at Los Alamos, so the map is distributed as Sigma datafiles as well.

Another national laboratory, Lawrence Livermore, is responsible for chromosome 19. A high-resolution, cosmid-based map assembled by restriction analysis and FISH mapping also contains ~400 STSs and many genes. The map is available at Livermore's Web site in the form of a series of large images. Raw mapping data does not yet seem to be available on the Internet.

Human chromosome 22 is represented by two centers. The University of Pennsylvania's map consists of somewhat more than 200 STSs ordered on the CEPH YAC library (Bell et al., 1995). The complete data set, along with search pages for querying it, is available at the Web site. In addition, the Sanger Centre in Cambridge, England, is actively engaged in mapping this chromosome in preparation for large-scale sequencing. Available at Sanger's Web site is an STS content map based on CEPH YACs. It can be downloaded as a series of PostScript pictures, or in a format that can be used with the ACEDB database (see end-of-chapter list). In addition, Sanger is in the process of constructing clone maps of the chromosome using a variety of cosmids, fosmids, BACs, and PACs. This data is not currently available on the Internet.

The Baylor College of Medicine is developing an STS content map of chromosome X based on the CEPH YAC library. The STS screening data set is searchable from a series of pages located at Baylor's Web site. In addition, Baylor provides an interface to search STS screening information published by a number of other sources.

Last, maps based on the complete human mitochondrial sequence are available at the Department of Genetics and Molecular Medicine, Emory University, as part of the MITO-

MAP database (Kogelnik et al., 1996). This site makes available a series of clickable image maps showing mitochondrial genes, variations, and rearrangements, along with the complete nucleotide sequence.

MOUSE MAPPING RESOURCES

Currently the major focus for mouse physical mapping activity is at the Whitehead Institute/MIT Center for Genome Research, where a murine STS/YAC content map is being constructed. The map, which will ultimately contain 10,000 STSs mapped on 24,000

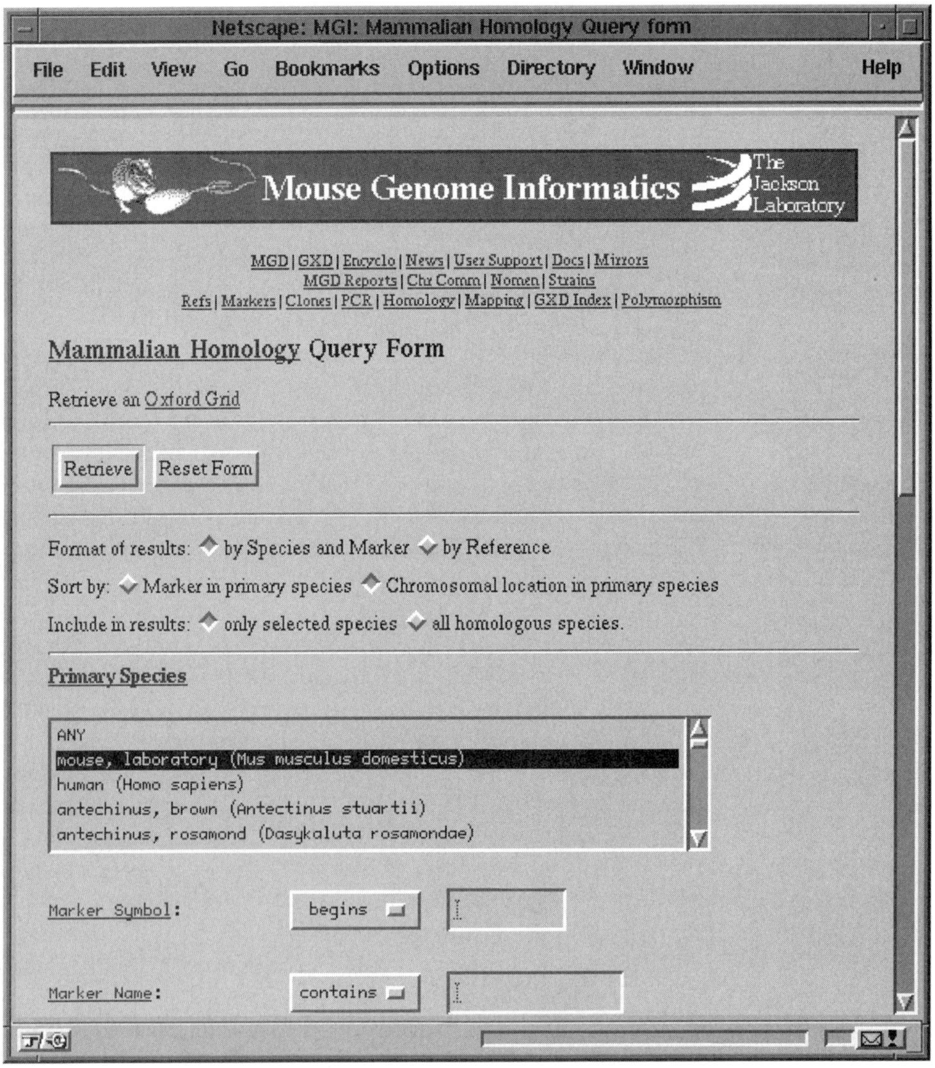

Figure 12.10   The MGDB synteny search form. This long form prompts the user to select two species and other search criteria, with the goal of generating a syteny map.

YACs, is currently at the three-quarters point, with somewhat more than 7500 STSs as of May 1997.

The MIT physical map can be browsed online at the Whitehead home page. First follow the links to Mouse Genetic and Physical Mapping Project; then scroll down to the section labeled STS Physical Map of the Mouse. This section has the same search options and user interface as the Whitehead human physical map, although no radiation hybrid mapping data is available.

Also available at the Whitehead site is a genetic map of the mouse based on 6331 simple sequence length polymorphisms, as well as an integration between this map and the Copeland/Jenkins restriction fragment length polymorphism maps. These RFLP maps, described in Dietrich et al. (1996), have a resolution of 1.1 cM. A higher resolution genetic map of the mouse is being prepared by the European Collaborative Interspecific Mouse BackCross project. This map, which has a maximum theoretical resolution of 0.3 cM, is available online at the ECIMBC home page. Five chromosomes had been completed as of May 1997.

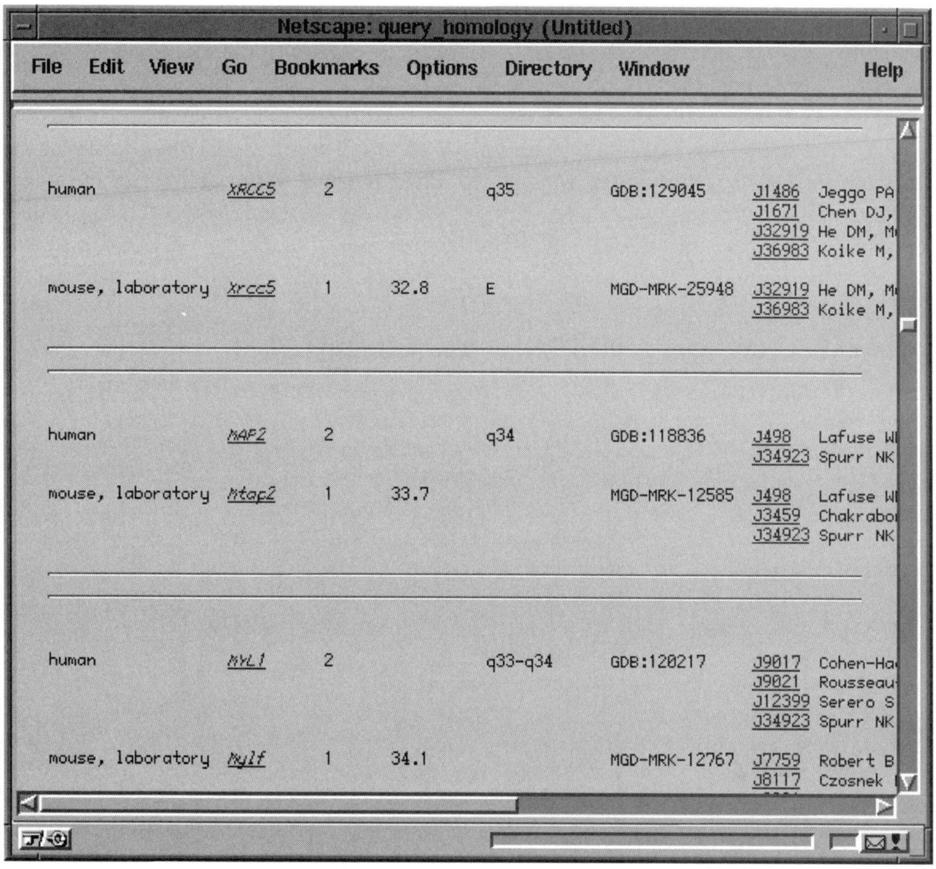

Figure 12.11 Output from an MGDB synteny search is a table showing genes in common between the selected organisms and their chromosomal positions, along with links to other information about the retrieved genes.

The Mouse Genome Database (MGD) is a large community database of mouse genetic information maintained by the Jackson Laboratory in Bar Harbor, Maine. Although primarily a genetic mapping repository, MGD contains some physical mapping information as well, including cytogenetic maps and synteny maps. More will be added in the future as the data becomes available. The MGD is also the definitive source for nomenclature information on murine genes. The MGD can be accessed via the Jackson Lab's home page. Follow the link labeled Mouse Genome Informatics, and then the linked labeled The Mouse Genome Database, to a page that serves as a jumping-off point for a variety of searches. Among the options listed here are bibliographic searches, searches for gene and marker symbols, and searches for polymorphisms.

Of particular interest are two links to mapping data. The first, labeled Maps and Mapping Data, leads to a page from which access to a large number of mouse genetic maps is possible. A cytogenetic map is also available. The second link, labeled Mammalian Homology, provides an interface to the MGD's synteny maps. These maps, based on the location of known genes, provide a low-resolution comparison between the chromosomes of two or more mammalian species. When this link is selected, the long page shown in Figure 12.10 appears. There are two scrolling lists on this page: Primary Species and Comparison Species (the latter is scrolled out of sight in Figure 12.10). Each list contains a series of mammalian species names. In addition, a large number of fields allow the user to limit the search by chromosome, by cytogenetic band, or by a number of other database fields that are mostly irrelevant (such as author names).

To use the form, simply select the names of the two species to be compared. To limit the search time, selection of a chromosome or cytogenetic band in either the primary or the comparison species is strongly recommended. Press Retrieve. After an interval of up to a minute, a tabular list of genes shared among the two species and their comparative map positions will appear. In the example output shown in Figure 12.11, a search for mouse chromosome 1 detects a large area of synteny with human chromosome 2 (third column).

Internet Resources for Topics Presented in Chapter 12

CEPH YAC map	*http://www.cephb.fr/ceph-genethon-map.html*
CHLC map	*http://www.chlc.org*
ECIMBC home page	*http://www.hgmp.mrc.ac.uk/MBx/MBxHomepage.html*
Entrez home page	*http://www.ncbi.nlm.nih.gov/Entrez/*
Entrez overview page	*http://www.ncbi.nlm.nih.gov/Entrez/nentrez.overview.html*
GDB home page	*http://gdbwww.gdb.org/*
GDB resource page	*http://gdbwww.gdb.org/gdb/hgp_resources.html*
Genethon FTP site	*ftp://ftp.genethon.fr/pub/Gmap/Nature-1995*
I. M. A G. E. Consortium	*http://www.bio.llnl.gov/bbrp/image/iresources.hrml*
Jackson Laboratory	*http://www.jax.org/*
NHGRI resource page	*http://www.nhgri.nih.gov/Data/*
Science transcript map	*http://www.ncbi.nlm.nih.gov/Science96/*
Stanford home page	*http://shgc.stanford.edu/*
Stanford RH protocol	*http://shgc.stanford.edu/Mapping/rh/procedure/*
Whitehead home page	*http://www.genome.wi.mit.edu/*
Whitehead FTP site	*ftp://www.genome.wi.mit.edu/pub/human_STS_releases/*

C. elegans	ACEDB	*http://probe.nalusda.gov:8300/other/*
E. coli	University of Wisconsin	*http://www.genetics.wisc.edu/*
D. melanogaster	FlyBase	*http://flybase.bio.indiana.edu:82/*
S. cerevisiae	SGD, Stanford	*http://genome-www.stanford.edu/Saccharomyces*

REFERENCES

Adams, M. D., Kelley, J. M., Gocayne, J. D., Dubnick, M., Polymeropoulos, M. H., Xiao, H., Merril, C. R., Wu, A., Olde, B., Moreno, R. F., Kerlavage, A. R., McCombie, W. R., and Venter, J. C. (1991). Complementary DNA sequencing: Expressed sequence tags and human genome project. Science *252,* 1651–1656.

Anuff, E. (1995). *Java Sourcebook* (New York: Wiley).

Bell, C. J., Budarf, M. L., Nieuwenhuijsen, B. W., Barnowski, B. L., Buetow, K. H., Campbell, K., Colbert, A. M. E., Collins, J., Daly, M., Desjardins, P. R., DeZwaan, T., Eckman, B., Foote, S., Hart, K., Hiester, K., Van Het Hoog, M. J., Hopper, E., Kaufman, A., McDermid, H. E., Overton, G. C., Reeve, M. P., Searls, D. B., Stein, L., Valmiki, V. H., Watson, E., Williams, S., Winston, R., Nussbaum, R. L., Lander, E. S., Fischbeck, K. H., Emanuel, B. S., and Hudson, T. J. (1995). Integration of physical, breakpoint and genetic maps of chromosome 22: Localization of 587 yeast artificial chromosomes with 238 mapped markers. Hum. Mol. Genet. *4,* 59–69.

Boguski, M., Tolstoshev, C. M., and Bassett, D. E. (1994). Gene discovery in dbEST. Science *165,* 1993–1994 (letter).

Chumakov, I., Rigault, P., Le Gall, I., et al., and Cohen, D. (1995). A YAC contig map of the human genome. Nature *377* (suppl.), 174–297.

Cohen, D., Chumakov, I., and Weissenbach, J. (1993). A first generation physical map of the human genome. Nature *336,* 698–701.

Cox, D. (1992). Radiation hybrid mapping. Cytogenet. Cell Genet, *59,* 80–81.

Dib, C., Faure, S., Fizames, C., Samson, D., Drou, N., Vignal, A., Millasseau, P., Marc, S., Hazan, J., Seboun, E., Lathrop, M., Gyapay, G., Morissette, J., and Weissenbach, J. (1996). A comprehensive genetic map of the human genome based on 5,264 microsatellites. Nature *380,* 152–154.

Dietrich, W. F., Miller, J., Steen, R., Merchant, M. A., Damron-Boles, D., Husain, Z., Dredge, R., Daly, M. J., Ingalls, K. A., O'Conner, T. J., Evans, C. A., DeAngelis, M. M., Levinson, D. M., Kruglyak, L., Goodman, N., Copeland, N. G., Jenkins, N. A., Hawkins, T. L., Stein, L., Page, D. C., and Lander, E. S. (1996). A comprehensive genetic map of the mouse genome. Nature *380,* 149–152.

Doggett, N. A., Goodwin, L. A., Tesmer, J. G., Meincke, L. J., Bruce, D. C., Clark, L. M., Altherr, M. R., Ford, A. A., Chi, H.-C., Marrone, B. L., Longmire, J. L., Lane, S. A., Whitmore, S. A., Lowenstein, M. G., Sutherland, R. D., Mundt, M. O., Knill, E. H., Bruno, W. J., Macken, C. A., Torney, D. C., Wu, J.-R., Griffith, J., Sutherland, G. R., Deaven, L. L., Callen, D. F., and Moyzis, R. K. (1995). An integrated physical map of human chromosome 16. Nature *377* (suppl.), 335–365.

Hillier, L., Lennon, G., Becker, M., Bonaldo, M., Chiapelli, Chissoe, S., Dietrich, N., DuBuque, T., Favello, A., Gish, W., Hawkins, M., Hultman, M., Kucaba, T., Lacy, M., Le, M., Le, N., Mardis, E., Moore, B., Morris, M., Parsons, J., Prange, C., Rifkin, L., Rohlfing, T., Schellenberg, K., Soares, M. B., Tan, F., Thierry-Mieg, J., Trevaskis, E., Underwood, K., Wohldman, P., Waterston, R., Wilson, R., and Marra, M. (1996). Generation and analysis of 280,000 human expressed sequence tags. Genome Res. *6,* 807–828.

Houlgatte, R., Mariage-Samson, R., Duprat, S., Tessier, A., Bentolila, W., Lamy, B., and Auffray, C. (1995). The Genexpress Index: A resource for gene discovery and the genic map of the human genome. Genome Res. *5,* 272–304.

Hudson, T. J., Stein, L. D., Gerety, S. S., Ma, J., et al., Lander, E. S. (1995). An STS-based map of the human genome. Science *270,* 1945–1954.

Kogelnik, A. M., Lott, M. T., Brown, M. D., Navathe, S. B., and Wallace, D. C. (1996). MITOMAP: A human mitochondrial genome database. Nucl. Acids Res. *24,* 177–179.

Lichter, P. C., Tang, J., Call, K., Hermanson, G., Evans, G., Housman, A. D., and Ward, D. C. (1990). High resolution mapping of human chromosome 11 by in situ hybridization with cosmid clones. Science *247,* 64–68.

Marynen, P., and Kucherlapati, R. (1995). Report of the Third International Workshop on Human Chromosome 12 Mapping. Cytogenet. Cell Genet. *73,* 1–24.

Murray, J. C., Buetow, K. H., Weber, J. L., Ludwigsen, S., Scherpbier-Heddema, Manion, T. F., Quillen, J., Sheffield, V. C., Sunden, S., and Duyk, G. M. (1994). A comprehensive human linkage map with centimorgan density: Cooperative Human Linkage Center (CHLC). Science *265*, 2049–2054.

O'Connell, P., Leach, R. J., Rains, D., Taylor, T., Garcia, D., Ballard, L., Holik, P., Weissenbach, J., Sherman, S., Wilkie, P., Weber, J. L., and Naylor, S. L. (1996). A PCR-based genetic map for human chromosome 3. Genomics *24*, 557–567.

Schuler, G. D., Boguski, M. S., Stewart, E. A., Stein, L. D., et al., and Hudson, T. J. (1996). A gene map of the human genome. Science *274*, 540–546.

Vollrath, D., Foote, S., Hilton, A., Brown, L. G., Beer-Romero, P., Bogan, J. S., and Page, D. C. (1992). The human Y chromosome: A 43-interval map based on naturally occurring deletions. Science *258*, 52–59.

13

ACEDB: A Database for Genome Information

Sean Walsh and Mary Anderson

Nottingham Arabidopsis Stock Centre
School of Biological Sciences
University of Nottingham
Nottingham, United Kingdom

Samuel W. Cartinhour

Crop Biotechnology Center
Department of Biochemistry and Biophysics
Texas A&M University
College Station, Texas

GENERAL FEATURES OF ACEDB

Background

ACEDB (**a** *C. elegans* **d**atabase) is one of the most widely used organizational tools for managing and presenting genome data. It was released in 1991 by Richard Durbin and Jean Thierry-Mieg, who developed it to support and coordinate large-scale sequencing and physical mapping efforts in the *C. elegans* community; see items 1 and 2 in the list of Internet resources and other materials at the end of this chapter.[1] Subsequently the software was refined and extended by Durbin and Thierry-Mieg, with code contributed by many others. During this time, ACEDB was adopted by a variety of animal and plant genome projects [3]. The software has also become useful for projects interested in "non-genome" information such as ethnobotanical data, gene nomenclature, and specialized bibliographies [4,5].

Bioinformatics: A Practical Guide to the Analysis of Genes and Proteins
Edited by A.D. Baxevanis and B.F.F. Ouellette
ISBN 0-471-19196-5, pages 299–318.   Copyright © 1998 Wiley-Liss, Inc.

[1] Items containing URLs, e-mail addresses, literature references, and amplifying notes are designated hereafter by bracketed numbers.

While it is difficult to count the number of public ACEDB-based resources precisely, a conservative estimate [3] as of spring 1997 was 25–30.

The popularity of ACEDB is due to several factors. The software is free and runs under Unix and the Macintosh OS, and a Windows version may soon be available. The database presents information using a rich graphical interface, including specialized displays for genetic maps, physical maps, metabolic pathways and sequences. The interface relies on hypertext to link related information and can be navigated easily using a mouse. Data is organized in an object-like fashion, using familiar categories such as bibliographic references, genes, alleles, and cloned DNAs. Perhaps the most important factor is the ease with which ACEDB can be reconfigured for new information. The simple schema definition language and the quick turnaround time for data loading make ACEDB appropriate for the construction of "throwaway" databases, which can be used for private analysis of data, as well as for more permanent data collections. Moreover, people do not need extensive training in computation or databases to run ACEDB. For projects with limited resources, this is often a critical component in the decision to use ACEDB.

This chapter focuses on ACEDB as a sequence data management tool rather than as a means of data presentation to the scientific community. These are not mutually exclusive tasks, but the emphasis here is on the usefulness of ACEDB early in the data-gathering and annotation process for a primarily in-house audience. Among the sites that have used it for managing sequence data or other project support tasks are The Sanger Centre in Cambridge (U.K.), The Genome Sequencing Center at Washington University, the *Aedes aegypti* genome project at Colorado State University, the *Arabidopsis* physical mapping project at Massachusetts General Hospital, and the malaria genome project at the Walter and Eliza Hall Institute (WEHI).

Readers will appreciate that software for managing and presenting biological data is evolving rapidly. ACEDB itself has been developed in the UNIX environment and was first released as an X-Windows application, but is now accessed by most users on public data servers via its World Wide Web interface. The future will probably see ACEDB connected to new families of displays constructed using Java or other "Internet-friendly" languages. However, this chapter emphasizes the X-Windows version (xace 4.3) and its sequence-related features.

Interface

The following conventions are used to describe mouse operations:

Left mouse: LM
Middle mouse: MM
Right mouse: RM

The casual ACEDB user interacts with the database by browsing its hypertext links. This mode of exploration is illustrated in Figure 13.1, a montage consisting of several ACEDB windows obtain from GrainGenes, a database for the Triticeae [6]. The windows were generated by a series of mouseclicks as the user navigated between different categories of information. The ACEDB main window is in the upper left and appears as soon as the software is launched. It contains a list of data categories ("classes") available for perusal. Pick-

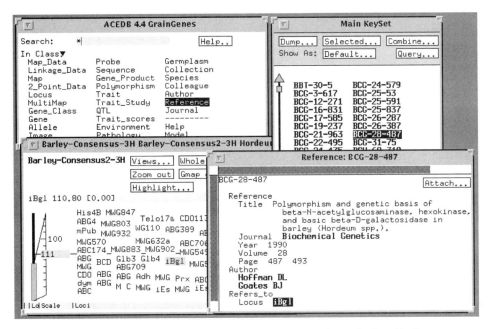

Figure 13.1 ACEDB display of data from GrainGenes. Details can be found in the text.

ing the Reference class (double-clicking LM) opens a KeySet window containing a scrollable list of members of the Reference class (top right). The members of a class are known as "objects." Picking a reference object such as BCG-28-487 opens a third window (bottom right) showing bibliographic details such as authors and title. Any of the boldface items can be picked to open additional windows.

Figure 13.1 also contains a genetic map (bottom left), opened as a result of picking the locus symbol iBgl in the reference window. This is one of several specialized displays designed to show data in a graphical form. The locus symbols on the map are also hypertext links and can be activated by picking (LM). The data underlying the genetic map is viewable in a text window similar to the one used for references. However, in this case the database curator has set the default for locus to show a genetic map if one is available and the appropriate data is present.

Several online tutorials for ACEDB are available. We particularly recommend the one by Bruno Gaeta at the Australian Genomic Information Centre in Sydney [7]. Dave Matthews at Cornell University has also prepared a tutorial for the genetic map display [8]. Sequence display features are described in more detail later.

Data Models

At the heart of the ACEDB system are the "data models" (or schemas), which determine how information is organized in the database. The models are expressed in a terse language that allows the database curator to define, for example, the kinds of data to be associated with classes such as sequence, gene, and reference. The models are stored exactly as they appear in Figure 13.2 in a text file called models.wrm within the wspec directory of the data-

```
//this shows partial models for the Sequence,
//Locus and Paper class

?Sequence DNA UNIQUE ?DNA UNIQUE Int
          Structure Length UNIQUE Int
          Properties Pseudogene
                     CDS
                     Genomic_canonical
          Locus ?Locus XREF Sequence
          Paper ?Paper
          Remark Text

?Locus Sequence ?Sequence XREF Locus
       Paper ?Paper

?Paper Title Text
```

Figure 13.2 Example models.wrm file.

base. ACEDB offers complete flexibility with respect to models designed for data displayed in text windows. However, other ACEDB displays [9] require models that include certain predefined structures. This topic is discussed later in the context of the sequence display. Note that a very detailed introduction to models and modeling for ACEDB is available [10]. The reader can survey models from different databases to see the range of possibilities [11].

To illustrate some of the features of a model, we can look at part of three models for sequence, locus, and paper information. This example does not show the full expressive power of the models language, but it illustrates several important features.

Models have a hierarchical tree structure and, like an outline, represent data starting from generalities and proceeding in the direction of more and more detail. From the root of the tree, each branch point represents a further subdivision of the data within the class. The branches are constructed from a series of tags (outline headings) optionally ending in zero or more fields, which can be filled in by data. Structure, CDS, and Paper are examples of tags, while Int and ?Paper are fields.

Starting at the top left and working down and right through the sequence model example, we can see that the model allows the DNA content of the sequence to be associated with a DNA object, its length, and the type of properties a sequence has (here the Properties branch subdivides into three branches); it also can be determined where the sequence has been published, whether there is a locus associated with it, and whether any special comments can be made about it.

The first field in this class (?Sequence) serves as a container for the name of the object. The object name is a unique identifier to which other sequence-related information can be attached. Other kinds of field are Text (accepts free-form text), Float (for floating-point numbers), DateType (for dates), and Int (for integers). A field's type can restrict the kind of data that can be loaded into it. For example, a length could be entered as 100 but not one hundred. By default, a field can reproduce itself to accept multiple values if they are entered. This often makes sense; a sequence might be associated with multiple papers, loci, or remarks. However, UNIQUE can restrict a field to one entry per object. In this example, a sequence object can have only one length. More sophisticated field restrictions are also possible but are not covered here.

Information is interlinked within ACEDB through the use of fields that accept object names. The "?" prefix identifies such fields. Consider the branch in the sequence model that associates a sequence with a publication:

```
Paper ?Paper
```

When data is entered into the ?Paper field for a particular sequence, a connection will be established between the sequence object and the named paper object. The connection is manifested in the user interface by a clickable link such as those shown in Figure 13.1. This is a one-way connection. Although browsers will see a clickable boldface Paper field in the sequence object, the corresponding Paper object will not contain a link back to the sequence. However, most curators prefer to provide two-way connections for their users. These can be established automatically through the use of XREF (cross-reference). One example of XREF in the sequence model is

```
Locus ?Locus XREF Sequence
```

An XREFed field has two parts. Preceding the XREF is the "target class," in this case ?Locus. This has to be a class—XREFs cannot be used for Int, Text, Float, or DateType. Following the XREF is the "target tag." The tag specifies which field within the target class will be used to create the reciprocal link. For the XREF to operate, the Locus class must be able to support the link. This means that within the ?Locus field a branch must contain both the sequence target tag and a field specifying a sequence object. The branch:

```
Sequence ?Sequence
```

satisfies this requirement. The XREF will create the reciprocal link as soon as the ?Locus field in the sequence object is filled with data. For the curator, this greatly simplifies the management of two-way links. A further refinement is to establish a fully reciprocal two-way XREF so that data entered into either field will establish a two-way link. To do so, we could modify the Locus model as follows:

```
Sequence ?Sequence XREF Locus
```

Models can be annotated by using the standard comment // (where anything on the same line but to the right of // is ignored when the models.wrm file is read into the database). Commenting is extremely useful and is used to document the models.wrm file and datafiles.

Data Entry

Data is entered into ACEDB using the models as a template. Datafiles can be loaded from the X-Windows interface or via a text-only command line interface to the database [12]. The command line interface, though not covered here, can play an important role in automating data collection from other processes. It is also possible to edit individual objects directly while the database is running. The choice of method depends on curator preferences and the amount and nature of the data being added. Small changes are conveniently made interactively, while bulk data is most efficiently loaded from a file. When files are used, the data format is straightforward, with one "paragraph" describing one object (blank lines delimit the paragraphs). The first line in a paragraph is always the class name followed by the name of the object. Thereafter, fields are identified by the tags immediately preceding them. To add sequence and paper objects, we might load the data in Figure 13.3.

Note that we are not obliged to fill every possible field, nor are we required to use tags in the exact order in which they appear in the model. However, tag–field combinations must correspond to the models and the database will signal an error if this rule is violated. Thus Genomic_canonical in the model is not followed by a field; it would be incorrect to enter data in which this tag was followed by other information on the same line. A tutorial describing data loading procedures in more detail [13] includes information about the preparation of large datafiles, deleting data, renaming objects, and other topics.

Queries and Tables

ACEDB uses a query language tailored to take advantage of its object-like qualities and the links between data categories. Several query interfaces exist: a text-only version (not described here) a "raw" query tool in which the user directly enters commands in the query language, a "query by example" tool, which functions like a fill-in form, and a "query builder," which assists users in formulating complex queries. The response to a query is always a list of object names (technically a KeySet as in Figure 13.1) that meet the specified criteria. Query syntax is fixed, but legal queries must be compatible with model structure. Thus

```
Find Sequence ATHF001; Follow Locus
```

is a legal query corresponding to the models and data discussed earlier. The response to this query will be a list of the loci associated with this sequence. However, the query

```
Find Sequence Age > 10
```

although legal syntactically, will signal an error because the Sequence class does not contain an Age tag or corresponding field. The database curator could modify the models to add such a field if desired.

ACEDB also includes TableMaker, a tool to construct relational tables. The interface is complex but powerful and allows the user to extract and relate information from interconnected classes. In contrast to the queries described above, the TableMaker is able to retrieve and display information from within objects, not just provide an answer as a list of object names. Tutorials for the query language and TableMaker are available [14–16].

```
Sequence "ATHFOO1"
Length 3879
Remark "A very strange Arabidopsis thaliana DNA."
Locus "FOO1"
Genomic_canonical
Remark "A second remark"

Locus "FOO1"
Paper "smith_1997_aahmt"
```

Figure 13.3 Example ACEDB datafile.

Availability and Installation

ACEDB is freely available from several anonymous FTP sites [2]. The standard distribution contains an installation script for Unix. The source code is also available for those who might need to recompile. Details about FTP and supported platforms can be found in the FAQ list referenced earlier [3]. This chapter documents ACEDB version 4.3, the current version at the time of writing. New releases are made periodically and are announced to the ACEDB newsgroup [17].

SEQUENCE ANALYSIS IN ACEDB

Introduction

Graphical displays allow users to rapidly assimilate and analyze genome data within ACEDB. We focus on sequence analysis, although there are Map and Clone Grid displays, which support genetic and physical mapping projects, and a display that allows biochemical pathways to be represented schematically.

The sequence display is known as the Features Map (Fmap), which is linked to a set of tools including GeneFinder [18]; Blixem, a BLAST [19] multiple alignment viewer [20]; and DOTTER, a dot-plot program [21]. Together these tools provide a fully graphical environment for the analysis of sequence data.

The Fmap was initially developed to support the *C. elegans* genome sequencing project, although the generic nature of the design has allowed sequences from major model systems, pathogens, and humans to be analyzed in an analogous manner.

The Features Map

The Fmap is a highly configurable display. Figure 13.4 shows a configured view of *rhp6* from *Schizosaccharomyces pombe,* which illustrates the general structure of the display: a header consisting of buttons and text, and a series of columns below. The columns have been numbered in red and are described from left to right:

1. *Locator* The green box shows the portion of the complete sequence (black bar) displayed. Moving is achieved by (a) the Zoom In, Zoom Out, and Whole buttons, (b) picking the green box and sliding (LM), and (c) picking to the right of the locator bar (MM) centers. Picking to the left of the locator bar (LM) allows scrolling and zooming.

2. *Sequence and ends* The white-filled box and sequence object name (EM:Z50728). White-filled boxes indicate overlap in contigs built from a number of sequence objects (no overlap in this example).

3. *Summary* Patches of color are overlayed on the yellow bar to highlight certain features. The blue bars delimit the "active zone."

4. *Scale* Numbering may be reset to start at an arbitrary point in the sequence using the Origin text entry box in the header.

5. *Genes* "Gene" is used here as a synonym for a complete or partial transcript [e.g., mRNA or Coding Sequence (CDS; translation initiation codon through stop

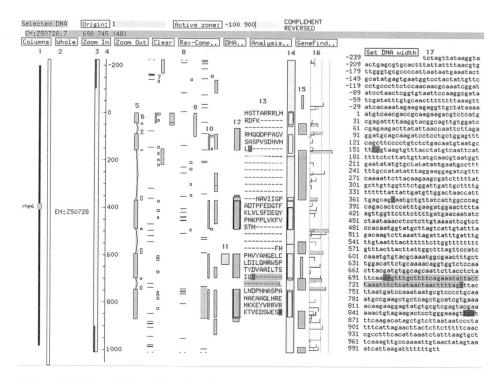

Figure 13.4 Fmap display of *rhp6* from *S. pombe*. Details can be found in the text. (See color plate.)

codon), which have a defined exon structure], Exons (blue outlined boxes) and introns (lines connecting exons) are shown.

6. *Features* Dark red outlined boxes correspond to features other than genes found in the feature table of EMBL or GenBank records (e.g., `misc_feature`).

7. *ATG* The small yellow boxes indicate potential methionine translation initiation codons in each reading frame. Provision for initiation by other codons is made by configuring GeneFinder tables.

8. *ORFs* Black horizontal lines indicate stop codons in each open reading frame. The second reading frame is shown here.

9. *GeneFinder Coding Segments* Grey boxes are regions showing a high probability of coding for protein.

10. *Coding Frame* The blue outlined boxes indicate the reading frame from which each of the exons is derived.

11. *Pssearch* The cyan box represents a match to a motif in the PROSITE database.

12. *BLASTX* Blue boxes represent locally maximal segment pairs (MSPs) (called HSPs in BLAST, see Chapter 7) from a BLASTX search of a protein database.

13. *Gene Translation* The gene is dynamically translated and colored by picking a gene (RM), which activates a menu; the options Show Translation and Colour Exons have been chosen.

14. *BLASTN*   Yellow boxes represent MSPs from a BLASTN search of a nucleotide database.

15. *INTRON_HMM*   Pale orange boxes represent the results of an intron prediction program.

16. *GeneFinder Splice Sites*   Upward pointing lines are splice acceptors, downward pointing lines are donors. Sites colored identically are in the same phase. Green features (splice sites, an ATG codon, and a stop codon) were used in the prediction of this gene.

17. *DNA Sequence*   Nucleotide sequence and coordinates. Base 1 has been set to A of the translation initiation codon (methionine, ATG). Exons are highlighted in yellow, codons created by splicing in purple, and the stop codon in red by choosing Colour Exons from the menu activated by picking a gene (RM). The sequence runs 5′ to 3′. The opposite strand is viewed by picking the button Rev-Comp (LM). The Rev-Comp menu (RM) has options to independently reverse or complement the sequence.

The view of a sequence object is mainly configured by picking the Columns button, which reveals a list of toggles turning columns on or off. Not all the available columns are displayed in Figure 13.4. The availability of columns depends on the database setup. Some columns are generic (e.g., ATG, ORFs, and DNA sequence), some depend on GeneFinder installation (e.g., GeneFinder Coding Segments and GeneFinder Splice Sites), and others depend on the curation of a particular database. Curators are able to add columns that represent the results of sequence analysis using external programs (BLASTX, BLASTN, INTRON_HMM, etc.).

Picking a feature (LM) highlights the corresponding sequence in pink and information associated with feature is displayed on the blue bar within the header. In Figure 13.4, the final exon in the CDS has been chosen. A second click (LM) spawns a text window if the feature is an object in the database. In this way, the data underlying the Fmap display can be browsed.

Efetch and Blixem

Picking a box (RM) that represents the result of a BLASTN or BLASTX database search activates a menu with two options, Efetch and Analyse in Blixem. Efetch [22] is a program, external to ACEDB, that retrieves as needed records from databases such as EMBL or GenBank. It is of course possible to store all database records within ACEDB, but the number of homologs renders this option unwieldy for distributing the ACEDB database if it contains large amounts of sequence. Fetching records also eliminates redundant storage of data on a user's system if access to the major sequence databases already exists. If sequence databases are indexed with other software such as the Sequence Retrieval System (see Chapter 5), Efetch behavior can be emulated with simple scripts, as indicated in the program's documentation [22].

The second option from the menu activates Blixem [20], a tool for viewing BLAST alignments. Figure 13.5 again shows part of the *S. pombe rhp6* gene in BLIXEM called from a BLASTX box. At the top of the display, a graph is drawn of sequence position versus percentage identity of MSPs to the sequence. MSPs are represented as horizontal lines,

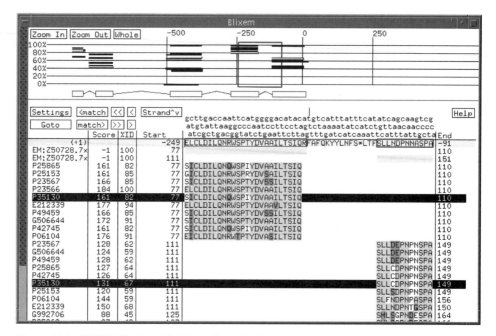

Figure 13.5   BLIXEM display of *rhp6* from *S. pombe*. Details can be found in the text. (See color plate.)

and a box highlights the limits of the alignment, which is expanded below to show the full detail of the alignment of MSPs to the sequence. By default the alignment shows identities (dark blue), conserved substitutions (light blue), and differences (no shading). Picking an MSP (LM) from the graph or the exploded view highlights all the other MSPs from the chosen sequence. This facility helps to gauge the quality of a match, as the distribution of MSPs along a gene can be readily assessed. Matches can also be inspected in the context of any functional information from database records; two clicks (LM) on a sequence in the expanded view retrieves the sequence record. The Blixem display can be configured to show both strands of the Fmap sequence, to highlight differences in the alignment, merge MSPs from the same sequence onto a single line, modify colors, or display a graph of low-complexity regions.

DOTTER

DOTTER is accessed from within the BLIXEM display (RM on the background) [21], a dot-plot program for detailed comparison of two sequences. Both DOTTER and BLIXEM are available as stand-alone programs [20,21]. Figure 13.6 shows the self-comparison of the *S. pombe* hypothetical protein C8A4.02C with a three-frame translation of genome sequence containing the corresponding locus, SPAC8A4.02C. The protein sequence is plotted along the *y* axis, the translated genome sequence and a box representing this single exon gene along the *x* axis. The longest diagonal is the perfect self-match, while other diagonals, arranged symmetrically about this, reveal six imperfect 36 amino acid repeated units. Moving crosshairs (LM and keystrokes) over a diagonal displays the alignment in a separate window.

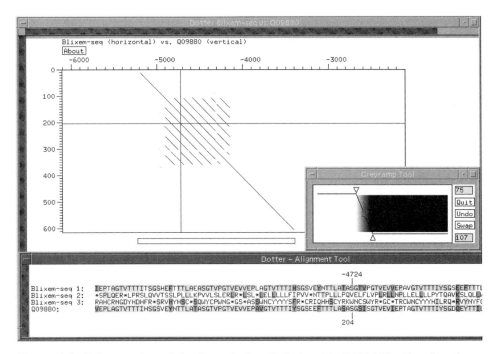

Figure 13.6 Self-comparison of the *S. pombe* hypothetical protein C8A4.02C with a three-frame translation of genome sequence containing the corresponding locus, SPAC8A4.02C.

To generate a plot, the DOTTER algorithm first computes a two-dimensional matrix of scores of all pairwise residue comparisons: that is, every residue in the horizontal sequence versus every residue in the vertical sequence. To increase signal-to-noise ratio of a plot, a window (default 25 residues) is stepped along the diagonals, which assigns a new score calculated by averaging all the points within the window. Each point in the matrix now has a value in the range 0 to 255 (one byte per point). Each point corresponds to a grey-scale dot proportional to its score. The Greyramp tool (see Figure 13.6) provides two thresholds, which can be set with the mouse. Scores below the minimum are displayed white while scores above the maximum are black; only scores between the thresholds are displayed as grey-scale tones. This facility allows the dotplot thresholds to be changed dynamically, to help detect the pertinent diagonals.

DOTTER called from within ACEDB can compare either DNA or protein sequences displayed in BLIXEM, or it can make a self-comparison (DNA/DNA). Options are available to compare just BLAST HSPs, or to highlight HSPs against a full comparison. The latter option is useful for detecting very weak similarities which BLAST may have missed. For an example, see Figure 2 in the literature reference cited in [21].

GeneFinder

The GeneFinder [18] program has been adapted and included within the ACEDB system. Both stand-alone and ACEDB versions use essentially the same algorithm (see Chapter 10 for a discussion of this). Here we concentrate on GeneFinder's graphical interface within ACEDB.

GeneFinder relies on a set of organism-specific configuration files located in the wgf directory of the database; without these, GeneFinder will not operate. Tables are generated by means of a set of utility programs supplied with the stand-alone version. Instructions on making tables are supplied within the GeneFinder distribution [18].

The GeneFinder button (RM) on the Fmap activates a menu. Choosing the GeneFinder Features option causes splice sites, blocks of coding potential, and translation initiation codons to be marked on the Fmap (see Figure 13.4). These features are calculated according to tables in the wgf directory, and each feature is allocated a score. Picking Autofind One Gene marks a predicted gene, named temp_gene, on the Fmap; sites used in the genes construction are highlighted in green.

When Autofind One Gene is selected, the GeneFinder algorithm generates a set of candidate exons. Exons belong to three groups: leading exons, which start at a translation initiation codon and end at a splice donor or stop codon; internal exons, which start at a splice acceptor and end in a splice donor, and trailing exons, which start at a splice acceptor and end in a stop codon. Note that GeneFinder does not predict the 5′ or 3′ untranslated region of a gene; a predicted "gene" in this context is just the coding portion. Exons are scored by summing the individual scores of the delimiting sites and the score of any block of coding potential encompassed by those sites. Introns are scored negatively according to length. The predicted gene is the highest scoring valid combination of exons and introns.

To examine a gene's score, pick the gene and choose Gene -> Selected; this highlights gene features in green. A table of scores is displayed by choosing Show Selected (see Table 13.1 for an example).

Parameters can be modified interactively to tune gene predictions. The menu option Parameters displays two sets of variables, Assembly parameters that relate to building genes from introns and exons and GeneFinder parameters that determine thresholds and ranges of features available for building exons. These parameters are listed in Table 13.2.

The parameters can be saved as a Method object, allowing database curators to define an optimal set of parameters. This is done by modifying the parameters of a training set of genes with known structure until a maximum number of predictions are in agreement with the training set. Inspecting score tables (see Table 13.2) during the training process will help to determine why particular genes are predicted in preference to others and will suggest parameters to modify. Nevertheless, in practice many of GeneFinder's predictions will contradict evidence available from Fmap columns (e.g., BLAST similarities). The Fmap provides a mechanism to specifically modify gene predictions in light of such evidence. Picking

TABLE 13.1   The GeneFinder score of *S. pombe rhp6*[a]

ATG/3′	5′/STOP	feat1	coding	feat2	Exon	Intron	Total
-11604	-11563	2.89	0.63	1.03	4.55		4.55
						-4.50	
-11515	-11451	1.58	3.20	2.90	7.69		7.74
						-8.60	
-11237	-11117	0.94	3.90	2.48	7.32		6.46
						-5.70	
-11011	-10908	1.75	1.26	1.59	4.60		5.36
						-4.50	
-10859	-10736	2.15	4.02	0.00	6.17		7.03

[a] The scores of five exons and four introns are summed to 7.03. Note that stop codons always score 0.00.

TABLE 13.2   GeneFinder Parameters

ASSEMBLY PARAMETERS

Minimum intron length and Minimum exon length[a]

Intron base cost	The cost to the gene score for including each intron
Intron rate	Used to calculate an additional cost for including an intron above the "Intron rate minimum"[b]
Intron rate minimum	See above
Inter gene cost	Cost of starting a each new gene using AutoFind Genes
Coding:intron score ratio	The coding score is multipied by this factor

GENEFINDER PARAMETERS

Features range	GeneFinder features are limited to a region of this length (bp)
3-splice cutoff	Minimum score threshold for a splice acceptor
5-splice cutoff	Minimum score threshold for a splice donor
ATG cutoff	Minimum score threshold for a translation initiation codon

[a] Parameter does not apply to first and last exons,

[b] additional cost = Intron rate * log (intron length - Intron rate minimum)

(RM) a GeneFinder feature (translation initiation codon, splice site, or stop codon) activates a menu with options to Select, Antiselect, or Unselect a feature. Using these options allows a gene to be fully stipulated, or to be required to specifically include or exclude a feature. Setting the "active zone" is another mechanism that excludes all GeneFinder features outside the region specified; the excluded regions are marked in blue on the Summary Bar (see Figure 13.4). As a last resort, a prediction can be modified manually by displaying the temp_gene object in a text box and choosing Update from the pull-down menu (RM). In these cases, setting Origin (see Figure 13.4) to base one of the translation initiation codon is advised. After editing it is necessary to redraw the display by choosing Recalculate from the pull-down menu (RM over white Fmap background). Options from the GeneFinder menu can be selected to save gene predictions as Sequence objects within the database. However, both saving and editing objects require write access to the database.

Importing Sequence and Magic Tags

The Import Sequence option from an Fmap display (RM on background activates menu) can be used to import sequences onto an Fmap without write access to the database. However, analyzing a sequence will generally require write access to the database and importation of the sequence as an ace file, as in the following example.

```
Sequence "MyShortSeq"
DNA "MyShortSeq"

DNA "MyShortSeq"
cacacacaccacacccacaccacaccacaccacacccacacccacacacaccacacccac
acaccacacccacaccaactctctctcatctacctttactcgcgctgtcacaccttaccc
ggctttctgaccgaaattaaaaaaaatgaaaatgaaatcctgttctttagccctacaaca
```

This file creates a sequence object and a DNA object. Selecting the sequence object MyShortSeq displays both the sequence object and the DNA object on the Fmap. Although this is very intuitive behavior, it is important to note that somehow the database knew that a sequence object needed creating and that the nucleotide sequence had to be displayed along with the sequence object. If the sequence object `MyShortSeq` is displayed as text it will look like this:

```
MyShortSeq
    DNA MyShortSeq 180
```

The length of the sequence has been calculated and inserted automatically into the Int field following the DNA tag in the object. DNA in this context is a "Magic Tag." These special identifiers are written into the database engine and are used mainly for display purposes. One implication of Magic Tags is that database developers and sequence analysts need to know which tags are used to generate elements of ACEDB displays. A description of how Magic Tags are used is available [9].

Programs are available to convert GenBank and EMBL records into ace format [23]. These programs greatly reduce the effort involved in importing a sequence if it is publicly available. An ace file produced from a GenBank-to-ace parser is shown in Figure 13.7. This example illustrates some aspects of sequence modeling in ACEDB. The nucleotide sequence and transcripts (e.g., CDS and mRNA) are linked to the sequence object `GB:ATAB11G`. Although the transcripts are sequence objects in their own right, they are modeled as subsequences of `GB:ATAB11G`. This sequence/subsequence modeling also allows sequence contigs to be built by specifying overlaps between sequences in another sequence object. This hypothetical example joins two sequences that overlap by 81 bases:

```
Sequence "LINK_MySeqs"
Subsequence "MyShortSeq" 1 180
Subsequence "MyLongSeq" 100 20000
```

BLAST Analysis and MSPcrunch

The Fmap, BLIXEM, and DOTTER support the display of results from the BLAST suite of programs (see Chapter 7). Projects that use ACEDB will typically perform the following database searches to obtain maximum homology information ("x" refers to the sequenced organism):

BLASTX	Translation of nucleotide query versus all available protein sequences
BLASTN	Nucleotide query versus ESTs from organism "x"
TBLASTX	Translation of nucleotide query versus translation of ESTs not from organism "x"
BLASTN	Nucleotide query versus all available nucleotide sequence other than ESTs

The actual database searched depends on a number of factors (see Chapter 2 for a discussion of publicly available sequence databases). The results of BLAST searches are typically filtered through the BLAST postprocessor MSPcrunch [20,24]. MSPcrunch performs a number of useful functions:

1. Regions of biased composition are given spuriously high scores by BLAST. MSPcrunch reduces these scores appropriately.

```
Sequence GB:X78886
Title "A.thaliana (Landsberg erecta) ABI1 gene."
From_database GENBANK
DB_annotation GENBANK GB:X78886
Identifier GENBANK ATABI1G
Accession GENBANK X78886
Nucleotide_id GENBANK g509418
Keyword "ABI1 gene"
Species "Arabidopsis thaliana"
Paper meyer_1994_a1452
Subsequence GB:X78886.1_mRNA 1 2244
prim_transcript 1 2244
gene 1 2244
Subsequence GB:X78886.2_cds 401 1998


Sequence GB:X78886.1_mRNA
mRNA
Source_exons 1 949
Source_exons 1020 1310
Source_exons 1442 1547
Source_exons 1640 2244
Locus "ABI1"


Sequence GB:X78886.2_cds
CDS
Source_exons 1 549
Source_exons 620 910
Source_exons 1042 1147
Source_exons 1240 1598
Locus "ABI1"


Paper meyer_1994_a1452
Title "A protein phosphatase 2C involved in ABA signal transduction..."
Author "Meyer K."
Author "Leube M.P."
Author "Grill E."
Journal "Science"
Year 1994
Volume 264
Page 1452 1455
Medline_ID 94255767


DNA GB:X78886
gaacaaggcacattagaactcttcttttcaactttttttaggtgtatatagatgaatctag
aaatagtttatagttggaaattgattgaagagagagagatattactacaccaatctttt
sequence truncated
```

Figure 13.7 Output from a GenBank-to-ace parser.

2. Regions similar to large protein families or with a high content of frequently occurring amino acids will generate a large number of MSPs. MSPcrunch removes redundant MSPs in these congested regions.

3. MSPcrunch tests for adjacent MSPs from the same database sequence. This test retains low-scoring MSPs, which are consistent with a gapped alignment.

4. MSPcrunch parses BLAST output and generates ace files.

Operations 1–3 effectively make BLAST more sensitive. If, however, all MSPs from a database search are required, MSPcrunch can be used simply as an ace file generator with the -w switch.

In-house BLAST searches of all sequences in the public domain require a significant investment in computational resources because of the size of sequence databases, the time needed to search them, and the effort required to maintain a database that is growing daily. However, small amounts of sequence can be analyzed by means of BLAST services provided over the Web [25]. The BLAST output can then be extracted from e-mail and MSPcrunch used to generate ace files.

Adding Results Columns

In the analysis of a region of sequence, it is often necessary to consider results from a number of database searches and predictive programs. Any results that define regions of nucleotide sequence can be imported into ACEDB and viewed as a column of colored boxes on the Fmap.

When an Fmap of a sequence object is displayed, a column of results is drawn for each unique "Method" referred to by the sequence object. Methods are objects that determine how a column of results is displayed and treated by Blixem. Here is an example of a BLASTN method object:

```
Method BLASTN
Colour LIGHTBLUE
Score_by_width Score_bounds 100 400
Right_priority 5.2
Blastn
Blixem_N
```

Method objects use a variety of Magic Tags, as described elsewhere [9].

The section of the sequence model which refers to methods is as follows:

```
Homol  DNA_homol ?Sequence XREF DNA_homol ?Method Float Int UNIQUE Int Int UNIQUE Int
       Pep_homol ?Protein XREF DNA_homol ?Method Float Int UNIQUE Int Int UNIQUE Int
       Motif_homol ?Motif XREF DNA_homol ?Method Float Int UNIQUE Int Int UNIQUE Int
Feature ?Method Int Int UNIQUE Float UNIQUE Text
```

Homol is a Magic Tag used to locate the data for drawing columns that represent the results of database searches. The model allows for homologies with DNA, proteins, and motifs (e.g., PROSITE motifs: see Figure 13.4, column 11).

Here is an example ace file written by MSPcrunch from a BLASTN search:

```
Sequence MyShortSeq
DNA_homol Z47047 BLASTN 900 1 180 1 180
```

The DNA_homol line defines a BLAST MSP; base 1–180 of MyShortSeq is similar to base 1–180 of Z47047 with a score of 900 using the method BLASTN.

The results from predictive programs (those that do not result in coordinates from another sequence: e.g., Hidden Markov Model prediction of introns in Figure 13.4, column 15) are stored under the "Feature" Magic Tag. An example ace file is as follows:

```
Sequence MyShortSeq
Feature INTRON_HMM 100 120 10.12
```

MISCELLANEOUS ANALYSIS FUNCTIONS

The DNA Analysis window is activated by picking the Analysis button (LM). The window presents a number of useful analysis functions that may be applied to the DNA Window (Fmap) or to a KeySet of objects. Only the functions that are generally useful are described here.

Finding Motifs and Artificial Gels

Motifs can be located in sequences by entering a search string in the text box of the DNA Analysis window and choosing either DNA (to search nucleotide sequence) or AA (to search the translated nucleotide sequence). Pressing Enter starts the search. Searches on KeySets return a new KeySet of sequences containing the motif, while searches applied to the DNA Window color the motif on the Fmap. In both cases a search report is added to the DNA Analysis window.

The motif search string can include ambiguity codes for nucleic acid bases. The on line Help file "DNA and amino acid nomenclature" lists amino acid and nucleotide ambiguity codes. Motifs can also be saved in the form of a Motif object and thereafter addressed by name. Here is an example ace file:

```
Motif "Branch"
Match_sequence yTrAy
Remark "Splice branch site consensus"
Remark "Y is pYrimidine, R is puRine"
DNA

Motif "HaeI"
Match_sequence "wGGCCw"
Offset 3
Cleavage "wGG'CCw"
Overhang 0
Remark "unpublished observations"
DNA
```

Note that `Match_sequence` is a Magic Tag within the Motif model. Once this file has been loaded, both motifs can be searched for simultaneously using the query:

```
Branch ; HaeI
```

It is also possible to make a KeySet of motifs and search for each match sequence simultaneously by toggling the Motif KeySet button and starting the search with nothing in the text box.

Fuzzy searching is also possible by specifying a number of allowed mismatches using the Max MisMatch button.

An agarose gel simulator is available from the Analysis menu (RM). Motifs are used to cut the Fmap sequence, and an image of a gel is displayed. This facility has an online help page called Agarose-gels.

Other Supporting Sequences and Software

Dump Sequence   The user can dump the Fmap Active Zone sequence or all the sequences in the KeySet in FASTA format.

BLAST Submission   Executes the `blast_mailer` script, passing the arguments `acedb_submission` and the nucleotide sequence.

Fastamail Submission   Executes the `fastamail_mailer` script, passing the arguments `acedb_submission` and the nucleotide sequence.

Splice Consensus   Calculates weight matrices around 5′ and 3′ splice junctions. The results are displayed in the DNA Analysis window.

Codon Usage   Calculates codon usage from all the sequences in KeySet.

Sequence Lengths   Generates a histogram of sequence lengths from KeySet and reports the total sequence length in the Analysis window.

Data Export   The Fmap pulldown menu (RM over white background) gives access to a series of data export facilities that write a file of features (exons, splice sites, etc.), sequence or CDS translations (FASTA formatted). The region exported corresponds to the Active Zone.

EMBL Dump   Writes the sequence and features to a file in a format for submission to the EMBL database.

Acembly   Although this chapter has concentrated mainly on sequence analysis, ACEDB also offers support for the management of raw sequence data. Acembly is an ACEDB-based program for displaying and editing sequence reads from an ABI sequencer. It is being developed by Ulrich Savauge and Danielle and Jean Thierry-Mieg. The software is designed to view and interpret trace data from sequencing runs and to assemble contigs by aligning individual sequencing runs. Various editing functions allow the user to identify problem areas, make or change base calls, annotate the data, and so on [26]. The Acembly package (Unix only) is distributed along with ACEDB and has a similar interface. Data from Acembly can be moved to other ACEDB databases easily.

ACKNOWLEDGMENTS

We thank Richard Durbin and Jean Thierry-Mieg for their help in the preparation of the chapter.

Online Resources and Literature References to Topics Presented in Chapter 13

1. The *C. elegans* genome project:
   http://www.sanger.ac.uk/worm/C.elegans_Home.html

2. Durbin, R., Thierry-Mieg, J. (1991–). A *C. elegans* Database. Documentation, code and data available from anonymous FTP servers at:
   lirmm.lirmm.fr, cele.mrc-lmb.cam.ac.uk
   ncbi.nlm.nih.gov

3. ACEDB FAQ. A text version is available via anonymous FTP at machine *rtfm.mit.edu* as:
   pub/usenet/news.answers/acedb-faq.
   For those whose Internet searches are restricted to e-mail, the FAQ can be retrieved from:
   mail-server@rtfm.mit.edu.
   The Web version is at:
   http://probe.nalusda.gov:8000/acedocs/acedbfaq.html

4. See, for example, the Plant Reference Databases at:
   http://probe.nalusda.gov:8300/related/index.html
   and the Insect Reference Databases at:
   http://probe.nalusda.gov:8300/insect/index.html

5. Beckstrom-Sternberg, S. M., Reardon, E., and Price, C. The Mendel Database, at:
   http://probe.nalusda.gov:8300/cgi-bin/browse/mendel

6. Anderson, O., and Matthews, D. GrainGenes, a database for small grains and sugarcane, at:
   http://wheat.pw.usda.gov/

7. Gaeta, B. Tutorial introduction to ACEDB, at:
   http://probe.nalusda.gov:8000/acedocs/angis/TOC.html

8. Matthews, D. The genetic map display, at:
   http://greengenes.cit.cornell.edu/acedoc/GMAP.html

9. Magic Tags and ACEDB displays at:
   http://probe.nalusda.gov:8000/acedocs/magic/index.html

10. Cartinhour, S. Exploring models design and structure, at:
    http://probe.nalusda.gov:8000/acedocs/exploring/toc_models.html

11. Selected models at:
    http://probe.nalusda.gov:8000/acedocs/models/models.html

12. Morris, J. Tace, at:
    http://probe.nalusda.gov:8000/acedocs/tace.html

13. Matthews, D. and Lewis, S. Loading data into ACEDB, at:
    http://greengenes.cit.cornell.edu/acedoc/aceloading.html

14. Matthews, D. and Lewis, S. Searching an ACEDB database, at:
    http://greengenes.cit.cornell.edu/acedoc/query.syn.html

15. Matthews, D. Using TableMaker, at:
    http://greengenes.cit.cornell.edu/tablemaker.html

16. ACEDB documentation library, at:
    http://probe.nalusda.gov:8000/acedocs/index.html

17. One of many newsgroups in the bionet hierarchy is *bionet.software.acedb*. Current and past postings can be accessed at:
    http://www.bio.net:80/hypermail/ACEDB

18. Green, P., and Wilson, C. GeneFinder, at:
    ftp://genftp.biotech.washington.edu/pub/
    To be added to mailing list, send e-mail to Colin Wilson at:
    colin@u.washington.edu

19. Altschul, S. F., Gish, W., Miller, W., Myers, E. W., and Lipman, D. J. (1990). Basic local alignment search tool. J. Mol. Biol. *215,* 403–410. Extensive help on BLAST is available at:
    http://www.ncbi.nlm.nih.gov/BLAST/blast_help.html

20. Sonnhammer, E. L. L., and Durbin, R. (1994). A workbench for Large Scale Sequence Homology Analysis. Comput. Appl. Biosci. *10*, 301–307. See also:
    http://www.sanger.ac.uk/~esr/blixem.html
21. Sonnhammer, E. L. L., and Durbin, R. (1996). A dot-matrix program with dynamic threshold control suited for genomic DNA and protein sequence analysis. Gene *167*(2), GC1–GC10. See also:
    http://www.sanger.ac.uk/dotter.html
    http://www1.elsevier.nl/journals/genecombis/preview/articles/0378111995007148/Menu.html
22. Efetch was written by Erik Sonnhammer. See:
    ftp://ncbi.nlm.nih.gov/lsn/MSPcrunch+Blixem/efetch.tar.Z
23. Data conversion tools are available at:
    http://probe.nalusda.gov:8000/acedocs/conversion.html
24. Sonnhammer, E. L. L., and Durbin, R. (1994). An expert system for processing sequence homology data. Proceedings of ISMB, *94*, 363–368. See also:
    http://www.sanger.ac.uk/~esr/MSPcrunch.html
    For latest documentation of MSPcrunch, see the file:
    ftp://ncbi.nlm.nih.gov/pub/esr/MSPcrunch+Blixem/
25. Basic Local Alignment Search Tool (BLAST), at:
    http://www.ncbi.nlm.nih.gov/BLAST/
26. Morris, J. Acembly, at:
    http://weeds.mgh.harvard.edu:80/acembly/ACE-mbly.html

## 14

Submitting DNA Sequences to the Databases

Jonathan A. Kans and B. F. Francis Ouellette

National Center for Biotechnology Information
National Library of Medicine
National Institutes of Health
Bethesda, Maryland

INTRODUCTION

DNA sequence records from the public databases (DDBJ/EMBL/GenBank) are essential components of any computational analysis in molecular biology. Accurate and informative biological annotation of sequence records is critical in every attempt to determine the function of a disease gene by similarity to a gene that was isolated and sequenced because of its biological function. The names or functions of the encoded protein products, the name of the genetic locus, and the link to the original publication of that sequence (why was it sequenced?) make a sequence record of immediate value to the scientist who retrieves it as the result of a BLAST or Entrez search.

This chapter is about getting these sequences and their annotations into the public databases, with an emphasis on the nucleotide sequence databases involved in the International Nucleotide Sequence Database Collaboration: DDBJ, EMBL, and GenBank. We present two different approaches for submitting sequences to the databases, one World Wide Web–based (e.g., using BankIt), and the other using Sequin, a multiplatform program that can use a network connection to great advantage but does not require one. Sequin is also an ASN.1 editing tool that takes full advantage of the NCBI data model (see Chapter 6) and will become a platform for many sequence analysis tools that NCBI will incorporate in the years to come. Because of this, Sequin is the update tool of choice.

Most journals no longer print full sequence data, and it is now the rule to submit sequences to a public database when an article is submitted for publication. The genome

Bioinformatics: A Practical Guide to the Analysis of Genes and Proteins
Edited by A.D. Baxevanis and B.F.F. Ouellette
ISBN 0-471-19196-5, pages 319–353.   Copyright © 1998 Wiley-Liss, Inc.

sequencing era (the period during which ESTs and genomic sequences are deposited at great speed, which we historically mark by the beginning of the EST project in late 1992) has already affected the scientific community in many ways. For example, many scientists release their sequences before the article detailing them is in press. This practice is now the rule for large genomic centers, and although some individual laboratories still wait for acceptance of publication before making their data available, others consider the release of a record as a publication in its own right.

As outlined in Chapter 2, the growth of the databases has been exponential. Most of the sequence records in the early years were submitted by individual scientists studying a gene of interest. A program suitable for these submissions must allow manual annotation of arbitrary biological information. However, the databases recently have had to adapt to new classes of data, and to a substantially higher rate of submission. Not long after the beginning of EST sequencing, it became clear that a separate submission protocol was going to be necessary for receiving these records, which would be coming into the databases at the rate of thousands per day, with some peak submission periods reaching 100,000 per week. Fortunately, these records are fairly simple and uniform in content, and thus amenable to automatic processing. The bulk submission protocol is discussed later. The submission process is also part of an international activity, and it is noted again that sequences submitted to any one of the three international collaborative databases (see Figure 2.1 in Chapter 2) will appear in the other two databases within a few days. Sequence records then are distributed worldwide by various user groups and centers, including those that reformat the records for use within their own suites of programs and databases (e.g., GCG, see Chapter 4). Thus by submitting a sequence to only one of the three database researchers can avoid any possible duplication of work for the database staff at these three locations, and also avoid the possibility that redundant records will be released. Also, most journals expect that all nucleotide sequences presented in a publication, and of central importance to the publication, will be referenced by an accession number provided by one of the international collaborative databases (see Chapters 2 and 6).

WHERE TO SUBMIT?

Historically, investigators would submit to a specified database, depending on the journal in which they wanted to publish. This is no longer true, although some journals still improperly indicate a preferred database. Rather, one should submit to whichever database is most convenient. This may be the database in the closest geographical area (if, for example, a telephone conversation will be required); it may be the repository one has always submitted to; or it may be simply the place one's submission is likely to receive the best attention. All three databases have knowledgeable staff who are able to help submitters throughout the process. Under normal circumstances, an accession number will be returned within a workday, and a finished record in 5–10 working days, depending on the state of things that work week, and the state of the submitted sequence.

Presently, it is assumed that all submissions of sequences are done electronically: via the World Wide Web, by electronic mail, or (at the very least) on a computer disk sent via regular postal mail. The URLs and e-mail addresses for electronic submissions are shown in the list at the end of the chapter. These two modes of submission replace the earlier method using the Authorin software, which is now outdated. Submissions prepared with Authorin are nonetheless still accepted and processed (at the time of this printing), but users of Authorin should be aware of its limitations, and of the availability of superior alternatives.

WHAT TO SUBMIT?

All three databases want the same end result: a richly annotated, biologically and computationally sound record, one that allows other scientists to be able to reap the benefits of the work already performed by the submitting biologist and affords links to the protein, bibliographic, and genomic databases (see Chapter 5). The databases are a repository of all experimentally derived sequences, and so the newly determined sequence of an mRNA or of a genomic region can be submitted to a database, whose staff will assist the submitter in providing sufficient information to make the sequence useful for others. There is available a rich set of biological features and other annotations, but the important components are definitely the ones that lend themselves to analysis. These include the nucleotide and protein sequences; the CDS (coding sequence, also known as coding region), gene, and mRNA features (i.e., features representing the central dogma of molecular biology); the organism from which the sequences were determined; and the bibliographic citation that links them to the information sphere and will have all the experimental details that give this sequence its *raison d'être*.

DNA/RNA

The submission process is quite simple, but care must be taken to provide information that is accurate (free of errors and vector contamination) and as biologically sound as possible, to ensure maximal usability by the scientific community. Here are a few matters to settle before starting a submission, regardless of its form.

Nature of the Sequence   Is it of genomic or mRNA origin? Users of the databases like to know the nature of the physical DNA that is the origin of the molecule being sequenced. For example, although cDNA sequencing is performed on DNA (and not RNA), the type of the molecule present in the cell is mRNA. The same is true for the genomic sequencing of rRNA genes, where the sequenced molecule is almost always genomic DNA. Copying the rRNA into DNA, like direct sequencing of rRNA, although possible, is rarely done. Bear in mind also that since the sequence being submitted should be of a unique molecular type, it must not represent (for example) a mixture of genomic and mRNA molecule types that cannot actually be isolated from a living cell.

Is the Sequence Synthetic, But Not Artificial?   There is a special division in the nucleotide databases for synthetic molecules, sequences put together experimentally that do not occur naturally in the environment (e.g., protein expression vector sequences). The DNA sequence databases do not accept computer-generated sequences, such as consensus sequences, and all sequences in the databases are experimentally derived from the actual sequencing of the molecule in question. They can, however, be the compilation of a shotgun sequencing exercise.

How Accurate is the Sequence?   This question is poorly documented in the database literature, but the assumption that the submitted sequence is as accurate as possible usually means at least two-pass coverage (opposite orientations) on the whole submitted sequence. Equally important is the verification of the final submitted sequence. It should be free of vector contamination (this can be verified with a BLASTN search against the vector database: see Chapter 7 and later in this chapter), and possibly checked with known restriction maps, to eliminate the possibility of sequence rearrangement or to confirm correct sequence assembly.

Organism

Having the proper organism assigned to a record is of crucial importance, although in most cases this is easily done. All DNA sequence records must have an organism assigned to them. Many inferences are made from the phylogenetic position of the records present in the databases. If these are wrongly placed, an incorrect genetic code may be used for translation, with the possible consequence of an incorrectly truncated protein product sequence. Just knowing the genus and species is usually enough to permit the database staff to identify the organism and its lineage. NCBI offers an important taxonomy service, and the staff taxonomists maintain the taxonomy that is used by all the nucleotide databases and by Swiss-Prot, the protein database.

Citation

As good as the annotations can be, they will never surpass a published article in fully representing large amounts of biology. It is therefore imperative to ensure the proper link between the research publication and the primary data it will cite. For this reason, having a citation in the submission being prepared is of great importance, even if it consists of just a temporary list of authors and a working title. Updating these citations at publication time is also important to the value of the record. (This is done routinely by the database staff, and will happen more promptly if the submitter notifies the staff upon publication of the article.)

Coding Sequence(s)

A submission of nucleotide also means the inclusion of the protein sequences it encodes. This is important for two reasons:

1. Protein databases (e.g., Swiss-Prot and PIR) are almost entirely populated by protein sequences present in DNA sequence database records.
2. The inclusion of the protein sequence serves as an important, if not essential, validation step in the submission process.

Proteins include the enzyme molecules that carry out many of the biological reactions we study, and their sequences are an intrinsic part of the submission process. Their importance, which is outlined in Chapter 6, is also reflected in the submission process, where this information must be captured for representation in the various databases. Also important are the protein product and gene names, if these are known. There are a variety of resources (many present in the lists that conclude these chapters) that offer the correct nomenclature for a given organism's gene nomenclature. (See Genetic Nomenclature Guide, Trends in Genetics, 1995, Elsevier.)

The coding sequence features, or CDS, are the links between the DNA or RNA and the protein sequences, and their correct positioning is central in the validation, along with the correct translation table. The nucleotide databases now use 13 different genetic codes (see end-of-chapter list), which are maintained by the taxonomy and molecular biology staff at NCBI. Because protein sequences are so important, comprising one of the main pieces of molecular biology information on which biologists can compute, they receive much deserved attention from the staff at the various databases. It is usually simple to find the correct open reading frame in an mRNA (see Chapter 10), and various tools are available for this [e.g., NCBI's ORF finder (see end-of-chapter list) and also as a function within Sequin (see below)]. Getting the correct CDS intervals in a genomic sequence from a higher eukaryote is a little trickier: the different exon-coding sequences must be joined, and this involves a variety of approaches, also described in Chapter 10. (The Suggest Intervals function in Sequin will calculate CDS intervals if given the sequence of the protein and the proper genetic code.) What a submission includes will be validated by the database staff, but even more appropriately, by the submission tool used, as well, on the WWW or with Sequin. Validation checks that the start and stop codons are included in the CDS intervals, that these intervals are using legal exon/intron consensus boundaries, and that the provided amino acid sequence can be translated from the designated CDS intervals using the appropriate genetic code.

Other Features

There are a variety of other features available for the feature sections of a submitted sequence record, and many of these will enhance the record. The complete set of these is represented in the Feature Table documentation, which is available on the WWW or as PostScript files available by anonymous FTP. While many features are available, there is much inconsistent usage in the databases, mainly due to a lack of consistent guidelines and poor agreement among biologists as to what they really mean. Getting the organism, bibliography, gene, CDS, and mRNA correct usually suffices, and makes for a record that can be validated, is informative, and allows a biologist to grasp in a few lines of text what biology is there to be captured. Nonetheless, the full renditions of the feature table documentation are available for use as appropriate, but with care taken as to the intent of the annotations.

Population, Phylogenetic, and Mutational Studies

The nucleotide databases are now accepting population, phylogenetic, and mutational studies as submitted sequence sets, and although this information is not adequately represented in the flatfile records, it is appearing in the various databases. This new type of submission allows, if only for a practical reason, the submission of a group of related sequences together, with entry of shared information required only once. Sequin also allows the user to include the alignment generated with a favorite alignment tool, and to submit this information with the DNA sequence. At the time of writing, NCBI was the only database accepting this information, although it is clear to all databases that the information is important for a great number of records now on hand. New ways to display this information (such as Entrez) should soon make this kind of data more visible to the general scientific community.

Protein-Only Submissions

In most cases, protein sequences come with a DNA sequence. There are some exceptions—people do sequence proteins directly—and such sequences must be submitted without a corresponding DNA sequence. SWISS-PROT presently is the best venue for these submissions, which can be processed at the EBI which will accept them for submission into SWISS-PROT.

HOW TO SUBMIT ON THE WORLD WIDE WEB

The decline in the usability of Authorin led the three databases to decide to use the forms-based approach on the World Wide Web. This new medium lent itself well to the submission process. Each of the three repositories engineered a form for the submission of DNA sequences to its database: Sakura (cherry blossoms) at DDBJ, WebIn at EBI, and BankIt at GenBank. The WWW is the preferred submission path for simple submissions (Figure 14.1), or those that do not require complicated annotations or too much repetition (i.e., 30 similar sequences, as typically found in a population study, would best be done with Sequin). The WWW form is ideal for a research group that makes few sequence submissions and needs something simple, entailing a short learning curve, or none. The WWW forms will be appropriate, sufficient, and more than adequate for the majority of the submissions: some 60–80% of submitters make their DNA or RNA sequence submissions via the WWW at NCBI. The alternative addresses (or URLs) for submitting to the three databases are presented in the list at the end of the chapter.

Although this part of the chapter emphasizes NCBI's BankIt submission tool, submission to any one of the principal databases will ensure that a sequence is appropriately processed and will be deposited in the two others, as well.

Upon entering a BankIt submission (Figure 14.2), the user is asked about the length of the nucleotide sequence to be submitted. This is because a WWW browser limitation makes it impossible to enter more than 29,000 nucleotides (characters) in a given window. If it is necessary to submit 40,000 base pairs (a common size for people submitting cosmid sequences), BankIt presents two windows, so that by copying and pasting 20,000 characters per window, the 29,000 characters/window limit can be accommodated.

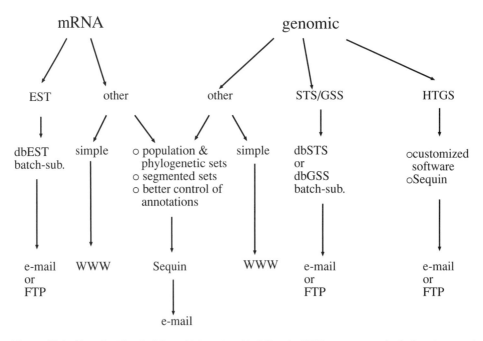

Figure 14.1 Flowchart for deciding which protocol to follow for DNA sequence submissions to one of the DNA sequence databases. WWW is BankIt, WebIn, or Sakura. For URLs and e-mail addresses, see the list at the end of the chapter.

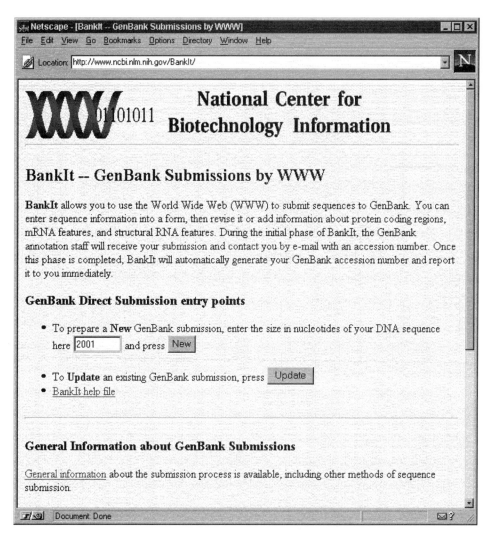

Figure 14.2   BankIt, the GenBank World Wide Web submission page. Entry point for the new submission (enter length of sequence and press New) or for an update of a record already submitted to GenBank.

The next BankIt form is also straightforward (Figure 14.3): it asks about the contact person (the individual to whom the database staff may address any questions), the citations (who gets the scientific credit), the organism (the top 100 organisms are on the form; all others must be typed in), the location (nuclear vs. organelle), some map information, and the nucleotide sequence itself. At the end of the form, there is a BankIt button, which calls up the next form. At this point some validation is made, and if any necessary fields were not filled in, the form is presented again. If all is well, the next form asks how many features are to be added (see Figure 14.4) and prompts the user to indicate their type(s). If no features were added, BankIt will issue a warning and ask for confirmation that not even one CDS is to be added to the submission. The user can say no (0 new CDS) or take the opportunity to add one or more CDS. At this point structural RNA information or any other legal DDBJ/EMBL/GenBank features can be added, as well.

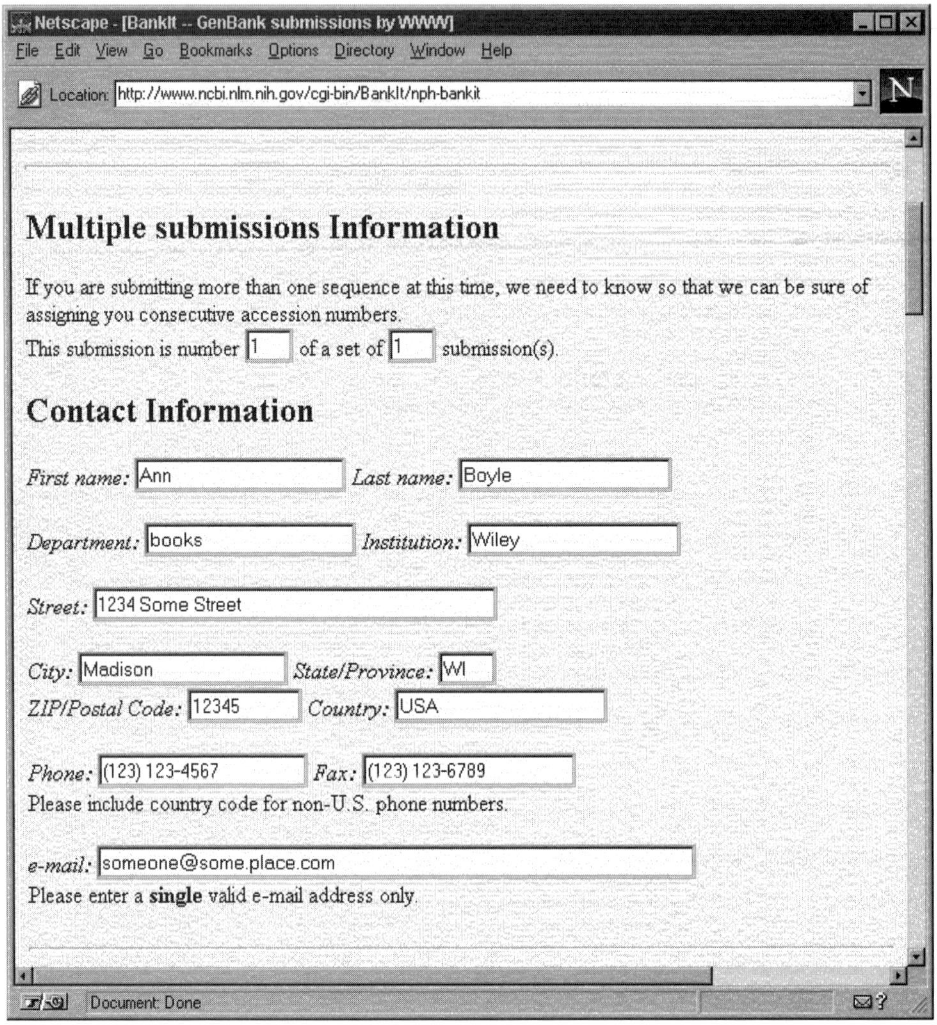

Figure 14.3 BankIt, the GenBank World Wide Web submission page: designation of contact person.

To begin to save a record, press the BankIt button again. The view that now appears (Figure 14.5) must be approved before the submission is completed: that is, more changes may be made, or other features added. To finish, hit BankIt one more time. Then the final screen (Figure 14.6) will appear; toggle the Update/Finished set of buttons and hit BankIt one last time, and the submission will go to NCBI for processing. A copy of the submission just finished should arrive promptly via e-mail; if not, contact the database to confirm receipt of the submission and to make any correction that may be necessary.

HOW TO SUBMIT WITH SEQUIN

Sequin is a program that is designed to assist scientists in preparing new sequence and update data for submission to DDBJ, EMBL, and GenBank. It is a tool that works on most

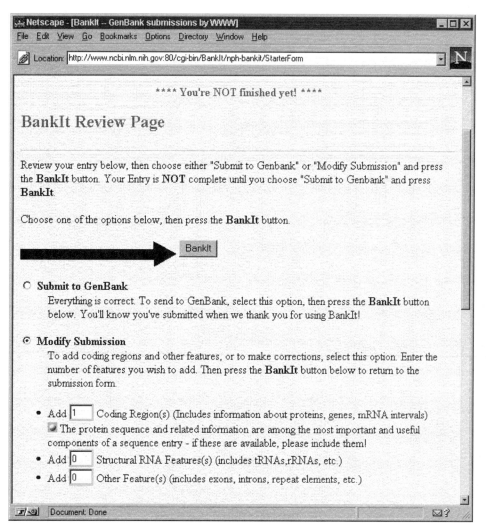

Figure 14.4 BankIt, the GenBank World Wide Web submission page: request for the number of features to be added before BankIt generates a new form with the appropriate number of feature form boxes.

computer platforms and is suitable for a wide range of sequence lengths and complexities, including traditional (gene-sized) nucleotide sequences, segmented entries (e.g., genomic sequences of a spliced gene for which not all intronic sequences have been determined), long (genome-sized) sequences with many annotated features, and sets of related sequences (i.e., population, phylogenetic, or mutation studies of a particular gene, region, or viral genome). Many of these submissions could in practice be performed via the WWW, but Sequin is more practical for more complex cases. Certain types of submission (e.g., segmented sets) cannot be made via the Web unless explicit instructions to the database staff are inserted.

Sequin also accepts sequences of proteins encoded by the submitted nucleotide sequences, and allows annotation of features on these proteins (e.g., signal peptides, transmembrane regions, or cysteine disulfide bonds). This is in contrast to the common view of most scientists when submitting a DNA sequence. The new concept here is that proteins are

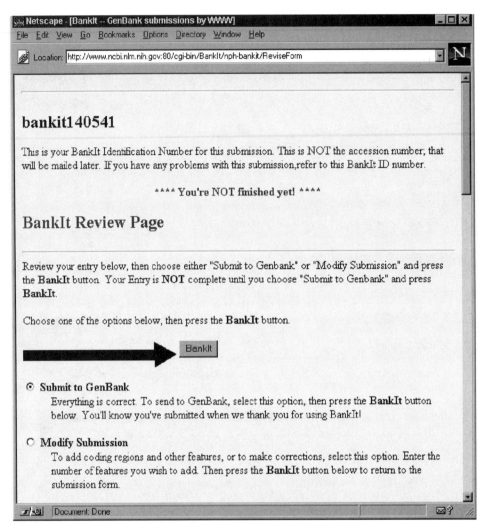

Figure 14.5 BankIt, the GenBank World Wide Web submission page: the penultimate screen. This is a toggle between adding or changing some of the features and indicating that the entry is complete as it stands.

annotated directly, not as a by-product of the DNA that encodes them. For sets of related or similar sequences (e.g., population or phylogenetic studies), Sequin accepts information from the submitter on how the multiple sequences are aligned to each other. Finally, Sequin can be used to edit and resubmit a record that already exists in GenBank, either by extending (or replacing) the sequence, or by annotating additional features or alignments (see below).

Entering a New Submission

Sequin has a number of attributes that greatly simplify the process of building and annotating a record. The most profound aspect is automatic calculation of the intervals on a CDS feature given only the nucleotide sequence, the sequence of the protein product, and

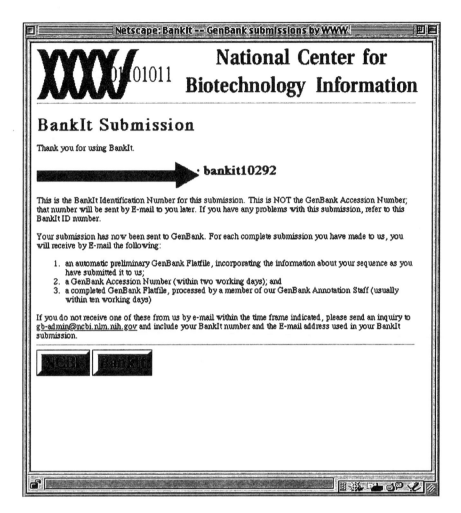

Figure 14.6 BankIt, the GenBank World Wide Web submission page: the final BankIt screen, indicating that the BankIt submission form has been successfully finished.

the genetic code (which is itself automatically obtained from the organism name). This "Suggest Intervals" process takes consensus splice sites into account in its calculations. Traditionally these intervals were entered manually, a time-consuming and error-prone process, especially on a genomic sequence with many exons, in cases of alternative splicing, or on segmented sequences.

Another important attribute is the ability to enter relevant annotation in a simple format in the Definition line of the sequence datafile. Sequin recognizes and extracts this information when reading the sequences, then puts it in the proper places in the record. For nucleotide sequences, it is possible to enter the organism's scientific name, the strain or clone name, and several other source modifiers. For protein sequences, the gene and protein names can be entered. (If this information is not present in the sequence definition line, Sequin will prompt the user for it before proceeding. But annotations of the Definition line can be very convenient, since the information stays with the sequence and can't be forgotten or mixed up later.) In addition to building the proper CDS feature, Sequin will automatically make gene and protein features with this information.

Since the majority of submissions contain a single nucleotide sequence and one or more coding region features (and their associated protein sequences), the functionality just outlined can frequently result in a finished record, ready to submit without any further annotation. And with gene and protein names properly recorded, the record becomes informative to other scientists, who may retrieve it as a BLAST similarity result or from an Entrez search.

Validation

To ensure the quality of data being submitted, Sequin has a built-in validator that searches out, for example, missing organism information, incorrect coding region lengths (compared to the submitted protein sequence), internal stop codons in coding regions, mismatched amino acids, or nonconsensus splice sites. Double-clicking on an item in the error report launches an editor on the "offending" feature.

The validator also checks for inconsistent use of "partial" indications, especially among coding regions, the protein product, and the protein feature on the product. (Unless told otherwise, the CDS editor will automatically synchronize these separate partial indicators, facilitating the correction of this kind of inconsistency.)

Viewing the Sequence Record

Sequin provides a number of different views of a sequence record. The traditional flatfile can be presented in FASTA, GenBank, or EMBL format. (These can be exported to files on the user's computer, which can then be entered into other sequence analysis packages.) A graphical view shows feature intervals on a sequence. This is particularly useful for viewing alternatively spliced coding regions. (The Graphical view's style can be customized, and these views can also be copied to the personal computer's clipboard, for pasting into a word processor or drawing program that will be used in preparing a manuscript for publication.) There is a more detailed view that shows the features on the actual sequence. For records containing alignments (e.g., alignments between related sequences entered by a user, or the results of a PowerBLAST search, see Chapter 7), one can request either a graphical overview showing insertions, deletions, and mismatches, or a detailed view showing the alignment of sequence letters.

The above-mentioned viewers are active. Clicking on a feature, a sequence, or the graphical representation of an alignment between sequences will highlight that object. Double-clicking will launch the appropriate editor. Multiple viewers can be used on the same record, permitting different formats to be seen simultaneously. For example, it is quite convenient to have the graphical view and the GenBank (or EMBL) flatfile view present at the same time, especially on larger records containing more than one CDS. The graphical view can be compared to a scientist's lab notebook drawings, providing a quick reality check on the overall accuracy of the feature annotation.

Advanced Annotation and Editing Functions

The sequence editor built into Sequin automatically adjusts feature intervals as the sequence is edited. This is particularly important if one is adding a 5' sequence to a record submitted earlier. Prior to Sequin, this entailed manually correcting the intervals on all biological features on the sequence, or, more likely, redoing the entire submission from scratch. The sequence editor is used much like a text editor, with new sequence being pasted in or typed in at the position of a cursor.

A major class of submissions involves multiple related sequences (i.e., phylogenetic, population, or mutation studies). These records are most informative if the user submits information on how the sequences align to each other. This alignment can be entered with the sequence data (e.g., in PHYLIP, NEXUS, or FASTA+GAP format) or calculated by Sequin after the sequences have been read. See Appendix II for examples of the various formats.

For these records, Sequin allows annotation of one sequence, whereupon features from that sequence can be propagated to all other sequences. (In the case of a CDS feature, the feature intervals can be calculated automatically by reading in the sequence of its protein product, rather than having to enter them by typing.) To do this, feature propagation is chosen (from the alignment editor). Selected features are then copied onto the remaining sequences, with feature intervals adjusted using the alignment information. The result is the same that would have been achieved if features had been manually annotated on each sequence, but with feature propagation the entire process can be completed in minutes rather than hours.

Feature propagation and the sequence editor combine to provide simple and automatic methods for updating an existing sequence. The Update Sequence functions allow the user to enter an overlapping sequence or a replacement sequence. Sequin makes an alignment, merges the sequences if necessary, propagates features onto the new sequence in their new positions, and uses these to replace the old sequence and features.

Sequin as an Analysis Workbench

Sequin also provides a number of sequence analysis functions. For example, one function will reverse-complement the sequence and the intervals of its features. New functions can easily be added. These functions appear in a window called the NCBI DeskTop, which directly displays the internal structure of the records currently loaded in memory. This window can be understood as a Venn diagram, with descriptors (see below, and Chapter 6) on a set (such as a population study) applying to all sequences in that set. With the DeskTop, the user can read the results of a PowerBLAST analysis, then drag and drop this information onto a sequence record, thus adding the alignment data to the record. The modifications are immediately displayed on any active viewers. Note, however, that not all annotations are visible in all viewers. The flatfile view does have its limitations; for example, it does not indicate that alignments are present.

The NCBI data model supports sets of sequences, and Sequin allows complete navigation around these sets, for purposes of display or annotation. For example, Nuc-prot sets contain a nucleotide sequence and its protein products. The nucleotide sequence can itself be segmented. In this case, a Seg set contains the segmented sequence and a Parts set, which in turn contains the raw sequence data for the individual segments. And the Population, Phylogenetic, and Mutation sets can contain multiple related sequences or Nuc-prot sets. The NCBI DeskTop is the quickest way of examining the internal structure of a record at a glance.

Consequences of Data Model

Sequin is an ASN.1 editor. The NCBI data model, written in the ASN.1 data description language, is designed to keep associated information together in descriptors or features (see Chapter 6). Features are typically biological concepts (e.g., genes, coding regions,

RNAs, proteins) that always have a location (of one or more intervals) on a sequence. Descriptors were introduced to carry information that can apply to multiple sequences, eliminating the need to enter multiple copies of the same information.

For example, the BioSource descriptor contains an organism's scientific name, preferred common name, taxonomic lineage, and GenBank division, as well as modifiers (e.g., strain, clone, chromosome, map location) specific to a given entry. Collecting this information in one place in the data specification makes it easier for the user to enter or edit this information. And placing a single BioSource descriptor on a Nuc-prot set satisfies the validator's desire (and the databases' policy) to have biological source information applying to each sequence, including the proteins.

Double-clicking on a paragraph in the GenBank flatfile view, or on a feature in a graphical view, launches an editor that can edit all pertinent information on that item. In some cases, particularly BioSource or Publications, the items may be descriptors or features, and discerning which is which from looking at the flatfile may be difficult. (It is easy to tell what is a descriptor and what is a feature in the NCBI DeskTop. And only features and sequences are shown in the Summary, Graphic, Alignment, and Sequence views.)

The data model results in conventions that may not be obvious to the casual user (looking at the GenBank or EMBL flatfile views) but can, in fact, simplify entry of biological information. For example, a publication, which appears in the header section of the GenBank flatfile, can contain a Remark subsection. Text explaining the biological conclusions of the reference, as these pertain to the sequence record, can be entered here. The text always remains with the reference in the report. In contrast, putting explanatory information in a large Comment section and referring to publications by number (e.g., "[5]") is a risky practice because the numbering may change (e.g., due to addition of new publications), making the numbers out of synch with the publications.

Similarly, citations on features (e.g., justifying ribosomal slippage in a coding region) internally reference the publication, not a publication number, even though in the flatfile a number is displayed. This is another convention that allows the publication numbering to change without "breaking" the integrity of the citations. And it means that there is only one full copy of the citation, which makes updating any information on the publication easier.

Nevertheless, literature references on sequence records should be used sparingly. A sequence record is not meant to be a review of the subject. Using links and neighbors in Entrez (and in Sequin with a network connection) is a much more reliable method of collecting relevant information, and of making original discoveries using the sequence databases.

For the simplest case, that of a single nucleotide sequence with one or more protein products, Sequin allows the user to work without needing to be aware of the data model's structural hierarchy. The CDS feature editor can be used to enter the protein sequence (or translate it from an entered location), and to enter or edit the protein feature (which supplies the protein name) on that sequence. The user can access the (single) protein feature without having to "navigate" to the protein sequence. And the CDS editor can also create a separate gene feature with the gene name.

Navigation is necessary, as is at least a cursory understanding of the data model, if extensive annotation on protein product sequences is contemplated. Many proteins have cysteine disulfide bonds, binding sites, active sites, glycosylation sites, signal peptides, or transmembrane regions. Annotating these can make a record more informative to biologists who come across it as the result of a BLAST or Entrez search. Setting the Target control to a given sequence changes the viewer to show a graphical view or text report on that sequence. Any features or descriptors created with the Annotation submenus will be packaged on the currently targeted sequence.

Although Sequin does provide full navigation among all sequences within a structured record, building the original structure from the raw sequence data is a job best left to Sequin's "create new submission" functions. Sequin asks up front for information (e.g., organism and source modifiers, gene and protein names) and knows how to correctly package everything into the appropriate place. This was, in fact, one of the main design goals of Sequin. Manual annotation requires a more detailed understanding of the data model and expertise with the more esoteric functions of Sequin.

A finished submission can be saved to disk (File -> Prepare Submission) and e-mailed to one of the databases. It is also a good practice to save frequently throughout the Sequin session, to make sure nothing is inadvertently lost.

Submitting a Single Sequence

The simplest submission contains a single contiguous nucleotide sequence and one or more protein product sequences. These records typically come from the traditional gene-based biological research, and such submissions can in most cases be done on the Web (e.g., see BankIt above) or with Sequin. Sequin offers the advantages of numerous validations as well as independence from the vagaries of network access.

Sequin begins with a window that allows the user to start a new submission or load a file containing a saved record (Figure 14.7). After the initial submission has been built, the record can be saved to a file and edited later, before finally being sent to the database. If Sequin has been configured to be network aware, this window also allows the downloading of existing database records that are to be updated.

A new submission is made by filling out several forms (Figures 14.8–14.15). The forms use folder tabs to subdivide a window into several pages, allowing all the requested data to be entered without the need for a huge computer screen. These entry forms have buttons for Prev(ious) Page and Next Page. When the user arrives at the last page on a form, the Next Page button changes to Next Form.

Starting a new submission begins with a request for a tentative title (Figure 14.8). Then the program asks for information on the contact person (Figure 14.9), the authors of the sequence (Figure 14.10), and their institutional affiliations (Figure 14.11). This form is common to all submissions, and the contact, authors, and affiliation pages can be saved by means of the Export menu item. The resulting files can be read in when starting other submissions by choosing the Import menu item. However, since even population, phylogenetic, or mutation studies are submitted in one step as one record, there is less need to save the submitter form pages.

The Sequence Format form (Figure 14.12) asks for the type of submission (single sequence, used in this example; segmented sequence; or population, phylogenetic, or mutation study). For the last three types of submission, which involve comparative studies on related sequences, the format in which the data will be entered also can be indicated. The default is FASTA format (or raw sequence), but PHYLIP, NEXUS, PAUP, and FASTA+GAP formats are also supported. These latter formats contain alignment information, and this is stored in the sequence record.

The Organism and Sequences form (Figures 14.13–14.15) asks for the biological data. On the Organism page (Figure 14.13), as the user starts to type the scientific organism name, the list of frequently used organisms scrolls automatically. (Sequin holds information on the top 800 organisms present in GenBank.) Thus after typing a few letters, the user can fill in the rest of the organism name by clicking on appropriate item in the list. Sequin now knows the scientific name, common name, GenBank division, taxonomic lineage, and,

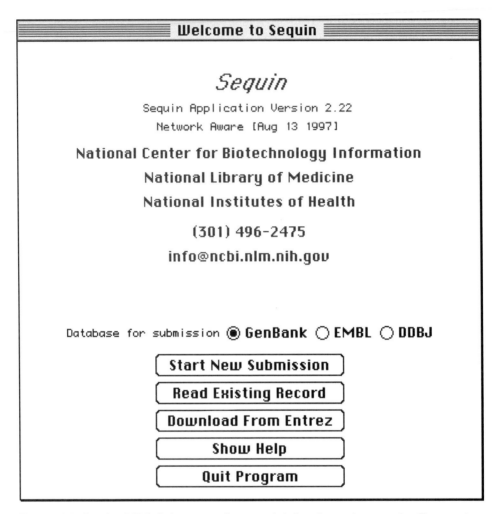

Figure 14.7 Sequin's initial window, presenting several choices for starting a session. To generate a submission from raw sequence files and a minimum of other information, select Start New Submission. As soon as the initial record is built, it can be saved to a file. To read in the file that was saved, or any other ASN.1 record saved to a file, select Read Existing Record. When Sequin has been configured to be network aware, it will show the Download from Entrez button, which is then used to download a record for updating.

most importantly, the genetic code to use. (For mitochondrial genes, there is a control to indicate that the alternative genetic code should be used.) For organisms not on the list, it may be necessary to set the genetic code control manually. Sequin uses the standard code as the default.

On the Nucleotide page (Figure 14.14), activating the Import Nucleotide FASTA button will read in the sequence. Set the molecule control to Genomic DNA or mRNA [cDNA], as appropriate. There are 5′ partial and 3′ partial checkboxes as well, which must be set if appropriate. The sequence can have a FASTA Definition line. This line precedes the sequence and begins with a left angle bracket (>); a "local identifier" may be specified as the first word after the angle bracket. If you do this, check the "FASTA definition line starts with sequence ID" box before importing the sequence. The local ID takes the place of an

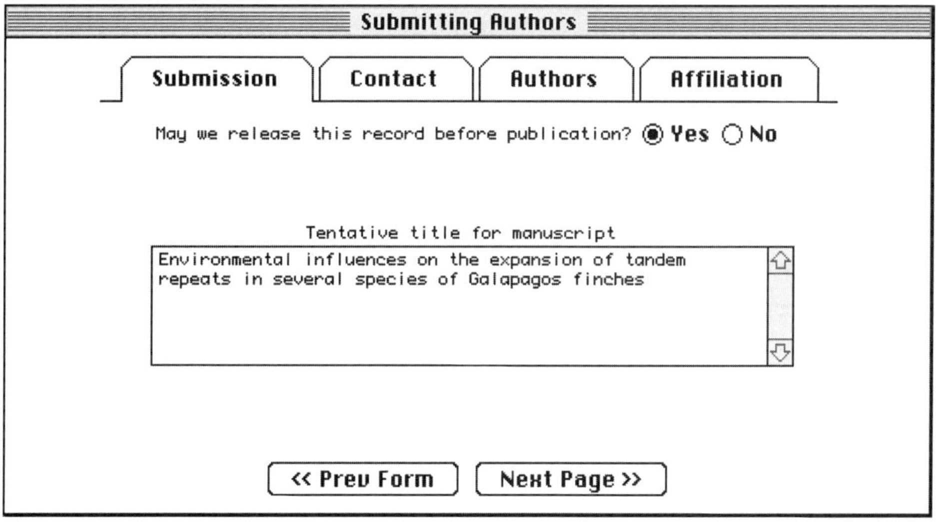

Figure 14.8 The Submission page is used to enter into Sequin a tentative title for the manuscript; this description of the submission is required even if the paper is not written, or even intended for publication. This page also allows the submitter to ask that the record not be released until the article has been published, or to specify the date of release.

accession number before one is assigned by the sequence database staff. Organism and strain information can be embedded in the Definition line, if desired. A sample definition line is as follows:

```
>TK [org=Mus musculus] [strain=BALB/c] thymidine kinase gene
```

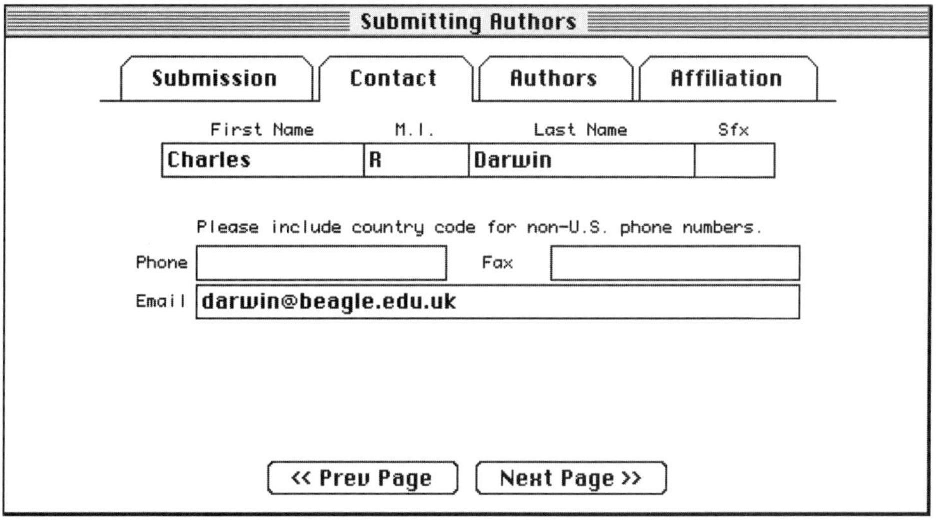

Figure 14.9 Sequin's Contact page records the name and contact information of someone who can respond to inquiries from the database staff (usually the person doing the submission, but not necessarily someone who actually did the sequencing). The Sfx field is for name suffixes (e.g., Jr., III) and not honorifics or academic degrees (e.g., Ph.D., M.D.). This information is not made public when the record is released, but is only maintained within the databases.

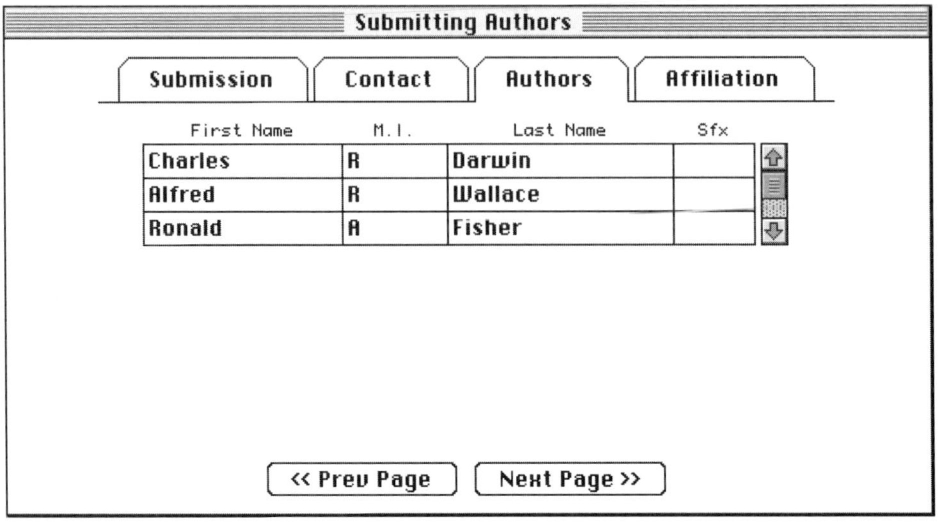

Figure 14.10 The Sequin Authors page names the authors of the manuscript describing the sequencing, (i.e., the people who get scientific credit for the sequencing). This page has a spreadsheet that accommodates as many author names as necessary. To move to the next field horizontally, press the Tab key. To moves down to the First Name column in the next row, press Tab from within the Sfx column. If anything is typed in the last row, a new row is appended to the spreadsheet. (The immediate visual indication of this will be a change in the scroll bar.) Pressing the Return key from anywhere in a row will add a new row just below the current one. Sequin will ignore any line in which the Last Name field is blank.

A summary report, shown after the nucleotide file has been read, gives the length of the sequence, the local ID, any organism name, strain, or other modifier parsed (extracted) from the definition line, and the remaining title (Figure 14.14). The summary also shows any illegal characters not in the nucleotide alphabet. If, for example, an amino acid sequence was accidentally imported, many of the letters will not be in the nucleotide alphabet, and the report will point out this error. In this case, choose Clear from the Edit menu, and then import the correct sequence.

Segmented nucleotide sequences can be entered by concatenating the individual segments in the same file. In this case, the definition line above each sequence indicates to Sequin that there are multiple segments. Each segment must have a unique local ID (e.g., made unique by basing it on the exon number encoded by that segment).

The Protein page (Figure 14.15) allows the protein sequence to be entered. It is much easier to enter this sequence, and let Sequin construct the record, than to manually add a CDS feature (and associated gene and protein features) later. This is especially true with segmented sequences. The NH_2 and CO_2H partial flags also should be set, if appropriate. The Protein page has a control to indicate that its local ID is in the definition line. It also allows gene and protein names to be encoded. For example:

```
>TKp [gene=TK] [prot=thymidine kinase] thymidine kinase protein
```

The local ID, TKp, must be different from all other local IDs, which in this case is TK, the local ID for the nucleotide sequence.

The Protein page also has a checkbox for creating an mRNA feature with the same intervals as the (to-be-created) CDS feature. The user would then be expected to double-click on the resulting mRNA, and to extend the 5' and 3' intervals on this feature via the mRNA

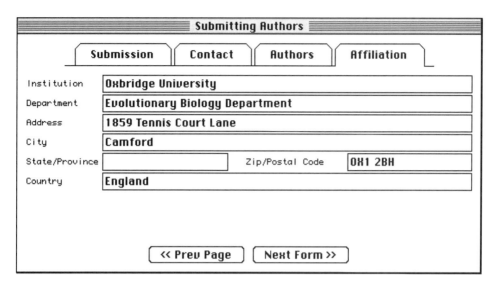

Figure 14.11 Sequin's Affiliation page is for the institutional affiliation of the primary author of the manuscript. When the record has been processed by the database staff, this will appear in the reference that cites the submission itself. On this page the Next Page button is now entitled Next Form; Sequin automatically checks the form when this button is pressed and notifies the user if any essential information is missing. If the information entered is satisfactory, Sequin will proceed to the next form.

editor. (Sequin's editors are designed to ensure that the overlapping gene feature will also be extended, relieving the user of the need to remember to extend its range separately.) Multiple protein sequences (e.g., alternative splice products) can be entered by concatenating them in the same file. As with nucleotide sequences, the Definition line above each protein sequence indicates to Sequin that there are multiple sequences.

Reading in the protein also causes a report to appear (Figure 14.15), giving the length of the sequence, the parsed local ID, the gene and protein parsed from the definition line, and the remaining title. The report also shows any illegal characters not in the protein alphabet. Choosing Clear from the Edit menu works for making corrections on this page as well.

At this point, pressing Next Form will cause Sequin to start assembling all the entered data into a submission record. For each protein sequence, Suggest Intervals is run against the nucleotide sequence (using the entered genetic code, which is usually deduced from the chosen organism). A Coding Region feature is made with the resulting intervals, as is an initial mRNA feature. A Gene feature is generated with a single interval spanning these intervals. A protein product sequence is made, with a Protein feature to give it a name. The organism (BioSource descriptor) is placed on the record, as is the publication descriptor. (These latter two are placed on the Nuc-prot set, so they apply to all nucleotide and protein sequences within this set.) Appropriate molecule information descriptors are placed on all the sequences.

A viewer form is then created that displays the GenBank flatfile form of the record (Figure 14.16). This viewer has menu items for saving the record to a file, validating it, and adding new features and descriptors. Perhaps the only remaining step is to double-click on the mRNA to launch its editor, click on the Location folder tab, and extend the 5' and 3' end points using the location spreadsheet. Pressing Accept will put the new feature location into the record, and immediately update all viewers on the record. The Graphical view (Figure 14.17) permits visual comparison of the CDS and mRNA intervals, and confirmation that

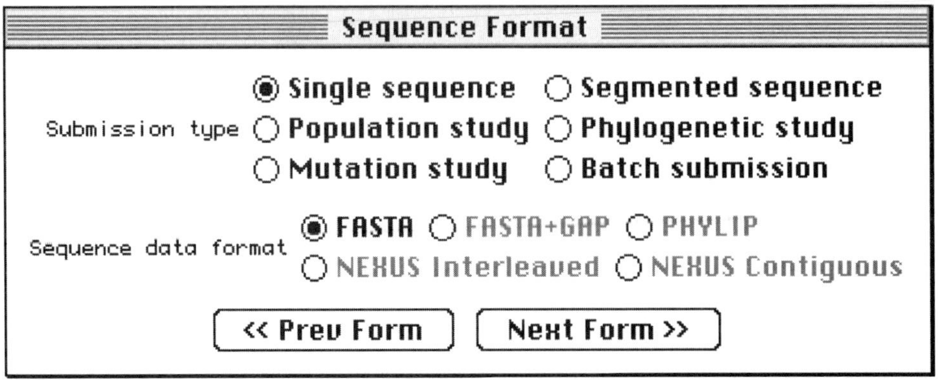

Figure 14.12 Sequin's Sequence Format form lets the user indicate the kind of record being submitted and the format of the raw sequence data. The majority of submissions are of a single (nucleotide) sequence. (There may be one or more protein product sequences.) Another class of submission is of segmented sequences. For example, in some genomic records, the exons are sequenced, but the introns are not completely sequenced. By segmenting the record, one can annotate Coding Region and mRNA features. Phylogenetic, population, and mutation studies all involve submission of more than one related sequence. These are packaged into the appropriate sets by Sequin. Batch submission is for sets of sequences not related by sequence similarity that are submitted together for convenience. Single and segmented sequence data must be in FASTA format. Population, phylogenetic, and mutation studies can also be in formats that contain alignments. These alignments are assertions of the submitter about how the sequences relate to one another. Sequin currently supports FASTA+GAP, PHYLIP, NEXUS Interleaved, and NEXUS Contiguous formats.

the gene feature is a single interval spanning these regions. Sequence view (Figure 14.18) shows the range of features, and translations of CDS features, on the actual sequence. Choosing Prepare Submission will run the validator, save the record to a file, then display the e-mail addresses for submitting that file to GenBank, EMBL, or DDBJ (whichever was chosen in the opening window).

Submitting an Aligned Set of Sequences

A growing class of submissions involves sets of related sequences: population, phylogenetic, or mutation studies. A large number of HIV sequences come in as population studies. A common phylogenetic study involves RUBISCO (ribulose-1,5-bisphosphate carboxylase), a major enzyme of photosynthesis and perhaps the most prevalent protein (by weight) on earth. Submitting such a set of sequences is not much more complex than submitting a single sequence. The same submission information form is used to enter author and contact information.

In the Sequence Format form, choose the desired type of submission. Population studies are generally from different individuals in the same (cross-breeding) species. Phylogenetic studies are from different species. In the former case, it is best to embed in the Definition lines strain, clone, isolate, or other source-identifying information. In the latter case, the organism's scientific name is embedded. Multiple sequence studies can be submitted in FASTA format, in which case Sequin should later be called on to calculate an alignment. Or, better yet, indicate the alignment information by encoding the data in PHYLIP, NEXUS, or FASTA+GAP formats. Selection from among these data formats is also done in the sequence format form.

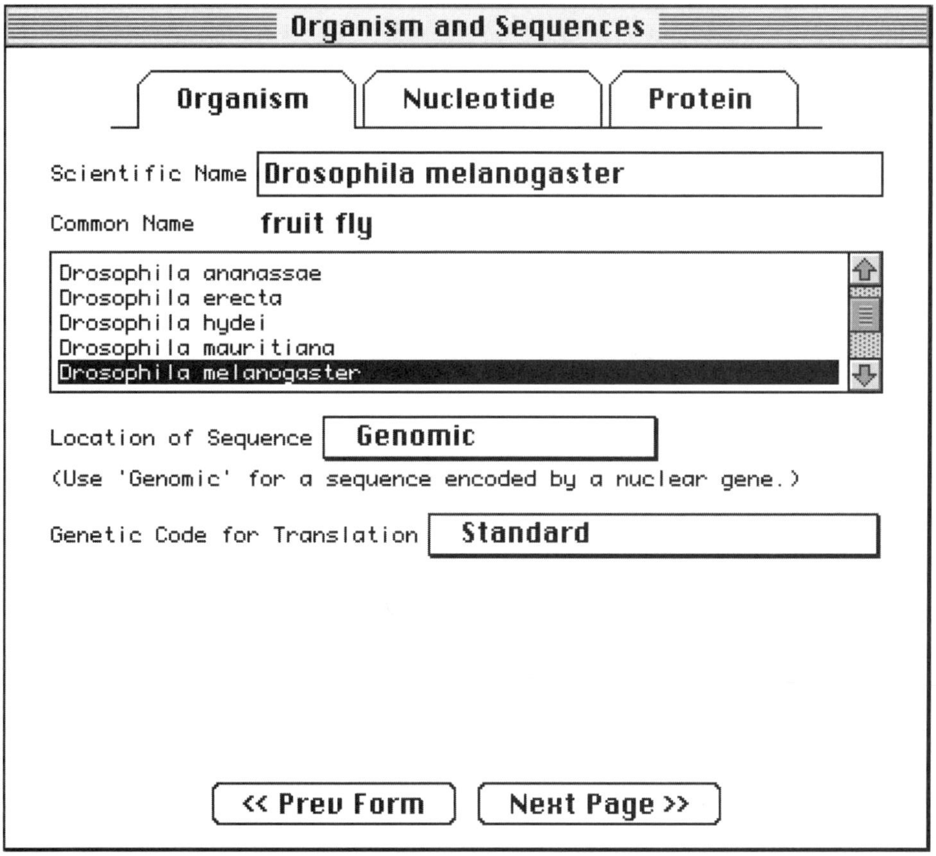

Figure 14.13 Sequin's Organism page asks for the scientific name of the organism being sequenced. For the 800 most commonly used organisms, the common name, full taxonomy, GenBank division, and genetic codes are stored. For organisms not in that list, the user must enter the proper genetic code. The Location of Sequence pop-up allows the user to indicate a mitochondrial encoding. In this case, the alternative genetic code for the specified organism is used for translation. In the case of phylogenetic studies, which involve different organisms, the organism selection list is hidden, the individual organism names are expected to be encoded in the datafile, and the genetic code control is a default for organisms that are not in the list.

The Organism and Sequences form is slightly different for sets of sequences. The Organism page for phylogenetic studies allows the setting of a default genetic code only for organisms not in Sequin's local list of popular species. The Nucleotide page differs only in the name of the Import button, which reflects the actual format selected (e.g., "Import FASTA" or "Import PHYLIP").

Instead of a Protein page, there is now an Annotation page (Figure 14.19). Many submissions are of rRNA sequence or no more than a complete CDS. (This means that the feature intervals span the full range of each sequence.) The Annotation page allows these to be created and named. A Definition line (title) can be specified, and Sequin can prefix the individual organism name to the title. More complex situations, where sequences have more than a single interval feature across the entire span, can be annotated by feature propagation after the initial record has been built and one of the sequences has been annotated. This is discussed in detail below.

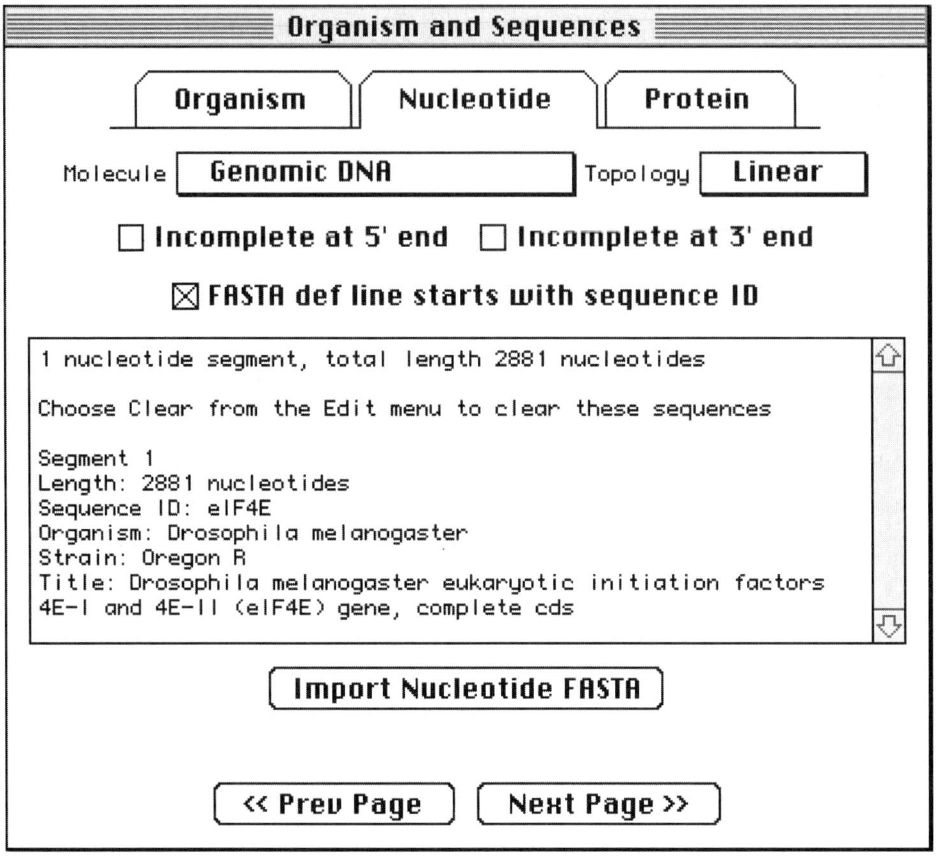

Figure 14.14 Sequin's Nucleotide page allows entry of the nucleotide sequence files and specification of the molecule type (e.g., genomic DNA, genomic RNA, mRNA, tRNA). mRNA is used even if the molecule sequenced was actually cDNA. Pressing the Import Nucleotide FASTA button puts up the standard file Read Dialog on the user's computer. When records are in separate files, as may happen for segmented sequences or studies of multiple sequences, this button must be pressed multiple times. However, it is more convenient to place all sequences in a single file. A report of how the sequence files were interpreted is displayed, along with a warning if any illegal characters were detected.

To proceed, pressing Next Form puts up an editor that allows all organism and source modifiers on each sequence to be edited (or entered if the definition line was not annotated). Upon confirmation of the modifiers, Sequin assembles the record into the proper structure.

When the viewer appears, the Target control is set to the first component in the set. Setting the Target to ALL SEQUENCES will produce a concatenated flatfile view of all sequences. The Graphical view, however, can show features on only one sequence at a time. And Sequence view will compare the sequences at the individual base level.

Annotating by Feature Propagation

Suppose a study of several alcohol dehydrogenase genomic regions is to be submitted, along with an alignment asserting the submitter's view of their relationship. The sequences

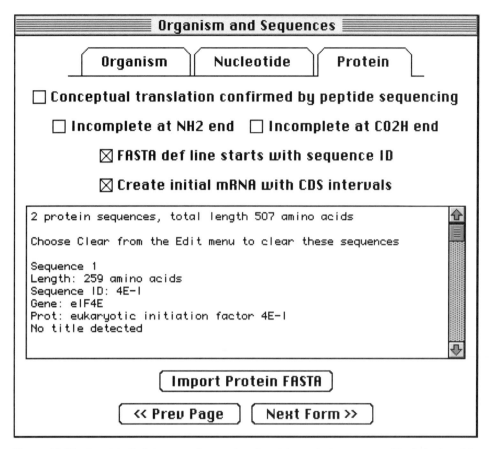

Figure 14.15 Sequin's Protein page allows entry of protein product sequences. The behavior of its Import button is identical to that in the Nucleotide page. As the last page in the form, it has a Next Form button. Pressing it will prompt the user to supply any essential information missing in the form. If the form is complete, Sequin will start processing the sequence data. If gene and protein names have not been annotated in the protein sequence FASTA Definition lines, Sequin will put up a form asking for these names. Sequin will then proceed to build an initial record based on the data supplied so far.

include 5′ and 3′ untranslated regions as well as the alcohol dehydrogenase exons and introns. Suppose that the protein sequence encoded by the first nucleotide is also available. The following steps will use feature propagation to annotate all sequences in the study.

First, target the first sequence. Then choose CdRgn from the Coding Regions and Transcripts submenu in the Annotate menu. Go to the Product subpage (in the Coding Region page) and import the protein sequence file (Import Protein FASTA in the File menu). If the protein and gene names are not annotated in the Definition line, enter these in the Protein subpage and the General page of the Properties subpage, respectively. Importing the sequence automatically runs Suggest Intervals, so the Location page should now have three intervals on the first nucleotide. And the genetic code should have been set from the BioSource on that nucleotide. Press Accept to complete the addition of the feature.

Target ALL SEQUENCES, choose Edit Alignment from the Edit menu to launch the alignment editor, and choose Propagate from the Features menu. Select the CDS feature in the first

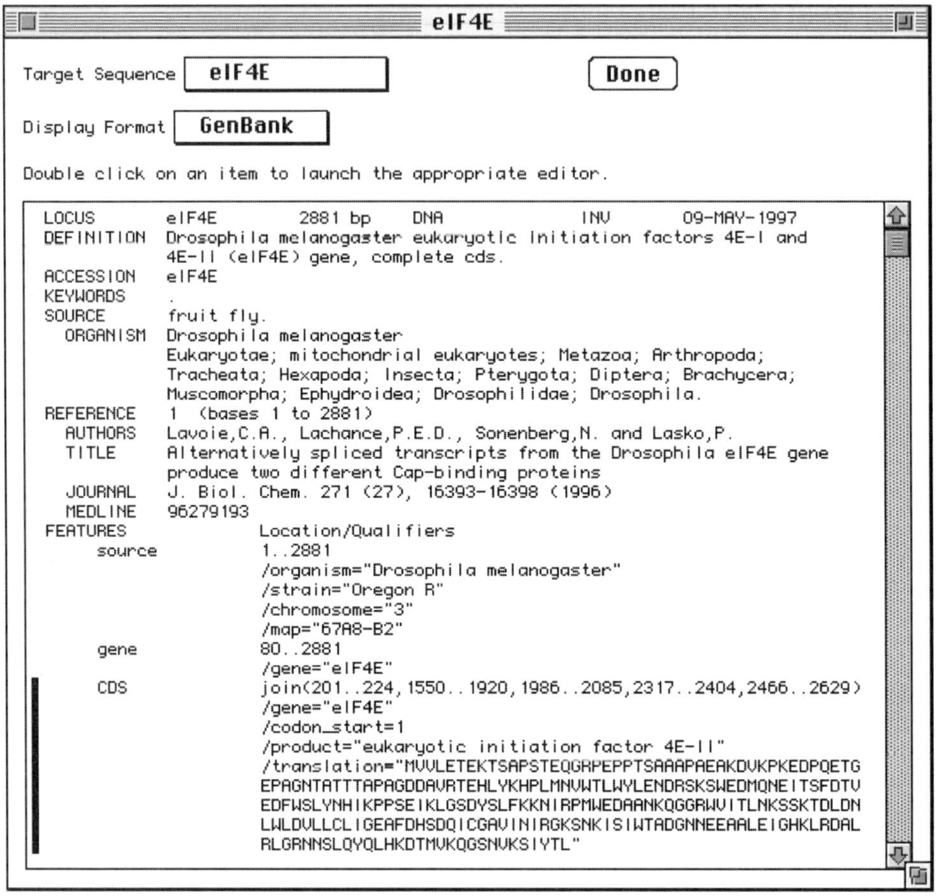

Figure 14.16   The sequence record viewer comes up by default in GenBank format. In this example, Sequin's CDS feature has been clicked, as indicated by the bar next to its paragraph. Double-clicking on a paragraph will launch an editor for the feature, descriptor, or sequence that was selected. The viewer can be duplicated, and multiple viewers can show the same record in different formats.

box, and all but the first sequence in the second box. Finally, press the Propagate button. (To see how the structure of the record is changing, keep the NCBI DeskTop open at these steps.)

Using Sequin as a Workbench

The NCBI DeskTop (Figure 14.20) allows drag and drop of items within a record. Clicking on an up arrow in a record expands the level of detail shown. If you drag a feature from its record onto the DeskTop, it is removed from the record, but is still available to the DeskTop. It can then be dragged back into the record, perhaps to a different packaging location. (Features can be dragged onto bioseqs, Bioseq sets, or existing feature tables. This does not, however, change the feature location. For descriptors, though, changing the packaging level does change the scope to which the descriptor applies. And a separate Seq-loc on the DeskTop CAN be dragged onto a feature, in which case it does change the feature location.)

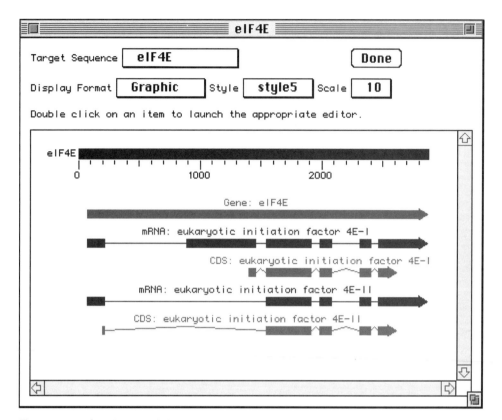

Figure 14.17 Sequin's graphic format shows segmented sequence construction and feature intervals. These can be compared to drawings in laboratory notebooks to see, at a glance, whether the features are annotated at the proper locations. Different styles can be used, and new styles can be created, to customize the appearance of the graphical view. The picture can be copied to a personal computer's clipboard for pasting into a word processor or drawing program.

Other ASN.1 data can be read from the DeskTop's Open menu. There are submenus for reading ASN.1 text form, ASN.1 binary form, and nucleotide or protein sequences in FASTA format. These will then appear as separate entities on the DeskTop, but they are suitable for drag-and-drop or for analysis with the DeskTop's filter functions. For example, the Seq-align output from PowerBLAST can be read in and dragged onto a sequence record. (PowerBLAST can also be run from within Sequin when it is configured for a network connection; see below.) It then becomes part of the record, as reflected by the viewers. Thus any program that can write ASN.1 output—for example, Gene features from a gene finder program—can have its output read by Sequin and its results added to a record by the user, and the analysis program does not need to understand the data model or how to package its results.

An exploded view of a complex record, illustrating some of what would be seen with the DeskTop, is shown in Figure 14.21. In this example, a phylogenetic study contains five components, each of which is a Nuc-prot set. There are two descriptors (Create-date and Publication) on the Phy set, and these apply to all components. The first Nuc-prot set is "blown up" to show more details: it contains nucleotide and protein bioseqs, and a

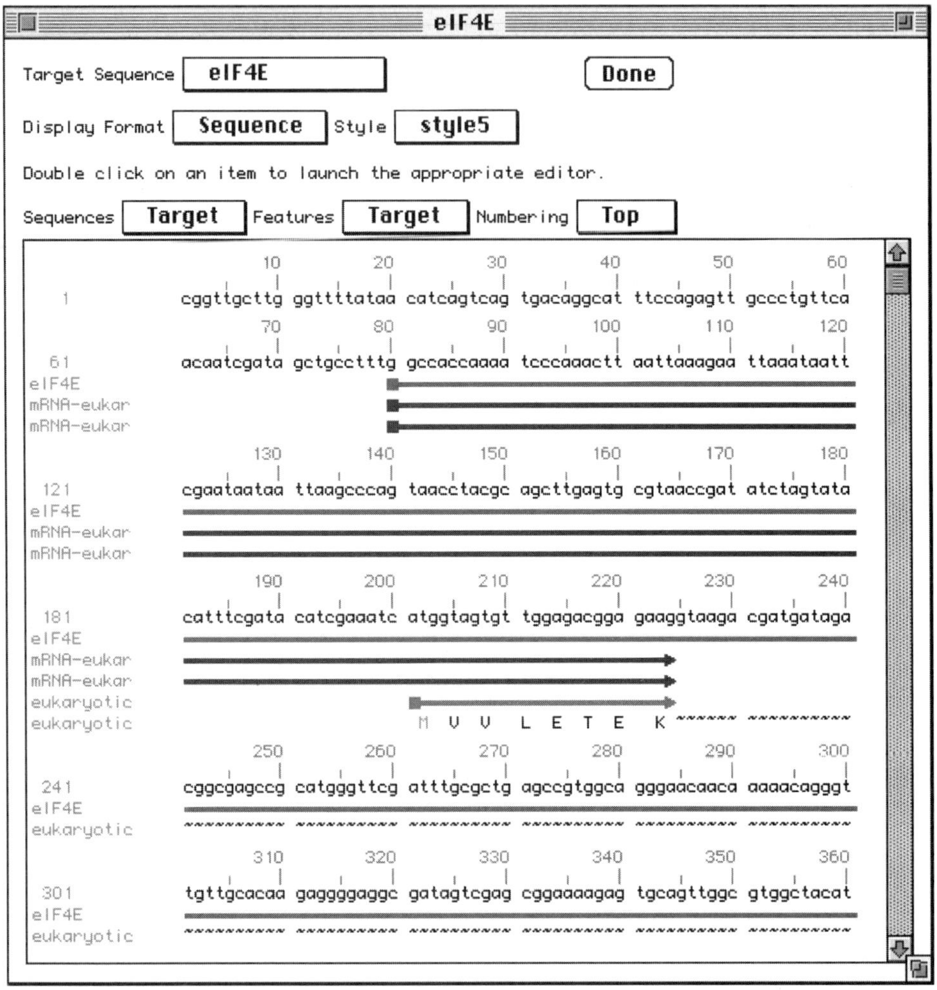

Figure 14.18 Sequence view is the display form of Sequin's sequence editor. It shows feature intervals on the sequence itself.

BioSource descriptor applying to both. (The other components of a phylogenetic set would have BioSources for different organisms.)

Both bioseqs are of type "raw," meaning that the actual sequence data is encoded in the bioseq. ("Segmented" bioseqs contain sequence identifiers that refer to the actual raw segments. This is how the Entrez Genomes division is built; see Chapter 6.) The nucleotide bioseq has a MolInfo descriptor, which says that the molecule sequenced was genomic [as opposed to mRNA (cDNA), or tRNA or rRNA]. The protein bioseq's MolInfo states that it is a peptide and that it is an author-supplied conceptual translation (as opposed to having been directly sequenced by Edman degradation or other methods).

Features in a DeskTop view show a text label and information on the feature's location and optional product. For example, the CDS feature location points to intervals on the

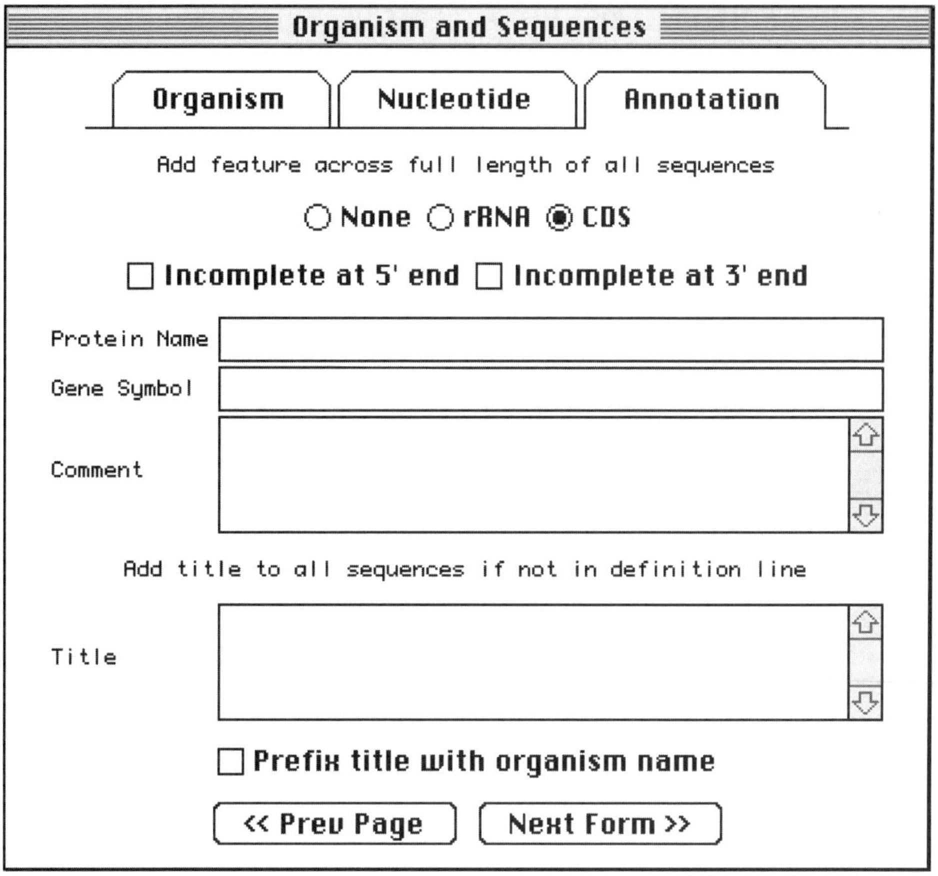

Figure 14.19 For population, phylogenetic, or mutation studies, the Annotation page replaces the Protein page. The most common submissions are of a CDS or rRNA from multiple sources. When all the CDS or rRNA intervals completely span the sequences, Sequin can automate the annotation of these features. The protein product name for CDS features or the RNA name for rRNA features can be entered, as well as the gene symbol, a comment on each CDS or rRNA feature, and a title for each sequence. It is also possible to prefix the title with the organism name in each record, which makes proper Definition lines for each of the records automatically.

nucleotide bioseq. Its product points to the entire protein bioseq. The text label ("alcohol dehydrogenase") is in fact taken from the Protein feature on the protein bioseq. This can easily be verified by editing the protein name in the Protein feature. (The GenBank flatfile view does the same kind of mapping, with a CDS taking the Protein feature's name for its /product qualifier, and the protein bioseq's sequence data for its /translation qualifier.)

Those who want to become familiar with the NCBI data model will find that viewing records of different kinds with the NCBI DeskTop is a good way to see bioseq sets, to discover the levels at which various descriptors are packaged, and to learn how the set hierarchy works. This understanding is not necessary for the casual user submitting a simple sequence, but for the advanced user it can immediately take the mystery out of the data.

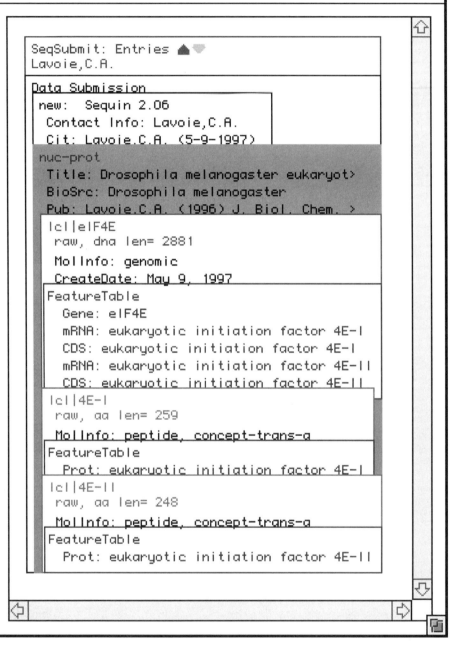

Figure 14.20 The NCBI DeskTop displays a Graphical overview of how the record is structured in memory, based on the NCBI data model (Chapter 6). It is less useful to a biologist, more useful to a software developer or database sequence annotator. In this example, the submission contains a single Nuc-prot set, which in turn contains a nucleotide and two proteins. Each sequence has features associated with it. BioSource and Publication descriptors on the Nuc-prot set apply the same organism (*Drosophila melanogaster*) and the same publication, respectively, to all sequences.

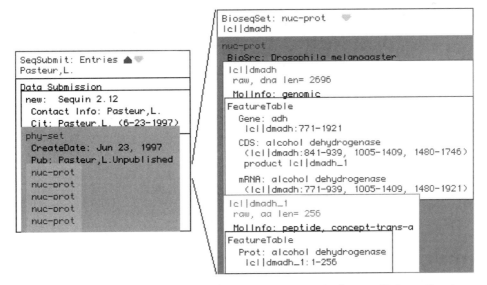

Figure 14.21   DeskTop views of a Phylogenetic set. In this composite figure, a Phylogenetic set contains several Nuc-prot sets and applies the same publication to all components. One of the Nuc-prots is expanded in further detail. It contains a BioSource for *Drosophila melanogaster,* a nucleotide sequence with Gene, mRNA, and CDS features, and a protein sequence with a Protein feature that provides the name of the product.

Sequin with a Network Connection

When configured for a network connection, Sequin includes the functionality of PowerBLAST, Network Entrez, and the ability to do MEDLINE/PubMed lookups as well as Taxonomy lookups. Choose PowerBLAST from the Search menu and a dialog box appears, offering the choice of running BLASTN or BLASTX with a nucleotide query; in addition, one can choose to search the nr database or several subset databases, including est and vector. The results are automatically added to the sequence record and will appear in Summary, Graphic, Alignment, and Sequence views.

Double-clicking on an alignment in one of these views will retrieve the corresponding sequence record from the Entrez network service. At the bottom of the window of the resulting viewer will be neighbor and link controls. So a user who sequences a disease gene and runs PowerBLAST within Sequin can immediately view the database "hit" and in one step will be able to retrieve the MEDLINE article that discusses its biology. Or sequence neighbors of that record can be retrieved, then passed (with the Refine button) into the Entrez Query window, where, for example, the results can be refined by selecting for or against any taxonomic category.

To configure for network usage, choose Net Configure from the Misc menu. The "Outgoing connections only" checkbox is used if the network has a firewall. In general, unless there is a temporary problem with the network, the "Test connection during configuration" checkboxes should be set.

At the time of writing, numerous enhancements were being added to Sequin. The best way to stay abreast of new developments (e.g., new versions of Sequin; bug fixes) is to visit the Sequin Web page and register as a Sequin user. The Sequin home page also contains information about the latest enhancements and complete documentation and FAQ listings.

EST/STS/GSS

Expressed sequence tags (ESTs) are short RNA sequences that are the result of cloned mRNA sequencing survey projects (see glossary for more extensive definition). Although these sequences represent the bulk of present nucleotide database content, ESTs comprise only a small fraction of the investments of submission processing from the databases' point of view. Only the automation of this process has made the processing of ESTs possible. Because the EST submission files are simple in format, they lend themselves quite conveniently to rapid processing, and can be loaded to the databases to the order of thousands per day. ESTs are usually produced in large amounts and represent more than two-thirds of the records present in GenBank release 102. Simply because of their numbers, the various nucleotide databases have had to design a new system for the submission and processing of records of these types. Fortunately the structure of these records is rather simple, and apart from the sequence itself only a few important data types need to be incorporated in the submission. These include information about the library (which includes the BioSource), as well as the citation information. In addition, the databases have developed a simple way for mapping groups to submit mapping information that may be known about a specific EST. The simple structure of this information lends itself very well to a relational database model, where simple data items can be loaded and from which various reports can be created. For example, in the simplest case a submitter need submit only one Publication information file, one Contact information file and, one Library information file. These can be submitted with hundreds (or thousands) of EST files (see Figure 14.22), which contain tags to link each sequence to an appropriate file of the other type. The files are normally built by customized programs, ensuring that the information is constant between the various records. The files are then submitted by e-mail (if the numbers are in the hundreds) or by FTP (if the numbers are in the thousands). Current addresses and contact information with the databases for submitting these records are indicated in the list at the end of the chapter.

This submission model was so successful that it was cloned for the Sequence Tagged Sites (STS) and Genome Survey Sequences (GSS) database submissions process. Here again the same simple file format is used with a few variants. The finer details of how to submit these records are also included in their respective Web pages.

GENOME CENTERS

Centers that specialize in sequencing large segments of DNA (hundreds of thousands to millions of base pairs per year) have their own information-handling systems. Not only have they designed their own database systems, but their programmers maintain software and databases that keep track of the various sequencing projects and will organize this information to allow assemblies to be tracked, performances followed, and problems spotted at an early stage. The genome centers format their results in a variety of ways, often including the WWW pages, making the information they produce available directly to the community as a whole or to their customers. If these genome centers want their sequences available in the public databases, they communicate with one of the databases to ensure that correct data exchange can take place. All three database centers (DDBJ, EBI, and NCBI) have extensive experience in working with the various genome centers to ensure timely and effortless (insofar as is possible) exchange of information. This includes the setting up of automatic exchange of data, the creation of special FTP accounts so that data can exchanged in a most

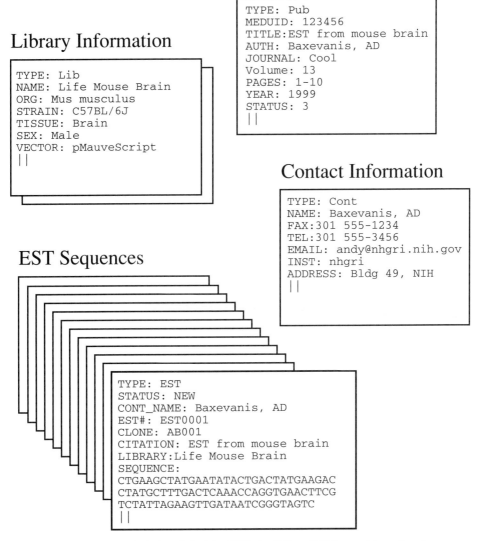

Publication Information

```
TYPE: Pub
MEDUID: 123456
TITLE:EST from mouse brain
AUTH: Baxevanis, AD
JOURNAL: Cool
Volume: 13
PAGES: 1-10
YEAR: 1999
STATUS: 3
||
```

Library Information

```
TYPE: Lib
NAME: Life Mouse Brain
ORG: Mus musculus
STRAIN: C57BL/6J
TISSUE: Brain
SEX: Male
VECTOR: pMauveScript
||
```

Contact Information

```
TYPE: Cont
NAME: Baxevanis, AD
FAX:301 555-1234
TEL:301 555-3456
EMAIL: andy@nhgri.nih.gov
INST: nhgri
ADDRESS: Bldg 49, NIH
||
```

EST Sequences

```
TYPE: EST
STATUS: NEW
CONT_NAME: Baxevanis, AD
EST#: EST0001
CLONE: AB001
CITATION: EST from mouse brain
LIBRARY:Life Mouse Brain
SEQUENCE:
CTGAAGCTATGAATATACTGACTATGAAGAC
CTATGCTTTGACTCAAACCAGGTGAACTTCG
TCTATTAGAAGTTGATAATCGGGTAGTC
||
```

Figure 14.22 The EST submission. Submitting ESTs (or STS and GSS records) requires the generation of simple files from which the database staff will build the GenBank and dbEST records. Single contact information, publication information, and one or more library information files will be joined with the many sequence files that will result in as many complete EST records. All these files start with a TYPE line and end with || on the last line.

accurate and convenient way, and the generation of tools to ensure data exchange in the most useful format. At NCBI, for example, FTP accounts have been set up for all genome sequencing centers that submit to the organization, and a variety of tools for accelerating the submission of high-throughput genome sequences (HTGS) have been created. These HTGS records are found in two different divisions of GenBank, depending on their status of completion (see Chapter 2). Unfinished records (phase 1 or 2) are in the HTG division of Gen-

Bank, and finished records (phase 3) are in the taxonomic division to which they belong. Throughout their existence, HTGS records keep the same DDBJ/EMBL/GenBank accession number. One of the tools devised by NCBI to build these records is fa2htgs, a command line program that can easily be incorporated in scripts and allows the user to generate HTGS submissions from FASTA files and a Sequin template. As for all other NCBI products, this program is available for most computer platforms.

High-throughput genome sequencing also implies a change in the way the sequences are used. This is why sequences generated by these centers are marked with an HTG keyword, making it possible for users of the data to selectively use it in their analyses, or to simply be aware of its origin. Data so tagged should not be confused with the unfinished records, which not only have the HTG keyword but are in the HTG division of GenBank. This is examined in more detail in Chapter 2 and by Ouellette and Boguski (1997). The database a genome centers wishes to work with will ensure appropriate handling of the HTGS data via the latest guidelines and tools.

UPDATES

Updating DDBJ/EMBL/GenBank records probably represents one of the most unrewarding tasks that could be imposed on any scientist. There is little incentive for doing it, there is little scientific credit, and it appears that few pay attention. This activity is, nonetheless, one of the most important steps after the submission process, and it ensures that the information in the record is still correct. The most important aspect of updating a record is to inform the database of publication of the citation associated with the record. This allows the database staff to update the citation in the record, which in turn permits it to be linked to the appropriate bibliographic reference (see Chapter 5). Then the record can link to the great mass of related references and the full scope of knowledge available with Entrez.

Another important piece of information is the correct name of each protein and gene present in a record; again, an update here allows appropriate linkage of that information with comparable material in the databases. The databases have specialized e-mail and WWW addresses to which record updates can be sent, and Sequin can also be used to do this task. Sequin is designed to update sequence records that are already in the public databases. To download the existing record, it is necessary to configure Sequin for a network connection. (The Net Configure menu item contains dialogs for making this connection.) When Sequin is then restarted, a Download from Entrez button (Figure 14.7) will appear in the startup window. This allows an accession number to be entered and retrieved directly from the ID database (see Chapter 6). The record can be edited by updating the citation (which may be available by MEDLINE/PubMed lookup) or by adding features, or new sequence can be added with the sequence editor. In the latter case, the Update Sequence function may be more convenient than pasting directly into the sequence editor. New updating features are still being added, and Sequin users are well advised to visit the Sequin WWW page to make sure they are aware of the latest developments.

The database staff at all three databases welcome all suggestions on making the update process as efficient and painless as possible. People who notice that records are published but not yet released are strongly encouraged to notify the databases as well. If errors are detected, these should also forwarded to the updates addresses; the owner of the record is notified accordingly (by the database staff) and a correction usually results. This chain of events is to be distinguished from third-party annotations, which are presently not accepted by the databases. The record belongs to the submitter(s); the database staff offers some curatorial, formatting guideline suggestions, but substantive changes come only from a listed submitter.

CONCLUDING REMARKS

The act of depositing records into a database and seeing these made public has always been an exercise of pride on the part of submitters, a segment of the scientific activity from their laboratory which they present to the scientific community. It is also a step that has been imposed by publishers as part of the publication process. In this process submitters always hope to provide information in the most complete and useful fashion, allowing maximum use of their data by the scientific community.

Very few users are aware of the complete array of intricacies present in the databases, but they do know the biology they want to represent. It has become the task of the databases to provide tools that will facilitate this process. The database staff also provides expertise with their indexers (some databases also call them *curators* or *annotators*), who have extensive training in biology and are very familiar with the databases, ensuring that nothing is lost in the submission process. The submission exercise itself has not always been easy, and was not even encouraged at the beginning of the sequencing era, simply because databases did not know how to handle this information. Now, however, the databases strongly encourage the submission of sequence data and of all appropriate updates. Many tools are available to facilitate this task, and together the databases support Sequin as the tool to use for new submissions, in addition to their respective WWW submissions tools. Submitting data to the databases has now become an enjoyable task, and scientists no longer have good excuses for neglecting it.

ACKNOWLEDGMENTS

Sequin is built on the NCBI Software Toolkit, to which a reasonably large number of people have contributed. However, several people at NCBI deserve special mention, since their roles have been central to its success. In addition to one of us (JAK), these include Colombe Chappey, Jinghui Zhang, Tatiana Tatusov, Jim Ostell, and Greg Schuler. The Suggest Intervals function was written by Webb Miller of Pennsylvania State University and then modified by Warren Gish (now at Washington University), Karl Sirotkin (NCBI), and Yuri Sadykov (now at Netscape). The BankIt submission form was designed by David Lipman and implemented by Brandon Brylawski, Sergei Shavirin, and Tatiana Tatusov.

Communication Resources for Topics Presented in Chapter 14: Internet and Postal Addresses; Telephone and Fax Numbers

General contact information and points of entry for submissions of DNA sequences to DDBJ/EMBL or GenBank.

DDBJ (Center for Information Biology, NIG)
    Address   DDBJ, 1111 Yata, Mishima, Shiznoka 411, Japan
    Fax   81-559-81-6849

E-mail
    Submissions   *ddbjsub@ddbj.nig.ac.jp*
    Updates   *ddbjupdt@ddbj.nig.ac.jp*
    Information   *ddbj@ddbj.nig.ac.jp*
World Wide Web
    Home page   *http://www.ddbj.nig.ac.jp/*
    Submissions   *http://sakura.ddbj.nig.ac.jp/*

EMBL (European Bioinformatics Institutes, EMBL Outstation)
    Address   EMBL Outstation, EBI, Wellcome Trust Genome Campus, Hinxton
                    Cambridge, CB10 1SD, United Kingdom
    Voice   01.22.349.44.44
    Fax   01.22.349.44.68
    E-mail
    Submissions   *datasubs@ebi.ac.uk*
    Updates   *update@ebi.ac.uk*
    Information   *datalib@ebi.ac.uk*
    World Wide Web
    Home page   *http://www.ebi.ac.uk/*
    Submissions   *http://www.ebi.ac.uk/subs/allsubs.html*
    WebIn: *http://www.ebi.ac.uk/submission/webin.html*

GenBank (National Center for Biotechnology Information, NIH)
    Address   Gen Bank National Center for Biotechnology Information,
                    National Library of Medecine, National Institutes of Health,
                    Building 38A, Room 8N805, Bethesda MD 20894
    Telephone   301-496-2475
    Fax   301-480-9241
    E-mail
    Submissions   *gb-sub@ncbi.nlm.nih.gov*
    EST/GSS/STS   *batch-sub@ncbi.nlm.nih.gov*
    Updates   *update@ncbi.nlm.nih.gov*
    Information   *info@ncbi.nlm.nih.gov*
    World Wide Web
    Home page   *http://www.ncbi.nlm.nih.gov/*
    Submissions   *http://www.ncbi.nlm.nih.gov/Web/GenBank/submit.html*
    BankIt   *http://www.ncbi.nlm.nih.gov/BankIt/*

Other resources, in order of presentation in the chapter

Taxonomy browser
                http://www.ncbi.nlm.nih.gov/Taxonomy/tax.html

Genetic codes used in DNA sequence databases
                http://www.ncbi.nlm.nih.gov/htbin-post/Taxonomy/wprintgc?mode=c

Find ORF: Open reading frame finder linked to BLAST page
                http://www.ncbi.nlm.nih.gov/gorf/gorf.html

DDBJ/EMBL/GenBank Feature table documentation are available on the WWW or as PostScript
files on the FTP server of EBI or NCBI
                http://www.ncbi.nlm.nih.gov/collab/FT/
                http://www.ebi.ac.uk/ebi_docs/embl_db/ft/feature_table.html
                ftp://ncbi.nlm.nih.gov/genbank/docs/
                ftp://ftp.ebi.ac.uk/pub/databases/embl/doc/

Release notes for EMBL and GenBank databases
  EMBL   *ftp://ftp.ebi.ac.uk/pub/databases/embl/release/relnotes.doc*
  GenBank   *ftp://ncbi.nlm.nih.gov/genbank/gbrel.txt*

Sequin: The submission and update tool for the DNA sequence databases
                http://www.ncbi.nlm.nih.gov/Sequin/

EST, STS, and GSS home pages. Information on retrieval and submissions to these specialized
GenBank databases
  EST   *http://www.ncbi.nlm.nih.gov/dbEST/*
  STS   *http://www.ncbi.nlm.nih.gov/dbSTS/*
  GSS   *http://www.ncbi.nlm.nih.gov/dbGSS/*

HTGS home page: High-Throughput Genome Sequences resource, tools, and information
                http://www.ncbi.nlm.nih.gov/HTGS/

REFERENCES

Boguski, M. S., Lowe, T. M., Tolstoshev, C. M. (1993). dbEST—database for "expressed sequence
    tags". Nat. Genet. *4:* 332–333
Ouellette, B. F. F., and Boguski, M. S. 1997. Database Divisions and Homology Search Files:
    A Guide for the Perplexed. Genome Res. *7,* 952–955

APPENDIX 1

GLOSSARY

algorithm   Any sequence of actions (e.g., computational steps) that perform a particular task.

browser   Program used to access sites on the World Wide Web. Hypertext markup language (HTML) enables browsers to represent a Web page the same way regardless of computer platform.

characters and character states   In phylogenetics, characters are homologous features in different organisms. The exact condition of that feature in a particular individual is the character state. For example, the character "hair color" might have the character states "gold," "red," and "yellow." In molecular biology, the character states can be one of the four nucleotides (A, C, T, G) or one of the 20 amino acids. Some authors define "character" to mean the character state as defined here.

client   A computer, or the software running on a computer, that interacts with another computer at a remote site (server). Note the difference between client and user.

descriptor   Information about a sequence or set of sequences whose scope depends on its placement in a record. A descriptor is placed on a set of sequences to reduce the need to save multiple redundant copies of information.

domain name   Refers to one of the levels of organization of the Internet; used to both classify and identify host machines. Top-level domain names indicate the type of site or the country in which the host is located (see Table 1.1).

download   To transfer a file from a remote host to a local machine via FTP.

e-mail   Electronic mail. Refers to messages that can be composed on the computer and transmitted via the Internet to a remote location within seconds. [*Ant:* snail mail, postal mail.]

EST   Expressed sequence tag. ESTs are usually short (300–500 bp) single reads from mRNA (cDNA) which are usually produced in large numbers. They represent a snapshot of what is expressed in a given tissue, and/or at a given developmental stage. They represent tags (some coding, others not) of expression for a given cDNA library. These records usually are very poor in annotation and have only library and BioSource information. They are represented in a variety of databases, notably DDBJ/EMBL/GenBank, dbEST, and Unigene (see Chapters 2 and 14). For more information, see: *http://www.ncbi.nlm.nih.gov/dbEST/*

FAQ   A computer file of frequently asked questions. Exactly what it sounds like: a compiled list of questions and answers intended for new users of a computer-based resource, such as a mailing list or a newsgroup.

feature   Annotation on a specific location on a given sequence.

firewall   Refers to the separation of a company or organization's internal network from the public part, if any, of the same network. Intended to prevent unauthorized access to private computer systems.

FTP   File transfer protocol. The method by which files are transferred between hosts.

Gopher   A document delivery system allowing the retrieval and display of text-based files.

GSS   Genome survey sequences. This DDBJ/EMBL/GenBank division is similar in nature to the EST division, except that its sequences are genomic in origin, rather than cDNA (mRNA). The GSS division contains (but will not be limited to) the following types of data: random "single-pass read" genome survey sequences; single-pass reads from cosmid/BAC/YAC ends (these could be chromosome specific, but need not be); exon-trapped genomic sequences; Alu PCR sequences. For more information, see: *http://www.ncbi.nlm.nih.gov/dbGSS/*

GUI   Graphical user interface. Refers to software front ends that rely on pictures and icons to direct the interaction of users with the application.

heuristic algorithm   An economical strategy for deriving a solution to a problem for which an exact solution is computationally impractical or intractable. Consequently, a heuristic approach is not guaranteed to find the optimal or "true" solution.

homologous   In phylogenetics, describing particular features in different individuals that are genetically descended from the same feature in a common ancestor. In molecular biology, often "homologous" simply means similar, regardless of genetic relationship.

homoplasy   Similarity that has evolved independently and is not indicative of common phylogenetic origin.

host   Any computer on the Internet that can be addressed directly through a unique IP address.

HTGS (HTG)   High-throughput genome sequences (HTG is the HTGS division in DDBJ/EMBL/GenBank). Various genome sequencing centers worldwide have begun the large-scale sequencing of human and other higher eukaryotic genomes. The databases have deemed it beneficial to put the unfinished sequences that are the result of such sequencing efforts in a separate division. These unfinished records, in most cases, are notable for important numbers of gaps in the nucleotides, low accuracy, and no annotations on the record. These sequences do not achieve the high standard expected in the standard DDBJ/EMBL/GenBank records. For more information, see: *http://www.ncbi.nlm.nih.gov/HTGS/*

HTML   Hypertext markup language. The standard, text-based language used to specify the format of World Wide Web documents. HTML files are translated and rendered through the use of Web browsers.

hyperlink   A graphic or text within a World Wide Web document that can be selected by means of a mouse. Clicking on a hyperlink transports the user to another part of the same Web page or to another Web page, regardless of location.

hypertext   Within a Web page, text that is differentiated by color or by underlining and functions as a hyperlink.

indel   Acronym for "INsertion or DELetion." Applied to length-variable regions of a multiple alignment when it is not specified whether sequence length differences have been created by insertions or deletions.

Internet   A system of linked computer networks used for the transmission of files and messages between hosts.

IP address   The unique, numeric address of a computer host on the Internet.

intranet   A computer network internal to a company or organization. Intranets are often not connected to the Internet or are protected by a firewall.

Java   A programming language developed by Sun Microsystems that allows small programs (applets) to be run on any computer. Java applets are typically invoked when a user clicks on a hyperlink on a Web page.

LAN   Local area network. A network that connects computers in a small, defined area, such as the offices in a single wing or a group of buildings.

molecular clock   The hypothesis that nucleotide or amino acid substitutions occur at more or less fixed rate over evolutionary time, like the slow ticking of a clock. It has been proposed that given a calibration date and a constant molecular clock, the amount of sequence divergence can be used to calculate the time that has elapsed since two molecules diverged.

mutation studies   In Sequin, a set of sequences for the same gene in the same species, perhaps the same individual, in which several different induced mutations are isolated and sequenced.

orthologs/orthologous   Homologous sequences are said to be orthologous when they are direct descendants of a sequence in the common ancestor (i.e., without having undergone a gene duplication event). See also homologous and paralogs.

PAM matrix   PAM (percent accepted mutation) and BLOSUM (blocks substitution matrix) are matrices that define scores for each of the 210 possible amino acid substitutions. The scores are based on empirical substitution frequencies observed in alignments of database sequences and in general reflect similar physicochemical properties (e.g., a substitution of leucine for isoleucine, two amino acids of similar hydrophobicity and size, will score higher than a substitution of leucine for glutamate).

paralogs/paralogous   Homologous sequences in two organisms A and B that are descendants of two different copies of a sequence that was created by a duplication event in the genome of the common ancestor. See also homologous and orthologs.

phylogenetic studies   In Sequin, a set of sequences for the same gene in individuals of different species. The presumption is that the individuals cannot interbreed. Sequin does not allow a single organism name, but expects the organism to be encoded in the Definition line. It does, however, present a control for setting the proper genetic code.

platform   Properly, the operating system running software on a computer (e.g., Unix or Windows95). More often used to refer to the type of computer, such as a Macintosh or PC-compatible.

population studies In Sequin, a set of sequences for the same gene in individuals of a single species. The presumption is that the individuals can interbreed. Sequin allows entry of a single organism name, though some distinguishing source information, such as strain, clone, or isolate, must be entered for each sequence if the program is to function properly.

protein name In a sequence record, the preferred field for a Protein feature.

protein description In a sequence record, used if the protein name is not known.

server A computer that processes requests issued from remote locations by client machines.

site An individual column of residues in an amino acid or nucleotide alignment. The residues at a site are presumed to be homologous.

spam Postings to newsgroups or mail broadcast to a large number of e-mail accounts that usually are irrelevant or not of interest to the recipients. Analogous to postal junk mail.

STS Sequenced tagged site. STSs are operationally unique sequences that identify the combinations of primer pairs used in PCR assays that generate mapping reagents, each of which maps to a single position within the genome. Variations on this definition are also present in this division. This division of GenBank is intended to facilitate cross-comparison of STSs with sequences in other divisions for the purpose of correlating map positions of anonymous sequences with known genes. For more information, see: *http://www.ncbi.nlm.nih.gov/dbSTS/*

Telnet An Internet protocol or application that allows users to connect to computers at remote locations and use these computers as if they were physically operating the remote hardware.

URL Uniform resource locator. Used Web browsers, URLs specify both the type of site being accessed (FTP, Gopher, or Web) and the address of the Web site. See also Table 1.2.

user The person using client–server or other type of software.

World Wide Web A document delivery system capable of handling non-text-based media of various types.

SAMPLE SEQUENCE FILE FORMATS

FASTA FORMAT

```
>eIF4E [org=Drosophila melanogaster] [strain=Oregon R] ...
CGGTTGCTTGGGTTTTATAACATCAGTCAGTGACAGGCATTTCCAGAGTTGCCCTGTTCA ...
>4E-I [gene=eIF4E] [prot=eukaryotic initiation factor 4E-I]
MQSDFHRMKNFANPKSMFKTSAPSTEQGRPEPPTSAAAPAEAKDVKPKEDPQETGEPAGN ...
>4E-II [gene=eIF4E] [prot=eukaryotic initiation factor 4E-II]
MVVLETEKTSAPSTEQGRPEPPTSAAAPAEAKDVKPKEDPQETGEPAGNTATTTAPAGDD ...
```

FASTA FORMAT FOR ALIGNMENTS

```
>Sequence 1
GATATAATCAGTTTATGGGATCAAAGCCTAAAGCCATGTGTAAAATTA
ACCCCACTCTGTGTTACTTTAAATTGCACTAATGCGACGTATACTAAT
>Sequence 2
GATATAATCAGTTTATGGGATCAAAGCCTAAAGCCATGTGTAAAATTA
ACCCCACTCTGTGTTACTTTATGCACTAATGCGACGTATACTGAT
>Sequence 3
GATATAATCAGTTTATGGGATCAAAGCCTAAAGCCATGTGTAAAATTA
ACCCCACTCTGTGTTACTTTAACTAATGCGACGTATACTAAT
```

FASTA FORMAT, CONTAINING GAPS

```
>Sequence 1
GATATAATCAGTTTATGGGATCAAAGCCTAAAGCCATGTGTAAAATTA
ACCCCACTCTGTGTTACTTTAAATTGCACTAATGCGACGTATACTAAT
>Sequence 2
GATATAATCAGTTTATGGGATCAAAGCCTAAAGCCATGTGTAAAATTA
ACCCCACTCTGTGTTACTTTA---TGCACTAATGCGACGTATACTGAT
>Sequence 3
GATATAATCAGTTTATGGGATCAAAGCCTAAAGCCATGTGTAAAATTA
ACCCCACTCTGTGTTACTTTA------ACTAATGCGACGTATACTAAT
```

PHYLIP FORMAT

```
     3    96
Sequence 1 GATATAATCAGTTTATGGGATCAAAGCCTAAAGCCATGTGTAAAATTA
Sequence 2 GATATAATCAGTTTATGGGATCAAAGCCTAAAGCCATGTGTAAAATTA
Sequence 3 GATATAATCAGTTTATGGGATCAAAGCCTAAAGCCATGTGTAAAATTA

           ACCCCACTCTGTGTTACTTTAAATTGCACTAATGCGACGTATACTAAT
           ACCCCACTCTGTGTTACTTTA---TGCACTAATGCGACGTATACTGAT
           ACCCCACTCTGTGTTACTTTA------ACTAATGCGACGTATACTAAT
```

NEXUS CONTIGUOUS FORMAT

```
#NEXUS
BEGIN DATA;
DIMENSIONS NTAX=3 NCHAR=96;
FORMAT MISSING=? GAP=- DATATYPE=DNA ;
MATRIX

Sequence 1
GATATAATCAGTTTATGGGATCAAAGCCTAAAGCCATGTGTAAAATTA
ACCCCACTCTGTGTTACTTTAAATTGCACTAATGCGACGTATACTAAT
Sequence 2
GATATAATCAGTTTATGGGATCAAAGCCTAAAGCCATGTGTAAAATTA
ACCCCACTCTGTGTTACTTTA---TGCACTAATGCGACGTATACTGAT
Sequence 3
GATATAATCAGTTTATGGGATCAAAGCCTAAAGCCATGTGTAAAATTA
ACCCCACTCTGTGTTACTTTA------ACTAATGCGACGTATACTAAT
```

NEXUS INTERLEAVED FORMAT

```
#NEXUS

[!This data assembled using Sequencher™, from Gene Codes
    Corporation.]
begin data;
    dimensions ntax=3 nchar=96;
    format datatype=dna gap=: interleave;
    matrix


Sequence 1    GATATAATCAGTTTATGGGATCAAAGCCTAAAGCCATGTGTAAAATTA
Sequence 2    GATATAATCAGTTTATGGGATCAAAGCCTAAAGCCATGTGTAAAATTA
Sequence 3    GATATAATCAGTTTATGGGATCAAAGCCTAAAGCCATGTGTAAAATTA


Sequence 1    ACCCCACTCTGTGTTACTTTAAATTGCACTAATGCGACGTATACTAAT
Sequence 2    ACCCCACTCTGTGTTACTTTA---TGCACTAATGCGACGTATACTGAT
Sequence 3    ACCCCACTCTGTGTTACTTTA------ACTAATGCGACGTATACTAAT
```

NBRF FORMAT

```
>DL;Sequence
Sequence 1, 96 bases, 750EDA48 checksum.
 GATATAATCA GTTTATGGGA TCAAAGCCTA AAGCCATGTG TAAAATTAAC
 CCCACTCTGT GTTACTTTAA ATTGCACTAA TGCGACGTAT ACTAAT*

>DL;Sequence
Sequence 2, 93 bases, D557AE5C checksum.
 GATATAATCA GTTTATGGGA TCAAAGCCTA AAGCCATGTG TAAAATTAAC
 CCCACTCTGT GTTACTTTAT GCACTAATGC GACGTATACT GAT*

>DL;Sequence
Sequence 3, 90 bases, B916B9DB checksum.
 GATATAATCA GTTTATGGGA TCAAAGCCTA AAGCCATGTG TAAAATTAAC
 CCCACTCTGT GTTACTTTAA CTAATGCGAC GTATACTAAT*
```

MSF FORMAT

msf.seq MSF: 90   Type: N January 01, 1776 12:00 Check: 6718 ..

Name: Sequence   Len: 96 Check: 3504 Weight: 1.00
Name: Sequence   Len: 93 Check: 5512 Weight: 1.00
Name: Sequence   Len: 90 Check: 7702 Weight: 1.00

//

```
        Sequence  GATATAATCA GTTTATGGGA TCAAAGCCTA AAGCCATGTG TAAAATTAAC
        Sequence  GATATAATCA GTTTATGGGA TCAAAGCCTA AAGCCATGTG TAAAATTAAC
        Sequence  GATATAATCA GTTTATGGGA TCAAAGCCTA AAGCCATGTG TAAAATTAAC

        Sequence  CCCACTCTGT GTTACTTTAA ATTGCACTAA TGCGACGTAT ACTAAT
        Sequence  CCCACTCTGT GTTACTTTAT GCACTAATGC GACGTATACT GAT
        Sequence  CCCACTCTGT GTTACTTTAA CTAATGCGAC GTATACTAAT
```

INDEX

AACompident, 247–248
AACompSim, 248
Accession number:
  GenBank flatfile record, 26–27, 129–130
  NCBI data file, 132
Accession.Version combined identifier, NCBI data
    model, 131–132
ACEDB (a *C elegans* database):
  analysis functions:
    artificial gels, 316
    finding motifs, 315–316
  availability, 305
  background, 299–300
  data entry, 303–304
  data models, 301–303
  installation, 305
  interface, 300–301
  popularity of, 300
  queries and tables, 304
  sequence analysis:
    BLAST analysis, 312–314
    Blixem, 307–308
    DOTTER, 308–309
    Efetch, 307
    features map (Fmap), 305–307, 311
    GeneFinder, 309–311
    Import Sequence, 311–312
    Magic Tag, 312
    MSPcrunch, 312–314
    results column, 314–315
  supporting sequences and software, 316
Acembly, ACEDB database, 316
Algorithms, alignment, 173. *See also specific types*
    of algorithms
Aliases, 6
ALIGN, 192
Alignment(s), *see* Sequence alignment
  classes of, 140
  multiple, 145, 172–188
  optimal methods, 150–151
  pairwise, 145
  seq-align, 139–140
  statistical significance of, 155–156
Alignment block, 179
ALSCRIPT, 185–187
Alu, repetitive elements, 167–169

Alzheimer's disease, protein sequences, 161–163
America Online (AOL), 3–4, 11
Ancient conserved regions (ACRs), 234
Andreesen, Marc, 11
Arabidopsis thaliana Database (AtDB), 116
ARPANET (Advanced Research Projects Agency of
    the U.S. Department of Defense), 1–2
Articles, in databases, 127
ASN.1 (Abstract Syntax Notation):
  information retrieval, 103
  MMDB structure database, 59–60
  NCBI data model and, 124–125
  sample record, 36–42
  SEQUIN program, 331–332, 342–343
Atlas of Protein Sequences and Structures, 18
Authors, in databases, 126–127

Background frequencies, 153
Bacterial artificial chromosomes (BACs), 269
Bairoch, Amos, 7
BASEML, 224
BASEMLG, 224
Bayesian pseudiscount method, 180
BEAUTY, 169
BIOSCI newsgroups, 6
BIOSEQ, 132–135, 344
BIOSEQSETS, 135–136
BioSource, 141, 143, 332, 345
BITNET ("Because It's Time"), 2
BLAST (Basic Local Alignment Search Tool):
  CDS features, 122
  database similarity searching, 160–162
  information retrieval, 101, 109, 117
  NCBI data model, 142–143
  parameters, 164
  query sequence, 142
  recent improvements to, 162–165
  sequence analysis, 89
  SEQUIN program, 332
  STS content maps, 283
  submission process, ACEDB database, 316
BLASTN, 24, 347
BLASTX, 233, 347
BLITZ, 260
BLIXEM, 169, 307–308
BLOCKS, 178–179

BLOSUM:
  progressive alignment, 175
  substitution matrices, 154–155
Bootstrapping, phylogenetic tree evaluation,
    215–216
BoxShade, 184
B-pleated sheet, 252, 257
Branch-and-bound method, phylogenetic tree
    searches, 211
Browsers, overview, 10–12
B-strand, 252–253

CENSOR, 232–233
CEPH map, YAC overlap, 290
CEPH YAC:
  clones, 293
  library, STS/YAC content map, 283–284
  map, overview, 289–291
Character-based methods, phylogenetic tree-
    building, 209–211
Chemistry rules approach, 48
Chime, 69
CHIP gene, 32
Chromosome X, STS content map, 293
Circular dichroism spectroscopy, 246
Citation(s), in database:
  components of, 127
  submission process, *see* Submission of DNA
    sequences to public databases
ClarkNet, 4
CLUSTAL W, 173–176, 185, 192
Cn3D, 69, 110
Coding measure, 234
Coding Region (CDS), seq-feat, 138–139
Coding sequence(s):
  database submission process, *see* Submission of
    DNA sequences to public databases
  defined, 19
Codon detection, bias in, 234–236
CODONML, 224
Codon Usage, ACEDB database, 316
COILS algorithm, 257–258
Comment, GenBank flat file record, 29
CompuServe, 4, 11
Compute pI/MW, 250
Computer-aided design (CAD), 62, 70
Computer domain, 2
CON division, GenBank, 24
Consensus sequence, 236
Constraint tree searches, 217
Cooperative Human Linkage Center (CHLC) map,
    278
Correlated disorder, 67
Coutinho, Pedro, 14
COVELS, 240

DALI algorithm, 58, 263
Databases:
  primary and secondary, 19–20
  similarity searching, 156–159

submission process, *see* Submission of DNA
    sequences to public databases
Data Export, ACEDB database, 316
Data submission, electronic, 128
Definition line, GenBank flatfile records, 25
Delta bioseq, 133
Describe tree, 203
Discontinuous alignment, 140
Discriminant analysis, 234
Distance, phylogenetic tree-building, 191, 223
Distance-based methods, phylogenetic tree-
    building, 206–209
Distributed document delivery system, 8
DNA Database of Japan (DDBJ), *see* GenBank
    Sequence Database
  components of, 16, 18, 21, 26, 33
  NCBI data model and, 124
  submission process, *see* Submission of DNA
    sequences to public databases
DNA sequence databases:
  historical perspective, 18. *See also* GenBank
    Sequence Database
  submission process, *see* Submission of DNA
    sequences to public databases
DNA sequence records:
  format *vs.* content, 20–21
  primary, 19–20
  secondary, 19–20
DNA sequences, submission process, *see* Sub-
    mission of DNA sequences to public
    databases
DNADIST, 218
DNAML, 218
Domain name servers, 2
DOTTER algorithm, 148–149, 308–309
Drosophila, 117–118, 162, 173
DUMP Sequence, ACEDB database, 316
Dynamic programming, 151

EBI BioCatalog, 14
Electronic mail, *see* E-mail
E-mail:
  addresses, 5
  advantages of, 4–5
  newsgroups, 6
  sending, 5–6
  servers, 6–7, 99
EMBL Dump, ACEDB database, 316
EMBL Nucleotide Sequence Database, 75
Entrez system:
  chromosome maps, navigation guidelines,
    272–275
  information retrieval:
    overview, 101–110
    query server, 111–115
    sample applications, 105–110
  NCBI data model and, 143
  overview, 17–19, 57–58
Eudora, 6
Eukaryotes, 236

European Molecular Biology Laboratory (EMBL):
  DNA sequence records:
    NID line, 26
    overview, 16, 18, 21
    popularity of, 33
    sample, 42–44
    segmented sequence, 124
    submission process, *see* Submission of DNA
      sequences to public databases
Exhaustive method, phylogenetic tree searches, 211
ExPASy database, 178
ExPASy server, 247–248
Expressed sequence tag (EST):
  database similarity search projects, 156
  submission process, 348–349
Expressed Sequence Tags (EST) division, GenBank,
  24

FASTA format:
  database similarity searching, 159
  defined, 20–21
  genome-wide maps, 280, 283
  information retrieval, 114
  Molecular Modeling Database (MMDB), 57
  multiple sequence alignment, 176
  NCBI data model, 142
  samples:
    for alignments, 359
    containing gaps, 360
    generally, 359
  SEQUIN program, 333–334
Fastamail Submission, ACEDB database, 316
FastDNAml, 222–223
File transfer protocol (FTP), 7–8, 117
Fitch-Margoliash (FM) method, phylogenetic tree-
  building, 207–208
Fluorescence spectroscopy, 68
FlyBase, 117–118
Fragment Assembly System, 89
Frequently Asked Questions (FAQs), 6
Fully qualified domain name (FQDN), 2

Gap penalties, 151–155
GCG (Genetics Computer Group, Inc.), sequence
  analysis, *see* SeqLab, sequence analysis
GenBank Data (GDB), genome-wide maps, 279,
  281
GenBank flatfile (GBFF):
  CDS feature, 30–32, 122
  feature table, 29
  gene feature, 32–33
  general consideration, 29
  header, 22–29
  overview, 18, 20
  RNA features, 33
  SEQUIN program, 332, 337
  source feature, 30
GenBank Sequence Database:
  codon bias detection, 236
  components of, 22

data, *see* GenBank Data (GDB)
  defined, 98
  file format, 20, 142
  historical perspective, 18, 98
  integrated gene parsing, 238
  NCBI data model, 142
  overview, 16–17
  sample record, 35–36
  submission process, *see* Submission of DNA
    sequences to public databases
  summary file, sample, 44–45
  warning sequence, 169
Gene(s), *see specific types of genes*
  -finding, integrated, 234
  parsing, integrated, 238
  seq-feat, 137–138
Gene Wars (Cook-Deegan), 18
GenEMBLPlus, 75–76
General dialog box, 184
Genethon genetic map, 278–279
Genethon genotyping information, 290–291
Genome, genetic maps of, 278
Genome centers, submission of DNA sequences to,
  348–350
Genome Data Base:
  genome-wide maps from large communities, 271
  navigating chromosome maps, 275–277
GenPept format, 17, 21
GENSCAN, 237
gi number, in NCBI data model, 130–131
Gilbert, Don, 21
Global alignment, 140
Gopher, 8, 117
Gopher holes, 8
GRAIL program, 235, 28
Graphical user interfaces (GUIs), 7, 12
Gribskov method, 180
Groups dialog, 184
GSS (Genome Survey Sequences), submission
  process, 348–349

Hadamard conjugation, 212
Hard links, information retrieval, 103–104
High Throughput Genome sequences (HTG) divi-
  sion, GenBank, 24, 133
Hit list, 156
Hosts, 3
HPGL™, 82
Human genome, transcript map, 278
Human Physical Mapping Project, 283–284
Hyperlinks, 9–10
Hypertext markup language (HTML), 11
Hypertext transfer protocol (http), 10

IBNR, 50
Indel regions, phylogenetic tree-building, 195
Information retrieval, from biological databases:
  integrated, Entrez system, 101–111
  medical databases, 118–119
  query server, 111–115

Information retrieval, from biological databases
  (Continued):
  retrieve server, 99–101
  sequence databases, beyond NCBI, 115–118
International Nucleotide Sequence Database Collab-
    oration, 16, 131
Internet, generally:
  basics, 1–3
  connecting to, 3–4
  electronic mail, *see* E-mail
  hosts, 3
  Intranet *vs.,* 12–13
  phylogenetic analysis, resources for, 225–226
  repeat analysis, resources for, 242
  World Wide Web, 10–15
Internet Explorer, 11–12, 104, 275
Internet service providers (ISPs), 3–4
Intranet, 12–13
Intron splice sites, in DNA, 237

Keratin, 258
Key terms, information retrieval, 102–103
Keyword, GenBank flatfile record, 27
Kinemage, 50, 70
Kishino-Hasegawa test, 217, 222
Kringle domain, 148

LALIGN program, 151, 159
Likelihood ratio test, 217
Local area network (LAN), 6
LOCUS line, GenBank flatfile record, 23, 122, 129
LOOK, 263
LookSmart, 14
Low-complexity regions (LCRs), 166
Lynx, 12

MACAW, 192–193
MacBoxShade, 184–185, 187
MACCLADE, 217, 223
Mage, 69–70
MALIGN, 192–193, 197
Map bioseq, 133–134
Maximum likelihood (ML), phylogenetic tree-
    building, 191, 195, 203, 209–211, 217, 221
Maximum parsimony (MP), phylogenetic tree-
    building, 191, 195–196, 203, 209, 211, 217
MAXTREES, 221
Medical databases, 118–119
MEDLINE database:
  article citations, 128–129
  components of, 28, 57
  information retrieval, 101, 103, 105–110, 116
  NCBI data models, 126–128
  unique identifier (MUID), 128
MEGA, 208
MEGA plus METREE, 223–224
MetaCrawler, 14
Meta-search engines, 14
METREE, 208
Microsoft, *see* Internet Explorer
Microsoft Exchange, 6

Minimum evolution (ME), phylogenetic tree-
    building, 208–210
MITO-MAP database, 293–294
mmCIF (MacroMolecular Chemical Interchange
    Format), 55, 59
MMDB (Molecular Modeling Database at NCBI):
  application programming interface (API), 60
  database services, 57–58
  defined, 49
  overview, 56–57
  structure file format, 59–60
  viewers, Cn3D, 69
Molecular populations, visualization of, 62–63
MolInfo, 141, 344
MOLPHY, 224
Molscript, 69
Mol type, GenBank flatfile record, 23–24
MoST, 179–181
Mouse Genetic and Physical Mapping Project, 295
Mouse Genome Database (MGD), 296
MOWSE (Molecular Weight Search) algorithm, 250
mRNA:
  repetitive elements, 167
  sample GenBank flat file record, 25
  seq-feat, 137
  sequence analysis, 86
MSF format, sample, 361–362
MultAlin, 175–176
Multiple alignment, *see* Multiple sequence align-
    ment
  database searching, 145
  phylogenetic tree-building, 192–195
Multiple representation styles, structure databases,
    60–62
Multiple sequence alignment:
  motifs and patterns, 176–184
  presentation methods, 184–187
  progressive alignment methods, 173–176
Multivariate statistics, 235
Myosin, 258

National Human Genome Research Institute
    (NHGRI), 291
NBRF format, sample, 361
NCBI (National Center for Biotechnology Informa-
    tion):
  BankIt forms, 324–326
  Citation Matching Service, 127
  Data Model:
    articles, 127
    ASN.1, 124–125
    authors, 126–127
    BIOSEQ, 132–135
    BIOSEQSETS, 135–136
    defined, 121–122
    examples of, 122–124
    electronic data submission, 128
    MEDLINE, 128
    patents, 127–128
    publications, 125–126
    PubMed UIDs, 128

purpose of, 125
SEQ-ANNOT, 136–140
SEQ-DESCR, 140–141
SEQIDS, 129–132
usage of, 141–143
DNA sequence records, 21, 24–28
Entrez, navigating chromosome maps, 272–275
genome-wide maps, 271
Transcript map, 278–281
NCBI DeskTop, submission process, 331, 342, 344–346, 349
Needleman-Wunsch algorithm, 151
Neighboring, information retrieval, 101
Neighbor Joining (NJ) method, phylogenetic tree-building, 207–209
NetGene, 237
Netscape, 69, 104
Navigator, 11–12, 275
Network Entrez, 104
Neural nets, 235
Neural network, 253
Newsgroups, 6
NEXUS format:
  samples:
    contiguous format, 360
    interleaved format, 361
  SEQUIN program, 333
NID line:
  GenBank flatfile record, 26–27
  NCBI data model, 131
NMR structure, models and ensembles, 63–65, 67
nnpredict, 253
Nonglobular regions, 262
Nuclear magnetic resonance, 246
Nucleotide databases, 323
Nuc-prot set, BIOSEQSETS, 136, 140–141, 343

Online Mendelian Inheritance in Man (OMIM), 118–119
Online services, 3
Optical rotary dispersion, 246
Organism, database submission process, *see* Submission of DNA sequences to public databases
Overlapping sequence fragments, sequence analysis, 88–89

Pairwise alignments, 145
PAM (point-accepted-mutation):
  progressive alignment, 175
  substitution matrices, 153–154
PAML, 224
Parametric bootstrap, 216–217
Parents persist, 108
Partial alignment, 140
Patented sequences, 127–128
Path graph, 149–150
PAUP™:
  defined, 87
  phylogenetic analysis:
    data format, 220–221

development of, 217–218
program availability and compilations, 220
tree building, 221
tree evaluation, 221–222
phylogenetic tree-building, 192, 195–196, 203, 206, 212–213, 225
SEQUIN program and, 333
PCR primers, 23
PDB (Protein Data Bank, Brookhaven National Laboratories):
  chain identifier, 55
  database services, 49–50
  implicit sequences, 55
  information sources, 70
  structure file format, 58–59
  structure records, sequences from, 50, 55
  validating sequences, 55
Pearson format, 20–21
Pedro's Biomolecular Research Tools, 13–14
Pending/Waiting List, 70
PeptideMass, 250–251
Permutation tail probability test (PTP), 213
Permutation tests, 213, 215
Pfam, 176
Pfscan, 176
PHYLIP format:
  applications of, generally, 192, 217–218, 223–225, 333
  sample, 360
PHYLODENDRON, 192, 222
Phylogenetic analysis:
  data model, alignment, 191–197
  model elements, 190–191
  practical considerations for, 225
  software programs, 217–225
  steps in, overview, 191
  substitution model, 191, 197–206
  tree building, 191, 206–211
  tree evaluation, 191, 213–217
Phylogenetic BIOSEQSET, 136
Phylogenetic trees:
  building, 191, 206–211
  evaluation of, 213–217
  rooting, 212–213
  searching for, 211–212
  SeqLab analysis, generally, 87
Physical mapping databases, public, *see* Public physical mapping databases
PID line, NCBI data model, 131
PileUp, 192
Polyadenylation termination signals, 237
Population BIOSEQSET, 136
Position-specific scoring matrix (PSSM), 178
Position weight matrix (PWM), 236–237, 240
PostScript™ format:
  applications of, generally, 69, 82
  genome-wide maps, 278
PowerBLAST:
  sequence alignment, 169
  Seq.annot, 136–137
  submission of DNA sequences, 331, 343, 347

Predictive methods:
  using nucleotide sequences:
    codon bias detection, 234–236
    database searches, 234
    framework, 232
    functional sites in DNA, detection of, 236–237
    future prospects, 241–242
    gene parsing, integrated, 238
    masking repetitive DNA, 232–233
    tRNA genes, finding, 238, 240–241
  using protein sequences:
    physical properties based on sequence,
      250–252
    protein identity based on composition,
      247–250
    secondary structure and folding classes,
      252–257
    specialized structures or features, 257–262
    tertiary structure, 262–264
PredictProtein, 255
Primary databases, DNA sequence records, 19–20
Probability theory, 234
PROBE, 181–184
Prodigy, 4
Profile, defined, 164
ProfileScan, 176–178
Progressive alignment:
  CLUSTAL W, 173–175
  defined, 172
  MultAlin, 175–176
Prokaryotes, 237
Promotors, in DNA, 236–237
ProPack, 192–193
PROPSEARCH, 248–250
PROSITE, 89–90
PROTDIST, 218
Protein DataBase (PDB), *see* PDB (Protein Data
    Bank, Brookhaven National Laboratories)
Protein databases, components of, 22
Protein Information Resource (PIR) database, 19
Proteins, modular nature of, 148–150
Protein sequences:
  database submission process, *see* Submission of
    DNA sequences to public databases
  predictive methods using:
    physical properties based on sequence, 250–252
    protein identity based on composition,
      247–250
    secondary structure and folding classes,
      252–257
    specialized structures or features, 257–262
    tertiary structure, 262–264
Protein structure, multiple representation styles,
    60–62
PROTPARS, 218
PSI-BLAST (position-specific iterative BLAST),
    165
Public databases:
  data submission, *see* Submission of DNA
    sequences to public databases
  physical mapping, 269–294

Public physical mapping databases:
  chromosome-specific human maps, 291–294
  genome-wide maps:
    from individual sources, 278–291
    from large community databases, 271–278
  mouse mapping resources, 294–296
  physical maps, types of, 269–271
PUBMED:
  database, 28
  identifier (PMID), 128
  UIDs, 128

Query sequence, 86–88
Query server, 111–115
QuickMap software, 290

Radiation hybrid maps, 269–270, 286–289
RasMol, 55, 68–69
Raw bioseq, 133
REDSEQ, 21
Reference, GenBank flatfile record, 28
Relevance pairs model of retrieval, 102
Repetitive DNA, 232–233
Repetitive elements, 166–169
Residue-by-residue alignment, 147
Retrieve server, 99, 101
RNA, *see specific types of RNA*
  genomic records, 33
  seq-feat, 138
  sequences, submission process, *see* Submission
    of DNA sequences to public databases
Robison, Keith, 13
rRNA genes, 234
RSF (rich-sequence format) files, SeqLab, 85
R value, 180

Saccharomyces cerevisiae, 156
Saccharomyces Genome Database (SGD), 116
SAM, 193
SAPS (Statistical Analysis of Protein Sequences)
    algorithm, 252
SavvySearch, 14
Sayle, Roger, 68
Schizosaccharomyces pombe, 305–306
Search engines, 14
Search entry points, information retrieval, 104
Secondary databases, DNA sequence records,
    19–20
Secondary structure, 252–253
Segmented bioseq, 133
Segmented sequence, 124
SEQ-ANNOT, 136–140, 142
SEQ-DESCR, 140–141
Seq-feat, 137–139
Seq-graph, 140
SEQIDS, 129–132
SeqLab, sequence analysis, *see* Wisconsin Package
  adding entries, 77–79
  annotating sequences, 83–85
  applications of, overview, 85–90
  creating new sequence entry, 79

Editor, 79–80, 85
extending by including programs that are not part of the Wisconsin Package, 91
Job Manager, 83
Main Window, 76–77, 91
monitoring progress, 83
troubleshooting, 83
viewing output, 81–82
Sequence alignment:
defined, 145
evolutionary basis, 146–148
Sequence analysis, *see* SeqLab, sequence analysis; Wisconsin Package
Sequence-based alignment, phylogenetic tree-building, 193
Sequence database(s):
beyond NCBI, 115–118
searches:
BLAST programs, 160–165
FASTA program, 159
low-complexity regions (LCRs), 166
repetitive elements, 166–169
similarities, 156–159
Sequence file formats, samples:
FASTA:
for alignments, 359
containing gaps, 360
generally, 359
MSF, 361–362
NBRF, 361
NEXUS:
contiguous format, 360
interleaved format, 361
PHYLIP, 360
Sequence Length, ACEDB database, 316
SEQUIN:
advanced annotation, 330–331
as analysis workbench, 331, 342
annotation by feature propagation, 340–342
data model, consequences of, 331–332
editing functions, 330–331
entering new data, 328–330
NCBI data model and, 143
with network connection, 347
submitting aligned set of sequences, 338–340
submitting single sequences, 333–338
overview, 326–328
validation, 330, 333
viewing the sequence record, 330
Signal Peptides (SignalP), 261–262
SIM, 151
Sims dialog, 184
Skewness test, 213
snRNA genes, 234
SOPMA, 256–257
Source line, GenBank flatfile record, 27–28
Spam, 6
Splice, generally:
Consensus, ACEDB database, 316
junctions, 232
Split decomposition, 212

SP-TrEMBL, 76
SSPRED, 255–256, 260
Stanford University radiation hybrid map, 286–289
STATALIGN program, 191
Structure databases:
atoms, 48–49
bonds, 48–49
chemical graphs, 47
completeness, 48–49
coordinates, 47
defined, 46–47
information resources, 70
MMDB, *see* MMDB (Molecular Modeling Database at NCBI)
PDB, *see* PDB (Protein Data Bank, Brookhaven National Laboratories)
sequences, 47
structure viewers, 68–70
3-D molecular structure data, 47
visualizing structural information, 60–68
STS (Sequence Tagged Sites):
content maps:
characteristics of, 269–271, 275, 278, 282–283
chromosome-specific human maps, 291, 293
placement on Whitehead maps, 283
submission process, 348–349
STS/YAC content map, 282–285
Subject sequence, 156
Submission citations, 128
Submission of DNA sequences to public databases:
EST/STS/GSS, 348
genome centers, 348–350
SEQUIN:
advanced annotation, 330–331
as analysis workbench, 331, 342
annotation by feature propagation, 340–342
data model, consequences of, 331–332
editing functions, 330–331
entering new data, 328–330
with network connection, 347
submitting aligned set of sequences, 338–340
submitting single sequences, 333–338
overview, 326–328
validation, 330, 333
viewing the sequence record, 330
updates, 350351
what to submit, 321–324
where to submit, 320
on World Wide Web, 324–326
Substitution matrix, 151–153
Substitution model:
building, 191
determination of, 197–206
phylogenetic tree-building:
among-site substitution rate heterogeneity, 202–203
parameter dimensions, 203–206
substitution rates between bases, 199–202
Substitution scores, 151–155
SWISS-MODEL, 263

Swiss-Prot:
  applications of, generally, 18–19, 21, 55, 76, 86
  BLOCKS and, 179
  information retrieval, 99–100
  PredictProtein program, 255
  PROSITE and, 178
  warning sequence, 169

Target frequencies, 153
TATA box, 232
TBLASTN search, 162–163
TCP (Transmission Control Protocol), 2
TeeAlign, 193
Termination signals, in DNA, 237–238
Tertiary structure, 262–263
TGREASE algorithm, 251, 259
3DB Atlas, 50, 57
3D viewers, 69–70
TMAP, 260–261
TMbase, 259
TMpred, 261
TOPITS method, 264
Topology-dependent test (T-PTP), 213, 215
Translation, initiation site in DNA, 237
Transmembrane regions, 259
Tree bisection-reconnection (TBR), 212
TreeDraw, 192
TreeTool, 192
TREEVIEW, 192, 222
TREMBL, 18
tRNA genes, 238, 240–241
tRNAscan-SE, 240–241
Tropomysin, 258
TurboGopher, 8

Uniform resource locators (URLs), defined, 10, 14
UniGene, 278
UNIX, 6–7, 160. *See also specific software programs*
Unweighted Pair Group Method with Arithmetic Mean (UPGMA), phylogenetic tree-building, 207–208, 221

VAST (Vector Analysis Search Tool):
  information retrieval, 101–102
  NCBI data model and, 58
  predictive methods, 263
Virtual bioseq, 133
Virtual libraries, 13
Virtual Reality Modeling Language (VRML), 62, 70

Walther, Dirk, 69
Web crawling, 14
Web Entrez, 104
WebMol, 56, 69

Web page, 10
Web surfing, 10
WHAT-IF, 263
Whitehead Institute/MIT Center for Genome Research, 281–283, 294
Whitehead radiation hybrid map, 285–286
Wisconsin Package:
  accompanying databases, 75–76
  database reference searching, 93
  database sequence searching, 94
  editing, 94
  evolution, 94–95
  fragment assembly, 95
  gene prediction, 95
  importing/exporting, 95–96
  Map program, 80–81, 96
  multiple comparison, 93
  overview, 75
  pairwise comparison, 93
  pattern recognition, 95
  primer selection, 96
  protein analysis, 96–97
  publication, 94
  RNA secondary structure, 94
  System Support Manual, 76
  translation, 96
  viewing output, 81–82
Word hits, 159
Words, 159
World Wide Web (WWW), general overview:
  browser wars, 10–12
  database submission process, 324–326
  Entrez, 57
  finding information, 13–15
  FlyBase, 117
  Genome Data Base (GDB), 275
  Internet hosts, 3
  navigation, 9–10
  WWW Entrez, 104
WU-BLAST, 164
WWW Virtual Library, 13

XBLAST, 233
Xenopus laevis, 173
X-ray crystallography:
  PDB files, 65, 67
  protein sequences, 246
X-ray structures:
  correlated disorder, 67
  local dynamics, 67–68

Yahoo, 14
Yeast artificial chromosomes (YACs), physical mapping, 269, 271, 278, 281
Yeast Protein Database (YPD), 116–117